STAR

ALSO BY PETER BISKIND

Gods and Monsters:
Movers, Shakers, and Other Casualties
of the Hollywood Machine

Down and Dirty Pictures:
Miramax, Sundance, and the Rise of Independent Film

Easy Riders, Raging Bulls:
How the Sex-Drugs-and-Rock 'n' Roll Generation
Saved Hollywood

The Godfather Companion

Seeing Is Believing:
Or, How Hollywood Taught Us to Stop Worrying
and Love the Fifties

STAR

*How Warren Beatty
Seduced America*

PETER BISKIND

SIMON &
SCHUSTER

London · New York · Sydney · Toronto

A CBS COMPANY

First published in Great Britain in 2010 by Simon & Schuster UK Ltd
A CBS COMPANY

1 3 5 7 9 10 8 6 4 2

Simon & Schuster UK Ltd
1st Floor
222 Gray's Inn Road
London
WC1X 8HB

www.simonandschuster.co.uk

Simon & Schuster Australia
Sydney

A CIP catalogue copy for this book is available
from the British Library.

ISBN: 978-1-84737-837-8

Designed by Kyoko Watanabe
Printed in the UK by CPI Mackays, Chatham ME5 8TD

To Betsy and Kate with love

CONTENTS

STAR

WARRENOLOGY:
AN INTRODUCTION

"You know what I think about these histories that we do on DVD, it makes me think of what Winston Churchill said, 'History will be very kind to me, because I intend to write it.'"

— *Warren Beatty*

F INISHING THIS BOOK was like recovering from a lingering illness, although admittedly one that I had brought on myself. I had wanted to write a biography of Warren Beatty since I met him in 1989, when he was shooting *Dick Tracy*. I had admired his films for a long time. Like everyone else, I was undone by *Bonnie and Clyde* when I first saw it in 1967, vastly entertained by *Shampoo* and *Heaven Can Wait*, and stunned by *Reds*. A veteran of the antiwar movement and a documentary filmmaker myself for a time, I was used to ragged, 16 millimeter black and white agitprop and was astounded that the biggest Hollywood star of the 1970s had given the *Gone With the Wind* treatment to the Russian Revolution and the formation of the American Communist Party—and gotten a big studio, Paramount, to pay for it. During the reign of Ronald Reagan, yet.

Then came *Ishtar*, but I was unfazed. Everybody, even Beatty, has flops. As editor of *American Film* in 1987, I wrote about it myself, and even put him, Dustin Hoffman, and Isabelle Adjani on the cover, in costume, all looking impish, as if they'd just gotten away with something, which, as it turned out, they hadn't. I was besotted, even though he refused to talk to me while I was working on that piece, delegating his cousin David MacLeod to do the honors, and only later, when it was too late, did he say he wished he had. Very Beatty-ish, as I would learn.

I first met Beatty in person, as opposed to the characters he played,

or the simulacrum in the tabloids and gossip columns, when I covered
Dick Tracy for *Premiere* magazine in 1989. I was struck by how original
a film it was, flavored with a dash of Charles Dickens and a dollop of
Bertolt Brecht, in equal measure. Beatty actually allowed me on the set
for a couple of days, a rare privilege indeed, until one night, very late,
I was standing in the back of a soundstage, way out of his eyeline, I
thought, when he took a piece of chewing gum from his mouth, fashioned it into a little ball, and playfully flicked it at me. I'm in, I thought
to myself, somewhat prematurely. He was shooting countless takes of
Glenne Headly, who played Tracy's girlfriend, repeating the same line
again and again, still managing to flub it. After the twenty-fifth or so
go-round, he walked over to me and threw me off the set, saying I was
making her nervous. (I don't think she even knew I was there.) I spent
a couple of hours with him in his trailer while he explained to me that
he would be happy to talk to me about anything I wanted—except *Dick
Tracy*, again very Beatty-ish. Did I want to talk about *Reds*? Well, yes,
but I was actually doing a piece on *Tracy*. He even explained why he
didn't want to talk about *Tracy*: "It's fundamentally destructive to the
ability to look at a movie and have your own feelings about it, because
it's obliterated by all this chatter that comes from us about our work,
and—I always say it's like somebody coming into a kitchen where there
is a seven-thousand-pound soufflé, and stamping their foot." The next
day, I returned to New York. Eventually he was ready to talk to me
about *Reds*, for *Vanity Fair*, some fifteen years later! Beatty is not a man
who likes to be rushed.

After the movie had wrapped, I went back to L.A. and spent a good
deal of time with him, again trying to draw him out on the subject of
Tracy. It was almost impossible. He would parry questions, change the
subject, make a joke, lapse into silence, or answer a question with another question. In those rare instances when he did respond, he insisted
the answer was off the record. Sometimes he would tell me two thirds
of a story but withhold the punch line, so it made no sense. In 2008,
at the American Film Institute's Life Achievement Award ceremony,
his oldest friend, screenwriter Robert Towne, locked eyes with him
and complained, "In forty-five years you never opened yourself up."
He once told *The New York Times*'s Lynn Hirschberg, "If you have
something to hide, then hide it." Adds filmmaker James Toback, also
a close friend, "Warren has a theory. Never disclose to anyone what

isn't absolutely essential to disclose. There's very little accidental about Warren; if he says something, there's a reason for it." But, as Hirschberg once observed, acutely, "Even when he is saying nothing, he is saying something." What she didn't say is that the reverse is equally true; even when he appears to be saying something, he is saying nothing.

Still, his evasions were orchestrated with a light touch. It became a kind of game, with me asking, and him not telling, in a million different ways. It was frustrating, even infuriating, but it was also kind of fun. As writer-director Paul Mazursky once put it, "He's one of the strangest and shrewdest guys I ever met. Strange only in that he's [so] close to the vest. If you're in a relationship with Warren, he's running it on some level. But he makes you feel nice."

By that time in the course of my work I had met a lot of stars, but never met anyone quite like him. Indecently gifted, he acted, he wrote, he directed, he produced. A brilliant mind. Tough. Analytical. Inquisitive. Hoovered up everything and gave back nothing. Funny. Self-deprecating. And good, or reasonably good, politics. And he was classy, had style to burn. Nothing and no one ruffled his feathers. He was Captain Cool, Mr. Natural. It cost considerable effort to present a lacquered exterior like his, but he pulled it off with seeming ease. Grace. That was the magic of it: you never saw the gears grinding. Norman Mailer, when he wrote about Beatty in *Vanity Fair*, called it "charm," tried to define it, and gave up.

I had never been a big believer in vaporous concepts like "charisma," which I filed away with "karma," "vibes," and "auras," but I'm embarrassed to report that when I was in his presence I felt an almost palpable sense of well-being, as if I were a better person because Warren Beatty liked me, or pretended he did. When he came to New York, he would call me up, and we would have dinner. I never quite understood it, thought, I'm not even writing about him now. Why isn't he hanging out with Dustin, or Mike Nichols, or Elaine May? Why me, a mere journalist? Because I reminded him of Leon Trotsky, which he once told me?

Going to a restaurant with him was a sobering experience. We were often alone, because he never ate until nearly midnight, and the place would be kept open for him. The maître d's were all over him. It was "Mr. Beatty this," "Mr. Beatty that." Occasionally we would go earlier, mingle with ordinary mortals. There were always women at the next table who would stare at him. I might as well have been invisible. Or, as actor Marshall Bell, a close friend, once described the experience, "When he and I are standing really close together at a cocktail party talking out of the sides of our mouths, somebody will actually ease in between me and him, and I'm looking at the back of their head. It might even be a guy." He flirted mercilessly. I remember eating with him in a joint in the Valley (San Fernando), when he started a conversation with one such woman, cute, with one of those pert, Southern California noses, and asked her what she did. She gazed at him with a glassy, doe-caught-in-the-headlights look and said, in a small voice, "I'm an organizer." I could see his antennae go up, as he smelled a kindred spirit, maybe a union organizer, or at the very least, someone like him, a political junkie.

"What kind of an organizer?"

"Closets."

While I was still working on *Dick Tracy,* I once waited for him for two hours outside a projection booth in midtown while he showed the film to the editors of *The New York Times,* or some such prestigious print outlet, and then clambered into his limo headed down to SoHo for dinner. I figured that it was now or never. In the hushed confines of the limo, I said, "If you ever decide you're ready to sit for a book, I'd like to do it."

"What kind of book?"

"A biography."

"I'm still alive."

"I know."

He never really gave me an answer, never said yes, never said no. Again, very Beatty-ish.

WHY WARREN Beatty? It's distressing to have to make a case for his importance just because no one under forty (maybe fifty?) knows who he is. If you go to the blogs, you'll find they're merciless, nasty and mean, for no better reason than that he's getting old. Ours is an unforgiving culture.

When I finished my book on the New Hollywood of the 1970s, *Easy Riders, Raging Bulls,* back in 1998, I felt like a hummingbird, flitting from blossom to blossom, filmmaker to filmmaker, extracting the nectar and moving on. I knew there was a whole lot more to that decade, and any of those directors could be pulled out for the full biographical treatment. Of course, many of them have been. There are plenty of books about, say, Francis Coppola and Martin Scorsese. There are even a couple about Beatty, but his reticence has always defeated biographers, even so fine a critic as David Thomson, who was finally reduced to fiction in *Warren Beatty and Desert Eyes*, alternating between orthodox, fact-filled chapters and imaginative narratives. A certain amount is known, of course, but the same stories have been recycled again and again with little added, an astonishing feat for someone who has lived in the public eye for five decades while managing, for most of that time, to lead the life of a celebrated lothario.

"Celebrated lothario": that was the rub. No matter what he achieved in film, it was overshadowed by his reputation as a superman of seduction. But by dint of assiduous attention to his image, he finally shed the reputation he enjoyed in the early 1960s for being little more than a playboy, and by the year 2000, he had transformed himself into a Thalberg Award winner. Of course his transformation was the product of considerably more than image control: Joan Collins's boy toy turned out to be one of the most versatile and skilled talents of his generation, enjoying the distinction of being the only filmmaker since Orson Welles to be nominated in four categories by the Motion Picture Academy, as he was in 1978 for *Heaven Can Wait* and then again in 1981 for *Reds*. The first four films he produced (*Bonnie and Clyde, Shampoo, Heaven Can Wait,* and *Reds*) racked up thirty-five Oscar nominations — a signal distinction, if we consider the Oscars a measurement of something other than advertising dollars in the pockets of the networks.

But even if we don't, there's no arguing with the movies, which brings us back to the old parlor game: how many defining motion pictures does a filmmaker have to make to be considered great? Rather than argue this again, I will just give my opinion: very few. Just choosing filmmakers with towering reputations, almost at random: Orson Welles? One, maybe two: *Citizen Kane* and *Touch of Evil.* Jean Renoir? Does anyone know titles other than *Rules of the Game* and *Grand Illusion*? Elia Kazan? Two — *A Streetcar Named Desire* and *On the Waterfront.* Of course, other filmmakers — Scorsese, Coppola, Stanley Kubrick, Robert Altman et al. — have more, but two seems to be the minimum, even though there are exceptions, like Sam Peckinpah, with one — *The Wild Bunch.* In any event, Beatty can claim five as a producer—*Bonnie and Clyde, Shampoo, Heaven Can Wait, Reds,* and *Bugsy*; all those, plus *Splendor in the Grass, McCabe & Mrs. Miller,* and *Bulworth* as an actor; and three as a director: *Heaven Can Wait, Reds,* and *Bulworth.* You can quibble with any one of these, but all together, it's a full house.

But Beatty is not only one of the foremost filmmakers of his generation; there are other things that make him appealing as the subject of a book. He was a people collector, knew absolutely everyone, both in Hollywood and out. He is a star in the grand tradition of Clark Gable and Cary Grant, and one of the last living bridges between the Old Hollywood studio system and the New Hollywood of the 1970s. He knew moguls like Jack Warner, Sam Goldwyn, and Darryl Zanuck; agents, like Charlie Feldman, Abe Lastfogel, Stan Kamen, and Lew Wasserman. He started out with Elia Kazan, worked with Robert Rossen, and was friendly with Kubrick, Renoir, George Stevens, and William Wyler. He knew all the actors, the giants of that and bygone eras: Charlie Chaplin, Gary Cooper, Cary Grant, and of course Marlon Brando. And then his own generation: actors like Hoffman, Jack Nicholson, and Jane Fonda; executives like Bob Evans, John Calley, and David Geffen. And he knew all the political figures, from the old lefties—both friendly witnesses like Clifford Odets and Budd Schulberg, and unfriendly witnesses like Lillian Hellman—to Jack and Bobby Kennedy, Hubert Humphrey, and Ronald Reagan, as well as sundry foreign leaders.

Moreover, I was interested in the intersection between politics and popular culture, and Beatty virtually defined it. He had always been passionate about politics and had been active in George McGovern's presidential campaign in 1972, and both of Gary Hart's runs at the presidency, in 1983, and again in 1987, until Hart withdrew under a cloud of scandal. And Beatty is a great storyteller, can hold you spellbound for hours, or else have you on the floor laughing.

And then there were the women. He had courted Natalie Wood, Leslie Caron, Julie Christie, and Diane Keaton, to name a few—a very few. As much as Hugh Hefner, he was the embodiment of the sexual revolution of the 1960s, and as such he was, for many men, the single most persuasive argument against marriage and family, two pillars of American ideology. Despite his slash-and-burn love life, women adored him. And no wonder; he loved them in return. Of course he preferred intelligence, good looks, and a hot body, but in a pinch, for a casual encounter, almost any female in the known world would do—blondes or brunettes, long hair or short, thin or fat, young or old, shiksas or JAPs, good skin or bad, white or black and every shade in between. He liked full-breasted, voluptuous women with dramatic curves, as well as small-breasted women with bodies like boys. He scoured lingerie ads in *Vogue,* checked out bathing beauties selling sunblock on billboards, headshots from casting directors, and 8 by 10s from modeling agencies. This may be somewhat of an exaggeration, but not by much. He could always find at least one characteristic to admire—the slant of a cheekbone, the golden flecks in the iris of an eye, the highlights on a head of hair, and so on. He used to say, "Women are like a jar of olives. You can eat one, close it up, or you can eat them all."

OVER THE years, I repeated my request, but he never showed much interest, generally saying he planned to write his own book, which seemed right—why would he, a self-confessed control freak, turn over something as important as his own story, his legacy, to someone else? As the years passed, I wrote lengthy pieces about him several times, for *Premiere* and *Vanity Fair,* but I also went on to other books, and forgot about writing a Beatty biography. Besides, his career was waning, he was making fewer and fewer movies, and a lot of those were flops.

Then one day, around the year 2000, while I was working on *Down and Dirty Pictures,* a book about Miramax, Sundance, and the indie filmmakers of the 1990s, the phone rang. It was Warren. He said, "You know that book about me that you always wanted to write? Maybe now would be the time." I perked up. But after having made the initial contact, he then turned skeptical, and I found myself in the position of having to convince him. (This I would learn was a ploy he had put to good use in his negotiations with studios.) Initially his position was that he wasn't going to cooperate. He is suspicious and mistrustful, and had a million reasons why he shouldn't. He didn't want it to seem like it was a vanity book, written by a friendly journalist. I said, "Neither do I." But I had never wanted to do a book without his cooperation, because I wanted his voice in the book. None of the many articles and books about him had captured it, his sense of humor, his intelligence. I pointed out that I'd have a hard time getting a contract without his cooperation. But he retorted that people who agree to cooperate with books about themselves always regret it. Tom King's biography of David Geffen, a good friend of Beatty's, had recently been published, and no good had come of that from Geffen's point of view. Could I come up with a list of five biographies wherein the subjects cooperated that did not turn out to be hatchet jobs? I dutifully compiled such a list, which included the adoring William Shawcross book about Rupert Murdoch, a biography of George Soros, and I forget what else. We talked and talked, and talked some more. Time passed. These conversations often returned to the same subjects and rehashed them. At one point, months later, he again asked me for a list of five biographies where the subjects cooperated and were glad they did. Politics, his friend Pat Caddell once said in another context, "is a game where the winner doesn't get to take his chips home. You come back the next day and they're back on the table." That is a good description of how Beatty works. You'll argue and argue and argue, and you'll leave at the end of the day thinking the issue has been settled. Then you will return the next morning and you'll be back at square one, because he's raising the same points all over again, the ones you thought had been disposed of the day before. He is so slow to act that he makes Hamlet look rash.

I had forgotten the original list by that time and came up with another. We went over each book. I was fully aware of his reputation for procrastinating and for leading people along—writers, directors, producers—who wanted him to star in their projects, or filmmakers who wanted to do documentaries about him (he had just led actress Lee Grant, who had appeared in *Shampoo,* on one such merry chase)— and then backing out, leaving them high and dry. Finally he agreed to cooperate. He said, although not in so many words, that he wanted his children to be able to read something that gave him his due as a filmmaker.

On one occasion, I was sitting with him in an Italian restaurant in Beverly Glen, the Beverly Hills mini mall in which his office is located, delivering a speech I had prepared on a potentially sensitive issue, to the effect that although I was grateful for his cooperation, I couldn't give him access to the text, or allow him to tell me whom I could talk to and whom I couldn't. Gradually I noticed he was staring at a young woman at the next table. I said, "Warren, did you hear anything I said?"

"Sort of."

"Sort of?"

"I have the feeling she's very smart. And she's sad . . ."

When I managed to get his attention, I told him I would have to write about his romantic exploits, which were too notorious to ignore. Readers would expect it. He said that that was okay with him; it was like another lifetime, distant, behind him. So, on that basis, I convinced my publisher to give me a contract, and began the book.

THAT, AS it turned out, was the easy part. I went out to L.A. from New York, where I live, to begin the interview process. We sat down a few times, but he was clearly uncomfortable, watchful about what he said, dispensing his responses one grain at a time, telling me nothing I didn't already know. Finally, at lunch one day, he told me that the only reason he had agreed to do the book was because he thought that once word of my book spread, the other writers with books in progress, specifically Ellis Amburn and Suzanne Finstad, would just go away, which of course was ridiculous. In other words he was just using me to scare other writers off; I was no more than a pawn on his chessboard. I was so shocked I thought I had misheard him, especially since he didn't seem particularly apologetic or in any way acknowledged that he had manipulated me. My next thought was, I don't know why I'm so surprised. I had been hearing about this kind of behavior for years. Buck Henry always called him the "master manipulator." Wasn't I paying attention? Did I think I was special, that it couldn't or wouldn't happen to me? Then he told me he was too busy to do any interviewing with me at the moment, but not to take it personally. Maybe some other time. And so began several years of cat-and-mousing. I realized that this book would fall under the category of Be careful what you wish for.

Every book presents its own peculiar problems, and this one was no different, which brings us to the "illness" thing. This was not an easy book for me to research and write. It was difficult emotionally to return to a period I had already written about, not to mention the fact that some of the principals were very unhappy about the way they were portrayed in *Easy Riders, Raging Bulls*, and refused to cooperate, like Robert Towne. Lots of people who knew Beatty well, like Dick Sylbert, had died. Among the living, Beatty inspires such a potent mixture of respect, devotion, and lest we forget, fear, that his closest friends and even mere acquaintances feel obligated to honor the same constraints that govern him. He still maintains relationships of one sort or another with most of his former girlfriends, like Leslie Caron, who are all afflicted with a contagion of silence. Ditto his sister, Shirley MacLaine, ditto his good friend Jack Nicholson. Invariably courteous, Beatty himself was on and off, depending on which side of the bed he got up on in the morning.

While I was working on the book, I always had certain guidelines in my head. I decided that anything of a personal nature that occurred after he and Annette Bening married was off limits, because I didn't want to be in the position of writing anything that might embarrass them or their four children. Prior to that seismic event, on the other hand, anything goes. I agreed that when anyone said anything terrible about him—of a serious, as opposed to a trivial, nature—I would allow him to respond, which I thought was only fair. But Beatty has a way of turning things—even of a generous nature—against you. So when I went to him with some not so nice things someone had said about him and asked him to respond, he accused me of trying to draw him into controversy and refused. Or responded, off the record. With Beatty, you often find yourself damned if you do and damned if you don't.

Still, when reading the remarks of his detractors, it is always well to handicap them, that is, to remain mindful of the envy factor. To paraphrase producer Art Linson, who once sued Beatty, "How can you not hate a guy who's better looking than you are, smarter, and richer? Everything I say is from envy." His reputation precedes him: people rarely come at him without an attitude, preconceived and often negative, if for no other reason than he has been indecently fortunate in the gene department, which is the reason he has fine-tuned his skills at self-deprecation. He has a lot to deprecate.

Once I embarked on the book, I realized that trying to "explain" Beatty would be futile. It is all too easy to connect the dots between his childhood in Virginia and his behavior as an adult, especially since the tropes that have characterized his behavior throughout most of his life are not all that mysterious and manifested themselves early on: womanizing, ambition, compulsion, and indecision. But for me, such psychologizing holds little interest. It's too reductive, and in the end, what does it tell us? He's compelling because of the life he has lived—the films he has made, the people he has known, the tumultuous events that engaged him throughout the course of his long career—but not particularly for how he got there. He wasn't born poor, he didn't struggle against adversity, or at least not more than most actors do.

He wasn't self-invented, didn't have to translate himself from one culture to another, didn't have to overcome a drug habit or other vice or trauma. From the beginning, he put the gifts with which he was blessed to good use. Besides, he has jealously guarded the details of his family life growing up; the little we know about his childhood comes from his sister, who has her own axes to grind. I just wasn't interested in his difficult father and sainted mother, let alone his grandparents and forebears—even though I've tried.

Moreover, Freudianism, the most popular scaffolding available to biographers to make sense of their subjects, has been reduced to cliché by nearly a century of use and misuse. True, Freudian formulations—the Oedipus Complex, penis envy, castration anxiety, narcissism, etc.—played a prominent role in many of Beatty's films, especially in the early years, when the cultural sway of Freud was still pronounced. He himself spent several years in psychotherapy, as did many of those who influenced him, including Kazan and playwright William Inge. I even dipped, almost at random, into a couple of psychiatric texts on sexual obsession and addiction, supplied by a couple of friendly analysts, but they shed little new light on his family drama. Freud is important to Beatty's work, but not so useful as a lens with which to view his life.

In this book, then, I have satisfied myself with describing Beatty. "Explaining" him is beyond my modest powers. Life is too short, a phrase that often springs to mind in relation to the art or science of Warrenology. On the other hand, he has lived one of the exceptional twentieth-century lives, filled with a wealth of experience that should be sufficient to satisfy the most jaded reader, not to mention the extraordinary body of work with which he has enriched the cinema.

1

A STAR IS BORN

―――――

How Warren Beatty shined in *Splendor in the Grass,* but watched his star plunge when he followed it with two flops in a row, and became better known for his romances than his performances, seducing and abandoning Joan Collins and Natalie Wood.

―――――

"He was insatiable. Three, four, five times a day, every day, was not unusual for him. I felt like an oyster in a slot machine."

—*Joan Collins*

ON A HOT summer night, in 1959, Warren Beatty and Jane Fonda were having dinner at La Scala, on Little Santa Monica in Beverly Hills, when Beatty spied Joan Collins at a nearby table. Collins, a striking brunette, was a younger, svelter, later-model Elizabeth Taylor, with a British accent to boot. She had been dubbed "the British Open," for her parade of well-heeled boyfriends. But Collins was no bimbo—she had a biting wit, which she would occasionally exercise at Beatty's expense, as she would prove nineteen years later in her autobiography, *Past Imperfect.* Then twenty-six, she was four years his senior, and had been in Hollywood for five years, having appeared in a number of low-rent pictures, including *Land of the Pharaohs,* a sword and sandal epic wherein she lay recumbent while cradling a diamond (paste, of course) in her navel. At the time, she was training with

Candy Barr to play a stripper in *Seven Thieves*, and hoping to wrest the lead in *Cleopatra* away from Taylor.

As Collins tells it, she was brooding about her lengthy and increasingly unhappy affair with a handsome producer, George Englund, then married to Cloris Leachman, and forking cannelloni into her mouth (she was always a big eater and had to fight her weight), when she noticed the indecently pretty young man boldly eyeing her from a nearby table. He was twenty-two at the time, but he looked like he was barely old enough to drive.

Although he was precocious—dating senior girls when he was a freshman at Washington and Lee High School in Arlington, Virginia— sexually speaking, Beatty was a late bloomer. Born in Richmond, the "Cradle of the Confederacy," and raised a Baptist among Baptists, he had been a virgin until he was 19 and ten months, and had had only one or two relationships he considered "serious." Since he dropped out of Northwestern University in 1956, he hadn't had any. But he had discovered in himself a raging lust for women. He realized, too, that women were drawn to him. It was as if he heard them calling out to him where other men were deaf, the way canines respond to whistles inaudible to humans. Says writer Peter Feibleman, who would help polish some of his scripts in coming years, "Hollywood was candy land for him. I once asked him, 'Why is it that every time I put my weenie in something, yours has already been there?' He just had a tremendous appetite." A few years off, when his career was prospering and his horizons broader, no female would be beneath his notice—stars, starlets, and models, of course, but also TV newscasters, studio executives, journalists, hatcheck girls, waitresses, dental hygienists, even daughters of friends—any woman, in other words, who crossed his path, and many who didn't, the innocent bystanders grazing the stacks in a library, stopped at a traffic light in the next car, pulling bread off a shelf in a supermarket, or sitting, like Collins, at a nearby table. As Clint Eastwood is reputed to have said, "No matter how hot a girl is, there's always someone who's tired of fucking her," and that person always seemed to be named Warren on-to-the-next Beatty.

What accounted for this passion, outside of motive, means, and opportunity, is hard to say. To hear him tell it, his juvenile immersion in a sea of estrogen was formative. "My childhood was very strongly and very positively affected by women," he said. "My mother, my sister, my aunts, my great-aunts, cousins, all of whom were women—and I was fortunately not smothered by them." Indeed, with Beatty, it wasn't just lust. He had a romantic streak; he wanted to make a connection, wanted to fall in love. Collins was ground zero, as it were, for his seduction of the whole town, the women, of course, but the men as well, figuratively speaking. No shrinking violet herself, she returned his gaze with equal boldness. He raised a glass and smiled. Her dinner partner remarked, "That boy who's looking at you is Shirley MacLaine's brother, Warren something or other." She took a second look. He was wearing a blue Brooks Brothers shirt and a tweed jacket. She was struck by his clean-cut, Clark Kent good looks, Kirk Douglas dimple, and sensual mouth, which would be remarked upon shortly by no less an authority than Kenneth Tynan. There was nothing wrong with that picture but the "spots" (British for acne) that marred his face, and Fonda, his date, who was giving him her full attention.

Beatty had met Fonda earlier that year in February, when director Joshua Logan had asked him to test with her and a few other actors in New York for *Parrish*, a tortured teen picture set on a tobacco planta-tion in Connecticut. "I really thought I was hot shit and I had in fact turned down a couple of movies," says Beatty. "I was broke of course. But I thought, I really don't want to do something until I do something that's good." Working for Logan would have been an excellent start. A giant of the theater, Logan had won a Pulitzer Prize for co-writing *South Pacific*, and directed a number of hit plays.

The director had wanted Beatty to smother Fonda with passionate kisses, but the young actor merely pecked discreetly at her cheek. "I thought he was gay," Fonda recalled. "He was so cute, and all his men friends were gay, and brilliant. And he liked to play piano in a piano bar—I mean, what were the odds he was straight? Shows you how dumb I was." Underwhelmed by Beatty's tepid approach, Logan said, "Look, are you afraid of Jane or something? Grab her, boy, grab her. Don't be shy." Beatty leapt upon Fonda, kissing her with such ferocity that Logan had to yell, "Cut! Stop! Hey, Warren, we're all out of film. That's enough!" Recalls the actor, "Oh my God. We kissed until we had practically eaten each other's heads off." Later, Beatty would report-edly say that she gave the best blow job in L.A., due to her ability to virtually unhinge her lower jaw, like a python that swallows prey much larger than itself. Coming from him, for whom blow jobs were routine as breathing, this was high praise indeed.

Collins next ran into Beatty at a Saturday night party given by Tyrone Power's widow in the flats of Beverly Hills. He was playing the piano, doing impressions of Erroll Garner, George Shearing, Oscar Peterson, catnip to women, who gathered around to watch him finger the ivories. They exchanged smiles, but he appeared engrossed in the music, and she went home.

The following day, Collins went to the beach to work on her tan, knowing she would have ample opportunity to show it off later when she zipped herself into a too small black faille dress for a party that evening. Her date was Gardner McKay, the six-foot-four heartthrob starring in TV's *Adventures in Paradise,* who, in the considered opinion of *Life* magazine, was the handsomest man in America. She arrived home to find six messages from Beatty, instructing her to call him at the Chateau Marmont, where he was staying. When Beatty went after a woman, "nothing would stop him," as production designer Dick Sylbert, who would become a colleague and close friend, put it. Before she had a chance to oblige, the phone rang. A boyish voice said, "Hi, did you get my messages?" She was impressed by the fact that although they hadn't spoken so much as one word to each other, he had found her phone number and was so self-assured that he didn't bother to identify himself. He invited her to dinner that night. She accepted, which meant blowing off McKay. Beatty instructed her to meet him at a place on Rodeo Drive in Beverly Hills at eight, adding, "I can hardly wait."

After the party, Collins rushed back to her Shoreham Drive home, wriggled out of her dress into jeans and a shirt. She knew Beatty was a few years her junior, so she removed some of her makeup, hopped into her rented yellow Ford—he was driving a rented Chevy—and met him at the Casa Escobar for Mexican food and margaritas. She was pleased that he was an Aries, a sign compatible with her Gemini. He was pleased that she was—Joan Collins. They admired each other till well past midnight. He drove her to her car, said he would follow her home to make sure she arrived safely. As she entered her parking garage, with him right behind her, she weighed the pros and cons of asking him up for a nightcap. He got out of his car, and short-circuited her should-I-or-shouldn't-I? interior dialogue by saying, "I'm coming up for coffee."

This was the beginning of an intense, nearly year-and-a-half affair, during which he took over her life, evincing a need for control that would characterize his behavior in future relationships. He urged her to stop smoking and take vitamins as he did. He called her repeatedly, at her count eighteen times a day. And it wasn't just her. He lived on the phone, making two, three dozen calls between the time his eyes opened in the morning and the time he closed them at night. He had remarkably good recall and committed many of his most frequently dialed numbers to memory after hearing or seeing them just once. (Ten years after they would break up, she ran into him at a party, and he still remembered her number on Shoreham Drive.)

Once Beatty and Collins connected, they were always together. He haunted the set where she was shooting *Seven Thieves*. The love-struck couple whiled away the time languishing on the beach. He wrapped himself around her, licked the salt off her lips, her fingers, wherever, as the breakers gently lapped the sand. In the evenings, they went to restaurants, clubs, and piano bars, exchanged fond glances, held hands, kissed, and canoodled. He made love to Collins relentlessly, although every now and then he would accept calls while he was inside her. Unlike Jack Nicholson, with whom he would become fast friends, he was not subject to premature ejaculation, but on the contrary would become famous for his staying power, his ability to go on and on and on, giving his partner multiple orgasms before coming himself. But for Collins, it was too much of a good thing. One Sunday morning, exhausted, she stumbled out of bed. Dragging on a forbidden cigarette, she said, "I don't think I can last much longer. He never stops—it must be all those vitamins he takes. . . . In a few years I'll be worn out." Later, a skeptic asked her if they really had sex seven times a day. She replied, "Maybe he did, but I just lay there."

Some of her friends found their relationship strange and unhealthy. He was too callow, they said, unknown and impecunious, using her to kick-start his career. But she was deaf to their doubts, impervious to their warnings. As a teenager, Beatty had been struck with George Stevens's *A Place in the Sun* (1951), with its story about a handsome but penniless young man on the make who sees his pot of gold within reach when he secures the love of a beautiful heiress, but who has to get rid of his pregnant and very inconvenient lower-class girlfriend. One can only speculate about the significance this story had for him in the context of his romance with Collins, who was way above him on the ladder to the stars. "Warren was 21 [sic] when I met him," she observed. "He was just *desperate* to become famous."

True, Beatty was struggling, but his career had been showing signs of life. His agents at MCA, Music Corporation of America, toiling on his behalf, had succeeded in securing him a five-year nonexclusive contract at $400/week from MGM on the basis of his screen test with Fonda. "When I got out here you know. I didn't have any money," Beatty recalls. "Suddenly I was under contract to MGM. That was just tremendous. I rented a little one-bedroom house near Coldwater Canyon. I had a car, a convertible. There was an orange grove beside the house which I thought was amazing, to see oranges growing on trees. There was nothing to do at the studio. Nobody complained that I was picking up this check." He had been nearly incapacitated with a bad case of hepatitis—he lost thirty-five pounds—but thanks to a doctor who had put him on a nutritious diet and discouraged him from drinking, he had steadily improved. Not that he was inclined to drink anyway, having grown up with a father who had an alcohol problem. As MacLaine described their father, "He'd come home drunk, set something on fire, leave again until the wee hours, then return and sleep til noon."

The hepatitis scare, along with nascent hypochondria exacerbated by a wannabe actor's vanity, left him with what would become a life-long fascination with things medical. He even became a surprisingly good amateur diagnostician. "Can Warren talk medicine?" asks Dick Sylbert, rhetorically. "He can go on about cholesterol numbers the way racing drivers talk tread thicknesses. Obsessed. The amount of attention that these stars demand is extraordinary. Warren once had a little rash. He went nuts. He's so careful, he's got no dirt on him, no antibodies. He gets a cold, he's knocked down, goes out. Like a baby, for weeks."

Collins was still entangled with Englund, who was in Hong Kong with Marlon Brando, prepping *The Ugly American*. When he returned, he tried to reclaim her. She reluctantly agreed to meet him at the Cock and Bull, a faux-British pub on Sunset Strip. Beatty peevishly asked her how long it would take her to send him on his way. Trying to assuage his anxiety, she said she imagined no more than an hour. Nervously scribbling shapes on a scrap of paper, he sourly imagined she would decide it was Englund she loved, not him. Enfolding him in a warm embrace, she reassured Beatty, but he was already on the phone before she was out the door. Englund pressed her to dump him. He echoed her friends, reminded her that for all his self-assurance, Beatty was barely out of short pants, while she was a woman of the world, a movie star, for Christ's sakes! She wavered, thought, Warren is pushy, awkward. Englund reminded her that he was divorcing his wife for her, and gave her a week to make up her mind. After one hour had turned into three, she jumped up from the table and left. He followed her to her car and kissed her with some passion.

Minutes after Collins got back to her apartment, Beatty arrived, furious, by her account. Apparently he had been circling the restaurant in his car while she was with Englund, frantic with jealousy. Pulling off his glasses and tossing them on the sofa, he shouted, "I saw you, necking in the parking lot."

"We weren't. He kissed me goodbye, that's all."

"Oh, sure."

He tried to intimidate her, but sans glasses, he was so nearsighted as to be almost blind, and fell over a stool. They abused each other through the wee hours, shouting hurtful things. But the next day, following a session with her psychiatrist, she chose Beatty. They celebrated at La Scala with MacLaine.

BEATTY HAD arrived in New York City in 1956, when he was nineteen, after leaving Northwestern, where he was enrolled in the Speech and Drama Department. His big sister had made the same journey four years earlier, when she was eighteen. "I remember the morning I left home," she wrote. "Warren had skipped football practice. He sat down at the piano to beat the hell out of it. . . . He was tall and handsome by now and didn't need me any more to finish his battles. I wondered when I'd see him again. I wondered when he'd decide what he would do with his life. I didn't know then (because he was as shy about his inside self as all of us) that every afternoon . . . Warren was in the basement acting out his soul to every Al Jolson record ever made, and memorizing in detail every play Eugene O'Neill ever wrote." She continued, "Warren and I might have believed we were not from a show-business family, but . . . because we both lived out the unfulfilled fantasies of our parents, I think we had a greater inspirational motivation than the Barrymores or the Redgraves."

Beatty found a $13 a week apartment on West 68th Street, previously occupied by a junkie. He lived on peanut butter and jelly sandwiches, worked at odd jobs, including dishwasher, bricklayer's assistant, construction worker, sandhog (in the Lincoln Tunnel), and piano player at Claven's on W. 52nd Street. He even had something of a singing voice. When the hepatitis hit, he lay in bed for weeks. It was a dark time; he feared he would never get better, never work as an actor again.

One day, as Beatty recalls, "A friend of mine asked me if I would audition with him in a scene for CBS. Which I did. And I was offered a job on one of the dramatic religious shows they used to have on Sunday mornings. I did that. And then agents started to see me and offer me things and I began to work."

This led to that, as it has a way of doing. "I needed money, and I wasn't that good a piano player and I was not what you'd call the world's outstanding sandhog," he recalled. "It began to occur to me that I could make money acting and that I could find in the theater a tool for expressing myself." He worked his way through shows like *Studio One, Playhouse 90*, and the *Kraft Theatre*. He did summer stock. In the course of his education, he began to recognize the names that were on everybody's lips—Marlon Brando, James Dean, Montgomery Clift, who starred in *A Place in the Sun*. He heard that they mumbled, so he mumbled.

Beatty had done some TV show and was eagerly awaiting some response from his friends. In his words, "There was an ancient and very beautiful actress of twenty-six with whom I had become, let's say, friendly. I mean very friendly. She was in California, she called, and said, 'Hi.'

" 'Hi.' I waited.

" 'Well, you really looked terrific.'

"I said, 'What does that mean?'

" 'You're gonna be a big movie star.'

" 'Yeah, you thought I was good?'

" 'You just looked wonderful.'

" 'But what'd you think of my work?'

" 'Well, I had a little trouble understanding some of what you said. But you looked so good.'

" 'What do you mean you had trouble understanding what—'

" 'Let's not get into that. The thing is, this can all open up for you—'

" 'Just tell me, what do you mean, you had trouble understanding what I said?'

" 'I don't think that's productive.'

" 'What percentage couldn't you understand?'

" 'What percentage? Don't be ridiculous.'

" 'Just give me an idea.'

" 'Don't get me into this, because, you know, it's not fair.'

" 'How much, like 10 percent?'

" 'No.'

" 'What, 20 percent?'

" 'Don't do this. Take it from me, you looked terrific, and that's what's gonna be important for you.'

" 'What, 30 percent?'

" 'Don't do this!'

" 'So what are you saying, you lost half of what I said?'

" 'If you don't stop . . .'

" 'I'm not gonna stop.'

" 'Okay, 90, 95 percent.'

" 'You missed 90 to 95 percent of what I said?'

" 'Yes.'

" 'That's not possible.'

" 'Did I tell you there was no point in saying this?'

" 'Oh my God . . . ' "

Eventually, Beatty decided he might benefit from some formal instruction. He recalls, "A friend of mine saw me walking up Eighth Avenue one day in 1957, and said, 'Where'ya going?'

" 'I'm going to such and such an acting school.'

" 'You can't go there.'

" 'Why not?'

" 'There's only one person for you to study with. Stella Adler.'

" 'Who's Stella Adler?' "

Beatty enrolled in her class. "She was an amazing, flamboyant figure," he continues. "I came to the first day, and Harold Clurman, who used to be married to her, stood up and gave the opening speech, a sort of call to arms. It was mesmerizing. There was a seriousness of approach to the study of acting that came out of a resentment with the superficiality of the commercial theater of the 1920s and the early 1930s, as well as the influence of the revolution in Russia, of Chekhov, and Stanislavsky and the Moscow Art Theater, that worked its way into the Group Theatre, which Clurman presided over. And out of that came Stella and Lee Strasberg and Sandy Meisner. Stella used to tell a story about when she and Harold would be wrestling around in bed at night. She would punch him and say, 'Harold, don't sleep like a great man. Just sleep.' "

Despite his admiration for the politics and passion that drove the Group Theatre and its heirs, Beatty didn't last long with Adler, with whom he got off to a bad start. Adler, apparently convinced that he was getting by on his looks alone, took a dim view of him. One day, he was a few minutes late to class. When he walked in, she announced, grandly, "Here comes Mr. Broadway." He was embarrassed, did some shit-kicking, hemming and hawing, but she had an attitude toward him that she never got over and he never understood. He directed Rita Gam in a scene from *A Hatful of Rain.* When they presented it, Adler, in Gam's words, "criticized Warren for being mannered and uncommitted." Beatty lasted about eight months. He never went back, although he always speaks about Adler with admiration.

Logan had first glimpsed Beatty on stage at the North Jersey Playhouse in Fort Lee in December 1958, when the actor was playing Richard Loeb in *Compulsion.* The audience was packed with agents and casting directors trolling off-off-off Broadway regional theaters for the next big thing. A young Mart Crowley was assistant to the director. (He later went on to write *Boys in the Band.*) Crowley recalls, "Warren always wanted to discuss and discuss and discuss his part. And he didn't like people calling him 'Beetie.'" He was fond of saying that his name rhymed with "weighty," not "Wheaties." Even then, when he changed the spelling of the family name from "Beaty" to "Beatty," he revealed the caution that would govern his behavior throughout his life, as well as his taste for endless toying, tinkering, tweaking. Unlike his sister, who got rid of her father's surname entirely, exchanging it for her mother's, he merely fiddled with it.

Compulsion ran for two weeks. Beatty got good notices. Logan was close to William Inge. Inge, along with Tennessee Williams and Arthur Miller, was among the big three American playwrights in the 1950s. He had had four Broadway hits in a row: *Come Back, Little Sheba* (1950), *Picnic* (1953), *Bus Stop* (1955), *The Dark at the Top of the Stairs* (1957). He had a thriving Hollywood career as well; all of these plays had become wildly successful movies.

Inge, a nondescript middle-aged Midwesterner with thinning hair who looked like a dry goods salesman, was gay. Even more than his friend, he was captivated by Beatty. "Inge was in love with Warren Beatty on sight," Logan observed. "Warren's career was assured. 'I absolutely must have him,' Bill said." Wags used to refer to Inge as Beatty's "fairy godfather." Inge was looking for an actor to play the lead in a script he was writing for director Elia Kazan called *Splendor in the Grass,* and decided that the young man would be just the thing.

Inge invited Beatty to his home at 45 Sutton Place South, in Manhattan. The actor had just gotten out of a sickbed, down with food poisoning. When he finally made it to Inge's apartment, he introduced himself as MacLaine's brother, an indication of the state of his nerves, since he was determined to make his own way, not ride on his sister's coattails. Inge told Beatty that he would try to get him the lead in *Splendor,* and in his new play as well, *A Loss of Roses.* From the actor's point of view, there was no smarter career move than to attach himself to a writer like Inge, on the one hand, and hot directors like Logan and Kazan, on the other.

Beatty was most likely aware of his effect on Inge, and would exploit it, but it is doubtful that they had an intimate relationship. Says photographer Michael Childers, who was director John Schlesinger's partner and later shot stills on several Beatty productions, "How smart of Warren to become a little coquette in order to ingratiate himself with Inge and Logan. Of course they were in love with him. I think Warren was smart enough to play it for all it was worth. Why not, if it was gonna get him a better part, or make his life easier. No sex was involved."

Inge introduced Beatty to Kazan, who was favorably impressed. "I liked Warren right off," he said, adding, "Warren had never been in anything before. He had been a high school football player, uncertain but charming." Later, he wrote, Warren "wanted it all and wanted it his way. Why not? He had the energy, a very keen intelligence, and more chutzpah than any Jew I've ever known. Even more than me. Bright as they come, intrepid, and with that thing all women secretly respect: complete confidence in his sexual powers, confidence so great that he never had to advertise himself, even by hints."

Beatty arrived on the scene at an opportune moment. Rarely had the movie business been afflicted by such a scarcity of young leading men. The older generation of actors, men like Spencer Tracy, Gary Cooper, Kirk Douglas, and Burt Lancaster, was headed for the Motion Picture Home. James Dean had been famously killed in his Porsche Spyder in 1955, while Montgomery Clift was more or less sidelined with a disfiguring car accident of his own the following year. Marlon Brando was thirteen years older than Beatty and had already begun his descent into an auto-de-fé of self-parody. Paul Newman was twelve years older, and Steve McQueen, seven.

The late 1950s produced a sorry crop of new faces, the likes of Tab Hunter, Troy Donahue, and R. J. Wagner, as well as a slew of good-looking actors who failed to break out, like Michael Parks, John Philip Law, Richard Beymer, and Brad Dillman, but only Tony Perkins, five years older than Beatty, had any real talent, and he was a niche actor, insufficiently masculine to play romantic leads. Dennis Hopper was too crazy to make it until much later, when he settled for being a character actor. Even Robert Redford was buried in the pack, his star lagging Beatty's by nearly a decade. Clint Eastwood was struggling in B-movies, hoping someone would notice him. Rock Hudson was wooing Doris Day. Sean Connery, also behind Beatty, would become trapped in James Bond hell. "There was this period between 1960 and 1967, where I don't think there were any young actors that were bankable," says Beatty. "I didn't have a lot of company."

Kazan was looking for new faces. He liked to work with young actors, because they were hungry and full of enthusiasm. "They say that fighters come to fight. These guys—Dean, Brando, Beatty—they came to act. You couldn't stop them," he observed. Kazan appeared ready to give him the lead in *Splendor.*

Inge summoned Beatty to his apartment once again, this time to read for the lead in *A Loss of Roses.* It was set in a small Midwestern town in 1933. Beatty would play a young man, Kenneth Baird, deeply attached to his mother, but distracted enough by her old friend, an aging actress, to have an affair with her. Eventually, he leaves both behind for a life of his own. Inge thought Beatty was perfect for the role of Kenny, whom he described in a letter as someone who so luxuriates in his masculinity it was as if "he feels a wreath has been hung on his penis." Inge wanted Kazan to direct, but he begged off, and the playwright was obliged to put *Roses* on hold. Meanwhile, Logan failed to get Clark Gable and Vivien Leigh for *Parrish,* and dropped out, leaving Beatty high and dry. (Logan later made the film with Troy Donahue in the role slated for Beatty, while Claudette Colbert and Karl Malden played the parents.)

Beatty returned to L.A. in a fruitless attempt to snag a part in a *Playhouse 90* production. But his luck changed when he secured a recurring role in a hit TV series, *The Many Loves of Dobie Gillis,* with production set to begin in L.A. in mid-May 1959. But outside of his sporadic appearances on *Dobie Gillis,* Beatty had precious little to show for himself but promised parts that might—but more often might not—materialize. MGM, meanwhile, was offering him parts he didn't want, and withholding the ones he did want, arguing, with some reason, that he lacked experience. He was growing increasingly unhappy as a contract player.

Then *A Loss of Roses* came back to life with Daniel Mann directing. (Mann had directed the movie version of the playwright's *Come Back, Little Sheba* [1952], with Shirley Booth, as well as Shirley MacLaine in *Hot Spell* [1958].) Inge pressed Mann to let Beatty read, and in September, after five weeks of indecision during which the actor fretted, Mann gave him the part in what would be his first Broadway play.

Beatty was thrilled. "I thought, I gotta go do the play because I'm not doing anything that means anything," he recalls. "I felt that I was turning into a very large piece of citrus fruit. I knew I had to get out of the deal with MGM." The studio responded, "You can't do a play." He said, "I said, 'I can, too,' so I went back and did it." He borrowed $2,600 from Lew Wasserman to buy himself out of the contract.

Roses was due to open out of town at the National in D.C., where as a sixteen-year-old teenager Beatty was employed in the summer of 1953 to chase rats from the alley behind the theater. When he arrived in New York in late September to begin rehearsals, he found a profoundly troubled production. Shirley Booth, who was playing Kenny's mother, didn't think her part was big enough; Carol Haney, playing the actress whom Kenny seduces, didn't like Booth, who in turn was disdainful of Haney for being a dancer, not an actress, while neither they nor anybody much liked Beatty, who was a novice, and struck them as tentative and unsure of himself. Booth resented the attention the director lavished on the young actor, who peppered Mann with questions about his motivation. For his part, Mann regarded Beatty as a loose cannon, who might say or do anything when he got on stage. "Warren won't listen to me," he complained. "He's going to do nothing until opening night and then he'll play on the sex appeal and charm and all the crap and do something on stage we won't even *know* about." Mann apparently contemplated replacing Beatty and told his understudy to get ready. But Inge protected his protégé. He told Mann that although the actor was insecure and undisciplined, he'd be great when the curtain rose.

After Joan Collins finished up the instantly forgettable *Seven Thieves* in October, she took the red-eye to Washington, where *A Loss of Roses* opened on October 29, 1959. Beatty's notices were good, although the play itself got no better than mixed reviews. Beatty meanwhile introduced Collins to his parents, Ira and Kathlyn, who were living in Arlington, across the Potomac River. She was slated to do *Sons and Lovers* in England. According to her, Beatty not only thought the story was tacky, he wanted her close by. "Warren kept me selfishly with him," she said, bitterly. "Warren's number one priority, in those days, and for many years after, was Warren." He was getting a big publicity bonus from his connection to her, and with *A Loss of Roses* less than a sure thing, it was a bad time for her to disappear. "Don't go, Butterfly," she said he "begged. 'Don't leave your Bee.'"

Butterfly heeded his entreaties. Instead of going to London, she went to New York to be with him when the play opened at the Eugene O'Neill on November 28. It was slaughtered by the critics—Inge's first flop—and left a legacy of bitterness in its wake. Rex Reed, in a famously bitchy *Esquire* profile of Beatty published in 1967, quoted an unnamed cast member recalling that on opening night in New York, Beatty "changed lines, business, blocking, and completely screwed up Carol Haney so badly that she ran into her dressing room in tears." Beatty didn't care. He was having fun with Michael J. Pollard, also in the play. They had a short scene together. It "was written to be about two minutes long," Beatty recalled. "We turned it into seven and a half minutes." But Mann cared. He said, "In my forty-year career, I've directed some of our finest actors—Brando, Vanessa Redgrave, Anna

Magnani, Elizabeth Taylor—but I have to say, Warren was one of the few to give me a problem."

Roses marked the beginning of Inge's decline. But despite the caustic reviews, Beatty emerged smelling like, well, a rose. In *The New Yorker,* Tynan famously described him as "sensual around the lips and pensive around the brow." Walter Kerr called him "mercurial, sensitive, excellent," and he was nominated for a Tony. Best of all, perhaps, was that Kazan had caught one of the performances.

Roses closed after twenty-one nights. It would be the last play Beatty would ever do. His burnished reputation aside, it left a bad taste. "There's no more enervating experience in the world than to do a play for more than one performance with actors who don't work well together," he says. "It's torture." He added, "The New York theater's a mess," not worth enduring "just to win the approval of four critics who decide whether you're going to be allowed to keep doing the play. That's a bore." Once again, he set his sights on the movies.

BEATTY AND Collins moved back to L.A. in early 1960, where they lived at the Chateau. Her sister, future sex-and-shopping scribe Jackie, once visited her there in what struck Jackie as her sister's plush movie star suite. She recalled, "I said 'Oh this is lovely, great!' [Joan] snapped, 'Yes, you won't actually be sleeping here. There is a little room at the top of the hotel where you will be sleeping.' I found at night Warren would change places with me. He would sleep in the suite, and I would be in his little attic room. Like everybody else, I got propositioned by Warren. . . . But Warren would proposition a chair if it looked at him sideways."

Beatty and Collins ate at the Aware Inn, a health food restaurant on Sunset near Doheny. Beatty continued to pressure Collins to give up drinking and smoking. He consumed soy burgers, drank carrot juice. Afterward, they walked to Turner's drugstore and looked for pictures of themselves in the fanzines.

Beatty still had his sights set on *Splendor,* which was set up at Warner Brothers. It was the opportunity of a lifetime, especially for a first film. He was determined to work with the best directors (according to Jane Fonda, he'd made a list), and with Kazan he was starting near the top. A former member of the Group Theatre and proponent of the

Method, Kazan was a titan of the stage and screen. He had directed the
work of Williams, Miller, and Inge—as well as the greatest film actors
of his era, including Brando, Clift, and Dean. Along with Miller, Arthur
Penn, Lillian Hellman, Lee and Paula Strasberg, and most members
of New York's theater community, he was a child of the Depression
and man of the left, profoundly influenced by the Communist Party
USA—first as an acolyte, then as an antagonist—which lay wounded
and bleeding from the hammer blows administered by the House Committee on Un-American Activities and its ill-begotten child, the Hollywood blacklist. Kazan had not only testified before HUAC as a
friendly witness, wherein he sacrificed friends and associates on the
altar of patriotism, but he had infuriated them by groveling before
HUAC, and then added insult to injury by placing an ad in *The New
York Times* on April 12, 1952, in which he exhorted others to do the
same. Victor Navasky observed in his book *Naming Names* that "part
of the reason he left the Party was because they wanted him to confess
error and humiliate himself." The irony of it all was lost on no one.
"Kazan was a pariah," director Arthur Penn recalls. "Lillian Hellman
despised him. She frothed at the mouth."

Beatty was aware of this history, which was still very much an open
wound in 1959—the year the blacklist was broken when Otto Preminger hired Dalton Trumbo to write *Exodus* and Kirk Douglas revealed
that Trumbo had written *Spartacus*—but it wasn't his fight, and for an
actor coming up, the advantages of working with Kazan far outweighed
whatever damage might be incurred by flak from the angry but largely
impotent Broadway and Hollywood left.

Splendor told the story of star-crossed lovers from a Kansas oil
town. Bud Stamper, son of a self-made businessman, has little interest
in his father's ambitious plans for his career, and instead merely wishes
to till the soil, a humble farmer. He falls in love with Wilma "Deanie"
Loomis, daughter of the local pharmacist, whose wife is determined
to build a firewall around their daughter's virginity. Although lust
indeed bubbles just below the surface of their relationship, Bud and
Deanie's love burns with a pure blue flame. They wish for nothing
more than a simple happiness that nevertheless seems out of their reach.
It's Romeo and Juliet all over again. Verona becomes a tiny town in
Kansas, while the outsized aspirations of Bud's father and the pinched
Puritanism of Deanie's mother stand in for the Montagues and the

Capulets. The story unfolds on the eve of the Great Depression, so that history joins psychology to batter the characters into submission. Inge's story is inflected by the twin towers of 1950s American culture, Marx and Freud, whose stock always seemed inversely related. As Marxism waned in the chill of Cold War, Freud ascended, and Freudianism provided the lingua franca for the intellectual discourse of that decade.

Deanie's proper upbringing in some respects mirrored that of the Beaty children, as set down by MacLaine in one of her memoirs. To hear her tell it, their parents led lives of quiet desperation. "We were taught to respect all material possessions, because it took long, hard years of work to be able to afford such things. . . . The three Wedgwood bowls and the matching plates and ash trays, the antique Chinese vase, the reproduction of 'Blue Boy' in the gold plated frame always made me think twice before I invited someone to the house. I was afraid something would get knocked over."

Sexual hypocrisy was a subject that would become dear to Beatty's heart, and there was much for him to identify with in the character of Bud, whose 1920s was the actor's 1950s. Beatty always explained the sexual adventurism for which he would become renowned in the 1960s by referring to the famously timid Eisenhower era that preceded it: "I went through exactly the same sexual revolution as the country went through," he said. "In the Fifties when I was a kid, I was walking around in a mode of behavior that related to centuries of Protestant repression. Every cell and fiber around you was influenced by religious upbringings of the past. It was a very puritanical time." But the resemblance to his own story stopped there. There was no 1960s to provide a happy ending for Bud and Deanie.

For Deanie, Inge suggested Natalie Wood to Kazan. Wood was a former child star—she had made her debut at five and struck gold with *Miracle on 34th Street* in 1947—but by the fall of 1958, she was twenty and was having a difficult time making the transition to adult roles. Warners had not done her any favors by forcing her to do a series of lame pictures like *The Girl He Left Behind* and *The Burning Hills*, among others.

Moreover, Wood's private life was in disarray. She was needy and neurotic, with a controlling mother and an alcoholic father, both of whom looked to her to be the breadwinner. Recalls photographer Michael Childers, who got to know Wood well at a later date, "Her mother was the meanest motherfucking woman, this dark shadow in the background, the mother from hell. Natalie was unstable, a wreck by the time she was sixteen." She had married R. J. Wagner in 1957, just after Christmas. The couple quickly became yet another pair of "America's sweethearts" in the fanzines. Wagner too had come up through the contract system, at Fox. But his career had stalled before he achieved stardom. Their spacious home at 714 North Beverly Drive, with its saltwater pool, was heavily mortgaged. Wood was hooked on sleeping pills and uppers. Says Mart Crowley, who would be Kazan's gofer on *Splendor,* and later became Wood's confidant and assistant, "When they were sober they treated each other terrifically, but it was kind of Jekyll and Hyde when they drank. She wanted to go to a psychiatrist, mend the marriage. His family, and particularly his mother, a very la-de-dah lady, was totally against it. There was no craziness in the family, and she didn't want any divorce, either."

The director was dubious. "When Natalie was first suggested to me, I backed off," Kazan said. "I didn't want a 'washed-up child star.' " Nor was his first impression of her favorable. She was wearing ear-to-ear lipstick, a fur coat, and all the trappings of a star. He thought she was exactly what he didn't want, too Hollywood. But Jack Warner told him he could have her cheap because he needed her rehabilitated into an asset, and Kazan was smart enough to see beneath the facade. "When I saw her, I detected behind the well-mannered 'young wife' front a desperate twinkle in her eyes," he continued. "I knew there was an unsatisfied hunger there." He sensed there was a "bad girl" hiding inside the "good girl. . . . I could see that the crisis in her career was preparing her for a crisis in her personal life," he wrote. "Then she told me she was being psychoanalyzed. That did it. Poor R.J., I said to myself."

Wood signed in mid-January 1960, which ratcheted up Beatty's anxiety level. He had dumped MGM and quit *Dobie Gillis* for *Roses,* but nobody in Hollywood cared about his handful of laudatory theater reviews. Kazan was testing other actors, or at least one other actor who had captured his interest, Jody McCrae, son of Joel. But Beatty campaigned vigorously for *Splendor.* Inge also pushed Beatty on Warner, showing him the actor's reviews from *Roses,* while predicting that he was going to be bigger than Dean or Brando.

One day, Kazan told Beatty, according to him, "I saw a screen test of

you. I've got to be very honest with you. I don't know if I want you."
Beatty's stomach turned over.

"Well, what should I do?"

"Do you want to make another screen test?"

"Sure." Beatty tested with Wood at Stage 4 of the Warners lot on
March 3, 1960. He was nervous, but not so nervous that he didn't complain about this and that. When he objected to his lines, Kazan, giving
him a dark look, as if to say, Who's directing this, you or me? merely
grunted "Really," a noncommittal, slightly skeptical response that
Beatty would make his own. He recalls, "I made a suggestion where I
thought his blocking was a little off. I said, 'Why don't I go over here
and I'll play the piano a little bit. Because I play.' He said, 'Really?'
About twenty or thirty minutes after that, Karl Malden came in, and
Kazan said, 'Karl, you take over.' And he left. I thought, This is no good,
I've disappointed him. That night, we were all supposed to have dinner
together at Chasen's. We met at Natalie's house, about seven of us. As
we were leaving, again I thought, He's being distant with me. I guess I
didn't get the movie. Then suddenly, he grabbed me by the lapels and
shoved me up against a wall. He said, 'Look kid, you got the part, okay?
You know that thing where you said to me that that was not a good idea
that I had? That was good. I need that. Keep doing that.' I felt a chill
start at my heel that went up my back to the top of my head, because I
thought, Unless I'm stupid, I'm not going to be poor. I have a shot. And
I can do something with it." He was paid $15,000 for the movie, but no
expenses, which amounted to $19,000. He continues, "So I came out of
that movie broke. But elated, because I knew that it was a good movie."

Beatty's problems weren't over, however. At the beginning of April,
just after he had turned twenty-three, and right before he and Joan
Collins were due to fly to New York so he could begin rehearsals on
Splendor, she realized she was pregnant. "Pregnant?" Beatty exclaimed,
incredulously, she recalled, "in his little boy voice," gulping handfuls of
vitamin E. "How did that happen?"

"The butler did it. Or maybe it's an immaculate conception."

"This is terrible. Terrible!" Indeed, it was. Not only was he broke,
he didn't want to be tied down, least of all by a baby. For an actress
Collins's age—she was one year older than MacLaine, and worried she
was already over the hill at twenty-seven—motherhood was career suicide. Besides, they both knew they weren't ready for the responsibility.

Abortion was the only option, although years later Collins said, "I desperately wished I could keep the baby. . . . But the fact that he wouldn't even consider the possibility hurt me dreadfully."

They flew east. Beatty accompanied her to a doctor's office in New Jersey. In those days abortions were illegal and often dangerous, even fatal. He was sweating profusely, and seemed to have lost his ability to speak. She thought, He's more scared than I am. He sat in a nearby coffee shop listening to "Love Is a Many-Splendored Thing" on the jukebox, while she underwent the procedure. The deed done, she recovered reasonably quickly. They rented a small apartment on Fifth Avenue and tried to put the episode behind them.

Kazan went into production at Filmways Studios on East 127th Street at the beginning of May 1960. As always, he was on guard against making a "Hollywood" picture, which meant that he used actual locations—Staten Island, Riverdale, upstate New York—as much as possible. He couldn't have been happy when Wood arrived in New York on the *Twentieth Century Limited* in a $6,500 mink coat accompanied by Wagner, Eddie Fisher, and Elizabeth Taylor, who was about to shoot *Butterfield 8* in the city, along with a great many pieces of luggage. Crowley recalls, "Kazan said to me, in his macho, down-home way of not doing anything Hollywood—no limos, no great dressing rooms, no nothing—'I guess we've gotta have some kind of little welcoming party, here's some petty cash, go out and buy some liquor and some ice.' I stacked up some cardboard liquor boxes and put a white tablecloth over them to make a bar. They walked up to me at the same instant, like, 'What'll it be, Mr. Wagner and Mrs. Wagner?'"

Kazan immediately set out to deglamorize Wood, turn her into a normal person. Remembers Crowley, "He told her, 'Of course, the eyelashes have got to come off, the lipstick.' Whenever she tried to sneak some on, even lip gloss, he always knew it, and told her in no uncertain terms, 'Wipe that off!'"

Beatty admitted to *The New York Times* that he was "scared and worried." He was well aware that his brief stint with Adler hardly prepared him for something like *Splendor*. "I suppose I *have* a method . . . sloppy, I guess," he wryly explained, the following year. To make matters worse, he was still fatigued from the hepatitis, and napped in his dressing room between takes.

Kazan was the first in a string of major directors Beatty sought out, mentors or father figures from whom he wanted to learn. His own father was, in MacLaine's words, "a spectacular disappointment to himself." He had tried any number of professions—he was at various times a musician, teacher, high school principal, and Realtor—and tried to spare his children disappointment by discouraging their great expectations, insisting that they play it safe. At the same time, he was overbearing. Beatty didn't need Freud to point out that he was searching for an older man whom he could accord the respect he couldn't give his own father. But his attitude toward them was ambivalent. Guilty, perhaps, that he was betraying his own father, he was always testing them, and invariably, with the exception of Kazan, found them wanting.

The two men were wildly dissimilar—mentor vs. protégé, director vs. actor, immigrant outsider vs. native son. Kazan was armed with the confidence born of age and success, while Beatty was virtually aflame with the arrogance of youth. This made for a potentially combustible mix, especially at the start, before they decided they liked each other. Beatty thought that Kazan, who was short and physically unprepossessing, a veritable Caliban next to Beatty's Ariel, was jealous of him, "didn't like good looking guys," and indeed, Kazan went out of his way to needle Beatty over his looks, making him self-conscious about what the director called his "turkey neck." Beatty was mumbling his way through the dialogue until Kazan called him on it, according to Dick Sylbert, who designed the production. Kazan told Beatty, "Just shut up and do what I say. I invented mumbling. I want you to say the lines."

During the first week, the director did something that angered his star, who lashed out at the spot where he knew Kazan was most vulnerable, the director's friendly testimony before HUAC. He snapped, "Lemme ask you something—why did you name all those names?" Recalled Beatty, "In some patricidal attempt to stand up to the great Kazan, I arrogantly and stupidly challenged him on it." Kazan grabbed his arm, asking, "What did you say?" and dragged him off to a tiny dressing room where they had some privacy, whereupon the director proceeded to justify himself for two hours. Recalling this incident later, Beatty said he immediately understood "the terrible effect that what he had done had on his life." Beatty continued, "He still thought that he had done the right thing. . . . But of course I think he did the wrong thing. There were a lot of people that suffered. And they suffered badly. Arthur Miller was a friend of mine. Lillian Hellman was a friend of mine, as was Joe Losey, Adrian Scott, Carl Foreman."

But regardless of whatever judgment Beatty rendered upon behavior widely considered unconscionable, the two men reached an accommodation. Says Beatty, "I like the title that Robert Vaughn used on his book, *Only Victims.* There were only victims. There was just too much sadness. And fortunately that wasn't part of my generation."

Beatty was determined to learn as much as he could from Kazan, and the director was generous with his lessons, teaching him how to break down a script, how to think about acting, where to place the camera, and so on. He also helped Beatty with his performance. The opposite of Cal, the role Dean played in *East of Eden,* who fought his father, Bud "does not rebel against his father," the director explained. Kazan took him aside, and unburdened himself with tales of his difficult relationship with his own father, saying, "I'm still afraid of that little, bent over man," as if giving the actor license to submit.

Still, Beatty was having trouble. Perhaps his problems stemmed from the fact that Bud's issues with his father were the opposite of Beatty's with his. Both fathers seemed to disapprove of their sons, and in both cases the sons defied them—by doing more, in Beatty's case, and less, in Bud's—than their fathers wished. Bud's father oppressed him with his expectations, demanding that he do great things. Beatty's father discouraged his ambitions.

On the other hand, Beatty was able to draw on the relationship he had had with sometime actress Ellie Wood when he was at Northwestern. Wood was a junior when he was a freshman, and she had heard all about him from a dorm mate, his girlfriend in high school. Like Deanie, Wood was chaste. "It was never consummated," she recalled. "We never made love. We just kissed. The fear of hell had been put in me. I was too well brought up." He told her that his father was her mother, which is to say, that they both had authoritarian parents. Wood came to New York the same year Beatty did. They lived a block away from each other, but when she knocked on his door, he wouldn't respond. She recalls, "It was as if a curtain had come down."

By several accounts, the reputation for being difficult that Beatty earned on *A Loss of Roses* was proving prophetic. "Warren was a little 'snotty'—I don't know a better word for how he behaved and can't find one in my thesaurus," Kazan wrote in his autobiography, adding, "but he was to grow into a formidable man." According to Bob "B.J." Jiras, Natalie Wood's makeup man, who later became part of Beatty's regular crew, as well as a friend, "The enemy—who none of us liked—was Warren. It was as if Warren Beatty had *already* become a movie star, had already made twenty movies. That was his attitude." The crew didn't like him either, and nicknamed him "Mental Anguish," shortened to "M.A.," in honor of his propensity for obsessional overanalysis, and the torment he put himself and everyone else through getting his part down. Added Don Kranze, Kazan's assistant director, "Warren was a pain in the ass. He was very young, anyway, but his emotional maturity was about thirteen. . . . We all sort of felt about Warren that he's an immature boy playing a man's game."

Not unlike other leading men, Beatty paid close attention to his appearance. His acne was a plague that he tried mightily to get rid of, especially after it had flared up during *Roses*, as a result of the makeup he was wearing. Occasionally, the six-foot-one actor was known to wear lifts in his shoes and to pump up his arms lifting weights before scenes in which his biceps would show, not unusual among actors. Crew members made fun of him for his vanity, barbs he eventually learned to deflect by calling attention to it before others did, when he would play variations on the tune of, "I'm the vainest actor in Hollywood," or, "You'll never meet an actor who's as narcissistic as I am." Kranze liked to tell a story about Beatty sitting in front of a mirror separating his eyelashes with a pin. According to one possibly apocryphal story, Kazan had the mirrors in his dressing room covered up so that he wouldn't be late to the set. At the wrap party, the director needled him with the gift of a hand mirror.

Barbara Loden, who played Bud's louche older sister, was having an affair with Kazan while he was still married to his first wife, Molly Thatcher. (Kazan and Loden later married.) Loden diagnosed Beatty with surgical precision. She thought he was just scared, afraid of being a movie star, and concealing his fears behind a patina of arrogance. She concluded that he had contempt for Hollywood, while at the same time seeking entry. She feared that, like Brando, he didn't have much regard for the profession he had chosen, and therefore would never respect himself.

Collins haunted the set, alert for the errant spark she feared might ignite an affair between Beatty and Wood. She was due to leave for Rome in the middle of June to shoot *Esther and the King*, the kind of lavish sword and sandal spectacle that, along with *Cleopatra* and *The Greatest Story Ever Told*, was going to bury what was left of the old studio system before the new decade ended. Neither was looking forward to being separated, and Beatty tried to persuade her not to go. But this time she was determined. She had already been suspended several times by Fox for turning down assignments, and she didn't want to risk another suspension. Moreover, not only had *Sons and Lovers* (1960) turned out well, but Mary Ure, who played the role she turned down on his advice, would be nominated for an Oscar. She wrote, "I was not about to let him interfere with my career again."

Like Collins, Wagner spent his time monitoring the love scenes between Beatty and Wood. He didn't really know Beatty, outside of the fact that both men went to the same gym. Crowley couldn't help noticing that the tensions between Wood and Wagner were getting worse. "Their marriage was crumbling," he says. "R.J. and she were trying desperately to get it back together. Natalie was fit for the loony bin."

It wasn't long before the gossip mills started turning. Even Kazan believed that they had begun an affair. "It was clear to Natalie, as it was clear to me, that Warren was bound for the top; this perception was an aphrodisiac," he wrote years later in his autobiography. "All of a sudden, he and Natalie became lovers. When did it happen? When I wasn't looking. I wasn't sorry; it helped with their love scenes."

Still, most knowledgeable sources agree that they were not seeing each other during the production. "If they were kissing between the flats, I didn't know anything about it," says Crowley. "It's not true that Warren broke up the marriage between Wagner and her, that they started an affair during the picture. He was still going with Joan, and Natalie was crying her eyes out in the dressing room between takes, chewing her lip, just an emotional wreck. She would go home exhausted, not fit to have an affair with anybody. And she didn't seem like any person that Warren would have gone for. Especially with Joan around. Her career was on the brink of extinction, his was just beginning, they had everything riding on this to be good, they were two very ambitious people, so they didn't have time for each other, romantically."

Wagner concurs. "Beatty had nothing to do with our breakup, and

Natalie didn't begin to see him until after we split," he wrote. "If she had been sleeping with Beatty, she would have told me." He adds, "I would have known about it."

Beatty too has always denied that they began their affair on the set. "There's a lot of apocrypha about Natalie and I having something going on during *Splendor in the Grass*. It's utterly untrue. In fact it was a fairly distant relationship." They struck Loden as jealous of each other, each thinking the other was getting more attention from the director. Wood disparaged him by employing the crew's shorthand, as in, "Here comes M.A." Adds Crowley, "She had great disdain for Warren during that picture. She told me that during the love scenes she wished Warren would bathe more!" Contradicting Kazan, Loden said that the director worried that the coldness between the two was affecting their love scenes. According to her, "Warren wasn't coming through. Kazan said, 'Pretend it's Joan, Warren.'"

With the set a hothouse of marital dysfunction, Beatty scored a run for family values by springing a chopped liver surprise on Collins one Saturday afternoon on the eve of her departure. He directed her attention to the refrigerator in which was a small cardboard carton, not unlike the ones in which pet stores send goldfish home, filled with chopped liver. Buried inside was a gold ring festooned with diamonds and pearls. "Absolutely beautiful," she exclaimed. "What's it for?"

"It's your engagement ring, dummy. I figured, since you're going away soon and we'll be separated we should um, well, um, you know . . . get—well, engaged."

"Are you sure you really want to—I mean you're not just doing this to make me feel secure, are you?" She wondered if he had bought it out of guilt over the abortion.

Popping vitamin C tablets, he replied, "No, Butterfly, I'm not— you know I don't do anything unless I want to . . . and . . . um . . . well . . . um . . . I guess I want to." They set the date for January 1961.

When Collins finally left for Rome, she said Beatty, worried that she might fall into the arms of a handsome, hot-blooded Italian, overwhelmed her with phone calls, telegrams, and letters, all professing eternal love. She asked him to help her with her part in *Esther and the King*. He advised her to imagine how Jesus would say the lines, and proceed as He would. Collins swore she never wandered, went to bed early, and wore a gold butterfly pin he had bought her from Buccellati.

She even spent a weekend in London choosing fabrics for her wedding dress. He pressed her to visit. Finally, she flew to New York for a few days. She says he was convinced she was faithless, and nothing she said would dissuade him. They fought bitterly, and on the return trip, she began to wonder if he was so jealous because he and Wood were having an affair. She worked herself up into a fury, indignant at the thought that he dared treat her like his personal property, and chafed at her prodigious phone bills and hefty air fare she had paid to fly to New York. As she thought about her "pimply, bespectacled, white-faced" fiancé, as she put it, the Italian men she ran into every day looked better and better. The air had begun to leak out of their relationship.

Splendor wrapped on August 16, 1960. Two days later, Wood started rehearsals for *West Side Story*, which was already in production. Meanwhile, back in L.A., Beatty joined Collins in her rental house on Sunset Plaza Drive, which meant no more than he left his half-unpacked suitcase bursting with clothes, books, uncashed checks, and whatnot open on the floor, much to her annoyance. Beatty was edgy and anxious. He seemed to have trouble looking after himself, complained, "I'm terribly sloppy. I just can't take care of money." He did reserve duty for two or three weeks at George Air Force Base in Victorville, California, and worried about lining up his next movie. Inge was adapting a new novel by Leo Herlihy, *All Fall Down*, making sure it had a meaty role for the actor, and Kazan had signed him up for three more pictures, but he wasn't forthcoming about what they might be. Beatty knew those personal deals most often amounted to nothing, but he was flattered.

The change of scenery had not improved the relationship between Beatty and Collins. She thought he was insecure, aggressive, insisted on always having his own way, and increasingly secretive. "I think [Warren] hides behind his glasses a lot," she said. "You know, people who sometimes wear sunglasses even when the sun is not shining—they're hiding." She called him a "perfectionist," and thought he had been spoiled by the fact that his first picture was *Splendor*, now rumored to be a masterpiece. In his eyes, no other project could measure up, not for him, not for her. But she didn't relish cooling her heels, waiting for her agent to offer her the part of a lifetime, while Beatty tossed her scripts into the wastebasket. Meanwhile, her wedding dress hung mothballed in her closet.

Still, with the Kazan picture under Beatty's belt and a new self-confidence, life started to feel good. He rented a Thunderbird. He began partaking of Hollywood's frantic social scene, and cultivating relationships with the giants of the Old Hollywood, revealing an insatiable curiosity about everything and everybody. "During that time, everybody he met he met through me," says Collins. He was the "most incredible person I've ever known for networking and contacts."

"My first Hollywood party was at Romanoff's," Beatty recalls. "I wasn't dancing because I never dance much, but let's say I was working the floor." He always stood out at the parties. He towered over the women, diminutive Jewish agents, writers, and executives, as well as the other actors, often shorter than himself, who filled the room. His hair was neatly cut and brushed back in an Elvis Presley pompadour, still the fashion of the early 1960s. He continues, "I looked around, and I thought, Wow, that's Rita Hayworth. I walked over to her with my hands in my pockets and stared at her. She was dancing with a guy with funny shoes on. Strange shoes. She stared at me and I stared at her. I said, 'I'm sorry. I'm sorry, forgive me. But I just couldn't help it.'

" 'That's okay. What's your name?'

" 'Warren Beatty.'

" 'Rita Hayworth.'

" 'Yes, I know that.'

" 'And this is Clifford Odets.' That's who she was dancing with. I couldn't have predicted that I would lose interest in Rita Hayworth so quickly. By now Clifford Odets was a demigod. I said, 'You're Clifford Odets? I can't believe that I'm meeting you.' "

Beatty had listened hungrily when Clurman and Adler had waxed lyrical about the good old days with the Group Theatre—he was only four years old when it was dissolved in 1941—and by bonding with Odets, also a friendly witness, he was able to channel the high passions that animated it, so conspicuously absent from the tail end of the 1950s. Breathlessly, Beatty asked, "Could I talk to you?" Odets replied, "Well, you're talking to me." The writer invited him over that night, and the two became fast friends. Beatty had found another mentor. The actor recalls, "So I went over to Clifford's that night, and spent many nights drinking red wine and listening to Clifford rail on about a billion things. He was a genius who loved to talk. And obviously when he got to Hollywood he preferred talking to writing. He always ended up about 3:30 in the morning talking about his shoes, because he felt that his father hadn't bought him shoes that were big enough and that had damaged his feet so he had these corrective shoes that he wore all the time. The shoes were a major thing with him. There was nobody that Clifford didn't know. Male or female."

Beatty and Collins watched the 1960 presidential election returns at Odets's home. (Later he would bring Natalie Wood over. She fell asleep.) He met Jean Renoir there. "I was so stupid," he continues. "I didn't know who he was. I said, 'Who is that heavy guy over there?'

" 'That is Jean Renoir.'

" 'What does he do?'

" 'He's a pretty good moviemaker.'

" 'No kidding.'

" 'Well, he did a little picture called *Grand Illusion.* He did a movie called *Rules of the Game.*'

" 'Are they any good?'

" 'I think you should see them as soon as possible.' I did see these movies and they became immediately my favorite movies. Jean was a major influence on me. Still is."

But the relationship with Odets dissolved in acrimony in March of 1962. Beatty had set up one of his treatments at Fox, *Fifteen Doves in Flight*, which turned *Camille* into an interracial romance by casting a black actress in Garbo's role. But when the deal fell apart, Odets suspected that Beatty was trying to edge him out. The actor explained that the studio would not meet Odets's financial demands.

One night, when he was still new to Hollywood, he went to a party where he ran into Gary Cooper. Beatty always speaks admiringly about Cooper's touch with women, saying, "He chased way more pussy than I did." Cooper was standing next to Hayworth, his hand on her bottom, under her skirt. It seemed to Beatty that Cooper had his finger buried deep inside her butt. How Beatty divined this is not clear. He was becoming adept at interpreting looks and glances, reading people. Wizard of penetration that he was, perhaps he just parsed the language of the bodies, or maybe he was projecting his own fantasies.

Another pillar of the Hollywood establishment with whom Beatty became close was Charlie Feldman, the powerful agent turned producer, a bon vivant and ladies' man who bore a resemblance to Clark Gable. He had founded Famous Artists, and represented everyone from

Greta Garbo to John Wayne, Marlene Dietrich to Marilyn Monroe. As a producer, he had made countless movies, prestigious Serious Drama like *A Streetcar Named Desire* and mainstream comedy hits like *The Seven Year Itch*, as well as everything in between. He was romantically involved with Garbo, Hayworth, Hedy Lamarr, sisters Joan Fontaine and Olivia de Havilland, Ava Gardner, Capucine, Angie Dickinson, Ursula Andress, and many other women.

Beatty had met Feldman a few months back on a plane from L.A. to New York when the actor was on his way to begin *Splendor.* It was love at first sight. As *What's New Pussycat?* (1965) director Clive Donner puts it, "They spoke the same language." Beatty appreciated Feldman's joie de vivre. He frequented Feldman's home at 2000 Coldwater Canyon, where he soaked up the wit and wisdom of the Hollywood *alte kackers* who so fascinated him. "Charlie's patio was always an interesting lunch," he recalls. "There would be Orson, or Zanuck, Cooper, Holden, Wayne, or Stevens or Hawks. Billy Wilder. Not to mention some fascinating European actress."

Like Kazan, Feldman saw that Beatty was going to be big, and wanted him as a client, but the actor kept him at arm's length. "As nearly as I could tell, Charlie had no real interest in being an agent," he says. "But I liked that he hadn't been to the office in ten, fifteen years. He was more fun than almost anybody I had met in Hollywood of the older guys."

Feldman advised him not to make another multi-picture deal at MGM, which, recalls the actor, "turned out to be very good advice. I learned not to confuse [friendship] with business, not to expect people to act in other than their own best interests." He loaned Beatty money. Says Sylbert, whom Feldman also mentored, "Charlie taught Warren a lot, like you don't put anything in writing, you don't sign contracts, you can walk out at any time. If directors are not your friends, you soon enough make them understand that they wish they were. Charlie always wore a red cardigan when he was going to bullshit somebody. He'd call a guy up, say, 'Come on down,' and he'd sit in the shade, face the guy towards the sun, and the guy would be falling asleep as he's selling him the deal! He helped Warren to be Warren. Warren is not going to do it the way you want to do it, and he made Warren feel comfortable with that."

Feldman taught Beatty to be stingy with information. As producer

Bob Evans puts it, "Warren never answers a question, he only asks questions." By example, if nothing else, Feldman showed him that it was acceptable to say one thing to one person and another to another. If he were circumspect enough, no one could ever accuse him of a falsehood. And if he were accused, so what.

THE STUDIO was not particularly excited about *Splendor*. Boss Jack Warner, writing to his number two, Benny Kalmenson, worried that it was glum and uncommercial. Bill Orr, Warner's son-in-law, had fallen asleep watching it. (At one screening, Wood reportedly cried her way through the picture, while Collins laughed.) Aware of the studio's apathy, Beatty frantically tried to exploit the heat generated by the picture even before it opened. Hungry to work on another quality production, he learned that José Quintero, who had launched the career of Jason Robards Jr. directing Eugene O'Neill's *The Iceman Cometh* in 1958 off-Broadway, was going to direct a movie based on a novella by Tennessee Williams called *The Roman Spring of Mrs. Stone*. Recalls Beatty, "I wanted to play something that wouldn't be another what they would call at that time 'shit-kicking-American-stumbling-mumbling-Method part.' I thought that's a great opportunity to go do another nationality, another accent. That was something I knew nothing about but I thought that I would learn as quickly as possible. I was $15,000 in debt."

The script was written by Gavin Lambert, and told the story of Mrs. Stone, a wealthy, love-starved older woman on holiday, who finds herself alone in Rome after her husband has a heart attack on the flight over. She is introduced to Paolo, an Italian gigolo, and foolishly, as it turns out, falls in love. Although he didn't develop it, it touched on a theme that would become a hallmark of Beatty's career: innocence chastised by experience.

Vivien Leigh, forty-eight, had been cast in the role of Mrs. Stone. She was coming off a divorce from Laurence Olivier, who left her to marry a younger woman, actress Joan Plowright. A clinical manic-depressive, Leigh needed lots of tender loving care. Just short of a decade earlier, while married to Olivier, she tried to tear off her clothes on a flight from Ceylon to Los Angeles, and jump out of the plane. On the set of the film she was then shooting, *Elephant Walk*, she cried nonstop, then began yelling "Fire! Fire!" as loudly as she could, more or less quoting Blanche DuBois in *A Streetcar Named Desire,* the character she had played to wide acclaim two years before. (She was replaced by Elizabeth Taylor.)

Cast as the Contessa, who pimps out Mrs. Stone to Paolo, was Lotte Lenya, the Austrian-born actress married to composer Kurt Weill. *The Threepenny Opera*'s original Jenny, she would become best known to Americans as the sharp-toed Rosa Klebb in the James Bond picture *From Russia with Love.* Jill St. John, occasional Bob Evans girlfriend and future wife of R. J. Wagner, played the other woman.

Beatty had to be approved by Williams and Leigh. He was hardly a logical choice; sensibly, Williams was of the opinion that the role called for an Italian. When the playwright asked Lambert, "What's going to happen with Paolo; who's going to play him?" the screenwriter replied, "It's not certain, but I hear, because of the Warner's deal, that they're pushing Warren Beatty." Williams remarked, "Well, I don't think he's right." Recalls Lambert, "We did look at a couple of Italian actors, but they didn't have that sort of charisma and sexual dynamism that Warren had."

Williams was recuperating from bad reviews—they supposedly gave him an ulcer—for *Sweet Bird of Youth* at the Caribe Hilton in San Juan, Puerto Rico. "I said to myself, Is there anything that I could do to get Tennessee's approval for this part?" Beatty recalls. "I had never been to Italy. I thought, An Italian, he should be darker than I was, so I got something called Man-Tan. You put it on your face and you turned a sort of an orange-yellow. I found an Italian with an accent. I worked with him for two days. I got what I considered to be an Italian suit. I put on the suit. I put on the Man-Tan. I put on the accent, and I flew to San Juan. I walked into the casino just off the main lobby, and sure enough, hunched over a blackjack table was Tennessee, whom I had never met, but I recognized him. I asked the waiter to give me a glass of milk."

Ever ready with medical advice, Beatty recalls, "In those days, they treated ulcers with milk. My father had ulcers, and he drank milk all the time, which, by the way, is the worst thing you can do. Milk is very irritating to the mucus membrane of the stomach—Crohn's disease, and so on. Any Ashkenazi Jew who has a high level of stomach upset shouldn't drink milk. Seventy to 80 percent are allergic to milk products. I'm not an Ashkenazi Jew except in *Bugsy,* but I have this kind of an allergy, you sometimes start clearing your throat if you drink a lot."

Back on track, he continues, "So I wrote a note, that said, 'Dear Mr. Williams, Anything you want.' (Signed) 'Paolo.' Tennessee was kind of loaded. He looked up and he saw this geek of a young actor standing there. He recognized me from *Splendor in the Grass.* He threw up his hands and he said, 'All right, all right, you've got the part.'" Williams biographer Dotson Rader wrote that as a closer Beatty offered himself to Williams. The story went, in Beatty's words, "I put on a bathrobe and went to Tennessee's hotel room, and he said, 'You don't have to do this. You've already got the part,' which was bullshit." Lambert recalls, "Tennessee was very impressed that he came to see him, with Man-Tan on, looking very Italian, and was eager for the part." Williams himself observed, sadly, "He is so beautiful, just looking at him brings tears to my eyes. What a waste."

With Collins in tow, Beatty met Leigh at the Dorchester Hotel in London for tea. "He didn't say a great deal," says Lambert, who was present. "He realized that he was being auditioned, and he knew that he had to be charming, which was very easy for him. He didn't have to be good-looking, because he was. He was very polite, very well behaved, didn't show off at all. Vivien was very, very taken with him, and said, 'Yes, yes, he's charming, he's wonderful-looking, he seems to me to be absolutely right.'"

Roman Spring was shot at Elstree Studios, outside London. Beatty hung out with Stanley Kubrick who was shooting *Lolita* there. As Collins recalled, the actor looked "devastatingly handsome. There was little trace of the spotty boy I had first seen sixteen months ago. His hair had been darkened for the part of the Italian gigolo. He had a deep tan, which, although it was out of a bottle, looked as if it came straight from Portofino. He wore a beautifully cut beige silk suit from Brioni, a cream crepe de chine shirt from Battaglia, and a brown-and-beige Saint Laurent tie. No wonder half the females in the restaurant were tripping over themselves to get a glimpse of him. The Warren Beatty sex-symbol image was beginning to emerge. Women adored him. He was loving every minute of it." It was nastily reported that he took longer with his makeup than Leigh.

Lotte Lenya later told Rex Reed that Leigh was infatuated with

Beatty: "Like most women, Vivien had a tremendous crush on Warren," she said. "He kept her so preoccupied that she allowed me to steal our most important scenes together. One night, we were watching the day's rushes together and Vivien gasped, 'Oh, how could I let you *do* that to me?' And I said, 'But dalink, you were very busy this afternoon and had no time to rehearse.'" Richard Burton is reputed to have told a journalist, "They were at it in broom closets, across billiard tables, in telephone kiosks; you have to hand it to the pair of them." Lambert is skeptical. "I knew Lenya very well," he says. "She never mentioned anything like that. There are all these stories, that he fucked Tennessee, that he fucked Vivien, none of which are true, I don't think. I think Vivien fancied Warren. But I think he was much too smart to take her on. It would have been a very stupid move." (Three decades later, Madonna claimed he admitted it.)

The character of Paolo was a stretch for Beatty, but Lambert thought he did a good job. "I don't think that at that time, there was anybody better," he says. "He had the charm and the sexiness and the odor of sexual corruption, which he played brilliantly. The only thing he couldn't do was the Italian accent. It's a little closer to Tijuana than it is to Rome." Nevertheless, Quintero—unlike Kazan, Logan, and Arthur Penn to come—had no luck with movies. He was too tentative even to shout "Action." "It was a mess," said Beatty. "Nobody would tell him how [to make a movie]."

After the production wrapped in March 1961, Collins returned to Los Angeles and Beatty went to Rome. "It was the high tide of American power," Beatty recalls. "Colonial America. I was like that, a sexual colonizer. I was Mrs. Stone. Arrogant. I pranced and preened down the Via Veneto, in my phony Italian suit, going to the hotels of all the actresses, the Hassler, the Excelsior . . ." He was at a café with Inger Stevens, when he ran into Lee and Paula Strasberg's daughter, Susan. She found him "charming and intelligent, with a tremendous need to please women," and the next day, he moved into her apartment for the rest of his vacation. He was wearing Paolo's wool suit. The pants were so tight Strasberg wondered how he could sit down. In her memoir, she remembered an evening at the home of Luchino Visconti, who wanted Beatty for *The Leopard*. She described the great Italian director, who was gay, as a "salon Communist" surrounded by adoring young men. On this occasion, transfixed, he neglected them in favor of Beatty, who nevertheless kissed her discretely on the back of the neck as he withdrew to the bathroom with her at his heels. "When we returned to the living room twenty minutes later, we were greeted by six pairs of hostile eyes. To my embarrassment, I realized my blouse was still unbuttoned. I wasn't quite sure how to act, but Warren beamed at one and all an enchanting, ingenuous smile."

When Beatty returned to Sunset Plaza Drive in May, still sporting Paolo's clothes—in particular a beige Eisenhower jacket he never took off—he and Collins continued their downward spiral. She wryly remarked that he was the only man she knew "who could get to the mirror faster than me in the morning." Both knew the relationship was over, but neither seemed to have the willpower to end it.

Actor George Chakiris was quoted recalling seeing Beatty hanging out on the set of *West Side Story* at the end of April 1961. By early June, Natalie Wood had finished with the film, and Wagner was finishing up *Sail a Crooked Ship*. He reportedly threw a party on the Columbia lot. Wood had promised to be the hostess, but half an hour after the appointed time she hadn't shown up. They started without her. Later she waltzed in with Beatty. She went over to Wagner and kissed him. He asked her why she was late. She claimed she had been sitting for stills, and had run into Beatty. According to a Columbia producer, the tension in the air was palpable. She pressed flesh, then Wood and Beatty disappeared for an hour. When they returned, Beatty had Wood on one arm and Joan Collins on the other. After the party, both couples went to the Villa Capri for dinner. Collins and Wagner looked on as Beatty and Wood giggled. Wagner says he does not recall the incident.

In July 1961, Collins was offered *The Road to Hong Kong*, latest in the Bob Hope–Bing Crosby road series, which would take her to London. Beatty threw the script on the floor. "It's crap," he said. "Crap! Why do you need to do it?"

"Two reasons," she blurted out. "For the money—and to get away from you." There it was, out in the open. Finis. Explained Collins, "It was obvious I had to be the one to end it with Warren. He seemed content to let it drift sloppily along."

WOOD AND Wagner announced their separation on June 21, 1961. In July, she rented a house on Chalon Road in Bel Air. Beatty moved in and the two lived quietly together, usually eating alone. The actor always wore the same outfit, a loose shirt open at the collar, and gabardine slacks. He read omnivorously and played the piano for hours at a time. He struck Natalie's sister, Lana, as "silent, studious."

The gossip columnists couldn't believe their good luck when Beatty and Collins separated at the same time as Wood and Wagner, and Beatty took up with Wood. They blamed him for breaking up her marriage, but quickly jumped on board as the new romance blossomed before their eyes. That summer, Beatty and Wood became the new "it" couple. Syndicated gossip columnist Dorothy Kilgallen wrote, "The way Natalie Wood and Warren Beatty are carrying on . . . it's a wonder they have time to eat." Wagner, still very much in love with Wood, confessed, "I wanted to kill the son of a bitch." He went so far as to drive over to Beatty's, brandishing a .38. "I was hanging around outside his house with a gun, hoping he would walk out," he recalled. "I not only wanted to kill him, I was prepared to kill him." He was talked out of it by a friend.

On July 27, Beatty was Wood's date at a screening of *West Side Story,* their first public outing together. Collins, who had suspected there might be some truth to the rumors that the romance between the two had been kindled on the set of *Splendor,* didn't know what to think. She was aware that Beatty was fully capable of juggling more than one woman at a time, which is to say, he was secretive and compartmentalized. "Even as a kid, Warren had a private world no one could penetrate," wrote MacLaine. "He could shut everyone out."

Despite Beatty's attentions to Wood, he was by no means neglecting his career. *Splendor* had still not been released, but Inge had finished his adaptation of *All Fall Down,* expanding the character, Berry-Berry, intended for Beatty. (MGM was financing, and Beatty owed a picture to the studio for settling out his contract.) Berry-Berry is a selfish, violent, and misogynistic young man, who is nevertheless idolized by younger brother, Clinton, from whose point of view the narrative unfolds. His goal in life is to have sex with as many females as possible, among them Echo O'Brien, an older woman, whom Clinton also worships. Berry-Berry invites her love, gets her pregnant, and then spurns her. She commits suicide. Heartbroken, Clinton goes after Berry-Berry, only to find him collapsed in a heap. Clinton's hatred turns to pity, and he leaves Berry-Berry alone to face himself.

Despite the fact that none of his movies had yet been released,

Beatty was paid $200,000 to play Berry-Berry. The rest of the cast, an unusually strong one, consisted of Karl Malden playing his father, Angela Lansbury his mother, Eva Marie Saint as Echo, and Brandon De Wilde as Clinton. It was directed by John Frankenheimer, and produced by John Houseman. Like Kazan, Houseman was another icon of the theater. He had worked closely with Orson Welles, founding the Mercury Theatre and producing Welles's famous 1938 radio hoax, *The War of the Worlds.*

At the time, the young star was riding the crest of a fierce wave of publicity, which the producer derided as "an astonishing campaign of self-promotion." Beatty, he said, "had managed to get pictures of himself, together with articles, into every major magazine in the country. Using charm, sex, and unmitigated gall, he kept the nation's female columnists in a tizzy. Before we had shot a single frame of film, he had turned a tall, nice-looking but rather awkward and completely unknown young man into one of the hottest names in the business — completely eclipsing such well-established fellow players as Eva Marie Saint, Karl Malden et al." He complained that Inge had pushed Beatty on him "almost against [his] will."

Beatty finally made his deal for *All Fall Down* early in the summer of 1961, and began rehearsals on July 12. In his memoir, *Unfinished Business,* Houseman recalled, "Our most serious problem was young Mr. Beatty. With his angelic arrogance, his determination to emulate Marlon Brando and Jimmy Dean, and his half-baked notions of 'Method' acting, he succeeded in perplexing and antagonizing not only his fellow actors but our entire crew."

All Fall Down commenced production on July 27, 1961. At the end of September, Beatty flew to Key West for some location shooting. Worried that he would have an affair with Saint, Wood joined him. She invited Crowley to come with her. Once there, she realized she had forgotten her diaphragm. Recalls Crowley, "I said, 'Oh?' She said, 'Now listen. Here's the thing. I can't go in the drugstore and buy one myself in this town. Key West is a big tourist place. So you're gonna have to pretend like you're buying one for your wife!' We found the poorest-looking drugstore we could find, that had a gravel parking lot in front. She sat in the car, I went in, and said, 'I need to buy a diaphragm for my wife,' and there was no problem, I came out with the package, and we just looked at each other and died laughing."

It didn't take long before stories began to emanate from the set, all of which had a common theme: Beatty was impossible. According to Houseman, "Our veteran cameraman, Curly Lindon, became so exasperated with him that he flew a camera-bearing helicopter within a few inches of his head." Houseman went on to recall that "on the last day of shooting, in a secret agreement with the local police, Warren Beatty was left to languish in a bare cell of the Key West jail while the company flew back to California."

BY THE fall of 1961, as the opening of *Splendor in the Grass* approached, the studio whipped the press into a frenzy. John Springer, the head of the New York office of Arthur P. Jacobs and Co., was his East Coast publicist. An affable man who also handled Marilyn Monroe, he generated reams of gossip about his client, much of which made its way into the women's magazines, *Ladies' Home Journal*, *Redbook*, *Cosmopolitan*, and the like.

Kazan and Inge advised the young star to make himself less accessible, lest he become known exclusively as a playboy. Springer reassured him that he was not going to be photographed in a swimming pool with a starlet. Beatty figured he could satisfy the publicists as well as those who urged restraint by the simple expedient of agreeing to speak with every reporter who called him, while saying nothing. He was withholding and inscrutable. He canceled interviews at the last minute, kept journalists waiting, failed to show up at all, or if he did, he took phone calls throughout the session. He skillfully created an aura of mystery around himself, so that when he deigned to do a substantive interview, journalists were flattered to death, and thus unstinting in their praise. It was all about keeping them off balance. Eventually, however, this backfired, earning him the enmity of the celebrity press. "The press has beat the shit out of me since 1960," he still complains. "Nobody gets beat up like a twenty-two-year-old pretty boy."

Splendor was finally released on October 10, 1961. Beatty and Wood attended the premiere together. The reviews were mixed. *The New York Times*'s Bosley Crowther, then the most influential American reviewer, called it "a frank and ferocious social drama," primly adding, "that makes the eyes pop and the modest cheek burn." He praised Beatty as "a surprising newcomer, [who] shapes an amiable, decent, sturdy lad whose emotional exhaustion and defeat are the deep pathos in the film.

Except that he talks like Marlon Brando and has some small mannerisms of James Dean, Mr. Beatty is a striking individual." *Time* magazine
was unstinting in its praise for Beatty, predicting that he "should make
the big time on the first bounce. . . . He has a startling resemblance to
the late James Dean, and he has that certain something Hollywood
calls star quality." At the end of the year *Splendor* made *The New York
Times* Ten Best list.

But by 1961, the early films of Ingmar Bergman, François Truf-
faut, Jean-Luc Godard, and Michelangelo Antonioni were beginning to
make their way to the United States, and in comparison to these, *Splen-
dor* was puerile, which is to say, the high-brow critics sneered. Dwight
Macdonald trashed it in *Esquire,* Stanley Kauffmann compared it to an
"Andy Hardy story" in *The New Republic,* and Brendan Gill in *The
New Yorker* called it "as phony a picture as I can remember seeing."
The movie did no more than respectable business.

Still, Beatty's notices created a firestorm around the young actor.
He was staying at the Delmonico on 59th Street and Park Avenue, and
he likes to tell the story of the time he was walking out the door when
he came upon two girls leaning against a car. One of them exclaimed,
"Oh my God, you're Warren Beatty!" and regarded him with adora-
tion, until the other added, "God, you're . . . nothing!" Beatty chalked
up their disappointment to the fact that he wasn't thirty feet tall, as he
was on the screen, and thought, That's fame for you.

One woman called Beatty's talent agency, MCA, in New York
threatening to jump out of a window if he didn't phone her immediately. Alarmed, the assistant who took the call contacted him, saying,
"I hate to bother you, but I've got this girl on the other phone, and her
name is Mary Smith . . . and she's gonna jump! Could you call her?"
Beatty replied calmly, "No, no, no, this goes on all the time."

Splendor made him an instant star, a serious candidate for the Method
mantle so conspicuously worn by Brando, Clift, and Dean. Those who
mocked Beatty's mumbling and mannerisms as empty posturing were
silenced both by the reception of the film and his performance. He was
no longer just a pretty boy with a full dance card. Beatty had arrived.

Thematically speaking, *Splendor* is a true relic of the 1950s. Kazan
and Inge's quietistic work occupied a safe and sleepy interlude between
the militant drama that preceded it, say, Odets's plays—*Waiting for
Lefty, Golden Boy*—mounted by the Group Theatre in the 1930s, and

Beatty's own *Bonnie and Clyde* that followed. In the ending, Deanie, fresh from a stay at a mental institution, seeks out Bud, only to find him mired in domesticity and eking out a living as a farmer, not the captain of industry his father had wished him to be.

Often the best critic of his own work, Kazan said, "What I liked about this ending is its bittersweet ambivalence, full of what Bill [Inge] had learned from his own life: that you have to accept limited happiness, because all happiness is limited, and that to expect perfection is the most neurotic thing of all; you must live with the sadness as well as the joy. Perhaps this theme rings so true because Bill himself had come to a point where he had settled for less, a place not in the first rank of playwrights along with O'Neill, Williams, and Miller but on an honorable sub-platform." The characters capitulate to what is portrayed as inevitable. As Kazan further explained, one reason he wanted to make the film was because Inge told him, " 'I'd like to tell a story about how we have to forgive our parents.' Bill was in psychoanalysis then, he resented his parents, and he was right at the moment when he was forgiving them—when he saw what they were and let them go." In other words, the name of the game was no longer resistance to or rebellion against the stultifying values of a society grounded on money and sexual repression; it was forgiveness and reconciliation, whether political, generational, or personal. Freud, not Marx, ruled.

One night, at a club in L.A., Beatty and Wood were eating dinner. Beatty glanced over at the adjoining table and couldn't help noticing that John F. Kennedy, Peter Lawford, and assorted hangers-on were seated there. Lawford got up and made his way over to their table. He turned to Wood and said, "Number One would like to invite you to join his party." Wood accepted on behalf of herself and Beatty, but Lawford made it clear that the invitation extended only to her. She demurred. "But it's Number One," Lawford exclaimed. Not apparently in Hollywood.

The Roman Spring of Mrs. Stone opened on December 28, 1961, to generally tepid reviews, certainly the first personally bad reviews that the young actor had yet received. In *The New York Times*, Crowther wrote, "Mr. Beatty ... is hopelessly out of his element as a patent-leather ladies man in Rome. His manners remind one of a freshman trying airs at a college prom, his accent recalls Don Ameche's all-purpose Italian-Spanish one." As Nicholson, who labored in obscurity for many years observed, "It was much easier to do as I've done, with no one watching. Warren had to learn in front of everybody." The picture disappeared without a trace.

In February 1962, Wood was nominated for an Oscar for *Splendor.* Inge was nominated for Best Original Screenplay. Beatty was reportedly miffed that he didn't get a nomination as well. Wood lost Best Actress to Sophia Loren for *Two Women,* but Inge won.

That spring, the press reported that the pair had become engaged, which was untrue, and that he had given her a Chihuahua puppy instead of a ring. But that didn't prevent him from cheating on her when he had, or created, the opportunity. Beatty had a one-night stand with Cher, who was then sixteen. "When I was 16 years old, I fucked Warren Beatty," she told *Playboy.* "Just like that. Of course, I'm one of a long list. And I did it because my girlfriends were so crazy about him, and so was my mother. I saw Warren, he picked me up and I did it. And what a disappointment! Not that he wasn't technically good, or could be good, but I didn't feel anything. So, for me, I felt, There's no reason for you to do that again."

All Fall Down opened two days after the Oscars, on April 11, 1962. The reviews were mixed. Despite his upbeat take on *Splendor,* Crowther was no fan of Beatty's, and wrote starchily, "Everyone in this story is madly in love with a disgusting young man who is virtually a cretin. At least, Warren Beatty plays him so he seems like one. . . . Surly, sloppy, slow-witted, given to scratching himself, picking his nose, being rude beyond reason to women and muttering about how much he hates the world, this creature that Mr. Beatty gives us is a sad approximation of modern youth." Beatty was quoted as saying he hated the picture himself, but took on the *Times* reviewer anyway: "Bosley Crowther has never liked me, but I don't like him either. I told him so once at Sardi's." Stanley Kauffmann, writing in *The New Republic,* on the other hand, praised Beatty's performance: "Warren Beatty, whose two previous film appearances were at best promising, fares much better here with the restless, bored Berry-Berry. . . . Physically, Beatty has the requisite magnetism; emotionally, he has the coiled-snake tension of black lower-middle-class frustration."

On April 15, 1962, Wood filed for divorce, charging that Wagner "preferred to play golf than stay at home with me," and that he ridiculed her friends who didn't play golf. After she pleaded that she had to leave for Europe because *All Fall Down* was playing the Cannes Film Festival on May 13, the divorce was granted expeditiously. Beatty and Wood spent two months in Europe, including a week in Rome. The vacation was industriously exploited by the press. Wood appeared on the cover of *Life* magazine on June 15, and they were mobbed everywhere they went.

JUST WHEN Beatty thought he was embarking on his brilliant career, he had made two flops in a row, and worse, he was singled out for ridicule. He couldn't help but take the reviews personally, and basically stopped working for sixteen months. He was desperate to play the lead in Kazan's *America, America,* but the director didn't think he was right, not enough rough edges, and turned him down. Beatty was bitterly disappointed and went on to reject *Barefoot in the Park, The War Lover,* and Visconti's *The Leopard.* (He said he did not *do* costume dramas, and Alain Delon took the role.) He turned down *Act One,* a biopic of Moss Hart, *Twilight of Honor,* and most famously, *PT 109,* a film based on Robert Donovan's account of John Kennedy's World War II combat exploits. "The White House had asked Fred Zinnemann and me to please do *PT 109,*" the actor recalls. "Zinnemann didn't like the script, and I didn't like the script, so I said to the producer, Bryan Foy, 'This is crap. You gotta rewrite it.' I also said it to Pierre Salinger [Kennedy's press secretary], who told the president." Beatty adds, "Jack Warner knew that I told the president, and he got all upset. He essentially kicked me off the lot because I said, 'Not only will I not do it, when I talk to the president I'm gonna tell him that he should not allow it to be done because it's lousy.' Warner said I'd never work at Warners again. I saw the president three days before he died, at a party. He said, 'You were sure right about that one.'"

In 1962, he said that he had turned down a million dollars' worth of work. According to Louella Parsons, he turned down seventy-five scripts and $2 million in salary between *All Fall Down* and the beginning of 1964. He called it all "crap."

Looking back on this period two years later, Beatty confessed, "I was not prepared for it. I was not ready for the agony, the coarseness, the vulgarity, having to do things here, being pressured there until finally they rub out your talents. I was insecure. I'd lost the spark and I felt like I was being sold like a can of tomatoes."

Beatty was still looking to attach himself to the great directors. Odets had recommended him to Robert Rossen. Fifty-four in 1963, Rossen was the crusty grandson of a rabbi. He was a short, barrel-shaped man with close-cropped, sparse gray hair, and a voice like sandpaper. Like Odets and Kazan, he was yet another member of the small circle of lefty writers and directors who had saved their careers by informing on their former friends and colleagues in the early 1950s. Like Kazan and Odets, he still considered himself a man of the left. Also like them, Rossen was a romantic figure for Beatty, a hero of the political wars of the Red Decade, despite his subsequent capitulation, and another potential mentor. He had a long list of distinguished pictures to his credit, including *Body and Soul* (1947), *All the King's Men* (1949), which won an Oscar for Best Picture, and most recently, *The Hustler* (1961), with Paul Newman. He hired Beatty for a project called *Cocoa Beach* in July 1962, set in the world of the space program at Cape Canaveral.

Nineteen sixty-two and 1963 passed in a blur. As Beatty described them, they "blended into a series of very good times, good food, a lot of good-looking girls, and a lot of aimless fun.... I drank wine.... I was becoming an adult. I didn't want to pass up really tasting my early twenties in order to churn up momentum." One of the good-looking girls was Kim Novak, on whom he had a crush. Beatty met her at a party, and she invited him to accompany her up to the house she kept in Big Sur. She picked him up at his hotel in a sporty Jaguar XK140 or 150. In the car with her were a terrier, a parakeet, a parrot, and a St. Bernard. They drove up the Pacific Coast Highway and stopped at Nepenthe, the celebrated hotel built on the site of a cabin once owned by Rita Hayworth and Orson Welles. "I realized that she had something going with the bartender, and that I'd been invited to make the bartender jealous," he recalls, wryly. "I was the hot young male star. But she had absolutely no interest in me." Beatty took this as a challenge. "I went to her house with her, but I couldn't get to first base. I couldn't stand it, faked a phone call, and told her, 'I've got to go back to L.A., it's an emergency, can you get me to the airport before it closes?' She drove me to the airport, and we never spoke again."

Rossen never finished *Cocoa Beach,* but he did have an adaptation of a novel by J. R. Salamanca, called *Lilith,* which he asked Beatty to do instead. By 1963, broke and $10,000 in debt, the actor didn't have much choice and agreed. *Lilith* tells the story of Vincent Bruce, a war veteran who works as an occupational therapist in a posh mental hospital for schizophrenics. Lilith is what was known in those days as a nympho-maniac, voracious and indiscriminate in her choice of partners (women as well as men), an enigmatic and capricious heartbreaker, cruel in her disregard for those who orbit her star, driving them mad if they weren't already. In other words, a female Warren Beatty, give or take some. One inmate (Peter Fonda) spurned by Lilith commits suicide, hastening Lilith's collapse into gibbering lunacy, and Bruce, who has also fallen in love with her, ends up a patient himself, his fate up in the air.

The script contained all the ingredients necessary to pique Beatty's interest. His relationship with Wood was nothing if not a window into the world of a world-class neurotic. Like *Splendor*, *Lilith* was another installment in the Freud-ridden tradition of Hollywood films going back at least to *The Snake Pit* in 1948, and including the previous year's surprise hit, *David and Lisa* (1962). It was a downbeat drama about a serious subject, with a perfect, sensitive-young-man role for him, and an equivocal, read "European," as opposed to a happy, read "Holly-wood," ending.

Perhaps atoning for his sins of conscience, Rossen struck a somber note. "Society considers the person who is outside its norms as sick," he told *Cahiers du Cinéma* in 1967, sounding like R. D. Laing. "Now, my own feeling is that society itself is sick. . . . We have to say what is out of joint in our time."

In the spring of 1963, Charlie Feldman approached Beatty about starring in and co-producing a project that he had originally bought in the late 1950s for Cary Grant, based on a Hungarian play called *Lot's Wife*. He already had a script, by I. A. L. Diamond, who had co-written Billy Wilder classics like *Some Like It Hot*, *The Apartment*, and *Kiss Me, Stupid*. Beatty had a sharp sense of humor and a gift for comedy, although he had yet to find a satisfactory vehicle for it. He seized the opportunity to get away from the sober dramas that had so far defined his career. He was fascinated by "the plight of the compulsive Don Juan," as he puts it. "It always struck me as a pathetic and funny char-acter, a victim of himself or society or his conquests or whatever—but a victim." But the actor stipulated one condition. He knew that Feldman would find a part for his then girlfriend, Capucine, if allowed, and he wanted assurances that nothing suitable for her would find its way into the script. Feldman, who did not take dictation, retorted, "Fuck you," but eventually agreed, and work on the script proceeded.

Needless to say, *Lot's Wife* was not going to be the title of the movie. Feldman was looking around for something more suitable. When Beatty was staying at Feldman's home, the producer couldn't help but hear him on the phone giving his customary greeting to female callers, "What's new, pussycat?" One day, the light bulb went on. Feldman exclaimed, "Title!"

Feldman and Beatty were not happy with Diamond's script, which they didn't think was funny enough. They needed a good joke writer. One night Beatty went to the Bitter End, a club in the Village, to catch a kid he heard was funny, Woody Allen. Feldman was prepared to offer Allen, who had no film experience, as much as $60,000 to rewrite the script. Allen's agent, and later producer, was Charles H. Joffe. Allen recalls, "When he said, 'Aw, I'd like your guy to do a movie with Warren Beatty,' Joffe didn't believe it for a second. Joffe only asked for $20,000, and that's what I got." Later, Allen continues, "Feldman said to me, 'I want you to write a script where we all go to Paris. There's a lot of beautiful girls there, we can all have a wonderful time. You can have a small part in the movie.'" So a movie that was to star Warren Beatty, now starred him and Woody Allen.

Beatty gave Allen the script, which Allen recalls was written not by Diamond, but Claude Binyon, an old-timer whose first credit was back in 1932. The actor said, "This guy's no slouch." Allen rolled his eyes, and replied, "Yeah, but I've never heard of him," and not bothering to look at it, started from scratch. "I didn't have breathtaking interest in the project because I thought it was never going to happen. I thought it was just a lot of big talk. No one was going to take me off the stage and say, 'Go write a script with a part for yourself in a Warren Beatty movie. He was this big star. But he kept coming night after night to the Bitter End, and he'd hang out with me between shows, and on the street afterwards, and we'd talk. He was very encouraging, very supportive."

When Allen went to visit him at the Delmonico, where he was staying, Beatty was wearing a white terrycloth bathrobe and carrying a fistful of phone messages. "If we were going to go out and eat, he'd call the restaurant and say, 'Hi, I'm calling for Warren Beatty—I still don't know how he had the nerve to do that—and he would of course always get a wonderful table. He was very, very good-looking. He'd pass women on the street and they'd say, 'Hello,' and he'd say, 'Hello,' and you could see that he would light them up."

When he was finished, Allen read his script—which he says had "a million great jokes"—to Beatty and Feldman, and the honeymoon ended. "You could see right away that Feldman came from the old school of Hollywood," Allen said later. "I had named the lead female character Becky, a Jewish name. He didn't like it. And when she met the lead male, who was supposed to be Warren, she had confident dialogue, she would say, 'Well, you know, I'm gorgeous and I'm great-looking.' Charlie couldn't countenance that because it was immodest and against the cliché of what the heroine would say. He regarded me as a quote-unquote beatnik, the guy who was coming up there in sneakers and a T-shirt and giving them jokes about Charlie Parker and suicide. I think Warren was more in tune with me than Charlie was. He was trusting Warren's instinct that I had something to offer."

Meanwhile, Beatty had reservations about Rossen's script for *Lilith* as well. He turned around and took *Youngblood Hawke* instead, to be directed by Delmer Daves. Then, abruptly, he changed his mind. This was the last straw for Jack Warner, who kicked Beatty off the lot for the second time. Worried that he would never eat lunch in that town again, Beatty took *Lilith*.

2

ALL FELL DOWN

How Beatty peered into the abyss, as his tabloid love affair
with Leslie Caron blackened his reputation and he
staggered from one bad movie to another.

"It got to the point where I would have to make a good picture or
get myself into trouble. That's when we made *Bonnie and Clyde*."

— *Warren Beatty*

WHILE BEATTY DITHERED over his next project, his relationship with Natalie Wood was winding down. They
broke up, they got together, they broke up, they got together. Lana Wood remembers them in different rooms. "Natalie would
lie by the pool in the sun for an hour and then when Warren would
appear in his trunks, his usual book tucked under his arm, she
would get up and go into the house," she writes. "There was always a
distance between them." Beatty was not very good in the role of the
dutiful boyfriend. He was rarely where he was supposed to be when
he was supposed to be there, and if he did show up, he was liable to
be hours late, driving Wood crazy. As Shirley MacLaine once quipped,
he was a guy who couldn't commit to dinner, and it was literally true.
"After a few hours, [Natalie] began to look at her watch, and by evening, she became distraught and began crying," recalled Lana, describing an average afternoon. "She stammered, 'Warren.' Later that night,

hours after he had said he would be home and several hours after they had been due to arrive at a dinner party, Warren sauntered in. Then it started. Natalie and Warren fought, and when the screaming became too much, Warren slammed the door and left again and did not return that night. Natalie, weeping, went to bed." Despite the attraction, the chemistry wasn't there. "Natalie was a lightweight," says Dick Sylbert. Gavin Lambert, who first met Natalie in 1956 when he was director Nicholas Ray's assistant, and eventually became her biographer, observes, "My impression was that she was in love with Warren. And very focused on him, because she was always like that. When there was somebody important in her life, that was the one person. Natalie was very much a commitment girl, and he was not a commitment guy."

Recalls Natalie's assistant Mart Crowley, "The morning of the day she was going to go to put her handprints in the cement in front of Grauman's Chinese Theatre, she asked me, 'What am I going to wear?' I told her, 'No low-cut dresses, no push-up bras, a suit and some good jewelry, because remember, you're a star and you are going to be a lady.' But Warren wasn't going to Grauman's, he wasn't even going to get dressed up to be beside her, he was just at the house making mischief. He wouldn't let her get ready. The hairdresser would be trying to work on her hair, and he'd throw her on the bed, kiss her and roll her around, messing up her hair. I'd be screaming, 'We're going to be late.' He chased me around the bedroom to get me out of the room, and finally tackling me. I was just furious with him, because of how late he was making us. All for no reason. Just because it wasn't about him. She had a deep affection for Warren, but she also felt that it would never work." Wood, still in therapy, concluded that she was flagellating herself for divorcing Wagner by trying to make a go of a relationship that had no future.

In March 1963, Wood began *Love with the Proper Stranger* in New York, with Steve McQueen. Three weeks later, *Lilith* commenced principal photography, also in New York. Wood's therapist, Dr. John Lindon, had been pressing her about *her* inability to make commitments. She in turn had made it clear to Beatty that his sudden disappearances wouldn't do. He, on the other hand, made it clear that he didn't want to be pinned down. They both knew the affair was pretty much over and parted on friendly terms.

An alternative version has it that Wood returned to L.A. to shoot the last five days of *Love with the Proper Stranger* in late spring. On April 26, 1963, she was supposed to have dinner at Chasen's with friends, including director Alan Pakula and actress Hope Lange, whom the director was then seeing. Beatty showed up, but disappeared for a weekend with the blond hatcheck girl. After he had his way with her, he was supposed to have returned to Wood's house, only to find that she had burned his clothes. (She apparently told Joan Collins she had done so.) Beatty always denied the whole thing, the hatcheck girl and the burned clothes. Says Lambert, "Natalie told me she never burned his clothes, and as to the hatcheck girl, Warren could be unfaithful, but—he wouldn't do that kind of thing." Many years later, Wood said, "Warren goes through women on an industrial scale, [but] he does it with charm."

IN THE beginning, Robert Rossen welcomed Beatty's participation on *Lilith,* treating him more like a friend and collaborator than an actor for hire. He involved him in script revisions and casting. After the part was offered to Natalie Wood, who turned it down—the prospect of another picture with Beatty was apparently too much for her—the two men crisscrossed Europe, checking out Lilith wannabes, a casting couch dream come true for the actor, although which of the lucky women he had sex with is best known to himself. The list included Jean Seberg, who had made a splash in Otto Preminger's *Saint Joan* in 1957, and then again in Jean-Luc Godard's *Breathless* in 1960. Beatty and Rossen flew to Paris to see her, and then hired her.

Like Kazan, Rossen was a New York director with a distaste for studio production. Save for one week at Filmways Studios, Lilith was shot almost entirely on location. Production began on Long Island in late April 1963. It was a long shoot, twelve weeks or so in all, and no sooner had it begun than Beatty realized he'd made a serious mistake. The warmth he'd enjoyed with Rossen evaporated virtually over night. Recalled Seberg, "At the outset, Rossen and he had a relationship which was strangely fraternal, very intimate, very like accomplices, even. Oddly, this relationship of intimacy stopped at the first day of filming, and from then on, it did nothing but deteriorate more and more." Beatty wanted out, but of course it was too late, and he felt trapped.

Rossen was not a fan of Strasberg, Adler et al., which put him at odds with his star. As always, the actor showered Rossen with a thousand questions. "If the director was indecisive, Warren would absolutely destroy him," says screenwriter Robert Towne. "He'd ask so many questions—and he can ask more questions than any three-year-old—that the director didn't know whether he was coming or going." Beatty tried to engage Rossen in lengthy analyses of each of his scenes. The director's response was, "I hired you because I thought you knew how to act, for Christ's sake. Don't ask me how to play the part. You're supposed to know how to play the part." According to assistant cameraman Tibor Sands, who later helped Beatty shoot the Witnesses for *Reds*, "Beatty was extremely difficult on the set."

It was said that Beatty resented the attention Rossen lavished on Seberg. Sands felt that Rossen was too soft to deal with Beatty. He continues, Beatty's behavior "was getting worse and worse until Rossen slapped him in front of everybody. That calmed him down."

The camera was an old-fashioned Mitchell. It took fifteen to twenty seconds to get the camera up to speed, and when Rossen called "Action," Beatty prepared himself for the take "by taking deep breaths and squinting into the sun while the camera was rolling," Sands recalls. "By the time he was ready, half the roll was gone." Beatty also put off some of the actors, including Seberg. "I was intimidated by Warren Beatty," she said. "He talked a different language than I did in his work." She wrote to a friend, "Warren Beatty's behavior is just unbelievable. He's out to destroy everyone, including himself."

According to Peter Fonda, who had a supporting role in the film, and who credits Beatty with encouraging him to get into acting, Beatty threw all the actors off stride, "because we all had to work to a tune that Warren had in his head. Warren asked for more and more takes, and we were running into overtime, which really annoyed Rossen. Warren would change the lines, and Rossen felt that he was screwing with his script—he wrote it—although Warren was just doing what most actors do, make the lines speakable."

Beatty famously held up the production while he argued with Rossen over whether his character would say, "I've read *Crime and Punishment* and *The Brothers Karamazov*" as Rossen wished, or, as Beatty preferred, "I've read *Crime and Punishment* and *half* of *The Brothers Karamazov*." Adds Sylbert, who designed *Lilith*, "Warren was a man who was seriously smarter than the people he was talking to. And he

was just as resistant as he would ever be any time he had another director except himself. He was brutal on directors."

Beatty made no secret of the fact that he thought Rossen was making a mess of the movie, and told him so, which enraged the director.
The actor attributed some of the problem to Rossen's drinking. Finally,
in frustration, Beatty intentionally mucked up some of his scenes, as he
later confessed, by mumbling, so much so that he earned the nickname
of "Whispering Jack Smith," after a singer popular in the 1920s and
1930s.

Again, Beatty was aloof with the crew. "I don't think that anybody
liked him," Sands continues. On one occasion, his dressing room was
trashed, the door torn off the hinges. They made fun of his self-regard.

Fonda took it upon himself to protect Seberg from Beatty. In one
scene, the script called for Seberg to slap Beatty. Fonda recalls, "She got
him the first time. The second take, he stopped her by putting his hand
up in a karate-like chop. He did that several times, and she was starting
to get bruised. I said, 'If he hits her again, I'm going to slug him. I'll step
on his dick in the parking lot.' The next day there was a guy there from
Columbia, who said, 'If you hit him, we'll sue the fuck out of you.' I
wasn't really about to go fight him. I was this skinny 23-year-old kid,
and Warren was pretty buff." According to Sands, Fonda was so dis-
tressed by Beatty's behavior that during the wrap party, at the end of
July, "Peter was running around trying to enlist members of the crew
to throw Beatty in the pool, because they didn't like him."

Beatty irritated Fonda by trying to steal his scenes. "He was timing
himself for the camera to be on him, and not on me," Fonda continues. "Maybe he was competitive." But he liked Beatty, and excused
his behavior because "I thought he was in turmoil, feeling done in by
Hollywood." Surprisingly, Fonda says, "Most of his paycheck for that
film was being garnished by Kazan. Because Kazan had won a lawsuit
against Warren for pulling out of a part. I was told about it by the ac-
counting people. They showed me the check."

But Rossen was not forgiving. He later called Beatty "psychotic,"
and added, "There was nothing I could do about it, because he's so sick
that he brings his sickness into anything he does." But it was Rossen
who was sick. Speaking of her first impression of the director, Seberg
observed, "When he came to see me in Paris, he was already seriously
ill. He had a strange disease, a kind of infection of the skin that made

dark spots on his body and on his face." Beatty says he never noticed, but that seems implausible, especially for someone who practically lived in the Merck manual. And if so, he seemed to be the only one. "From day one on Rossen got worse and worse," says Sands. "It looked like a heart condition. Purple lips, and he was out of breath." According to Seberg, "At the end of the filming, he was in a complete state of exhaustion. . . . And the permanent confrontation that opposed him to Warren did not help matters; he even wanted to bring a lawsuit against him, and other childish things." Before his death in 1966, Rossen said, "If I die, it'll be Warren Beatty who killed me." Sands adds, "Beatty probably contributed to it. I completely agree with [Rossen]." And Sylbert, "Warren's vision of Rossen is that they had this wonderful relationship. Rossen wanted to kill him with an axe."

Shortly after *Lilith* wrapped, Beatty flew to New York, where he invited Arthur Penn to Delmonico's and asked him to direct *Honeybear*, a script he had been chasing, written by Charles Eastman. Penn was yet another entry on his list of Great Directors. A slightly built man of forty-one years and serious mien, he was fifteen years older than Beatty. When he came back from World War II, he wanted to make movies, but he discovered, in his words, that "Hollywood was a closed club. Back came Jimmy Stewart, back came Gable, all these people, and it was as it was before the deluge. Theater was equally closed, very much a gentleman's game, but in TV, you could get a job. And that's where we all started. We all shot up right through it." Penn distinguished himself in what later became known as the golden age of live television, doing shows like *Playhouse 90* and *The Philco Television Playhouse*. "TV just exploded in the face of the studios," he continues. "We were not the gentleman's club. We were arrogant street kids."

Eventually, Penn turned to live drama, where he had considerably more success, and by the time Beatty tried to recruit him to direct *Honeybear,* he had established himself as the premier Broadway director with a succession of hits: *Two for the Seesaw* (1958), *The Miracle Worker* (1959), *Toys in the Attic* (1960), and *An Evening with Mike Nichols and Elaine May* (1960). He even boasted of a big movie, the screen version of *The Miracle Worker,* which was released in 1962 and earned him an Academy Award nomination for Best Director, as well as Oscars for Anne Bancroft and Patty Duke.

Penn had no interest in *Honeybear.* Instead he showed Beatty a script called *Mickey One*, offering him the lead. "I found him very smart," Penn recalls. "He was smart enough to have said, 'Who are the best writers, I want to know them, I want to know Tennessee Williams, I want to know Bill Inge,' and he managed to do so. He was a young man determined to make it." Penn explained that he was trying "to push American movies into areas in which Fellini and Truffaut have moved," but Beatty wasn't impressed and said, "I don't understand this thing. What do you see in it?" Penn described the film as a metaphor for McCarthyism. "That didn't particularly fly with Warren," recalls the director. "He still didn't like the script, he didn't like the idea of it." Beatty kept saying, "It's too fucking obscure." But eager to work with Penn, Beatty finally said, "I'll do it. I'm gonna put myself in your hands."

MEANWHILE, IN a parallel universe, two men named Robert Benton and David Newman were toiling away at *Esquire*, then enjoying its moment in the sun. Benton was the art director, Newman an editor. Benton and Newman were an odd couple, a pairing of opposites, Benton the designer, Newman the wordsmith. Benton was the soft-spoken Gentile from Texas, the Felix Ungar of the two, finicky, precise, and orderly, while Newman was the Oscar Madison, a New York Jew, loud and opinionated. But they shared a love of movies. The early 1960s saw the tide of film culture crest in the United States, particularly in New York, which was awash with movies from all over the world—Italian, Swedish, Polish, Japanese, Brazilian—the kind of adult fare that had prompted the weekly and monthly reviewers to turn up their noses at *Splendor in the Grass*. Dedicated cineastes, pale as newts, threaded their way from tony venues like the Museum of Modern Art through seedy art houses like the Thalia or the New Yorker on the Upper West Side to railroad flats on the Lower East Side where a bedsheet could easily serve as a screen on which flickered an image thrown by a creaky 16 millimeter projector that sounded like a coffee grinder.

The New York Film Festival made its debut that year, 1963, showing, among others, Joseph Losey's *The Servant*, Roman Polanski's *Knife in the Water*, and Alain Resnais's *Muriel*. It was a time when unprepossessing critics—Pauline Kael, a tiny woman of fierce opinions (she was known as the "bird woman of Petaluma," an allusion to her diminutive stature and her place of birth, a chicken farm in Petaluma, California) who could easily have passed for a small-town spinster in one of Inge's plays, and Andrew Sarris, best known for popularizing the French auteur theory in America—could become culture heroes, commanding vast gatherings of glassy-eyed college students. Kael's collection of her reviews, *I Lost It at the Movies,* would become a best-seller in 1965, while Sarris would strike back (the two had a long-running feud) with *The American Cinema: Directors and Directions, 1929 to 1968,* which became the cineastes' bible. Sarris's acolytes termed themselves "auteurists," while Kael's, many of whom she placed in prominent positions in various publications, affected hearing loss when they were scornfully referred to as "Paulettes."

In any event, besotted though Benton and Newman may have been with, say, the bleak black and white visions of Ingmar Bergman or Michelangelo Antonioni's gnomic tales of the anomie that appeared to enervate the whole of Italy with chronic fatigue syndrome, or the bloody choreography of Akira Kurosawa's samurai spectacles, for them it was the French cinema that fascinated them most, defined by those twin giants of the Nouvelle Vague, the cold, austere, intellectually bracing Jean-Luc Godard, and the warmer, fuzzier, more sentimental François Truffaut. Both Godard and Truffaut wrote for *Cahiers du Cinéma* and had a taste for American studio films, particularly of the gangster variety, albeit refracted through French eyes. "All the time, everywhere we went, the only thing any of us talked about was movies," recalls Benton. He and Newman had just seen Godard's *Breathless* and couldn't get it out of their heads. Nearly as much, they loved Truffaut. "Within two months, I saw *Jules and Jim* twelve times," recalls Benton. (Newman and his wife, Leslie, named their daughter Catherine after Jeanne Moreau's character in that film.) Benton continues, "You cannot see a movie that often without beginning to notice certain things about structure and form and character." He and Newman educated themselves simply by watching movies. In the early 1960s, film schools virtually did not exist. At the Museum of Modern Art, a kid named Peter Bogdanovich was programming retrospectives of Hollywood directors. "Bogdanovich did two brilliant monographs, one on Hitchcock and one on Hawks," continues Benton. "Those were the closest things we had to a textbook."

By way of one of those cosmic coincidences that suggest there's no such thing as chance, Benton and Newman discovered that they were both reading the same book, *The Dillinger Days,* by John Toland, which in its footnotes touched on the escapades of Bonnie Parker and Clyde Barrow, who cut a swath of mayhem across five Southwestern states from 1932 to 1934. Benton was no stranger to the legend of the outlaw couple. He was born in Waxahachie, and grew up in East Texas. His father had gone to Clyde's funeral. "They were great, great folk heroes," he recalls, famous for their daring getaways against overwhelming odds. Although they had been dead for a good thirty years, in East Texas their memory was fresh. Clyde had at least one sister still alive, as did Bonnie, when the film would be shot in 1966.

In August 1963, Benton and Newman embarked on an outline. Working at night, with the banjo picking of Lester Flatt and Earl Scruggs' "Foggy Mountain Breakdown" on a Mercury record blaring scratchily from the stereo, they wrote a seventy-five-page treatment, which they finished by the end of November. With the nothing-to-lose bravado of neophytes, they set their sights on their patron saint, Truffaut, to direct it. After all, they felt they had written a European film. "The French New Wave allowed us to write with a more complex morality, more ambiguous characters, more sophisticated relationships," says Benton. By November they finished the treatment, or so they thought, and by January 2, 1964, their script ended up in the hands of the great man.

MEANWHILE, BEATTY was trying to nudge along *What's New Pussycat?* On November 22, 1963, he met with Stanley Kubrick in his Central Park West apartment in order to persuade him to direct it. "Warren used to go to school on Stanley stories," recalls Warners publicist Joe Hyams. " 'What did Stanley do on this movie? What did he do on that movie?' " Says Beatty, "Stanley was the best. He always liked to perpetuate the feeling that he was a mad genius, that he knew things other people didn't know. Although he was sitting in London, he would know what was happening in the balcony of the Grauman's Chinese."

Dr. Strangelove would not be released until the end of the following January, but Kubrick was afraid that it was so scornful of the Cold War pieties on which President Kennedy had campaigned—he alarmed voters with the so-called missile gap—that he would block its release. He asked Beatty to arrange a screening for the Kennedys, which the actor did, although his clout was not yet of the dimensions that would have enabled him to corral the president or his brother Bobby; he had to settle for wives, relatives, and hangers-on. Beatty was leaving Kubrick's on his way to meet with Feldman and Woody Allen, when he heard that Kennedy had been shot. (Allen recalls that on that day he was in L.A., working on the script at the Gene Autry Motel across Sunset Boulevard from the Interlude, the club at which he was performing.)

In February 1964, Beatty met Leslie Caron at a dinner party thrown by her agent, Freddie Fields, co-head of Creative Management Associates (CMA) at the Bistro, a popular Beverly Hills restaurant, to promote her Oscar prospects for *The L-Shaped Room* (1963). With her dark, bobbed hair, blue eyes, and lips forever pursed in an enchanting pout, Caron, born in 1931 and six years older than Beatty, was the star of *An American in Paris, Lili*, and particularly *Gigi*, in which she had starred opposite Louis Jourdan and Maurice Chevalier in 1958. Beatty had seen all her films and had a crush on her. "It was like lightning had struck," he told Sylbert. But there was a hitch: she was married to Peter Hall, the director of the Royal Shakespeare Company, with whom she had two young children, Christopher and Jenny. Still, husbands were never much of an impediment to Beatty, and he asked if he could see her home. She said yes, and the two embarked on a discreet but passionate affair. "That was it," says Sylbert. "It was like an explosion. Blew up the marriage, the children. You couldn't quite understand why. Who was Leslie Caron? He is in a certain way a fan."

From her point of view, Caron recalled later, "I was struck by his appearance and his personality. He had star quality: very good looks, a great smile, he was tall and athletic. Seduction was his greatest asset. Once he was interested in a woman, he would never let go. He enveloped her with his every thought. He wanted total control of her, her clothes, her makeup, her work. He took notice of everything." She added, "We practically did not leave each other for the next two years." Like the other women he saw seriously, he put Caron into psychoanalysis.

As Beatty was guiltless with regard to Wood and Wagner, so he was with regard to Caron and Hall. He did not deserve the reputation for being a home wrecker that was hung around his neck by the tabloids; their marriage was already fatally stressed. Both Caron and Hall were driven and ambitious. Their careers kept them apart, hers in Hollywood and his in England. "My tiredness, her anxieties and our per-petual separations chipped the marriage away," wrote Hall. "We both had affairs. By 1962 there wasn't much left but resentment."

That same month, Caron was nominated for Best Actress, along with Wood for *Love with the Proper Stranger,* and MacLaine for *Irma La Douce. America, America,* which Beatty had badly wanted and didn't get, was nominated for Best Picture, along with *Tom Jones, Lilies of the Field, Cleopatra,* and *How the West Was Won,* a lame bunch, save for *Tom Jones,* but consistent with the creative malaise that clung to Hollywood like smog.

Beatty, accompanied by Caron, returned to New York to begin rehearsals for *Mickey One.* On March 2, 1964, he flew to Chicago for the beginning of the shoot. Despite Penn's ambitions, *Mickey One* was about as far from Truffaut and/or Godard as Chicago from Paris. Sylbert derisively called it "Mickey One ½," as in, "Let's be a foreign film-maker, say, Fellini." A pretentious play by Alan Surgal, written under the influence of the Protestant existentialist theologian Paul Tillich, with whom the writer was infatuated at the time, became even more pretentious in the hands of Penn, who indeed turned it into a parable of McCarthyism, elliptically told, with other Big Ideas tossed in for good measure.

Shot in funky black and white, the budget was low, $1.1 million—the only way Penn could get it financed—but it wears its poverty on its sleeve, as if a threadbare look guarantees its authenticity. The plot, such as it is, presented the story of a not-yet-ready-for-prime-time stand-up comic on the run from the mob for reasons that remain opaque at best. The symbolic tableaux Penn scatters about the film like plums in a pudding were visually striking and might have worked had they been organic to the story, but they just come off as clumsy, portentous, and finally embarrassing.

To Penn, making a European film meant breaking up the narrative. "Movies didn't have to tell that story like a railroad track," he says. "They could go sideways, with self-referential tangents. That was a very liberating idea, which unfortunately I was unable to accomplish. Because my main storyline was not strong enough, the tangents became the dominant aspect of the film." Well put.

Beatty was fully aware of just how problematic the project was, but even though the two men were better matched than he and Rossen, *Mickey One* proved to be yet another fractious production. "We had a lot of trouble on that film because I didn't know what the hell Arthur was trying to do," the actor said later, with unaccustomed frankness. "I didn't know what Penn wanted. . . . I'm not sure that he knew himself. . . . [The picture is] unnecessarily obscure. It reaches further than it needs to. . . . Arthur felt that I never really trusted him on it, and he was absolutely right." He would complain to the director, "Nobody's going to understand this fucking scene. Why don't we just say what it's about?"

"No, Beatty, we're not going to say what it's about." Big mistake.

One of his major objections was that although he was playing a stand-up comic, his jokes didn't get any laughs. "I felt they were pretentious jokes . . . jokes about cosmic situations—you know, the danger of nuclear attack, the ownership of the military–industrial complex— they weren't very funny jokes. . . . I think I know when I've got a funny joke to tell and when I don't."

For his part, Penn was equally frustrated: "At that stage in the game, I don't think Warren was as adept an actor as he later became." He was embarrassed by acting, self-conscious and ill at ease. "He doesn't like strong displays of emotion and he knew that he had been getting along very nicely on his good looks and his persona," Penn observed. The director couldn't get the kind of performance out of Beatty that he wanted, in his words, "a certain flamboyance. I didn't know Warren well enough. I kept thinking, That's just an acting choice. He ought to be able to make another choice." Penn kept pushing and prodding, "Come on, you can do it better than that. Let's get out here and do it." But finally, he realized that it was not just an acting choice, "it was antithetical to Warren's personality. He's very wary, and moves very, very carefully. Understandably, in that he lives in a minefield. There were many love affairs that I didn't know about, that were potential stuff for the papers."

Indeed, this was one of the worst performances of Beatty's career. He seemed either stiff, or, under Penn's prodding, melodramatic, as if emoting in a silent movie. It feels as though he's acting. Beatty's character was supposed to be Polish, because Penn believed that the best comics are outsiders of one ethnicity or another, but that was clearly beyond the actor's range, and the director finally gave up. The lack of specificity accentuated the abstract, free-floating feel of the film, grounded in nothing.

The movie wasn't helped by a wooden performance by Alexandra Stewart, who played opposite Beatty. Before he signed her, Penn had consulted Truffaut, who told him, "Oh, she's wonderful, she's just wonderful." He goes on, "So, virtually sight unseen, I hired her. I didn't know that Truffaut was having an affair with her. She had no inner fire, and Warren didn't respond too well to that kind of passivity. When he didn't get the kickback from her that he was expecting, he would give me a look, as if to say, 'What did you get me into here?' So it was misbegotten from the outset."

Beatty's relationship with Caron was still under wraps, or so he thought. She visited the set in a "disguise"—sunglasses and a scarf—that fooled no one and amused everyone. The script supervisor even told her she looked like Leslie Caron!

Caron went on to Morocco with Hall on a brief vacation in a futile effort to salvage their marriage. Instead, she told him she was in love with Beatty. "'Yes, I was having an affair with Warren,' she said. 'Wasn't everyone?'" She told Hall she was moving to Los Angeles, leaving the children with him. Hall announced their separation on April 5. "I didn't blame Leslie; I didn't even blame Warren Beatty," he wrote later. "He was just the catalyst for a split that had long been inevitable." Eight days later, on April 13, 1964, Beatty accompanied Caron to the Oscar ceremony at the Santa Monica Civic Auditorium. Caron, Wood, and MacLaine all lost to Patricia Neal, who won for her role in *Hud*. *Tom Jones,* which was British-made, won Best Picture, which struck some observers as virtually un-American. "Wonder why we hate ourselves," wrote gossip columnist Hedda Hopper, off base as usual. The answer lay not in insufficient American amour propre, but in the sickness of the studio system.

Meanwhile, Beatty's relationship with Feldman was dissolving in acrimony over *Pussycat*. He bombarded his friend with a fusillade of telegrams full of questions about the status of the project. Feldman failed to respond, even though Beatty begged him to clarify the situation so he could focus on *Mickey One*. Despite Woody Allen's suspicions, Feldman liked his work. It was Beatty who now had the problem. He was supposed to play a womanizer trying to remain true to his fiancée, but who can't resist the bevy of females who throw themselves at him. His psychiatrist is useless. He's involved with one of his patients, who also lusts after the womanizer. As draft followed draft, the actor began to notice that his part was growing smaller, while Allen's was growing larger. "In the original script, Woody's part might have appeared on six pages," he recalls. "In his first rewrite, the part went to twelve or fifteen pages, and it was funny. Then it went to twenty or thirty pages. By the time we got to what Woody thought was an acceptable rewrite, his part was almost half the script. Mine was almost as large but not quite as good. Woody couldn't quite grasp what was funny about a compulsive, successful Don Juan." Besides that, Beatty felt that the characters had changed, Allen's for the better, his for the worse. Allen's started as a nebbish who hopped around on a pogo stick, and became "a lovable guy who found it hard to get laid and had all the really good jokes," he said. "My character had turned into some neo-Nazi Ubermensch who was unkind to women."

There were other problems between Beatty and Feldman. Beatty says he had been given various assurances regarding casting and director selection. He favored Groucho Marx in the part of a mad psychiatrist; Barbara Harris as the female lead, a part that was eventually split into three; and Mike Nichols, who had yet to make a film, to direct. None of them was happening. And worse, Feldman urged Allen to strengthen the part of the French girl. Beatty still feared that his friend was going to cast Capucine in the role.

When a gossip column item appeared on April 16, 1964, to the effect that Caron would appear opposite Beatty in *Pussycat*, Feldman exploded, concluding that the actor had planted it, trying to force his hand. In an angry letter to Beatty he wrote, "You seem to forget that this is a venture of mine and not yours, and until you straighten yourself out in this regard this picture will not start, nor will I assign a director. Either I will cast the picture my way and do this film my way, or the picture will not get going for some time. . . . I don't want you dictating to me how this picture should be done, or for that matter any picture with which I am identified." Feldman never sent the letter, but the damage had been done. With *Pussycat* in trouble, or at least Beatty's involvement in trouble, the actor began to look around for another project.

MICKEY ONE wrapped at the end of May 1964. Beatty flew to Caron's side in Jamaica, where she was shooting *Father Goose*, opposite Cary Grant. At night, in Caron's bungalow, she and Beatty fretted over his career problems. He couldn't understand why Brando, Dean, and Clift were taken seriously while he wasn't. He talked about quitting acting, going into directing or producing. She encouraged him.

In the beginning of June, Caron called Hall, informing him that she was flying to London to pick up the children and take them to Los Angeles, where they would live with her. Hall reacted angrily, and on June 8, 1964, he filed for divorce.

Beatty and Caron believed the affair was still their secret, but Grant invited journalist Roderick Mann, a friend, to the set. Mann published an interview with Caron on June 14, 1964, wherein he dropped a small bombshell, namely, that "for the past two weeks she has been enjoying the company in Jamaica of Warren Beatty, the handsome Hollywood actor, who flew down here amid great secrecy and promptly went to ground." Mann also mentioned that she had visited him in Chicago, and that she was undecided as to whether to settle in Hollywood, but would make a decision after her two children had spent the summer with her there. The response from Hall was swift. He charged Caron with adultery and named Beatty as a co-respondent. The judge granted him a restraining order preventing Caron from taking their children out of the country for seven days. Then Hall filed for custody.

Beatty's relationships with Joan Collins, who was single, and Natalie Wood, who was separated, were one thing, but appearing to break up the marriage of a mother with two children, even if it wasn't true, was something else, and when it became public, it was ugly. The British press in effect affixed a scarlet "A" to Beatty's chest. He himself wasn't happy with his behavior. As he once observed, "When you're falling in love you're a fascist. You lie, you cheat when you're with someone else, or you're breaking somebody up." It was only the year before that *The L-Shaped Room* had won a BAFTA award and only months before that Caron had been nominated for an Oscar, but it might as well have been another lifetime.

Beatty accompanied Caron back to London. He had just accepted $200,000 to star in and co-produce *Pussycat,* but confronted Feldman in his suite at the Dorchester. He accused him of reneging on their agreement—creating a role for Capucine, and letting Allen write him out of the script. Recalls Sylbert, who was associate producer, "Warren said, 'Charlie, I'm not going to do it.' Charlie was in shock. Furious. You didn't fuck with Charlie Feldman." Adds Beatty, "I finally walked out in a huffing bluff or bluffing huff, thinking they wouldn't let me go. But they were only too happy to let me go. He went around pretending that he was upset because I walked off the movie when in fact I think he was ecstatic, because he was able to go to these people who were much more important in getting money. And also he didn't have to deal with me." Peter Sellers, then the biggest comedy star in the world, came on board to play the Groucho Marx part, Peter O'Toole, fresh from *Lawrence of Arabia* and *Becket,* replaced Beatty. Beatty had invested a considerable amount of time and energy into *Pussycat,* and he was devastated. "I diva'ed my way out of the movie," he said. "I was wrong. And hurt. I was really hurt." He and Feldman didn't speak for four years, until just before Feldman was diagnosed with pancreatic cancer in 1968. The picture turned out to be a big hit, and a turning point for both Beatty and Allen. "Woody was very unhappy with the movie that was finally made," continues Beatty. "I was even unhappier, because I would have gotten rich off it. After that, Woody was always in control of whatever he did. And so was I."

IN MAY 1964, the neophyte brother-and-sister producing team Elinor Jones and Norton Wright paid Benton and Newman $1,700 for an eighteen-month option on their treatment that expired on November 27, 1965. Truffaut thrilled the writers by expressing interest in directing, then dashed their hopes with talk of a prior commitment (*Fahrenheit 451*), and kept them on tenterhooks while he plucked he-loves-it, he-loves-it-not petals off the *Bonnie and Clyde* blossom. He promised to make a decision by late July, and suggested a first-of-that-month deadline for the writers to turn in their script. When they got back to New York, they scrambled to transform the treatment into a screenplay, where description became dialogue. Like real screenwriters, they were late, failing to finish until early August, but when they handed in their draft, Wright and Jones were over the moon about it.

The script, with Truffaut attached, went out to the studios, most of which worried that the main characters—killers, after all—were unappealing, and that Truffaut was ill-suited to direct this material. Their chances were not helped by the fact that their screenplay featured a ménage à trois: Bonnie was in love with Clyde, and Clyde with Bonnie, but he needed the stimulus of C. W. Moss to get off. Rumor had it that Clyde had turned bisexual during a stint in prison, and they ran with it. After all, it was in keeping with Benton and Newman's notion that the couple were cultural outlaws, as well as with the experimentation that was becoming obligatory in the sexual revolution of the 1960s. Besides, *Jules and Jim* was built around a ménage à trois. But the studios weren't impressed. Benton and Newman were turned down all over town. Months passed. Benton thought that *Bonnie and Clyde* was dead.

A bad situation can always get worse, and on September 7, it did. In a letter to Elinor Jones, Truffaut informed her that although he too loved the script, he was unable to direct it, because he was due to begin *Fahrenheit 451* in the summer of 1965, and then direct *The Bride Wore Black.*

Benton was devastated. He thought, That's it. It's over. But with Truffaut out of the way, the path was cleared for Beatty, who, meanwhile, was having his own problems.

On Saturday, September 19, 1964, *Lilith* premiered to a shower of rotten tomatoes, figuratively speaking. It opened its commercial run in New York on October 1. The reviews were scathing. In *The New York Times,* Crowther heaped scorn on the young actor, writing, "a muddy performance by Warren Beatty doesn't help. Mr. Beatty has a sodden way of moving and a monotonous expression that suggests that his character should be getting treatment all the way through the film. He does not help to clarify matters or generate sympathy." Beatty called up Arthur Penn. The actor recalled, "I needed some confirmation, so I asked, 'Do you think I need to talk faster?' He said, 'Are you kidding? Everyone does. What have I been trying to tell you for years?'"

Beatty blamed Rossen for the picture's failure. His odd relationship with the director which skidded from admiration into a swamp of hostility, was not unlike his relationships with Inge and Odets, whom the actor wooed and then discarded. Odets speculated that his behavior—on the surface almost a parody of Freud's Oedipus Complex—was an echo of his connection to his father, whom he revered as a youngster but grew increasingly estranged from in later years as the older man descended into drink, anger, and self-pity. Beatty was himself enough of a child of the Freudian 1950s to refer repeatedly to his "patricidal" posture toward his older mentors, as he did with Kazan. Although there was undoubtedly some truth in Odets's characterization, it wasn't the whole story. Inge was in artistic decline and Odets had squandered his talent on talk and booze by the time Beatty met them, so one need not invoke Freud to figure out why Beatty might have moved on from them.

A year or so after the dinner at Chasen's marked the end of Beatty's relationship with Natalie Wood, she and her sister ran into him in New York. Lana, then seventeen, claimed he always used to throw inviting looks her way when he was living with Natalie. She said he came on to her after dinner at a restaurant when her sister had left. She recalled that "he told me I was always provoking him by running around Natalie's house in a bathing suit," and insisted that he come back with her to her hotel room. Lana, who says she managed to escape, never liked him, but changed her mind some years later when he caught her in the middle of a divorce, and they had a brief affair.

A few months later, there was a strange coda to his relationship with Natalie. As was often the case with his lovers, the embers burned on well after the blaze had been doused. In May 1964, Wood started *The Great Race,* directed by Blake Edwards, a project she hated and did only to satisfy her contract with Warners. Toward the end of the shoot, on Friday, November 27, 1964, she was having dinner with Mart Crowley at La Scala, in one of the red leather booths. She spent the meal bitching about Edwards, who was always dumping water on her and throwing pies at her. She was lonely, had no one in her life. Suddenly Beatty appeared at their table, virtually aglow with good health and fine spirits. He sat down for a moment, then left. After the dinner, Crowley drove her home to her place on Bentley Drive. On the way, she told him, "Warren's coming over for a drink." When they arrived, she went into her bedroom to fix her face. When she came out, she asked Crowley, "What are you doing?"

"Nothing, I'm going to go home."

"Why don't you spend the night here."

"Okay."

The bell rang, and she said, "That's Warren." Crowley let him in, said "Good night," and retired to the library, where there was a couch that doubled as a guest bed. He closed the door and went to sleep. Lana Wood later quoted Crowley saying that he had heard "raised voices" between Beatty and Natalie, after which Natalie tried to take her life, the implication being that the actor had tipped her into a suicidal funk. Lana recalled that Crowley, who didn't like Beatty either, directed several "expletives" his way, suggesting that he believed the actor was at fault.

Crowley denies that he told Lana, who was then still in high school, anything of the sort, and says he heard nothing until three or four in the morning, when he was awakened by a soft scuffling sound at his door. "It was just a miracle that she didn't collapse and die before she got to my room. In my jockey shorts, I stumbled to the door and unlocked it, and she just fell in on top of me, collapsed. Gone, out of it, not a word. I dragged her to the bathroom, turned the shower tap to freezing cold, and shoved her in there. I put her on her back on the floor—there was water everywhere—and I thought, She's gonna get pneumonia, so I massaged her hands and feet, and slapped her face. When she came to in the hospital, she said, 'You son of a bitch, my face is absolutely beat to shit, what were you doing?' "

She was taken to the old Cedars Sinai on Fountain Avenue, where George Gershwin, Judy Holliday, and many other celebrities had died. "It was really touch and go," Crowley continues. "They pumped her stomach, determined that she had taken Seconal. Meanwhile, Warren was calling, leaving messages on her phone machine at home. At first they were, 'Where the hell are you? What's going on?' Then it was, 'What is the matter? Are you angry? What is it? Call me back. Call me.' The calls from Warren just kept building up, with increasing urgency. I never returned any of them, because I was told by Natalie's agents, the William Morris people, 'This can't get out.' "

When Wood recovered, she went home, listened to more messages from Beatty, and finally called him back. "Nothing happened," she told him. "After you left, Mart and I suddenly decided to drive down to Palm Springs for the weekend." Wood told Crowley, "He didn't believe me, and asked if I'd been in the hospital. 'That's crazy,' I said, and stuck to my story." Crowley continues, "I saw him about two months later, in La Scala, and he backed me up in a corner, and said, 'You lied to me, you son of a bitch, you said you went to Palm Springs, I know where you were, you were at Cedars. That's why you didn't return my calls.' I said, 'No, Warren, what are you talking about? We had a great time, we went to Palm Springs!' " Crowley never asked Wood why she tried to commit suicide. "She was really, really fucked up in the head at this point in her life."

Speculates Lambert, "Maybe seeing Warren was herself grasping at this last straw. I think that she did have some idea of getting back with him, although she knew that by that time he was involved with Leslie Caron. One evening, after the suicide attempt, we were having dinner at La Scala, and at the end of dinner, she suddenly said, 'Let's go see Warren.' She really cared about him a lot, and I had the feeling again that she thought something might happen, and I knew that the deal was, if after half an hour, nothing was going to happen, I would get up and say, 'You've got an early call tomorrow,' and if it looked like something was going to happen, I would just leave. We parked in the garage, she got on the house phone, turned to me, and said, 'He wants us to come up right away.' So we did, and there was Warren, very cool, very charming, offering us a drink, offering us pot, whatever. He knew the score as well as I did. We talked about nothing in particular, and it was pretty clear after twenty minutes or so that it was not going to go any further. I got up, and said, 'Natalie, I think you have an early call.' She got up at once and said, 'Yes, I do.' And that was it. We drove home talking about other things, and I very pointedly did not ask her, because I knew if she wanted to say something, she would. I took that to mean that she'd given up any idea that they would ever get back together again. That was the last time I saw them together."

Still, there was nothing like a little competition to get Beatty's attention. Even though he and Wood were long over, he remained possessive of the women in his orbit. Wood met Henry Jaglom at a party in July 1965. Jaglom was a would-be actor from a wealthy family in New York who had studied at the Actors Studio. They started to date. He took her to a club, where they ran into Beatty, who watched them leave. When they walked into her house, she looked at the phone and said, "In ten seconds that phone is going to ring, and it's going to be Warren." In exactly ten seconds, the phone did ring, and it was Warren.

BY MID-DECADE, Beatty's once promising career had crumbled. *Lilith* was his third flop in a row, with a fourth, *Mickey One*, on the way. His romance with Caron had turned into a nightmare of litigation and bad press, while his relationship with Feldman had foundered on the shoals of *What's New Pussycat?*

"It was a very upsetting period, the first year or two years of being famous," Beatty observed. "Very, very upsetting." He was sufficiently concerned about his own state of mind to go into psychoanalysis with Vivien Leigh's doctor, therapist-to-the-stars Martin Grotjahn, a minor celebrity in his own right. Grotjahn treated everyone from Danny Kaye to David Geffen. It was in the waiting room of Grotjahn's office that Beatty first ran into Robert Towne. Three years Beatty's senior, Towne was born Robert Schwartz in 1934, and spent his early years in San Pedro, just south of L.A., where his father, Lou, sold ladies' clothes out of the Towne Smart Shop. Eventually, he moved from shmattas to real estate, changed the family name to Towne, and moved the family up and out to Brentwood. Young Robert grew up to be tall and athletic. But he had a scholarly bent, read voraciously, and could speak intelligently, even eloquently, about movies. He had a Talmudic stoop that came in handy in later years when he cast himself as a screenwriting guru.

Towne did a little acting, but quickly turned to screenwriting, then regarded as beneath contempt, a derelict cousin of playwriting. But with the demise of the studio system, writers began to get some respect, and Towne was actually good at it. "He had this ability to leave a sense of moisture on the page, as if he just breathed on it in some way," says Jerry Ayres, who was then an executive at Columbia Pictures and who would hire him to write the first of his three great scripts, *The Last Detail.* "There was always something that jostled your sensibilities, so that reading of the page gave you the feeling that something accidental and true to the life of a human being had happened there." But Towne liked to hear himself talk and could be numbingly verbose. Says David Geffen, who later produced *Personal Best,* which Towne would write and direct, "Bob was an extraordinarily boring man. He always talked about himself. He used to go to Catalina to write, and he would describe to you in endless detail watching the cows shit."

Towne had a script, a western called *The Long Ride Home* that Roger "King of the Bs" Corman wanted to direct. Beatty read it, thought about playing the lead. Recalls Towne, "He set up a meeting with Roger, which was unusual, because Roger was doing his quickies with five-day production schedules, and Warren had worked with Kazan. He asked to look at an example of Roger's work. Roger showed him *The Tomb of Ligeia* that I had written for him. This was not something that endeared Roger, as a director, to Warren. Warren said, 'Look,

I feel like I'm about to get married, and the bride is just beautiful, but then I learn she's been a hooker.' "

Beatty declined the picture, as he declined most pictures, but he liked Towne, and they became fast friends. Says Ayres, who was one of the few out-of-the-closet gay men in Hollywood at that time, "They were so intimate, they were twisted together like a knot. Traveled everywhere together, were on the phone all the time squabbling, carrying on like [lovers]. I'm not seriously suggesting they were lovers, but there was a sort of intermixing that was intense and as intimate as lovers."

As time passed, "Towne was like this shadow image of Warren," says writer Buck Henry. When Beatty grew a beard, Towne grew a beard. When Beatty took up cigars, Towne took up cigars. They sounded alike on the phone, the same whispery delivery, the same emphases, the same rhythms. They sounded so alike that Beatty was fond of calling Towne's wife, pretending to be her husband. Towne became Beatty's accomplice in hypochondria. Both men suffered from a variety of allergies, and they constantly compared notes. But most important, Towne would become the star's house writer, someone he could call at 3:00 A.M. and ask to write a new scene. Towne would do it, and well.

BEATTY RELOCATED to London to be with Caron. Director and Monty Pythonette Terry Gilliam met him there some time later. "He was great," says Gilliam. "His main problem was that he had to charm every woman that he saw, whether she was fat, ugly, tall, or old. If he got into a lift with a woman, he had to seduce her by the time they reached her floor. He can't stop himself."

Beatty was still looking for a project that they could do together. Perhaps influenced by his budding friendship with Cary Grant, he was on the lookout for a romantic comedy. He complained that he had done several "festival" pictures in a row, and was now looking for something popular. He seized on a cotton-candy script by William Peter Blatty, who would become best known as the author of *The Exorcist*, called *The Babysitter*, aka *Promise Her Anything*, in which he plays a bachelor who baby-sits for his neighbor, a single mother (Caron), in order to date her.

Caron had not contested Hall's divorce petition, and *Promise Her Anything* got underway in the shadow of the court proceedings. On

February 2, 1965, Hall was granted a divorce on the grounds of Caron's adultery with Beatty. The court awarded him custody of both children, and Beatty was ordered to pay the costs of the litigation.

The picture wrapped in May 1965. Meanwhile, Jones and Wright were still flogging *Bonnie and Clyde*. They had sent it to Penn that January, who turned it down for the second time. He was just about to begin *The Chase* and felt it was too similar. They took it to United Artists. Wright recalled UA chairman Arthur Krim's horror when he came across the ménage à trois. He asked, "Am I to assume that Clyde Barrow and this character C.W. are, well, being sexually intimate with Bonnie Parker?" Wright replied, "Oh, yeah, they're both balling her. And maybe each other! It's a ménage à trois." Krim shuddered. Continued Wright, "It was as if I'd spit on the flag."

At the end of May, Beatty and Caron had lunch with Truffaut in Paris. "I don't think Warren ever had lunch with anybody without an ulterior motive," says Benton. But accounts of what that motive was differ. According to Caron, who wanted Truffaut to direct her in an Edith Piaf film, Beatty was campaigning for the lead in *Fahrenheit 451*, but Truffaut was committed to Oskar Werner—Jules in *Jules and Jim*—and turned him down. (Beatty says he had no interest in *Fahrenheit 451*, didn't even read the script, nor was he looking for a project for the two of them.) In passing, however, Truffaut recommended *Bonnie and Clyde* as a vehicle for the actor, whom he apparently didn't like. Subsequently, he expressed himself on this subject in a note to Jones: "He seems to me an extremely unpleasant person. He and Marlon Brando, and several others, are on a little list that I've classified in my head as 'Better not to make films at all than to make films with these people.'" Benton speculated that he suggested *Bonnie and Clyde* in an effort to get the actor to stop pestering him about *Fahrenheit 451*. According to Beatty, "Truffaut was utterly bored by me. I think he really did not like me for some reason of principle." In any event, Beatty flew to New York the next day. "There was this funny thing that happened when I became a financible star in my first movie," he explains. "I was more prone to letting things be offered to me, taking it easy about going out and doing it myself." He was determined to be more proactive. He decided to contact Benton and Newman.

One Saturday in the middle of June 1965, Benton's phone rang. He picked it up, and a voice said, "This is Warren Beatty." Benton, thinking it was a gag, said, "Who is this, really?" The voice replied, "This is really Warren Beatty." Beatty said he wanted to read the script. Benton may have been a novice, but he knew he was a mere writer, and no star was about to come to his door. So he said, "I'll drop it off. What hotel are you in?" But Beatty replied, "No. I'll pick it up." Explained Benton, that's "what makes Warren great." Still, he thought that meant sooner or later, a couple of days, maybe a week, maybe never. But within twenty minutes, the bell rang. His wife, Sally, opened the door, and there was Beatty, who took the script and left. "My wife was in blue jeans and a shirt and her hair was in curlers," recalled Benton. "It was two weeks before she'd talk to me again." About a half hour later the actor called, said, "I want to do it." But Benton was worried about the ménage à trois, thinking Beatty would never buy it. He said, "Warren, what page are you on?"

"I'm on page 25."

"Wait till you get to page 40, then call me back." Beatty called back an hour or so later, and he spoke words Benton had been waiting years to hear: "I've finished the script. I understand what you mean, but I still want to do it."

Beatty returned to L.A., where he had moved into the tenth floor penthouse of the Beverly Wilshire Hotel. Having uncharacteristically acted on impulse, he started to second-guess himself. Stung by a swarm of question marks, he began to worry he'd made a mistake—the story had been told before on film, the gangster picture was dead, worse, it would be treated like a western, another threadbare genre, or just another killers-in-a-flyover-state gore fest—*In Cold Blood* was in the pipeline at UA—anything he could think of. Caron, who at the time thought she was going to play Bonnie, urged him on. Still, he worried. Says Towne, "He was walking around saying, 'Should I do it?' He asked everybody, including the operators at the Beverly Wilshire." Towne told him, "Go ahead."

Beatty was also uncertain about the nature of his relationship to the picture. He was by no means sure he wanted to star in it himself, something he neglected to tell Benton. The historical Clyde was very much a runt, and he imagined Bob Dylan in the role. He thought of his sister for Bonnie, but couldn't place her with Dylan. It's also possible that after four years of struggle he recognized that he was not nearly so good an actor as Marlon Brando—nobody was—nor was he going to posthumously profit from a fiery crash, like James Dean. Maybe it was time for him to take out some insurance. He had always been a sponge for information and obsessed by detail. He was finished ceding decisions to people for whom he had little respect. The lesson he took away from the *Pussycat* debacle was that, like Woody Allen, he must produce.

In a few short years, under the sway of European film and the French auteur theory, everyone would want to become a director. But not quite yet. And after his experiences with Quintero, Frankenheimer, Rossen, and Penn, Beatty was becoming weary of chasing directors. Rossen had produced *Lilith,* and Beatty heard him when he said, "For me, producing means . . . control of my material from the beginning to the end. . . . When I was in control as a producer, I did my best pictures." In the early 1960s, anyone who knew anything wanted to be a producer, move into the vacuum created by the fall of the studios, still run by an ancien régime of geriatric moguls, out of touch with the changing world around them.

Into the breach rushed powerful independent producers like Sam Spiegel, David Selznick, Sam Goldwyn, and the Mirisches, who usurped the functions that had traditionally belonged to the studios, and could lay claim to being "creative producers" who hired the directors. More often than not they saw the project through from beginning to end. Not only did superstar directors like Kazan and Rossen, as well as enterprising agents like Feldman and Ray Stark, turn to producing, even actors like Burt Lancaster, Kirk Douglas, and John Wayne were taking control of their destinies by setting up their own production companies.

Still, the actors who produced were established stars at the top of their games with decades of successful pictures behind them. "Pretty boys didn't really produce pictures," as Beatty himself put it, "certainly not at that age." (Orson Welles produced that young, but he had a glittering reputation as a wunderkind at the time.) Nor were they hands-on, as Beatty intended to be. They delegated the nitty-gritty details of production — and they were legion — to their producing partners. Beatty's friends warned him against it: "You're not actually going to call yourself a producer, are you?"

"No . . . Yeah, I'm actually going to say, 'Produced by.' "

"That's not very smart."

But Beatty had become comfortable thinking of himself in the role. "Up until the very last minute, I had intended to call in an outsider to actually produce the picture, because . . . it would be too much work," Beatty explained. "But I changed my mind. . . . I found, in other pictures that I have done, some trivial, some not, an awful lot of people were saying to me, 'What the hell do you think you are? A producer?'" The year before, Beatty announced the formation of his production company, Tatira, named after his parents, Ira and Tat, his mother's nickname when she was a little girl. But Jones and Wright's option still had five months to run, so Beatty had to sit tight and watch *What's New Pussycat?*, released on June 22, 1965, clean up at the box office, strengthening his resolve to control the pictures he developed.

Meanwhile, UA production head David Picker, who had dissented from Krim's decision to turn down the *Bonnie and Clyde* script, came back to Jones, telling her that UA would finance the picture if she and Wright could bring it in for $800,000. This in turn brought Truffaut back in, who wanted Alexandra Stewart for his Bonnie, and Terence Stamp for Clyde. Jones, like Benton and Newman, was thrilled that Beatty had shown interest, wrote to Truffaut asking if he would contemplate the American instead of Stamp. Truffaut wrote back "that it was out of the question that I would make it with Warren Beatty." A few weeks later, on August 25, Truffaut dropped out for the second time.

Mickey One landed on screen on September 27, 1965, with a resounding thud. Crowther, reviewing the picture in *The New York Times* when it played the New York Film Festival, called Beatty "affected and oddly amateurish." For once he was right.

Meanwhile, Beatty was still chasing Charles Eastman's *Honeybear*, as well as several other scripts, including a remake of Renoir's *The Lower Depths*, as well as *Kaleidoscope*, yet another attempt to exploit the runaway success of the James Bond pictures. He also started working with Towne on a script. Ever since *Pussycat* got away from him, Beatty had an itch to return to the same territory, the story of the compulsive Don Juan. Both men saw William Wycherley's *The Country Wife*, a Restoration comedy, at the Chichester Festival Theatre in England. "Warren and I were talking one day about what would be a current adaptation of *The Country Wife*," recalled Towne. "It's a wonderful play about a man called Horner who lets it be known throughout all of social London that his doctor, Doctor Quack, has rendered him a eunuch. Consequently, all husbands trust Horner with their wives, a big mistake. He's in fine shape. We talked about it, and Warren said,

'Well, what would be the contemporary equivalent? An actor?' I said, 'No, it would be a hairdresser.' And he said, 'You're right.'"

Towne had run into a hairdresser named Gene Shacove, who had a shop called the Razor's Edge. The writer stopped by one day and couldn't help noticing that the place was chock-full of stunning women—and one man, Shacove—a hip guy with a blow-dryer who rode a motorcycle. He thought, Wow. This guy has it made. The only rooster in the henhouse. And everyone assumes he's gay. Beatty had an ax to grind in this respect. "It was that period when we were all very infatuated with Freudian thinking, and analysis caused us to think that a rose is not necessarily a rose and a camel is a horse," he says, adding, "I wanted to challenge the fashionable assumption that the Don Juan is expressing self-hatred, self-love, hatred of women, excessive love of women, homosexuality, sadism, masochism, a wish for eternal life, and so on." Beatty never thought about himself as someone who was inordinately interested in sex, obsessed or addicted to it in any way. His attitude was, it was perfectly normal, and society was too puritanical to accept it. And indeed, if you looked like him and were gifted with the talent for seduction that was his, why not? He did it because he could, thank you very much, Dr. Freud!

Beatty hired Towne to write the script for $25,000. The working title was *Hair*. Later, it would become *Shampoo*.

ON NOVEMBER 27, 1965, Jones and Wright's option on *Bonnie and Clyde* finally lapsed. Beatty pounced, picking up the script for, he says, $7,500. Later, his company, Tatira, paid Benton and Newman a writing fee of $75,000. By this time, Beatty had decided to play Clyde himself, and hire a director. He was not enthusiastic about either Truffaut or Godard. He wisely told the writers that they had already written a European picture, so they needed an American director. His first instinct was to go with one of the giants he admired. He approached George Stevens and William Wyler. Luckily for him, neither was interested. Nor were a half dozen other directors. Beatty asked Penn, who turned down the film yet again. Meanwhile, the actor disabused Caron of her belief that the part was hers, although he says he never considered her for the role: "It's an outlandish thought that a French woman would play Bonnie."

With Beatty starring, MacLaine was out. She quipped, "That would be adding incest to injury!" Beatty was unamused by her attempts at humor at his expense. As in, "I'd love to do a kissing scene with him, to see what all the fuss is about. . . . I keep my daughter as far away from Warren as possible!" The two were estranged for years, whether because he was sensitive to the imputation that he owed his career to her, or because he disliked her husband, Steve Parker, who turned out to be a swindler, or for other reasons. "I only know what I read in the papers about Warren," she said. "We rarely see each other any more. I've tried to reach out to him, but he just doesn't seem to want to communicate with me."

Kaleidoscope was James Bond lite, a frothy confection of glamour, romance, with a dollop of derring-do set against the glamorous backdrops of mod London and jet-setting Monte Carlo. It went into production in January 1966, in London. But *Bonnie and Clyde* was never far from his mind, and when the production ended in March, he was free to focus exclusively on his new picture. On the 14th of that month, he sent the writers a note, imploring them to cut down the script for the purpose of resubmitting it to the studios. "Some of these clowns may forget that they've already read it," he wrote. "Please make yourselves really unhappy. Cut off arms and legs, etc. . . . Pick an image of some executive that Lillian Ross might have written about and try to make him happy." He assured them that the trims would be purely strategic, that they could restore them at a later date. Casually quoting "The Love Song of J. Alfred Prufrock," he continued, "I want to emphasize also that if you have any thoughts about a new girl that you might have seen, or a new director who's not well known, as Mr. T. S. Eliot said—it's time now, please. To be very realistic, the men at the studios are not writing home to their mothers about Godard doing a picture that costs (so) much. . . . Also, they're not holding their breaths until they get an unknown girl. This is one reason why I want the script that we submit to them to seem as unladen with problems as possible."

Around the same time, Beatty attended a royal premiere of *Born Free* with Caron, where he encountered Julie Christie for the first time. She was up for a Best Actress Oscar for John Schlesinger's *Darling* (1965), and had appeared the same year in David Lean's *Doctor Zhivago*. In the full bloom of her success, she had become a phenomenon in England, just "Julie," or "the face," or "the face that launched a thousand flashbulbs," the very embodiment of "swinging London."

Christie's father managed a tea plantation in Assam, India, where she was born in 1941. At the age of six, her parents shipped her to a convent school in England, where she was raised by an "Auntie Elsie." She missed her mother, hated the school. A nun once told her, "You are quite ugly enough as it is without making faces," and she was expelled for telling a dirty joke.

The movie world is no stranger to female beauty, God knows, but Christie was something special. Recalls Schlesinger's partner, Michael Childers, "When Julie walked in a room, she was dazzling." She was famous for her ripe lower lip, killer jawline, electric blue eyes, and chiseled features, later framed by a mess of blond ringlets. Waxing lyrical, Pauline Kael would write about her in *McCabe & Mrs. Miller* that "One wanted to see [her] on the screen not for her performances but because she was so great-looking that she was compelling on her own, as an original." Like Beatty, she became famous so fast that she became acutely aware of her slender training as an actor, which exacerbated her insecurities. She confessed to Oriana Fallaci, "I hate myself. I'm so afraid. Afraid of not being liked by other people, of being rebuffed. . . . I'm afraid of being a failure, madly afraid." She was honeycombed with anxiety. "I was always deeply anxious," she said. "I never felt that I was cool enough, or that I was dressed right. Silly things. I was fearful." Beatty observed, "Julie was the most beautiful and at the same time the most nervous person I had ever met. She was deeply and authentically left-wing, and making this fuss over royalty did not amuse her. She could not contain her antipathy for this type of ceremony."

The actor liked Christie for Bonnie and took her to lunch, but eventually decided that being English, she wouldn't work. The next month, back in L.A. on April 18, 1966, Beatty co-presented an Oscar for production design. Wearing a shocking mini-skirt, Christie won Best Actress for *Darling.* He ran into her again, months later, at Pinewood Studios, where she was shooting *Fahrenheit 451,* and he was having lunch with Charlie Chaplin. (Chaplin was directing *Countess from Hong Kong* with Marlon Brando and Sophia Loren.) It was in with the new, out with the old. Caron must have seen the handwriting on the wall. "Warren has an interesting psychology. He always falls in love with girls who have won or been nominated for an Academy Award," she said. He "had a subtle way of getting to know people. Like a detective, he would discover all about them."

Beatty set up a meeting with Godard, if only to appease Benton and Newman, in whose hearts the Nouvelle Vague bad boy still dwelled. Godard flew in to Heathrow, but the two never met, or at least that's what Beatty says. He recalls that he had the flu, 103 fever, and stood up the French filmmaker, later claiming that he hadn't realized Godard had come to London specifically to see him.

AROUND THE same time, Beatty saw *Promise Her Anything*, hated it, and if it hadn't quite penetrated before, he now realized his career had hit a brick wall. He'd made another entry into his oeuvre of stinkers, and he was in desperate need of a critical or commercial hit, hopefully both. He wasn't yet "Warren Beatty," or if he had been, for a brief moment at the beginning of the decade, he was no longer.

The actor redoubled his efforts to find a director, cast his picture, and set it up with a studio. Once again he approached Penn. He told Benton and Newman, "I don't know if Arthur is going to want to work with me again, but I'm going to lock myself in a room with him and not let him out until he says yes." The writers, still in love with the idea of Penn, agreed. They were even impressed by *Mickey One*, admired the fact that Penn had tried to do a "European-American film." They didn't much care that it was a mannered mess. Says Benton, "There were a lot of European movies that were messes—Truffaut made any number of messes, we've all made messes we don't want to be judged by. While *Mickey One* may or may not have worked, it's what was underneath it that was vital, a sensibility. We wanted somebody who spoke a kind of language. And I really believe that Arthur did. And that Warren did."

Beatty knew Penn was in Stockbridge, Massachusetts, sulking. "I thought I had come to the end of it," Penn says. "My confidence was shattered. I didn't know what direction to go, back to films or try the stage again. It was either put up or shut up, become a filmmaker or not." His Broadway pedigree and formidable intellect had afforded him poor protection against the kinds of humiliations routinely heaped on directors in those days. He had developed *The Train* in 1964, only to have it taken away from him by Burt Lancaster, whom he had persuaded to join the cast. Then there was the embarrassment of *Mickey One,* compounded by *The Chase* (1966), a Sam Spiegel production featuring Brando, Robert Redford, and Jane Fonda. While Penn was prepping a new play, *Wait Until Dark,* in New York, Spiegel cut the film behind his back. It was his first encounter with a producer, which he likened to the birth trauma.

Penn refused Beatty's offer. He told him, "I don't want to do any more movies." He was emotionally drained, bitter and demoralized. He thought, "I don't want to deal with those people again. I don't like that life out there. I just don't like it." Beatty called again. Again Penn said, "Warren, I just don't think so." But Beatty persisted. Penn gave a little ground: "Let me read it again," he said. But he was still not impressed. He gave the script to some friends, who told him, "Don't touch it, it's terrible." But the actor kept at it. "He punched every button that he knew, and he knew a lot of them," Penn recalls. "We'd been pretty close." Beatty flattered him, wheedled and needled. He continues, "Then he hit me with the personal stuff, said something like, 'You're hiding out up there, you're licking your wounds, that's not what you do. C'mon get off your ass and let's do it.' Warren is very persuasive."

According to Towne, "Penn was a court of last resort. Warren considered *Mickey One* highly affected and pretentious, but he thought quite rightly that Arthur was an immensely talented and intelligent man." Dick Sylbert claimed that Beatty found Penn useful because "Arthur was obviously very malleable," and the star could have his way with him. "Warren's just smart about movies, and he knew what he wanted from Arthur," he says. "He wanted somebody from the East, somebody who understood actors. After all, Arthur was the teacher at the Actors Studio."

Beatty would not be denied, and in June 1966, he invited Penn to lunch at Dinty Moore's with their common agent, Abe Lastfogel of William Morris. Penn was no match for the combined persuasive powers of the two men. But he remembered the endless arguments between himself and Beatty on the set of *Mickey One,* and negotiated an MO for *Bonnie and Clyde.* He recalls, "We made an agreement to tell each other very frankly what we thought of each other, violently if necessary. We also agreed that, in the case of total disagreement, it would be he who would give way and do what I wanted." For his part, Beatty told Penn, "Look, we're going to disagree every day. There are certain things about each other which we think are really phony, and we're going to deal with it every day until we make a good film." Penn finally agreed to direct it. Says Penn, "Beatty and I both had a sense that we were better than we had showed.

"Once I said, 'Okay,' I got enthusiastic," Penn continues. "Warren and I were not content with the script." Beatty asked him to do the next pass. The two writers drove up to Stockbridge to work on the script with Penn through May and June. Even though their story was set in the 1930s, Benton and Newman had written a script about the 1960s. As Newman explains it, "Being an outlaw was a great thing to want to be, whether it was Clyde Barrow or Abbie Hoffman. All the stuff we wrote had to do with *epaté le bourgeois*, shaking society up, saying to all the squares, 'We don't do that, man, we do our thing.' The thing we loved about Bonnie and Clyde wasn't that they were bank robbers, because they were lousy bank robbers. The thing about them that made them so appealing and relevant, and so threatening to society, was that they were aesthetic revolutionaries. In our view, what kills Bonnie and Clyde is not that they broke the law, because nobody liked the fucking banks—but that they put a tattoo on C. W. Moss. His father says, 'I can't believe that you let these people put pictures on your skin.' This is what the '60s turned out to be about. Arthur wanted to make sure that it was also about the '30s."

Penn told Benton and Newman that their notion of Bonnie and Clyde as radicals of style was "part of it, but only part. I'm telling you guys, I'm older than you are, you don't know what it was like during the Depression, and I do, and I want to get that in here. There's no social context." He was drawn to the Dust Bowl setting. "Instead of just a couple of gun-crazy kids, these two were going to rectify the [lopsided distribution of wealth by] robbing banks, which was where the money was. That was not in the film, and it belonged there." To him, it became less a tale about tattoos than one about foreclosures, with the thieving couple administering harsh populist justice.

They had written a scene where Bonnie and Clyde holed up in an abandoned house, and Clyde teaches himself how to shoot by blowing out the windows. Penn suggested that the old sharecropper who owned the shack return, with his family packed into an Okie truck, a nod to *The Grapes of Wrath*. The sharecropper says, "This was my house, the bank foreclosed on it." Newman explains, "Arthur suggested the whole notion that these were people who perceived the bank as their enemy. The idea was to hook up with what was happening to America in the Dust Bowl." Paradoxically, Penn also stressed the opposite, the timeless, folkloric dimension of the outlaw couple, as Newman puts it, "the myth of Bonnie and Clyde as two magic people whose reverberations, even in their own lifetime, touched deeply the secret fantasies of average Americans."

In the second week of June 1966, Beatty went over to Natalie Wood's home on North Bentley to persuade her to play the female lead in the new film. Penn vetoed her because, like Kazan, he didn't want a star. Alternatively, she declined. Wrote Lana Wood, "Two months in Texas meant dealing with Warren, too, and Natalie wasn't up to that, either, especially without her psychiatrist." Adds Michael Childers, "She had a lot of resentment towards Warren. He was a no-can-go-there subject with her." That same month, Beatty met Maya Plisetskaya, the Bolshoi Ballet's prima ballerina, at a reception at the Beverly Hills Hotel. Plisetskaya was married, and five years older than the American actor, who was then twenty-nine. He was smitten. She had the classic dancer's body, petite, with small breasts, and good bone structure. She dressed simply in plain blouses and slacks, and had no use for makeup or jewelry. Beatty told Sylbert that it was the most wonderful relationship he ever had: "She never understood a thing I said, I never understood a thing she said. We never talked."

Beatty and Plisetskaya occasionally double-dated with Jaglom and Wood. Wood, whose parents were Russian, translated. Beatty would ask her, "Tell her how you say, 'I love you more than life itself.'" On one occasion, the two couples drove together to a party Jack Warner was throwing for the Bolshoi. Beatty was giving her soulful looks, and saying things like, "You're exquisitely beautiful, you have lovely breasts," etc. She replied in kind: "You're fantastic, so handsome, so hot," and so on. He explained to her in detail his theories about how and why small breasts are sexy. Talk was always important to Beatty, a key element in his flirtations, seductions, whatever, and as they approached the Warner mansion on Angelo Drive, he diverted Wood into winding side roads and circuitous detours so that the talk could continue. Jaglom found all this peculiar. After all, she was Beatty's former lover. Finally he asked Wood, "How long are you going to do this?" She replied, "As long as it lasts. It's like phone sex without the phone."

FOR BENTON and Newman, the trip to Hollywood was like following the Yellow Brick Road to Oz. They went west in July 1966 for
ten days to continue working on the script. Beatty took them up to
his penthouse in the Beverly Wilshire, aptly called La Escondida (the
Hideaway). It was a small suite, consisting of two rooms furnished
with a piano surrounded by a disorder of books, scripts, records, half-
eaten sandwiches, and a slew of room service trays piled against the
door or buried amid a litter of phone messages, unopened envelopes,
and balled-up typing paper. Outside, there was a wraparound terrace covered with Astroturf on which he lay reading, getting his Bob
Evans reflector tan, or taking in the sweeping, 360-degree panoramic
view of Los Angeles from the airport to the southwest, to the hills
above Sunset Boulevard. He no longer went to a gym because he didn't
want to be bothered by fans, so he did his sit-ups on the patio, and always had a pair of dumbbells handy for the occasional muscle flexing.
Having sex with Beatty was like a rite of passage for aspiring starlets
who filed through the penthouse. Recalls screenwriter Peter Feibleman, who came to know him well, "Warren was the very definition
of a stud. He just held still, and they all passed through his door. He
wouldn't let the hotel operators screen his calls. Anybody who called
him got him. It didn't mean he would talk to them, but they could
get him."

Beatty used to hang out at MFK, the drugstore in the hotel. One
time, Richard Harris stepped into the elevator behind him. Harris was
drunk, not an uncommon occurrence, and belligerent. He muttered,
"You bastard," trying to get Beatty to turn around. Finally Beatty did,
abruptly kissing him on the mouth, surprising Harris and defusing
what could have become an ugly scene.

John Schlesinger and Michael Childers had taken a suite on the
floor below. "I'd watch the Warren Beatty show, the revolving doors,
all the girlfriends going up one elevator, and coming down in another
elevator at the end of the hall," Childers recalls. "He didn't have much
of an education, and he had an insatiable desire for knowledge. He was
always reading and reading and reading. Stacks of books on the table.
He sought out people who knew a lot—it didn't matter what field
they were in—and surrounded himself with them. And he loved gossip. From L.A., he'd call twenty people up in New York just to get the

daily dope." According to Sylbert, he was always on the lookout for spats, separations, and divorces, "because he was great with wounded birds." Sylbert adds, "He had *nothing* in his life in those days but pussy and movies, and since the movies were six years apart, there was a lot of pussy. And politics, which is the same thing to him, pussy in pants. It's power."

Beatty chauffeured Benton and Newman around town in his Thunderbird or his black Lincoln Continental convertible with red leather upholstery, two of four new cars furnished him by the Ford Motor Company every year. Every time he stopped at a light, he'd flirt with the female drivers in the adjacent lane.

Penn lobbied with the writers to get rid of the ménage à trois. "It just struck me as being way out of left field," he says. "I was older than Benton and Newman, and I knew more firsthand than they did about these gangsters. I remembered Dillinger and Pretty Boy Floyd as simple, redneck guys, bumpkins more than anything else. The FBI escalated them into these great big terrible figures, but they were small-town hoods. The idea of a ménage à trois, in a situation like this, just seemed to me to be so sophisticated and so out of where the energy was that I said, I don't think so, and when it came time for the casting, I steered them away from a hunk, which was what he was originally."

According to Newman, Beatty didn't go for it either. He said, "Let me tell you one thing right now: I ain't gonna play no fag." He thought the audience wouldn't accept it. "They're going to piss all over my leg," he said, using one of his favorite locutions, meaning that he would lose their sympathy, such as it was, jeopardizing the picture's chances at the box office.

Beatty, on the other hand, says he had no problem with it. "Newman was skeptical that this was a decision that Arthur had made on his own. But it was totally [untrue] that I wanted to play a more conventional character. I was very enthusiastic about going against convention, and when Arthur made this suggestion, I was slightly disappointed, but I also thought that if Clyde had been gay, then that would have been the subject of the story. That takes up a lot of space. Arthur's point of view, and it certainly was mine, is that the picture was more socioeconomic than it was sexual. I thought the picture was totally about the Depression, the 1930s."

Benton and Newman still didn't get it. Truffaut never blinked at the ménage à trois, and if it was good enough for him, why wasn't it good enough for Beatty and Penn? It was nonnegotiable. But in a long story meeting, Penn managed to awaken them from their francophile trance. Towne, who was kibitzing from the sidelines, agreed that the ménage à trois had to go. "None of us felt we had to avoid a taboo," he says. "We just felt we couldn't dramatically resolve relationships that complex, and still rob banks and kill people. You just run out of time. You look at *Jules and Jim*, and it takes a whole movie to go from Tinker to Evers to Chance. Without the action and the violence." The writers gave in. Says Newman, "We were so excited that somebody wanted to make this movie, that I'm sure we would've done it in blackface if Warren had suggested it."

With the ménage à trois on the writing room floor, they all thought, There's a piece missing from the puzzle. And, Newman, continues, "with us being good Freudians, we came up with Clyde's impotence." Impotence was fine with Beatty, so long as Clyde overcame it in time for the end credits.

There remained the small matter of securing financing. Even with the ménage à trois pared down to a ménage à deux, the studios' reflex reaction, in Towne's words, was that "the characters are not sympathetic, its violence is gratuitous." Many of them looked askance at Beatty the producer. As *Time* magazine sized up the situation, he was "an on-again, off-again actor who moonlighted as a global escort."

Nevertheless, he and Penn flew to Texas in August to scout locations. They found most of what they needed in the scattering of small towns that pocked the flat, desolate land around Dallas, most of which had remained unchanged since the 1930s. It was so dry and the people so spare and sparse, it seemed as if any errant gust of wind might blow them away, like tumbleweed.

UA made a bid, but it wasn't high enough, and Beatty found himself back at Warners, which, by 1966, resembled a wax museum more than a bustling studio. "The lot seemed to me to be abandoned by then," says Penn. "It was like a ghost town." Jack Warner was on the verge of selling his studio to Seven Arts. He was anxious to retire. Throughout the 1950s and 1960s, he gradually liquidated the company. He sold off the pre-1948 library to Associated Artists Productions in 1956, and got rid of the real estate holdings. "If they hadn't done that, if they'd had to rely on the films that were being made during that period, they would not have survived," says Dick Lederer, then head of advertising and publicity. "He was in business to maintain an incredible lifestyle, like the Shah of Iran."

With a surprisingly sure hand, Beatty shepherded Penn, along with Benton and Newman through Warner's executive suites. "Warren said, 'He's going to say this, I'll say that, then he's gonna say this, then Arthur will say that,'" recalls Newman. "It was like *The Twilight Zone.* We went in, and it went exactly the way Warren said it would go." Except that Beatty couldn't get a deal.

Warner had never forgiven Beatty for turning down *PT 109* and backing out of *Youngblood Hawke* at the eleventh hour. "He always hated me," Beatty recalls. "He said he was afraid to have a meeting with me alone because he thought that I would resort to some sort of physical violence." Warner always made sure his desk was between him and the star. Adds Joe Hyams, who worked for Lederer at that time, "I used to think so too, that Warren was gonna hit him. 'Make sure I'm not in the room. I don't want any part of it.' Warren used to lay for him, but Warner wouldn't let him in the office."

Beatty, who had been known to make theatrical gestures in the past, prostrate himself on the floor when he thought it would get him what he wanted, finally managed to trap Warner in his office. All he needed were a few crumbs from Warner's table. He fell on the rug, grabbed him around the knees, and pleaded for his movie. "Colonel!"—everyone called him "Colonel" or "Chief"—"I'll kiss your shoes here, I'll lick them."

"Yeah, yeah, get up, Warren."

"I've got Arthur Penn, a great script, I can make this movie for one six; if nothing else, it's a great gangster movie."

"Get up, get up!"

Warner was embarrassed. He barked, "What the fuck you doin'? Get OFF THE FUCKIN' FLOOR!"

"Not until you agree to make this movie."

"The answer is NO!" Warner paused, caught his breath. With a $1.6 million budget, *Bonnie and Clyde* was inconsequential, no more than a flea on the back of his pet project, *Camelot.* Why not indulge the meshuggah guy. He gave in.

Beatty now insists that none of this ever happened, but Hyams swears he witnessed it with his own eyes (Lederer says it was the feet of Jack Warner aide Benny Kalmenson that he kissed), and in 1971, when asked if it was true, Beatty said, "Probably. Possibly. I used to do all sorts of crazy things with Jack. He thought I was a little crazy. Well, I am a little crazy."

Beatty and his lawyer, Jack Schwartzman, worked out the terms with production head Walter MacEwen. MacEwen's hands were red and crusted from psoriasis, eczema, or shingles, nobody quite knew which, and he wore white cotton editing gloves to conceal them. He was an old-school, courtly man, the good cop to Jack Warner's bad cop, but he refused to meet Beatty's price. Beatty said, "Look, just give me $200,000, and I'll take a percentage of the gross."

"How much?"

"Well, 40 percent."

"Fine." MacEwen agreed, and by the end of August, they had a deal. The budget was set at a meager $1.8 million. Although Beatty's bite of the back end would become an embarrassment for the studio, Warners didn't expect there would be much, if any, back end to bite. Modestly budgeted pictures like *Bonnie and Clyde* were breaking even at about two times their cost, and according to the terms, the star wouldn't see any money until the movie made almost three times the negative cost, leaving a small cushion of profit for the studio.

At the last minute, Penn sheepishly tried to withdraw. He asked Beatty, "Would I be letting you down terribly if I didn't do this movie? I don't think we've accomplished what we needed to accomplish with the script." He felt that what he referred to as the film's "dramatic profile" flatlined. "There was a then-and-then-and-then quality to it," he says. But Beatty refused to let him go, saying, "I'm sure that we can do it." Penn suggested bringing in Lillian Hellman or Arthur Miller for a rewrite. Beatty didn't think they needed to roll out the big guns, and suggested Towne instead, who shared Penn's view that, in Towne's words, "It's too episodic. You knew how they die, so there was no mystery, no suspense. The only question was where and when. You have to build up to that." Says Penn, "Towne was a very helpful presence. He was a guy with whom I could talk about the subtextualized aspects of the film." Towne worked for three weeks. The extent of his contribution is still the subject of debate.

Towne was responsible for some small but telling touches. "When

I was a kid, I noticed four things about movies: the character could
always find parking spaces at every hour of the day and night; they
never got change in restaurants; and husbands and wives never slept in
the same bed. Women went to sleep with their makeup on and woke
with it unmussed. I thought to myself, I'm never going to do that.
In *Bonnie and Clyde,* Bonnie counts out every penny of change, and
C.W. gets stuck in a parking place and has a hard time making a getaway."

Benton and Newman were not thrilled by Towne's input. Newman
says, "Towne was Warren's buddy—they were as tight as you can be—
and Warren wanted him around. We didn't like that, but there wasn't
anything we could do. We had no power. Towne did three things: he
added three lines of dialogue to the makeout scene in the beginning of
the movie in the car, where Clyde can't get it up; he wrote a speech for
Bonnie's mother; and he rewrote the first scene with the sheriff, Frank
Hamer, where he spits on her, they put him in the rowboat and they
strand him in the water. I never liked that scene, still don't. That's all he
did. Nothing else."

Beatty started to gather his crew and cast. "In a very calculated way
Warren assembled a bunch of talented people who were either looking for their first break or looking to revive a flagging career," says
Newman. "Arthur was fired from *The Train,* so he was in the toilet.
Warren had done all those flops and had this reputation as a difficult
actor, or difficult person. Everybody was going to bust their humps
for that movie. It was a great tribute to Warren as producer." Theadora
van Runkle was a costume designer wannabe, a former illustrator who
wasn't even in the guild, and worked for scale. "When Warren Beatty
asked me how I was going to make Bonnie look sexy, he was pleased
enough with the answer that she shouldn't wear a bra—and gave me the
job," she recalled. Two exceptions to the young-and-cheap rule were
veteran cinematographer Burnett Guffey, who was sixty-one at the
time, and editor Dede Allen, who had cut Kazan's *America, America*
and Rossen's *The Hustler.*

Casting the picture turned out to be surprisingly difficult. It was
done out of New York, the site of a revolution in casting. Casting director Nessa Hyams recalls, "Most of the casting people were in L.A., and
were middle-aged, ex–service men, functionaries. Their idea of casting
was to call the agents, who brought all the kids in—they were very simi-

lar in look and style, sort of nondescript, blond hair, blue-eyed kind of thing. But there were a lot of young actors running around New York not yet discovered."

Penn and Beatty had both worked in the theater and live television—a rich gene pool for the New Hollywood. The cast was filled out with actors out of this milieu, like Estelle Parsons and Gene Hackman. Penn chose Parsons for Clyde's sister-in-law, Blanche. She got a paltry $5,000 for her trouble. "I didn't have much interest in doing films," she explains. "I was devoted to theater." She thought, I'm not interested in this, it's a secondary-type role. But as she read through it, she found it more compelling, and changed her mind. "I was quite surprised when I realized what the message was: the bad guys are good!"

Parsons says it was she who suggested Hackman, who played Clyde's brother, Buck. Beatty had had one scene with him in *Lilith* and liked him, so he hired him. Michael J. Pollard, who would be C. W. Moss, was an old friend of Beatty's who had appeared with him in *A Loss of Roses*. "I was doing a TV show, a western," he recalls. "I ran into Warren in a clothing store when he was living at the Beverly Wilshire. We both said, 'What are we doing here?' The next thing I knew I was in *Bonnie and Clyde*." Even then, Beatty did the producer shtick like a veteran. He told Pollard, "We're going to get you a nomination for an Academy Award!"

Outside of Beatty and Faye Dunaway, who would be hired to play Bonnie, none of the cast remotely resembled movie stars. With his Midwestern Everyman features, you'd be hard pressed to pick Hackman out of a bleacherful of Cubs fans. Parsons was no Elizabeth Taylor, and Pollard had a face that looked like it had been fashioned out of Silly Putty.

Beatty and Penn had a picture of Bonnie in their heads, someone who could have walked out of a Dorothea Lange photograph, with a pale, gaunt, and hungry look (albeit beautiful, of course), appropriate to the Dust Bowl where she was born and raised. But it wasn't like every actress in town was beating down the door for the opportunity to work for next to nothing. Says Benton, "Warren believed in fly-fishing and trolling and casting. So, the net was wide open." After Wood, Jane Fonda was his first choice. She recalled that Beatty was so elliptical she wasn't sure whether he had offered her the part or not. (Penn felt her look was too sophisticated for the role.) According to Beatty, Fonda didn't want to work with Penn again after *The Chase*. Her other objection was, " 'You can't mix comedy and violence like this.' She implored me not to do the movie." He went on, "We got turned down by every living actress for the part of Bonnie." They included Jean Seberg, Carol Lynley, Ann-Margret, Sharon Tate, and Tuesday Weld.

One day, back in New York, Beatty, Benton, and Newman went over to Frank and Eleanor Perry's editing room in the Newsweek Building, at 444 Madison Avenue, to look at photos of Janet Landgard, whom the Perrys had cast in *The Swimmer*, their new film with Burt Lancaster. Beatty and the writers were standing in the lobby having a lively conversation about Bonnies, "We like this girl," "She's not right," etc., etc. Beatty was animated, focused, engrossed in the subject, but suddenly, as if a switch had been thrown, his eyes wavered, and he tuned out. Following his gaze, they were barely able to make out a tiny figure at the other end of the cavernous lobby, some forty feet away. The figure resolved itself into a girl, an actress or a model, carrying a portfolio. Beatty walking slowly toward her looking over the top of his glasses, pointing his finger at her, a cobra and its prey, with the writers following in his wake. The girl seemed mesmerized, and started edging away, until her back was flat against a wall. He stopped right in front of her. Her eyes welled up with tears. He said, "Hi, I'm Warren Beatty." She replied, "I know," and started to weep. Solicitously, he put his arm around her shoulder, and took her off to a quiet corner, writing down her phone number. By the time the three men got back to the elevator, he was all business again, resuming the conversation where they had left off, without missing a beat. Newman and Benton were dumbstruck. "Shit," says Newman. "This guy really is amazing."

Beatty was close to settling on Sue Lyon, who had made a splash in Stanley Kubrick's *Lolita*, when Faye Dunaway's name floated to the top of the pool. Dunaway had done several plays, and only two movies, neither of which had yet been released: Otto Preminger's *Hurry Sundown* (1967) and Elliot Silverstein's *The Happening* (1967). Penn had seen some of the former, and asked her to come to L.A. "We were getting pretty close to the wire here," he recalls. "And I said to Warren, 'You gotta meet Dunaway.' But Warren had heard some bad things about her," and he added, "Faye was not his first choice, by a lot." She was known as "the Barracuda" even to her friends. When she appeared at the Beverly Wilshire, she had gained upward of twenty-five pounds for her role in *Hurry Sundown*. She did come from a modest background, but she looked like she'd attended Brearley.

That evening, Beatty and Penn, Benton and Newman had dinner with her. Benton recalls, "When we left them, David and I both said, "That's her. That's Bonnie." Beatty was still against her. He wasn't impressed by her appearance, and said, "She doesn't look like much." Specifically, he didn't think her face was right. Her cheekbones were so sharply defined she could have planed a plank of wood with them. Towne thought, Fuck, man. She looks like something you put on the prow of a ship. Later, back in the penthouse, Penn remembered that the star was obdurately set against her, but was outvoted by him and the two writers. According to her, she was paid $30,000. Dunaway was thrilled. "This was the first, big feature I got my hands on," she said. "This script was amazing. It was the role which was most like me, closest to me. I was from North Florida, which is very Southern. I grew up with those kinds of people."

But Warner, who had never read the script, was unhappy that Penn and Beatty had populated the cast with unknowns, and tried to cancel the film at the last minute. On September 19, 1966, he memoed Mac-Ewen, writing, in Beatty's words, " 'Who wants to see the rise and fall of a couple of rats? Am sorry I did not read the script before I said yes. . . . guess we can't get out of the *Bonnie and Clyde* deal. We're going to lose every nickel.' He said, 'I don't know what Warren Beatty has on his mind.' He said, 'These pictures went out with Cagney.' " He added that *Bonnie and Clyde* would lose the studio every penny it made on *Kaleidoscope*. When Warner said, "We're not going ahead," Lastfogel countered: "Oh yes, you will. 'Cause we have a deal."

Kaleidoscope premiered on September 22, 1966. To keep Warner happy, Beatty flew to New York to do publicity, most prominently the *Today* show, co-hosted by Barbara Walters. In her book *How to Talk with Practically Anybody About Practically Anything*, she confessed, in effect, that in Beatty she'd met her match. "He answered me in monosyllables with an expression of extreme boredom bordering on distaste," she wrote. "Finally, I resorted to the hackneyed but spoil-proof, 'Tell me, Mr. Beatty, what is your new picture about?' " According to her, Beatty went quiet, and after an endless pause, he said, "Now, that's really a very difficult question." She continued, "I'd had it. Right on the air, in front of ten million, I am certain, very sympathetic viewers, I said, 'Mr. Beatty, you are the most impossible interview I have ever had. Let's forget the whole thing and I'll do a commercial.' "

The reviews of *Kaleidoscope* were abysmal. In a mercifully brief notice, the indefatigable Crowther wrote that it was "empty of narrative substance," while Beatty and his co-star, Susannah York, were "forced and flat, fumbling like a couple of dressed-up amateurs." Again, he was right. Jack Warner needn't have worried about *Bonnie and Clyde* eating up *Kaleidoscope*'s profits. There weren't any.

3

THEY ROBBED BANKS

How Beatty electrified the country with *Bonnie and Clyde*,

met his match with Julie Christie, and fell out

with Robert Towne over *Shampoo*.

"If Warren never did anything but *Bonnie and Clyde*, it wouldn't matter. That was such a superb motion picture, and he was great in it."

— Woody Allen

*B*ONNIE AND CLYDE couldn't have come along at a more propitious moment. Another picture like *Kaleidoscope*, and Beatty would have gone the way of Troy Donahue. It went into production in October 1966. Of course, Warner Brothers wanted Beatty to shoot on the lot. But Beatty had absorbed the lesson taught by Kazan, who, as far back as the late 1940s and early 1950s in films like *Panic in the Streets* and *On the Waterfront*, had embraced location shooting for the authenticity it afforded. Although somewhat older than they were, Beatty shared the impatience that the fledgling film-school, movie-brat generation would show for Hollywood artifice. He fought to shoot the picture in Texas, which had the added advantage of enabling him to get far from the heavy hand of the studio. Speaking of this production, Towne recalled, "Warren said one day, 'It's a war against unreality.' Without things like crab grass, telephone poles, pimples, poorly patched asphalt in the streets—you've got the back lot and you've already begun to lose your battle with all the artificial elements you fight against in trying to make what appears on film look real, or credible."

Preoccupied with other things, like feathering his nest by selling his company, Warner gave in. Later, while the shoot was in progress, he would rail against it, complain, "Why aren't they on the lot? Why do they have to be in Texas? Mike Curtiz could shoot on the lot! Mervyn LeRoy could shoot on the lot! What's wrong with these guys?" But by that time, it was too late.

As the star and first-time producer of a picture that he hoped would rescue his career, Beatty was under tremendous pressure. Not surprisingly, he found it difficult to chew gum and walk at the same time, that is, produce and perform at once. *Bonnie and Clyde* was "the first time I'[d] produced a film, so I was constantly faced with the anxiety of knowing that in almost every area I was ignorant," he said shortly after the film was released. Unlike the executives who laughed in his face, the crew snickered behind his back. Hackman recalled that they thought he was no more than a dilettante. Penn remembered that "they were appalled that this snot-nosed pretty boy was making a movie when it was clear he had no idea that everything he was doing was completely wrong."

But Penn found Beatty had changed for the better since *Mickey One*. Authority became him, which is to say, as Penn puts it, "He was the producer, so he had a kind of proprietorship over it, where I think he felt that he had to set a good example, too. So he was not the actor personality of *Mickey One*. He was much more in charge." The director continued, "He was a freer actor, by a long shot," adding, "Clyde came from the South, a part of the world Warren was more familiar with than urban Polish Chicago. He really understood Clyde, he knew him."

For once in his life, Beatty was the one on the receiving end of a flurry of questions. The number of details was overwhelming. "It is all detail, detail, detail. A hundred million, thousand, billion details," he complained. "When it's raining and your girlfriend or your wife is saying, 'Why aren't you doing such and such?' and the person you are working with has to go home and return a call to his press agent, and lunch is being served, and the head of the union says, 'Well, you have to stay out there for another ten minutes because they have to have coffee,' and then the camera breaks down, and there is noise, a plane flying over, and this wasn't the location that you wanted . . . are you going to have the energy to devote to the detail of saying, 'That license plate is the wrong year'? That's where the stamina, the real fight comes in. That is what's tiring."

Beatty was dismayed by how much energy and time he had to spend on politicking. "By the time you get any kind of personal statement on film, you've accomplished something in public relations, in union relations, and there's the Screen Actors Guild, the makeup men's union, the sound engineers, the teamsters, the caterers," he observed, sourly. "It's a business where the prime requisite is strength. Strength. [But] that's not how strength should be ideally expended. I mean, it's better to expend strength rattling around your hotel room all night because you can't clarify an idea or a way to get your idea across or figure how you will deal with a point in a story."

Although Beatty prided himself on never losing his cool, he was stretched to the breaking point, and every once in a while, he snapped. Toward the end of the film, just before the fatal ambush, he is supposed to be eating a peach, which squirts a spray of juice when he bites into it. During a rehearsal, the prop master announced, "There's no peaches."

"Why not?" Beatty asked.

"'Cuz they're not in season."

"What the fuck am I going to do, use apples?" yelled Beatty. "With fuckin' peach juice? There's gotta be peaches in season somewhere. I don't give a fuck what you have to do. I want those peaches here." Says Towne, "Warren went nuts. But the guy did not have time to find the peaches. What we got was pears, and we injected water into them with a hypodermic, so the pear would squirt. It was that insistence on detail and attention to detail [that made him a great producer]. At twenty-eight years old, Warren was an impressive guy."

To everyone's surprise, it turned out that Beatty was good at producing. Dede Allen visited the set on several occasions. "There wasn't a car that was driven, or anything, that Warren hadn't personally checked out," she recalls. "He was involved in every tiny detail of every shot. You learned to respect his brain very, very fast 'cause he's so friggin' smart. What a producer he was." Added Dunaway, "Warren just wrote a new chapter in the book of Hollywood. I once said to him, 'You were the first actor-producer, weren't you?' He said, 'No, but I was the best!'"

Still, he hadn't changed entirely. When Beatty put on his acting hat, he reverted to form. As was his wont, he insisted on knowing the whys and the wherefores of everything Penn did, and didn't care how much time it ate up to find out. "Warren questioned everything that was being done," says Parsons. "He and Arthur argued about every shot. They were yelling at each other. We would go to our dressing rooms and wait and wait. When Gene Wilder came to the set, it was like, 'What's happening here? Are they ever going to make this movie?' He wondered if this was the end of the film. We had gotten used to it." Pollard recalled the four of them—himself, Dunaway, Hackman, and Parsons—stuffed in the hot car waiting while "Warren would be talking to Arthur for hours on how the scene should be done." As Towne once put it, according to Dunaway, " 'Whoever gets tired of arguing first, loses.' "

Beatty once admitted, "I can be obnoxious. I knew I would be hard to take in a one-on-one dialectic with Arthur, that finally he would say, 'I just can't take it anymore.' " So it was that Towne, who had developed a bond with Penn, acted as a buffer between the two men. "For example, Arthur had this scene that he wanted to do with Bonnie and Clyde pretending what it would be like when they were dead," he recalls. "Warren came to me and said, 'You can't write that fuckin' scene, 'cause it's a fuckin' pretentious piece of shit.' I thought, Well, maybe I'll try and make it work; it's only paper. But Warren kept yelling at me about it. 'We can't pamper him! How can you do this?'

"My theory about that was—there's this joke about the guy who gets VD during the Korean War. The American doctor says, 'This particular form of VD is just untreatable, and the only thing we can do, 'cause you're going to get gangrene, is amputate it.' The guy says, 'You can't do that.' He hears about some medicine man in the hills, finds him and shows him his problem. The medicine man says, 'The American doctors, they say cut?' He says, 'Yeah, yeah. No cut?' The medicine man says, 'No, no, wait two weeks, fall off by itself.' What I felt was, in two weeks it would fall off by itself. Once Arthur had a chance to see the dailies and gain some confidence, he would not want to shoot the scene. And he didn't."

Although Beatty was always careful to pay obeisance to Penn in public, it seems that their battles were at least in part rooted in a basic disagreement over whose movie this was, which played itself out as an abstract argument over the auteur theory, which is to say, how movies are made, who controls them, and whether they reflect a single sensibility or a group process. Beatty had been burned chasing directors. As he put it in 1967, "I am just beginning to climb out of this cavalcade of crap that says, 'Just do what the director says. Do anything he tells you.'" Not yet a director himself, as a star and now producer, Beatty had a stake in overthrowing their authority. According to the French auteurists via Andrew Sarris, the director "comes in with eighteen cans of film under his arm the way that Sinclair Lewis would come in with a novel. Well, that's bullshit," he continued. "Suddenly, it's Otto Preminger's *Hurry Sundown*. The directors are the stars. Then it becomes stylish to say that a film must be the expression of a single man's vision. Twenty million dollar visions. You don't hear much about Fellini's writers, do you? They're there."

Penn, needless to say, saw the process differently. He subscribed to the auteur theory in "that film is really one man's form," he claimed. "Warren's concept of the group as such is a way of making good, successful pictures. [But] I would put the emphasis on successful. . . . People in the entertainment world . . . work together and make a good show. But a movie may be a very bad show and be a wonderful movie. . . . Godard's films are not good shows, in that they are not consistently high level in entertainment. . . . But they are damn good movies." Indeed, Penn is sensitive to the imputation that Beatty, not he, directed the picture, or even the suggestion that Beatty had an inordinate influence over it. "No, it's just plain not true," he says, hotly. "I make my own movies. Good or bad, I directed *Bonnie and Clyde*."

Sylbert, on the other hand, says, "When Warren makes a picture—I don't care who else is involved, I don't care what they call themselves—it's his picture. *Bonnie and Clyde* is Warren. Arthur's never been that good, but you got near Warren at the right time, he's going to make you better. Not merely better, but dramatically better. There would be no Bob Towne if there were no Warren Beatty, or Dick Sylbert, or whoever it is."

Penn, who wore dark glasses to ward off the blazing Texas sun, and invariably had a cigar clenched between his teeth (he'd learned something from the Old Hollywood, after all), enjoyed working with

Beatty. "Warren was wonderful," he says. "He was playing a man who was impotent. He embellished on that, bumped his head on a car door when she accused him of not performing. He brought this to rehearsal. He's a damn creative actor. He was learning all the time, camera angles, techniques. A man that intelligent is not going to sit there like a mushroom on a log."

Several sources say that Beatty was so focused that he surprised them by swearing off women, or nearly so, over the course of the production. He once told screenwriter and future friend James Toback, "You should not have sex at all. . . . The film will be better if you never come. On *Bonnie and Clyde,* I never fucked once." However, according to the *Dallas Morning News* film critic, recalling the shoot many years later, "Even in the SMU campus newspaper office, word filters down that women are visiting the *Bonnie and Clyde* set."

But the testosterone level on the set was so low that Beatty felt comfortable inviting his parents, Ira and Kathlyn, to visit. His mother was then a two-pack-a-day smoker. "So here was this dignified, lovely woman coughing up a storm, with a cigarette dangling from the side of her mouth," Beatty recalled. "And I asked her, 'Do you love me?' My mother looked embarrassed. She said, 'Well, of course I do. Why do you ask such a thing?' I said, 'Then do me a favor. Put out that cigarette and never smoke again.' She paused. Then she said 'OK.' She put out the cigarette and never took another, in front of me or anyone else."

Still, it was a tense production, if for no other reason than it brought together a group of unusually gifted, ambitious people around a film they believed in, and dumped them into a pressure cooker of financial and scheduling constraints. "I don't think anybody got along very well," recalls Parsons, who complained that Hackman made her cry. "Everybody on that film was beginning movie stars. They all wanted to get somewhere with it. Except me. It was beyond my comprehension that anybody could be as good an actor as Gene Hackman was on the stage and want to be a movie star. I think he was in some sort of competition with Warren. He wanted to be noticed."

Beatty had little patience for Dunaway's behavior, his responsibilities as a producer for keeping the picture on schedule and budget outweighing his natural sympathy for actors. All the tics that later drove Roman Polanski crazy during the *Chinatown* shoot, the constant summoning of hair and makeup just as the camera was ready to roll, were already in place. Bob Jiras, who did Wood's makeup on *Splendor in the Grass*, did the same for Dunaway. "[After every take,] she yelled, 'Hey, B.J.!!' at the top of her voice. He yelled back, 'Falling in,' with a little lisp, and rushed over, carrying a big tray with the puff. She was slowing down the pace of the production."

Having difficulty shedding 25 pounds to get the lean and hungry look she needed for the Depression drama, she was in torment. Recalls Penn, "The first days of *Bonnie and Clyde* were hell. She was testy, no question about it, testy. She and Warren had a hard time. Because she was quite heavy, and she was on a total fast. She really ate nothing for several weeks, just drank water." Even a former hog farmer who had built a soundstage used by the production, Bill Stokes, reported that Dunaway was difficult. "She wouldn't ride out to the set in the same car with Warren. She was really something else."

Towne didn't have much patience for her either, and he shared Beatty's aggravation. One day Penn corralled the two of them, said, "Sit down, we gotta talk. I had a conversation with Faye, and told her she was having an adverse effect on the crew. She's just frightened, and sensitive, and you've been very unfair, very insensitive to her needs. I'd urge you, please, please, to support this woman." He made them feel awful. A couple of days later, he took them aside again, said, "Remember what I said the other day? Do you mind if I take it back?"

Given the dynamics of the set, it was unlikely that Beatty and Dunaway would have become lovers, and by all accounts, they didn't. When it came time to shoot the love scene, where Clyde finally manages to deliver, Beatty found Dunaway the night before, and said, casually, "We need to talk about the before-fuck and the after-fuck." It didn't get any more intimate than that.

Next to managing Dunaway, Penn's biggest challenge was the DP, Burnett Guffey, a veteran of dozens of pictures. "Bernie fought everything that he was being forced to shoot," remembered Dede Allen. Like most studio cinematographers of the day, his goal was to light it so they could show it at the drive-ins, from which the studios raked in a good income. That meant blowing the light out as if *Bonnie and Clyde* were a Rock Hudson-Doris Day comedy. Like all the Hollywood craftsmen of his generation, Guffey was a practitioner of the well-made film. Anything less he dismissed as sloppy work. As director Curtis Hanson, then a journalist who was on the set, recalled, "I was there when they shot the scene in the cornfield. There were these enormous dark clouds that kept passing by. Bernie wanted to wait for continuity's sake, so the weather would be one way or the other, and Arthur said, 'Let's shoot it, and not only was it beautiful, but it also felt like what was happening to those characters, that a dark shadow was coming over their lives." Finally, Guffey just threw up his hands and quit (everyone was told that he had had a heart attack). He was replaced by someone even more conventional, and had to be persuaded to return. Subsequently, after MacLaine saw the film, she asked him to shoot *Sweet Charity*, saying, "I'd like you to shoot it the way you shot *Bonnie and Clyde*." He replied, "Like *Bonnie and Clyde*? Get somebody else!"

The historical Bonnie and Clyde had been killed thirty-two years earlier, on May 23, 1934, in an ambush orchestrated by Sheriff Hamer and the Texas Rangers. The two were caught in a hail of bullets on a deserted stretch of road near Gibsland, Louisiana. Bonnie died with a movie tabloid at her feet, a bacon and tomato sandwich in her mouth, and a Browning automatic rifle across her lap. Clyde was driving without his shoes. He never even reached the pistol he had concealed in the car's door. When the law examined the car afterward, they found a second Browning rifle, three submachine guns, six automatic pistols, a .38 caliber revolver, two sawed-off automatic shotguns, a couple of thousand rounds of ammunition, fifteen automobile license plates, and Clyde's saxophone. She was twenty-three, he was twenty-five.

Beatty and Penn, Benton and Newman, downplayed the historical outlaws' vast arsenal, and instead blamed the violence on the lawmen. With the Vietnam War very much on their minds, they wanted to dramatize both the inordinate firepower at the disposal of the authorities, and its asymmetrical, that is, disproportionate use against those who were (relatively) harmless, B-52s, say, against black-pajama-clad peasants. Says Penn, "The Vietnam War is not immaculate and sanitized. It's fucking bloody. *Bonnie and Clyde* had to be in-your-face."

In the movie, the outlaw couple is mowed down in a hail of slow motion bullets like grotesquely tumbling marionettes. Penn explains, "There's a lot more to this medium than was being used, so let's not just repeat what the studios have done for so long. Remember, this was the time of Marshall McLuhan. The idea was to use the medium as a narrative device. I wanted to take the film away from the relatively squalid quality of the story into something a little more balletic. I wanted closure." He added, "I thought we had to launch into legend, we had to end the film with a kind of pole vault, you know, some kind of great leap into the future, as if to say, 'They're not Bonnie and Clyde, they're two people who had a response to a social condition that was intolerable.'"

Penn wanted to heroize Bonnie and Clyde, killers yes, but more sinned against than sinning. Struggling to find a visual equivalent to the larger-than-life charisma of the outlaw couple at the moment of their death, their apotheosis, Penn drew variously on the much admired slow motion choreography Akira Kurosawa employed in *The Seven Samurai,* Jean-Paul Belmondo's protracted, spastic death scene in *Breathless,* and even the Zapruder film, which he mimicked by blowing away a fragment of Clyde's scalp in the manner of JFK's assassination. This may seem like a stretch, but the national trauma was only three short years behind them.

The principals agreed that the film's violence—unexpected, sudden, and abrupt—should jolt viewers out of the complacency that protects mere voyeurs, spectators. The bullet hits were intended to hurt not only the characters, but the audience as well. "How do you make a picture about Bonnie and Clyde and not make it violent?" wondered Beatty. "It upsets people, but that's good that it's upsetting. I think the danger is violence that *doesn't* upset people." The best example is the famous sequence juxtaposing a comic scene in which C. W. Moss has trouble extricating the getaway car from a parking space, with one in which a bank officer hops on the running board. Panicked, Clyde shoots him in the face in close-up, splattering his blood all over the window. "In the [Production] Code, you could not fire at somebody and have them get hit in the same frame," explained Penn. "You had to have a cut. I designed that scene so you didn't have a cut."

Speaking about the ambush, which they called "the Jack Kennedy scene," Beatty says, "In those days, people were not getting their heads blown off with hundreds of thousands of squibs in every scene. It was as violent a piece of film as had ever been in movies." When the squibs were tripped by a current sent through wires under their clothes, they exploded like blossoms of blood. Four cameras were yoked together right next to each other, all going at different speeds—24, 48, 72, and 96 frames per second. The slower the motion, the faster the film moves past the gate, drastically limiting the length of each take. Penn continues, "The speed of some of the cameras was so great, that I was worried about running out of film, so I couldn't say, 'Okay, action'! It had to be split second. So we determined that the cameras would roll when Warren squeezed the pear. On the first take, he squeezed the pear, and then froze. Boom, boom, boom, boom—everything was going off, and he was just standing there while his squibs blew off, grinning at the camera. It was funny, but it wasn't funny to me at the time." Penn was at it for three or four days before he was satisfied. "That was one of those felicitous moments where I saw it just as it is on the screen," recalled Penn. "I could not explain it to anybody. There was a lot of head shaking on the set, what the fuck is going on here?"

The relationship between Beatty and Dunaway was so tense that Penn had to resort to sleight-of-hand to get the response he wanted from the actress. Bonnie and Clyde exchange a last look before they die, but Beatty and Dunaway were not looking at each other, rather at Penn, who says, "I told her: 'Look at Clyde'—in the direction where Warren was supposed to be. At the last moment, I made Warren move to one side, and put myself there instead, so that she has this sweet, kind look." He adds, "There was closer contact between me and Faye and me and Warren than there was between those two."

BY THE time *Bonnie and Clyde* wrapped its location shooting and returned to Los Angeles in December 1966, the production was weeks over. The arguments between Beatty and Penn, the multiple takes, Dunaway's vapors, the Guffey hiatus, and the four days it took to shoot the ending all took their toll. The picture went approximately $700,000 over budget, ending up at about $2.5 million, making Jack Warner apoplectic.

Beatty was exhausted. Little did he know the worst was yet to come. Still, wrapping the location work gave him a brief respite from the all-consuming picture, and freed him up to turn his attention to future projects. Towne, who punched up the script in the evenings and played tennis during the day under the hot Texas sun, had done little on *Shampoo*. Beatty, meanwhile, who had an affinity for things Russian, was toying with the idea of making a film about John Reed, whom he stumbled upon in 1964. He says, "When you're very, very young, you hear, 'John Reed, Harvard guy gets over [to Russia] and ends up being buried in the Kremlin wall,' and then you find out later that he traveled with Pancho Villa, so after you read *Ten Days That Shook the World*, you read *Insurgent Mexico*." Penn recalls that Beatty asked him to read *Ten Days That Shook the World* before *Bonnie and Clyde*, and Dede Allen remembers that Beatty mentioned putting Reed's life on film while he was making it. They were having lunch in a Chinese restaurant when he asked, "Have you ever heard of Jack Reed?" Allen had been a labor activist during the union strife that rocked Hollywood in the mid-1940s, and her husband, Steve Fleischman, a TV writer, had been blacklisted, so Reed's name was familiar. She replied, "Yes."

"I'm going to do his story one day."

Against the wishes of the studio, *Bonnie and Clyde* was edited in New York, at 1600 Broadway, the old Studebaker Building, in a corner room on the tenth floor. With copper-colored hair, milkmaid complexion, rose-colored lipstick, and glasses that hung from her neck, Dede Allen was a striking woman with a bigger-than-life personality. Then forty-one, she started her career as a messenger at Columbia Pictures in the mid-1940s, and clawed her way up through sound editing to picture editing, for which she got her first credit in 1948. She had come up as a woman in a man's business, and had no patience for the ways things had been done in the past.

Penn and Beatty wanted to achieve the jagged, kinetic style of a filmmaker like Godard, who used taboo devices like jump cuts to create the kind of jack-rabbit velocity they wanted to drive *Bonnie and Clyde*. Both men kept pushing Allen to quicken the pace, admonishing her, "Cut it down, make it go faster, take another five minutes out of it, go deeper." Allen hadn't seen many Nouvelle Vague films, but she didn't need to. She had supplemented her feature work by editing commercials and industrials. "You had 30 seconds to tell a story and sell the product," she recalled. "The only way to do it was to break all the rules, pull out all the stops and use any trick you could think of to get the message across."

Allen recognized that audiences were literate in film grammar and didn't have to be led by the nose. Her assistant, Jerry Greenberg, explains, "Dede was the first person I knew who jumped people through doors. Before her, you had to show somebody on one side of the door, opening the door, cut to the inside, and see that same person enter. She knew she didn't have to show the door opening up. She was unapologetic."

On *Bonnie and Clyde,* she not only snipped and trimmed, she prelapped the sound, that is, began the sound before the cut, which had the effect of shoving the audience into the next scene. She nearly dispensed with leisurely dissolves, the traditional way of getting from scene to scene, instead favoring direct cuts, which also served to speed up the pace and jolt the audience. She continues, "That made it jumpier, more the style of this ragamuffin group of bank robbers." Some of the cuts consist of no more than a few frames. There are over sixty cuts in the scene in which the gang is surprised by the cops in their garage apartment. The staccato pace mimics the machine-gun style of the Barrows themselves. Sarris called it "shock cutting"—"wild contrasts from one shot to the next, which give the film a jagged, menacing quality."

Meanwhile, Allen recalls, "There was a lot of tension between Warren and Arthur at that time, and very often I was in the middle. Warren was sitting on the steps with his head in his hands. It got so bad I burst into tears to stop them." When he wasn't arguing with Penn, she continues, "Warren was sitting on the couch making phone calls. He had all these numbers in his head." He was seeing Juliet Prowse, as well as Maya Plisetskaya, among others. His relationship with Leslie Caron gradually petered out. She blames his preoccupation with the picture, which took him to Texas, and then to New York, while she was in England. Caron was bitter, and made no bones about it. She was quoted in the press saying, "The way he discarded me after I got him to buy *Bonnie and Clyde* was rather ruthless. . . . Anyone who has come close to Warren has shed quite a few feathers. He tends to maul you."

Like Joan Collins, she found his attentions to be a mixed blessing. "Warren was wonderful, but the difficulties of living with him were too great for my constitution. He lived a professional life 24 hours a day, and everything had to fit in with his public image." She had found him egotistical and narcissistic: one morning he called at 5:00 A.M., waking her. According to her he said, "You're sleeping! You're not thinking about me!" If he was teasing, the humor was lost on her. Worse was the cheating. She said, "He could not pass a girl without trying to seduce her. His role model was Casanova really; he wanted to be admired by the whole world." She told a reporter, "I will not tolerate unfaithfulness. That's why I left Warren. He was unfaithful. So it was over."

Beatty had by no means forgotten Julie Christie, who was just finishing *Far from the Madding Crowd,* which wrapped in mid-February

1967, for Schlesinger. When she was offered *Petulia* by Richard Lester, she took it, even though she had sworn not to bite into the Hollywood apple. She told herself that Lester, an American who spent the Vietnam War years in England, where he did hip films like *The Knack*, as well as *A Hard Day's Night* and *Help!,* both with the Beatles, was hardly Hollywood, which was true.

Earlier in the summer, the Summer of Love, appropriately enough, she flew to San Francisco, rented a place in Sausalito, and started work. Beatty knew that Lester had hired Dean Tavoularis as his production designer, and used him as a go-between with Christie, who was engaged to marry a British artist named Don Bessant. She had just purchased a flat on Selwood Terrace in London, where the two planned to set up housekeeping. She took her commitment to Bessant seriously and met Beatty's advances without enthusiasm. The more he flattered her, the more she withdrew. His reputation as a womanizer didn't help. Recalls Beatty, "A Hollywood movie star was silly to her." She explained, "I was always attracted to people who appeared to think you were dross, people who I felt thought I was really stupid and frivolous, and who really didn't give a toss what I looked like." She refused to be his date for the premiere of *Camelot* that fall, the third week of October 1967, refused to see him at all.

But Beatty finally persuaded her to let him visit her. "I got to San Francisco and tried to rent a car, but I realized that my driver's license was expired, and they wouldn't let me," he recalls. "I hired a limo. This was at the height of the '60s. I showed up in Sausalito at this hovel she was living in—the idea that she was in Sausalito was socialist enough—and I didn't realize the buzz saw I was driving into. She was appalled. She gave me a hard time about everything." When he would acquire one of the first car phones in Los Angeles sometime later, she made fun of him for using it.

The two were very different. She, as Goldie Hawn once remarked, would have been more comfortable milking a cow than making small talk at a Hollywood party, while he, Christie assumed, was one of those Hollywood playboys like his pal Bob Evans, with the fake bronze tan, shirt unbuttoned to the waist, and gold chain around his neck. He took her to dinner in Sausalito and disarmed her with his intelligence and charm.

Meanwhile, back in the cutting rooms, Dede Allen was fielding worried calls from Rudy Fehr, who was the studio's head of editing. On one occasion, she recalls, he complained about the love scene. He said, " 'Miz Allen, you can't have that scene'—it was where she goes down on him—he was shocked and horrified.

" 'You'll have to speak to Mr. Beatty about that.'

" 'You just have to put your foot down. You know we can't have a scene like that in a Warner Brothers movie.' And of course we had a scene like that in a Warner Brothers movie."

In June, with the editing nearly done, Beatty, accompanied by Penn, showed a cut of the entire film to Warner in the screening room in the mogul's palatial home. Warner wouldn't sit in a warm seat, so if the room were used before he used it, his chair was off limits. He was famous for his reviewer's bladder. "I'll tell ya something right now," he said, turning to Penn. "If I have to go pee, the picture stinks." The movie was about two hours, ten minutes. They still had to take about fifteen minutes out of it. Finally the lights went down, the film started, and five or six minutes in, Warner excused himself. He returned to his seat for another reel, and then he relieved himself again. And again. Finally the lights came up. There was a dead silence. "What the fuck is this?" asked Warner. Silence. "How long was that picture?" Son-in-law Bill Orr, sitting with him, said, "Chief, it was two hours and ten minutes." Replied Warner, "That's the longest two hours and ten minutes I ever spent. It's a three-piss picture!" Beatty and Penn didn't know whether to laugh or cry. Beatty struggled for something to say. Finally, speaking with painful deliberation, his sentences swallowed by the ominous silence that filled the room, he said, "You know what, Jack? This is really kind of an homage to the Warner's gangster films of the '30s, you know?" Warner replied, "What the fuck's an homage?"

Beatty showed the film for Father Sullivan of the Catholic Legion of Decency, who swore Dunaway didn't have any panties on in the opening scene where she charges down the stairs. Recalled Beatty, "Faye was wearing a sheer blouse and no bra. Father Sullivan kept saying, 'Run it again, that's her breast, that's a nipple.'

" 'No, no, no. That's a button.'

" 'No, no, no, run it again.' " *Bonnie and Clyde* was locked later that month. By that time there was so much animus against the picture at the studio that the few old hands who were impressed were hesitant to say so. Allen had been spreading the word that the head of trailers was

enthusiastic. He came to her, terrified, and whispered, "Don't tell anybody I liked it, or I'm gonna get fired." Dick Lederer knew they were
going to bury it. It wasn't even on the release schedule. The head of distribution was a man named Morey "Razz" Goldstein. Without having
seen the picture, he decided to release it on September 22 at a drive-in
in Denton, Texas. "September, in those days, was the worst time of the
year to send out a picture," says Lederer. "It was just throwing it away."
One day in New York, Lederer got a call from a fan of the movie at
the studio who said, "I just saw a rough cut of *Bonnie and Clyde*; it's
dynamite, a special movie." Encouraged, Lederer went to Benny Kalmenson, said, "Benny, listen. Don't lock in *Bonnie and Clyde* just yet.
Let's take a look at it before we make our decision. There's a rough cut
available. Warren will scream, but I can get it sneaked in overnight."
Kalmenson, a former steelworker, ran Warner's New York office. He
was a squat, heavyset man who dressed and behaved like one of James
Cagney's bad guys, from *Public Enemy* or *White Heat*. "He was always
saying, fuckin' Warner this, fuckin' Warner that—every other word was
fuck, fuck, fuck," recalls Lederer. As Beatty observed, his "language
made Jack Warner sound like Mother Teresa." In this case he replied,
"Fuck it, if you want to do that, fucking do it."

The next afternoon, Lederer screened the picture for himself and
his staff. He was bowled over, but it made no difference. He went over
to Goldstein's office, found the four division managers in a meeting.
Goldstein said, "Dick, we've seen the movie, and we're sticking with
our original schedule. But I tell you what we'd like to do, one of those
great country premieres in Denton. You get the old cars and raise hell,
and you bring Warren, and Arthur and Faye, and we'll have a great
time." Lederer was furious. He turned to the division managers and
said, "Listen. No problem getting the old cars, but that's about all I
can get. The only place Warren is gonna go when he hears what you're
doing is into this office with a knife, to cut off your balls, one by one."
He walked out. Lederer was right; Beatty wasn't happy. He fought for
better play dates. Goldstein was unmoved, said, "You guys are all crazy
with this movie, give up on it already."

The August 1967 issue of *Esquire* contained more bad news. Rex
Reed, who was building a formidable reputation with his snarky interviews and razor-sharp celebrity profiles, published a bitchy piece
called, "Will the Real Warren Beatty Please Shut Up." In it, Reed

quipped, "Interviewing Warren is like asking a hemophiliac for a pint of blood," which was true enough, if a writer was lucky enough to catch him in a hemorrhagic mood. But Reed also wrote that he was "the most enfant of the enfants terribles," and worse.

Beatty was humiliated and depressed by Reed's piece, which served to exacerbate his already active distrust of the press. He screened the picture at the old Directors Guild building in July. He invited the giants of Hollywood, the men he had cultivated—Feldman, Spiegel, Renoir, Stevens, Wilder, Fred Zinnemann, Sam Goldwyn, Bill Goetz, and so on. His friends advised him against it; *Bonnie and Clyde* was hardly a film geared to a geriatric demographic. He was sticking out his neck, asking to have his head chopped off. Beatty was barely able to watch the film, acutely conscious of the mistakes, of how it must look through all those pairs of seventy-year-old eyes. His mind wandered. Seated in the back, he got up, sat down, got up again. As the "Jack Kennedy" scene ended, and the tail credits rolled, a deathly silence settled over the theater. Then the audience exploded. Through the din, he overheard somebody near him say, "Well, Warren Beatty just shoved it up our ass."

Beatty was buoyed by the screening. "People who I really wanted to impress, Wyler and Stevens, and Renoir and Zinnemann, were really impressed," he recalls. He was receptive when Joe Hyams suggested that the Montreal Film Festival was the appropriate place for the premiere. "I remembered they had a picture called *Mickey One*, a piece of shit, and the only place in the world it succeeded was in Canada," Hyams recalls. "I said, '*That* picture made it in Canada! *This* picture can make it in Canada!'" *Bonnie and Clyde* premiered worldwide at the opening night of the Montreal International Film Festival at Expo '67, on Friday, August 4.

"What a reaction. It was incredible," recalls Lederer. "There were fourteen curtain calls for the stars, there was a standing ovation. After it was all over, Warren was on the bed in his suite with a girl on either side, dressed, but cuddling up to him. There was this nice young French girl who was the macher of the film festival. Warren said to this girl, 'Listen, honey, where is the wildest spot in Montreal? I want to go there tonight.' She said, 'Mr. Beatty, *this* is the wildest spot in Montreal!'"

Beatty's bad luck was that Bosley Crowther was in the audience. "I knew Crowther," Penn recalls. "He disliked *Mickey One* intensely, and I took him to task for it when we were on a panel together at Lincoln

Center. One time during the festival, he gave me this terrible look, just, 'I'm going to get you.' And he did."

Bonnie and Clyde opened in New York on Sunday, August 13, at the Murray Hill and the Forum, when flower children were still celebrating the Summer of Love and blacks were burn-baby-burning the inner cities of Detroit and Newark. Crowther's review, better described as a mugging, was even worse than anyone expected. In words that he would probably wish he had never written, he called it "a cheap piece of bald-faced slapstick that treats the hideous depredations of that sleazy, moronic pair as though they were as full of fun and frolic as the jazz-age cut-ups in *Thoroughly Modern Millie.*"

Those were the days before movies opened in four thousand theaters and lived or died by the first weekend. They dipped their toes in the New York and L.A. waters and only gradually waded further out into the treacherous depths of the hinterlands. Pictures could be damaged if not killed by a bad review from Crowther. Lately he had been on a tear against violence in movies, attacking brutal films like Robert Aldrich's *The Dirty Dozen* and John Boorman's *Point Blank.* But Crowther saved his best for *Bonnie and Clyde,* savaging it on two successive weekends in the Sunday Entertainment section. "I was scared to death of his power and the fact that his review made me look bad," says Lederer. "It really hurt me."

Benton and Newman had rented a house in Bridgehampton for their families for the summer. Benton told his wife, Sally, "Look, it's just another movie. It's been a big part of our lives, but you can't expect anything." Then he read Crowther's attack, thought, "It's not even going to last two weeks." But the *Times* began to receive letters from people who had seen the film and liked it. Recalled Penn, "Then Crowther wrote another attack, a Sunday piece, and more letters poured in, and Crowther responded again, and the more he frothed, the more he created support for the film." (Eventually, Crowther frothed himself out of a job.)

Bonnie and Clyde became a tipping point, to use Malcolm Gladwell's phrase, marking a shift in mass culture of tectonic proportions, away from the proper, morally and aesthetically conservative official culture of the Eisenhower era toward the anything-goes, let-it-all-hang-out counterculture of the 1960s, with its massive antiwar demonstrations and fighting in the streets. After *Bonnie and Clyde,* nothing would be the same. Says Beatty, "Everything was different in another year. It was the death knell of the studio system, and the rise of anarchy in the troops. I don't think they realized at Warner Brothers how much the movie business was going to change."

What's more, *Bonnie and Clyde* became the occasion for the emergence of Pauline Kael from the obscurity of San Francisco art house buffery into the glare of the New York media, where she flourished. She unleashed a lengthy review in *The New Yorker*, dated October 21, in which she not only praised the picture to the sky, but jeered at its detractors, accusing them of stupidity, Philistinism, and worse. She wrote that "*Bonnie and Clyde* is the most excitingly American movie since *The Manchurian Candidate*. The audience is alive to it." Kael's review amounted to a nine-thousand-word gloss on a line by Bob Dylan, who put it a bit more succinctly: "something is happening here, But you don't know what it is, Do you, Mister Jones?" Says Towne, "Without her, *Bonnie and Clyde* would have died the death of a fuckin' dog."

But Kael's readiness to pick up the flag and lead the charge on behalf of beleaguered filmmakers, to inject herself into the cultural fray and become a player herself, led her to disregard the cardinal rule of reviewing: Thou Shall Not Consort With Thy Subjects. In her own version of the joke wherein the actress, too dumb to know the pecking order on the set, has sex with the writer (instead of the director or the star), she took Benton and Newman to lunch, during which they were only too happy to unburden themselves of their intentions to a sympathetic ear. "Her review was the best thing that ever happened to Benton and myself," recalls Newman. "She put us on the map. This was a genre gangster film in its broad outline, not a highly respected genre. What she did was say to people, 'You can look at this seriously, it doesn't have to be an Antonioni film about alienated people walking on a beach in black and white for it to be a work of art.'" Snubbed, Penn groused that she regurgitated their remarks in the guise of her own insights. Likewise, she dismissed Beatty with faint praise. The actor called Kael, both chided and charmed her. When she finally met him sometime later at a screening of a documentary on Penn, she says, "He came on very strong to my daughter, who was then a teenager."

Kael's review may have made an impact on the New York intelligentsia, but it had no effect on the studio. When Kalmenson finally saw the picture, he rendered his own verdict in characteristically blunt language: "It's a piece of fucking shit!" Beatty was desperate. He followed Kalmenson into his office, and said, "Let me pay you for this negative." Kalmenson was incredulous. No one spent their own money on a movie, especially one that looked like it was going into the toilet. Rolling his eyes and regarding Beatty as if he were an alien life-form, he replied, "Ah, get the fuck outta here, Warren, where the fuck are you gonna get two fuckin' million dollars?" Beatty had no idea where he could get $2 million, but retorted, "I can get it, don't worry." Later, he thought, They're beginning to take me seriously. They know they can get out of it if they want to. He redoubled his efforts, virtually camping out in Lederer's office. Lederer referred to him as the "mosquito," because he was always buzzing around.

Bonnie and Clyde did no better than fair business in New York. Lederer went to Kalmenson, again, implored him to pull the rest of the September dates and delay the roll-out to give word of mouth time to build. "I really think this man was beginning to have an inkling that the business was passing him by," he recalls. "This was a watershed movie for him, 'cause he knew he blew it. But he was stubborn, a man of iron will. I thought he'd kill me. He cursed me—'I don't want to hear any more about this fuckin' *Bonnie and Clyde*, I'm not taking anything out of release, I've got eighteen pictures to put out, it's gonna stay where it is, goddamn it!' And it did."

Bonnie and Clyde opened in Denton, Texas, on September 13, 1967, went wide through the South and Southwest the next day. Beatty was like a man possessed. "He was like a bulldog that got his teeth in this thing," says Hyams. "The passion he had then, checking sales contracts, and distribution—we all used to say that he'd be a much better producer than an actor." He tracked the box office, visited theaters himself. Rumor had it that he tried to replace an older projectionist at a Chicago theater with a younger one because he thought a youthful man would get the picture and show more care. Recalled Guy McElwaine, then his West Coast publicist, "Warren had the studio send a memo to all the theater managers telling them to raise the sound level of the picture. Then he wrote personal notes to all the projectionists and stuck them in the film cans, with the projectionists' names on each one. If a normal film was played at 15 decibels, he wanted *Bonnie and Clyde* played at

22 decibels." Beatty intended the sound of the gunshots to startle the audience, as they had in *Shane*, directed by the man he so admired, George Stevens, fourteen years before.

Meanwhile, Beatty was flying to San Francisco to campaign for Christie, with whom he was making considerable progress. An accomplished storyteller, he held her spellbound with his tales about the stupidity of the Warners executives. She was impressed by the fact that he was trying to do something about it, and realized that far from being an apologist for Hollywood, he was as anti-studio as she was. Eventually, she returned to London and the new house she was going to share with Don Bessant, and to all appearances, resumed her relationship with him. "Bessant was still her guy," recalled a friend, Irish actor Kevin McHugh. "But word was out that Beatty had already 'happened,' that he was going on in the background. . . . No one in the circle spoke about it, it was just known." It wasn't long until Bessant moved out. "I don't think the split had anything to do with Warren Beatty," reflected Bessant's mother. "She was becoming very famous. It did make things a little difficult and Don wasn't into that kind of life." Beatty and Christie became an item. Those who had a stake in her, like John Schlesinger, worried that he would take over her career, even "closing the Christie corporation down altogether," so that she could devote herself to him.

As it turned out, the London opening on September 15 was a smashing success. He had organized midnight screenings every night for five consecutive nights the week before the premiere, making it the hot ticket that the hip influentials—John Lennon, Mick Jagger, Mary Quant, Vidal Sassoon, the photographers, the designers, the theater people, the press—fought over. Recalls Lederer, "He ran roughshod over everything to get this done."

Beatty likes to tell the story about how he stunned a projectionist by appearing in the booth of the Warner Theatre in Leicester Square because he could barely hear the gunshots. According to the star, the projectionist said, " 'You're the producer of this picture?' and I said, 'Yeah.' And he said, 'Well, I've really helped you out in the sound here. I've made a chart, and I turn it up here and down here, and so on. It's the worst mixed picture. I haven't had a picture so badly mixed since *Shane*.' "

The movie became a hit in England, more than a hit, a phenomenon. The Bonnie beret was all the rage. Quipped Hyams, "It helped start the no-bra trend, because Faye didn't wear a brassiere in the film. That's a contribution Warren made that nobody gives him credit for." Magazines in New York that ignored the picture when it opened were overwhelmed by calls from their London stringers. *Life* woke up and did a fashion layout on Dunaway.

In June, Warner had gone to New York, where he announced the sale of his controlling interest in the studio to Seven Arts Productions, for a sum variously reported at $32 million and $95 million. The new owner, Eliot Hyman, retained him temporarily, as well as Kalmenson, Lederer, and Hyams. He made his son, Kenneth, head of production. But the groundswell that was building for the picture was too late to affect the bookings in the U.S. According to Penn, "Once the word came down from somebody like Benny Kalmenson to the exhibitors that it's a dog, they booked it for a very short period and then they booked another film in afterwards. It was customary for a picture to have a five-week guarantee, but we didn't."

According to Beatty *this* was the real problem, not the grosses. "They were very happy with it," he recalls. "It had done very nicely. Much better than they had hoped." But *Reflections in a Golden Eye,* a turkey starring Marlon Brando and Elizabeth Taylor that Seven Arts had made before it purchased Warners, was booked in right on its heels, pushing *Bonnie and Clyde* out on October 11. "In effect," continues Beatty, "to have kept *Bonnie and Clyde* going would have lost them the theaters for *Reflections,* which cost three times what *Bonnie and Clyde* cost, or more."

Lederer continues, "I was discouraged by that September opening, after we'd broke our asses, I just gave up on the picture. I had done my best, and it died anyway. I never felt it could be resurrected. I really didn't." He added, "It had played 2,000 play dates, which at that time would normally account for 90% of the revenue that you would obtain, and the film only had $2 million in rentals." Bitter, Penn observed that Americans discard movies the same way they do paper cups.

The apparent failure of *Bonnie and Clyde* stung Beatty, not in the least because he had to watch Mike Nichols's picture, *The Graduate,* get the kind of box office that he felt belonged to *Bonnie and Clyde.* Beatty was intensely competitive. Although he would never say a bad word to the press about another movie, another person, another anything, in private he was cutting. Buck Henry, who wrote *The Graduate* and would later collaborate with Beatty on *Heaven Can Wait*, recalls, "He said to me, 'I saw your guy's movie the other night,' meaning *The Graduate*, 'and I was really pissed off and worried until you guys fucked up at the end.' He meant the driving sequence, which he thought was lame. In effect, he said, 'I was so relieved that you didn't make a great film.' It was so purely Warren that I laughed. 'Cause when I remembered it years later, I thought, I've never heard him say so-and-so made a good movie. 'Got a lot of laughs out of *Airplane*'—that's about as good as it gets. He's looking for the flaws: 'Is their film better than mine?' I've only heard him say a good word about one movie in all the time I've known him, and that was *Doctor Zhivago*. To have that movie as a touchstone is somewhat limiting."

Five weeks or so after *Bonnie and Clyde* had been given up for dead, *Time* magazine plastered the picture on its December 8 cover as Exhibit A for a story bannered "The New Cinema: Violence . . . Sex . . . Art," by Stefan Kanfer. Kanfer was heralding the revolutionary decade to come, in which Hollywood filmmaking would not only become thoroughly Europeanized, it would be revitalized by the energy and iconoclasm of the new youth culture spawned by the antiwar movement. He cited the jarring shock cuts in *Point Blank*, the lesbian scenes in *The Fox*, the violence of *Bonnie and Clyde*, and the fractured narrative of films like *Blow-Up*, to make his point that studio-backed films were changing in ways unimaginable a few short years before. He defined the characteristics of the New Cinema: sexual boldness, unfettered by the Code; disregard for time-honored pieties of plot, chronology, and motivation; a promiscuous jumbling together of comedy and tragedy; and a new, ironic distance that withholds facile judgments based on conventional morality, which in turn blurs the distinction between heroes and villains. *Time* lavished particular praise on *Bonnie and Clyde*, calling it "the best movie of the year," a "watershed picture," bracketing it with the likes of *The Birth of a Nation* and *Citizen Kane*. Kanfer even compared the climactic ambush to Greek tragedy.

After the magazine hit the newsstands, Beatty paid a call on the new Warners head. He said, "Eliot, we have to rethink this. The movie's been mishandled. I want you to rerelease it." Hyman looked at him as if he were crazy. It was a bold demand. Studios didn't rerelease pictures.

To do so was to admit a mistake, acknowledge that they had botched the initial campaign. "There's a conflict of interest in your booking *Reflections in a Golden Eye,* a Seven Arts movie after *Bonnie and Clyde,*" continued Beatty, undetered. "I'm going to make trouble for you." Hyman refused again. He had been shocked when he discovered the size of Beatty's profit participation. It was so large Hyman had no financial incentive to put the movie back in theaters were he so inclined, which he wasn't. Finally, Hyman said, "I'll release the picture if you reduce the size of your cut."

Now it was Beatty's turn to refuse, and he did so, saying, "I'm gonna sue you, Eliot." Hyman regarded him coldly, figuring the odds, as he nervously flipped his pencil up in the air, caught it, threaded it through his fingers.

"What the hell would you sue me for?"

Beatty was bluffing, didn't have the foggiest idea what he would sue him for, but familiar with Hyman's past, which he knew included some questionable associations, he thought, Eliot knows more than I could possibly dream of. So he returned his gaze, smiled thinly, and said, "I think you know." Adds Beatty, "With a man like Eliot, that was, of course, the best thing to say, because whatever it was he knew, it frightened him." Within a couple of weeks Hyman had rebooked the picture.

On February 20, when the Oscar nominations were announced, Beatty had good reason to feel encouraged. *Bonnie and Clyde* got a staggering ten, including two for him personally—for producing, with his film up for Best Picture, competing against *In the Heat of the Night, Guess Who's Coming to Dinner, The Graduate,* and *Doctor Dolittle*—as well as Best Actor, where he faced Dustin Hoffman for *The Graduate,* Paul Newman for *Cool Hand Luke,* Rod Steiger for *In the Heat of the Night,* and Spencer Tracy for *Guess Who's Coming to Dinner.*

Also nominated were Penn for Best Director, Dunaway for Best Actress, Hackman and Pollard both for Best Supporting Actor, Parsons for Best Supporting Actress, Benton and Newman for Best Original Screenplay, and on and on. Dede Allen was slighted, despite her editing tour de force. "The reason why I never got recognized for that picture by my peers was because they really thought it was the worst cut picture they had ever seen," she says. "Until they began to imitate it!"

Beatty called Christie, inviting her to be his date to the Oscars. She would fly to Hollywood, share his penthouse at the Beverly Wilshire, and stay on well after the ceremony was over. He gave her a Yorkshire terrier, which she took wherever she went.

Eventually, Christie moved into the Malibu beach house rented by Schlesinger and Childers. Initially, Schlesinger was leery of Beatty, referring to him as someone who "gets through women like a businessman through a dozen oysters." In April 1968, in a letter to a friend, he wrote, "But one can't interfere in these matters, even though [Beatty] has tried his best to do so with her career." He wondered whether the actor was "very good for her future."

Nevertheless. Beatty charmed everyone, finally moving in himself for a few months, taking over the lease after Schlesinger left to prep *Midnight Cowboy*. "The Julie and Warren thing was magical," Childers recalls. "He was demented about her. I knew sixteen other girls he dated, but Julie was special." Beatty always credited her with freeing him of his sexual inhibitions. She never made judgments about what practices were right or wrong, good or bad. She was open to everything.

"They couldn't keep their hands off each other," Childers continues. "It was hot, hot. She would sit on his lap and they would kiss. There was a lot of fucking going on. Noisy fucking. Julie was smitten. Never in love, or at least I never heard the L-word. I think he certainly was with her. He told me that he always wanted to marry her. But she was a very independent lady and never wanted marriage. This was before women's lib, but she was the epitome of the new free girl. Rich—rich in life, passionate, political, a hippie. She really loved her pot. And she hated Hollywood, hated the bullshit, the parties, the premieres. She wouldn't go to film festivals, openings, anything. She said, 'I give the best performance I can, and that's all I'm gonna do.' She didn't like Warren's whole quest for power."

It was a heady world to which he introduced her, and it exacerbated her insecurities. "Often I didn't feel clever enough," she said. "He is very clever. . . . I felt uninformed." But she appreciated the doors he opened for her. "I had access to politics through Warren—and power. . . . It is very useful to know and see how people you might loathe and despise and hate operate as human beings."

Although Christie was appalled by the Old Hollywood establishment in which Beatty moved freely, she had no trouble fitting into the hip New Hollywood scene. She was often stoned. Although he would take the occasional toke, he was too vain, too protective of his looks and his body, too afraid of losing control to do drugs with any regularity. She would dash through the lobby of the Beverly Wilshire in a diaphanous white cotton sari with little underneath, trailing five-figure residual checks that fluttered from her handbag onto the floor as she rummaged around for her keys. Money meant little to her; one day she shocked Beatty by losing a $1,000 check in the street.

Christie took her politics seriously, and indulged her profession only to support the myriad of causes with which she was involved. Says Towne, "If ever a movie star existed for whom stardom meant nothing, it was Julie. She was genuinely a blithe spirit." But by March of 1967, with an Oscar for *Darling,* there was no denying, however much she disdained the movie world, that she had become a star herself.

When Christie was elsewhere, Beatty was on the phone with women. He kept the proverbial black book, even though his memory for phone numbers made it superfluous. Never identifying himself on the phone, speaking in a soft, insinuating voice rarely raised above a whisper, flattering in its assumption of intimacy, enormously appealing in its hesitancy and stumbling awkwardness, he asked them where they were, with whom, where they were going next, and would they be sure to call him when they got there. His appetite for control and thirst for information were as voracious as his appetite for sex, and it seemed that inside his head was a GPS indicating the whereabouts of every attractive young woman in Los Angeles. He told them that yes, he was in love with Julie, but he wanted to see them anyway. Not in the least put off, they appeared to find this reassuring. He explained his MO: "You get slapped a lot," he said, "but you get fucked a lot, too."

"Julie's smart, and she knew there were other girls around," says Childers. "That was part of the turf. But it used to piss her off. You could always tell when there'd been a falling out. She would curl her lips and pout. She was a screamer, volatile. They'd break up, she wouldn't see him, the phone would ring, and she'd say, 'If that's Warren, tell him I'm not here.' I'd say, 'Warren, she's baking bread and doing yoga today. She doesn't want to talk to you.' Six days later they'd be back together." For the first time, it seemed that he had met his match.

The day after the Oscar nominations, Warner Brothers put *Bonnie and Clyde* into 340 theaters, including many from which it had originally been pulled. The word of mouth was such that the same exhibitors who had fled from the picture when it was first released as if it were radioactive were now clamoring to show it. But "by the time it got into the theaters again, the studio could not get very good terms, because they had screwed the release up so badly," says Beatty. Still, the box office was impressive. In September, it had grossed $2,600 for a week at one theater in Cleveland; it played the same theater in February and grossed $26,000. By the end of 1967, *Bonnie and Clyde* had netted $2.5 million in rentals. When it was rereleased the following year, it netted $16.5 million in rentals (about $40 million in grosses) momentarily making it one of the top twenty grossing pictures of all time. According to *Variety*, Beatty walked away with somewhere around $6.3 million from the first and second runs.

Bonnie and Clyde went from triumph to triumph. As Joe Hyams reflects, "There was so much done to kill this picture, but it was really hard for the company to destroy it, that's how good it was." When the film opened in movie-mad Paris in February 1968, Beatty was treated like the prophet of a new era. He was just about to cross the generational divide (activist Jerry Rubin had famously said, "Don't trust anyone over thirty"), giving him, perhaps, a historical perspective, of sorts: "I would be seated at a table with Maurice Chevalier on one side, Artur Rubinstein on the other and Mr. and Mrs. Pompidou across the candlesticks. There were old men with beautiful young girls—not one but clusters of them. There were women dripping jewels, and somehow I felt, this time will never come again."

One day, Truffaut caught up with Benton and Newman. He was dismissive of the picture, told them he was disgusted by the decision to eliminate the ménage à trois. "Beatty had no genuine innocence, no authenticity," he complained. "He distorted the script out of fear of being ridiculed."

Bonnie and Clyde, meanwhile, won awards from the New York Film Critics, the National Society of Film Critics, and the Writers Guild of America. The Oscars were scheduled for April 8 at the Santa Monica Civic Auditorium. On April 4, Martin Luther King, Jr., was assassinated at the Lorraine Motel in Memphis, Tennessee, sparking riots across America, sometimes in cities that had not recovered from the urban conflagrations of the previous year. Beverly Hills liberals acknowledged the occasion by driving with their lights on. King's funeral was set for April 9, and five Academy participants—four of them black (Louis Armstrong, Diahann Carroll, Sammy Davis Jr., and Sidney Poitier, plus Rod Steiger)—threatened to withdraw if the show were not postponed. The Academy reluctantly agreed to reschedule the event for April 10. Even so, a lot of people, including Penn, still stayed away.

The competition shaped up to be one between the Old Hollywood—represented by two mild, bleeding-heart pictures, Stanley Kramer's *Guess Who's Coming to Dinner* and Norman Jewison's *In the Heat of the Night*, in addition to an inept musical, *Doctor Dolittle*, that had bombed at the box office, nearly finishing the job *Cleopatra* had started at Fox—and the New, in the form of *Bonnie and Clyde* and *The Graduate*. Estelle Parsons, a reluctant attendee, gave expression to the suspicion with which New York regarded Hollywood, and vice versa. "The idea at the time was that films like *Bonnie and Clyde* might get nominated, but they couldn't win, because they were not Hollywood films," she says. "Most people who voted lived in Hollywood, and they voted for the bigger movies where the jobs were."

The host that night was Bob Hope, who joked about President Lyndon Johnson's recent decision not to seek reelection. The Old Hollywood laughed. The New Hollywood, including Beatty and Christie, Hoffman and his date, Senator Eugene McCarthy's daughter Ellen, and Mike Nichols, sat stone-faced through Hope's patter. Martha Raye read a letter from General William Westmoreland thanking Hollywood for raising the morale of U.S. troops in Vietnam through its work with the USO. Through it all, the Barrow gang was confident, expecting to clean up. "We were so fucking sure we were going to win the Oscars," recalls Newman. "Ken Hyman came up to us in the lobby, and said, 'Got your speech ready, boys?'"

Benton and Newman indeed had their speeches ready. When Steiger and Claire Bloom announced the nominees for the writing awards, Newman was halfway out of his seat. Benton buttoned his jacket and straightened his tie. As he heard the words, "And the winner is . . ." he actually stood up. Sadly for him, the lucky man was William Rose, for *Guess Who's Coming to Dinner*. Benton fell back into his seat like he'd been clubbed. Newman, meanwhile, couldn't believe his ears. "They gave it to this English twit, William Rose!" he complains. "As the guy came back down the aisle with his Oscar, I had the impulse to tackle him and scream, 'It's mine! Give me that God damn thing!" (Memory plays tricks. Rose wasn't present, and director Stanley Kramer accepted the award for him.)

Despite its clutch of nominations, *Bonnie and Clyde* was for the most part passed over, as Parsons predicted. It lost Best Picture to *In the Heat of the Night*. Ironically, Leslie Caron presented Best Director, and seemed visibly relieved when it went to Nichols, for *The Graduate*. After all the Sturm und Drang, *Bonnie and Clyde* won only two awards, Parsons for Best Supporting Actress and Guffey for Best Cinematography, ironic in view of his reluctance to do as he was told. "You know the really great thing when Guffey won the Oscar?" Beatty recalled. "He got up there and he thanked . . . Jack Warner." At the time, he (or Dunaway to whom the quip was also attributed) said, "We're all disappointed. As a bunch of bankrobbers, we wuz robbed."

"There were people in Hollywood who just hated that movie," remembers Benton. "The thing that ticked off Crowther is that there was banjo music while they were shooting people. It was perceived to be a thumbing-your-nose attitude, a moral flipness, an arrogance, because nobody in this movie ever said, 'I'm sorry I've killed somebody.' "

"WE DIDN'T know what we were tapping into," said Penn. "The walls came tumbling down after *Bonnie and Clyde*. All the things that were in concrete began to just fall away." Contradictory though they may have been, due to the different agendas of the various contributors, the film embodied several of the decade's intellectual preoccupations. If the 1950s saw American culture turning away from the 1930s infatuation with Marx toward Freud, the second half of the 1960s reflected a fatigue with the insistent navel-gazing and pop psychologizing of the postwar work of Williams and Inge, and a rebirth of interest in social relations. "The Freudian nature of their own relationship puts me to sleep," said Beatty, referring to the outlaw couple. "I've seen too much of that." Towne too went out of his way to dismiss the Freudian interpretation of the story. "The feeling was, If he could only fuck, he wouldn't shoot people," he says. "In the end he can fuck, and she says, 'What would you do if you had to do it all over again?' 'I wouldn't do it in the same state!' So you realized, that wasn't going to make any difference."

Still, the picture did come out in the middle of the sexual revolution, and it was hard entirely to escape the long arm of psychoanalysis, or deny the conclusion that if Freud were dead, it was long live the post-

Freudians: Wilhelm Reich, Norman O. Brown, and Paul Goodman. *Bonnie and Clyde* was a sequel, of sorts, to *Splendor in the Grass.* Instead of the pathos of young lovers capitulating to small-minded adults, here the children would have their revenge against the grown-ups, and then some. What a difference six years would make. *Bonnie and Clyde* carried a message of sexual liberation. Sex would make you free. In its clumsy libidinal economy, Clyde's gun does what his dick can't, and when his dick can, there's nothing left for his gun to do, so he dies. It was all summed up by that ubiquitous antiwar bumper sticker: Make Love, Not War.

If Freud was out, at least in its orthodox form, Marx was back in, courtesy of Beatty and Penn. The beating heart of *Bonnie and Clyde* is best detected in the picture's populist embrace of bank robbing as a blow against plutocracy, as well as the transformation of the outlaw couple into modern-day Robin Hoods. From the moment Clyde introduces himself and his partner, saying, "I'm Clyde Barrow and this is Miss Bonnie Parker. We rob banks," the movie throws down a gauntlet: the unapologetic, unabashed romanticization of bank robbers and killers. In the crucible of the Vietnam War, the good guys were stepping over the line that separated them from the bad guys, and vice versa. In *Dr. No* (1963), James Bond casually exercised his "license to kill" by executing a larcenous metallurgist, coldly counting each shot until he knows the man's gun is empty. By making villains of traditional authority figures—bankers, cops, parents—*Bonnie and Clyde* went considerably further, turning conventional morality on its head. The film legitimated violence against the establishment, the same violence that seethed in the hearts and minds of hundreds of thousands of frustrated opponents of the Vietnam War.

Beatty had no trouble embracing Penn's populism. As he put it, "The political message in 'Bonnie and Clyde'? You better give the have-nots some money, or they'll shoot you." That was the commonsensical foundation upon which he would base his liberalism in the years to come. "Warren's fundamental belief about politics is that the world is a safer and better place for everybody if nobody gets shit on too bad," explains Jeremy Pikser, who would work on *Reds* and co-write *Bulworth* with him. "He doesn't want anybody in the world to be so poor, miserable, and so pissed they want to kill rich people. 'Cause that's bad for him. [He readily admits that this is the point of view of] a rich, selfish, self-interested individual. He realizes that his life is an embarrassment of riches, so envy is not a good thing for him."

But populism was only part of the *Bonnie and Clyde* story. The misfits of the Everyman-on-the-run films of the 1930s and 1940s like Fritz Lang's *You Only Live Once* and Nicholas Ray's *They Live by Night* are victims; they just want to be normal, but society won't let them. Those pictures took that yearning and milked it for pathos. Here, it's the reverse. Until the final ambush, Bonnie and Clyde aren't victims. They freely choose to do what they do; they like robbing banks. Except for a few fleeting moments when they dream about living like other people, they disdain normalcy; it makes them vulnerable. They would much rather live fast, die young, and leave good-looking corpses than reel in the years rocking away on the back porch. Theirs is not a moral journey. *Bonnie and Clyde* flays bourgeois morality; there is a straight line from it to the brutality of *Taxi Driver*, nearly a decade later.

It was not only the violence of Bonnie and Clyde, not only their refusal to say they were sorry that antagonized "them"; it was the flair and energy with which the film pits the hip and the cool against the old, straight, and stuffy. Beatty not only "shoved it up the asses" of a generation of Americans that was on the wrong side of the generation gap, the wrong side of the Vietnam War, but also a straitlaced generation of Motion Picture Academy members of whom Bob Hope was the public face, that hoped to go quietly, with dignity. *Bonnie and Clyde* wouldn't let them. It unceremoniously pushed them out the door, and they understood that perfectly. On some level, Crowther, Hope et al. must have seen themselves in Sheriff Hamer, Dylan's Mr. Jones who didn't understand what was happening there, didn't get the joke, and must have been angered by it. By discarding the way things had always been done, by daring to do them differently, and in most ways better, Beatty and Penn, Benton and Newman, flipped the bird at the people who had come before them and cut a fresh path through the tangled undergrowth of convention. If there is such a thing as cinematic patricide, *Bonnie and Clyde* would have to plead guilty to the crime. Newman was right. Like *The Graduate*, young audiences recognized that *Bonnie and Clyde* was "theirs."

The real originality of *Bonnie and Clyde*, however, lay in the fact that it recognized that in America by mid-decade, both Marx *and* Freud were dead, not to mention God—as memorialized on the April 8, 1966, cover of *Time* magazine. But if the kings were dead, it was long live the king, in this case Andy Warhol. Fame and glamour, as the Beatles recognized, had become more potent than sex, class, or religion. "Warhol was giving parties at the Factory with Viva, Edie, Candy Darling, the fifteen minutes of fame bit," says Newman. "None of those people did anything; they just wanted to be celebrities. Likewise, our take on *Bonnie and Clyde* was that *they* wanted to be celebrities. They saw in each other the mirror of their own ambitions. Although they were both at the bottom of society, in each other they saw someone who validated an image of what they could be. Clyde creates for her a vision of herself as a movie star, and from that moment on, even though he couldn't fuck her, he's got her." And similarly, near the end, when Bonnie reads him her "poem," "The Story of Bonnie and Clyde," published in the newspaper, he tells her, "You told my story. You made me somebody they're going to remember." It is then that he's finally able to perform sexually; fame is an aphrodisiac.

For all the talk about the Depression and the Vietnam War, *Bonnie and Clyde* is a paean to coolness, to the right of the young and the beautiful, of movie stars, of celebrities, to write their own rules, to do as they please. This was something Beatty understood. Bonnie and Clyde were not so different from him when he started out, famous before he'd made a movie, a celebrity because he wanted to be a celebrity, acted like a celebrity, and was packaged like a celebrity by his publicists. He was the Paris Hilton of the late 1950s; he anticipated Andy Warhol's celebrity factory by a good half decade. And indeed, in the first blush of his stardom, and later as he gained enormous power, he did do as he pleased, he did write his own rules.

Still, as the hollowness of that became increasingly evident to him—he wasn't reading T. S. Eliot for nothing—as the gossip columns and magazine interviews turned yellow and brittle before the ink was dry, Beatty struggled to give his celebrity some substance, to realize, to concretize, to incarnate himself in the only way he could: to make, finally, a great movie.

Beatty was both puppeteer and puppet, a trope that appears in many of his movies, *Bonnie and Clyde* being the first. Seducing Bonnie by, in essence, promising to make her a star, Clyde does a casting couch number on her. In other words, he becomes the producer inside the movie, Beatty's fictional alter ego. This makes *Bonnie and Clyde* a movie about itself, as movies often are, a representation of its own journey to the screen, an act of aesthetic narcissism, a mirror held up to itself. There was a whole lot more to the outlaw couple than there was to the somnambulists who glided, like exotic fish, through Warhol's films. Bonnie and Clyde were like the performance artists of the 1960s, or the outsider artists of today. Their legend was their art. They were their own subjects, and their medium was crime. *Bonnie and Clyde* offers up a metaphor of art as an offense against official culture, not unlike Godard's oft put analogy between the camera and the gun, or Scorsese's portrait of himself as a killer seated in the back of the cab in *Taxi Driver.* As such, the subject of the movie—transgression against the status quo—replicated and foretold its reception. Like its eponymous heroes, the picture was nearly killed in return.

NINETEEN SIXTY-EIGHT was a year of unprecedented upheaval in the United States. The spirit of hope that had launched the Summer of Love the previous year had curdled, giving way to a roller-coaster ride of highs and lows through a blasted landscape of war, assassinations, political protests, and police brutality. On Wednesday, January 31, at half past midnight, North Vietnam and its guerrilla allies in the South launched the Tet Offensive, sending seventy thousand troops out of the jungles to brazenly carry the war to the cities. The Johnson administration had been insisting for months that there was light at the end of the tunnel, that the endless escalations, the Phoenix program, the strategic hamlets, the electronic battlefield, the carpet bombings and rain of Agent Orange would inevitably bring the insurgency to its knees. But now the scale, audacity, and synchronicity of the attacks provided a dramatic indication that this was no more than wishful thinking, turning an increasing number of Americans into doves.

The killing of Martin Luther King in particular changed the tenor of American politics. While it may be an exaggeration to say the "dream" was dead, suddenly the struggle for racial justice and against the war grew uglier. Beatty was drawn to the turmoil in the streets. Two weeks after King was assassinated, Columbia University in New York City erupted into violence, became the scene of a widely publicized confrontation between student protesters and police. He visited the Columbia campus with Julie Christie. But whereas many in the antiwar movement had given up on electoral politics and regarded themselves as revolutionaries, Beatty, who underneath it all was deeply conservative, both aesthetically and politically, as always, leavening his idealism with a bracing dose of realism, was more comfortable working inside the system. Unlike Godard, in whom he had little interest, he would never have embraced Maoism, or any other "ism." And with Johnson out of the race, it wasn't unreasonable to look to the 1968 presidential election as part of the solution, not the problem. Reviewing the presidential politics of that year, Hunter Thompson wrote in *Fear and Loathing on the Campaign Trail '72*, "it was clear that the next president would be Gene McCarthy or Bobby Kennedy, and The War would be over by Christmas."

Throughout the Democratic primary campaign that pitted Kennedy against McCarthy, Charlie Feldman lay dying of pancreatic cancer. Beatty reconciled with Feldman shortly before he was diagnosed in January 1968. "It was *Bonnie and Clyde* that caused me to reconcile with him because I realized that it was my relationship with him that made me produce my own pictures," he says. "I made a lot more money from *Bonnie and Clyde* than I would have made on *Pussycat,* and it was a better movie. Plus, if I had done *Pussycat,* I doubt that I would ever have done *Shampoo,* so in a way both *Bonnie and Clyde* and *Shampoo* came out of *Pussycat.*"

Beatty sat at Feldman's bedside throughout his final days, spelling his new wife, Clotilde Barot. She recalls, "Warren would stay with me until four o'clock in the morning." He told her, "I'll take over, I'll read a script, I won't make any noise." She adds, "When Charlie started to throw up blood, Warren was there." Feldman died on May 25, 1968.

Eleven days later, on June 5, the hammer fell again. Kennedy, who had just handily defeated McCarthy in the California Democratic primary, was assassinated at the Ambassador Hotel in Los Angeles, just after he gave his victory speech. With the killing so close on the heels of King's death, the hope inspired by Kennedy's campaign—the contagious image of the smiling, golden-haired prince embracing and embraced by those less fortunate, farmworkers, wounded veterans, poor blacks and whites—gave way to a pervasive feeling of doom, a dark, foreboding sense that the times had become unhinged. As a political figure, Bobby didn't have nearly the gravitas that King did, but in many ways his death was more cataclysmic, changing the face of American politics—for the worse—for years to come in ways that could barely be imagined. Shortly after the assassination, in a note to Jean Howard, former Ziegfeld girl, Hollywood photographer, and Feldman's former wife, Beatty wrote, "I have never been so depressed. It was the worst thing that's ever happened to this country and the saddest. God, will it ever end."

Politically speaking, Beatty was just getting his feet wet, and wasn't taken seriously as an asset by the Kennedys, even though he had campaigned for RFK in Oregon. They were not in the market for charisma, having more than enough of their own. Bobby's brother-in-law and Southern California campaign manager Steven Smith, who died in 1990, "thought Beatty was full of shit," says a source. "Steve was a backroom guy who was pretty tough. He didn't like the whole actor thing. He thought Beatty was a lightweight. Beatty really wasn't in that Kennedy loop. He wasn't close to any of them, and still isn't." Nevertheless, the star admired Bobby. As he put it some time later, "JFK was a very impressive figure to me, and the atmosphere that surrounded him was dazzling. But Bobby was a much stronger influence." In the late 1990s, he described himself this way: "I'm a Bobby Kennedy Democrat, or where I think a Bobby Kennedy Democrat would be now."

In the immediate aftermath of the assassination, Beatty, like many others, was preoccupied with, as he puts it, "picking up the pieces." He campaigned for the Anti-Ballistic Missile Treaty, as well as several candidates for public office, like Adlai Stevenson III, in Illinois. He trod the hustings on behalf of Senator John Glenn's Emergency Committee for Gun Control, and in support of a gun control bill sponsored by Senator Joe Tydings of Maryland. On July 6, 1968, he addressed the crowd at a Giants-Cardinals baseball game at Candlestick Park in San Francisco and was booed. "I loved the way, say, that he would go to baseball matches and stand up in the interval and talk about getting rid of guns," recalled Christie. "He would be this little tiny figure in this big baseball stadium, and I would be looking down at him. I thought he was wonderfully courageous for doing that." Later that day, he put in an appearance at a Sonny Liston fight at the Cow Palace. "They asked me to get up and say some words in favor of the Tydings bill between rounds," he recalls. "Because it seemed like everybody in the Cow Palace had a gun, you know. And they threw hot dogs at me. It was hilarious, in retrospect only." The heckling he received at the two events helped to convince him that perhaps he would be more effective behind the scenes.

Despite his activism on behalf of Democratic Party issues, Beatty managed to maintain friendships with many prominent Republicans whose views he abhorred. Politics was never personal with Beatty. A decade later, Beatty had occasion to meet General Douglas MacArthur's wife. He recalls, "One night I got a message at my hotel, 'Mrs. Douglas MacArthur would like to have dinner with you.' I thought it was some friend of mine making a sick joke. I called the number, and it was John Kluge, who I didn't know. I said 'Mr. Kluge, this is Warren Beatty. Did you call me?' And he said, 'As a matter of fact, I did. I'm having a little birthday celebration for Mrs. MacArthur and she would like you to come.'

" 'Mrs. *Douglas* MacArthur?'

" 'Yes, she's a wonderful woman.'

"I came to the dinner. Sinatra was there, and various well-known people. I was seated next to Mrs. MacArthur, who was an extremely beautiful woman of ninety-two, I think. We got along very well. By dessert, we seemed to be old friends. I said 'Let me ask you a question.'

" 'What?'

" 'I'm just so interested. I can't help asking you this question.'

" 'What's that?'

" 'When you were with your husband in moments of extreme intimacy—'

" 'You mean when we were fucking?'

" 'Yes. What did you call him?'

" 'What did I call him when we were doing that?'

" 'Yes.'

" 'General.' "

Beatty liked older women, in fact, very old women. In the mid-1990s, he would work ferociously to get Katharine Hepburn into *Love Affair*. He was good friends with Diana Vreeland, the former editor of *Vogue*, when she was in her seventies. Ditto Lillian Hellman, who was certainly no beauty. "I met Lillian at the opening night of *Barefoot in the Park* in 1964 at a party at Tavern on the Green," he recalls. "She was a compulsive smoker. Julie Christie and I spent Christmas with her years later. As a present I gave her a box of the biggest Nicaraguan cigars I could find. They were huge, about half a foot long. I also gave her an incredibly elaborate box that contained every kind of snuff known to man. And then I gave her a course at Schick Center to stop smoking. Inside of two weeks she smoked all the cigars, sniffed all the snuff, and never went to the Schick thing once. She just could not stop smoking. She had all kinds of problems, emphysema and her carotid artery was all blocked up."

Peter Feibleman, who was a sometimes lover and longtime friend of the playwright—and wrote a wonderful book about her called *Lilly*—brought her out to L.A. when she was in her late sixties. "Lillian hated actors, hated theater people," he recalls. "She liked Maureen Stapleton, that's about it, and Warren. He took her out to dinner. To a big fancy restaurant where she dropped her teeth into her spaghetti. She was almost dead. When he got back, he said, 'She's a fascinating woman. I'd rather have dinner with her than with any woman I know.' But it went no further. He had sense enough not to dive into the La Brea tar pits, and that's what having an affair with Lillian would come to. He'd be dead. She had an enormous jealous streak."

Years later, Feibleman also introduced Beatty to Kitty Carlisle Hart when she was about ninety. "I made the mistake of thinking, Poor little old lady," he says. "But that flirtation was visible across the street. There was no little old lady, and there was no man doing anybody a gracious favor. They *liked* each other on a sensual level. Yes, he does love older women."

The last week of August 1968, Beatty and Christie went to the Democratic National Convention in Chicago. At one point, the actor was summoned to an audience with Hubert Humphrey, the presumptive Democratic candidate. Even though Beatty had supported Bobby, he never bought the vilification of the Johnson-Humphrey regulars by the Kennedy wing of the party. "We were taught to hate them," he says. "If it weren't for the Vietnam War, LBJ would have gone down as a great president." Beatty had a more nuanced appreciation of party veterans like Humphrey, and were the vice president nominated, Beatty was inclined to support him.

"I was in the park being gassed, I looked at my watch, it was 6:15, and I had to cross the street to the Hilton Hotel to have the meeting," Beatty recalls. "Humphrey was impressed by *Bonnie and Clyde,* and he wanted me to make a campaign film for him. I told him that I could only do that if he came out against the war. He looked at me and said,

'You wait, in the next few days, you'll be surprised, I'm going to make a statement.' 'Course he didn't make it until the last week of the campaign. But I remember having the sense that an actor had the luxury of spanning both sides of the river, and how much access films gave you to the levers of power in the country."

In September 1968, about a month after Soviet troops had invaded Czechoslovakia, Beatty and Christie flew to the USSR to explore the possibility of making the John Reed film there. He knew some Russian, and had written a script called *Natural State* about a romance between an American man and a Russian woman that took place during the Cold War, presumably inspired by his relationship with Maya Plisetskaya. Nobody knew who Beatty or Christie was. They stood on line waiting for tables at restaurants in Soviet Georgia, the birthplace of Joseph Stalin, like everyone else. "You couldn't believe the atmosphere there," he says. "Everybody was bugged, every telephone call was recorded." He went with the intention of seeing whether he could get official cooperation, and whether he could cast a Russian actress in the part of the woman in his Cold War script. The answer was no on both counts. He asked to meet a particular actress and was told, "She can't really meet you yet because she has a broken leg."

"Is it in a cast?"

"Well, they're putting it in a cast. You can see her in a few days." A few days went by, and he asked again, "Can I meet her?"

"Not quite yet, but in a few days." Not knowing their man, they were thinking he would give up and return to the United States. But a few days later he called again, said, "I don't understand, why can't I meet her?"

"Well, she broke the other leg!"

Says Beatty, "They didn't want her to be in a Western film."

The Soviet director Sergei Bondarchuk, who had just directed *War and Peace*, also wanted to make a movie about Reed. He had seen *Bonnie and Clyde*, thought Beatty looked like Reed, and asked the actor to do it. But Beatty didn't like the script, thought it was "anti-American," and turned Bondarchuk down. "I didn't want to spend five or six or eight months over there having coronaries and not come back here with anything," he says. Nevertheless, he put *Natural State* aside, and instead asked, "Can I talk to some people who might have known Reed?" They said there was a woman who claimed to have had an affair with him. He said, "Can I meet her?" As in the case of the actress with the two broken legs, the response, at least initially, was nyet. He insisted, turned it into a confrontation, and finally they took him to her apartment on the seventh floor of one of those drab postwar buildings that looked like—and probably were made of—cinder blocks stacked like Legos. Eleonora Drapkina was about eighty. Her mother had been close to Nadya Krupskaya, Lenin's wife, and there is a photograph of Eleonora at the age of fifteen, an incredibly beautiful girl, standing next to Lenin. Drapkina examined Beatty with interest, and told him he was the worst-dressed millionaire she'd ever met. He asked her his stock question that told him how candidly people would speak of the regime: "What do you think of Solzhenitsyn?" Says Beatty, "The party line on him around the film ministry was, He's a wonderful writer but very crazy. I had just finished reading *The First Circle*, fantastic about the labor camps, and I thought he was a great writer, and anything but crazy. But nobody would say a good word about him." She replied, "Without doubt, he is the greatest living writer in the world." He thought, Ahh, this is getting interesting, and asked, "Did you have a romance with John Reed?"

"A romance? I fucked him!"

"Were you ever in a labor camp?"

"Oh yes."

"Where was it?"

"Ummm. North of Minsk."

"How long were you there?"

"Oh, sixteen years."

"How do you feel about Stalin?"

"Only hate. But of course the revolution was in its early stages."

He recalls, "It was at that moment I thought, I have to make a movie about that kind of passion. I'm going to make it without the Russians. And just the way I want to make it. I felt some sort of need to protect this poor American who was buried in the Kremlin wall. His ideals were not solely the property of the Soviets."

Adds Jeremy Pikser, whom Beatty hired as a researcher on *Reds,* "Old women are Warren's biggest fetish. I don't think he actually had sex with old women, but he has a major soft spot for them. From the moment he met this old woman who said she'd fucked Jack Reed, he wanted to make a film about him."

BASKING IN the afterglow of the success of *Bonnie and Clyde*, an enormous personal triumph, Beatty became, if not necessarily an auteur in the French sense, one of the most powerful figures in the industry, a serious actor and a canny producer who had accomplished the unthinkable: forced a studio to eat crow. He said at the time, "If I went to someone now and said I wanted to make a musical of the Last Supper, they'd probably say, 'Okay, let's talk about it.'"

Beatty rented a second suite in the Beverly Wilshire, just under his penthouse, and hired an assistant, Susanna Moore, a nineteen-year-old sometime model who grew up in Hawaii and later became a novelist. She went up to see him, nervous, the phone ringing off the hook, Warren very flirtatious. At the end of the interview, as she was about to leave, he stopped her, walked over and said, "There's one last thing I haven't checked yet—I need to see your legs. Can you lift up your skirt?" Moore duly lifted her skirt. "Okay, you got the job." Moore recalls, "Warren has to control and dominate. He would say, 'I had a script for you to read, you weren't there.' He'd want to know where you were the night before, are you fucking him, and so on. He was willing to get into conversations about women's clothes or their makeup: 'You shouldn't wear that color, you're too beautiful to wear green.' Women love that, because men are so frequently not paying attention."

Hits like *Bonnie and Clyde* always raise the ante, the "what's next" question, and the actor cum producer was tired, suffering from postpartum *Bonnie and Clyde* depression. By December 1968, Beatty couldn't even talk about the film. He would tell the press, "I don't think it's so revolutionary or different. It's a well-made film. We worked hard on it. It came out nicely. But after all, it's only a movie." Instead of developing another picture himself, he thought it might be easier just to act in someone else's movie. "I'm kind of exhausted," he confessed. "*Bonnie and Clyde* took a long time." But even that seemed beyond him. He never liked anything, couldn't make up his mind. He was offered every script in town. But few of the projects that came in over the transom piqued his interest, and he was very good at just saying no. He had a million reasons for turning down scripts, ranging from the ridiculous to the sublime, as in, "I'm just lazy" to "it's not important enough," which at least had the virtue of making him sound like a serious person.

Ultimately, Beatty did nothing. "People were dying in Vietnam, and the immediacy of that problem, and the racial problems that were underneath it, these were very immediate things," he recalls. "It was very hard in 1968 to go into a soundstage and find that more interesting than what was happening outside. Making movies next to [participating in] that was boring. Boring." He continues, "There was a wish to act, and to feel identity through that action. People took chances and risked their lives. Martin Luther King put it very well when he said, If you don't have something to die for, you don't have something to live for."

Despite fatigue, depression, and distractions of one sort or another, Beatty did find time to labor over the script of *Shampoo* with Towne. But it was not a happy collaboration. Over the course of a few months in 1969 they met repeatedly for lunch, usually at the Source or the Aware Inn, eating radishes and downing cup after cup of chamomile tea. After these sessions, Towne would go home and write. "Warren and I had some arguments over the script," he recalled. "He wanted to have one strong woman's role for Julie Christie, and I ended up writing two strong women's roles, or two roughly equivalent women's roles. His view was that neither role was strong or good. He was very angry about it, and I was very angry about his being angry about it, because I thought the script was really pretty terrific."

But beyond their disagreements, it soon became evident to Beatty that something else was wrong; the script wasn't happening. Towne suffered from writer's block. "Bob would love to work for money on rewrites on which he got no credit, and would do it quickly," says former Columbia executive Jerry Ayres. "Over three weeks, he'd have a whole new script ready. But something that had his name on it would become all involved in the neurosis of completion and failure, and take forever." Bob Evans, who later hired him to write *Chinatown*, says, "Towne could talk to you about a screenplay he was gonna write and tell you every page of it, but it never came out on paper. Never. You know why? He's on the phone with Warren half the day. He's really Warren's nigger."

Towne had two weaknesses. He had difficulty with structure, a real liability for someone who often turned in massive scripts the size and weight of doorstops. Then too, for all his artful dialogue and clever set pieces, storytelling was not his strong suit. "Robert had written a script that was very good in atmosphere, and in dialogue, but very weak in story, and each day the story would go in whatever direction the wind was blowing," says Beatty, referring to *Shampoo*. "He would just never finish. It has to do with talking, an unwillingness to make choices. It's symptomatic of depression."

Towne would complain to friends about how difficult Beatty was. From his point of view, his friend was too linear. "He would not allow me to stop and think about everything and nothing," he says. "Nietzsche or Blake said, 'The straight roads are the roads of progress, the crooked roads are the roads of genius.' Warren will not knowingly go down a crooked road."

Finally, Beatty lost patience. He was tired of sitting around munching carrot sticks and tossing around ideas that evaporated into thin air. He said to Towne, "Look, I don't wanna keep waiting for what you're gonna do. Finish by December 31 and show it to me. If you don't do it, let's forget it. I'm gonna do it myself." December 31 rolled around and there was no script. "He missed that date by something like three weeks, and we just sort of lost contact," Beatty says. "I was angry. Julie was angry. Because we had set time aside for this movie." Towne thought *Shampoo* would never be made.

BEATTY HAD turned down a myriad of better scripts and more compelling projects than *The Only Game in Town*, but when George Stevens called him in August, while the actor was in Chicago, and asked him to replace Frank Sinatra opposite Elizabeth Taylor, he said yes. By the time Beatty had met Stevens, the director's best films—the light comedies of the early 1940s and two films in the 1950s—were behind him, and no one but Beatty thought he was a great director. Astonished, Dick Sylbert told him, "You can't possibly want to do that movie." But Sylbert realized, "He did it to watch Stevens direct. You know what he found out? Film is the cheapest thing there is. You can shoot as much as you want." Or, as screenwriter Jeremy Pikser once observed in a different context, Beatty perversely and repeatedly adopted his friend Muhammad Ali's rope-a-dope tactic, as if he couldn't do good work without willingly putting his career in jeopardy beforehand. Or perhaps it was the opportunity to seduce Taylor, the very avatar of unattainable glamour and fortune in *A Place in the Sun*, now within reach, after a fashion, if he cared to spar with Richard Burton. Or maybe Beatty was telling the truth when he said he had lost interest in movies, that he was bored, and it really didn't matter what kind of junk he made. Or perhaps it was his salary. It was an open secret that Taylor was getting $1.25 million. Not to be outdone, Beatty asked Darryl Zanuck for the same, and it was rumored that he got it, making it by far his largest payday to date, and astronomical for the period. (Some accounts say he got $750,000.) The decision made little sense, except that it put him in commuting distance to Christie, who was in Geneva shooting a picture called *In Search of Gregory,* directed by Peter Wood. Schlesinger sent Wood a letter advising him how to direct Christie, which read, in part, "give her a kick up the arse and keep Warren off the set."

Set in the seedy underbelly of Las Vegas—albeit cleaned up for PG consumption—*The Only Game in Town* concerned two losers, Joe Grady (Beatty), a gambler cum piano player, in love with Fran (Taylor), a show girl infatuated with a married man. The picture was a two-hander with a tiny cast. Beatty anticipated that it would be a short shoot. But there was no such thing as a small Elizabeth Taylor picture. She was coming off a hysterectomy and in poor health, with chronic back trouble. She insisted on moving the production to Paris for tax reasons and to be near Burton, who was starring in *Staircase,* another forgettable movie, with Rex Harrison.

Production started on September 26, 1968. Knowing Beatty's proclivities for British brunettes and older women—Taylor was seven years his senior—Burton was suspicious. Confiding in his diary on October 20, he wrote, "I am ridiculously (I hope) jealous of E. nowadays because I suppose she's working with a young & attractive man who obviously adores her. She tells me I'm a fool & that he's like a younger brother. Ah, I say, but there have been cases of incest." And again, "Wouldn't it be ironic if Eliz fell in love with her leading man on this pic? It would be an ironic ending to our love affair, wouldn't it? I think I may fire a warning shot over the bows of our young Mr B." When Burton visited the set, he described needling them both: "I say, Eliz. Don't you think you should be a bit closer to your lover? And W . . . you look a touch bashful. Is my presence making you nervous?" Whether it was because Burton warned him off, or because Burton and Taylor were such press bait that an affair with her might as well have been conducted in the windows of Bon Marché, or for some other reason best known to himself, Beatty claims he declined to press his advantage.

Paris's haute société provided the young star with more than enough women to distract him. Taylor would amuse (or alarm) Burton by reciting a litany of names of titled and untitled females who swarmed around the set and frequented Beatty's hotel, including Brigitte Bardot, an SAS stewardess, and Princess Elizabeth of Yugoslavia, whom he'd met through Burton and Taylor. They also introduced him to Maria Callas, who was heartbroken over the news, splashed about the tabloids, that her ex—Aristotle Onassis—was to marry Jackie Kennedy. One can only imagine Christie's take on the world in which Beatty was so comfortable, given that the city had almost been consumed by the flames of revolution a scant four months earlier in the upheaval known as May '68, which nearly closed down the Cannes Film Festival and transformed the work of French filmmakers like Jean-Luc Godard. Finished with her film and back in London, Christie joined two thousand or so demonstrators at an anti–Vietnam War action chanting "U.S. murderers" in front of the American embassy in Grosvenor Square on November 23, at which an American flag was burned.

On November 5, 1968, Humphrey had narrowly lost the popular vote to Richard Nixon. Bobby Kennedy, had he lived, would undoubtedly have won. Beatty observed, "It was the end of a lot of dreams of the early '60s, and the morning after that election, for me the prospects were pretty grim."

Plagued by delays, *The Only Game in Town* dragged on and on. Production spilled over until the next year, and the marathon shoot didn't wrap until March 3, 1969. Beatty and Christie promptly left for an around-the-world holiday. The issue that agitated the press was whether or not the lovebirds would marry. Beatty scandalized the women's magazines by ridiculing the venerable institution of marriage, joking (perhaps) that the best time for a wedding was noon, because if the marriage didn't work, you haven't screwed up the entire day.

When they returned, Beatty and Christie spent a considerable amount of time in London at her Selwood Terrace flat. She was so disorganized her friends had to take her to the supermarket when the cupboards were bare. The couple fought continuously. One of her housekeepers in London recalled, "There I was, poised between them, making up the bed, lips sealed, while this furious row raged. I didn't want to know [what it was about]. I just recall feeling how absolutely farcical the situation was. And Julie could shout!" Christie complained to friends, "Warren doesn't drink, doesn't smoke, doesn't swear. That makes it a bit hard on me—because I can't do any of those things with him either!"

Beatty (now joined by Christie) still had trouble making commitments of any sort. Walking down New Bond Street one day, he passed a tailor, and broke stride, as if he'd forgotten something. His companion shot him a quizzical look. "About a year ago I went in and had the first fitting for a suit but I've never wanted to go back to him for the second fitting. I just can't . . . go back." Another quizzical look, to which he explained that he would then have to return a third time to pick it up. One Los Angeles hostess only served buffet if they were invited because she never knew if they would show up.

On the night of August 8 and 9, Charles Manson and family ventured forth from the Spahn Ranch and murdered Sharon Tate, Roman Polanski's wife, who was eight months pregnant, and four other people in the Benedict Canyon home they were renting. Polanski flew from London to L.A. Despite the relative obscurity of the victims, the murders hit home. No one was untouched. Everybody in Hollywood knew them, had had their hair done by one of the victims, Jay Sebring, as Beatty and Towne had, or had been invited up that night and had begged off because they were too tired, too stoned, or had something better to do, like Bob Evans. Just a few months earlier Polanski had tried to get Beatty to take over his lease. Beatty recalls, "I went up to look at the house, and thought, Yeah, I'll stay here for a while, because I wanted to get out of the hotel, but then a couple of people walked out from another part of the house, and said that Roman had told them to take the house. They said, 'There's plenty of room for everybody,' but I thought, No, I don't want to be in a house with anyone else."

L.A.'s entertainment community was paralyzed by fear. With the perpetrators still at large—the cops suspected Polanski—people looked at one another and wondered. The chaos wrought by the war, the assassinations, the riots, had come home to roost in Hollywood. If the 1960s had ended the year before, when Nixon was elected, they ended again on August 9, 1969. As Sylbert put it, "All over town you could hear the toilets flushing."

Says Beatty, "Roman did a press conference at the Beverly Wilshire, so everybody came up to my place beforehand. Then he went down to talk to the reporters, and told them he hadn't killed his wife. They were dubious. It was impossible to escape it in this town, even if you were not friends with the people involved. The original version of *Shampoo* was strongly influenced by the killings. The story was stretched out over a period of months, got into drug running, and was headed towards an apocalyptic ending."

4

EASY WRITER

How Beatty went to school on the script for *McCabe & Mrs. Miller,*
and then took a year-and-a-half leave from movies to work
on the George McGovern presidential campaign.

"Had I been the producer I would have killed Robert Altman."
— *Warren Beatty*

BEATTY ALWAYS WANTED to make movies with his lovers, either because he regarded them as his muses, or simply because, as Joan Collins had discovered, he was a possessive man and, all too familiar with on-the-set romances, wanted to keep an eye on them. Now, having given up on *Shampoo,* at least for the moment, he said to his new agent, Stan Kamen, "Let's find a picture I can do with Julie." Kamen replied, "What about Robert Altman? He's got a script called *The Presbyterian Church Wager.*" Beatty replied, "Who's he?"

In fact, there was no reason Beatty would have heard of Altman, who had done a lot of television, directing shows like *Maverick,* *Bonanza,* and *Combat* in the late 1950s, early 1960s, as well as one obscure feature, *That Cold Day in the Park.* Even his agent, George Litto, a short, pugnacious man, didn't particularly like him. "Nobody wanted to make a picture with Bob Altman," says Litto. "He was this bombastic rebel, bomb thrower, crazy son of a bitch. He was confrontational. He would get in your face and tell you to fuck off. He could be a miserable prick."

Like director Hal Ashby, Altman was one of those men, older than the flower children and a maverick in the 1950s, for whom the 1960s was invented. After he got high on his first joint, he never came down. He let his hair—what there was of it—go long, grew a beard, wore turtlenecks, caftans, ankhs, and beads, whatever the head shops had to offer, although he never neglected his first love, Cutty Sark.

The Presbyterian Church Wager was controlled by a first-time producer named David Foster, a former publicist, who instantly recognized the tremendous media dividend the picture would reap by yoking together Beatty and Christie for the first time.

Beatty read the script at the beginning of the new year, 1970. He screened *M*A*S*H*, which featured Donald Sutherland and Elliott Gould, the director's breakout picture, as yet unreleased. Like *Bonnie and Clyde,* it would be that singular thing, a commercial hit that broke creative ground. Beatty got it right away. He applauded Altman's irreverence and antic style. If Penn was an iconoclast, Altman was more so, made Penn look positively prim. With zero patience for the conventional wisdom of the this-is-the-way-it's-always-been-done old-timers, he subverted the star system by favoring ensemble casts. He used overlapping sound that often made dialogue unintelligible. He undermined plot with episodic narratives that refused to tell a coherent story. He disregarded cinematographic conventions with generous use of the zoom lens. Altman was always reminding the audience it was watching a movie. Like Penn, he was interested in the relation between the medium and the message, but whereas Penn could often be portentous, Altman was playful, sprinkling narrative and visual puns throughout his pictures. As Beatty puts it, "He did not wear his seriousness on his sleeve, which Penn did."

Best of all, *M*A*S*H* was irreverent. It disrespected religion and with its liberal use of raw language transgressed the boundaries of accepted filmmaking practice. "It was the first time you saw guys during an operation covered with blood saying, 'Nurse, get your tits out of the way,'" says Litto. It was the first major studio movie in which "fuck" was used. In short, again like *Bonnie and Clyde,* it was a wise-ass "up yours" from the cool to the uncool.

Based on a book by Edmund Naughton called *McCabe,* McKay's script was very much a conventional western, the story of a mysterious gunslinger riding into a godforsaken turn-of-the-century town in the Northwest. Beatty was worried about what Christie would think about the part. "Julie never wanted to do anything," he recalls. "She was the most selective actress I've ever met. She tested for *Doctor Zhivago* in a five-day screen test. She was totally unknown, they gave her the picture and initially she turned it down!" He thought to himself, I just don't know if Julie will want to do this. It's an American woman, and really isn't anything at all like her. As he predicted, she was reluctant. "Julie really didn't want to do it, and I had to really push her, because I thought she could be very funny in it."

Beatty called Altman from New York, said, "Don't do anything until I come to town," and then flew to L.A. to meet him. The two men hit it off, or seemed to. Beatty agreed to do the film, and finally convinced Christie as well, but there can only be one genius on a picture, and there was trouble ahead. With the two stars on board, Warner Brothers, now under new ownership (Steve Ross had bought the company from Seven Arts and installed Ted Ashley as chairman and John Calley as head of production), agreed to finance it. The business was in such bad shape that even though Beatty was in great demand, he had to forgo his customary salary up front in lieu of a cut of the back end gross.

The Only Game in Town was released on March 4, 1970, and expired on arrival. Referring to Stevens, Beatty, and Taylor, Vincent Canby, Crowther's replacement, wrote in *The New York Times,* "Assigning those three to the film version of Frank D. Gilroy's small, sentimental, Broadway flop is rather like trying to outfit a leaky Central Park rowboat for a celebrity cruise through the Greek islands. The result is a phenomenological disaster." The picture grossed a mere $1.5 million, and Fox, which lost an estimated $10 million on the film, and probably a whole lot more, pulled it without further ado. Beatty compared it to telling a joke underwater.

The Presbyterian Church Wager, soon to become *McCabe & Mrs. Miller,* wouldn't go into production until late 1970 at the earliest. Christie was restless. Joseph Losey, yet another blacklisted director, offered her *The Go-Between,* based on a novel by L. P. Hartley, which was a sort of pre-*Atonement* story set in Edwardian England. Christie, who was living on the beach in Malibu in a house rented from actress Gayle Hunnicutt, decided to squeeze it in before *McCabe*, and arrived at the location in Norfolk in the beginning of July, after which Beatty occasionally joined her. The couple, now being touted as the new Burton-Taylor, was mobbed by press and fans. Christie hated being hounded every time she poked her head out the door, said that she had begun to "feel like Lassie the Wonder Dog." Reporters were still speculating on the likelihood that the couple would marry. Irritated, often as not she would turn on her heel, and stalk off, leaving an expletive in her wake.

While Christie was making *The Go-Between*, Beatty met Britt Ekland for the second time at a dinner party that year given for Roman Polanski in London, from which she noted that Christie was "foolishly absent!" As she described the encounter, "Warren's gaze descended on me, and the moment our eyes met I knew we committed physically." She fell "madly" in love with him. "No man had made me happier than Warren." Describing his technique in bed, she famously wrote, "Warren could handle women as smoothly as operating an elevator. He knew exactly where to locate the top button. One flick and we were on our way." She thought he loved her too, but was disabused by overhearing too many "whispered phone calls to Julie."

When she flew to L.A. to do *The Dean Martin Show*, he followed, and she stayed with him in the penthouse. Beatty insisted that he didn't want Christie to know about the affair. "She'd hit the roof if she knew," he told her. "But I guess that is one of the gambles we're going to have to take." He stroked her face, assured her that "London was dead without you," and told her how much he missed her. They watched porn together in a theater. She wondered, "How can cinema audiences be turned on by simulated sex? I will never make a porno film unless it's for real and only with you." Amused, he replied, "In that case we had better get a camera crew to film our activities in the penthouse." Ekland had to go back to London for a TV show. He seemed relieved. "I realized that Warren was incapable of lasting love," she concluded when the relationship ended after two months. "When he picked a bloom, it was only for a season."

The Go-Between wrapped in early September. Back in L.A., Beatty and Christie resumed their tempestuous relationship. Hunnicutt would get notes from her from time to time, alerting her to irreparably damaged articles of furniture.

The cast and crew of *McCabe & Mrs. Miller* flew up to Vancouver in the bitterly cold fall of 1970, arriving in mid-October. Beatty and Christie rented a glass house on Horseshoe Bay in West Vancouver. Altman looked like a hippie Civil War officer—bearded, with love beads draped around his neck. He was pictured in *The New York Times* wearing a battered, Humphrey Bogart fedora and a coat colorfully embroidered with strange, organic-like shapes topped by a fur collar. He had never worked with a star like Beatty. Sutherland and Gould complained and bitched, but finally did what they were told. Beatty wasn't about to do anything he didn't want to do. He was stubborn, would wear people down. On the other hand, Beatty had never worked with a director quite like Altman before, freewheeling and irreverent, also used to getting his own way, resistant to his charm, and moreover enjoying the confidence of coming off the huge hit that *M*A*S*H* had become.

Touted as a genius by the critics, with Pauline Kael leading the charge, Altman was shedding collaborators like dandruff. He was in the middle of a falling out with McKay, a longtime friend who knew him when. Suddenly, as often happens, the script that had been good enough to attract Beatty and Christie and in turn get Warners to commit, was good enough no longer. Altman never had a high regard for writers. They were just nuisances, their scripts impediments to his creative process, which was heavily dependent on improvisation. He dismissed this script, as he did others, as no more than a "selling tool," to secure financing for the picture. "It was one of the worst western stories you've ever heard," said Altman. "It had all the clichés. This guy was a gambler, and she was a whore with a heart of gold, the three heavies were the giant and the half-breed and the kid." Litto was skeptical. Altman "and Brian McKay had a falling-out, so he wanted to make the script irrelevant to Brian's contribution," he said. "It was better in Brian's version. In my opinion, he should have stayed closer to it."

But that was not to be, since Beatty too turned against the script. He says he never met McKay, but at a studio meeting for which he had flown in from London, he was quoted shamelessly flattering the writer: "Your words brought me seven thousand miles." Now he felt differently. Nor was Beatty comfortable with free-form improvisation. "It was pretty clear that Bob didn't want to shoot that script," Beatty recalls. "And it was pretty clear that he expected us to go and improvise throughout the movie. And I just wasn't going to do that. I believe in improvising, but I don't believe in improvising from nothing. So I had to write a script." He added, "We started frenetically taking it apart scene by scene. . . . I had to go down into the basement of this house, where I worked, to make sure there was something we could say to each other every day." He adds, "I would take these aphorisms from my father's family in Virginia and combine them in the dialogue between McCabe and Mrs. Miller."

He continued, "I worked quite a bit more on the script than he did. I think Altman was much more happy with a kind of hit and miss approach. My approach was more linear. . . . I wrote most of the scenes that I was in." At first, he resented it, but after it was all over, he changed his mind. It built his confidence as a writer. "It was good for me," he says. "The picture had to be written, so it was like, write or die. When it was all over, I realized that I had written a movie, certainly co-written a movie." So it was that Beatty was angered when he saw Altman take screenwriting credit for himself, after apparently trying to get his former friend McKay's credit removed. Beatty felt that if anyone deserved credit, it was himself.

Christie was in the same position. As Dick Sylbert puts it, "Warren was not gonna let anybody do what they wanted with mein Julie." She wrote her lines as well. Bob "simply turned Julie's stuff over to her," says Joan Tewkesbury, the script supervisor. "She had a companion who knew all the different kinds of dialects, and they would go off and take these scenes and redo them as a woman would do them in this position."

In the hands of Altman and Beatty, any resemblance to a traditional western evaporated the moment McCabe rode through the drenching rain into the town of Presbyterian Church. The character became a flummoxed antihero, in keeping with both Altman's cinema of helplessness and Beatty's inclination to play with and subvert his own star persona. "I like to play schmucks," he said. "Cocky schmucks. Guys who think they know it all but don't. It's been the story of my life to think I knew what I was talking about and later find out that I didn't." Clyde Barrow and McCabe "shared a sort of foolishness," he continues. "They were not heroes. I found that to be funny, and Altman found it to be funny; we really agreed on that."

Altman says he told Beatty, " 'Let's have him convey his whole back-story without ever telling it.' And Beatty got frightened of that. Those opening shots, when he's coming into town and he's talking to himself, mumbling—where he's saying, 'I got poetry in me. . . . ' Beatty was nervous about doing it that way, but I said, 'Just do it, what the hell, it's just another lousy movie.' "

Recalled Christie, "We didn't have a clue what we were making because [Altman] would get ideas overnight, or somebody would do a brilliant improvisation that just went on and on and he'd suddenly incorporate that, though it had nothing to do with any story or anything."

The town became a character in its own right. Altman had the cast and crew live in the settlement in which the drama would unfold as it was being built. Says Beatty, "Bob had a talent for making the background come into the foreground and the foreground go into the background, which made the story seem a lot less linear than it actually was."

One Altman touch was the picture's mellow yellow hue. He says, "One of the big problems was that the lenses were so sharp, and the stock was so good, that it was going to look like a Christmas card." He used to walk around the set with a Polaroid Land camera, as big as a loaf of bread, wearing an old yellow velour sweatshirt. One day he pointed the camera toward his stomach, snapped a picture, then took another of the set, creating a double exposure with a yellowish cast. He went to the DP, Vilmos Zsigmond, and told him that that was what he wanted the film to look like, and that he wanted to flash the film." Says Beatty, who nearly used the technique on *Reds* before deciding it was too risky, "It was considered a very bold thing to do. You flash the positive, but you don't flash the negative, because then you can't do anything about it if it's fucked up."

Altman also experimented with the sound, creating layered soundtracks. He disliked dubbing dialogue later in the studio: it undercut the feeling of spontaneity for which he strove. But the weather in and around Vancouver at that time of year was punishing, and hell on the sound recorders, who lost syllables, sentences, and whole pages of dialogue in the howling wind. Altman thought the sound was just fine, he'd gotten what he intended. One weekend, during the shoot, editor Lou Lombardo, who had been in L.A. editing Altman's previous picture, *Brewster McCloud*, put in an appearance on the set. According to

Altman agent George Litto, "Bob had a lot of guys that just said, 'Yes.' Lou had no fear. When Bob did something he didn't like, Lou would say, 'It's shit.'" Lombardo worked for Sam Peckinpah as well as Altman, and once a pert, fresh-faced young entertainment reporter asked him to compare the two directors. He leaned back with a look of mock profundity, and said, "Sam Peckinpah is a prick, and Robert Altman is a cunt!" Altman showed him some rushes. Lombardo loved what he saw, but hated what he heard, or rather, didn't hear; the sound, he said, was "fucked." Altman blew up. "He stormed off into his bedroom, slammed the door, and never came out," recalled Lombardo. "I was [just] trying to tell him the fucking sound is bad." How bad no one would know until it was too late.

As the production proceeded, the relationship between Altman and Beatty began to fray. John Schlesinger's companion, Michael Childers, shot stills on *Nashville, 3 Women,* and a couple of other pictures for Altman. "Bob was crazy," he recalls. "Smoked too much goddamn dope. He could never make up his mind. It was 'Why don't you improvise, and I'll come back, we'll film it in a half an hour.'" Neither, of course, could Beatty make up his mind. Adds Childers, "Talk about an actor who could not make up his mind screaming at a director who could not make up his mind!"

Trained in television, Altman shot quickly from the hip and was satisfied with one take, for the same reason he preferred to use the sound recorded on the set to dubbing later. This in itself put him on a collision course with Beatty, who was used to big budget productions where money was no object. He invariably did take after take, slowly working his way into his performance. Altman complained about Beatty's "nitpicking, the way he pushed and bugged me." The actor wanted to know the purpose of every setup, of every camera move, entrance, exit, and bit of business. As Jack Nicholson once put it, "He'll chew something til the cows come home." Every so often, Beatty had to put Altman in his place, remind him who was boss. In one instance, he nixed Altman's planned trip to the Astrodome in Houston, Texas, for the premiere of *Brewster McCloud,* on the grounds that the director needed to be fresh for his Monday morning call.

According to Altman, the issues were related to Beatty's and Christie's disparate ways of working. He says, "Warren wouldn't start rehearsing until the camera was rolling on take four or five. Julie was always the best on her very first take, and after a while, she started losing interest, and you could see it. So I had one actor who was getting better, and another who was getting worse. Finally I tried to put the camera on her first, and then try to get him in.

"Warren was great in the film, and there were no bad relations, but it was a touchy situation. He once said, 'Tell anybody this and I'll call you a liar, but this picture is about me as a movie star and Julie second, and then all the rest of the people in this picture, who don't count.' And he was a little upset that I was spending so much time building up an atmosphere. Because he had never made films that way. Warren is basically a control freak. He wants to run the show."

Eventually, Altman learned to go around Beatty, rather than through him. There is a brief scene in which the actor is sitting in his office drinking, nothing complicated. As he reaches for the bottle, he knocks it over, catches it, and pours himself a drink. As first assistant director Tommy Thompson recalls it, "We shot it once, we shot it again, we shot it about eight or nine times. After take ten, Bob said, 'That's good for me, print 2, 5, 10.' Everybody was ready to go, it was one in the morning, and Warren said, 'Wait, wait, wait a minute. I'm not happy with it.'

" 'No, no, it's fine.'

" 'I want another one.'

" 'Okay.' Did another one. 'You happy with that, Warren?'

" 'No, I want another one.' "

According to Jim Margellos, the unit production manager, "It was like a test of wills. There was so much tension between the two of them you could cut it with a knife." Continues Thompson, "Finally, Bob said, 'Look, I'm tired, and I can't tell the difference anymore. Tommy will stay here with you, and you can shoot until you're happy with it. Good night guys, I'll see you tomorrow morning,' and he left. I don't know how many we did, thirty, forty, till Warren finally said, '2, 5, 10, 18, 27, 34, and 40,' and we wrapped. It was four in the morning, but Warren was happy and Bob was happy." Adds Joan Tewkesbury, "The path to success is sometimes the one of least resistance: 'You wanna shoot the Taj Mahal? Fine. I don't give a shit!' "

For his part, Beatty says, "A lot of times, Bob would wonder why I was working so hard. I'm just a person that thinks, when you go to all that trouble to set up a movie and build a set and get dressed and go there, I don't see any harm in doing a number of takes."

Altman got his revenge in the scene that ends the movie. McCabe, pursued through a blizzard by the company's hired gunslingers, is fatally wounded and falls into a snowdrift. Recalls Margellos, "Warren was buried up to his ears, with snow blasting into his face from the wind machine. It was colder than hell. Bob kept saying, 'Okay, one more time.' They dug Warren out, put him back, and did it again. He must have done it twenty-five times." As the film would evolve in the editing, Altman underlined his message. He cuts away from McCabe to the townies frantically trying to save the burning church, and to Mrs. Miller stoned on opium. As the wind howls and snowflakes slowly cover McCabe's fallen figure to the doleful sound of Leonard Cohen on the soundtrack, they are all oblivious to the drama of his death. The cross cutting at once makes a bleak commentary on the foolishness of heroic aspiration, and underlines Altman's contempt for stars.

Some observers say that the *McCabe* shoot was a happy time for Beatty and Christie, but others think the relationship was winding down. They were affectionate with each other, and so relaxed that it seemed as if they were married. It was said that they secretly were; Christie was coy with the press, refused to confirm or deny. To gossip columnist Joyce Haber, she said, tartly, "If we are, we are, and if we're not, we're not."

Alternatively, it was reported that he repeatedly asked her to marry him, and she turned him down, not because she objected to marriage herself, but because she knew he was promiscuous. "Warren never allowed anybody to control him," says Sylbert. "He'd cheat on them, fuck anybody he wanted to. Julie began to learn from Warren that there was no such thing as faithfulness." Free spirit though she may have been, exposure to Beatty seems to have made her more inclined toward the virtues of monogamy, or at least that's what she said. "Infidelity destroys love," she observed. "If you love someone and it's good, you've got to have the sense to stick with it." Sounding as if she were referring specifically to Beatty, she continued, "You can't just go swanning off with everyone who attracts you. It's greedy and selfish. It sounds great to do whatever you want at a given time. But it never works out in real life—only in the movies."

Altman observed that during the parties that punctuated the shoot, she sat apart, apparently bored with the gossip, and perked up only when the subject turned to politics. "She used to sit on the edge of those parties, while Warren mingled," he said. He continued, "It's not easy to counter that pillow talk. The only bad times we had were when the two of them obviously had fought over something or other the night before. I could feel the tension." Beatty did reportedly say, generously, if somewhat ominously, "If ever we split up, I'll pay her alimony—that's if she wants or needs it."

The show finally wrapped at the end of January 1971.

McCabe HAD been a physically exhausting shoot. Beatty and Christie went off on Sam Spiegel's boat, where he began his own draft of *Shampoo,* unhappy with the version Towne had finally turned in the previous January. Beatty didn't get back to him for months, Towne claimed, and then said it wasn't funny. "That script didn't work. I had felt bound by some sort of decorum not to step in and write it myself," Beatty recalls. "After *McCabe,* I felt, This is sort of enjoyable, so go ahead and write it. I decided to start fresh. I'd become more and more active in politics, and the apocalyptic Manson killings had long gone by the boards, so I wanted it to be the political apocalypse of 1968, which had a profound effect on me. I set my script on election night. The earlier script went over weeks or months or years, you couldn't tell what it was. I had it wind up at a series of parties, and the aftermath of those parties." Beatty wrote, in effect, a satyrization of Jean Renoir's corrosive portrait of the haute bourgeoisie in *Rules of the Game,* which fiddled while Hitler prepared for World War II.

Towne was ambitious, had his sights set on directing himself, and was unwilling to dwell in the reflected glory of his friend forever. He was acutely aware that writers, for all their importance, were far down the Hollywood totem pole. Towne used to joke about his dependent position, called Beatty "Badge," borrowing from Natalie Wood, as in, "Badge can get me into the A-list parties," and referred to himself as "Sharecropper." He says, "I always felt like one of those parrots at Hefner's. They would clip their wings so they could fly a little, but not beyond the grounds of the Playboy Mansion." But to Towne, it was far from funny. According to Sylbert, he complained that "Warren was a terrible bully." Sylbert goes on, "Warren treated him like a donkey. He didn't listen to him, told him what to do, 'Write this,' 'Write that.'" Says Buck Henry, "Like so many of us writers, Bob suffered from that thing about wanting to be rich and famous, and knowing that we're never going to be as rich and famous as the guys we're doing the work for. It makes a kind of tricky thing of gratitude and resentment in some people."

Although Towne was way too politic to trumpet his friendship with Beatty, he couldn't resist dropping his friend's name when he was trying to impress. He'd disappear for a week, then confide in a conspiratorial tone, "Don't tell anybody, but I was in a hotel room in Houston rewriting Beatty's picture." The implication was, he was indispensable to the star. But, says Bob Evans, who would have a falling out with Towne over *The Two Jakes*, "Bob claims to have done a lot more writing for Warren than Warren says he did. If I had to bet, I'd bet on Warren. He has a clearer head." Occasionally Towne let others overhear his end of a phone conversation with the actor, in which he made it clear Beatty couldn't push him around. He would say, "You cunt . . . you're just being a cunt . . . that's more cunt stuff," and so on for half an hour.

Says screenwriter Jeremy Larner (*The Candidate*), who was one of the lucky few who had the privilege of overhearing Towne on the phone with Beatty, "Towne was tremendously turned on by these conversations. He had a certain relish for dealing with [Beatty]." On the other hand, Towne took Jack Nicholson for granted, perhaps because they had known each other longer and had come up together through the Roger Corman ranks. Larner continues, "His attitude towards Nicholson was that Jack was this brilliant boy who you had to let indulge himself in any way he wanted to, but with Beatty, here was somebody who was capable of being crafty, somebody more worthy of Towne's mettle. Towne probably thought a lot more about Beatty than he did about Jack, he was more in love with Beatty. Most guys in Hollywood are more turned on by each other than they are by the women they fuck." According to Evans, "Towne treated Jack as an equal, but looked up to Warren as a messiah. That's the power Warren has."

For his part, Beatty wanted Towne at his beck and call to doctor every script he might give him, regardless of his other commitments. At the same time, he paradoxically resented Towne for making Beatty so dependent on him, even though the actor demanded it. He knew that Towne had his own ambitions to direct, and worried that eventually he would go his own way. Referring to his friend, he would quote Elia

Kazan: "Never underestimate the narcissism of a writer." At that point in their respective careers, each still needed the other, and eventually they patched up their differences.

After he got back from his break on Spiegel's yacht, Beatty went right into $, aka *Dollars,* directed by Richard Brooks, an instantly forgettable heist movie, yet another ill-considered choice. The film was shot on location in Hamburg, with some time spent in Norway. It is notable only because Beatty met co-star Goldie Hawn in the course of it, who became a lover and lifelong friend. Beatty was almost killed filming a scene in a railroad yard. He slipped and fell on tracks, nearly failing to get out of the way as a freight train bore down on him. His ankle was badly torn up. *Dollars* wrapped in April 1971.

BEATTY WAS back and forth to London with Christie. The two of them frequented Leonard of Mayfair on Grosvenor Street, run by Leonard Lewis. It was the hair salon of choice for everyone from Twiggy to the Beatles, including, bizarrely, the Krays. Even in this crowd, Beatty stood out. He struck Lewis as "one of the most conceited men I'd ever met. He loved to be pampered with facials and massages and thought of himself as Mr. Immaculate." According to the hairdresser, the actor took Christie to a fashionable plastic surgeon, Phillip Lebon, to have her breasts enhanced. (So much for the anti-establishment hippie. She once lost the opportunity to be the first Bond girl in *Dr. No* to Ursula Andress because her bust was insufficient.) "Phillip told me how devoted Warren was while Julie was recovering from the operation. He would sit beside her bed for hours on end, just stroking her hair and holding her hand."

Still, Beatty's relationship with Christie was not what it once was. Christie discovered that his girlfriends, past and present, were everywhere, like houseflies. Reportedly, he would have dinner with Christie at Chasen's, then return later that evening to have dinner with another woman. Still, says Sylbert, "He was very possessive. If I went out with Julie in London, I would get a call the next day. He would say, 'You can take the girl out in London, but you can't take the girl out of London.' He would know. He should have worked for the FBI. He was always worried about me. Warren always knew there was nobody he fucked that, if I put my mind to it, I couldn't fuck too. It's one of the reasons I got a lot of respect from him. In a way, as he said, 'We're all cousins.' "

Making up for lost time, when Beatty returned from Hamburg, he saw a slew of women, including Twiggy, Liv Ullmann, model/actress Carole Mallory, and singers Joni Mitchell and Carly Simon. Simon had cut a swath through the high-profile studs of the period, including Nicholson, Mick Jagger, Kris Kristofferson, and Cat Stevens. She conceived a real passion for James Taylor, but she always made time for Beatty, whom she described as "very persuasive, very, very persuasive." When she wrote "You're So Vain" in 1972, there were many claimants to that particular crown. Beatty always seemed most persuasive, or at least he thought so. In 1999, he said, "Oh, let's be honest, that song is about me, it's not about Mick Jagger, it's about me." According to Simon herself, "It certainly sounds like it was about Warren Beatty. He certainly thought it was about him—he called me and said thanks for the song. At the time I met him he was still relatively undiscovered as a Don Juan. I felt I was one among thousands at that point—it hadn't reached, you know, the populations of small countries." Her line, "You gave away the things you loved, and one of them was me," might well have referred to his and Nicholson's habit of trading women back and forth. Said screenwriter Jake Brackman, who was a close friend of Simon's and wrote many of her lyrics, "They find a new girl and then they want to share her as a male bonding thing, that passed-on feeling."

Jennifer Lee, then in her early twenties, was a statuesque beauty who grew up in an upper-middle-class home in the Berkshires, and seems to have had sex with every man in the movie and music worlds before she married Richard Pryor. Of all the bimbographies that litter this period, hers, called *Tarnished Angel* and based on her diaries, is one of the best. In the spring of 1971, having dropped out of Finch College and living in New York City, she was doing some acting and modeling when actress Nancy Allen, future wife of Brian De Palma, introduced her to Beatty. They dropped in on him at the Carlyle. He opened the door wearing a white terrycloth robe, and welcomed them with, "I just got out of the shower." As Lee wrote, despite the fact that he was thirty-three, old, to her, "he's very warm and sweet and adorable . . . like a young boy, with a strong, tight body, and lots of energy." Allen made her excuses and left. Lee thought to herself, I know what he had in mind for the three of us, and now there's just us chickens. Do I want to be alone with this knockout? She said, "Maybe I should go home, too."

"Aww, come on. I'm not going to bite you."

"Nancy's messed up your plans, huh?"

"Yeah, but I always have a back-up. I don't think I'll use it tonight. We'll save that for later." When the phone rang, it was Christie, whom Lee referred to as the "ball-and-chain main squeeze." He politely excused himself and took the call in the bathroom.

Beatty and Lee became friends. She knew he was seeing a great many women, but consoled herself that she was at the front of the line. He offered to pay for her first term at Stella Adler's. Of his skills in bed, she recalls, "For all his reputation, he's not a particularly great lover. (He's not that well endowed.) In fact, it's almost as if his reputation gets in the way. His need to be 'great' in bed transcends any true consideration of his partner's needs, so it all boils down to *his* experience, *his* conquest. When he tries to relate intimately it's too hard—it's like crossing a line into serious narcissism. He likes to give directions, not only about positions, but about how you should feel and react. The pressure to have the biggest most earth-shattering orgasms can get a little relentless. I've definitely had to fake a few."

If Ekland and others are to be believed, Lee was in a minority. How many women were there? Easier to count the stars in the sky. But devotees of the Guinness Book of Records want to know. Beatty used to say that he couldn't get to sleep at night without having sex. It was part of his routine, like flossing. This was who he was. As the evening progressed, he would disappear with his little black book, looking for a phone. Simple arithmetic tells us that if he had no more than one partner a night—and often there were several—over a period of, say, three and a half decades, from the mid-1950s, when he arrived in New York, to 1991, when he met Annette Bening, and allowing for the stretches when he was with the same woman, more or less, we can arrive at a figure of 12,775 women, give or take, a figure that does not include daytime quickies, drive-by blowjobs, casual gropings, stolen kisses, and so on. (Of course, this figure is only a tad more than half of the 20,000 women with whom Wilt Chamberlain claims to have had sex, but it's impressive nevertheless.)

There were so many women that it's hard to characterize his sexual preferences by how he behaved with any particular one. Different women served different purposes. He compartmentalized sex the same way he compartmentalized everything else, and it would take a prodigy of empirical research, no less than an Alfred Kinsey, to draw a comprehensive sexual profile. There was nothing particularly outré about Beatty's sexual practices. He enjoyed oral sex, both giving and getting. He liked anal sex as well, giving not getting. He was not averse to spanking, in which he played the spanker, not the spankee but he did not appear to be much interested in exploring the exotica of, say, the *Kama Sutra*.

Doubles and triples, i.e., more than one woman at a time, were de rigueur in those days, although some women weren't thrilled by the idea. For Lee, it worked, more or less. "The extra person becomes just an object in the process, one that guards against the dangers of intimacy, but during these sessions Warren and I can connect in a way that we can't when we're alone," she writes. "This [second] woman, whoever she may be—a top model, a wealthy married lady—becomes *our* object, *our* device. So a strange thing happens, beyond sexuality, Warren and I become freer to communicate. We enjoy another kind of intimacy, one that's born out of complicity: shared glances, private jokes, awkward moments. If I drift, even if only for a moment, he gets concerned, asks if I'm okay, and pulls me back into this mad reality. Although he's the ringleader in our sex games, he's imbued me with an ego-gratifying authority and a sexual savvy, often allowing me to take charge. After our lady leaves, we discuss the experience, compare observations and personal moments. And the silence is filled with tenderness and relief, if only for a brief time."

According to another woman with whom he had a lengthy relationship, Beatty liked to watch two women make love, and "then have sex with each one of them." She speculates that he believed that every woman is a lesbian at heart, reflecting, "There was this funny thing [he did] of encouraging one woman to sleep with the other woman, because that would reveal—he told me this—their real hidden desire and love, which of course he could never participate in because he's not a woman. It was clear that that act would have been betraying him—in a way that he cannot compete with. Another man he can compete with, a woman he can't. I always got the feeling that he needed women to betray him, [that he] set up the woman to betray him, so that it made it okay for him to then do what he needed to do, orchestrate the breakup."

One woman he knew suggested adding another man to the mix for variety's sake. Beatty would never say no; in fact, he once supposedly said, "What do I care whose mouth it is?" But it never happened, which led her to believe that this was not something he wanted to do. She knew that had she suggested adding another woman, it would have happened that night. Years later, during the 1980s, he would tell one woman that he had never had sex with a man, giving her the impression that he wasn't opposed to it in principle—he'd try anything—but in the midst of the AIDS crisis, it was too dangerous.

In the 1970s, a stunningly beautiful transvestite named Richard made the rounds of some of the hipper Beverly Hills parties. You had to be very sharp to realize that he wasn't a woman. Unaccountably, Beatty was taken in. He was dancing with him for some time when to the amusement of those who noticed, he suddenly stiffened—as if touched by the tip of a red hot poker—when he realized that "she" had a penis.

Of course, Beatty was into phone sex before there was phone sex. He would call a woman in the middle of the night, asking softly, in his silky voice, "What's new, pussycat," or using another of his favorite openers. Then came the questions: "Where are you?" "What are you doing?" "What are you wearing?" He asked when she last had sex and with whom, and encouraged her to describe it. He asked if she'd like to see him with another girl, would she let another girl go down on her, or another man, even wondering how many men she could handle at a time. He might mention a friend of his who found a picture of her mother in which she was having sex with five men simultaneously. He told a strange tale about driving into the Bois de Boulogne in Paris at night with whomever he was seeing at the time. The Bois de Boulogne was filled with dark, woodsy areas and was famous as a trysting place for gay men. It was in one of those leafy groves that he stopped the car and opened the windows. The vehicle was immediately surrounded by men who put their penises through the window. His companion sucked them off, one after another, while he watched. Why gay men wished to be fellated by a woman is anybody's guess, but these were, after all, just fantasies, intended to arouse his female audience. "It was a power trip," observed one woman. "I felt like a puppet, but I was a willing puppet. I didn't mind."

Sexually, he put the women first, their pleasure before his. He was rumored to "double bag," i.e., use two condoms, which makes a certain amount of sense; it relegated the risk of pregnancy virtually to zero, and it reduced the stimulation that might have made him come during the long, grueling sessions in which he worked his magic. But after women started taking birth control pills in the 1960s, men rarely wore condoms (until AIDS came along), and some women report that he wore no protection at all. One, who had a lengthy affair with him, when asked if he employed tricks to distract himself—reviewing alternate takes in his head, going over deal points—just laughed, and said, "That's where he lives." She invoked the Aesop's fable about the scorpion that stung the frog that carried it across the river. When asked why, the scorpion said, "It's my nature." In Beatty's case, she explained, "He's Mr. Withholding. That's where he lives. He's lucky he can come at all." The immortal words of *Dr. Strangelove*'s General Jack D. Ripper spring to mind: "I do not avoid women, Mandrake . . . I do deny them my essence."

WITH BEATTY away in Hamburg, Altman had a free hand with *McCabe* during postproduction. When the actor finally screened the picture, he wasn't happy with what he saw, or rather, heard—or, to be even more precise, didn't hear. "I couldn't hear what people were saying," he recalls. "The sound in the first couple of reels, in which one would ordinarily expect that the exposition would be laid down and had to be clear, was not clear. That sort of irritated me." Beatty was upset, not to say furious, over the muddy track. Recalled Sylbert, "The soundtrack was a mess. Warren thought Altman was a total slob."

Never one to admit a mistake, Altman just dismissed Beatty's complaints, a star bitching: "Warren was infuriated. He still is, and he'll just have to stay infuriated." First AD Tommy Thompson took Altman's side: "The principals thought every word out of their mouths was a pearl, and they didn't want music, let alone other dialogue, obscuring it." Editor Lou Lombardo, on the other hand, who had raised the issue with the director when he was on the set, sided with Beatty and reiterated this conclusion after he heard the mix. "It still is bad," he said. "[Bob] never changed it. I think he accomplished what he wanted to do with sound in *M*A*S*H*—where it was audible but it was overlapped. . . . But on *McCabe*, it was recorded in there—a dirty track, a muddy track. It was like trying to get an out-of-focus picture in focus."

According to Altman, Beatty asked Warner Brothers to withdraw the picture so that the sound could be rerecorded, but the studio refused. The new Warners regime had virtually nothing in the pipeline and was eager to get the film into theaters. Besides, they were reluctant to tangle with Altman and get a reputation for being director-unfriendly. "You think we could've gotten him to redo it?" says Ted Ashley. "This was an individual who presumed himself to be an artist." Beatty adds, "Things had progressed to such anarchy in the studio system, and film-makers were treated with so much respect, if we had photographed the movie in darkness, they would have thought that was an interesting approach, and hoped they could exploit it in the marketing." He had to be satisfied with looping—rerecording—a handful of his lines, which only angered Altman without making the track any cleaner. Said Altman, "I can hear it every time I see the picture." Nobody was happy, not Altman, not Beatty.

McCabe & Mrs. Miller opened on June 24, 1971, at the Criterion and the Academy theaters, in New York and L.A., respectively. Apparently, Beatty's contract obligated the studio to a summer release. According to Patrick McGilligan's biography of Altman, the Technicolor lab in L.A. was booked solid, and a Canadian lab was used instead, which quickly turned out four flawed prints. Even Altman acknowledges that there was a problem: "There was something wrong with the soundtrack," but claimed he was not at fault. "It wasn't checked by my editor and I was told that it had been checked," he says. "And so that bad soundtrack, on top of the design of the sound, really made it impossible to hear. I screamed, 'You've got to shut it off, there's something wrong with the soundtrack.' They said, 'Oh, that's the way you did it.' Well, it wasn't the way I did it. I left the goddamned theater and went someplace and had a steak. I was ready to get on a plane and go to Alaska."

The press screenings were a disaster. The daily reviewers generally panned the movie. Vincent Canby in *The New York Times* wrote, "The intentions of *McCabe and Mrs. Miller* are not only serious, they are meddlesomely imposed on the film by tired symbolism . . . [that] keep[s] spoiling the fun of what might have been an uproarious frontier fable."

Pauline Kael, who was a fan of Altman's, if not Beatty's, quite rightly raved, calling it "a beautiful pipe dream of a movie," went on *The Dick Cavett Show* and talked it up. But the picture died, and Beatty's efforts to revive it, as he did *Bonnie and Clyde,* failed. Although *McCabe & Mrs. Miller* shares *Bonnie and Clyde*'s distaste for authority and cynical mistrust of the "system," as well as its unhappy ending, standard for any New Hollywood movie, it went further than *Bonnie and Clyde* in undermining the romance between the two leads, and concluding the film with an anticlimax photographed in cold long shots that distance the audience and minimize whatever feelings McCabe's death might otherwise have evoked. Like the post–*Bonnie and Clyde* Arthur Penn, Altman was going down the road of genre deconstruction, which, it seemed, the box office would not support. "It still hasn't grossed much money," said Altman in 1996. John Wayne, no fan of genre-cide, denounced the picture for subverting the western. According to Altman, Beatty "was really a bit of an asshole. He was quite brutal about it when it came out, and of course blamed me for its defects. Warren is a very self-oriented person. Many people think it's his best film, but it didn't succeed, so he didn't like it. He'll never mention it."

Indeed, Beatty blamed the inaudible soundtrack for the picture's failure to perform. "It prevented it from having a tremendous commercial potential because the audience was confused," he says. "If it hadn't had to meet a certain date in the summer, it would have been remedied by Altman. I don't think he intended to screw it up." But once again, Beatty paid a price for not producing. As he puts it, "Had I been the producer I would have killed Robert Altman."

Over the four decades that have passed since *McCabe & Mrs. Miller* was released, its reputation has grown, and it often finds a place on the "best westerns of all time" lists that critics fondly compile. Despite Beatty's unhappiness with the picture, *McCabe* had a significant impact on *Shampoo*, which is much more an ensemble piece than he had made before, much less plot-driven than even *Bonnie and Clyde*. It gave him the confidence to write his own version of the *Shampoo* script. It also served, in the spirit of John Wayne, to strengthen his conviction to steer clear of the kind of genre deconstruction practiced by Altman and Penn. As a producer and star, Beatty had a much more robust commercial sense than many of the directors of the 1970s, and in the same way that he gave a cold shoulder to the New Hollywood love affair with the French *Nouvelle Vague* and the cinema of Antonioni and Fellini, he recognized that there was a limit to the degree to which American audiences would indulge the zeal with which these directors flouted the conventions of the studio film.

BEATTY HAD feared the worst when Richard Nixon beat Hubert Humphrey in 1968, and he was not disappointed. While 1971 was free of the catastrophic assassinations that cast a shadow across the American landscape three years earlier, the storm clouds gathering then had burst into a hard rain of death and destruction. The peace talks between Henry Kissinger and the Hanoi government were deadlocked, and the Nixon administration launched an invasion of Laos in February 1971. On June 13, *The New York Times* had published the Pentagon Papers after the Supreme Court rejected an attempt by John Mitchell's Justice Department to quash it.

On September 9, 1971, some ten weeks after the opening, while *McCabe* was still in the theaters, about one thousand convicts protesting the subhuman conditions in New York State's Attica prison (one shower per week, one roll of toilet paper per month) and the shooting of George Jackson by guards at San Quentin the previous month, seized the facility, taking some thirty guards hostage. Four days later, after Governor Nelson Rockefeller ordered troopers and sheriffs to storm the prison, ten guards and thirty-two prisoners lay dead.

It was evident that Beatty's heart wasn't in his career. He was still rejecting scripts faster than they were being offered. "I've spent . . . something like seven years just turning down movies," he said. "Obviously, there's something uncomfortable for me about making them." He said no to the pictures that made Robert Redford a star: *Butch Cassidy and the Sundance Kid, The Sting,* and *The Way We Were.* He also turned down David Lean's *Ryan's Daughter* (1970), *Bob and Carol and Ted and Alice* (1969), *The Godfather, The Great Gatsby,* and *Last Tango in Paris.*

Beatty decided to shelve movies and plunge into the presidential campaign of George McGovern, a well-regarded but obscure senator from South Dakota whom the millions of Americans opposed to the Vietnam War hoped would become the new Eugene McCarthy, the new Robert Kennedy, and seize the Democratic presidential nomination from the boys in the smoky back rooms who controlled the party machine. "The McGovern campaign was at the center of the '70s," says Beatty. "It laid the foundation of everything that happened in the Democratic Party afterwards. The Democratic Party was at its lowest point, and the establishment guys said, 'Oh, fuck it, we're just giving up,' and that's when the real interesting guys moved in, and they were all young, because McGovern couldn't tolerate anybody who was older. Gary Hart happened because of the McGovern campaign. Bill Clinton."

McGovern was the very definition of an underdog. His numbers in the polls failed to exceed 5 percent, and no one but his immediate family, and possibly a couple of cows in South Dakota, recognized his face. He was severely challenged in the charisma department, "painfully earnest," as Hunter Thompson described him, going on to call him the "Willy Loman of the Left." Beatty himself, in a rare unguarded moment, compared him to "Mr. Peepers."

After the horror show of Chicago 1968, reform Democrats had rewritten the byzantine rules that governed the selection of delegates to the convention, boosting the importance of the primaries at the expense of the party bosses. The process became more reflective of the will of the voters, but it also turned the primary campaign into a free-for-all, with all kinds of candidates tossing their hats into the ring. Maine's Ed Muskie was the odds-on favorite, a shoo-in who had locked up the endorsements of the Democratic Party power brokers, with Humphrey, the candidate of Big Labor (how quaint that sounds today), also expected to make a strong showing, trailed by Washington senator Henry "Scoop" Jackson—the "candidate from Boeing," as he was known—stubbornly holding aloft the banner of Cold War anti-Communism. Finally, three antiwar liberals brought up the rear, McGovern, New York City mayor John Lindsay, and Brooklyn congresswoman Shirley Chisholm. And then there was former Alabama governor George Wallace, who was truly beyond the pale.

Beatty met with McGovern's campaign manager, Gary Hart, a bright, articulate lawyer and policy wonk from Colorado. There were some coincidental similarities between Hart and Beatty. They were about the same age (Hart was six months older), and shared the same middle name: "Warren." (Beatty's actual first name was Henry.) Both had tinkered with their last names, Beatty adding the "t" to "Beaty," Hart dropping the last syllable from "Hartpence." Hart had tried his hand at acting, and both were avid readers, fascinated by Russia. Beatty had already made several trips to Moscow, while Hart was a student of Leo Tolstoy, particularly *War and Peace*, although, as things turned out he should have paid more attention to *Anna Karenina*. Loosely speaking, Hart's model for McGovern's campaign was the same as that of General Kutuzov, who turned back Napoleon with his live-off-the-land guerrilla strategy that depended on cunning, perseverance, and organization to defeat an adversary who was better armed and financed.

Like Beatty, Hart was good-looking in that tousled Jack Kennedyesque sort of way. (Thompson wrote that he looked like a "ski instructor.") During the campaign, people—particularly those unschooled in
fandom—confused the two men.

In any event, it was love at first sight. Later, when Hart himself ran
for president and the two became even closer, friends would say, glibly,
that each wanted to be the other, have what the other had. Both scoffed
at the idea, probably because there was more than a little truth in it.
Observes journalist/politico Bill Bradley (not to be confused with the
former New Jersey senator), who befriended both men and worked
in various capacities on Hart's presidential campaigns, "The potential
of women, and the glamorous lifestyle was something that intrigued
Gary, obviously, but if it had only been that, Gary would not have
stayed friends with Warren. With Jack Kennedy, Sinatra did not bring
a lot of intellectual chops to the party. With Gary, on the other hand,
Warren did. When you're with Warren in that context, you feel you're
at a very high level, and that's where Gary wanted to be. Warren would
say, 'Let's call Senator so and so, and see what he thinks of this,' 'cause
Warren could get anybody on the phone. It was that as much as the
glamour component."

With charismatic figures like Jack and Bobby Kennedy dead, and
Ted sidelined by Chappaquiddick, the Democrats were glamour-
challenged, and McGovern realized he needed more than a little of
that Hollywood stardust. Beatty was of two minds as to how public
a role to play, but in the early days of the campaign, he traveled with
McGovern, introduced him at rallies in Iowa and New Hampshire,
states whose early caucus (Iowa) and primary (New Hampshire) led
the pack. He did whatever needed to be done, whether it was knocking
on doors, chatting up Tupperware ladies in tract-house living rooms,
speaking to boisterous audiences of antiwar students on college campuses or union halls sparsely filled with assembly-line workers. But
an unpleasant public appearance at the University of Wisconsin at
Madison in September 1971, around the time of the Attica riots, helped
him decide his role. This was one of the most radical campuses in the
country. Beatty had just had a tooth pulled, and then flown in from
London to attend the rally. "It was a howling mob," recalls McGovern.
"The first battle cry was a boozy 'Bullshit!' coming from the first row.

The marijuana smoke was pretty heavy, and the potheads heckled him, shouting him down for his wealth, his social position: 'What do you have in common with ordinary people?' He didn't handle it well, got flustered, probably because he'd never heard that kind of heckling before." Said Beatty later, "It was not only an embarrassing encounter, but it made me think about my role in the campaign." He added, "I felt that the advertising aspect of the participation made me feel silly. I think the public is innately suspicious of the self-forwarding, publicity-seeking, capricious artist who would like to attach some mood of seriousness to his persona by participating in public affairs. I guess it was hard for me to risk that kind of criticism." Beatty started to worry about the erosion of the firewall between politics and entertainment, which in the future would become one of his favorite themes. On his way back from Wisconsin, he decided to play a less public role.

For Beatty, the McGovern primary campaign was punctuated by the opening of *Dollars,* which premiered on December 12, 1971, and released two days later, to tepid reviews. Meanwhile, the British press reported in March 1972 that Beatty and Christie had finally parted ways. She had called him from the beach at his Beverly Wilshire penthouse one night, told him it was over. He hung up the phone, thought, She's in bed with somebody, I can tell, and he muttered out loud, mournfully, "They've all dumped me." She went off to Venice to do a supernatural thriller, *Don't Look Now,* directed by Nicolas Roeg and co-starring Donald Sutherland, with whom she had an affair.

Hart told Beatty about a twenty-one-year-old wunderkind named Pat Caddell, a volatile black Irish-American pollster he had recruited straight from Harvard. Caddell's brain worked faster than his mouth, if that were possible; he spoke in machine-gun bursts, chopping off sentences in midcourse as new thoughts thrust their way to the forefront. He spritzed ideas and favored dramatic gestures. *Newsweek* called him "the permanent enfant terrible of the Democratic Party, a connoisseur and exploiter of voter anger, alienation and fear. He specializes in protest candidates who try to win by running against the party." Aflame with the arrogance of youth, brash and acerbic, and in later years angry as well, Caddell had little patience for those who disagreed with him. He fought with numbers, marshaling them to crush his opponents; they enabled him, like every pollster in every campaign, to assume the mantle of a shaman. Best of all, he delivered. He would call the primary results to the decimal point. He recalls, wistfully, "I was so young, I had no enemies. It was the only time I would never have any enemies."

Caddell, of course, had heard about Beatty as well. He finally met him in Miami for the Florida primary, on March 14, 1972. The two men hit it off immediately. They would sit next to each other on the campaign bus, take adjoining hotel rooms. "I was like his kid brother," says Caddell. Unlike Beatty and Hart, theirs was a friendship of opposites. "Warren was nice to everybody," the pollster continues. "He was never arrogant, a great people person, made everybody feel important, never exaggerated, never called attention to his role, what he was doing. He didn't want any credit, didn't want any attention. Plus, Warren is really smart about issues. He's well read, he thinks. He was a much beloved figure. But it was the most ego-depressing thing in the world to be around him. There were droves of women, and they'd ignore you. You didn't exist."

Beatty threw himself into the arcana of campaigning—he asked a lot of questions and listened to the answers, soaking up information—and then confined his input to dispensing behind-the-scenes advice in the areas he knew best—media, public opinion, networking. He never demanded limos, but rather rode the campaign bus like the rest of the staff, catnapped on sofas, ate fast food, pizzas, and hot dogs. When Beatty did make suggestions, they were often bold and dramatic. "Other people were going about their jobs," Caddell continues. "Warren thought about big things." Gradually, Beatty gained more influence with the McGovern campaign than any other Hollywood figure had before him in a comparable situation, with the possible exception of Arthur Krim, who advised Lyndon Johnson. According to author Ron Brownstein, "Beatty operated at the heart of the campaign, a ghost in the machine."

Despite the exhausting pace, Beatty was enjoying himself, and retained his sense of humor. During the Wisconsin primary, Frank Mankiewicz checked into his hotel and was given a message from Beatty. In those days, in order to return a long distance call, it was necessary to call back a specific operator. Mankiewicz did so, and while he waited, she got Beatty on the line and asked, " 'Mr. Beatty, what is your special billing?' 'Well,' he deadpanned, 'always above the title, in a size of type no smaller than that of the director.' "

McGovern won the Wisconsin primary on April 13, a stunning victory that surprised even his staff. Muskie dropped out after the Pennsylvania primary on April 25, leaving McGovern and Humphrey—now the front-runner—to duke it out, with Wallace the wild card. Beatty quickly became indispensable. In addition to figuring out ways to spend money, he proved to be surprisingly effective at raising it. In Cleveland, one starstruck contributor wrote out a check for $50,000. Beatty told him, "I won't take that money. People of your standing—if you can't give six figures, we want nothing from you." The man tore up the check and wrote another for $125,000. With that money, McGovern ads went on the air the next day. McGovern made a strong showing, losing Ohio to Humphrey by only nineteen thousand votes, and his staff was convinced that the primary election had been rigged by the state Democratic machine. By some accounts, roughly ten thousand of those votes were sacrificed to his relationship with Beatty, who offhandedly told a reporter that he favored the legalization of marijuana, an admission that was picked up by Scoop Jackson and exploited for all it was worth.

Beatty's biggest contribution to the party coffers came from the proceeds of the rock concerts he organized, the first time that anyone had systematically tapped performers for a political campaign. As Bill Bradley puts it, "Warren invented the rock political benefit concert." He called in favors, twisted arms, cajoled, guilt-tripped, and just plain inspired the likes of Barbra Streisand, James Taylor, and Carole King to play five concerts, starting on April 15 at the Forum in L.A., where Nicholson, Christie, Burt Lancaster, Gene Hackman, and Sally Kellerman, among others, did usher duty, another one of Beatty's ideas. The concert injected $300,000 into the campaign in California, before making its way to major cities across the country. All in all, according to McGovern, Beatty raised more than a million dollars. Beyond the money, the concerts introduced scores of Hollywood stars to direct participation in American politics, finally ending the legacy of the HUAC years, which had discouraged them from involvement with politics for fear of blacklisting.

Beatty and Christie attended the Democratic convention in Miami Beach from July 10 to July 13, despite their reported breakup. It was a fractious affair. The party was badly split. It seemed to the old guard, the back room crowd that included Chicago's Mayor Richard Daley, the AFL/CIO's George Meany, both of whom backed Humphrey, that the lunatics—antiwar activists, feminists, black power militants— had taken over the asylum. Indeed, voters watching the proceedings on TV might have been excused for mistaking it for an SDS convention, with formations of every stripe doing battle. The Miami Beach Convention Center was atremble with the cries of "ABM" ("Anybody But McGovern"). The "Stop McGovern" forces spearheaded by Jimmy Carter, among others, coalesced around Humphrey, much to the displeasure of the insurgents.

Bill Clinton, then a long-haired twenty-six-year-old McGovern volunteer, recalled trying to twist the arm of a recalcitrant female member of the Arkansas delegation in an effort to secure her vote on an arcane parliamentary point. "I said, 'Is there any way in the world I can convince you to vote with us?' She said, 'Yeah, if you get Warren Beatty to walk on the beach with me,'" Clinton recalled. "As God is my witness, 30 minutes later I get on an elevator and there he is. I explained the deal to him. He said, 'Sure I'll do it.' He walked 100 yards on the beach. That woman voted for us on every single thing."

McGovern finally mustered the delegates he needed to capture the nomination. His "Come home, America," acceptance address was a stirring call for the country to return to the ideals from which it had strayed, lost, as it had become, in the steaming jungles of Vietnam. But McGovern had slipped in a gratuitous lump of undigested Emersonian verbiage, like a basketball swallowed by the proverbial snake, or so it seemed to speechwriter Bob Shrum, who was desperate to get rid of it. The candidate, however, dug in his heels. Shrum enlisted Beatty, whom he had just met, in his cause. Beatty "looked at the draft and the two of us headed for McGovern's suite," he recalled. "Once there, Warren offered a pithier, more persuasive argument than I'd thought of. 'Look, George,' he said, 'you can't do this to this speech. It would be like making love to a beautiful woman—it's wonderful, it's as good as it's ever been—and then at the last minute pulling out and saying, 'I'll let Ralph finish for me.' McGovern laughed and the Emerson quote was gone."

McGovern had won the day, but he had lost the war, which is to say, the fight had so inflamed passions that he found himself presiding over a badly divided party, ill-equipped to win a national election against an incumbent president, even one as dubious as Nixon. Then, in the middle of the convention frenzy, McGovern made a fatal error, and compounded it by dealing ineptly with the fallout: he selected Missouri senator Tom Eagleton to be his running mate. The bombshell exploded in the press about ten days later: Eagleton had a history of mental illness, including depression, for which he had had shock treatment or, as Caddell succinctly puts it, "Eagleton went out without his shorts."

But Beatty believed that within every defeat lies an opportunity, and in this case, the Eagleton fiasco offered McGovern another chance to reach out to his enemies within the party. Beatty thought that McGovern-Humphrey would constitute the strongest ticket the Democrats could field, appealing both to the young, disaffected antiwar activists as well as the Democrats' traditional base, who were older and more conservative. Despite Humphrey's equivocation on the Vietnam War four years earlier, Beatty had a good relationship with the senator. He was, in fact, the perfect emissary to the Humphrey camp. Beatty went to persuade him to replace Eagleton. But Humphrey had already served as vice president under Johnson, had run for president against Nixon, and had just been on the losing side of the brutal Anybody But McGovern fight. His amour propre would not allow him to accept. Still, Beatty also knew that Humphrey lived and breathed politics and would run for dog catcher if he were approached in the right way. The actor spent four hours applying salves and unguents to Humphrey's bruised ego, and finally came up with a scenario that would allow Humphrey to accede to the wishes of the Democratic candidate without losing face. He maneuvered him into a corner by asking, "Don't you think that anybody—if the party called him—would have to serve? How could anyone turn the party down?" Humphrey found himself agreeing that yes, no true-blue Democrat could refuse if he were drafted by the Democratic National Committee.

Excited, Beatty went to McGovern and told him, "You can get Humphrey if you go before the DNC and say you want whomever the party thinks is the best candidate, meaning Humphrey, and Humphrey will take it. But what you cannot do, George, is you cannot call him yourself, 'cause he'll say no. 'Cause who wants to be number two on the ticket? He's sticking his head into oblivion." But knowing that McGovern was too much the gentleman to have the DNC make Humphrey an offer he could not refuse, he told Caddell, "You know what? I've just told him not to, and you watch—he's going to call him."

Sure enough, McGovern did call Humphrey, and Humphrey turned him down. Says Caddell, "Swear to God. We were that close to having it done." Whether Humphrey's presence on the ticket would have prevented the Nixon landslide and changed the course of history is questionable, to say the least, but McGovern believed that had he put together a Democratic slate that would have appealed to the conservatives within the party, the election, in his words, "would have been very close."

In the event, Nixon slaughtered McGovern at the polls, amassing a plurality of 23 percent of the popular vote. McGovern's collapse enabled the old guard to retake the Democratic party in December. Texas senator John Connally's protégé Robert Strauss was installed as chairman of the DNC, moving the party to the right, and thereby setting the stage for three decades of Republican rule, briefly interrupted by Democratic me-too centrists like Carter and Clinton.

The Nixon landslide buried the hopes of everyone who sought a quick end to the Vietnam War; his apparent mandate, bellicose and overwhelming, spawned an atmosphere of gloom best expressed by Hunter Thompson's overheated but prescient prose. Nixon "represents that dark, venal, and incurably violent side of the American character," he wrote. He is "America's answer to . . . the Werewolf in us. . . . At the stroke of midnight in Washington, a drooling red-eyed beast with the legs of a man and a head of a giant hyena crawls out of its bedroom window in the South Wing of the White House and leaps fifty feet down to the lawn . . . pauses briefly to strangle the Chow watchdog, then races off into the darkness . . . towards the Watergate, snarling with lust, loping through the alleys behind Pennsylvania Avenue."

Such was the mood of unease and apocalyptic paranoia that shaped the script of *Shampoo*, and permeated Beatty's next film, *The Parallax View*, directed by Alan J. Pakula in the spring and summer of 1973.

REGARDLESS OF the outcome, as the campaign ended, Beatty was pleased with himself. Says McGovern, "He was one of the three or four most important people in the campaign. And he never sought credit." Years later, in a rare moment of public self-regard, looking back on his participation he said, "I'm real good at it. I'm discreet. I don't kiss and tell. I don't tell secrets about, y'know, political things. I try to be shrewd. . . . I think my interest in politics has saved my . . . soul. You've gotta have a life. You've gotta relate to people. Otherwise, you'll make movies about movies and it just won't be very interesting. So you've gotta make movies about life, and my avenue into life, my way of getting to know people, has been political."

Beatty's immersion in the campaign had opened his eyes. If he had any ideas about throwing his own hat in the ring, he gave them up, for the moment, at least. He turned back to film. He had a lot of projects still in the air, scripts half finished, ideas floating around his head.

One of them was *The Parallax View,* set in contemporary America, still in the shadow of the assassination of John F. Kennedy. Based on a novel by Loren Singer, adapted by Lorenzo Semple Jr. and rewritten by David Giler, *The Parallax View* told the story of the murder of a presidential candidate, followed by the suspicious deaths of nine of the ten witnesses. The final witness is a journalist who begins his own investigation of the previous deaths, and uncovers a vast conspiracy. Alan J. Pakula, who had directed *The Sterile Cuckoo* (1969) and *Klute* (1971), and would go on to make *All the President's Men* (1976) and *Sophie's Choice* (1982) was attached. He was considered a hot up-and-coming director, and he was one of the people Beatty was eager to work with. *The Parallax View* was set up at Paramount.

The picture featured Paula Prentiss and Hume Cronyn. It was shot by the gifted Gordon Willis, who had already done *The Landlord* for Hal Ashby, *Klute* for Pakula, and would shortly become celebrated for the moody, golden hues that infused his work on *The Godfather.* Known as the Prince of Darkness, Willis was one of the new breed of DPs who liked to work in low or available light. Most of the picture was shot in and around L.A., with exteriors shot in Seattle.

Beatty found the theme appealing. The preoccupations of the story—conspiracy and attendant cover-up—couldn't have been more topical, and were being played out in real life as the movie was being shot. The Watergate hearings, broadcast live by the networks, had begun on May 17, 1973, and riveted the nation. They were still in progress when production began. Almost every day there were new, startling revelations that shed light on the duplicity and lawlessness of the Nixon administration. During breaks, cast and crew would gather around a TV on the set or crowd into Beatty's trailer to watch the hearings on his. Explained Pakula, *The Parallax View* "brought out all my personal pessimism—I heard the first Watergate and CIA rumblings on the car radio daily as I was driving to work on it. It suggested that man is doomed."

To make matters even more interesting, Hollywood was in the grip of a nasty writer's strike that had closed down the town. The rewrite of the script was finished a scant six weeks before the start of production. No one was happy with it, but the decision was made to go ahead anyway, at least in part because Beatty had a pay-or-play deal. But Pakula didn't mind starting without a script. "He liked chaos, he liked to create a situation where he could come in and pull it all together at the last minute," recalls Jon Boorstin, an intern on the film who was Pakula's nephew by marriage, and son of Librarian of Congress Daniel Boorstin. "Alan thrived creatively on that sense of uncertainty. He would shoot a movie and not know how it was gonna end. But Beatty wouldn't do it."

Despite his dismissive remarks about his movie career, the actor knew that after his disappearing act, following three flops in a row, he couldn't risk another. He knew the script needed work. According to Howard Koch Jr., first AD, whose father had been head of production at Paramount, and who would work with Beatty again on *Heaven Can Wait,* "We always said, 'How come we're getting new pages if there's a writer's strike,' and literally, nobody else in town was shooting, except this movie." It was acceptable under Writers Guild rules to work on the script, but not to hire a writer. Yet, it seemed like one or more writers were indeed plying their trade. He goes on, "We were able to continue because we said we weren't making any changes to the script, but there were tremendous changes made to the script, by a scab writer. Every day, either I or someone else would pick up some pages from [the writer's] house." Says Frank Yablans, who was then head of distribution at Paramount, a former booker, scrappy and belligerent, "It was done sub rosa. Beatty was the greatest mind-fucker who ever lived, period. He always held himself above it all. He was the king, and the instigator. I'm sure Evans had something to do with it. Towne went along too. He wanted to be one of them. They were all very close." (Towne denies that he worked on the script during the strike.)

Living on a steady diet of new pages was hardly unprecedented for a production, but it is not a recipe for speed. Continues Boorstin, "Every morning during the shooting, they would sit around for two or three hours and talk about the script, rewrite, and then they'd go to work. As an intern, I thought everyone did this. I didn't realize that with eighty people standing around waiting, this would drive them crazy. It was unheard of in a Hollywood production." Koch adds, Pakula would "call me and say, 'We're shooting at the marina.' The trucks would pull out, and we'd go to the marina, but there was nothing to shoot. The scenes would come in, there'd be phone calls back and forth, and then Warren and Alan would work on a scene, and if there were scenes with Hume, he would come in and the three of them would work for hours and hours on the pages they had just gotten until they finally got the scenes right."

Koch had mixed feelings about Beatty. Like others, he experienced Beatty as a black hole, a maw of antimatter that swallowed everything and gave nothing in return, neither light nor heat. He says, "We were friends in the way that you're allowed to be friends with Warren, which is, he wants to know everything you're doing, everything you're thinking—'I'm maybe gonna do a movie at Fox, what do you think of the head of Fox? Or d'ya think Paramount might be better?'—and then you say, 'Well, Warren, what's goin' on with you?' 'Naaah, nuthin' much.' 'C'mon Warren,' and maybe he'll give you a little—'Dating a girl, but it's no big deal.' And you never get there with him. Because he's closed. It was very difficult to work with him. Everybody was subservient to him. He will suck you dry of all your creativity, your craftsmanship, and then once all of that is done, then maybe he'll feel comfortable for a minute, but then he'll come back and ask for a little bit more."

This was the first acting Beatty had done since *Dollars* wrapped in April 1971, and he was rusty. Pakula didn't mind indulging his penchant for shooting double-digit takes. Like Beatty, he would say, "It's only film." One of the director's strengths was his ability to deal with difficult actors, which would shortly see him through *All the President's Men*, with Redford and Hoffman. "Both Allan and Warren are very canny, very crafty, very manipulative people who know how to charm someone and get them on their side," says Boorstin. "That whole process of the rewriting I'm sure was as much about managing Warren as it was about changing the script. Because I didn't see the script doing a lot of changing around."

In one scene, Beatty does nothing more complicated than sit at a table stirring soup. The actor did take after take to get just the right amount of steam coming off the soup. Charlie Maguire, the production manager, whom Beatty had first met on *Splendor in the Grass* and who went on to work on many of his films, took the slate used to mark the start of each take and kept it as a souvenir. It said, "Warren Stirs Soup. Take 98"!

Beatty is a self-confessed obsessive-compulsive, the kind of person who straightens up a picture hanging on the wall, squares up a coffee table, moving it a fraction of an inch to the left or to the right so that it lines up with the walls. It's a clinical term for a perfectionist, and the behavior is fairly common, but it merely labels, doesn't "explain" his behavior—the serial takes, the return to and reopening of subjects already aired and seemingly closed, even his dating habits. What's more interesting is the uses to which he puts his compulsive behavior. Instead of trying to rein it in, he let it range free, probably because he could—and yoked it to his purposes, whatever they happened to be at any given time, for better or for worse. These included breaking actors down, getting his way with writers—and often, making good movies.

With little of Pakula's patience, DP Gordon Willis was another story. He was a tough, gruff customer who even at the beginning of his career liked to take control of the set. "Gordon had no patience with actors," Boorstin recalls. "He would get pissed off. He thought [all the takes were] just a waste of time. How many times can you stir the soup? After six or seven takes, it wasn't getting any better anyway."

According to Boorstin, Willis ruined Beatty's best moment in the movie, which profoundly disturbed the actor. It was a shot in a shabby motel room that Willis lit with just one bare bulb, no fill light. In the rushes, the scene was so dark that the performance was lost. "Alan was really upset when he saw the dailies," Boorstin remembers. "He thought he was directing an actor, and he was directing a shadow." Willis, who was used to working on the edge of light and darkness, was contrite, admitted that he'd gone too far. But sometimes he confessed that he didn't think Beatty was a good enough actor to pull it off, and he underlit the scene on purpose, to protect him.

Sometime during the shoot, Mike Medavoy, then an agent at Creative Artists Agency who seemed to handle virtually all the New Hollywood players, visited Beatty on the set. He represented director Hal Ashby and writer Carole Eastman, both of whom had films coming up with Beatty, the former *Shampoo*, and the latter *The Fortune*. Medavoy wanted Beatty to buy Eastman's script. He recalls, "Mike Nichols wanted to do it, and Warren wanted to do it, and Jack Nicholson wanted to do it, so I knew I had a lot of leverage. I went to his trailer. Warren asked, 'What do you want for the script?' I said, 'I really don't know. What you should do is ask around town and find out what's the most ever paid for a script, and give me more.' Eventually Carole got a lot of money for it, a little more than $400,000. It took forever for me to confirm the deal with Warren. I think he wanted to direct *The Fortune* himself, although he never said that." According to Beatty, he didn't buy *The Fortune*. "Medavoy," he says, "is fuckin' senile."

Beatty tried to seduce his co-star Paula Prentiss, but she wasn't having any of it. She said, "Obviously, it's very tempting to go to bed with someone as pretty as that, and the temptation is always there. But it's totally just a quickie high, and when you get close you realize it's all packing with nothing lasting underneath."

Boorstin, who remembers Beatty "as a charmer, not a bully—he wanted people to like him"—recalls girls lining up outside his trailer. The intern had an attractive Indian girlfriend at the time. One day, Beatty's assistant pulled Boorstin aside and said, "Warren wants to know how serious you are about her. Because he's interested. But if you're serious he'll lay off." Beatty was punctilious, and Boorstin responded in politically correct fashion: "It's not up to me, it's up to her." But he thought, Warren's poaching the intern's girlfriend! The star of the movie! What is he thinking?

Boorstin recalls being puzzled by the fact that some of the girls outside Beatty's trailer who got past the door were not particularly attractive, especially since Julie Christie, who was doing *Uncle Vanya* on Broadway, was flying in to spend every weekend with him. Some were chubby, some had hints of mustaches on their upper lips. Some had the errant pimple or mole or other blemishes. "A lot of it is the chase—it invigorates him," Boorstin says, concluding that the prey, once trapped, often became irrelevant.

Indeed, Beatty was eclectic. A man for whom the sweet perfume of supermodels and actresses was no more exotic than the air he breathed, Beatty was interested in more than looks. Late in 1971, he implored singer-songwriter Carole King, who was pregnant at the time, to sleep with him because, he explained, he'd never been with a late-term woman and wanted to see what it was like. (She refused.) One night he got a phone call from a woman he didn't remember, who was married and lived in Colorado. She'd had breast cancer and a mastectomy. Her husband didn't want to sleep with her anymore. Beatty was outraged, told her, "I'd fuck you in a second, fly out here." Says a woman to whom Beatty told the story, he would have fucked her in a second, "because he wouldn't care about that. Obviously beauty is important to him on some level, but it so wasn't about that for him."

Of course, this was Beatty's story. Carly Simon had a different one. One day, after her mastectomy in 1997, she was sitting with a female friend in the bar at the Carlyle when Beatty walked in. "Oh, how wonderful that you're in town," he said. "Why are you here?" Simon told him she was on her way to see her oncologist. "She felt the warmth in his voice disappear," said the friend, and he made his excuses and left. Subsequently, Simon wrote a song called "Scar" about her cancer, in which there was a line that presumably referred to Beatty: "that poor little puppy, so scared of misfortune and always on guard."

LATE IN 1973, Beatty was staying at the Beverly Hills Hotel. He noticed two beefy men in dark suits, narrow ties, and crew cuts seated in front of a TV screen in a room down the hall from his suite. Cables snaked along the floor of the corridor. Every time he went out, there would be a new pair of men, almost identical to the previous set, dark suits, narrow ties, and crew cuts. He was concerned about the press, apprehensive that they were spying on him. He called the desk, said, "This is Warren Beatty. There are two men in a room down the hall from me. Can you tell me who they are?"

"I'm sorry, Mr. Beatty, we can't give out that information."

"I need to know who those guys are."

The man excused himself, came back on the line, and said, "Confidentially, Mr. Beatty, they work for Mr. Hughes."

"Howard Hughes?"

"Yes."

"Which suite is he staying in?"

"I don't know. Mr. Hughes has reserved six rooms."

"Why doesn't he take a bungalow? They're more private."

"Oh, yes, he's taken four bungalows. That's where he puts the girls." Beatty was impressed, and that became the seed of a decades long interest in doing a movie about Hughes.

By the end of 1973, Beatty was able to give *Shampoo* his full attention. Although the script was not finished, the story, such as it was, focused on George Roundy, the hairdresser, and his attempts to raise money to start a salon of his own while in the meantime sleeping his way through the great beauties of Beverly Hills, primarily Jill, his current girlfriend, or at least so she thinks; Jackie, his former girlfriend; and Felicia, with whom he's having an affair on the side.

Beatty had planned to direct *Shampoo* himself, but he'd never directed before, and eventually changed his mind, started looking for someone else. He always wanted at least one more set of eyes looking at what he was looking at, but he worried that it wouldn't be worth the agony, the energy drain of hashing out differences of opinion. Finally, he decided, "As long as I had control over what went in and what stayed out and what the film is, why not take advantage of the talents of another person."

Several directors turned him down, but he kept looking. Hal Ashby had won an editing Oscar for *In the Heat of the Night*, and had received considerable recognition as director for his previous three films: *The Landlord, Harold and Maude,* and *The Last Detail,* in the course of which he had worked with Beatty's friends Nicholson and Towne. Beatty knew him slightly, and liked him. Ashby was a stoner; he smoked dope morning, noon, and night. Not only did this not bother Beatty, it may have been a plus, since it would quickly become apparent that he did not intend to let Ashby do much in the way of directing, anyway.

The two men met for dinner in November. "We talked about different ideas and he asked me if he had ever mentioned *Hair* which was *Shampoo*'s original title," Ashby recalled. "He said he and Bob Towne had worked on it when they were doing *Bonnie and Clyde* and that when Towne had finally written the script and given it to him to read, he was so angry with it that he sat down the next day and wrote his own version." He explained that *Shampoo* was a film à clef, a satiric swipe at the Hollywood community in which everyone has too much money, too much time, too much everything.

Beatty showed Ashby each version. Knowing that he might well be working with both of them, Ashby diplomatically told him that he thought it best to meld the two. Soaked in sex as it was, he knew *Shampoo* would be a hit, whereas his own movies were too quirky to do much business. For all his dislike for the Hollywood system, he was eager to hitch his wagon to a star of Beatty's magnitude. Says Jerry Hellman, who would produce *Coming Home* in 1978, which Ashby directed, "Warren was a giant star, and Hal looked up to and cherished his friendship with Warren."

Towne had problems with Ashby going back to *The Last Detail*. Recalls Beatty, "Hal and Towne never liked each other very much. Towne felt that Hal was a little lax. Hal was never a person to fight to get it right, exactly the way it was on the page." But for Beatty, those aspects of Ashby's style that were anathema to Towne made him attractive, just as the director's taste for weed did. Beatty knew that Ashby would be open to "guidance." Beatty continues, "Towne said, 'I implore you not to use Hal Ashby, use Mark Rydell.' I said, 'I'm using Hal Ashby.'" He paid him $125,000 and 7.5 percent of the net.

Beatty, who did not yet have a studio deal, went ahead and lined up key members of the crew and cast. He filled the production slots with his own people, leaving Ashby with none of his regulars, save for editor Bob Jones, who had cut *The Last Detail*. Anthea Sylbert, married to Dick Sylbert's identical twin brother, Paul, designed the costumes. She had never worked with Beatty before. Her first impression was, "He's always answering a question with a question, and he already knows your answer."

As his line producer, Beatty hired Charlie Maguire instead of Ashby's Chuck Mulvehill. Ashby wanted to hire Haskell Wexler as his DP, but Beatty resisted and hired Laszlo Kovacs, who had shot *Easy Rider, Paper Moon*, and a slew of other New Hollywood films. Dick Sylbert was the production designer, instead of Bob Haller, who had done several of Ashby's films. Sylbert was one of the few allowed to read Beatty's script: most of the actors received only their lines. "Everything is very secret," he said, attributing Beatty's guardedness to pressure, overwork and "paranoia. . . . Everybody's against him. Everybody's trying to harm him."

Using himself as a magnet, Beatty set about attaching key cast, calling in favors from people he had worked with or had relationships with. He usually managed to get them for very little money, especially on a production like *Shampoo,* which was essentially an ensemble piece. He himself was the single biggest above-the-line cost, and he would defer his salary, as he did on *Bonnie and Clyde*. In this way he was able to keep the budget down while assembling a marquee cast, practically guaranteeing any studio—not to mention himself—a fat profit. It was a shrewd strategy and nearly foolproof. "Anyone who can get people to work for him for nothing without any contracts, like Julie and Goldie, is a brilliant producer," says Bob Evans, although Don Devlin, who would shortly co-produce *The Fortune* and disliked Beatty, took a dimmer view. "He exploits everybody," says Devlin. "On every picture he makes he cajoles and charms and gets people to work for incredibly low amounts of money, and they all think they've done him this extraordinary favor, and he will make it up to them, but as soon as he's completed one picture, he's off doing that to the next guy, 'cause that's just the way he operates."

It was a foregone conclusion that Christie would play Jackie, George Roundy's ex-girlfriend. Goldie Hawn played Jill, his current one. For Lester, the fat-cat GOP fund-raiser George hits up to invest in his business despite the fact that he's sleeping with his wife, Felicia (Lee Grant), and his daughter, Lorna (Carrie Fisher), Beatty settled on actor Jack Warden. Tony Bill played a TV commercials director, Johnny Pope.

It was Fisher's first film role. Her father was singer-actor Eddie Fisher and her mother Debbie Reynolds, the pert, squeaky-clean star of *Singin' in the Rain* and 1950s comedies like *The Tender Trap* and *Tammy and the Bachelor*. Beatty's old friend George Furth brought her to the set and introduced her to him. Beatty, who didn't believe in auditions, just chatted with her. Fisher was then seventeen and still a virgin. Nevertheless, she was thoroughly infected by the counterculture, and worried that she'd be tarnished by her too-straight mother's sunniness. She took pains to distance herself from Mom, which she demonstrated with her potty mouth—she took pride in being the virgin who talked like a truck driver, which Beatty appeared to enjoy. She recalled that Beatty hired her, not Ashby.

Because she was underage, Beatty had to obtain the blessing of her mother. The part called for Lorna to say to George, "You wanna fuck?" But Reynolds was squeamish about it, and according to Sylvia Townsend in her book with Dick Sylbert, *Designing Movies*, she wanted Fisher to say "screw" instead. Beatty drove over to their rented home in Brentwood, and played the piano for her. Said Fisher, "Warren could get anybody to do anything. Even my mother, 'Tammy,' who was really conservative then, he even got her to agree to have me say the 'F' word."

Beatty even began to build the sets with his own money before he had a deal. He would have had to pay hefty penalties to the actors out of his own pocket if the production didn't start on schedule. In order to hold the actors, Beatty and Ashby had to begin shooting in six weeks, by the end of January.

Although Towne was again on board, he was still dragging his feet. He was tired of the script and angry with Beatty, who was more than impatient. Says Beatty, "Robert's failure to deliver on time kept a host of highly paid people on contract waiting."

Meanwhile, *Don't Look Now* was slated for a December 9 release. Paramount owned the U.S. rights. It contained a hot scene between Christie and Sutherland, and rumor had it that they actually had had sex. There may have even been a reel floating around town that everyone was looking at. According to Dick Sylbert, he threw a party at which Beatty ran into the director Nic Roeg. "Warren saw Nic, said, 'Nic, come outside, I wanna have a talk with you.' They went outside. Warren was gonna beat the shit out of him."

Evans, who at that point was nearing the end of his tenure as head of production, recalls, "I got the picture at my home, and we ran it on a Saturday night. Warren grabbed my arm, said, 'You can't show that picture.'

" 'What are you talking about?'

" 'He's fucking her! He's fucking her in the movie!'

" 'What can I do about it?'

" 'Nic tricked her into it. She'll go crazy.'

" 'Whaddya mean she'll go crazy, she did it!'

" 'Bob, you . . . can . . . not . . . let this picture come out this way.'

" 'I have no control over it.'

" 'Bob, she'll have a nervous breakdown.'

" 'Warren, don't be naive. She did the scenes. She didn't have a double do it.'

" 'Well, Nic used to go with her, and he talked her into it. He said it would only be subliminal.'

"He called Julie and made her fly out here. She saw it, and got hysterical, crying, [and said to me,] 'I'm losing my mind.'

" 'Julie, look. You didn't have a body double . . .'

" 'Well, Nic, he promised. . . . You've gotta help me.'

" 'How can I help you?'

" 'I don't know, but you've got to get that scene out of the movie.'

"I did it. I called the guy at the rating board, and said, 'You're gonna get a picture. Give it an X.' 'Cause in the contract it had to get an R. I could'a been fired for doing that. They gave it an X. Nic Roeg was furious with me, because he knew it was a setup. I did this as a favor for Warren. Pretty big favor, I'd say. Did he thank me?" (Roeg has no recollection of these incidents.)

HAL ASHBY was pleased to have gotten the plum director's slot in *Shampoo,* but he quickly found himself in the middle of the stormy relationship between Beatty and Towne, during which a few drags on a joint might have come in handy. Once he had hired the director, Beatty claimed pride of place and sat down with him to work on the two drafts. Ashby instructed his assistant, "*Don't* tell [Towne] I'm working with Warren."

Beatty recognized that there were a lot of good scenes in Towne's draft, so with the help of Ashby and Helen Feibelmann, Beatty's secretary (no relation to Pete Feibleman), he combined his draft with Towne's and showed the hybrid to the writer, saying, "I'm gonna make this picture whether you like it or not, do you wanna do it?" Towne read it, agreed to come back on board.

In December, Beatty, Ashby, and Towne got together at the Beverly Wilshire for ten days or so to crash the script. They were all aware that the January start date, a mere six weeks off, was bearing down on them. They started at nine in the morning and worked till eleven at night. They talked—or rather shouted—through the pages, and then Towne, who was not happy, went into the next room to write. He says, "Warren used his political power to control creative situations," and he recalled that the process was fueled by "adrenaline and rage." He and Beatty hurled abuse back and forth, as in, "You motherfucker!" Then they would turn to Ashby, who would say quietly, "Well, what if you did it like this?" Beatty said the script never would have been finished were it not for Ashby's placid demeanor.

Given the volatility of the sessions, they were all surprised that the result was as good as it was. Beatty called them "the most creative ten days of my life, probably." Towne gave Beatty credit as well. "Warren is the kind of person who, once he makes up his mind to do something, after procrastinating seemingly forever, is hysterically committed to it. He's like a sergeant blowing his whistle and going over the top and leading the troops into the machine guns."

According to Towne, one morning over breakfast Beatty casually asked for a co-screenwriting credit. He felt he had been shortchanged by Altman on *McCabe & Mrs. Miller*. Without missing a beat, Towne said, "Okay," agreed not to go to arbitration. A friend to whom Towne told the story was outraged, asked him, "Did Warren really write any of it?" The writer said something like, "Naa, ya know, what he did was cross out a lot of stuff that I wrote, and he told me to do this and that, and we usually fought about it, and sometimes he really fucked things up."

"How could you let him get away with that?"

"Oh, you know Warren. Unless you do things like that, you're not gonna get the other stuff you can get from Warren."

Since the days of *Bonnie and Clyde*, Beatty had operated as an independent producer on his personal projects. He realized that if he used his own money to develop his films and hire the talent, he could both maintain control over them and get a better deal from the studios by playing them off against one another. Beatty had spent $1.4 million without having a deal. "He was so courageous at what he did, taking these tremendous risks," says Dick Sylbert. "He could'a really come a cropper, and he almost went into the shithouse on *Shampoo*. He nearly outsmarted himself."

Shampoo was a hard sell, and Beatty was having a difficult time setting it up. Lester "the Investor" Persky was putting together a package of films he was financing for Columbia. He says, "It was very hard-hitting, and the studios didn't think a film named *Shampoo* about a hairdresser who was pretending to be gay, and was making out like a bandit with all the wives and girlfriends of his friends, was a sympathetic character, or believable. They thought it was awful." Evans, on the other hand, would have bought belly button lint from Beatty and Towne, and the actor knew it. He took it to Paramount first. Evans was staying at the Carlyle in New York. Beatty flew in with the script, sat there while he read it. It was about the world Evans knew well. He was eager to do it and named a figure. But Beatty had no intention of taking the first offer he got. He brought the project to Warners, where he already had a deal for *Heaven Can Wait*, a remake of *Here Comes Mr. Jordan*, with Muhammad Ali attached as the boxer. He talked numbers with then president Frank Wells, who topped Evans. Meanwhile, says Evans, his boss, Frank Yablans, overruled him and yanked his offer. Beatty cannily went after executives new to their posts who had, as was the custom in Hollywood, wiped their predecessors' slates clean and consequently were desperate for product to fill the pipeline. "Warren knows how to ingratiate himself with any new administration," says Evans. "He would do it with Diller [on *Reds*], then Katzenberg [with *Dick Tracy*] when Katzenberg went to Disney. Most of his pictures are made with new administrations." Evans claims that Beatty called him and said, "Look, Bob, I'm bringing it to [Columbia head] David Begelman, and I want to tell him that you want it. He offered me three million four. I want to tell him that you offered four million." Evans says he demurred.

"I can't do that Warren, because we have a deal amongst the guys that we can't lie—"

"Hey, come on, Bob, it's me. Begelman calls you, I want you to tell him you're offering $4 million for it."

Indeed, Beatty would not be denied, and Evans, a star-fucker before he was anything else, says he gave in. Begelman made an extremely sweet offer, almost twice as much as Warners, way more than was prudent given Columbia's parlous financial condition, and given the fact that Begelman hated the script, thought it was cynical and offensive. By the time the endless backing and forthing was over, buyer's remorse set in, and Begelman welshed on the deal. Recalls Beatty, "He turned out to be off his trolley," adding, "People thought Columbia was going into Chapter 11 at that point, and he simply reneged on it, because the deal was bigger than he should have offered." Towne added, "Up to a week or so before we were shooting Warren had literally assumed the burden of the picture himself. At that point, because of very complex difficulties with Columbia it appeared as if he was going to have to pay personally for a $4 million movie."

Beatty continues, "When Begelman reneged, I went back to Warners." But Wells knew that Columbia had fallen through and that

Beatty had nowhere else to turn. The actor recalled, "I had to go back on my hands and knees. [Beatty said], 'I think you were offering such and such.'

" 'Yes, but that was then.'

" 'Oh, what is it now?'

" 'Half of that.' "

Beatty was in deep trouble; as Sylbert said, he had nearly out-smarted himself.

On the other hand, Beatty says "it's not true" that Yablans nixed Evans's offer. Yablans recalls, "Everybody hated *Shampoo*. The girl saying, 'I wanna suck your cock'? Oh my God! They didn't under-stand it. I didn't understand it, but it was a movie I would have made. I would have made anything with Beatty. As an actor, a hired gun, he had a tendency to walk through. But when he believed, there was no one like him."

Wells and Begelman may have been putting the screws to Beatty, but, according to Medavoy and Persky, he had an ace up his sleeve: *The Fortune*. Begelman was desperate to get the film, with Beatty *and* Nich-olson, *and* Mike Nichols attached. If Begelman wanted *The Fortune*, he would have to take *Shampoo* as well. But Columbia didn't have nearly enough money to do either film, much less both, and in what turned out in hindsight to be a move of stunning stupidity, Begelman laid *Shampoo* off on Persky.

"I said, after reading the two scripts, I would forgo *The Fortune* and do *Shampoo*," Persky claims. That was the reason they suddenly said they would do *Shampoo*. So it was a terrific, no-lose deal for them. Except that Warren made a very rich deal, 10 percent of the gross from first dollar. After the presumed break-even point, which was some-where between $12 and $13 million, his share rather quickly went up to 40 percent of the gross."

Beatty denies buying *The Fortune*, or yoking it to *Shampoo*. Ac-cording to him, he bearded Begelman at a Democratic fund-raiser. The Columbia executive knew that Wells had stiff-armed Beatty, knew that the star had already spent a lot of his own money, thought that he had the upper hand. He blandly told Beatty, "I never made you any prom-ises." Beatty poked his finger into Begelman's considerable chest, hard, backing him across the room, while saying in a loud voice, "You're a liar. *I* know you're a liar, *you* know you're a liar, but we're gonna forget that, and we're gonna do this deal. You have zero, you need this picture. Just match my original deal with Warners." Begelman, who was nothing if not self-possessed, was nevertheless getting red in the face. Flustered and defensive, he finally gave in. But Begelman was willing to offer only half of what he originally offered, indeed approximately equal to the original Warners deal. Pace Persky, Beatty says he couldn't even get first dollar gross, and had to settle for a cut of the gross after the "rolling break," or break-even. Nevertheless, he had his deal.

5

DON JUAN IN HELL

How six words—"I want to suck his cock"—turned *Shampoo*

into a $60 million hit, while Beatty took up with

Michelle Phillips, and finally bought a home.

"One-third of the audience walked out on Julie Christie's line.
Columbia thought they had the greatest disaster in their history."

—Don Devlin

J UST BEFORE *Shampoo* was slated to go into production, Beatty
astonished gossip columnists who had long scolded him about his
nomadic living arrangements by finding a home, after a lengthy
search conducted by Helen Feibelmann. It sat on five acres at the top
of Mulholland Drive, and formerly belonged to Danish tenor Lauritz
Melchior. "The Viking," as Melchior had called it, was a simple, white-
washed structure in the Bauhaus style, commanding a panoramic view
of the San Fernando Valley. Beatty, who was being harassed by stalkers,
explained that too many people knew he lived at the Beverly Wilshire,
and that he needed more privacy. He complained that the recent new
addition to the hotel enabled guests to look down on his patio. He
may also have decided that his penthouse pad was no asset to a man
with political ambitions.

The house, along the stretch of Mulholland dubbed Bad Boy Drive
because it also boasted the homes of Brando and Nicholson, came with

a pool and a guesthouse that Beatty initially intended to tear down to make way for a screening room, gym, and sauna. But he ultimately tucked the screening room into the lower level of the main house. (It had its own entrance, which was used, on occasion, by Orson Welles, who was too large to get through the front door.) After pondering his purchase, and inviting his friends, including Christie, to look at it, he paid $167,000.

What with the uncertainty over the financing, *Shampoo* didn't begin principal photography until March 11, 1974, on Stage 7 of General Services Studio. Ashby may have been the director of record, but Beatty ran the show. As he had on *Bonnie and Clyde*, he found it difficult to do two jobs, much less three. "Being the producer and star is almost impossible," he liked to say. "A good actor has to be childlike and maintain a feeling of make-believe. He has to learn to put himself out of control and respect that state. A good film-maker needs to be in complete control, so in doing both you pay a price." Anticipating a sixty-day shoot, he felt the pressure too intensely to enjoy the process. Throughout, he rarely looked happy; his brow was always furrowed, his mouth set in a grimace of anxiety.

Feelings were raw, and tempers frayed. Says Lee Grant, whom Beatty had started calling two years before he actually began production, "We had a rough start. He put twelve years into that script, and he had very strong opinions." On one occasion, she almost quit. There is a scene in which her character, Felicia, walks into her teenage daughter's room to find her on the bed, while George is coming out of the bathroom. Beatty didn't like her performance. "He said that I had a look on my face, as if I knew that he had slept with my daughter," she remembered. "He said that women don't know, that they immediately go into denial. Well, I got a migraine and went home for two days, and when I came back I told the director, Hal Ashby, that I couldn't work like that and I had to quit. No one ever told me before what I was thinking." Ashby's response was, characteristically, "Okay." Grant continued, "I started to leave. Warren saw my face and he asked what was wrong. So I sat down and I told him. He threw up his hands and said, 'Play it your way. What do I know? I'm a man.'"

Even Hawn, who was a loyal friend and placid of disposition, said later, "I was not happy with Warren." She explained, "He's a multi-talented individual but he's very demanding. You learn a lot from

Warren, but it can be very time-consuming. I didn't have a lot of laughs making *Shampoo*."

Carrie Fisher had her own problems, somewhat different. She remembered that as the producer, Beatty could do whatever he wanted with her, ask her to try on this bra, that bra, no bra. She felt he was just messing with her, treating her like a doll. Even though she felt objectified, she found it hard to be offended because Beatty's manner was so playful. He was having fun, if she wasn't. Beatty teased her for being a virgin in front of the crew and cast, embarrassing her, making her feel like a moron. She recalled, "He offered to relieve me of the huge burden of my virginity. Four times."

Beatty marked his thirty-seventh birthday on March 30. The cast and crew threw him a party. As he was cutting the cake, a redheaded go-go dancer streaked across the room, threw her arms around him and gave him a birthday kiss. He was locked in an embrace with her before he realized she was naked. His face turned red.

Beatty made it clear that he was in charge. Anthea Sylbert recalled that he asked to see her sketches for the costumes. "I said, 'You're the producer, what am I going to show the sketches to you for? I'd rather show them to Hal.' And he said, 'I want to see the sketches.' So from the beginning, it became clear that it wasn't going to be like what I was used to, that Warren was a different kind of producer and Hal was a different kind of director, and that it was going to be a Warren Beatty film no matter how Ashby felt." Adds Lee Grant, "Warren treated him like any other member of the crew. But Hal *had* to stay around; it was like his bargain with the devil because it was going to be a big hit."

Beatty used Ashby as a surrogate director, but he preferred to work around and through him instead of running right over him. This was the era of the auteur, after all, and Ashby could make a fair claim to that distinction. Beatty was not insensitive to the complexities of the situation, and tried to exercise his influence with some delicacy. Anthea Sylbert recalls, "One day, Warren said to me, 'I want you to watch that scene there.

" 'Well, how was it?'

" 'Okay.'

" 'Just Okay?'

" 'Just Okay.'

" 'Go tell Hal.'

" 'I'm not telling Hal anything. You go tell Hal.' "

She explained, "I found it very embarrassing at first. Because I didn't think it was my job to be telling Hal Ashby, 'It's not funny enough.' " But after a while she fell into the habit of doing things Beatty's way. Nevertheless, she was unable to quell her discomfort and felt sorry for Ashby. She said, "I hate even talking about it. In some ways, I'm [still] embarrassed that I did it."

Ashby was sandwiched between Beatty, who stood next to him, and Towne, who crouched under the camera. Beatty would often show Ashby how he wanted scenes shot, like one in the shop, where he demonstrates seduction by hair styling. In costume, wearing tight jeans, a half-unbuttoned blue silk shirt, an iridescent green scarf looped and knotted around his neck, and lots of Indian jewelry, he told the director, "I'll show you how I see this scene." Facing a customer, and virtually sitting on her lap, he pushed her head forward, toward his crotch, and massaged her scalp. Turning to Ashby, he said dryly, "I want this to be a totally asexual scene."

To Carrie Fisher, Ashby was invisible, not really directing. He didn't direct the actors, didn't direct her. He was smoking a lot of pot, and at the wrap party, he was presented with a large joint. To her, that said a lot. In practice, it was rough on the actors. Recalled Hawn, "We'd get three different directions, one from the director, one from Bob, and one from Warren. There were times when we'd say, 'Guys, get together, can one person give me a note?' So it became difficult."

On the other hand, Ashby may have brought some of it on himself, through his passivity, his drug habit, and his training in the cutting room, which taught him that it wasn't necessary to get things just right on the set, because he could shape the film later, in post. As a friend put it, "Hal would never judge a take. To him, they were all good. He was an editor." Ashby created a vacuum into which Beatty, already inclined to grab the reins, was more than happy to rush.

Still, Ashby's friends were irate. Haskell Wexler visited the set on a number of occasions. "Warren just chewed Hal up and spit him out," he recalls. "Hal was like an office boy on that, and he's not used to being treated that way, Warren telling everybody what to do, just taking over." According to Bob Jones, Ashby's editor, who says Beatty threw him off the set one day when he was hanging around, "It was tough for Hal. I'd go on the set, and Warren and Towne would be off whispering in the corner. Hal would be sitting in the other corner. I purposely stayed away. It was uncomfortable seeing what was going on."

One day, Ashby walked up to Sylbert, who was dressed, as always, in his "uniform"—a safari jacket from Abercrombie & Fitch, khakis, a beige (his twin, Paul, wore blue) work shirt, and a red bandanna twisted around his neck—and said, as Sylbert recalls, " 'I can't take it anymore. These guys won't let me alone.' He hated it, because we'd have meetings, and we'd go, 'All right Hal, this is what we're gonna do . . . ' We beat the shit out of him, had him boxed in—Warren, Towne, myself, and Anthea. Actor, script, set, and costumes. We'd make him reshoot, do takes he didn't want to do, coverage he felt he didn't need. But he was wacked most of the time. And generally he was smart enough to just go with the flow. He was the best person Warren could have hired, because Ashby's feelings about people were very good. To do that movie, you couldn't be mean, you couldn't do an Altman: 'Schmucks, schmucks, schmucks.' "

Indeed, Ashby did manage to capture George's sweetness, his innocence, the flip side of his narcissism. He tried, in his words, "not to be too harsh on [the characters] . . . because their bullshit is so inherent that it'll come out anyway. In other words you can humanize a little bit more with the character because all that stuff's going to come out whatever it is. You know, make him a little bit more believable hopefully and not make him a caricature."

About a year and a half later, Ashby admitted, "It was very difficult because I was working with an actor who was the producer of the film and we spent a little bit of time trying to differentiate between that, never with much success."

Beatty, however, made no apologies. After all, he had incubated the project. It was his, without a doubt. "I'm not a hired actor in *Shampoo*," he explained, by implication alluding to Ashby, who was in his view a director-for-hire.

Shampoo became an early laboratory for Beatty's notion of "hostile intelligences," ultimately refined to three. Essentially, it was an insurance policy that works this way, to paraphrase him: If one person runs the show, he is hostage to his own mistakes, originating in ego, stupidity, or plain bad judgment. If two people share the responsibility, one is going to dominate the other, so in effect you still have only one person making decisions, or worse, neither will prevail and there will be a standoff. With three, he says, "usually the right thing prevails." In practice, this meant that Beatty, Sylbert, and Towne, who was rewriting as they went along, with Ashby playing catch-up, argued a lot while the cast and crew stood around and waited. Often, the outcome was productive, the way it was supposed to be.

Dick Sylbert claims credit for the celebrated scene between George and Jill (Hawn), wherein she asks, "Were there other women?" and he replies, "Well, there were a few times at the shop—let's face it, I fucked all of them." He says he told Beatty, "You're fucking whining all the time. You need a scene where you say, 'I love fucking pussy.'" Warren went to Towne and said, 'We need a scene where I finally say how I feel about pussy.'"

Towne recalled, "Warren was towering over Goldie, so it seemed like he fucked everybody, and then was lecturing her about it. Hal thought it was okay, but I called for a reshoot. Warren, being the prudent producer, was reluctant. I insisted, and then he got mad at me for not having realized that it was fucked up before we shot it. I went for a walk with my dog Hira, and realized that Warren had to be sitting down and Goldie towering over him, and that this speech had to be personal. It had to be torn out of him, so I did a rewrite." And indeed, as Towne wrote it, it was personal, maybe too personal, and has always struck Beatty watchers as words from the heart: "I don't know what I'm apologizing for, I go into that shop and they're so great looking, you know. And I, I'm doing their hair, and they feel great, and they smell great. . . . It makes my day. Makes me feel like I'm gonna live forever . . ."

Both Beatty and Ashby liked to shoot a lot of film. But, according to Jones, the resemblance stopped there. "The difference between a Beatty set and an Ashby set is incredible," says Jones, who worked for both of them. "They shot film for different reasons. Hal would create a feeling of freedom, where people would contribute. He loved to liberate other people's creativity, and he wouldn't judge it, he'd just be open to it. And he would go for lots of different coverage. Warren shoots little coverage, hundreds of takes on everything, and kind of wears the actors down."

Beatty liked Ashby, and always spoke well of him. And, to hear him tell it, the director-in-waiting learned a lot by watching him. "Hal understood something that I had trouble with, which was the value of passivity. A lot of times people will look at a person who seems passive as a guy who doesn't know what he wants and doesn't know what he's doing. Rather, it's the value of not pushing it, the receptive potential of directing, allowing of things to happen, which is a big gift for a movie director. Of course, Hal's great teachers were Stevens and Wyler."

To Dick Sylbert, *Shampoo* was the opposite of *Chinatown*, which he had just finished. If *Chinatown* was about concealment, *Shampoo* was about display, vanity, narcissism, which were "what the seventies turned out to be," he said. "What you hide in *Chinatown*, you show in Beverly Hills. It's about showing everything. 'You know what I got? This is what I got. You want to see my house? This is what's in it.'" Sylbert had a method, which consisted of distilling the movie's theme, choosing visual metaphors reflective of that theme, and then making each and every design element a slave to those metaphors. In this case the visual equivalents were mirrors. There were mirrors everywhere, two hundred or so, according to the designer. The mirrors made Beatty nervous, not because he didn't like admiring himself (he always had "one eye in the mirror," to quote "You're So Vain"), but because they smacked of "I'm-here-too-ism," a cardinal sin in his book. "When you have a shot in the mirror, you usually think about who's shooting it," Beatty reflected. "Sometimes shots in mirrors will overly complicate a shot, and when you overly complicate a shot, some people will say, 'Gee, what an interesting way of shooting something.' . . . We were not a group of people that liked to draw attention to the way something was shot." As Sylbert put it, "You get a mirror shot if you have a real scene, and there happens to be a mirror there. It's not because the mirror's there that you make the shot." Perhaps the only exception to Beatty's proscription of "I'm-here-too-isms," was himself, to whom it did not apply. For him, it wasn't "I'm here, too," it was just, "I'm here," and truly, without him, there would have been no *Shampoo*.

The production continued into May, when they shot for three days in the Bistro restaurant on Rodeo Drive and also did the party in a Holmby Hills mansion. The notorious fellatio scene, where Christie, at the election night dinner, dives under a table to perform the nasty on Beatty, was shot during the last week on a closed set.

Shampoo wrapped on June 12, 1974, only a couple of days shy of two weeks behind schedule. Beatty planned to go to the wrap party with Christie, but he asked her if she minded if he brought along Michelle Phillips, formerly of the Mamas and the Papas. Outside of her music career, she was perhaps best known for her action-packed eight-day marriage to Dennis Hopper, and subsequent romance with Nicholson, which lasted about two years, from 1972 to 1974. They split up before *Shampoo* began. Phillips and Nicholson were not getting along. She told him, "One day I'm going to leave you and you'll never know why." Nicholson had a safety razor in which the blade consisted of a ribbon of metal advanced by turning a knob. One day he walked into the bathroom, grabbed the razor, and discovered that the ribbon had been used up. He accused her of being the culprit. She said, "I can't stand living with someone who complains all the time," and walked out. He never knew why.

Phillips had called Towne, asked him to let her be an extra in the party scene. She went into Beatty's trailer to say hello. "I started seeing Warren towards the end of *Shampoo*," she says. "It was just a kind of weird, surprising attraction. Because I was not attracted to him when I first met him. It was just something that happened. It was funny, because he was still kind of going with Julie. When he asked her, 'Is it okay if Michelle comes along with us?' she said, 'Sure.' She didn't care. I think her indifference about how he behaved made him love her more." Christie's equanimity could have stemmed from the fact that they had more or less broken up, or she was unaware that Beatty and Phillips were involved, but Phillips doesn't think so: "I think she did know. We didn't make any secret about it. She just wasn't jealous, she just wasn't possessive."

Phillips was familiar with the gossip that swirled around him. She had to be; everyone in Hollywood was; everyone in America was. "I was concerned about his reputation, but I was drawn to him," she goes on. "I don't think women walk into the trap without thinking, I can change him. Warren is the great seducer. He makes every woman he is with feel that she is the One—Maybe I really am the one." But "you could never get that close to Warren." Phillips felt "He was very cautious with his emotions. Because I'm sure he didn't want to feel used either. Let's face it, he was a star, and a big star."

The Parallax View was released on June 14, 1974, two days after *Shampoo* wrapped, to tepid reviews. Wrote Vincent Canby in *The New York Times*, "You're likely to feel as cheated as I did." Beatty felt cheated because Paramount opened it right next to *Chinatown* at Manhattan's prime exhibition site, the twin Coronet and Baronet theaters on Third Avenue and 58th Street.

Beatty felt *Parallax View* was not getting the full attention of distribution and marketing. He objected to the fact that it was released only a week before *Chinatown,* in effect having to compete with it. Yablans admits, "It was a major film for us, a big summer movie. I didn't believe in *Parallax View.* It was heavily flawed. We didn't have time to finish the picture in a proper fashion, because the writer's strike came right when we were shooting the film, and the script needed an enormous amount of work."

According to Evans, who produced *Chinatown,* Beatty complained to Bluhdorn. He felt Beatty had stabbed him in the back. He says, "My closest friend, he tried to kill me."

BEATTY BARELY had time to catch his breath. He wrapped *Shampoo* on a Friday, and started rehearsals on *The Fortune* the following Monday. Production started in early July. He was leery. He realized yet again, that every time he wasn't in control, there was trouble. "Had I produced *The Fortune*, we wouldn't have started shooting for another couple of months," he says. "In truth I should'a had [at least] a month off, but I wanted to work with Mike and I wanted to work with Jack." But Mike Nichols, who was co-producing, and directing, assured him it would be all right. It wasn't.

The Fortune was based on the script by Carole Eastman. Eastman, who died in 2004, had written Nicholson's first hit, *Five Easy Pieces* (1970). An exotic flower, even by the standards of the day and place, she managed to stand out among the parade of freaks cruising Sunset Boulevard in their flamboyant plumage — wild hair, colorful bandannas, vintage clothing, hammered silver bracelets. A former dancer and actress, she was tall, blond, rail-thin, with a swan's long neck. In fact, she was very like a bird, high-strung, startled into flight by the rustle of a leaf.

Born in 1934, she came from a working-class background, and made something of a specialty of characters who did the same. She had a great ear for the rhythms of blue-collar speech. Her reputation rested on her script for *Five Easy Pieces*, directed by Bob Rafelson and released in 1970. "Jack was always wild about Carole," says Harry Gittes, an old and close friend of his. "She was the first person to understand how brilliant he was, and wrote a character for him—a blue-collar intellectual, which is what he is—and he never, ever forgot that."

Eastman was a recluse, an agoraphobe, wouldn't leave Los Angeles, rarely went to places with which she was not already familiar, wouldn't let anyone else drive her car, and insisted on taking the wheel when she was in someone else's. "Carole was born to be an eccentric old lady," recalls writer Buck Henry. "She was severely strange. She wouldn't set foot in a plane if you put a gun to her head." She refused to ride in elevators, was phobic about having her picture taken, obsessed over food and wouldn't eat meat at the same time that she, as *The Fortune* producer Don Devlin, who died in 2000, put it, "was coughing herself to death on cigarettes," which she chain-smoked.

Eastman's sexual orientation provided fodder for endless rumination; she dipped her toe into both genders, but she never seemed to make up her mind, or have a lover of either sex for any length of time. She often hid behind dark glasses, and even disguised her screen credit with a pseudonym, Adrien Joyce, as she did on *The Fortune*, although this may have been an attempt to disavow the pictures made from her scripts, with which she was never pleased.

Devlin, for one, couldn't understand why Nicholson "deferred to her wisdom," why he didn't recognize her limitations. But Nicholson prided himself on his eye for talent, and Eastman for him was the mother lode. According to Dick Sylbert, unlike Beatty, "Jack had no first class writers around him. He didn't have niggers, he had schmucks." Sylbert's wife, Susanna Moore, was working for Nicholson at the time, and read the script for him. She said, "What is this arch piece of shit?" But if she told Nicholson, he didn't listen. Continues Devlin, "Jack is a kingmaker. He gets enthusiasms for people, and he had such great enthusiasm for Carole that he put his faith in her, as opposed to [the script], whether or not he really understood it. Jack often confuses badly written material with complex material. It was that faith in Carole that might have gotten Warren to that table, plus his desire to do a movie with Jack."

Beatty also seemed to have a high opinion of Eastman's intelligence. Before she died, she told one of his biographers, Suzanne Finstad, that as she was getting into her car after having dinner with him at a restaurant, Beatty grabbed "her arm so tightly he left bruises," exclaiming,

"I want to take you up to show you this property up on Mulholland. Because you're going to live there."

"Why am I going to live there?"

"Because I'm going to marry you." Eastman didn't know what he was talking about, until he explained, "This is a gonadal matter," and she realized that he wanted smart children. "Certain men do think that way," Eastman concluded. "They are thinking genetically of how to breed up, as they say in the animal world." As Beatty himself put it, "I have theories about the DNA's need to replicate itself, and let's face it, it replicates itself in a romantic way."

Five Easy Pieces was the only decent script that Eastman ever wrote, or had produced at any rate, but Devlin's jaundiced view of her talents may have taken shape in the shadow of the fiasco *The Fortune* became, because he believed in her enough at one time to rent her a room at the Chateau Marmont along with a typewriter so she could write the script. It was then that he became attached as producer.

Set in the late 1920s right before the Crash, and based on two news stories from the period, the script told the story of the heiress to a sanitary napkin fortune named Fredrika Contessa 'Freddie' Biggars. (Rule #1: Beware of scripts in which the characters have whimsical names.) It was originally called *The Mousebed Heiress*, after a laboriously explained conceit in which Freddie recalls that "mousebeds" were her euphemism for Kotex. Beatty and Nicholson play two dim-bulb friends, Nicky and Oscar, who try to kill her for her inheritance. It was a premise just nutty enough to be promising, but when Eastman got it down on paper, to use a favorite epithet of Nicholson's from those days, it was "lame-o." Says Devlin, "I hated the script. It was terrible." Eastman was not one to embrace criticism, and when he confided his doubts, "she went through the fucking roof."

According to Nichols, he read half the script, given to him by Nicholson, on the first leg of a flight to Poland, and the second half sitting on his suitcase in the Warsaw airport waiting to get through customs. In those circumstances, the phone book would have been entertaining.

With Nichols in the cab of the locomotive, there was no stopping the train. As Devlin points out, "In those days everybody supported everything directors wanted. Directors were auteurs. Nobody knew what an auteur was, but it sounded pretty good. Don Siegel used to go around calling himself an auteur. He would go into these meetings, get into a fight with the executives, and he always said, 'Yeah, but there's only one auteur sitting in this room, and I'm that guy.'"

Devlin not only went way back with Eastman, but with Nicholson as well. (He was one of several, including Gittes, who were considered "Jack's Best Friend.") He had a reputation for being a decent man in a business not always known for decency. "Don is extremely honorable," says Hank Moonjean, a veteran line producer whom Nichols and Nicholson brought in to do the picture. "Whatever he says I would take for gospel." Buck Henry also testifies to his probity: "I'm sure if Devlin said [something], it's true." But this virtue may not have served him well on *The Fortune*. When the project got the green light from Columbia, Devlin was appalled. "I was the voice of doom," he remembers. "I said, 'What are you doing? You have 240 pages, two acts, and no third act.' But I was the only person there saying, 'This script is nowhere near ready, this is ridiculous.' And of course, that did not endear me to anyone."

Beatty had been devoting himself to *Shampoo*. "I didn't read *The Fortune* until the day I showed up to work," he recalls. Nicholson, who was on location in Spain with Michelangelo Antonioni for *The Passenger*, and went right into *Chinatown* when he returned, had apparently not been able to focus on it, either. Devlin continues, "None of them had studied the thing, and all of a sudden they were beginning to ask the questions that should have been asked six months or a year earlier." It seemed as if the three principals, Beatty, Nicholson, and Nichols, were all so excited by everyone else's excitement, that they didn't notice the script wasn't finished.

Beatty's reputation for being a tough, even ruthless, negotiator, was well deserved. Sometimes Devlin found himself identifying with Freddie, *The Fortune*'s mousebed heiress. He thought that Beatty and Nichols were trying to kill him. "Warren of course wanted to produce it," recalls Devlin. "And Mike had produced, or at least co-produced every movie he ever made, so it was like, 'Who the fuck is this friend of Carole's who's the producer?' From the moment the three of them decided they were going to make this movie, it was a total nightmare for me, because these guys with their power and their influence simply took over the project, and were continually trying to get rid of me. Warren can't resist exploiting everyone, even when it's not putting the extra dollars in his pocket. He does it for the joy of screwing people. He calls it 'going to war.' This left-wing intellectual uses military expressions when you're strategizing: 'Well, you'll be the point man.' 'We'll kill them.' Warren is simply a man who exults in doing people in. His behavior is not based on his getting richer, it's based on his making sure nobody else does. If he were brilliant and nice, what a combination that would be, but he's just a prick." But Devlin hung in, and got co-producer credit with Nichols.

Beatty disputes Devlin's account of these events in every respect. "I had no control over *The Fortune* at all," he says. "If anything, I was in the fourth position. It was Jack and Carole, and then Mike came into it, and then me." Indeed, he does not have a producing credit.

Anthea Sylbert suggests that Nicholson, who often observed ugly battles between old friends going on around him—*The Fortune*, *Chinatown*, and later *The Two Jakes*—seemed to be amused by them. Says Devlin, "Part of it in truth is that many of Jack's close friends are real egomaniacs, ambitious, nasty people. There's no such thing as a picture that Towne makes, where there's not all kinds of trouble. There's no such thing as a picture Carole Eastman is involved with where there's not endless amounts of trouble. It was very, very brutal, being so massively screwed by his partners, with his proxy. Certainly I would not recommend doing business with Warren and Mike to any friend of mine, if they could possibly avoid it."

SHAMPOO WAS edited in the Mulholland house, before Beatty started renovating it. Bob Jones, who aspired to be a writer and later would win an Oscar for the script for *Coming Home,* hadn't formed much of an impression of Beatty. "I stayed away from Warren as much as I could," he recalls. "I felt I was on Hal's side, I was about the only one. I didn't like Warren, just for what was going on at different times. I didn't want to have much to do with him so any chance I'd get to avoid a screening that Warren had, I'd do it."

Still, according to him, Beatty, now preoccupied with *The Fortune,* mostly stayed away, letting Ashby do what he did best, supervise the editing. "There was another whole ending," the director recalled, "as opposed to what we ended up with. Much harder and harsher. In fact, the last line was, 'A fuck is a fuck, it's not a crime.' Which was really heavy; it came down too hard."

In addition, the intention was to end with an epilogue, set in the then present, giving a glimpse of the characters six or so years after the events that transpired in the film. In both Beatty's and Towne's versions, the characters had continued to make messes of their lives, each in his or her own way. As usual, the two men could not agree on which one to use and finally ran out of time. By necessity, the film defaulted to the ending they had shot, with George having dropped all the balls he had in the air: Felicia, Jill, and finally Jackie, who is, he realizes belatedly, the only one he ever loved. Standing by his motorcycle at the top of Mulholland Drive, he watches her being collected by Lester below, George's own future a question mark. Ashby preferred it, perhaps some small reward for the patience he had displayed over the course of the production. "I like to leave a little bit of an enigma there about exactly what it is," he said, "because I think that's what makes it not a totally down kind of an ending."

According to Jones, Beatty spent no more than a week in the editing room, at the end, when Ashby was finished. Outside of wanting to pick up the pace, he basically approved of Ashby's cut. "When Warren wanted to screw with the film, Hal stayed away," says Jones. "After Hal left, and I started working with Warren, I liked him a lot. Then he wanted me to do *Reds.* Luckily I was writing." According to Jones, Beatty asked Ashby to direct *Dick Tracy.* It never happened, but Beatty and Ashby parted on good terms, and remained friends more or less, until just before Ashby died.

When *Shampoo* had wrapped, Beatty hired Tim Vreeland, son of his friend, former *Vogue* editor Diana Vreeland, and head of the UCLA architecture department, to renovate the Mulholland house. Needless to say, the renovation took forever. According to Dick Sylbert, Beatty, a stickler for details and always changing his mind, drove Vreeland crazy. The architect executed an exotic black and white Italian marble floor for one of the rooms. Each piece was different, and fitting them together was a task worthy of crossword puzzle guru Will Shortz. When it was completed, Beatty had it torn out, because he decided that it didn't fit his profile as a Democrat, a man of the people. Beatty spent months agonizing over furniture. Then he rented some. People speculated that it was for the same reason that he had rented his penthouse for so many years: he was able to charge the rent to the studios.

Beatty had moved Phillips and her daughter, Chynna, then six, into his new home, just before he was slated to begin *The Fortune.* Among other things, it bestowed an aura of solidity and permanence on their relationship, or so she thought. They camped out in the house during the renovation. Phillips took over the interior decoration, such as it was. Director Glenn Gordon Caron, who would direct Beatty in *Love Affair*, visited the house many years later. "I noticed there was no art on the walls," he recalls. "It seemed odd given Warren's intelligence, and his inquiring mind, so one day I asked him, 'Warren, where's the art?' He looked at me and pointed to himself. You could almost imagine that he had thought out the room as the perfect display case for himself, where he was standing." Beatty was undoubtedly making a joke on himself—sort of. He did have a spare, less-is-more aesthetic. "He won't show you his life in a house," says Sylbert. "It looks like an ice cube with a piano in it."

Phillips furnished the house in Art Deco—then the rage. Beatty also bought a car, a Mercedes coupe. It didn't take too long for him to turn the inside into a mess, the penthouse on wheels. They lived like a family, but he kept the penthouse and would go there to work. He quickly adapted to his new domesticity, driving Chynna to school in the morning. "He really loved Chynna," Phillips says. "He tried to help her learn how to read, and enjoy reading."

Phillips continued, "When Warren is in love, he is a very generous person. I don't mean that financially, I mean that in a sense that he devotes himself to you. The woman in his life comes first. When he is with you, he's with you 100 percent. You go everywhere together. If you have to go to New York, you go to New York together. If he has to open a movie in Australia, you pack your bags. He loves companionship, and we had a lot in common in that sense. We both loved to travel." She adds, "For a very long time, I did desperately want it to work between us." Jennifer Lee, who saw Beatty on and off throughout the 1970s, recalled being asked to join him and Phillips in a threesome, which Lee declined.

Beatty repeatedly raised the possibility of their doing a movie together, but despite his "carrot dangling," it never happened. Reportedly they would fly to Bali to be married in the summer of 1975, which never happened either. She remembered, "I wanted to have another child, and we talked about marriage a lot, but he was very noncommittal." She thinks he would have married her had she gotten pregnant. But "I never pressured him to marry me," she continued. "I waited for him to ask."

Phillips complained that he "never really knew how to have fun. . . . He could make me feel so childish and guilty for wanting to stay in bed all day eating ice cream and making love. He, too, felt guilty about doing things like that—just doing nothing. His idea of a good time is five hours on the phone."

MEANWHILE, THE start date of *The Fortune* was fast approaching.

The problem with the ending of the script was not that it didn't work, but that it didn't exist. Says Henry, "The legend is Carole has never written the end to a film. That was true of *The Fortune*. It made Mike crazy. He could never get the ending out of her." Says Nichols, "The script was like 345 pages, and it had no ending nor did it ever get an ending from Carole. I had to carve a story out of all those pages. Sort of like a butter sculpture at a wedding. As a result, I wasn't too warmly inclined toward Carole Eastman."

Nichols, who was coming off *Day of the Dolphin* (1973), an expensive flop, had dropped a lot of his team. Now he changed his mind. According to Devlin, as preproduction proceeded, "Mike got more and more frightened, realizing he had no movie, no idea what the fuck the movie was about, and he began firing people in order to bring back all the people he had that he hoped would save his ass." Many of those he brought back were also Beatty regulars, like Dick Sylbert. Reassembling the old gang may have reassured Nichols, but it served to exacerbate the bad vibes on the set. The lines were drawn between the Beatty Bunch (Nichols, Nicholson, and Sylbert) on the one hand, and those who had never worked with them before, like Devlin and producer Hank Moonjean, on the other. And as often happens in these cases, the insiders disliked the outsiders, and vice versa. Says Devlin, "They and only they were the cool ones."

The first choice for the mousebed heiress had been Bette Midler, but she kept Nichols waiting, and that was the end of that. Nicholson suggested Mama Cass Elliot, to whom he was devoted, but Nichols wryly reminded him of the scene in which he and Beatty stuff the heiress into a trunk and throw her into the ocean. He quipped, "She'll never fit inside it." Eventually, Stockard Channing's name surfaced. She had had virtually no film experience (it would be her second movie, and first credited role), but Nichols liked her and cast her as Freddie.

When Nichols was finished cutting the script down, he had no choice but to say, "We're never going to have a complete script, we're gonna start anyway." It was shot in Culver City on Forty Acres, the old Selznick lot, the site of Tara of *Gone With the Wind* fame. According to Devlin, Beatty and Nichols immediately quarreled over their approach to the movie. "There was a tremendous disagreement, on the first day of shooting," he recalls. "As soon as Warren and Jack started to perform, everything that had been said about what the film was about went right out the window." Nobody agreed. Eastman thought she had written a Preston Sturges comedy, but Nicholson was playing it for slapstick, and making Nichols laugh. According to Moonjean, "Jack was doing Laurel and Hardy, while Stockard was doing sophisticated Carole Lombard comedy." Devlin continues, "Mike hated what they were doing, because it was so different than what he had anticipated, and they wouldn't do it the way he asked them to do it, so for the first several days they shot A and B versions, Mike's and theirs. They came to despise each other.

"Mike tried to get Warren off the film. I was in the room when he was storming and frustrated, and trying [to get him fired]. He called the lawyers and he found out he couldn't do that, 'cause Warren was one of the owners of the project." Beatty says of Devlin's account, "It's insane. Utterly insane. Just crazy. Truly bizarre. This is something constructed by somebody who might have felt left out. Jack never had any disagreements with Mike. I never had a moment's unpleasantness on the movie."

Devlin claims Beatty was casually offensive to Channing. He recalls, "Warren turned to Mike, and said, 'Would anybody believe that I would fall in love with this piece of shit?' Right in front of Stockard! It was just as sickeningly rude to say it in front of the actor." Adds Moonjean, "This was her first big role. She was a nervous wreck. Warren can be very cruel. I've known Warren a long time. I know [strangers] better than I know Warren. I try to avoid [working for] him. I don't like him. He's not a nice person." Channing herself said that Beatty and Nicholson acted "like jerks" to her.

Phillips was a frequent visitor. "Mike Nichols had to bar me from the set, because I would show up and disappear into the bungalow with Warren, and it was terribly painful for Jack," she said. "She just ignored him and came anyway," recalls Devlin. Phillips explains, "I was madly in love with Warren."

On July 29, Mama Cass died. Nicholson was distraught, and production was suspended for a day. Initially, it was reported that she choked on a sandwich. The joke, tasteless as it was, and probably originating with Sylbert, who had a tongue like an asp (he once said of someone that he was so uptight you could "sharpen a pencil in his asshole"), was that had she given the sandwich to Karen Carpenter (who died of anorexia), both women would be alive.

Eventually, despite the rough patches in the beginning, the production settled down. The weight of *Shampoo* lifted from his shoulders, Beatty regarded *The Fortune* as a walk in the park. He and Nicholson enjoyed each other, and set the tone, or tried to. Unless there is a real disaster in the making, everybody's a "genius," on a movie set, and this film was no exception. The principals were relentlessly upbeat.

The Fortune wrapped at the end of August 1974.

THE FALL of 1974 and winter months of 1975 were given over to planning the marketing of *Shampoo,* which Beatty supervised with his customary zeal and meticulous attention to detail.

Begelman saw *Shampoo* for the first time at a screening room at Goldwyn. He was appalled by "the line," or rather, the notorious exchange in which B-movie producer William Castle, who plays the fat cat sitting next to Jackie at a Republican election-eve dinner, says, "I can get you anything you'd like, what would you like?" and she says, "Well, first of all," looking at George Roundy and diving under the table, "I'd like to suck his cock." He asked Beatty to remove it, a request the producer rejected out of hand. (When Towne was asked what was "behind" that scene, he cracked "$30 million in film rentals.") To Beatty, it was the very point of the movie. "It wasn't just a dirty moment where she says a dirty line," he says. "The subject of *Shampoo* is hypocrisy, the commingling of sexual hypocrisy and political hypocrisy. The reason Julie's line made for such an explosive moment was because it shredded that hypocrisy."

The early screenings were not encouraging. *Shampoo* was previewed in Santa Barbara early in the new year with disappointing results. "The audience was fairly conservative, the screening went very badly," Beatty recalls. "We all felt awful, the cards were terrible." Says Devlin, "One third of the audience walked out on Julie Christie's line. The studio had never had anything like that happen. Columbia thought they had the greatest disaster in their history. This did not surprise David Begelman, who still hated the picture."

Beatty drove back to L.A. with Begelman, who gave him a little pat on the knee and a pep talk. He said, "They can't all be hits, so you go on to the next." The next night, the picture was screened at the Directors Guild without a single change. "The roof came off the theater," says Beatty. Lester Persky says that superagent "Sue Mengers hated it, came up and said, 'It won't do $4 million.' That's because it struck home to her, she was reacting to the woman's position." Ashby also couldn't help noticing that the women in the audience, mostly spouses of the directors, were not happy. They felt insulted and demeaned by the picture's portrait of the sex-starved Hollywood wives who were putty in George's hands. "All of them were getting up-tight," he recalled. "One person said to me afterwards that his wife said, 'I know what that asshole [Beatty] is out doing all the time.'"

Shampoo opened on February 11, 1975, one of the worst times to release a picture, months too early for Oscar awareness. Devlin, who had another movie with Columbia (*Harry and Walter Go to New York*), happened to be in Begelman's office "when the Teletypes started coming in with the critics' reviews of *Shampoo*. They loved it. He should have been elated—the studio was saved, he was going to be thrust into the limelight as this great executive—but he was totally shocked and depressed because his judgment was wrong. He had put all of his bets on the other horse, *The Fortune*."

The reviewers were mostly ecstatic, but under the sway of auteurism, and showing how little they knew about how films were actually made, they reflexively treated *Shampoo* as a "Hal Ashby" film. Vincent Canby wrote in *The New York Times*, "Hal Ashby's *Shampoo* remains the American film comedy of the year. A witty, furtively revolutionary comedy of manners." Writing in *The New Yorker*, Pauline Kael, a closet auteurist herself, raved, "*Shampoo* is the most virtuoso example of sophisticated kaleidoscopic farce that American moviemakers have ever come up with." Beatty and Towne had been courting her, and it worked. "Warren and Bob Towne recognized her value, and they were going to snow her, work her," says Paul Sylbert. "They could smell that this woman was a perfect setup for this kind of thing. It was very conscious." She was susceptible to the blandishments of stars, especially star-auteurs and glib writers who practiced on her vanity, dazzled her with their attention. "Everyone knew that Kael was feedable, that if you sat next to her and got her drunk, and fed her some lines, you could get it replayed in some other form," says Buck Henry. "There's a trick that Warren and Jack had with intellectual women. They would turn them on by suggesting that they were hot for them. If any woman had shown up from the *Partisan Review,* they would have commented on how beautiful she was. Rose Bird was the chief justice of the California Supreme Court, widely condemned for her liberal death penalty decisions, and ultimately run off the court. Warren and Jack told her she was glamorous and sexy, a hot babe, and if that isn't a turn-on to a woman who has spent most of her life in law school, nothing is. They seduced Pauline Kael with ideas, with their scripts."

Beatty arranged a special screening for Kael, along with Towne, Michelle Phillips, and Kael's friend, Richard Albarino. According to him, they sat around and discussed the movie afterward, and then went out for drinks. "She'd take out her notebook and say, 'Oh, that's really good,' and write it down. She'd be very bald about it." When she came to L.A., Towne took her out to Trader Vic's. "Towne had Kael wrapped around his finger," says Henry. Indeed, Towne, the co-writer, rather than Beatty or Ashby, was the focus of her review, just as Benton and Newman were the focus of her famous piece on *Bonnie and Clyde.* Towne has a cameo in the picture, and she flattered him by writing that he looked like Albrecht Dürer. He started dropping her name in conversation in a way that suggested that he and Kael were intimates, that he had explained his views to her—that *Shampoo* was a version of Renoir's *Rules of the Game* and Bergman's *Smiles of a Summer Night.* When her review came out, it was sprinkled with references to Bergman's film. No one could prove it of course, but people were suspicious. "You think Kael recognized what was behind *Shampoo?*" continues Henry. "He told her."

According to Beatty, Towne called Kael almost every day when she was at *The New Yorker,* and dropped her when she retired. Towne got to all the critics, he says, except for Canby. Beatty claims that the writer never liked the ending of *Shampoo,* and called *Time* magazine critic Jay Cocks to discuss it with him before Cocks wrote his review—in which he criticized the ending, to wit, "The ending is a betrayal of all that is best in the film, revealing that the film makers have been interested in apologizing for George, not satirizing him."

Despite the glowing reviews it received at the time, *Shampoo* has never gotten its due, probably because it is a comedy — comedies have always been undervalued in Hollywood — and worse, an adult comedy, that is, a satirical comedy of manners. The script and the performances are across the board superlative, and the picture is chock-full of brilliant scenes and small, throwaway touches that are gone almost before they're registered.

Beatty was uncharacteristically doing a lot of press to promote the picture, but he was typically ambivalent about it. "You can kill a movie just by turning up in magazines and newspapers and on talk shows until you make people sick of you," he worried out loud. "I'm not even sure this press tour was a good idea." He considered each request carefully and turned down a lot of them. Inevitably, the *Today* show came up. "I don't think I can do that," Beatty said. "Ms. Barbara Walters has made a public statement of the fact that I am the most difficult subject she ever tried to interview." Going over the invitation list for the premiere, he stumbled over the name John Dean, of Watergate fame. Without missing a beat, he vetoed it, saying, "I don't think so. It'd turn into John Dean night."

Beatty had long been both amused by and discomfited by his reputation — self-created, of course — as the Playboy of the Western World, as Diane Keaton would later call him. He was aware of the difficulties that he faced with the press. "I know that movie actors are over-rewarded in our society and that the press has to cut people like me down to size," he told critic Frank Rich. "They make me into an insane eccentric with an incredible fear of losing my youth who lives in a bomb shelter, who contemplates or is going through plastic surgery and who has devastating relationships with women. It goes through cycles. . . . My tide goes in and out."

Shampoo turned out to be a huge hit. According to Persky, it pulled in about $22.6 million in rentals in its initial domestic run (or about $60 million in grosses), five times its negative cost ($4.5 million). It became the fourth highest grossing film of 1975. Tickets cost only $3.50 in those days, so tripling the grosses to bring them in line with 2010 prices, and adjusting for inflation, gives us a $204 million grossing domestic blockbuster, with $100 million in rentals. According to Persky, Beatty made about $6 million in 1975 dollars. Other reports put the figure as high as $15 million.

If *Shampoo* had an auteur, it was probably Beatty rather than Ashby. "I don't see it as a Hal Ashby movie," says producer Jerry Hellman. "I see it as being much more a reflection of Warren's sensibilities. If you look at the film now, it looks very much like a commercial piece of that time, and designed to be shocking, but it didn't have any of the quixotic, bent, off-center way of looking at life of Hal's best movies."

Shampoo helped everyone connected with it, although some more than others. At least that's what those on the shorter end of the stick felt. Ashby grumbled that he hadn't made as much on *Shampoo*—which nobody in the industry considered his picture—as he should have. And he rarely mentioned the film, even to his close friends.

For Towne, *Shampoo* was the last gasp of a phenomenal burst of creativity. He would be nominated for an Oscar again, as he was for *The Last Detail* and *Chinatown*, his third in a row. But he felt shortchanged. He received a fee of $125,000, and was entitled to 5 percent of the gross from the point at which the picture earned four times the cost of the negative, which was $16 million, or so he understood. Since the movie cost a little over $4 million, he figured that he was owed in the neighborhood of $1 million, but he hadn't seen anything near that. Beatty reportedly acknowledged to a third party that he never explained the deal to the writer, said simply, "There are some things you can't talk to Towne about."

About a year after the picture was released, Beatty met with Towne at the Beverly Wilshire. According to Towne, Beatty explained for the first time that Begelman had forced him to accept a rolling break even deal, which meant that the payouts to gross participants, like Beatty, as well as other new charges, were added to the negative cost—thus, the "rolling break even"—meaning that net participants like Towne would seldom see any money. (Since Beatty produced, Towne, like Ashby, Hawn, and Christie, were paid by his company.) According to Towne, Beatty blamed the anemic payday on Begelman. He said, "Begelman fucked us."

"He fucked you, he didn't fuck me," Towne replied. "My deal was with you, and you neglected to tell me that this deal was worth less than half of what I thought it was."

"You know what they say about Hollywood: You don't get rich on your last picture, you get rich on your next picture."

"That may have been true when I worked on *Bonnie and Clyde* for

$8,000, but the future is now, as far as I'm concerned. I'm not gonna sue, and I'll still be your friend, but I'm never gonna work with you again. This is absolutely chickenshit."

Still, according to Beatty, Towne's deal, which was made when he was still writing for Roger Corman, was doubled twice, and his cut was bigger than Ashby's, Christie's, or Hawn's. His agent must have known what kind of deal he had, and for his account to be true, it must be assumed that his agent never told him and he never asked. Adds Beatty, "Towne talking about [the rolling break even] as a surprise—that's sort of insane. It was not a surprise, it was the deal."

Despite the fact that Towne was making $1 million a year throughout the second half of the 1970s, he repeatedly took sizable, six-figure loans from Beatty, apparently with little intention of paying him back because he felt Beatty owed him for *Shampoo*. Says Dick Sylbert, "Bob thought he had it coming to him, that Warren had fucked him."

The co-screenwriting credit also rankled. Says David Geffen, "Bob always said that Warren extracted credit from him that he didn't deserve. I interceded on Bob's behalf with Warren, and it was one of the most embarrassing things that ever happened to me. I said, 'You know, Warren, I really think that you're out of line,' and he went crazy, said, 'Who told you this?'

" 'Bob.'

" 'I want him to tell you this in front of me.' At a party that Goldie Hawn had, Warren was so furious that he grabbed me, and he grabbed Bob, and he said, 'Okay, he's telling me that you said all this shit, say it in front of me.' And with me standing there, Bob said he didn't do it. And the reason he didn't have the guts was because it wasn't so. Warren called me up that night, and said, 'Don't ever do that again.' "

Says Beatty, "Robert has some serious problems. It was he that offered *me* the screen credit. I would have been happy to go to arbitration. Look, I wrote the fuckin' story. The story had no political context with Robert, no Nixon, no nothing. All of that is 99 percent me, my work. I've always said, because I wanted to say nice things about Robert, that Robert wrote the first draft, but it was written by me and Robert. We used to meet every fucking day and I'd have to tell him the goddamn story. It's absolutely not true that every line of dialogue is his. It's an outrageous lie. Both party sequences were written by me, none of those were in Towne's original draft at all. That's half of the movie. Because there was so much really good writing in the first script, I very inventively combined the two, with Hal and my secretary, Helen Feibelmann, and then I took it to Towne. When he read it, he was rather amazed. I've always said, because Robert was a close friend of mine, 'Of course, the best writer is Robert, of the three of us, but if you don't write it, if you don't put words on the paper, you can't be.'" He adds, "This idea of his being upset about credit is insane. Half the fuckin' time the guy didn't show up on the set, he'd be at the doctor."

BEATTY WORRIED that his reputation as a ladykiller was coloring the reception of *Shampoo*. "Half the audience thought I was showing off how sexy I am," he says. "Nobody understood that it was about politics." Consequently, he hammered home the politics whenever he had the chance. "Vietnam polarized the town," he explains. "*Shampoo*'s audience was the audience that didn't want to go to war, that used every means to end the war. Then Watergate destroyed authority in the country, ended trust in politicians. What *Shampoo* had to say was what our generation at that time had to say about America, which was, We're not being honest about the way we're governed, our leaders are not being honest, we're not honest about what we stand for. I don't think that people today remember very clearly the heat of political passion that existed during this period. Now, nobody gives a shit."

Beatty indeed had an agenda for *Shampoo*, in fact, several. Politically, he wanted to expose American gobbledygook about sex, while ridiculing the narcissism and self-absorption of the overprivileged who stuck their collective heads in the sand while Vietnam was being bombed back into the stone age abroad, and the U.S. was burning at home. True to its avatar, *Rules of the Game*, it presents a rogues' gallery of material guys absorbed by money and goods, along with narcissistic women immersed in their feelings, their love affairs, and their looks. *Shampoo* was a gloss on Steely Dan's "Hollywood Kids." "Basically the upper class is full of shit, man," said Ashby. "You know, they don't give a fuck about anybody." He added, "They were all whores. . . . Everybody was selling out all through that picture."

But Beatty had a more personal agenda as well, revealed in the self-reflexive nature of the film, with its slew of inside jokes—Lester is undoubtedly named after Lester Persky, who financed the movie; Christie in the role of an old girlfriend, which is what she was by that time; and the cast is filled out with Beatty's friends and acquaintances. Beatty is playing it close to the bone, so that it feels like we're peering behind the curtain of his own life, at no more than a fragile fictional remove, so much so that it's tempting to regard it, as Nicholson observed, as a specimen of autobiography. There is so much of him in the character that the film becomes an echo chamber of his own quirks and habits—the picture begins with George under the covers with Felicia, hopping up to take phone call after phone call, and like Beatty, he seems to be a rolling stone, living nowhere and owning nothing, save for a motorcycle and a hairdryer.

As Nicholson once put it, wisely, "It's my point of view that all movies are either literally or symbolically autobiographical." Consequently, after making an unusually personal film, Beatty moved swiftly to distance himself from George, accentuating the differences between himself and his hairdressing, head-fondling doppelgänger. In the one-step-forward-two-steps-back dance at which he was so adept, he claimed that he identified more with Lester, a rich entrepreneur, than he did with George—the very same Lester whom Beatty wryly observed Christie thought he was when she "rejected" him in real life. In Hollywood, the skein of relationships, both genuine and fictional, linking "reel" life and "real" life is always tangled, but in this case it would have taken a Houdini to have undone the knot. Beatty is, of course, George *and* Lester, the sybarite and the businessman, which is perhaps why he identified so closely with Howard Hughes. And Christie, by accounts other than Beatty's, rejected him more for his affinity with George than with Lester—or, perhaps, both.

How like Beatty was George? It's true that for your garden-variety, unobsessed male, Beatty seemed to spend an inordinate amount of time on matters of the heart—he, of course, would just call it living his life—when, it might be argued, in view of his slender output, he could have been more profitably concerned with setting up his next picture. But he rarely let sex, or at least the sex act, interfere with his work. One woman reported that when they were having sex in the morning, after insuring that she came frequently enough to face the rest of the day with a smile, he pulled out, explaining that he had a lot of writing to do, and if he came himself he would be too wasted to concentrate, and would just fall asleep.

Beatty was not going to lay himself bare for all the world to see without a purpose—or purposes. One was obvious—as he had so often said—to bury Freud's notion that Don Juans are misogynists or latent homosexuals, as if there were something unnatural and unhealthy about chasing women. As George confesses to Lester, he went to beauty school to get girls. As Hawn put it, *Shampoo* was "a message [Warren] wanted to get out, a part of his story that he wanted to talk about."

But that was only the beginning. As he repeatedly made clear when he distanced himself from George, he also wanted to bury, once and for all, his reputation for being a sexual predator. Unlike Harry Horner, in Wycherly's *The Country Wife*, George is not a libidinal con man so much as a passive beneficiary of the prejudices of others. He almost never pretends to be gay; rather, he's a blank canvas on which others paint their fantasies—incorrect fantasies, as it turns out to their chagrin. They assume whatever it is they assume, and he merely refrains from setting them straight.

George is Paolo, the 1950s gigolo in *The Roman Spring of Mrs. Stone* transported to the era of *Playboy*, when sex had become benign, not destructive, or so it seemed. He is softer and more appealing than Paolo, and unlike him, George's goal is pleasure, not money, so much so in fact that he can't help jumping into bed with Lester's wife and daughter while he's trying to get a loan from him. As Towne once said, he's a naïf, an innocent, a natural child, the dumb blonde. Or, as Dick Sylbert once wittily observed about Beatty's screen persona, he always plays the girl. Despite his toughness and self-assurance, he also displayed traits traditionally associated with women, like his insatiable appetite for the telephone, his ability to listen, his taste for manipulation and indirection instead of forthright displays of power, and his capacity for empathy—when he chose to employ it. Moreover, the attention he lavished on himself provided him a window into the world of female vanity, as it was conventionally defined. Throughout his career he not only eschewed action roles, he has avoided any kind of physicality at all. (He was even dubious about riding a motorcycle for *Shampoo*.) His characters never get into fights, and despite his athleticism in high school, he only twice played an athlete—in *Heaven Can Wait* and *Love Affair* (a retired athlete).

George is rarely moved to seduce anyone; rather, he lets himself be seduced and used by everyone else. He's passive and reactive, juggling his women, true, but often as not dropping a ball. He tries to manipulate his girlfriends, but he's too clumsy, and they end up manipulating him. Again, Beatty mocked his off-screen image, as he did in his other films, worked against it, underplaying his intelligence by impersonating limited, not-so-bright men. Despite the fact that he was tall, and used his body to intimidate when he wanted to, here he needed to appear vulnerable, unthreatening, as Towne understood when he tweaked Beatty's scene with Hawn so that he delivered his lines sitting down instead of looming over her. Women wanted to take care of him. He massaged the behavior he displayed in real life to make it more sympathetic. As Ashby recognized, the innocence and vulnerability he so skillfully projected, using the tics and mannerisms he fostered—the soft-spoken, hesitant speech, the downward cast of the eyes, the aw-shucks shit-kicking dance with the feet—combined to create the impression that he was no more than an overgrown kid, rubbing the edges off what might otherwise appear to be an unappealing character. The film renders George nonthreatening by portraying him as a hapless, not-too-bright bumbler who, if he hurts those around him, hurts himself more. He is his own worst enemy. As he is left standing on the side of Mulholland Drive, staring despondently at the distant expanse of the city beneath him watching Jackie go off with Lester, we feel sorry for him.

With George (and Beatty—innocent by association) firmly established as a victim, less predator than prey, the star then moves on ingeniously to turn feminism to his advantage by arguing that women are exploiting him, not the reverse, all demanding their pound of his flesh. As he put it, "Men over thirty have a hard time accepting *Shampoo*'s easy acknowledgment of the fact that there are women today to whom men are merely sex objects. They're upset, unsettled by the theme that says promiscuity is no longer just for males, that there are women who enjoy uninvolved, unemotional sex encounters. . . . Feminists are delighted at having a stupid male sex object that they can talk about."

By 1975, fierce feminist manifestos like Germaine Greer's *The Female Eunuch* and Kate Millett's *Sexual Politics* were starting to gather dust, but the fires they ignited still burned hot. Feminists were repudiating the sexual revolution of the 1960s as no more than another instrument of male domination. Always a formidable dialectician, and thus armed, Beatty blithely applauded women's right to turn the tables on their oppressors, and used it to defend the Don Juans of the world. Far from being a male chauvinist, George was performing a crucial service by becoming a sex toy for emancipated women.

Beatty's sleight-of-hand wasn't entirely hypocritical; at times he undoubtedly felt like a sex toy, even if a self-created one. He complained about the burden of having to live up to women's expectations. He felt that they anticipated that he would flirt and flatter, and that they would be disappointed, slighted, even angry if he didn't come on to them. They expected that he would take them home, and give them the sexual satisfaction of a lifetime. He felt that he had to be user-friendly. "Many times I'm called upon to perform," he sighed. "And it just won't happen. I'm busy, I'm thinking about other things, I'm worried about Julie . . ." or Joan, Natalie, Leslie, Michelle et al. He had a stock excuse for those occasions when he just wasn't up to it. He would say to a complete stranger, "I'd love to fuck you, except that—" and then he would come up with an excuse that got him off the hook. He fortified himself with vitamin therapy—B complex, E, and lecithin—to pump up his thyroid. Imagine Bill Henrickson in *Big Love*, amplified a thousand times. It wasn't easy being Warren Beatty.

But at the same time that *Shampoo*, like *Splendor in the Grass* fifteen years earlier, waged a campaign against libidinal repression, and rescued the sexual revolution from feminist backlash, it shows some sympathy for civilization, if not its discontents. If George is not the predatory spider at the center of a web of seduction, he is a wild child who has so rent the fabric of the domestic contract—as loosely woven as it had become in the 1960s—that he can't control the consequences. Beginning as a metaphorical apologia for Beatty's own conduct, *Shampoo* evolves into an auto-critique, as George devolves from a thoughtless hedonist to a plaything of others, to his own victim. As Beatty himself put it, rather unforgivingly, George "has an unsublimated libido, and is approaching middle age with no economic future. He is a product of the generation that believed in making love not war. He is ignorant politically and doesn't participate in the forensics of national survival. . . . He has scattered his sexual energies. Then, when things get tough, he tries to return to the nuclear family, but discovers he can't." In that same penultimate scene, when he's staring down at Jackie leaving in

Lester's limo, any sympathy we may feel toward him is leavened by the recognition that he is merely getting his just deserts. The film renders a judgment as harsh as any feminist might wish.

Tempting though it may be to take *Shampoo* as the star's mea culpa, his admission that he was on the wrong course, that his life of promiscuity, or serial monogamy as he preferred to call it, was bankrupt, Beatty watchers did so at their own peril. They forgot that Beatty is an actor who had drawn on his own life before, and that other films had ended with his character chastened or dead. In spite of the autobiographical elements in *Shampoo,* it is well to remember that the humbled George Roundy was not Warren Beatty. *People* magazine reported, when he got the Man of the Year Award from Hasty Pudding club at Harvard, that when asked for his opinion of monogamy by a fetching female reporter, he intimately fingered her necklace, while his other hand was on Michelle Phillips's knees. Phillips "hissed," "Warren, get your hand off of her!" He withdrew it quickly, as if he'd been burned, while Phillips turned to another reporter and answered for him: "He likes monogamy just fine." But he would not marry her, and *Shampoo* did not leave him a broken man, but an enormously powerful force in Hollywood, more so than anyone else, with the possible exception of Francis Coppola. (Had Power Lists been the currency of entertainment magazines then as they are today, Beatty would have been at or near the top.) Retribution, comeuppance, what have you—was for the movies.

Still, Beatty's was a precarious balance, and sometimes he overplayed his hand. He boldly participated in a panel during the second Women's Film Festival with Penn and Jeanne Moreau, moderated by feminist critic Molly Haskell. "I don't know what I was doing," he recalls. "Sometimes the urge to self-destruction just overwhelms you. Molly was wearing this flowing scarf, and suddenly I found myself wiping my glasses on it. I couldn't believe what I was doing. The audience was filled with feminists, and of course they started to hiss and boo." She was humiliated. Beatty, however, defused an ugly situation by offering to read their scripts—which of course was nonsense. At the end, they rushed the stage and swarmed all over him. Haskell recalls, "There was a lovefest with Warren Beatty."

Beatty and Phillips went to London for the British premiere of *Shampoo.* He wanted her out of sight of the British tabloids and shut her up in the hotel, which she didn't appreciate. She went back to L.A. in a snit while he continued the tour. He returned to New York, went to L.A., and was back in London in August. He was still occasionally seeing Christie, with whom he dined on the 25th at Leith's, a hip restaurant in Notting Hill. They sat at a prominent table under a spotlight. He was dressed all in white, she in a Gypsy outfit with a large shawl. They had a dignified argument. A week later they both returned to L.A., she to her Malibu house, and he to the Beverly Wilshire. "It's very strange," observed Phillips, "because I don't think they even like each other any more."

MEANWHILE, *The Fortune* had been screened for Columbia in New York, at 711 Fifth Avenue, the company headquarters. The audience was packed with every warm body in the building, the secretaries and kids from the mail room, as well as the executives. The lights went down, and the opening scene flashed on the screen, a long shot of Freddie (Channing) climbing out a window of her mansion and descending a ladder, while Nicky (Beatty) drives up in the foreground to collect her. There was nothing funny about it; in fact, it's too early in the film to know what's going on. But one member of the audience began to guffaw loudly. The others, some embarrassed and most puzzled, turned around to see who it was. It was Columbia CEO Alan Hirschfield, who actually stood up and apologized, said, "I'm sorry, I'm sorry, it's just in anticipation—and fear of course."

Hirschfield was right to be afraid. *The Fortune* was released on May 20, 1975, only three months after *Shampoo*. The actors acquitted themselves as well as could be expected. The problem was the script. Ostensibly a comedy, there isn't a single belly laugh from beginning to end. Despite the appealing premise, the film is so sluggish and unfunny it makes *Ishtar* look like *Tootsie*. Every once in a while the tedium is punctuated by pratfalls that have all the humor of a burst balloon. According to Dick Sylbert, "Warren told me he knew how to fix it, but nobody would listen."

The reviews, save for *The New York Times*, were dismal. In *Time* magazine, Jay Cocks wrote, "*The Fortune* is a bleak, frostbitten farce, desperate for invention and rather a sham." It grossed under $12.5 million. According to Devlin, "Mike was shattered by *The Day of the Dolphin*. Now he was shattered again when *The Fortune* fell on its ass after one week." He continues, "Warren was laughing, because in the course of making it, he came to detest Mike. And of course he was exulting in the success of *Shampoo*."

The Fortune proved that even the star-kissed Beatty Bunch could stumble. It seemed that the lavishly talented participants—geniuses all—not only believed their own press, but their friends' as well. As Frank Rich, who had been on the set in August, remarked in a dour postmortem published in *New Times*, "I heard the word 'wonderful' more times in ten days than I had heard it in my entire life. Everything was 'wonderful,' and some things were 'very wonderful' or even 'extremely wonderful.'"

IN 1975, Paul Schrader struck a deal at Warners to do a project called *Hardcore*, about a small-town girl who runs away from home to L.A., where she disappears into the squalid underworld of pornography, with Schrader writing and directing, and John Milius producing. On Thursday, February 26, 1976, Warners announced that Beatty would star as the father who searches for his runaway daughter, as well as produce and possibly direct. Once Beatty came on board, Schrader realized right away that he was in trouble. For starters, the star wanted to recast the script. "He felt that he was too young to have a daughter," says Schrader. "He wanted me to write it as his wife." The two men fell into bitter disputes almost at once. "I would go up to the Beverly Wilshire where he was staying, every morning, and then write every afternoon," he continues. "I'd argue with him in the morning, batter him down and win. I'd go home, and go back the next morning. He would start right where we left off. The same argument. I'd win again. And I'd go home. After about four or five meetings, I realized that I was going to have the same argument over and over until he won it. As for me, I just felt defeated. It got to the point where I wanted to throw the typewriter and say, 'Look, you write the fucking thing, you know?'" When it was all over, Beatty asked him, according to Schrader, "'Do you want to write *Reds*?' and 'Do you want to write *Howard Hughes*?' And boy, I thought, I just want to go home. Get me out of here." Ultimately Schrader did direct the picture, with George C. Scott in the Beatty part.

By August, when Beatty withdrew from *Hardcore*, it was reported that his friends in politics warned him not to do the picture, and some interpreted Beatty's departure as an indication that he was planning to run for office. Meanwhile, his affair with Michelle Phillips was winding down. Like some of Beatty's other women, Phillips came to feel the relationship was one-sided. "Two people cannot both live for one person," she says. Phillips felt suffocated. She wanted a career in movies, but "Warren didn't want me to act. He wanted me to be with him all the time. . . . [After a while,] I couldn't live under the same roof with him; we were fighting all the time." She was offered a part in *Valentino*. "Warren would tell me, 'You can't do [the] film because we'd be separated at Christmas,'" she continues. "It didn't seem to occur to him that he'd cheerfully spent Christmas alone for years when he lived in a hotel." She adds, "When I told him I was going to do *Valentino*, he said, 'Well, that's probably the end of our relationship.'" She added, looking back, "I knew that [it was over] when I came back after doing *Valentino*, but it took us a while to finalize the breakup." In 1978, she explained, "The last year was very difficult. The relationship became so neurotic. . . . I was with somebody who didn't make me happy and I didn't make him happy. But there was this terrible need to clutch at each other. We were both terrified it was going to be another failure and we were both acutely aware that people would say we could never make it with anybody because we were too selfish to care about anybody. Which is what they do say about Warren now. Then came the day when I finally realized that Warren was never going to tell me it was over. He'd much prefer me to do it. He doesn't want to take the responsibility of anything not working out. I realized it would always be a part of his personality to evade the issue, and I'd have to make the decision." When he failed to renew the lease on a beach house they had together, "I finally faced up to it and got out." She moved into a small apartment. Phillips added, "Warren never reacted at all."

One of Beatty's friends commented, "Warren is not a cruel person, but he does start to get careless. He doesn't try to hide restlessness or boredom. He's a hint-dropper, and he gets less and less subtle until the message hits home. He has a thing about leaving on good terms, so he never wants to be the one to walk out." Characteristically, he manipulated the women into such untenable positions—often by being flagrantly promiscuous—that they had no choice but to leave. Continued Phillips, "That is what Warren makes his women do." She adds, "When Barbara Walters asked him about all the women in his life, he said, 'Well, they always broke up with me, I never broke up with them.'

While I was watching the interview, I was holding my stomach laughing so hard [I fell] on the floor. That certainly is the strategy that works for some men. But you can't go with a hundred different women and a hundred different women reject you, over and over again when you're such a wonderful person." Phillips thinks he manipulated women into leaving him because he was worried about his reputation. "He's always tried to have the image of a very serious person. I'm sure that he didn't want to be looked upon as a predator. But once Warren and I broke up, we did break up. I left him, don't forget. I got to save a little face too."

On this subject, Beatty was quoted as saying, "The decision to end an affair is never mine. And it's never without considerable cost. Where sex is involved, you become very vulnerable and when separation takes place—God, the pain. Even the promiscuous feel pain." In regard to his inclination to play the victim in these relationships, writer Peter Feibleman says, "He was the best-looking, most successful stud in Hollywood for a very long time. He has to say, 'She was right, I was wrong.' He has to be the girl in the relationship. You have to denigrate yourself a little. Because otherwise they will bury you. That's the correct position for any gentleman. And above all, Warren Beatty is a gentleman."

Sometime after Beatty and Phillips had ended it, she encountered filmmaker James Toback on a plane. Speaking of Nicholson and Beatty, she told him, "'One liked to watch football the whole day and one liked to make love the whole day,' and I'll leave it to you to figure out who was who," he recalls. "She told me how much in love she'd been with Warren, and how addicted she'd been to him. So addicted and dependent on him that she couldn't get away. Still, she felt she had to, and when it was her birthday, and he asked her what she wanted, she said, 'Since I can't say no to you whenever you call, but I know I really should, what I would like as a present is for you not to call me and ask to see me anymore.' And he didn't."

Singed by her passage through the Beatty flame, it took Phillips a considerable amount of time to get over it. "I was emotionally churned up when Warren and I split. . . . and for the first time in my life I finished up on a psychiatrist's couch. I was terrified I was going to end up in therapy for years." In 1978, she said it took her a year to realize that when he said, "I want to marry you . . . I want you to have my babies," he was just being agreeable, saying things he thought she wanted to hear. "I think he's probably emotionally crippled for life.

Warren knew that he would never live up to my expectations. It wasn't that he couldn't. He just didn't want to. He feels that marriage, or a one-woman relationship isn't a happy, productive life. He feels that it's shallow, meaningless, and boring. So he has a stream of shallow and meaningless relationships all the time. He makes a point of not getting too close to you. The closer he gets, the more afraid he gets. And so he goes off and has another meaningless affair. . . . He thinks they're healthier, or at least the only kind he can have."

It has always been said, even by Phillips, that Beatty raised Chynna like his own child, but she also disputed this. "He loves people thinking that he's really concerned about children," she said, also in 1978. "But it's just an image. He never really put himself out to care, only when it was convenient to him. . . . They did like Warren, but only so far as they knew he couldn't give them much. So they didn't expect much from him."

Phillips's state of mind was suggested by the title of her first and only solo album, *Victim of Romance*, released in February 1977, as well as several of the cuts: "Paid the Price," "Baby as You Turn Away," "Having His Way," and "No Love Today."

Years later, Phillips has mellowed. "I don't have bad memories of our time together," she says. "I grew a lot through my relationship with Warren. I learned a lot about myself, a lot about human nature. It was a great experience for me, and we're still very good friends."

BEATTY HIRED his first cousin, David MacLeod, to help him with *Reds*. MacLeod was the son of his uncle, Alex MacLeod, his mother Kathlyn's brother, who had been hit by a car and killed. MacLeod senior had enjoyed the distinction of being the only Communist Party member of the Canadian parliament. Among other things, David had been a speechwriter for Canadian prime minister Pierre Trudeau. He was six feet tall, slender, with fair hair, thinning, and glasses. MacLeod watched Beatty's back. He was everywhere and nowhere, the only person Beatty fully trusted. If the star was secretive and suspicious, MacLeod was more so. He was loyal, energetic, and detail-oriented, but he used to say about his cousin, somewhat enigmatically, "Warren's gonna be the most interesting guy you could ever talk to, and he will walk you right up to a big pit, and will get more even more interesting as you get closer to that pit. But it's up to you to make your way around it."

Friends like Towne tried to discourage Beatty from making *Reds*. The star ran it by Gary Hart, who responded, "Give me a break." The great cinematographer Néstor Almendros, a Cuban exile and bitter foe of all things red, told him, "Listen, you can make pictures about homosexuals, you can make pictures about murderers, but you cannot make them about Communists!" Beatty, who listened to everyone and no one, was undeterred.

Reds would be a sprawling, three hour and twenty minute homage to the high passions that animated the largely forgotten American left in the years before, during, and after World War I and the Russian Revolution, two upheavals that changed the course of the twentieth century. The resulting film is an achievement nearly unparalleled in the history of American cinema—ambitious, complex, and entertaining in equal measures. It is partly a biopic, centered on the short but eventful life of the writer and radical John Reed, one of the few Americans buried in the Kremlin, whose account of the bloody birth of the Soviet Union, *Ten Days That Shook the World*, is a classic of political journalism. The film is partly a love story, re-creating Reed's tumultuous relationship with fellow journalist Louise Bryant, partly a historical drama that chronicles, among other things, the rise of Bolshevism and the birth of the American Communist Party, and partly a documentary, one that rescues from obscurity thirty-two survivors of that period who knew or knew of Reed, and serve as a kind of Greek chorus.

Born to comfortable circumstances in Portland, Oregon, in 1887, Reed went to Harvard. Once he cast off the remnants of his bourgeois background—says Beatty, "It took me quite a while to get over the fact that he was a cheerleader"—he found his calling as a would-be poet, journalist, and rebel, torn between his aspirations to art and to political activism—a conflict with which the star was intimately familiar. And, like Beatty at the beginning of his career, when the actor's dating games made him a fixture of the gossip columns, he had something to prove. He was too much fortune's child—too good-looking, too well off, too talented—to be taken seriously. Upton Sinclair once dismissed him as "the playboy of the revolution," a phrase some applied to Beatty as well, fairly or not. (Walter Lippmann, however, once described Reed as someone with "an inordinate desire to be arrested," a charge no one could have made of Beatty.) Reed wooed the bold and the beautiful of his time, like salonista Mabel Dodge, famous for bringing D. H. Lawrence to Taos, New Mexico. He was an adventurer, inexorably drawn to the action. And in the teens of the last century, the action was on the left, among American unions like the Wobblies (the Industrial Workers of the World), and in Mexico, where peasants were breaking eggs with their machetes, and even more so, in the seething cauldron that was czarist Russia. The love of Reed's life was Louise Bryant, the dentist's wife he lured to New York from Portland to join the ranks of the artists and revolutionaries who peopled Greenwich Village, among them Eugene O'Neill, Edna St. Vincent Millay, Emma Goldman, Max Eastman, Dorothy Day, and so on. Bryant too had large appetites; she had an affair with O'Neill, among others; covered World War I from the trenches of France; and accompanied Reed to Russia, all the time struggling to carve out her own career.

Reed went to Russia three times, first in 1915 to cover the Great War, then in 1917 as a participant-observer in the Russian Revolution—he was in Petrograd when the workers seized the czar's Winter Palace—and again two years later to plead for Bolshevik accreditation for his newly formed Communist Labor Party. While he was away in 1919 the infamous Palmer Raids decimated the ranks of the American left. Reed wished to return to America regardless, but the Soviets refused, arguing that he could better serve the revolution in Moscow than sitting in a U.S. jail. He persisted, tried to cross into Finland, and ended up in a Finnish prison. (There is some evidence that the Bolsheviks colluded with the Finns to stop Reed from leaving.) With phony papers and in disguise, Bryant made the perilous journey to Russia to find him. But by the time she got there, he had been released to the Soviets, and spent what little was left of his life working in the propaganda ministry, writing and making speeches. The couple was reunited, but Reed died on October 17, 1920, three days before his thirty-third birthday, of typhus and a stroke. Bryant succumbed much later, in 1936, a drug addict, boozer, and pauper.

The night after George McGovern was nominated by the badly divided Democratic convention in Miami in 1972, Beatty holed up in a hotel room for four days and wrote. Eventually he produced about twenty-five pages and a step outline, but he had gone about as far as he could go on his own and needed a proper writer. The star would finance script development out of his own pocket, as he did *Shampoo* and would also do with *Heaven Can Wait*. He considered collaborating with Lillian Hellman, Budd Schulberg, and/or Paddy Chayefsky, but decided against all of them for the same reason: "It can be very hard for one generation to collaborate with an older generation," he says. "You owe it a certain level of respect and when you're collaborating you have to be able to take the gloves off.

"I realized that I had to get back before Stalinism and get into a frame of mind that had to do with a much more idealistic period that was Marxist and early Leninist, you know, pre-NEP [New Economic Policy]. That I had to get into a much more naive state of mind about it. I wanted to collaborate with someone who would hold my tendency to be sentimental in check and would keep up my interest in what some people undoubtedly would call 'the minutiae' of the movement."

In 1976, he met Trevor Griffiths, a successful British playwright whose London hit, *Comedians*, Mike Nichols was then taking to Broadway. A prominent left-wing intellectual, Griffiths wasn't about to get his head turned by a celebrity. He was burly and pugnacious. According to Jeremy Pikser, a protégé of Griffiths's, "Trevor felt, 'I'm a Marxist historian, a playwright. You're a Hollywood movie star. What do you have to tell me about how to do the story of John Reed?' I couldn't imagine two less likely people to have an effective collaboration."

It was clear to Griffiths that Beatty identified closely with the subject. "Warren spoke as if he was the reincarnation of Jack Reed," Griffiths says. "Reed was a golden boy, and I would get the sense as we talked, that he thought he'd been born to play him. Or, Jack Reed had been born so that Warren could play him!"

Jerzy Kosinski, whom Beatty would cast as a Soviet official, Grigory Zinoviev, said the same thing. "Warren saw himself as John Reed. . . . Beatty's *Bonnie and Clyde* was like Reed's book about Pancho Villa — gangsters shooting at one another. And Beatty's *Shampoo* was about the morality of the middle class, like John Reed's little articles about the minor failings of America. Political fellatio. . . . Warren looked for a big subject, just as Reed also looked for something big to report. . . . The project of making a movie about John Reed became what going to Russia was for Reed. It would affect his life."

Beatty courted Griffiths, offered him a ride (with Candice Bergen) up to Connecticut for Nichols's wedding to Annabel Davis-Goff, an

Irish-American writer. "He asked me in the car if I knew anything about John Reed," Griffiths recalls.

"'Well I know a bit, what do you want to know?'

"'I don't want to know anything, I know everything about Jack Reed.'

"'Oh, you're Warren Beatty, I'd forgotten.'"

Beatty understood why Griffiths might be sarcastic and was undeterred. He called Griffiths again at Nichols's place a week or two later. "We were sitting down to dinner," Griffiths continues. "Mike answered it, and said, 'It's Warren Beatty, he'd like a word with you.' I said, 'Jesus Christ, I'm eating.' Mike said, 'If I were you I'd talk to him.' I went to the phone, and Warren said, 'Now look, I actually started making a movie about this guy ten years ago. And people tell me that I would be an idiot not to ask you to do it.'"

The two men huddled in New York a couple of weeks later. Beatty says he showed Griffiths everything he had written. "He could tell that I was somewhat willful, that is to say, not as malleable as many screenwriters maybe are," Griffiths continues. "So he was very careful in suggesting that there was plenty of room for my own creativity. That was the wooing stage, where [he] said, Listen, you're the writer. There was never any question of co-writing, it was just a question of my doing it."

Beatty wasn't exaggerating when he told Griffiths that he knew all there was to know about Reed. Before returning to London to work on the script, Griffiths made a pilgrimage to Widener Library at Harvard, which housed the Reed Collection. He opened the visitor's book. "And there, ten years previously, right at the beginning was 'Warren Beatty,'" he recalls. "It was a bit unnerving that he had done that kind of research." Indeed, Beatty loved researching his pictures, especially one like *Reds*, probably because he dreaded actually starting production. (He also picked the brain of historian Robert Rosenstone, who was writing a biography of John Reed. When Beatty first met him, he opened with, "Let's trade John Reed fuck stories.")

Beatty was devoted to making his life and his work appear effortless, and he would rarely admit that it wasn't, but one stressful day a few years later when he was preparing *Dick Tracy*, screenwriter Bo Goldman recalls him doing "this strange kind of—it was almost balletic—cave-in as he twisted himself downwards until he collapsed on the floor. I said, 'What's the matter?' He told me how depressed he would get when he was beginning to shoot a picture, and he wanted to lie down and die. He said, 'There's a hundred people out there who think they can do it better than you.' "

Griffiths and Beatty started work on the script in the fall of 1976. The playwright didn't know how to type, and Beatty did, sort of, so the star sat at the typewriter pecking out dialogue. The playwright explains, "It wasn't the best way of working in my view. But it was the only way we had. He certainly didn't want me to go away and do it myself. He took scene after scene and used another argot, the language of Manhattan, 1977, '78, '79, employed by certain sorts of stylish intellectuals, very much of our time, nothing at all to do with the 1910s and the 1920s. What he finally wrote was what he wanted."

One day, Goldman spied Beatty and Griffiths having tea at Rumplemeyer's on Central Park South in the dead of the afternoon. The two men did not appear to be speaking, and Goldman thought, That poor sonofabitch, I'm never going to work with Beatty. I'm never going to be in Griffiths's shoes, and of course soon I was.

6

ORSON WELLES, C'EST MOI

How Beatty directed his first film, *Heaven Can Wait*,

hustled the cover of *Time*, began dating Diane Keaton,

and embarked on *Reds*, the greatest challenge of his career.

"When he discovered that he could direct, he didn't need Buck Henry anymore. Warren pushed him into the background and just took over."

—*Paul Sylbert*

WHILE GRIFFITHS WAS working on "The John Reed Project," Beatty's mind wandered. But he kept returning to the idea of a romantic fantasy, because that's what he wanted to see himself. He was depressed at the time. A couple of his friends had died. Appropriately enough, the romantic fantasy he kept returning to was a comedy of resurrection, namely, a remake of a 1941 picture, *Here Comes Mr. Jordan,* with Robert Montgomery, Evelyn Keyes, and Claude Rains. Montgomery improbably played a prize-fighter named Joe Pendleton, who is nearly killed in a plane crash. An overly zealous heavenly gofer harvests his soul prematurely, but his body is cremated before the error can be rectified. Joe's soul is temporarily parked within a shady millionaire named Farnsworth, who has just been drowned by his wife, Julia, and his male secretary, her lover. Eventually, it moves on to a more appropriate home in the body of another boxer, enabling him to win the big fight at the end of the picture. "Something about the theme didn't seem small," Beatty said. "It was dealing with death and reincarnation. That made me want to see it particularly." Beatty bought the rights from producer Jed Harris for $25,000, and hired Elaine May to write the script.

Albeit a much more gifted writer, May was in some respects the East Coast Carole Eastman. Or, more accurately, she was to Beatty what Eastman was to Nicholson. "They were very different," says Buck Henry, who would polish the script and co-direct with Beatty. "Carole was scared of everything; Elaine was fearless. But they had some of the same problems in their writing, an inability to condense and get it organized."

May was best known for being one half of Nichols and May, the celebrated stand-up comedy team that had performed *An Evening with Mike Nichols and Elaine May* on Broadway from October 8, 1960, to July 1, 1961. She was a full-blown eccentric, brilliant and wacky in the extreme. Someone once said of her, "She knew the subtleties of Scandinavian drama, but she didn't know if Mexico was north or south of the United States," and it was true. She could get lost in a closet. Richard Burton is reputed to have remarked, "Elaine May is the most fascinating, maddening girl I have ever met. I hope never to see her again." Screenwriter Bo Goldman remembers May from the early days of live television: "She was very, very difficult, very crazy. I was associate producer on a *Playhouse 90* thing called 'A Pane of Glass,' about a mental institution, and she was playing a catatonic. Elaine was supposed to say one word, but she refused to say it. John Frankenheimer directed it, had enough of her meshuggena behavior, and fired her."

In 1969, May directed her first movie, *A New Leaf*, with Walter Matthau, Jack Weston, and herself. She went over budget and tried to remove her name from the picture. She followed that with a modest hit, *The Heartbreak Kid* (1972), from a Neil Simon script, with Charles Grodin and her daughter, Jeannie Berlin, but in 1973 she shot a disastrous caper movie, *Mikey and Nicky*, with John Cassavetes and Peter Falk. *Mikey and Nicky* proved fertile soil for the full flowering of her looniness. The film went way over schedule and over budget, and ended in a series of lawsuits. Paul Sylbert, who worked for Elia Kazan (*A Face in the Crowd*), and Alfred Hitchcock (*The Wrong Man*), was her production designer, and likes to tell a story that has become the stuff of legend. "It was two o'clock in the morning, and we were still shooting on South Street in Philadelphia," he recalls. "She'd already fired the cameraman, and the operator was now the new cameraman. We were shooting a scene between the two guys, and we were shooting for an hour, two hours. Finally John went off this way, Peter went off that way, and the camera was still running. And running, and running. Finally, the operator figured, I gotta call 'Cut!' Elaine hit the roof. 'Whaddya mean, "Cut?" I'm the director, I'm the one who says "Cut"!' The operator said, 'But there's no one in the frame.' She replied, 'But they might come back!'" As one wag put it, "Elaine May is a woman of many words. However, the word 'cut' does not happen to be among them."

Beatty first met May in 1964. May was attractive, but, as Paul Sylbert says, "There's nothing sexual about Elaine. 'I did that already,' was her whole attitude towards sex. It was almost English." According to May's friend, Peter Feibleman, May and Beatty never had an affair. "If you were a female, and you were seen with Warren, it was just assumed," he explains. "She liked him, but Elaine was too savvy to be one of those girls on Warren's list. The minute sex got into it, she would have been dead in the water. She became the person he talked to. She was like a guy when the three of us were together." He recalls once sharing a joint with Towne in Beatty's kitchen. Towne said, "'You know, I've got a little boat, a sailboat. Do you like sailing?'

"'I love sailing. I grew up on Pontchartrain,'" Feibleman replied.

"'You wanna come sometime, you're welcome. But there's one rule I'm ruthless about: If you come aboard, you have to bring pussy. Otherwise you're gonna hit on the pussy that's there, and there's going to be unpleasantness, and a fight, and I won't have it. I'll leave you on the dock if you're alone.' He was stoned and he kept saying, 'You have to have pussy, you have to have pussy.'

"'All right, all right, what about Elaine?' I was living with Elaine, which he didn't know.

"'Naaah, she doesn't have to bring anybody!' It was like that. Elaine was a guy!"

Beatty was well aware of her foibles, especially glaring when she got behind a camera. But he also recognized her gift, liked her, got her. As Paul Sylbert puts it, "Ideas fly off her like lint." And he was only hiring her to write. He had asked her to polish *What's New Pussycat?* back in

1964, but she declined. When he asked her again, more than a decade later, to work on *Heaven,* she accepted.

Beatty put her up at the Beverly Wilshire. One day his assistant got a call from the hotel, "Where is Warren? Elaine May has just left the hotel, we want him to see the room." May was notorious for her slovenliness. Her lipstick was smeared. Whatever she had eaten that day was all over her clothes. She looked like someone else had dressed her, buttons mismatched with button holes. She smoked cigarillos and couldn't be bothered with ashtrays, so the ashes just fell anywhere, usually on herself or the floor.

In addition to May, Beatty also hired Feibleman to work on the script. "All directors think they're writers, but most are not," Feibleman says. "The ones who think they are are usually the ones who are not. But talking to Warren was not like talking with a Hollywood director. It was like talking to another writer."

Beatty set up *Heaven* at Warner Brothers. But once again, as with *Shampoo,* there was trouble. Business Affairs began to nickel-and-dime him. Says Paul Sylbert, whom Beatty hired to design the picture, "Warren wasn't happy, at Warners. Elaine couldn't get the script finished. She had a draft, and he was trying to make it work, so he was writing, plus whatever he got in from other people. Plus, Warners was bugging him to turn it in." There were other issues as well. The estimated budget was reported at $6 million. "Perfectionist" is the scariest word on a studio lot, one that sends executives running for the hills, and Beatty's reputation for getting things just right just didn't sit well with the Warners front office. CEO Ted Ashley felt, in his words, that "Warren, who was among the most finicky, obsessive people, might take a picture that we thought was commercially marginal, and bring it to the point where we'd lose a bunch of money." According to one source, Beatty wasn't coming up with a budget for the heaven scene. President Frank Wells pressed him, Beatty procrastinated. Wells pressed him again, Beatty put him off again. Wells and Beatty were both tough negotiators; they pushed each other's buttons. Finally, Beatty met with the Warners brass shortly before they were scheduled to begin production. Wells asked him again for the numbers on the heaven scene. Beatty was evasive. When the star looked away, Wells mouthed "asshole" for the others to see. Irritated, Beatty said, "Do you want to make a budget, or do you want to make a movie?" Characteristically, Wells, an attorney and a numbers guy, wanted to make a budget. Recalls Beatty, "They just kept irritating and irritating me, finally they wouldn't let me have a water cooler, and I said, 'Look, if I can't have a water cooler, lemme try to make this picture somewhere else, and if I can't make it I'll bring it back. Give me one day.' They did, and I made a deal somewhere else." Wells appeared happy to let him go. He and Towne had gone to the same school, played water polo. Wells had been the goalie. Towne quipped, "He's still a goalie. He won't let anybody score."

Wells would live to regret it. Beatty always had a backup. He hadn't forgotten that Charlie Bluhdorn had been a stand-up guy when Beatty was trying to get backing for *Shampoo*. He had devoted his considerable charm to wooing Barry Diller, whom Bluhdorn had just installed as the head of Paramount. Beatty knew that few were immune to his charm, and most often it got him what he wanted. He had known Diller through Democratic campaign politics since the executive's days at ABC. Diller had assembled a team of exceptionally able young Turks, some, like him, recruited from television—Michael Eisner, Don Simpson, and Jeffrey Katzenberg. Beatty understood that Diller, like David Begelman when he got to Columbia, would be desperate for product.

Bob Evans was in Atlanta with Diller and Eisner, at a test screening of *Black Sunday*. According to him, Beatty called, said, " 'I got in a big fight with Warners today, fuck'em, I'm not gonna make the picture there.' I told this to Barry, right after the preview, he took the corporate plane, and flew back. He was with Warren all day Saturday, all day Sunday, and by Monday morning, *Heaven Can Wait* was a Paramount film. That shows how hungry Diller was at the time." The studio agreed to give Beatty $3.5 million, payable in three stages, plus a percentage of the gross, with escalators at specified levels of profitability. The picture was announced in the trades on March 4, 1977. The budget was about $9.5 million, excluding Beatty's fee.

By July of 1977, Beatty had squeezed as much out of May (and Feibleman) as he could. To him, no script was ever finished, every script needed work, and this one wasn't any different. He also needed a director. He had still never directed himself—officially, at any rate—and even though he was edging up to it, he was still not his own first choice for the job. "I just think Warren didn't want to try this first one all by himself," says Paul Sylbert. "Maybe he thought that the studio would be happier with a directing team." He approached Arthur Penn and

Mike Nichols. Both declined. He gave the script to Peter Bogdanovich, who also turned it down.

In a flash of inspiration, Beatty realized that Buck Henry might be able to do both, rewrite the script and co-direct—and even do some acting. "I wanted a writer on the set, and I didn't think it would be rewarding enough for him to follow a number of other screenwriters, and so I said, 'Come in and co-direct,'" Beatty recalls. "He was very smart in the way he dealt with me. Because when I would obsess about certain things, he would be amused by it, tolerate it, not get upset by it. He'd sit there reading *The Nation* or *The New Republic.*"

Henry was a military brat, believe it or not, the son of an Air Force general. He went to Dartmouth. "Buck was into every scene imaginable," recalls a friend. "He was incredibly funny, very repressed, very prurient, almost like an adolescent. He was always interested in fringe people, strippers and weirdos." He lived in a basement apartment on 10th Street in the Village that he shared with a life-sized stuffed gorilla that made its home on the living room floor. Henry never took off his pajamas, simply flinging his street clothes over them when he went out.

Henry had a dry and unforgiving wit that he wielded like a rapier. It cut so fine his victims didn't even know they'd been sliced until well afterward, when a gout of blood gushed from the wound they didn't know they had. He quickly made a name for himself on *The New Steve Allen Show, That Was the Week That Was*, and *Get Smart*, with Mel Brooks.

Henry was smart and levelheaded, a gregarious man who had to be at every gallery opening, every new theater piece, every concert, every party. Best of all, Henry was needy. After being profiled as "the hottest writer in Hollywood" in *The New York Times Magazine* in 1970 for *The Graduate* and *Catch-22* (he also wrote *The Owl and the Pussycat*, and rewrote Peter Bogdanovich's hit *What's Up, Doc?*), Henry was marking time. Once a year he hosted *Saturday Night Live*, then in its heyday, and did some occasional writing for the show. Despite the fact that Hal Ashby had been extremely unhappy on *Shampoo*, Henry, knowing that his days as flavor of the week were over, had no qualms about co-directing with Beatty. "I knew Warren a little bit, liked him," he says. "Except for actors, everybody [who works with him] ends up so bitter that they have a skewed vision of what actually takes place, and you never can quite piece it together. Much as I loathed some of the script—because I don't believe we come back—I knew that it was going to work." He added, "Warren gets me real cheap all the way around, because it was my big chance. I accepted immediately." There was no discussion of ground rules, what to do if they disagreed. As Henry puts it, "We both knew that he had final say, that was a given, and as Warren said, quite sensibly, 'It doesn't matter who says "Action!" Or who says "Cut!" Anyone can do it.'"

The day Henry set foot on the Paramount lot, he was flattered by a banner draped over the front gate that said, "Welcome to Paramount, the Home of Buck Henry." He continues, "Of course, a few days later, there was a sign that said, 'Welcome to Paramount, the Home of Charles Grodin.' Warren seduces the actors. He is a master manipulator."

Henry did not share Feibleman's high opinion of Beatty's skills as a writer. "My sense is that Warren orchestrates," he says. "He doesn't like writing that sounds like writing. He thinks that it has to sound like behavior. He doesn't like subtext in dialogue. Let the actor provide whatever subtext there is. So he's very big about scenes where people say, 'I feel like having a hamburger.'

" 'Well, I don't.'

" 'Okay, then we can eat later.' "

As Beatty began to cast the picture, he thought of Muhammad Ali for the role of the boxer, and first Cary Grant, then Eugene McCarthy for Mr. Jordan, the heavenly host. Dyan Cannon turned down the role of Julia Farnsworth three times, but Beatty wouldn't take no for an answer, and accompanied by Henry paid a call on her at her home, where they finally persuaded her to take it, despite the fact that she referred to something Henry had done, he recalls, as "that piece of crap." Elaine May persuaded Beatty to hire Charles Grodin to play Farnsworth's secretary, Julia's co-conspirator and lover. Jack Warden, whom Beatty had used to such good effect in *Shampoo*, played the trainer, Max Corkle. Ali's schedule apparently precluded his participation, and both Grant and McCarthy declined the role of Mr. Jordan, which eventually went to James Mason. Henry was cast as Mr. Jordan's assistant, aka the Escort, and Beatty played the lead himself, now a quarterback instead of a boxer. The big fight became the Super Bowl.

Beatty hired William Fraker to shoot the picture. Fraker had shot

Rosemary's Baby (1968), *Bullitt* (1968), and had recently finished *Looking for Mr. Goodbar.* He also asked Bob Jones, who had cut *Shampoo,* to edit this one as well. He called Howard Koch Jr., who had been first AD on *Parallax View,* and since then had worked on *Chinatown.* Koch told him, "Warren, haven't heard from you in a couple of years. What's goin' on?" Characteristically, Beatty replied, "Um, nothing much. But I want to talk to you about something."

Koch met with him at the Hideaway, a little bar on El Camino tucked into the Beverly Wilshire, where, along with the Hamburger Hamlet on Sunset, Beatty liked to hold meetings. According to Koch, he said, "I'm gonna do a remake of *Here Comes Mr. Jordan,* and I'd like you to work with me on it." Beatty asked him to be first AD and executive producer.

"Why me?"

"Because I don't think there's anybody else in town who could put together the Super Bowl the way you could. I want you to be the AD and the executive producer on the movie." A little flattery does wonders, and such was Beatty's gravitational pull that Koch overlooked his reservations. "Warren was a great producer," he says. "He had taste, style, and power within the studio system. In 1977, as tough as Diller or any of those guys were, Warren could walk into any studio head's office, and they wanted to be seen with him, they wanted to do a Warren Beatty movie. No one could say no to him. So he was able to squeeze more out of tight-fisted executives than anyone. And not only could he talk to studio executives, he could talk to people all the way down to the lowly guy in craft service, and get him to do the job the way he wanted it done. That doesn't necessarily mean you come in on schedule and on budget. It means you deliver a great movie, and then nobody cares. And he really wanted to make great movies."

Koch knew that Beatty was famous for his parsimony. He had a habit of inviting people to lunch and forgetting his wallet. Says Paul Sylbert, "Warren never spends a dime. His secretary, Helen Feibelmann, said that in twenty years he had never given her so much as a birthday card." So Koch was encouraged when Beatty picked up the check.

With all the other parts cast, only the female lead, Betty Logan, the earnest, ecologically minded feminist with whom Pendleton falls in love, remained. Every actress in town wanted the role. Beatty and

Henry tested them all, including Diane Keaton, who was hot off *Annie Hall* and had *Goodbar* coming up. "She was my idea for the part," says Henry. "I thought we needed an all-American non-glamour-puss who should be able to do bits of comedy, which she can do. Warren barely knew her when she came into the office. His first remark about her was, 'Did you look into her mouth? Fort Knox'—meaning, a mouth full of gold fillings. Which was very Warren-like, peremptorily rude. It's not intentional, and it's not unintentional, it just is what it is."

After every test, Beatty would turn to Henry and say, wistfully, "She's no Julie." He and Christie were not on particularly good terms. She had no interest in acting in the picture, but Beatty wanted her. Recalls Henry, "We did this pretend search for a lead actress, and I didn't realize this was a pretend search until late in, after hearing, 'But she's no Julie' for the fiftieth time." There were two months of, "Is it going to be Julie or is it not going to be Julie." Beatty had to send David MacLeod, whom Christie liked and trusted, over to Wales, where she was living in a farmhouse in Cefn-y-Coed, Montgomery, to intercede for him.

Continues Henry, "It was part of David's job to pacify Julie, keep her happy. Eventually, she gave in. I know I'm ascribing master mechanics to Warren, but I think he always knew it was gonna be Julie. But they were so edgy that he also knew—he's so weirdly smart about this kind of shit—that at the end of this movie, he wasn't going to be able to say, 'Julie, I want you to look me in the eyes in this scene,' without her getting irritated. He needed a buffer, a go-between with her, somebody who could take the place of the director, and say, 'Just stare at him while he's talking.' That was me." (It didn't hurt that Beatty is said to have secured her services by making her a very rich offer.) Adds Koch, "When he finally got her, he was ecstatic. He thought she was the right person for the movie, but he wanted to get back with her in the worst way, so it was also, 'Do I have a chance to get her back?' And she was the one he could never get back."

Once Christie had been cast, her character had to be rewritten as a Brit, which was Henry's job. He also wrote dialogue for himself, James Mason, and the servants. "I think he had more confidence in Elaine than he did in me," Henry remembers. "Perhaps rightly so, because Elaine's stuff was brilliant, off-the-wall brilliant. Warren was always yelling at me, 'Will you finish the fucking scene and stop writing jokes!' Then we'd tear it up. I would write a scene, and then Warren would say, 'This is just a joke, isn't it?'

" 'Yes. It will make the audience laugh.' "

In May 1977, Beatty had hired a twenty-three-year-old bushy-tailed assistant fresh out of the University of Chicago graduate school named Hal Lieberman. Lieberman was about to wed, and Beatty, whose opinion of the institution of marriage had not improved since he had split up with Michelle Phillips, tried to discourage him, saying things like, "I'm not going to let you do that, it's worse than a funeral, you're an idiot."

Rubbing his eyes, as if to make sure he were fully awake, the young assistant instantly found himself transported from the musty stacks of the Regenstein Library to Beatty's inner circle, which consisted of MacLeod and Helen Feibelmann. Lieberman, who later became president of Universal Pictures and is now a producer (*Terminator 3: Rise of the Machines*), recalls, "I've never met anybody so fuckin' self-involved. I liked Warren, but he was the sun, and everything around him was a satellite. Everything, everything—was all about Warren Beatty, whatever his needs were, minute to minute, day to day, whether it would be a cup of tea, or whatever—your needs, other than illness needs, were secondary. He did have kindness in him, but he had a side of him where you didn't really exist in his world. He meant everything to himself.

"I was on call twelve, sixteen hours a day, seven days a week. He told me, 'Whatever I need you're going to get for me. And you better get it.' Once he wanted fresh cranberry juice. It was out of season, and I said, 'I can't find this.' He said, 'That's not what I want to hear.' It was like, My God, this is a guy who expects to get what he wants. Eventually, the prop master got it for him. It was a lesson to me: for a guy like this, you had to dig deeper.

"Every morning before we went to the set, we'd take a schvitz. They closed down a health club, the two of us would go, and sit there, looking at each other, for an hour, in the steam. He had a nice body, and he wasn't uncomfortable being naked. He wasn't modest. But he wasn't an exhibitionist either. His dick was normal, not ridiculously big."

Both on the Paramount lot, and on location at Filoli, the Georgian mansion near Palo Alto designed by Willis Polk in the early twentieth century, where the exteriors of the Farnsworth scenes were shot, Beatty was besieged by girls. Lieberman continues, "There were always a handful of women who were circling. I never knew where the fuck they came from, from Warrenville. He'd ask, 'Who am I fucking right now?' Warren enjoyed messing with your head." Beatty would part the curtains on the windows in his office, peek through and say, "That one's pretty, bring her in." Lieberman went outside, and asked, "Do you want to meet Warren Beatty?" He recalls, "When Warren would be busy, part of my job was entertaining the girls. Keeping them company while they were waiting for an audience with him. They would always say, 'I won't sleep with him.' Then they would be with Warren, and—bang! Because he definitely has that thing. He just turns on the spotlight, and you're on stage. Even when he met my wife, he got up in her grille. It was like, 'Dude, turn it off. I'm married to her!' He didn't want my wife; this is just who he is." Beatty continued to needle Lieberman about being married. "He'd say, 'Don't you want to fuck this one, don't you want to fuck that one?' 'Why'd you get married, are you insane?'" Depending how busy he was, the girls would file in and out at odd hours of the day. If he was asked, "So, how's the day going?" he was liable to say, "Another day of fucking and sucking and coming in their hair."

Not everyone Beatty invited in looked like Christie. One person who watched this scene unfold, fascinated, observed, "I think that Warren could have been choosier. Some of the women weren't worth running after. They were less than plain, overweight, and mustachioed." Lieberman once said to Beatty, "You're Warren Beatty, why don't you get some standards? How can you let some of these girls blow you?" Beatty looked at him blankly, as if he were speaking a foreign language, and replied, "Why not?"

HEAVEN CAN WAIT began production late in the summer of 1977. Directing for the first time, Beatty was, as Koch describes him, "like a kid in a candy store." First and foremost an actor himself, he liked actors, trusted them, and was good with them. If ever there were a filmmaker to whom the axiom "casting is nine tenths of the job" applied, it was Beatty. He cast the best, and empowered them, gave them the permission to go for it, made them feel comfortable, beguiled them, and then goaded them beyond all reason, drove them, infuriated them, bored them, broke them. He didn't impose his vision on the actors so much as squeeze them until they wept with frustration and gave up whatever it was they were holding back.

As a director, Beatty often behaved as if collaboration was the heart of the directorial process. If he trusted his lieutenants, he delegated, let them do their jobs, and nothing was too insignificant for him to require their input. Paul Sylbert says that he never needed to either intimidate nor manipulate Beatty the way he did Elaine May and other directors he worked for: "I never tried to block Warren from doing something. Because he never did anything that would hurt the movie. He just lets you do your job. Kazan did the same thing. Hitchcock did the same thing. He's not a Hitchcock, and he's not a Kazan, but he's up there with these people. His mistakes—and we all carry the seeds of our own destruction—come from the fact that he is what he is, but that's also what produces the good stuff."

Nevertheless, no one was more aggressive about asserting his directorial prerogatives than Beatty; no one exercised more control over every single aspect of making and marketing a movie than he did. And no one was more relentless in accumulating credits.

Acting, directing, and producing, all at the same time, took its toll. It tired him out, made him irritable. Koch continues, "Warren doesn't come off frightened. You don't see that side of him. Even if he doesn't have an answer for something, or doesn't know what he wants, he's not going to let on. He would do it in other ways, by not giving us answers. But he was a frightened guy. Who isn't insecure? He is human." Paradoxically, wearing so many hats offered him some protection, allowed him to indulge his customary elusiveness. As Henry puts it, "When you take on that many functions—dealing with the cast, the money, the studio, there was all this stuff on top of where do we put the camera and what do we put in front of it—you can always be somewhere else. You can always say, 'I'd like to discuss this with you, but I gotta go see to that.'"

All of this took time. "He agonizes over decisions, so you can imagine how slow this process is," says Sylbert. "Sins of omission are his biggest fears. His whole life is done that way. Very careful. Cautious. I've always thought he has two brains. Just like a cow has got two stomachs. He ruminates. It goes from one to the other."

Video assist, a new toy that enabled directors to watch the scene they have just shot instead of waiting days for the rushes to come back, was intended to speed things up, but for Beatty, it just provided more cud to chew on. "*Heaven Can Wait* was one of the first movies where you could actually come back and watch yourself on video," says Koch. "Warren likes to look at himself, and he likes to look at all the other actors, and the fact that he could not only be in the scene as an actor, watch the scene live as the director, and then watch it again on video, took an awful lot of time. I used to say, 'Do three or four takes, then come back and look, because every time you go back and forth, all of a sudden it's an hour. And we're way behind schedule. Warren didn't care."

Grodin defends Beatty's slow pace. "I was sitting in on a scoring session with Warren on *Heaven Can Wait*," recalls Grodin. "The music techies said to him, 'You should spot the music and how long.' Warren replied, 'We're not making hamburgers here. I can't just snap my fingers. I'm not sure.' The techies rolled their eyes. A lighting crew will think nothing of spending five hours setting up lights, but if the director spends more than a minute talking to the actors, it's indulgent. It's no coincidence that people like Warren make the better movies. If you want forty pictures a year, you don't go to him. If you want something that's going to be around for a decade, you do."

Still, says Koch, "I had to put up with a lot of shit from Warren. When you're making a film, your director needs to make decisions. I would say, 'Okay, Warren, we're movin' outside, we're gonna shoot out in front of the big tree.' Because we had discussed it. He'd get out there and say, 'I don't know, do you really think we should be out here in front of this big tree? Maybe we should be inside.'

" 'Warren, we're here, the whole company's here, the light's right, we're ready to go—'

" 'I don't know, maybe we should be inside.' The reason he's difficult is you can't get inside his mind. I want that man who's my boss, the number one creator, to tell me what he's thinking so that I can tell the DP to light it the right way, whatever. Warren is someone who keeps everything to himself. A lot of times, when he does a lot of takes, he may not even be paying attention, he's thinking about something else. Or he wants to see how far he can go. So the difficulty with Warren is not just one thing."

Koch's pièce de résistance, the scene for which he was hired to orchestrate, was the Super Bowl sequence in which the Rams were ostensibly playing the Steelers. In fact, it was shot during halftime of a preseason game between the Rams and the Chargers at the L.A. Memorial Coliseum on September 1, 1977. The production was given a grand total of fourteen minutes to shoot everything that was needed. "I had to get two football teams, cheerleaders, coaches, referees, all out there," he recalls. "I had to have all six cameras in the ready positions, and Warren had to be in the scene. But we were thrilled, because therefore he couldn't control it. Billy Fraker and I controlled it. Warren caught the immaculate reception—he threw the ball, it got tipped, popped up in the air, he caught it behind the line, ran down the field for the winning touchdown and got put up on everybody's shoulders—at least seven or eight times."

When those fourteen minutes had elapsed, the Rams and the Chargers returned to the field. Beatty came up to Koch and said, "No, no, no—I want to shoot more."

"We're done here, Warren. We're done."

"No, no, no, we can't be done, we didn't get enough." Koch continues, "He was so upset, he was seething through the whole second half that I had let him down, because I couldn't hold back the NFL! After the game was over, we kept shooting all night long. When he saw the dailies, he was thrilled. The difficulty was, he never wanted to let any day go, any scene go, any anything go, and he'd hold it as long as he could, before giving it up, say, to the editor to edit."

Despite Buck Henry's upbeat attitude, co-directing with Beatty was no picnic, and the arrangement did not last long. It was *Shampoo* redux. Says Koch, "Warren was the director. It was very difficult for Buck, very difficult. It wasn't about what Buck needed from the movie, or what Buck could give to the movie, it was about what Warren could suck Buck dry for, all the humor, all the far-out ideas that Buck would have that Warren would use and probably call his own."

Henry had the otherworldly detachment of an extraterrestrial, and it helped him take adversity in stride, but irony, even in the hands of a master like Henry, goes only so far. The more power Beatty got, the more he indulged in his penchant for perfection. "Certainly Warren is the only director I've ever really had fights with," Henry says. "They weren't so much about aesthetics as about tactics: the camera's here, but maybe if it were just two inches over there—that stuff. He liked to worry things to death. We used to fight about a lot of dumb things—

they weren't dumb to him—it's midnight, he'd say, 'I don't like take 32. Let's do another.'

" 'It's fine, we don't need any more.' I think shooting an overly high number of takes tires out the actors. He feels that everybody who's working for him is on call twenty-four hours a day, all the time. So it's, 'Let's do another two hours.'

" 'Fuck you, we've got to get up at six.'

" 'What, you're going to bed now? We're not going to talk about tomorrow? We need to work on this. I want to talk more about it.'

" 'I don't. We'll talk about tomorrow, tomorrow. I'll see ya later.'

" 'Wait, stick around, don't leave the set yet.'

" 'Everyone else has left the set. I'm leaving the set!' Very often, he wants you to argue with him so that he can pick the opposite of what you're arguing: Should I wear the gray pants or the black pants? I think you should wear the gray pants. I know he's going to pick the black pants. After a while I used to think that the way to get him to do something was to argue the opposite. It's like when you're driving, and you just know when you choose to go west, you should have gone east. So you go east, and it's the wrong choice. It's that double think. I would never know what his original opinion was when these arguments came up.

"At one point, Warren said, 'I think we should get rid of the character actors.' We were in the middle of shooting. I said, 'What the fuck are you talking about? Are you crazy? They're all wonderful. They're all doing exactly what we want them to do.' 'Course, almost all of them were friends of mine that I'd cast, servants in the house. I think he was testing me, but I don't know what the test was for. Maybe how much power he had over everyone, which he always liked to do."

Henry had a couple of bad weeks in Palo Alto while they were working at the Filoli mansion. James Mason used to drawl softly, in his amused, world-weary way, "Poor Buck, what a burden he has to carry. He just has to get used to being treated that way." Henry continues, "It was always about, 'Defend your position. You really think that blah blah is true?' " Beatty had a way of leaning in while he was arguing that Henry found intimidating or, as he puts it, "He was climbing up on your shoes, moment by moment. Then sometimes Warren expressed real anger at being at odds with whomever it was he was having a disagreement with. He does not like to be crossed, even about simple, stupid things."

According to Dick Sylbert, "Warren beat the shit out of him. Humiliated him every day. Just like he humiliated Bob Towne. Warren said to me after *Heaven Can Wait* that he hated Buck because he works very hard, and Buck doesn't. Buck reads a magazine. You're shooting a scene, and he's reading *Scientific American*."

At one point, Henry thought, Let's not pretend anymore that we're co-directing this. I should just go home. But he couldn't go home because he was still acting in the picture, and some of his scenes were yet to be shot. He was frustrated, unhappy, and very angry, very suspicious: "Warren'll put the heat on and turn it up as high as he can to the point where people either almost quit or actually quit. They get exhausted and walk away. Whether it's just a concomitant of the way he works, or whether he likes to make people walk away — 'cause in the worst-case scenario, some people believe it's so he can take the credit. I don't know whether he does it consciously — he doesn't do much unconsciously — or not." (Henry did get co-directing credit, although he did not get writing credit. The script was attributed to Elaine May and Warren Beatty.) Henry was never sure about Beatty's motives. He said to himself, That prick will not make me quit. I knew if I quit, my credit would go with me. At other times, he thought, No, it's just his style, just unnecessary attention to a kind of detail that buries the bigger picture. He continues, "The other side of it would be that sometimes he would make a mistake that was so wrong that when it showed up on screen, he would just laugh hysterically at the idea that he'd been thinking the way he'd been thinking, something that dopey. That's always endearing. He has a fabulous sense of humor. If he didn't, he'd be unbearable. You'd have to kill him."

WRITER-DIRECTOR Jim Toback would fill the locker room buddy slot vacated by Towne. He wasn't as good a writer as Towne, didn't have the range, but he was just as bright, just as grandiose, and like Towne, talked a great movie. He grew up wealthy on the East Side of New York. Toback went to Harvard and graduated magna cum laude. He worked as a journalist, writing on Norman Mailer for *Commentary*, among others, and shared Mailer's posture: the tough guy intellectual. He eventually secured a contract to write a book about Cleveland Browns superstar running back and actor Jim Brown. Toback was a compulsive gambler, often putting six-figure sums on the table. He would shift fistfuls of hundreds from his "unlucky" pocket to his "lucky" pocket.

Like Beatty, Toback had an active mind, knew a lot about a lot of things, was well read, loved Mahler, etc. etc. In short, he was good company, and kept Beatty entertained. Better, Toback was not going to compete with Beatty. If anything, he already had his own reputation as a dedicated womanizer, possibly even more skillful than Beatty, because he needed to be; he had less to work with. The two of them were companions in mischief.

Fingers was the first film Toback directed. It was based on his own script, starred Harvey Keitel, and was released on March 2, 1978. Pauline Kael gave it a rave. Toback had known Kael slightly, but her review turned the acquaintance into a friendship, cemented in part by their mutual loathing of Andrew Sarris, who had given *The Gambler,* which Toback wrote, a bad review. "When he walked into a room, she would actually flush," recalled her friend Richard Albarino. "Like a schoolgirl. Like she had a crush on him." (Toback says he never slept with her.)

Toback ran into Beatty at a party thrown by actress Lucy Saroyan in Beverly Hills. Saroyan drew him toward the actor, saying, "You might not believe it, but this guy gets as many girls as you do." Beatty replied, "Oh, I would believe it very easily." Flattered, Toback thought, Boy, does this guy know how to seduce people. He called Beatty at his office the next day and said, "We met at Lucy Saroyan's party last night, and I have a script that I'd like you to do."

"Well, send it over."

"I'll read it to you."

"I know how to read. You can send it over."

"I know you know how to read, but you'll only see it if I can read it to you first."

"Well, that's ridiculous."

"Well, that's the way it is."

"What have you directed?"

"I wrote *The Gambler* and I directed this movie called *Fingers.*"

"Let me see *Fingers.*"

"Okay, I'll arrange a screening for you."

"Fine. How about tomorrow?"

"Fine." For eight days in a row, Beatty canceled the screening. Finally, on the ninth day, Toback told him, "You know, if you don't want to see it tonight or can't see it tonight, then let's just forget this and I'll just move on, because this has gone on too long."

"I'll see it." That night Toback showed it to him and Ali MacGraw. After the movie ended, Beatty paced around the screening room, excited. According to Toback, he asked, rhetorically, "Do you know how good this movie is?"

"Of course I know how good it is."

"How did you get Keitel to do these things?"

"It wasn't difficult. He's a bold actor."

"Let's go out to dinner." The three of them left the screening room, heading for the Four Oaks on Beverly Glen. Beatty led the way in his chocolate Mercedes 450, driving fast, so fast that Toback thought he was trying to lose him. Over dinner, Toback read him and MacGraw the script, called *Love & Money*. Beatty told him, "I'm going to buy it."

Beatty couldn't decide whether or not to produce *Love & Money*. His relationship to Kael was prickly; he resented the condescending way she treated him in her reviews, and privately he disparaged her and the Paulettes, referring to them as "Ma Barker and her gang," but he flattered her by asking her advice about Toback. He recalls, "I thought he was off his trolley, and I was going away to do *Reds*. She said, 'Do *Love & Money*. Forget *Reds*. Why make a film on the Communist Party?'"

A lot of Beatty's friends couldn't understand what he saw in Toback, and why he, who had never produced a film for someone else, and took years to get his own off the ground, suddenly decided to launch *Love & Money*. "Jimmy made him laugh a lot," says Henry. "I think that's mainly what it was about. I'm not convinced Warren thought Toback was as skillful a director as Toback thinks he is. But then nobody could be."

Moreover, Beatty liked bad boys. Toback was someone with whom the star could share the joy of cruising, reveal his dark side, if that's what it was, someone to whom he could expose the unsanitized Beatty, the part of himself that he took great pains to conceal from all but his closest male friends, like Towne, Nicholson, Evans, Polanski, and Dick Sylbert. Overweight, slovenly, and profane, Toback was Falstaff to Beatty's Prince Hal.

Toback worked out of Beatty's office at Paramount with him on the script intermittently for a couple of months through the production of *Heaven Can Wait*. "I got to hear the endless spieling about what this secretary or that would allow him to do," recalls Henry. " 'If I could just come on her leg, that's all I really need, is to play with my nipples and just . . . ' Hilarious." One day, Toback picked up a young woman and talked her into coming back to the office with him. According to him, he had her up against the wall and was jerking off on her, when he sensed someone behind him. Turning his head, he discovered Henry, watching him. Henry met his gaze without embarrassment, and calmly said, "Proceed." (Henry has no recollection of this episode.) In this three-ring sexual circus, Beatty's act, however impressive, seemed positively mundane, even boring.

NEEDLESS TO say, the script work on *Heaven Can Wait* continued into and through production. "The script was Elaine's, but it was doctored, changed, fooled with, rewritten, all of which went on for the entire production," recalls Paul Sylbert, who had a novel under his belt and wrote a couple of scenes himself.

Like others, Sylbert registered Beatty's vanity with amusement. As he puts it, "When Carly Simon writes a song called 'You're So Vain' about him, you have to accept the fact that he's vain! He didn't pussyfoot around it, he just said, 'I'm what's important!' "

Beatty was a student of the camera. He understood the impact of different angles and lighting on his looks. Early in the movie, he clashed with Fraker—they later became fast friends—because he didn't think the DP was showing him off to best advantage. "He was tough on Fraker," says Henry. "It always came down to the same thing: Warren asking for a little more, a little more, a little more. Their fights would end in yelling. They were 'Fuck you,' 'No, fuck you' fights."

Sylbert recalls, "Warren would see the dailies, and if there were kicks of highlights off the banister rail when he was coming down the stairs, like Joan Crawford he got very upset. Because it took the attention away from him."

There is one scene, after Pendleton has been reincarnated as Farnsworth, where Beatty is standing in front of a triple mirror in Farnsworth's dressing room, he is getting into his polo gear. The door out of the dressing room is to the right. He's looking in the mirror, the camera is slightly behind him, off his left shoulder. You see him in three quarters figure, and you see his reflection. He has to say, "Okay, I'm leaving." Recalls Sylbert, "Any human being would turn to his right and go towards the door. Warren, on the other hand, turned to his left, made a complete pirouette, a circle into the camera, and then went out the door!"

But says Henry, "The dividing line between vanity and camera understanding is thin. You do things for the camera that you wouldn't do in real life. It's like when you're on stage, you're trained, if you're facing the door, to turn to the audience on the way out. Warren knew that his success was at least partly due to the fact that the camera really liked looking at him. It's the same thing Cary Grant knew."

Adds Sylbert, "Cary Grant and Warren were pretty close, and he learned from Grant too, picked up these do's and don'ts from hanging around these people and seeing how they operate. Like, he was using mascara on every movie. It accented his eyes, made them prettier. My ex-wife, Anthea, had to talk him out of it on *Shampoo*." Another trick involved putting the camera twenty-five feet away, and shooting his close-ups with a long lens, which supposedly took four years off his age. While Sylbert was working on *Heaven Can Wait*, he was moonlighting on a project for Marlo Thomas, who was a friend of Beatty's. He recalls, "He gave her a list of the Ten Commandments for Being a Movie Star—how you deal with interviews, what you do with makeup, how you act in this situation, questions about appearance—and he stuck to them."

Beatty's hair, which was thick, long, and dark, was one of his best features. He washed it with a six-pack of beer every morning to make it glossy, give it luster and body. But male pattern baldness prevailed among the men in his family, and he had a bald spot on the crown of his head the size of a silver dollar. His hair was so thick that he was able to conceal it for the most part, but if anyone alluded to it, it made him crazy. Losing his hair was one of his worst nightmares. For Hal Lieberman, it humanized him. "He was an unbelievably great guy," he recalls. "The fact that he was a human being made him a greater guy. Who wants to be absolutely perfect? But maybe he did."

Beatty suffered from hypoglycemia, which made his face swell. Lieberman kept ice packs ready to calm the pouches that popped up like toadstools under his eyes every morning. The cameras couldn't roll until they subsided.

"There was a lot of waiting around," Henry says. None of the actors appreciated it. Grodin explained, "Warren Beatty believed in having everybody made up and in costume for what seemed like just about every day. He had worked with Robert Altman, and Altman did it because he might at any moment decide to put one of the actors into a sequence where the script didn't have them. Warren, on the other hand, never did anything like that, but had us all made up and in costume anyway because of the possibility he *might*." Years later, when Grodin was in the Bay Area and trying to decide whether to visit Filoli, the scene of all that waiting, or San Quentin, a high-security prison, he quipped, "I'll take San Quentin . . . maybe because *Heaven Can Wait* was filled with so much waiting, that the estate is scarier than the prison."

David MacLeod tended to Julie Christie, driving her around, doing her errands. Says one source, "David used to bring around all these pretty boys." Christie brought a group of friends with her from England, and they rented a house near Palo Alto, played a lot of volleyball, topless, except for her, although Grodin remembered going to a pool party there where she was "walking around bare-breasted." The rumor was that she and Beatty weren't speaking. "The worst battle I ever saw was between Warren and Julie," says Sylbert. "God! Ranting. Screaming. He finally walked out [of her dressing room] raging, He said to me, 'I just raised my voice in there. I *hate* that.'"

"Warren took the position of slightly ignoring her," says Feibleman. "Once he was looking at something on TV in his trailer on the Paramount lot. There were six, eight people there. He picked up the TV and put it where everybody could see it except Julie. She was sitting with her face to the back of the set. She just giggled, and got up and moved her seat. Their fighting was playful. And sullen. He was like a child whom you've displeased."

"I'm not sure Julie ever wanted to make this movie," says Sylbert. "Through the whole thing she was not happy. She had no great regard for him as a director. She didn't trust him." Adds Koch, "She didn't like the character, she didn't like anything. And then she broke her arm roller-skating right near the end of shooting, which really pissed him off, 'cause he wanted to finish the picture. There was this great moment with Julie and Warren, where they were at the limousine. It's goodbye, because he knows James Mason's gonna pull him away. He was saying to her, 'Look, somebody might come up to you someday, it may even be a quarterback, ya know, but give 'em a chance.' He gives her a kiss. Well, in the first rehearsal, it was just a peck. And Julie said, 'Warren, you're supposed to be in love with me, goddammit, what kind of a kiss is that?' He said, 'All right, Julie,' so in the second rehearsal, he gave her—I mean, a *kiss*. Julie said, 'You don't have to fuck me in front of everybody, just give me a kiss like you love me!' With that, Warren broke out in hives. I swear. Because nobody could get to him the way Julie could get to him. And we couldn't shoot. But he got back at her, with the famous close-up of her at the end of the picture, where the quarterback, Tom Jarrett, says, 'You wanna get a cup'a coffee or somethin'?' And she recognizes him, and replies, 'You're the quarterback.' Eighty-five takes. It was, Warren going, 'One more.' 'Whaddya want, Warren?' 'One more.' 'One more.' 'One more.' To the point where she was crazed." According to Michael Childers, whom Beatty had hired to take stills, "She was crying, she was in hysterics for days. Warren would never tell her what to do, what to change, just, 'Do it again, do it again, do it again'"

Christie complained to Henry about having to look Beatty in the eye, ironic in that looking Joe Pendleton in the eyes, seeing into his soul, into his essential self, no matter the material husk in which it is hidden, was essential to the plot. He'd ask Henry, "Would you please tell her to look me in the face when we're saying this stuff, and not look off into the corners." She, on the other hand, begged Henry, "Pleeease, don't tell me to look him in the eyes. Pleeease don't make me have to." Henry recalls, "I said, 'You have to. You have to look in his eyes to see who that person is.' They displayed this peculiar sort of affection, but at its best it was like Beatrice and Benedict."

Indeed, there is a scene in the movie in which Beatty and Christie are walking through the rose gardens of the Filoli estate. He is wearing a stylish leather jacket, and she the haircut she hated, the one she sneeringly called her "dolly girl" hairdo, which made her look like Little Orphan Annie, at best obscuring her face, and at worst making her look foolish. In the film, romantic music is swelling up on the soundtrack, drowning out their conversation, wherein Christie was saying, in her clipped British accent, "I can't believe you're still making these fucking dumb movies when, I mean, there are people all over Europe making fabulous films, about real things, Fassbinder and so on, and you're still doing this shit," and then she'd smile at him as if butter wouldn't melt in her mouth. Beatty just laughed, but there it was again, the old itch that needed to be scratched: Was he a serious filmmaker?

"EVERY NOW and then in my life, I would run into a woman—particularly in foreign countries—someone I'd always dreamt about, and very often, one of the first things they would say is, 'How's Warren Beatty? Have you seen him lately?' And a deep depression would fall over me," says Henry. "I know dozens of women that [Warren had sex with that] nobody knows about. One of the reasons we had such a good time, in between the times we didn't have such a good time, is that, I would say a name of someone, from maybe twenty, twenty-five years before, that I knew in New York that no one else I knew knew, and Warren would either say a word, or do a physical thing that allowed me to know that he knew exactly who I was talking about and knew her as well as I did. And these were not movie stars. These were strange people. He is the Pro."

While the production was shooting at Filoli, Henry won a football pool worth around $500. He was friendly with the Mitchell brothers, notorious San Francisco pornographers best known for their film *Behind the Green Door* (1972), with Marilyn Chambers, the former Ivory Snow girl (it was made for $60,000, and grossed $25 million). Henry, who took sex seriously, or as seriously as he took anything, had a girlfriend who worked at their theater, the O'Farrell at 895 O'Farrell Street. "I rented a couple of buses and took a few cars, and almost the whole crew on Buck's Magical Mystery Tour," he recalls. "The Mitchells gave me their theater, girls included. Everyone had a great time, watched fifty or sixty girls doing live shows, really spectacular stuff."

Dubbed "the Carnegie Hall of public sex in America" by Hunter Thompson, a longtime patron, the O'Farrell contained five different rooms, in Henry's words, "the famous Wall Dancing Room where you stood in little glass booths and looked at an arena type stage in which girls would whip each other, play with toys, and perform various unspeakable acts." In the famed Kopenhagen Room, about twenty people would sit at tables arranged around the perimeter, drinking, snorting coke, and smoking dope. The girls would hit the deck, performing at the feet of the spectators, who were given flashlights to shine on them. The girls backed up onto the tables, bent over, and offered up their butts to the guests. "I was surprised Warren came, because he was very careful about public stuff," Henry continues. "But he did, and he enjoyed it very much." Recalls Lieberman, who was sitting next to Beatty, "The music was blaring, the booze was flowing, and there was probably some blow as well. The girls were all over us, and you could eat them as well. Warren was egging me on like crazy." Henry goes on, "Some of the girls came back to Palo Alto with us. Several days later, my girlfriend told me that the clap was running through the theater, and that any of us who cared to might do well to take a shot of penicillin." Recalls Koch, "Warren came up to me about a day and a half after our visit to the Mitchell brothers, and said, 'You gotta find me a doctor and get me a penicillin shot, and fast.' He was already sick." (The brothers went out of business in 1991 when one killed the other.)

Heaven Can Wait wrapped, after about eighty-five days, running just a little over. It cost about $11 million. "I vividly remember the very last night of the shoot," says Henry. "We were back in L.A. on a set at Paramount, it was late, two, three in the morning, the last scene, everyone was saying goodbye to everyone, and Warren was sitting at an editing machine over in a dark corner of a dark stage, looking at takes. He stayed there as everybody drifted out and went home. It was like a movie, the artist in the gloom, looking at take after take, not saying goodbye, just letting everybody just sort of walk off into the night and dissolve. Of course it kept him from having to be sentimental about anything. I think he likes to avoid those moments. For me, it was a telling tableau, about his reluctance to fit into the kind of friendly set culture of it all. Although when he wants to he can be more charming than French presidents."

Knowing how angry Henry was at the time, people always asked him if he would work with Beatty again. He once said, "I can't imagine that anyone would ever direct him twice," but, having mellowed (or needing work), he also said, "I know that he can make one miserable, but it doesn't matter in the long run because the work is usually interesting, and that makes up for it." Christie, on the other hand, returned to England and didn't do another film for several years, devoting herself to "de-celebritisation." She recalled, "I'd rather talk to my ducks than some of the freaks I met in Hollywood." She added, "I thought I was going mad there."

Again, Beatty left some people feeling shortchanged, not only in regards to money, but in the credit department as well. According to a source, Koch's contract stipulated his name and title had to be displayed on the ads and the poster. He saw early in-house mock-ups of the posters, and his name wasn't on them. He asked Beatty, "Warren, where's my name?"

"Oh, it's a mistake, I'm sorry. It'll be on the next ones." The next version appeared, and he said, "Warren, my name's still not on the poster."

"Don't worry, it'll be there." When the poster was finally off the presses, his name wasn't on it. Beatty didn't return his calls. Koch had his attorney call Paramount. The studio said, "Warren Beatty told us not to put your name on the poster. The only name on the poster is supposed to be his." Koch was so desperate that his father, who was then president of the Motion Picture Academy, asked Lieberman, "Kid, I need you to get this done for my son, I need you to get into Warren's head." Says Lieberman now, "I couldn't fathom that Howard Koch Sr. would come to me, the gofer. Talk about going down the scrotum pole! But he knew I was with Warren all the time."

Heaven Can Wait was the first movie Koch had a piece of, and Beatty paid him the money he was due. Time passed. Koch was getting ready to do *Greystoke* with Towne. One day, he was in a bedroom of Towne's house at the beach, talking to Shirley MacLaine about something or other, and Beatty walked in. According to someone who was there, when he saw Koch, his face turned red. He said, "Oh, hi."

"Warren, why did you fuck me?" Koch asked. "Why do that to someone who worked so fucking hard for you, and why did you lie to me and say, 'Don't worry, it's a mistake?'"

"I never planned to have your name on the poster!"

"Why would you do that? Why did you want me on the film?"

"Nobody else could have done the Super Bowl like you did it."

As the production drew to a close, Lieberman's responsibilities grew weightier. "He was having me read scripts for him, do coverage," he recalls. "One day, he came back from New York grumpy, and he said, 'I want you to write down what you did last week, and I want you to write down what you're going to do next week.' I said, 'I'm not doing that, I know what I do, and you should know what I do.' So I walked out, and literally cried on the ride home, 'cause it was over. I thought I was special to him. He was like an older brother."

There's a scene at the end of the movie where Joe Pendleton, now in the body of Tom Jarrett, is in the locker room, cleaning up after the Super Bowl with his trainer and friend, Max Corkle, who is in on the secret. But Mr. Jordan has wiped Joe's memory clean, and he no longer recognizes Corkle. It's a sad moment, a death of sorts, and for anyone who knows Beatty, has felt the warmth of his attention, and then experienced the cold as it is withdrawn and turned elsewhere—the Liebermans of the world, the old flames, former friends—this scene has extra poignancy.

"Warren was always calculating exactly what he wanted to put out," Lieberman says. "There were those moments when he would hug me, but not many of them. My takeaway when I was done with Warren was that he was the loneliest person I'd ever met. He was able to disengage so easily, he was so detached."

Beatty evidently overcame his aversion to Keaton's gold fillings, because he started seeing her in the spring of 1978. Oscar night often marked the debut of a new flame. Keaton had won the year before for *Annie Hall*, when she beat Jane Fonda (*Julia*) and Shirley MacLaine (*The Turning Point*). Even Beatty—especially Beatty—was not above wanting a trophy girlfriend.

Slender, pale as porcelain, radiating an air of nervous intelligence, and displaying a quirky talent for comedy, Keaton was an original. She had an elliptical way of speaking in which sentence fragments bumped up against one another like cars in gridlock without ever hooking up into sequences that made a whole lot of sense. The eldest of seven children in an Air Force family from Southern California (her mother was once a "Mrs. Los Angeles"), Keaton came to New York as a teenager, got a part in the original stage version of *Hair* in 1968, and was the only member of the cast who refused to take off her clothes for the naked climax. She appeared in Woody Allen's *Play It Again, Sam* and *The Godfather*, both in 1972.

Keaton was adorable as Woody Allen's neurotic girlfriend in *Annie Hall*, and singlehandedly started a fashion craze with her gender-bending mix-and-match wardrobe of men's ties and trousers with women's skirts. "I remember the first time I ever saw Warren—I must have been about twenty-six—at the Beverly Wilshire Hotel," she recalls. "They used to have a bookstore there, and I was inside, and I looked out and saw him in the lobby. I thought, My God, he's so beautiful. It was like there was a light. He looked at me for a second, and then [his eyes] passed me by. I thought, I'll never know him. He'll never be somebody in my life." She was wrong. By May 1978, *Time* magazine was reporting they were an item. "I wasn't the Warren Beatty type, but there I was," she continues. "He was just so . . . overwhelming in every way. I remember looking at his face and just going, 'How am I here with this?' The brilliance and the talent, you get caught up in it."

To Woody Allen, it made a lot of sense. "Warren always liked bright women, and she's pretty and very, very smart. She always had a weakness for guys who were beautiful. Warren certainly was beautiful and he's smart too. I always thought they would have a lot to talk about."

Meanwhile, there was a film to market and release. Evans, who had an office across the way from Beatty's on the Paramount lot, loves to tell the story about the one sheet in which the actor is facing the camera dressed in sweats and displaying a fine pair of angelic wings. Evans remembers, "I got a call. 'Could you please come over to my bungalow?' I walked in. He took out the one sheet, and said, 'That's it. Whaddya think?'

" 'Warren, the crotch.'

" 'Whaddya mean?'

" 'You have sweat pants on. There's no crease. It looks like you have a pussy.' He picked up on it immediately. He grabbed the phone, and it cost Paramount $250,000 to make new one sheets with a crease in the crotch. It was the most expensive crotch retouch in the history of cinema. Paramount was so angry with me they almost threw me off the lot. Warren couldn't have cared less."

Beatty was approached by *Newsweek* for a cover, but parlayed it into a cover for *Time,* which had a larger circulation, by playing one against the other. *Time*'s cover line read, "Mister Hollywood," meaning that he had become far from an outsider, if he ever was one. Inside, Frank Rich wrote, "Having already produced two smash hits in his only previous tries, *Bonnie and Clyde* (1967) and *Shampoo* (1975), Beatty must now be regarded as a major film maker as well as a star." He predicted that *Heaven Can Wait* would "be the most popular entertainment of the summer." Rich called his performance "likable and funny," adding, "The movie has everything going for it . . . and best of all, a touching (but PG) romance between the hero and Co-Star Julie

Christie, who communicate largely through passionate eye contact, the heat of which has not been felt since Clark Gable and Vivien Leigh met in *Gone With the Wind*."

Heaven Can Wait opened on Wednesday of the following week, June 28, 1978, in New York and L.A., going wide on Friday. Presumably, enthusiastic word of mouth would drive the picture into the all important July 4th weekend, then considered the best slot of the summer. Recalls Koch, "I was there opening night in Westwood, when we were at the National, and the Ali MacGraw, Kris Kristofferson movie, *Convoy*, was down the street. There were lines around the block for us, and nobody at *Convoy*. We did a huge opening weekend. And the movie just played and played." *Heaven Can Wait* grossed $3.7 million the first weekend on 540 screens. (By way of contrast, *Grease*, the box office pacesetter that year, grossed about $9 million in its opening weekend on nearly twice as many screens.) In total, its domestic gross was $82.1 million, with rentals of $49.4 million. The trades reported that Beatty walked away with $15 million-plus for himself.

The picture got generally good, not to say, enthusiastic reviews, but Kael, who buried it in a longer piece entitled "Fear of Movies," a defense of violent films that must have made Crowther turn in his grave—how much things had changed!—was unimpressed. As damning as Christie, she compared it invidiously to *Bonnie and Clyde* and singled it out as an example of "safe" cinema. Mocking Beatty for being a credit hog—he's "the star (who is also the producer and the co-director and even takes a co-writing credit)," she derided it as a "prefab" film. "It wasn't bad," she continues. "Why, then, does it offend me when I think about it? Because it's image-conscious celebrity moviemaking; Beatty . . . wants to be a nice guy, the same way Burt Reynolds does in *Hooper*. They go soft on themselves and act on one cylinder. They become so *dear*—Beatty the elfin sweet Jesus, and Reynolds the macho prince who hides his saintly heart—that they're not functioning as artists; they've turned into baby-kissing politicians."

Kael was ridiculing what she considered Beatty's inclination as an actor to pander to his audience. But from his point of view, he was just playing to his strengths. He knew his limitations and stayed within them. He wasn't a character actor like Al Pacino or Dustin Hoffman or Robert De Niro. He was a leading man, and leading men play themselves, or versions of themselves. As Henry puts it, "There are certain actors who never stray very far from a central figure that they create. There are certain things either he doesn't want to do or he knows he can't do, or shouldn't do, and he stays away from them. If you listened to Warren's voice in half a dozen of his major performances, from Clyde to Joe Pendleton, and in between, he is always this quiet, stumbling guy, who uses a basic vocabulary of maybe a thousand words at best, kind of like Henry Fonda. It's a quiet, middle-class, Everyman voice. And that's been his strength. But in some cases it has been his weakness, making him unavailable for certain other things. To my ear it makes all his dialogue sound like it came out of the same writer." Future roles like Bugsy Siegel would show that he was smart enough to know that as an actor he had it in him to do more and better.

But Beatty wasn't there yet. He was still doing very well with his aw-shucks shuffle. As Paul Sylbert puts it, "He was good in *Heaven Can Wait*, because he was doing that side of him that's boyish and innocent, eager and honest. He has a lot of those qualities." *Heaven Can Wait* does tug the heart strings—it's virtually impossible to watch the last scene with a dry eye. The film dances on the edge of mawkishness, but pace Kael, never stumbles. It is poignant, not smarmy.

In retrospect, it's not so puzzling that *Heaven Can Wait* connected as well as it did. It is, as Rich pointed out, about love, death, money, sports, success, and idealism, all subjects close to the hearts of boomers. So far as Beatty himself is concerned, at least on one level, the film, again, is about himself. After all, he started as a football player—in high school—and ended up a millionaire, the way Pendleton does when he enters the body of Farnsworth. And Betty Logan influences Pendleton (she radicalizes him) in much the same way, we have to imagine, that Christie affected Beatty. She's Christie the activist, all sharp elbows, frumpy and aggressively political. Pendleton even plays the clarinet the way Beatty played the piano, which is to say, like the star, he's a sensitive soul, an artist in a jock's body, which he used to say about himself: he was too susceptible to play football.

Heaven Can Wait is a movie about acting as well, inhabiting different roles. But more interestingly, it is about acting in a larger sense— trying on identities, looking for the right fit between inner and outer. It may have seemed perverse in the extreme for Beatty to snipe at his good fortune, gripe about his perfect features, and he didn't, exactly, but like Pendleton the poet-quarterback, Beatty was an intellectual born into the body of a movie star. He was always trying to prove, as a young college dropout, that he wasn't just a pretty face, that he was more intelligent, more sensitive than his good looks might indicate.

Beatty called *Heaven Can Wait* a comedy of reincarnation, but it's actually a fantasy of incarnation, of becoming. Beatty, remember, was the star before he was a star, the celebrity before he was a celebrity, and his struggle had been to fill the vessel. The historical Clyde Barrow was known as "the phantom of the Southwest," just as Gary Hart called Beatty "The Phantom" for his peek-a-boo, now-you-see-him-now-you-don't dance between presence and absence in politics. It was the same with movies—he couldn't commit, couldn't or wouldn't pull the trigger, and the same—dare we say?—with his relationships, sexual and emotional. The latter were always the hardest. He had shown that he could play every role—actor, producer, writer, director—and play them well, just as it all comes together for Tom Jarrett—sort of. Jarrett can win the Super Bowl, but can he reconnect with Betty Logan? The film suggests maybe, leaving unresolved the question of whether or not Jarrett (or Beatty) can find his way back to who he really was. Paradoxically, *Heaven Can Wait*, a light comedy, a remake no less, an "entertainment" in Arthur Penn's term, is at the thematic heart of Beatty's work.

But regardless of the buttons it pushed, there is simply the fact that, in Paul Sylbert's words, "*Heaven Can Wait* is very well made. Warren is a good director. Most directors don't have a grasp of what it is they're making. He does. He doesn't always explain it, but there is something going on in his brain that is telling him that this is right and this is wrong. He does have an idea of what he's doing, and why he's doing it."

That same summer, while Beatty was getting serious with Diane Keaton, he started to see Jacqueline Onassis. Uncharacteristically, his loose lips sank that ship. He reportedly boasted to Andy Warhol, Bianca Jagger, and others, among them Studio 54 owner Steve Rubell, who allowed as how Beatty had told him "that he'd fucked Jackie O." When it got back to Onassis, she dropped him. At an old boyfriends party she threw on December 20, 1978, the two reportedly had an argument, and she was overheard telling him that he'd done something "disgusting."

When the Oscar nominations were announced on February 20, 1979, *Heaven Can Wait* cleaned up with nine, including Warden and Cannon for supporting, Paul Sylbert for production design, and Fraker for cinematography. Beatty himself was nominated for four Oscars: Best Picture, Best Actor, Best Screenplay, and Best Director. He was the first person to be nominated in four categories since Orson Welles in 1941 for *Citizen Kane*. But it was a tough year, and ominously, Michael Cimino's *The Deer Hunter* also got nine nominations, while Hal Ashby's *Coming Home* got eight. (The other Best Picture nominations were Alan Parker's *Midnight Express*, and Paul Mazursky's *An Unmarried Woman*.)

The Awards ceremony was held on April 9. Beatty took Keaton, and the two were observed holding hands. But they were upstaged by demonstrations against *The Deer Hunter* by Vietnam Veterans Against the War. The expectation was, not unreasonably, that the two Vietnam-themed movies would cancel out each other, leaving the way open for *Heaven Can Wait*. "Warren was sitting in the aisle," recalls *Deer Hunter* producer Barry Spikings. "He actually had his leg out—ready to go." But *Heaven Can Wait* was virtually forgotten. When all the envelopes were opened, *The Deer Hunter* won Best Picture, Michael Cimino won Best Director, and Best Actor went to Jon Voight for *Coming Home*. *Heaven Can Wait* won only a single Oscar, Paul Sylbert's for Best Art Direction. Explaining why *Heaven Can Wait* didn't win, *L.A. Times* critic Charles Champlin quipped, "All the joking references to Warren Beatty's celebrated romantic swath raised the possibility that some voters may have felt that the man who has everything can get by on nominations and large grosses, while heaven waits."

TREVOR GRIFFITHS's wife had been killed in a plane crash, requiring that he return to London to look after his three children. He sent his first draft to Beatty from there at the end of 1977. "Warren rang me up and said, 'I've got to read it again, but this is wonderful. This is just terrific,'" he remembers. Griffiths was not used to dealing with producers and didn't know that this was Kid Gloving Writers 101, the Praise Stage, and therefore he put a sinister interpretation on the follow-up phone call. He continues, "When he rang me again a week later, there was a completely different tone to his voice. He told me he had shown it to Bob Towne, and gave me the sense that Towne had declared that the American people would say, 'How could John Reed get it so wrong, spend his whole adult life following a corrupt and lousy experiment in revolution. You simply cannot make a movie about a man who dies a

Communist. America will not accept this.'" It was indeed a dilemma, because if Reed, disillusioned, recants at the end, Beatty would be stuck with a movie that says, in Jeremy Pikser's words, "Everything you've just seen has been a big, stupid mistake. The guy's life has been point-less. Where's the movie in that?"

Griffiths continues, "Warren wanted to keep the outline, keep the shape, keep some of the characterizations, but start over. And indeed, that's what we did." Griffiths returned to New York in the early sum-mer of 1978 to hash out the rewrite with Beatty. Pikser met the star at this time, shortly after *Heaven Can Wait* had come out and Frank Rich had profiled him for the cover of *Time*. "Warren was huge, he was king," recalls Pikser, continuing, "The first draft was tendentious. Humorless. It was much more historical, in that the relationship be-tween Reed and Bryant was not nearly as modern. And Reed was more of a character than a vehicle for Warren. In one scene, Reed embraced Louise and said, 'Your hair smells like damsons.' Damsons are a kind of plum. They do exist in America; Reed might have been familiar with them, and as a poet, in a flight of fancy, might conceivably have com-pared them to the smell of her hair, but Beatty's reaction was, 'What the fuck is a damson? I sure as hell would never say that about a woman! What kind of an idiot is this guy Trevor Griffiths? It must be some sort of English thing.'" He adds, "But I don't think he hated Trevor's draft any more than he hates other first drafts. He never has a draft he likes. It's never, 'Okay, now the script is done.' It's like, 'Let's work on it.' You go into a film rewriting while it's being shot."

According to Beatty, "That draft had two serious problems. One is that it seemed too British, and the other was that both of these people were idealistic, committed Marxists who more or less drove off into the sunset on the back of a tractor at the end of the story. There was no tension between Bryant and Reed. What I needed to do was pit her feminism against his chauvinism, turn a woman who was in love with a man against that man. And for me, this movie had very much to do with the tug-of-war between an artist and a politician. The life of an artist is one that we say is uncompromised, while politics is the art of compromise. The constant conflict was, What can you do in art? versus, What can you do in politics?"

Beatty and Griffiths struggled with a new draft. "It was really painful, really unpleasant," Griffiths recalls. "I was sitting in a room for six or eight hours a day with a guy that I was increasingly growing to detest, and who was increasingly growing to detest me. That's the Sartrean version of hell."

If Beatty in his everyday exchanges is invariably polite, soft-spoken, often displaying flashes of dry wit, rarely allowing himself to get annoyed or irritable, script meetings are free-for-alls, extreme, no-holds-barred combat. Of his notion that the best work comes from the clash of "hostile intelligences," Pikser quips, "It's often more hostile than intelligent."

Pikser recalls that Griffiths told him Beatty once threw a chair across the room, but the playwright doesn't remember it that way. "Absolutely not," he says. "Halfway through our time at the Carlyle, he started taking his coat and shirt off, and began doing upper body exercises with these huge chairs that the Carlyle has. He would do curls, set them down, do curls on his back so his stomach would get some of it. I asked him what all this was about, and he told me he had a dream in which he had started filming *Reds,* and suddenly I appeared on the set, picked up a million-dollar camera and threw it at the wall. Smashed it to pieces. His subconscious was telling him a lot about the dangers of working with a guy who was as wild as me. So he was showing me that he was a big fella, a BIG FELLA."

According to Pikser, outside the script meetings, Beatty reverted to his default personality: "He was sweet as honey." But Griffiths disagrees: "It was not just in script conferences. I think he is a brute, I think he is a bully, there is something not terribly grown up about him that is smeared across his life. But it's not just personal, it's to do with being unimaginably wealthy within the superpower that is America. Movie stars are about power. Because they have power they believe they have authority, and it's a very hard realization they have to make occasionally that they don't have authority, they just have power. I knew that if I'd gone into production with him, it would have been bloody, physically bloody."

After four and a half months of struggling with the second draft at the Carlyle, Griffiths told Beatty in late August or mid-September 1978 that he had to go back to London. According to him, the conversation went like this:

"Listen, I have three children, they have no mother, and I need to be back home."

"You can't go home. Once you sign on with me, you surrender all rights to your life." Griffiths laughed.

"I don't know what you're laughing for," Beatty continued. "I'm serious."

"I'm laughing because you can't be serious. My life is my life, and nobody takes it away from me. I'm going home."

"I'm coming with you!" So they ended up together again, this time working at the Dorchester Hotel in London.

Beatty heatedly denies this account. As someone who now is the father of four children, he says, "Would I do something like this?" Maybe not now, but then he didn't have children and regarded them as impediments to his work. In answer to Beatty's question, Buck Henry says, "Absolutely! But he would have a rationalization. Not only was it good for him, it was good for Trevor Griffiths too. 'Cause it would advance his career, keep his mind occupied, give him something to think about other than the tragedy." Adds writer Bo Goldman, "Pure Warren Beatty. He'd say something like that, because he gets so obsessive about the work. The guy's wife had died, he has to let him go. So Warren's gonna fight about it. It's like something he couldn't control."

In any event, the chasm between the two men was too wide to bridge. "The atmosphere around us was poisonous," says Griffiths. "It was messy, it was vile, it was foul-mouthed on both sides. Towne's critique was much more fundamental than Warren realized. Because he was basically saying, 'Make another movie, don't do this one.'" There is a key sequence near the end of the script aboard the train on the way back from Baku, the capital of Azerbaijan in southern Russia, where Reed berates Zinoviev, the Soviet commissar, for rewriting his speeches. Suddenly, in the middle of a heated exchange, the counterrevolutionary White Army attacks the train. Griffiths complained, "Do we really need this scene? What is important is the argument, not the attack on the train."

"Listen," said Beatty. "One thing you have to learn—in a movie, one bullet is worth a thousand words."

"That's terrible, because I'm a writer, and all I've got are words," he roared, exasperated beyond understanding. "And then," he recalls,

"Beatty exploded, and I exploded again, and walked out of the room, packed my bag, and left. I never saw him again."

Of course, Beatty was right. *Reds* is not a novel or a play; it is a movie, a popular entertainment, or at least that was the hope. Would audiences go for it? "That's the great thing about Warren," says Pikser. "It's a gamble. That's what makes it fun. If he thinks there's no chance that people will hate it, he's not interested in doing it."

"It was a huge relief when we separated," says Beatty of Griffiths. "I thought it would be good for me to have a doctrinaire Marxist to keep me from [wandering off the straight and narrow]. But the truth is that I'm not a Communist, I'm not a Marxist, I'm a centrist. So we just couldn't continue."

"CASTING IS the whole ball game," Beatty says. "The character of Louise Bryant holds the movie together. When I do a movie I get an actor in my head, and then I better get them." Beatty had been planning to ask Julie Christie to play Louise Bryant. After all, as Buck Henry puts it, "He was making his *Doctor Zhivago,*" and she had played Lara in David Lean's film. But that didn't happen, ironic, in view of the fact that it would have been the role of her career, and *Reds* the serious picture suited to her politics she always wanted him to make. Instead, he asked Diane Keaton to be his Lara—that is, his Louise Bryant. It was announced in the trades on June 6, 1979. (Beatty did dedicate *Reds* "To Jules.")

Some thought Keaton was a mistake. The real Bryant was much tougher, brassier, opportunistic, and sexually voracious than the woman portrayed in the script that Keaton would play in the movie. But he seemed to regard Keaton as something of a muse, or at least that's what he told the press: "It sometimes seemed I had very little interest in making a movie until I was romantically motivated. You need and want that in order to build, to produce, to direct, to schedule, to act in, to finance . . . if Diane Keaton had not made *Reds*, I don't know what I would have done." For her part, Keaton says, "I didn't really believe it was going to happen. He would say, 'We're going to shoot now, and then we would not shoot now, and then he would say, 'Okay, the next few months,' but it kept getting put off and put off for what seemed like an endless amount of time. So it really wasn't a reality until we were actually in England, and we started to shoot. And then I believed we were doing it."

The other key role, of course, was Eugene O'Neill, who was a friend of Reed's but had an affair with Bryant. One day, Beatty invited Jack Nicholson to a casting session. Under the pretext of asking for advice, Beatty recalls, "I said, 'I've got to get an actor to play Eugene O'Neill and it's got to be somebody who leaves not a shadow of a doubt that he could take Diane away from me.' He said, 'Well, you have no choice. There's only one person—me!'" (There was some speculation in the press that Nicholson in fact took the part because he wanted to steal Keaton from Beatty after Michelle Phillips had made her way from him to his friend.)

According to AD and executive producer Simon Relph, Beatty "worried and worried about casting Jack, because he was too old. They were both too old. When we met Jack, he was doing *The Shining*. It was towards the end of the film, and Kubrick had got him into the most shambolic state. A kind of grotesque figure appeared at the hotel." Adds Dick Sylbert, "Jack gave up the idea of worrying about getting older. He looked at his hair, he looked at his stomach, and he said, 'Fuck'em.'" Relph continues, "Warren said to me, 'Do you think Jack can get in shape?' We only had three or four months. I said, 'If he wants to do it, I'm sure he can.' He did really want to do it. When it was time, he appeared, having shed a huge amount of weight, and all the years. He was fantastic."

Beatty rounded out the cast with Paul Sorvino, who played the fiery Italian-American Communist Louis Fraina; Gene Hackman, who had the small but memorable part of Peter Van Wherry, a magazine editor; and Maureen Stapleton, who would prove to be splendid as anarchist Emma Goldman. Stapleton was an eccentric, a heavy drinker who could memorize a play without trouble, but according to Nina Rosenblum, her son's partner and a documentary filmmaker, "did not know how to turn on the radio, the cold and hot water, or a light bulb."

Stapleton didn't like the character. She felt Emma Goldman was a self-righteous, humorless ideologue on a mission, and she just despised that in life, either on the right or the left. She turned Beatty down. Beatty came back, said, "Maureen, if you don't do the movie I'm going to kill you." Eventually, she gave in.

Beatty was largely using British locations to stand in for American

ones like Provincetown and Greenwich Village, but he worried the lo-
cales wouldn't be convincing to U.S. audiences, so he took care to populate the picture with veteran American character actors like Ian Wolfe,
R. G. Armstrong, Jack Kehoe, and Emmet Walsh, who were familiar
from dozens of movies. He also made strategic use of nonactors, such as
Paris Review editor George Plimpton playing a fashionable publisher
with an eye for the ladies, including Bryant; and writer Jerzy Kosinski
(*The Painted Bird*) who was marvelous as Zinoviev. An outspoken anti-
Communist, Kosinski initially turned Beatty down because he feared
he would be kidnapped in Finland (where Beatty planned to shoot the
Russian scenes) by the KGB. Kosinski told him, "You're crazy to do
this. . . . I can't." Beatty countered with, "Why don't we shoot you in
Spain? You'll have Franco to protect you!" Of course, Kosinski understood that Beatty was joking. Franco was dead, but shooting his scenes
in Spain did assuage his anxieties, and he agreed to do the movie.

Once again Beatty did not initially intend to act in or direct the film.
He knew how difficult it was simply to produce a picture of this size
and complexity, and as an actor he would have to appear in big chunks
of the movie. He briefly considered John Lithgow, who resembled
Reed physically, but eventually decided to do it himself, just as he became convinced there was no one else to hold the reins, save for him.
He told Dick Sylbert, "I can't trust anybody to direct this movie but
me. If Kubrick called me tomorrow I'd turn him down. But I hate the
idea. To be a director, you have to be sick."

To ease his way, he surrounded himself with confidants—MacLeod,
script supervisor Zelda Barron—as well as trusted collaborators, like
Dick Sylbert, who was fresh from three years running production at
Paramount, and was arguably the most skilled production designer in
the business. He hired Dede Allen, who since *Bonnie and Clyde* had
done *Little Big Man, Serpico*, and *Dog Day Afternoon,* and was the
doyenne of the New York editing world. He persuaded Stephen Sondheim to do the score. "Warren has enthusiasms that surprise you," says
Sylbert. "There's something that Stephen Sondheim does to Warren
that has him in tears. I never got it."

Vittorio Storaro, who was responsible for Bernardo Bertolucci's
stunningly photographed pictures, and had most recently survived
Apocalypse Now, was a master of lush lighting and the moving
camera—though Beatty, raised at the knee of George Stevens, who

never moved the camera unless he had to, had his own ideas about how the picture should be shot. Beatty recalls, "One day Vittorio came to me in tears. 'Warren, I want to please you, but the camera just sits there. You never move it.' His crew had pieces of dolly tracks in their hands." But in a concession, Beatty did agree to process all the film at Technicolor in Rome—which entailed lengthy delays—because it was the only place where they knew how to add silver, making for more saturated colors, which Storaro (and he) wanted.

No one knew better than Beatty that *Reds* was not going to be just a series of pretty pictures, and that presented a problem. As Pikser puts it, "We had an audience which didn't know the first fucking thing about any of this stuff, and if we were going to educate them with the dialogue, it was going to be deadly—it would ruin the film." For example, approximately ten to twelve minutes—an eternity in screen time—is devoted to internecine squabbles within the American left. "It's not like you think, Hey, let's make a lot of money with the breakup of the Communist Party and the Communist Labor Party, coming out of the Socialist Party," Beatty recalls. "The idea that anyone would be crazy enough to try to interest a movie audience for that long in something so arcane is pretty amusing. What a ticket to the candy counter that would seem like." When he saw *Reds* again after many years, he thought, I don't even know what the hell they're talking about, and I wrote it!

Some years earlier, Beatty had come up with an elegant solution to the problem: the Old People, aka the Witnesses, the talking-head interviews with thirty-two survivors of the period who knew or knew of Reed. Pikser recalls, "If exposition kills historical dramas, why not just take the bull by the horns, and say, 'We're going to make a little documentary that will provide the information we need, but it won't be purely didactic, it will be funny, it will have entertainment value.'" Mischievously, Beatty has the Witnesses, who are on display for their recollections, begin by contradicting one another, and talking about the fallibility of memory, its lapses, and tricks it plays.

The Witnesses included Roger Baldwin, a founder of the American Civil Liberties Union, along with writers Rebecca West (*The New Meaning of Treason*) and Henry Miller, whose *Tropic of Cancer*, published in the U.S. by Grove Press in 1961, struck an early blow for the sexual revolution when the Supreme Court ruled it literature, not pornography. Beatty had read an interview with Miller where the writer described himself as "the Warren Beatty of his day." Says Dede Allen, "Miller had nothing to do with Jack Reed, but Warren just wanted him." Pikser wrote him a polite letter. Miller wrote back saying, "You seem to be after the same kind of academic crap I've always hated my whole life, I think I would be terrible for you, there's no way you could make use of me, I don't think I would like to meet you, I don't think you would like to meet me." Pikser was crushed, wrote an abject apology, "You misunderstood me, we think you'd be great, blah blah." He showed it to Beatty, who said, "Throw that out, send him a telegram: PERFECT! WHEN DO WE ARRIVE?" Pikser did so, and the next thing he knew he had an invitation to dinner at Miller's house, with the novelist and his final (and platonic) girlfriend—an actress named Venus, of course, in her late twenties (Miller was a spry eighty-eight). Miller's only request was that Beatty find Venus a movie part. Beatty always spoke well of her, but wasn't going to have anyone telling him who to cast. He didn't give her a part.

After Griffiths walked out, Beatty continued to work on the script himself. He knew that he was going against the grain, and from the very beginning, according to Pikser, he said, "I have to make an absolutely conventional, corny love story. I want a puppy. I want American flags all over this movie. I want every hokey, old-fashioned Hollywood convention we can come up with so that we can hang the rest of the story on them." Pikser adds, "He knew he needed things like the dogs to make this thing not feel like an alien conspiracy of Russian Jews, to give it something that Americans could feel was American."

Beatty consulted and/or used other writers, including Feibleman, Towne, and Pikser, as well as Hellman, Schulberg, Chayefsky, but primarily May. Says Henry, "If you have the structure and need help, you can't get better help than Elaine." The brutal script meetings began again. "Warren functions creatively in a pugilistic manner," says Pikser. "He likes to fight. It's not fun to fight with a stupid person, so he likes to have smart people to fight with. You start working on a script, you can expect to be abused. Anybody who's ever worked with him who doesn't admit that is lying. That's how he is with Towne, that's how he is with Elaine, but they love it. They're extremely volatile. They throw things, they scream. They swear at each other. They feel that this is what it means to be creative. The first time I met Towne"—who only kibitzed on *Reds,* while May worked on it extensively—"he walked up to me and he said, 'I just want you to know something.' Right up in my face. 'I don't give a fuck about history.' I was like, 'What do you want from me, man, I'm just a kid here.'"

May focused on the relationship scenes between Reed and Bryant, and Bryant and O'Neill. Unlike Griffiths, she understood that Beatty was the star, that Reed was in large part a vehicle for him, and that the Reed-Bryant relationship had to have contemporary resonance, a modern flavor. The tension between the two, although rooted in the historical reality of the period, had to crackle with the passions that roiled the women's movement of the 1970s. But like Towne, she had no feel for or interest in the period in which the film was set. Echoing Towne, she said blithely, "I don't know anything about this history, and I don't particularly want to know anything about it." But somebody needed to, so she insisted that Pikser be part of the process. Holding up some pages, she would say, "Jack and Emma Goldman need to fight here. I don't know what the fuck they would fight about," and throw him a pad. He wrote a fight and showed it to her. She would take a line at the bottom and move it to the top, a line in the middle and move it to the bottom, and say, "Okay, that's great, do it again!" He recalls, "That's one of the things that she taught me. She'd always say, 'There's no such thing as writing, only rewriting. That's great, write it again!' Then she'd say, 'That's how Warren directs: "It's a great take, let's do it again."'"

To Pikser, Beatty's odd-couple approach to script development—May tossing Griffiths's historical drama into the pop culture blender—was incomprehensible. It would have made more sense to tap someone from the pool of ex-Communist or fellow-traveler screenwriters who knew the history and the movies. "Stitching together that kind of writer out of Warren and Elaine, Trevor and me, was stupid," he says. "Abe Polonsky could have done it, Waldo Salt could have done it. But Warren was so not interested in that. He's very smart about his own [limitations]. Any of those guys would have made him feel diminished as a contributor. He wanted it to be his vision." But it was also true that the finished script was very, very good, better, probably, than anything Polonsky or Salt could have written on their own, and in many ways the ripe fruit of Beatty's "hostile intelligences." One way of putting it is to say Griffiths provided the trunk, Beatty the branches, May the leaves—and Beatty again, rewriting on the set, the forest.

7

FROM RUSSIA WITH LOVE

———

How Beatty made a budget-busting epic about the

Russian Revolution at the height of the new Cold War,

and got Paramount to pay for it.

———

"After *Heaven Can Wait*, Warren could dictate what he wanted to
make. *Reds* was his come shot."

—*Robert Evans*

WAY BACK IN 1967, in the wake of *Bonnie and Clyde*,
Beatty had quipped that the picture was so successful
the studios would have backed him to make a musical of
the Last Supper. But they never in a million years could have imagined
that he would want to do a picture like *Reds*. It may not have been as
revolutionary as *Bonnie and Clyde*, as sharp as *Shampoo*, and it may
have been a good twenty minutes too long, but *Reds* is without question his masterpiece, his *Citizen Kane*, his *1900* or *Raging Bull*—the
fuck-you film, the go-for-broke film, the film toward which his career
had been building.

Coming off the box office success of *Heaven Can Wait*, Beatty
was probably the only star with the clout (or desire) to launch a major
motion picture that would dramatize the Russian Revolution from a
not entirely unsympathetic perspective—and get a studio to pay for
it. *Reds* not only pioneered the big screen blend of fact and fiction

that was known as docudrama, it lavished on this taboo subject the vast resources at Hollywood's disposal: a big budget, A-list stars, and, in this case, the brains, skills, and talents of that generation's best and brightest. All of this at a time that could not have been less hospitable to the subject. That *Reds* was made at all is almost incomprehensible, and all the more extraordinary for being a testimony to the vision and persistence of one man. As Dick Sylbert, put it, "Talk about obsessed! Warren's ability to will something to happen was mind-boggling." Simply put, no Beatty, no *Reds*.

By this time the studios had recovered from the wild-in-the-streets fever of the early 1970s, were sitting up in bed and beginning to eat solid food, especially Paramount, which had scored with *Saturday Night Fever, Grease*, and *Heaven Can Wait*. When the last got its nine Oscar nominations in February 1979, Beatty made his move. He did what he always did: he played the field, making the studios compete for his favors. After Warners had passed on *Shampoo* and *Heaven Can Wait*, a humbled Frank Wells told him that he wanted his next picture, whatever it was. But Paramount was Beatty's first choice. "I'd been hearing about *Reds* for years," says Barry Diller, the studio's chairman and CEO. "It's like remembering when you first heard about Santa Claus. It was pervasive. I was fascinated by it. I thought it was an impossible idea for a movie, but Warren created success with *Heaven Can Wait*, and if you create success, you are entitled to extra room."

Beatty knew that *Reds* was going to be a tough sell. He told Diller that it wasn't fair to submit this to him alone, so he went to New York to give what then passed for a script to Gulf + Western chairman Charlie Bluhdorn. "Charlie *really* loved Warren—he was such a star-fucker—and he's the one who committed," says then head of production Don Simpson, who died in 1996. "How much iz diz goyink to cost?" Bluhdorn asked, in the guttural accent of his native Austria, which Paramount executives used to mimic, calling him "Mein Führer" behind his back.

"I've got to be honest with you, I don't know," Beatty told him, "but it's a long, long movie. It's about a Communist who dies at the end, doesn't get the girl, and there's virtually no script. I would expect that it may be a very dodgy commercial subject, but if you want to do it, I gotta have an answer from you in a couple of days. I'm gonna lose Diane Keaton to another movie if I don't start. But if it's no, I'll take it elsewhere. And if somebody else makes it instead of you, I would be likely to bring to that other studio anything I did after that."

"Go outzide."

Beatty seated himself by the door to Bluhdorn's inner sanctum in what looked to him like a dentist's chair.

After a few minutes, the chairman poked his head out, and barked, "Cum ink."

Beatty recalls, "They were all looking at their shoes. Bluhdorn started talking about Castro, whom he knew because Gulf + Western was in the cigar business. Finally, he said, 'We're going to make it.' But it was clear they didn't really want to. He made the movie because he didn't want to lose the movie."

Indeed, a few days later, Bluhdorn came down with a bad case of buyer's remorse. Beatty explains, "Charlie went back and forth, probably because of the political nature of the movie. Rumors were flying that this was a pro-Communist picture, with a Communist hero, and that was very disconcerting for this big conglomerate. There couldn't have been more hostility to Communism at that time in history, with everything shifting to the right."

Again Bluhdorn asked, "Vat iz diz vilm goyink to cozt?"

"I can't really tell you."

"Name zee figure."

"Why would I do that? That would be dishonest."

"Letz zay diz vilm iz goyink to cozt twenty-fife million."

"Okay, $25 million."

"Do me a vayvor. Take diz twenty-fife million. Go to Mexico. Keep diz twenty-vor million vor yorzelf. Spent diz vun million on a vilm. Juzt don't make diz vun."

"Charlie, I have to make this movie."

Finally, Bluhdorn acceded to the inevitable. Then Beatty got a call from one of Bluhdorn's pals. (The Gulf + Western head was suspected of underworld connections, among them the attorney and mobbed-up Hollywood fixer Sidney Korshak, although Beatty says the caller was not Korshak.) The man said, "If you know what's good for you, you won't make this picture!" Beatty says he replied, "I'm making the picture and I'm going to pretend I didn't hear what you just said."

At that point, the budget was hovering in the low $20s. Recalls Diller, "It was really not possible to budget the movie. We did a kind of estimate, and we were of course terribly wrong, which is why Warren and I got into enormous difficulties later. I don't know what we would have done if we knew what the real cost was. I doubt we would have done it, but who knows?"

BEATTY WAS still mulling over *Love & Money*. One day, he told James Toback, "You need a producer regardless of whether I'm in the movie or not. And we need a third intelligence anyway, because you and I have pretty much said what we have to say. And since Pauline Kael's telling me how great you are and that I should work with you, let's see if she has the balls to quit her job and produce the movie." Beatty confronted her, saying, "You tell Fellini how to make movies—if you think it's so easy, you ought to try it yourself. Stop telling me how dumb I would be not to do a movie with Toback, quit your job and come and produce, and the three of us will work together." She replied, "Maybe I should." She felt that by the late 1970s, movies had become so awful that her job had lost its luster.

In early 1979, he hired her to produce *Love & Money* in a pay-or-play deal reportedly worth $200,000. She took a five-month leave of absence from *The New Yorker*, went to L.A., and brought along Albarino. This was a bold move. Warrenologists were mesmerized. Says Paul Sylbert, "Here was the Voice of Movies in America, and Warren addressed her ego with notions that she could do something about the business, how bad it was." Adds Paul Schrader, "Because of her power, executives used to be terrified of her. There was a feeling in the industry that Warren was the only one who could bring Pauline down. The ultimate smooth move was to flatter her to death, give her a little power and put her in an office until she was gradually exposed as being one of us and therefore not dangerous. I really believe he brought her out there to humiliate her, maybe not consciously, but some part of him did." Says Buck Henry, "The whole point of it was to keep her away from *Reds*. Warren knew he was going to make *Reds* and he knew that Kael was always incredibly patronizing towards him. He thought, If I put her together with Toback and make her think she's part of the company, even if I dump her in a year, she can't come back and slam me. Guys like Towne knew she was completely seduceable. Warren just took the next step. We're talking about manipulation on a level unknown to man. Even I can't quite believe it, except that it was Warren."

As the scenario played out, however, everybody failed. Beatty and Kael wrangled over *Reds*, which she still did not think he should make. "She would not give up on *Reds*," says Beatty. "She even called Diane Keaton, called my fucking girlfriend, to get her to persuade me not to do *Reds!*"

Then she read Toback's script for *Love & Money*. She told Albarino, "This is terrible." According to him, she was so powerful that she thought other critics were out to destroy her (which they were), and if she produced this film, she would just be handing them a club with which to batter her. "This will be a major embarrassment for me," she continued. "I'll be a laughing stock." She asked Albarino to do a page one rewrite that Toback hated.

Finally, Kael asked Beatty, "This is awful. What should I do? Should I give him the money?"

"Yes. You're the one who convinced me what a genius he is."

Says Toback, "Warren wanted to work it out, wanted the three of us to work together. But after six weeks with her, I said to him, 'That's it, either I'm going or she's going.'"

Beatty thought Toback was making a mistake, and told him, "You're being very stupid. What are you worried about? You get to the point where you're shooting and then you can do whatever you want. But if you unload her now, Barry will say, '[without Pauline,] I have been sold a false bill of goods.' And he will not make the movie."

"I'll have to deal with that."

By the middle of May 1979, Kael was out. Beatty told her, "Toback, against my wishes, feels this can't work." Later, Toback confessed, "I was polite in the press, making it seem as if it were a mutual decision, but it wasn't a mutual decision at all. I got rid of her."

Beatty felt some measure of responsibility for her, but he also knew that if and when she went back to *The New Yorker*, she would become a time bomb waiting to go off. He had to let her down easy. He told her, "Let's see if we can work something else out at Paramount." He got her an overall deal at the studio. Shortly before she died in 2001, Kael said, "Don Simpson had no interest in any projects of mine." Rumor had it that she would go over to director Richard Brooks's office, complain that she had been put out to pasture, and weep. Looking back on the sequence of events some years later, Beatty says, "Hiring her was the stupidest thing I've ever done."

ALONG WITH Keaton, Storaro, Simon Relph, Dick Sylbert, and others, Beatty made another trip to the Soviet Union in 1979 in a last-ditch effort to persuade the authorities to let him film there, and also to let Sylbert see the place, in case they had to shoot in Helsinki, their fall-back location, since it was designed to replicate St. Petersburg. "We sat in Moscow with these guys for days," Sylbert recalls. "They said, 'Comrade Beatty, we think it's very, very progressive, you making this picture about John Reed, but we have to see a script.' He said, 'I'm not going to show you a script.' 'But Comrade Beatty, then it's impossible to do.'"

Beatty was no more comfortable there than he had been ten years earlier, and didn't hesitate to bait the Soviets. When he visited the Museum of the Revolution, he asked the guide why there were no photographs of Trotsky! At a meeting with officials of Mosfilm, the state film company, Beatty recalls, "Everyone was in good humor, they were all smiling. I was talking really fast, and I made the mistake of referring to the 'Bolshevik takeover' instead of the 'glorious Revolution.' I saw their faces fall, and as the words came out of my mouth, I leaped forward to try to pull them back, and failed. I realized then that we weren't going to get permission to shoot anything there. But I knew that going in."

Principal photography began on or about August 8, 1979, in London. It could not have been a worse time to begin a picture that treated the birth of the Soviet Union in heroic terms, however qualified. This was the year the Russians invaded Afghanistan, and production and postproduction would spill over into the early 1980s, when the new U.S. president, Ronald Reagan, famously dubbed the Soviet Union the "Evil Empire," igniting yet another round of anti-Communist hysteria. The Iran hostage crisis was dragging on, and in Poland, the Communist puppet government was locked in struggle with Solidarity.

Reds was based at Twickenham Studios, aka "Twickers," but it wasn't big enough, and they built sets at every studio in and around London. The sheer size of the production—it sprawled over several countries—and the glacial pace at which it proceeded made it quickly apparent that *Reds* would stay neither on schedule nor budget, especially when Beatty was wont to say things like, "There are some movies that just can't be clarified on paper, and they make themselves as you go along. You know what you're going after, and then you adhere to Napoleon's battle plan.

When they asked him how he planned a battle, he said, 'Here's how I do it—first I go there, and then I see what happens.'"

Beatty would spend whatever he needed to get what he wanted. Says Relph, "The budget was actually quite low, given how ambitious a film it was, but it started to swell once we began shooting, and we more than doubled the production time. I think the original intention was probably fifteen or sixteen weeks. We actually shot the film over a whole year, some thirty-odd weeks, plus these 'hiatuses' where Warren went back to the drawing board."

Beatty had energy and stamina to burn, but he had already put in a herculean effort on this picture, the shoot was just beginning. There was so much name-brand talent involved that just slotting *Reds* into their busy schedules was like solving a Rubik's Cube. "We had to wait for Maureen Stapleton," remembers production manager Nigel Wooll. "She wouldn't fly. We wanted her in November, but in November there are no oceangoing liners across the Atlantic because it's too rough." Finally, she agreed to take an ancient Polish freighter. David MacLeod picked her up, along with her son, Dan Allentuck, and his partner, Nina Rosenblum, in New York, and squired them to Baltimore, where they would take the *Polowska* to Rotterdam, and then continue on to England on a hydrofoil. The freighter broke down in the middle of the Atlantic, turning a one-week trip into a two-week trip, during which they subsisted on tripe and cabbage. *The New York Times* reported, "Maureen Stapleton Lost at Sea."

When they reached Rotterdam, MacLeod met them, accompanied by a young boy who would be known as "Little David" and looked to them as if he were no more than twelve years old, although he was older than he seemed, maybe seventeen. MacLeod introduced him variously as his ward or his girlfriend's son. He was always rubbing his back, alarming Stapleton, who thought there was something peculiar about the relationship. "He was as good-looking a guy as I'd ever seen," says Toback, who met him through MacLeod. "He was in the Warren Beatty, Alain Delon category, better looking than James Dean. He had a magnetic physical presence."

Stapleton spent two months sitting by the phone in her rented London apartment waiting to be summoned to the set. Beatty would often appear in the evenings to take her out to dinner with the rest of the cast. He threw a boisterous party for Paul Sorvino when he arrived, during which the actor sang arias and told Woody Allen's famous joke about Beatty: "If I'm reincarnated, I want to come back as Warren Beatty's fingertips." No one laughed.

As it was on *Heaven Can Wait*, "Do it again" became the refrain. Beatty shot take after take, as if the best take were just around the corner. He was unapologetic. "It's axiomatic that the cheapest thing we have is film. It's the hours that people spend on the day that cost you money," he says. "But that's a hell of a lot less time than coming back and adding another shot. What you do is say, 'Do it again.' And you hire good actors."

Stapleton didn't have much patience for Beatty's "Do it again" habits. In one scene, shot in Manchester, she was addressing a rally of six hundred or so extras. It was raining hard, and Beatty was doing take after take, never saying what he wanted. At one point she exclaimed, "What do you want me to do? Take off my clothes?" She once recalled, "He was such a goddamned perfectionist. . . . We had done eight or nine takes, perhaps ten or eleven. I couldn't see anything wrong with it—they all looked the same to me. Anyway, he was way down the other end of the block and shouted for the umpteenth time through his bullhorn, 'One more time, sweetie.' I took the bullhorn from Simon [Relph], one of the unit directors, and I shouted back, 'Warren, are you out of your fucking mind?' And the whole crowd of extras cheered and clapped. So he comes back on the bullhorn: 'I may be, darling, but do it again, anyway.' So we did it again." Her son, Dan Allentuck, recalls, "After a while, she was just thinking, Over, over, over."

It wasn't just the big scenes that Beatty shot and reshot, or the complicated ones, or the intense ones that required a real performance. There was one scene in which he enters a room and tosses his hat onto a chandelier. He did something like 107 takes, even though he snagged the chandelier with his hat three quarters of the time. Customarily, a director will say "Cut" at the end of a take. The cast and crew break while the DP prepares for the next one. According to production manager Nigel Wooll, Beatty "wouldn't stop the camera. Instead of going to take 2, take 3, take 4, he'd do it all in one run until the load of film ran out after ten minutes." But this created its own peculiar problems. Wooll recalls, "We burned out three camera motors because they overheated. I've never, ever burned out a camera motor before or since. It was extraordinary."

Some of the actors welcomed the challenge. Recalls Paul Sorvino, who says Beatty had him do as many as seventy takes for one of his scenes, "It was a point of pride with me to do as many as Warren wanted. It was like, 'Yeah, you want another one? How 'bout ten more, how about twenty more?' It was that young macho thing in me that said, I can stand up to anything. I thought Warren felt he had to strip the actors down. A lot of directors do that in a cruel way, skinning them, flaying them. But Warren just wanted the best that I had, so I gave it to him."

Others were not so amenable. Says one source, "I saw several actors actually break down and start crying. Jack was almost in tears. In one scene with Diane, I remember him screaming, 'Just tell me what the fuck you want, and I'll do it!' Literally, his eyes filled with water from the frustration of not knowing why he was asked to do it again." Retorts Beatty, "Put it this way. It was a scene of great frustration, and a scene of great emotion. Maybe it just means I'm a good director!"

Whatever it was he was looking for, Beatty got what he wanted. The scenes between Nicholson and Keaton represent some of the best work either actor has ever done, helped enormously by Beatty's and May's dialogue, alternately passionate, biting, and just plain funny, as when O'Neill, who is in love with Bryant and using her in a pickup performance of *The Emperor Jones*, just can't resist complaining, "I wish you wouldn't smoke during rehearsals. You don't act as if you're looking for your soul, but for an ashtray."

One day, Dede Allen went up to Beatty and complimented him on the script. "The dialogue, the cadences, sounds very contemporary, very modern." He gave her a look as if to say "Duuh!" and then explained, "Dede, this is not Warren Beatty as John Reed, this is John Reed as Warren Beatty! That's what being a movie star is."

Keaton appeared in more scenes than any of the other actors, save Beatty, and many of them were scenes of great difficulty, where she had to assay a wide range of emotions from romantic passion to anger to sorrow, and deliver several lengthy, emotionally complex speeches. She too repeated her takes again and again, and reportedly broke down in tears of frustration. There was one scene, early in the picture, where Reed is trying to persuade Bryant to ditch her dentist husband, leave Portland, and move to New York, where the action is. Her hackles rising, she asks, suspiciously, "What as? Your concubine, your whore?" Finally Reed retorts, "It's almost Thanksgiving. Why don't you come as a turkey?" Says second AD Michael Green, "Warren did something like ninety takes. This was to make her paranoid, to get something out of her that she wasn't giving him. Keaton finally [blurted out,] 'How many ways can you say, "I'll come as a turkey"?'"

George Plimpton, who was offered the part of a lecherous publisher after he literally tripped over Beatty asleep on the floor of the Playboy Mansion, auditioned for it by kissing Keaton with so much conviction that Beatty yelled, "Stop it." Plimpton thought that Beatty was trying to break Keaton, turn her into what Bryant must have been like with Reed. Adds Relph, "It must have been a strain on their relationship, because he was completely obsessive, relentless."

Keaton had mixed feelings about Beatty's methods. She found that the great number of takes helped her discover resources she didn't know she had. "At the same time, though, I didn't exactly feel like I knew what I was doing," she says. "It was really Warren's performance, not my performance. He was never satisfied, and he pushed me and pushed me, and frankly I felt kind'a lost. And maybe that was his intention in some way, for me."

Gene Hackman's part was small, just two scenes. He was fond of Beatty, and still mindful that the producer had kick-started his career by tapping him for Buck Barrow. So when Beatty asked him to do what was essentially a walk-on, he agreed. "It was a pleasure to work for Warren, even though he did a lot of takes," Hackman says. "It was close to fifty. He didn't say a lot to me. There's something admirable about somebody who is that tough, and perseveres that way, so I hung in there. But all those takes—I was going blind. After take 5, I'm kind of finished. I had no idea how they would change, one from the other. I don't think that I ever verbalized anything to him in terms of my annoyance—I just sucked it up—but he must have known."

Assistant editor Billy Scharf, who would also work on *Ishtar*, explains Beatty's method best: "A lot of people say Warren overshoots. I know that not to be true. Directors who come back with insufficient material are doing a disservice to the opportunity. They get intimidated by stars. Warren does not. In the movie, when Reed wants to leave Russia and go back to America, Zinoviev tells him, 'You will never be at this place, at this time, again.' Warren felt that way when he shot. He believed that that was the time, and that was the place, and he had to exploit the opportunity to the hilt. He had the resources, and he wanted to use them, because he knew he would never get another chance."

Still, a lot of the crew were unhappy. Some of them used to call him "Masturbeatty," because of the degree to which he indulged himself. Pikser recalls, "He's reasonably affable if he doesn't feel under pressure, which is rare, so he's not smiling a lot. He jumps all over people. He gets really irritated if there's noise on the set. He worked them hard, made them wait, and was always pinching pennies. The crew hated it, the actors hated it. It's always hell on Warren's sets." Says Beatty, "That may be the attitude of a crew member or someone who is looking at his watch thinking, What time will we break for tea? But that's not my attitude, and it's almost always not the attitude of actors that I hire. This is not something where you say, 'What should we do, play Parcheesi?' There's got to be something about it that says, 'Hey, this is important!' Otherwise, it's a lot of fun, but no cigar."

THE DAYS dragged on. Not only did they have to wait on the actors' schedules, they would break for script work, for editing, for holidays. Production was held up for a week until Beatty's cold sore disappeared. As the bills piled up, the warm relationship between Beatty and Diller turned frigid. At the end of long shooting days, Beatty got on the phone with the Paramount head, and the two men screamed at each other until they were hoarse. "Within a week, we were a week behind," Diller recalls. "And it just went on from there. They had all sorts of problems. They had production problems, they had weather problems, they had fatigue problems, they had Warren and Diane problems. It was all done on the fly. Which is a dopey way to make a movie. It was just a mess, and it went on and on. And it would stop a lot, and then start again, and then it would stop, and everyone would go home, and then it would start again. It was one of those rough, rough shoots that made everybody unhappy."

But Diller was in a bind. "Here's the dumbassness of it all," he continues. "I should have forced him not to be Warren. But that would have been stupid. That's his process. That's how he functions." Finally, the Paramount head simply ceased returning Beatty's phone calls. He explains, "I was so angry with him, I thought it was just pointless to talk to him. I wanted to make him feel guilty. I thought that would have some effect. That was naive." Says Beatty, dryly, "I think there was probably a point when they would have preferred not to have been involved. And that lasted through July, August, September, October, and November. They were extremely not nice. We literally were not on speaking terms. I think they felt that it didn't hurt to have me over there in a state of anxiety. A very effective tool with me is the silent treatment, because then I feel that someone has taken his ball and gone home. And I didn't know how to cope with that." Then at Christmas, Diller and Eisner flew to London and saw a five-hour cut that Allen had specially prepared. Both men loved it; from that point on, Paramount was behind the movie.

When production resumed after Christmas, the show moved to Helsinki. Second AD Green was in charge of the Finnish extras. He recalls, "Around dinnertime, the night before we were due to shoot a sequence on the train in a little station an hour out of Helsinki, I got a call from Warren, who said, 'Hey, Michael, the Russian-looking woman we've got in that carriage, I want you to make sure that she can actually speak Russian because I've got a couple of Russian words that I want her to say.' So I called up the extras coordinator, said, 'Listen, that old lady we've got on the train, can she speak Russian?' She said, 'I think so, I'll check.' She called back and said, 'No, she can only speak Finnish.' 'You've got to recast her, then.' That was a big deal at that time of night, because you not only have got to replace her with someone who speaks Russian—in Helsinki, not many do—then you've got to have a costume made. By three o'clock in the morning we finally found two women who said they could speak Russian, their faces looked right to me, I showed Warren the photographs, he picked one, then they woke up the costume lady and got her dressed by eight o'clock the next morning. I was quite pleased with myself when I knocked on the door of Warren's trailer. I said, 'Here's your Russian lady.' He was standing in the doorway looking down at us, and he said, 'Good morning' to her, in Russian. The woman stared at him blankly. He looked at me, and he looked at her, and he said something else in Russian, and she kind of shrugged. He said, 'Michael, this woman doesn't speak Russian.' I said, 'Well, um . . . she told us she did, we thought she did.' I felt like a fool. You think you've pulled the rabbit out of the hat, where in fact you've done the reverse. Warren is an extremely clever man. With movies, things do go wrong, and usually you can double-talk your way around it, but you can't with him. If he asked someone a question, and they give him an answer, he would ask, 'Who told you that?' 'Were they in a position to know what they were talking about?' He'd nail it down. I learned fairly quickly that if I made a mistake, the thing to do was say, 'I screwed up,' because you couldn't get away with anything."

They had to wait for snow to fall in Helsinki and the rain to stop in Spain, their next location, where Beatty had to deal with an insurrection of the extras, about one thousand of them, gathered for a crowd scene. Ironically, it may have inadvertently been his fault to begin with, because he stirred them up by giving them his stock pep talk: "This is an important film, the first big studio film about socialism," and so forth. It was very hot, and they had been up since four in the morning. The caterers had failed to give them rolls, and by lunchtime they were starving, with little more to eat than fruit, as they watched the actors and crew chow down a three-course meal. "They came storming into where we were eating, banging trays, and turning over tables," recalls Wooll. Beatty was furious with him and Relph. But he handled the situation like the enlightened capitalist he is, in a manner calculated to make the author of *Ten Days That Shook the World* turn over in his grave, underlining the fact that for all the similarities, Beatty was not Reed. As Wooll recalls, he told the two ringleaders, " 'You're right. We apologize, we'll put you in charge of extras, and we'll pay you more money.' They both said 'Yes,' and from then on there was absolutely no problem at all. He took the sting out of the tail."

The degree to which Reed became disillusioned with the revolution had been an issue from the start, and would continue to be one through postproduction. To be sure, the historical Reed didn't like everything he saw in Russia, and did have issues with the Bolsheviks, but at the end of his life he wrote an article insisting that the revolutionary must subordinate his will to Party discipline. Besides, as Griffiths puts it, "He did not find, nor could he have, historically, the sort of full-blown Stalinism that you kind of smell in the second half of the film."

Reed's ambivalence toward the Bolsheviks was replicated on the set, in a milder vein, by a tug-of-war between Pikser and Jerzy Kosinski. Pikser had been cast, a trifle uncomfortably, in the role of commissar of political correctness. "Warren thought I was a Stalinist, a Lenin-loving, don't-pee-on-my-revolution defender," he recalls. "He used to call me to his trailer, and say, 'Start a political argument with me.' I would realize halfway through it was because he was going to have a fight in the scene he was shooting, and he wanted to get in that mood. He's a Method actor. But I think he gets something from that conflictual relationship that the other person may not get."

In the critical sequences on the train coming back from Baku, Reed becomes furious with Zinoviev because he discovers that the commissar has been changing his speeches. Reed thinks he's been inciting the Muslims of Soviet Asia to rise up in class war, but when he realizes they're chanting, "Jihad, Jihad," he understands that he's actually been recruiting them to a religious war. Beatty had been relying more on Kosinski for the script work than Pikser. To Kosinski, Zinoviev was an incipient Stalinist, changing and censoring Reed's speeches, but to Pikser, Reed was no more than a bourgeois writer defending his copy against his editor, a Hollywood filmmaker protecting his movie against the studio. Pikser felt he was being marginalized. "Eventually I said, 'Warren, I'm really not doing anything. Don't you think it's time for me to go home?' He said, 'You're quitting on me. There comes a point where everybody turns their back on you.' He wanted me to stay and fight—forever. It was as if I was betraying him." Beatty asked Pikser to be brutally frank about his opinion of the picture and put it in a memo. He did, and Beatty was furious. Recalls Pikser, "It's the only time he made me cry. By the end of the filming, we were not really speaking to each other. Still, these kinds of fallings out are never really personal. If I called him a week later and said I have a funny growth on my hand, he would say, 'I want you to go to this doctor, and I'll pay for the bill.' There's a tremendously loyal friendship from Warren. Regardless of any kind of work-related villainy."

Months passed, leaves flew off the calendar. The set was closed to journalists. A shroud of secrecy, dubbed "the Beatty curtain" descended on *Reds,* which only served to stir up a devil's brew of rumors. London insiders were quoted saying *Reds* was in trouble. The wrap date was pushed back from December 1979 to June 1980. One cast member complained, "Everyone appreciates the work except Warren." The press reported delays, rewrites, overtime, extravagance, and waste—actors with no more than two lines to deliver shuttling back and forth between the U.S. and England. The ratio of film shot to film used was said to have reached fifty to one. Several crew members left *Reds* to work on other pictures, then came back. Sylbert shoehorned

Partners into the *Reds* schedule. The budget reportedly skyrocketed to $30 million.

As the wrap date became no more than a vanishing point forever receding over the horizon, mordant jokes about the production were heard on the set, some of which found their way into the *Grabber News*, an occasional broadsheet put out by jaded crew members. For example, the sheet reported that *The John Reed—Louise Bryant Story*, the film's working title, was a popular term for Seconal sleeping pills, and suggested alternatives such as *The Longest Day, The 39 Takes,* and *Take the Money and Run.* It even published its own irreverent version of Reed's death, with Bryant at his side, that parodied both *Reds* and *Heaven Can Wait:*

> JACK
> You know, Louise, here I am dying.
> I'm only 33 but sometimes I feel at
> Least 10 years older. I
> Feel like I've lived every moment
> Of my life over and over again.
> Sometimes I feel like I lived
> Some moments over 30 or 40 times.
> I guess that would have killed anyone . . .
> Louise, if I was to come back,
> As somebody else . . . would you . . .
> Would you know it was me?

> LOUISE
> Come back? What as?

> JACK
> It's almost Easter. Why don't
> I come back as a ham.

Beatty always had to be careful of his health, and it suffered, especially when he was stressed. According to Kosinski, "He was drawn, puffy, overweight; his skin had lost its freshness." For a time, in Spain, Beatty shared a shack with Kosinski and wife. "Why was Beatty there?"

wondered Kosinski. "What helped me to become Zinoviev was questioning why this crazy American was doing this crazy thing. I honestly didn't think this was going to work. I thought he was going to be buried in the Kremlin wall again." Says Pat Caddell, his old friend from the McGovern days, now a political consultant whom Beatty would hire to work on the marketing, "He was coughing a lot. I used to say, 'You're going to kill yourself.'" Pikser recalls, "Warren felt isolated. He used to say to me, 'You and I are the only two people who give a fuck about what this movie is saying.' Which was true. He felt like he was bogged down in the Philippines fighting the Japanese. And nobody else cared if he was going to win or not."

James Toback thinks that there is a deep vein of depression or melancholia that laces Beatty's personality. "He's fighting off depression all the time," he says. "Churchill used to refer to depression as 'the beast,' and everything he did was a way of temporarily keeping the beast at bay. That accounts for his compulsion to make use of time, to be engaged—with work, with his house, with something—never to be sitting around doing nothing, never do what other people call relaxing, going on vacation, which he is almost incapable of." It's the same impulse Michelle Phillips complained about, his ability to make her feel guilty for lying in bed all day, having sex and eating ice cream. From this point of view, making films, doing take after take, sleeping with one woman after another are just other ways of keeping the beast at bay.

"We do have our ups and downs, we do go in cycles," Beatty confessed. "Like most people, I get tired when I'm trying to create. Sometimes when I'm all alone it just can be the most miserable thing in the world because I know that I don't have the answer to a creative problem. When I go into a down, at nine o'clock in the morning, for example, things are very bleak. At ten o'clock, they start to look a little bit less bleak. And about eleven o'clock, I'm thinking, I might even have an idea. By 11:30, when I've mapped it out and I think I'm just about ready to go, I rehearse it a couple of times, but now I'm at twelve o'clock or 12:30, so I think, We better break for lunch because I don't want to get halfway into it and then break. When I resume after lunch, I'm down again because my glucose isn't really where it should be. About three o'clock or 3:30 I've almost got it. From 3:30 to about 4:30, I might really have it, but I'm beginning to get close to the end of the day and getting tired. By five o'clock I know I better not try to get in too much more.

And by six, 6:30, seven, I'm ready to go home. I feel like I should be confined to some ward for catatonics.

"Not that everyone is manic-depressive, but everyone whose end results have to be an energetic expression of what they want to get across, whether they're filmmakers or politicians or preachers or athletes, is subject to downs. The importance of fun to filmmaking is like saying what is more important to the making of the film, the manic cycle or the depressive cycle? Well, it's gonna be the manic cycle, but the depressive cycle fuels the manic cycle. So I don't think it's good to think of this as an unhealthy condition. We try to do as well as we can do."

Needless to say, Beatty's relationship with Keaton, who was high-maintenance in the best of times, suffered. Indeed, it barely survived the shoot. Working with an actress with whom the star or director—both, in this case—has an off-screen relationship has always been a dicey proposition. Says Caddell, "Directing your girlfriend in something like this was insane." Beatty admits, "Making a movie together if you've got someone who is even moderately obsessive-compulsive, is hell on a relationship. It's like running down a street holding a plate of consommé and trying not to spill any."

Pikser recalls, "Warren was always trying to please Diane. Which was not easy. Which is why he wanted to do it so much. It's no fun for him if it's easy. He really likes women who kick his ass. He always moaned about it, but I think that's what drew him to her. It was a very contentious, volatile relationship. He bought her a pair of handcuffs, as either a Christmas or a birthday gift. I took that as an ironic comment on her feeling that he wanted to constrain her. Or, maybe they were just into that!" Says Beatty, "God help me, I've never been into that. The idea of handcuffs as sexual paraphernalia has always made me laugh. There would be about as much chance of Diane Keaton being into that kind of stuff as there would be of her becoming interested in skydiving."

"Warren didn't have an easy time, because of Keaton," says Peter Feibleman, who observed them together. "Any woman who's in love with him enough to be at his mercy will be angry with him the whole time. Not because he hurt her, but because he could hurt her. And Diane was. She's the opposite of what she seems to be on the screen. She used to slaughter Warren. She's a very unpleasant lady when she is angry. She's a rage rat. Unspeakable stuff. She had a kind of nasty flounce. She was the original snotty girl. She just clawed at Warren.

"Warren did the movie for her, but nothing he did seemed to please her. She was princessy enough that if you acknowledged her throne then you became her vassal. But he had to deal with a great number of other people. All she saw was that his attention wasn't on her. She lost sight of the fact that the whole fuckin' thing was being done around her. With great love. And it got worse and worse and worse. So many, many, many women would have been grateful for ten minutes with Warren, so he picked the one who was running away. There's a certain attraction in that. Julie was the opposite. She was out to please. When they fought, it was different, a sort of lovers' quarrel. You could sense the love with Julie, you could not with Diane. It was playful with Julie. It was hostile and awful with Diane."

Says Keaton, "I don't think we were much of a couple by the end of the movie. But we were never, ever to be taken seriously as one of the great romances. I was mad for him, but this movie meant so much to him, it was really *the* passion of his professional life, it was the most important thing to Warren. Completely, absolutely. I understood that then, and I understand it now." Translation: *Reds* was more important to him than she was.

Some people close to *Reds* thought that the relationship between Reed and Bryant echoed the off-screen relationship between the two stars way more than it reflected the historical couple. Says Caddell, "It was sometimes hard to tell the difference between what you're seeing on the screen and what you're witnessing in real life." In the picture, Reed and his circle—especially the heavyweights, like the anarchist Emma Goldman—don't take Bryant seriously. She's writing an article about the Armory Show—by then three years old—at a time when the world was going up in flames.

While *Reds* was in preproduction, Keaton was putting together a book of photographs of hotel lobbies. Pikser speculates, "Diane wanted to be serious in ways that Warren was ambivalent about. To really have been a partner in Diane's quirkiness, the singularity of her pursuit of the obscure and the avant-garde, which to me was a product of a restive and intelligent mind, for him would have been heavy lifting. There was a way in which he wanted to pay obeisance to her intellectual pursuits, but at the same time there was a sense on her part that he didn't really respect or appreciate them. So when Warren says in *Reds,* 'You're writing about the Armory Show, why should I take your work seriously if you don't take it seriously yourself—can you imagine what Warren really thought about her taking photographs of hotel lobbies?" Beatty rarely accompanied Keaton to gallery openings and would rarely visit her sets.

Says Buck Henry, "I don't think he understands the motivation for knowing about something or really loving it when it has no practical connection to oneself. The idea of Warren standing absorbed in front of a great painting or being in an opera house and being carried away, or even the theater—he could never understand how I could waste my time being in a play. We had mutual friends who were in the art world, who used to talk to me about art. I know Warren was suspicious of the conversations. Why would I really be interested? I'm not going to get anything out of it. For him, it's not about being overwhelmed by anything outside of himself. It's about how you get other people to respond in that way."

There was no real reason why the couple's on-screen relationship shouldn't have reflected their off-screen one. If Beatty saw himself as Reed when he started, his identification with him only intensified as the shooting progressed. He even took to wearing the clothes—wide wale corduroys and custom-made shirts—worn by his celluloid avatar. Likewise, Keaton felt she had an intuitive understanding of Bryant: "I saw her as somebody who really wanted to be extraordinary, but was probably more ordinary, except for the fact that she was driven. I knew what it was like not to really be an artist. I knew what it felt like to be extremely insecure. I knew what it was like to be envious."

Beatty merely did what all auteurs—even reluctant ones—must do, make an intensely personal film, in this case with a chunk of history that in other hands could easily have remained lumpy and undigested. But sensitive, perhaps, to the imputation of self-absorption, both Beatty and Keaton deny that the Reed-Bryant relationship mimics their own. Did Keaton feel she was in Beatty's shadow the same way Bryant felt she was in Reed's? "No," he responds. "She had just made one of the great, great movies, *Annie Hall,* she had won the Academy Award. She was very much in demand." Adds Keaton, "It was completely different. I didn't find myself dead in a stairway, drunk. Also I don't think that we're that important, historically. Warren and I. Sorry to say."

The simmering tensions between the two seem to have boiled over the day they shot Reed's death scene—he succumbs to typhus in a squalid Moscow hospital—with Bryant at his side. Says art director Simon Holland, "It was at the time when he and Diane were about to split. He couldn't concentrate on what was happening around him. He couldn't even see how Diane was acting. After it had been going for quite some time, Warren wouldn't say 'Cut,' he would just start again. Eventually, he stopped and he sat up and he looked at script supervisor Zelda Barron. He said, 'How was that, Zelda? Was she all right?' " Beatty says he was most likely concerned with continuity issues, but some on the set interpreted his question as an invitation to evaluate Keaton's performance, a breach of protocol. According to Holland, "Diane just went, 'W-a-r-r-e-n B-e-a-t-t-y, you'll never do that to me again!' And she walked out. And that was it." Adds location manager Simon Bosanquet, who was also there, "She went to the airport, and left. It was a real exit and a half, a wonderful way to end."

Of this anecdote, Keaton says, "Yes, it rings a bell; no, I'm not going to talk about that." According to Beatty, "It's completely not true" that he asked Barron to critique Keaton. "I have never asked that question of anyone. It's just not something you do. When we were shooting that scene, there were other matters between me and Diane that were personal. Nobody knew what was transpiring between us. No one knows what's going on between me and any of the actors. And often I don't know either."

According to Beatty, *Reds* finally wrapped at the end of February 1980. (According to *Variety,* it wrapped the last week of July.) When it was all over, Beatty described himself as a very tired man.

POSTPRODUCTION WAS a saga unto itself. It had already been underway for some time in London, and in the early spring of 1980, it moved to Trans-Audio on West 54th Street in Manhattan, next door to Studio 54. Cutting *Reds* was a factory operation that spilled out onto several floors, and virtually cannibalized the company. Rooms filled with editors and/or boxes of film branched off long hallways that bisected or trisected the spaces.

In those days, the editing of an average feature took a few months, at best. *Reds* was a long film, but postproduction lasted for over a year and a half, enough time to start and finish a picture, and then some. The size of the job required a veritable army of editors and support staff, some seventy people. The assistants had assistants, so that it seemed like every editor in New York who could walk and talk was hired. The structure of Dede Allen's army was strictly hierarchical, with Allen at the top, then co-editor Craig McKay, then Kathy Wenning, who was in charge of the Witnesses, on down to the assistants, apprentices, interns, and drones. Most of the staff was thrilled at the prospect of working on a Warren Beatty film, working for Allen, and getting a steady paycheck that might come in forever. But it quickly became clear that everything has a price, and Cindy Kaplan, Allen's first assistant, spoke for many when she says, "It was the greatest thing and the worst thing at the same time."

The most immediate problem Allen faced was organizing the vast amount of footage that Beatty had shot. "I was overwhelmed with film," she says. The party line, Allen recalls, was that *Reds* had not exceeded the benchmark recently set by *Apocalypse Now*: 700,000 feet of exposed film, or one hundred hours' worth. Allen continues, "It got to the point where I never discussed it with anybody. That was *verboten*. [But] I know it was more than 700,000 feet. Are you kidding?" According to Wooll, "We went through over 2.5 million feet of film." One source in a position to know claims Beatty shot three million feet, roughly two and a half weeks of screen time, with about one million feet actually printed.

There were so many dailies that Jill Savitt, an assistant editor, had trouble finding places to screen them. Adds Wenning, "I had a quarter of a million feet of the Witnesses alone. You would look at some simple shot, and there'd be fourteen takes. And that was just one angle on a given scene. My eyes would glaze over. I could see tiny differences, but eventually they stopped registering. We had to keep records of the infinite permutations of every scene, with everything duplicated so we could go back, and that alone kept assistants going forever." There was one person whose sole task was to transfer film to tape so that Beatty could look at it at the Carlyle Hotel, where he was staying.

Allen was famous for her memory and her work ethic. Despite the vast amount of footage, she knew every frame and where it was. To only exaggerate slightly, she would say, "Give me Diane saying 'and' "—one word. The editors groaned and began to scurry about in circles, mice lost in a maze, until Allen would suggest, "Try reel 3, scene 34," and so on. She threw herself into the editing, worked harder than anyone, and demanded that everyone do as she did. She even worked on Christmas Day. As Kaplan puts it, "She saw her role as being in service to the film 100 percent, and to the director, and anticipating everything that he needed. Her attitude was, whatever it took, it really didn't matter how hard it was, you just did it. Dede would be talking, and I would go to the bathroom, she would come running after me and stand outside the stall and continue talking." The mother of postproduction supervisor Terri Kane, who left before the film was finished, invited her for Thanksgiving.

" 'Are you kidding?'

" 'Just tell Warren it's Thanksgiving!'

" 'No, I can't do that.' I wasn't told I couldn't, I just didn't imagine that I could. I didn't even ask."

Yvette Nabel, an assistant sound editor, recalls, "I had a gallstone attack, and I was lying on the floor in agony, and I said, 'Can I go home?' The answer was, 'No, we may need you!' Either you worked on *Reds*, or you didn't work on *Reds*. You weren't allowed to have any kind of a life."

Kate Hirson, a looping editor, was a single mother. "Being a woman and having a child while working in film was just not okay," she recalls. "There were no allowances. And no sympathy. At seven at night, I would say to everybody, 'I'm just going to go out and grab a quick hamburger.' I'd jump in a taxi, race home, and kiss my son, jump in a taxi, and rush back. Although I couldn't mention that I had to take my kid to school, nonetheless there was this huge amount of leeway about seeing a therapist. 'Kate? Four times a week? No problem, just go!' "

Morale was terrible. "People were very angry," says apprentice sound editor Susan Lazarus. Recalls Hirson, "Dede was such a crazy person, you always had to be on call in case Warren needed you. He was a night person, so he would work from eleven to two. Everything was about Warren. Anything he wanted, any whim—he would cancel anything at the drop of a hat. He was the king. It was slavery. We were in *Reds* prison." Wenning adds, "According to Dede it was absolutely essential for one of us to be in the editing room on weekends to babysit Warren in case he came in. He'd show up late, or never at all. That's what I got paid for. Overtime."

The postproduction pressure cooker took its toll. "It was one of the hardest years of my life," Wenning continues. "I got divorced." One assistant editor tried to commit suicide with sleeping pills. Says Lazarus, "When it was over, I had to go to therapy because I felt that I'd lost my sense of self." Hirson gave up editing features and moved over to documentaries. So did Kaplan. She says, "I was working really hard, night after night, and one night I looked up at around 3:00 A.M., and I thought, We're not curing famine in Africa here. I realize this is going to be a good movie, but who cares? After a year and a half, you start to wonder about your own priorities.

"Making this film was like *Fitzcarraldo*, dragging a ship over a mountain. The thing wouldn't have happened without someone like him, and I have great respect for him for that. But on the other hand, he just wasn't a very nice person. Is it worth being inhuman to be able to get there?"

What made things more difficult is that Beatty ran hot and cold. There was a short list of people whose calls had to be put through, including certain women, close friends, and his parents. Recalls Kane, "Once his mother called, and I said, 'Do you want me to find Warren?' 'Oh, no, don't bother.' And when I told Warren, he got upset. MacLeod told me, 'You have to remember how Warren is with his parents, you always have to find Warren and put those calls through.' If Stephen Sondheim called, you'd better find Warren, because he was on the list. It was Sondheim, Sondheim, Sondheim. Then, all of a sudden, it clicked off—'I don't want to hear from Sondheim.' Very abrupt. It was like he had broken up with a girlfriend."

Beatty held this tinker toy assemblage of editorial talent together with the glue of his personality. He could inspire such dedication that some people didn't mind the long hours. "He had that charisma that just makes people want to do things for him," says assistant editor Billy Scharf. "You've been there all night long, and then you're asked to do it again, and you know you're being used in some way—you felt like a schmuck—but you do it. That's why he's a great producer." Eventually they got used to him, and relaxed.

The star was fully aware of his effect on the assistants, and wielded his charisma with intent. Wenning recalls, "All the women were trying to look good for him. One Sunday, I was in his office, the snow was coming down, and Warren was pacing back and forth in front of the window. It was like a scene from *McCabe & Mrs. Miller*. I was sitting on the couch, he had his back to me, and he was talking. I said, 'Warren, I can't understand you.' He said, 'When the film's over, go get your hearing checked.' He said it gently and kindly, not, 'Are you deaf? There's something wrong with your ears.' Sure enough, I had otosclerosis. It could have gone on undiagnosed. I thank him for that."

Beatty was full of contradictions. At the time he was arguably the biggest star in the world, just two years out from his *Time* magazine cover. Yet he didn't have an entourage, didn't insist on being treated like a movie star, knew people's names, invited them out to dinner. Kane recalls, "You didn't have to handle Warren. He did a lot of things for himself." She was impressed that he didn't require limousines. "I was a nobody, and he was Warren Beatty, and I'd be getting into a car I'd ordered from the service, while he would walk to the corner and hail a cab," she remembers. "It was always extraordinary to me"—until she realized he didn't want anyone to know where he was going.

Beatty was deceptive. He scored points for not requiring star treatment, but at the same time, he didn't because he didn't have to. Allen was savvy enough to create an environment in which he was treated that way regardless. Kane recalls, "One day, I sent a kid, a production assistant (PA), out for Chinese food for Warren. The kid came back, empty-handed. I freaked out. 'Where is the food?'

" 'I ran into Warren in the elevator and I gave him the bag.'

" 'You just handed him the bag? Of Chinese food? You can't just hand Warren Beatty a bag of Chinese food. You have to put it on a tray!' "

Every Beatty film is shrouded in secrecy, and *Reds* was no exception. Editing changes within scenes were recorded on continuity sheets so that there was a record of them. Once, an errant breeze coming through an open window carried some of these sheets of paper out the window down onto Eighth Avenue. Kane recalls, "Dede made us go down to the street and look for the sheets, because someone might find one and breach the secrecy."

MacLeod was an island of calm amidst the chaos. He had an office across the street, and people found excuses to hang out there and decompress. He was accessible and funny, and dispensed advice about how to deal with Beatty. MacLeod was sharing a loft belonging to actress Blair Brown with Little David. Recalls Kane, "Little David didn't know how to relate except sexually. He was extremely provocative. He'd sit on your lap and lick your neck. He'd always say, 'But I'm just a kid.'" MacLeod told people that Little David came from a poor family with many children. They credited him with helping a kid out of a bad situation. Little David always said that MacLeod was like a father to him, took care of him when nobody else would. But after work, the two Davids would go clubbing. "It seemed odd, and you kind'a wondered, because MacLeod was taking this boy out every night," says Kane. Adds Sherri Taffel, also a post-production coordinator, "You felt there was something slightly inappropriate, but you didn't exactly know what."

Little David was friendly with Michelle Phillips's daughter, Chynna. "Once, when Chynna was about twelve, we called Warren from Shanghai," Phillips recalls. "I had to go east from Beijing, and she had to go west through New York, back to L.A. I asked him, 'Is it okay if she stays in New York overnight, and then you can put her back on a plane to Los Angeles?' He said, 'Yeah, send her, I'll take care of her.'"

Taffel picked Chynna up at the airport and drove her to the Carlyle. "Chynna was wearing a blue Chinese shirt," she recalls. "She was stunning. Little David met her in the lobby, took her up to her room." According to Taffel, when Beatty arrived at the hotel, he asked, "Where's Chynna?"

"She's upstairs in her room getting settled."

"Where's David?"

"He's up in her room with her."

Taffel recalls, "Warren went nuts. Started screaming, 'What are you doing letting them up in the room together? Are you crazy?'" She wasn't certain that Beatty's concern was strictly paternal. Angrily, she told him, "It's your own fears about yourself that are at play here. Not everybody is the way you are. David is fine in the room with Chynna."

Despite a sizable contingent of smart, ambitious women — even the apprentices were documentary filmmakers — the culture of the editing rooms sharply contradicted the feminist politics — such as they were — of *Reds*. Beatty may have been in heaven, but Louise Bryant would not have been happy there. According to Wenning, during her interview he asked her, "Do you want to fuck?" She answered, "I don't think so," and he "just moved right along, and that was the end of that."

Kane remembers an incident that happened one day when she was sitting in her office, legs crossed, wearing a skirt. "He came by my desk and slipped his hand around my inner thigh. It really flipped me out. I was like Road Runner in the middle of the air. He was not coming on to me, just playing. There was this long hallway of editing rooms, and sometimes he would just go down the hallway from room to room to room, and he would do something like that to each woman."

There was a cultlike aspect to the whole thing. The *Reds* cutting rooms were about as close as it was possible to get to *Big Love*'s Juniper Creek, in midtown Manhattan c. 1980, although with Studio 54 next door, that's perhaps not such an exaggeration. Suffice to say that Beatty's playfulness, and his deeply held belief in his own entitlement, would lead him routinely to do things that today could get him brought up on charges of sexual harassment in the workplace, if any of the women wanted to press charges, which is unlikely. Adds Kaplan, "He was very flirtatious. Sometimes we'd be in the editing room, me, Dede, and Warren, supposedly watching a scene. He'd just pick me up and start laughing, while she was working at the Moviola. He thought it was funny, while everyone else was rolling their eyes."

Kaplan was involved in hiring personnel. "Warren complained to me that the women I was hiring weren't pretty enough," she recalls. He was joking—sort of. Recalls Hirson, "Once one of the temps was Xeroxing something, and Warren came up and just stood behind her, like, Notice me, notice me, notice me! She looked up, and she said, 'Uhh, did you want something, sir?' She didn't have a clue who he was. When he realized that, his face dropped, and he walked away. It was a typical Warren moment. He was just relentless in his focus on a young apprentice on the picture side, in this very predatory way. Wherever she was, he would track her. We were all waiting—how long was it gonna take before this poor girl gives in? Then finally he wore her down. He just did it 'cause he could. I was very offended by it."

But a lot of the women on the staff either overlooked Beatty's behavior or appreciated it. Says Lazarus, "He really loved women. He loved talking to women, he loved working with women. You didn't feel he was exploitive, even though you knew he would jump into bed with anybody." Adds Wenning, "I had a great time with Warren. He was always interesting, he knows so much about so many subjects, and when you got past his nonsense with women, he was just fun. And, he gave great neck rubs." As researcher Judith Evans, who was often at his side during postproduction, points out, flirting was almost therapeutic for him. "He had this overwhelming responsibility on this movie," she explains. "The flirtations were a relief in this context. He needed that kind of response from women. Men like Warren who seek power are only alive when someone is looking at them with admiration or desire. It's almost a chemical thing. And that became more true as the film was coming to an end and becoming very difficult."

THERE WAS enormous pressure to finish and release the film because of the hefty interest payments Paramount was making on the loan. As head of the whole operation, Allen bore the brunt of the pressure. Her relationship with Beatty was fraught. His practice of bringing his friends around to look at the film and offer suggestions rubbed her and the editors the wrong way. From their point of view, they were hardworking professionals, while Beatty was rounding up amateurs and outsiders to gum up the works.

The visitors ran the gamut from Michelle Phillips to George McGovern. Says Wenning, "What would be frustrating was not the visitors, but the people who came around and hung out. Towne and Caddell occupied a lot of Warren's time, and it was during periods like that that he ignored Dede. He's a towering intellect and artist, and I was surprised that at his age, he'd still be a kind of a high school locker room type guy. He'd get with these guys and it would be like Animal House. There was a lot of talk about girls, and Dede being an older woman, was really cut down by that."

The kibitzers often confused more than they clarified. Says Judith Evans, "People were pulling him in all directions. He would have these screenings with Nicholson et al., and everyone had different things to say. He would come in the next day and say, 'Why did I do that?'"

Keaton was a frequent visitor as well, dubbing her dialogue, or just there. She was always early to the looping sessions, Beatty was always late. Recalls Kane, "We'd go through a session, and they would leave, and half an hour later they'd still be standing in front of the elevators, arguing, walking away from each other, and coming together again. Then we'd go back to Trans-Audio, and there they'd be in the lobby still arguing, and it would go on all the time." One day Beatty and Keaton got into a screaming fight in the lobby of the building that lasted for what seemed like hours, while people just brushed past them pretending not to notice. According to Judith Evans, "A lot of time was spent waiting around while Warren and Diane were involved in some 'Where is our relationship going?' discussion."

To Allen, Keaton was just another distraction. Her left-wing history seemed to give her a personal—even proprietary—stake in Reed and Bryant's story. Possibly she was competitive with Keaton for Beatty's attention as well. In any event, she disparaged the actress, patronized her as a lightweight, a Valley Girl whose histrionics diverted Beatty from his work. From Allen's editing room, she could hear or watch Beatty, one office away, talking on the phone—often several phones at once—flirting with various women. The tenor of Allen's feelings could be judged by the fact that, when Beatty's office was being furnished, she dourly suggested a Naugahyde couch, "so we can just hose it off."

More than anyone, she was flummoxed by Elaine May, the most influential of Beatty's pals. He felt that she was one of the few people in the inner circle who didn't have her own agenda, and he wanted her at his beck and call. Once she hurt her ankle, couldn't walk without a cane. It was late, and she wanted to go home. He grabbed her cane, while she screamed, "Give me back that cane, I want to get out of here." Phillip Schopper was a young editor who played the role of a gadfly on the film, a sort of roving critic who evaluated other people's work, which didn't make him too popular. (He would later become romantically involved with May, and remain with her for thirteen years.) He says, "Elaine is probably the best editor there is. She has an amazing ability to go from the beginning of the project to the end of the project, and watch it every time as if she is seeing it fresh."

But to Allen and the other editors, she was just an irritant. The editors couldn't understand why Beatty excluded Allen from the very conversations with his friends in which important decisions were made that crucially affected her work. When May (or Towne) was in with Beatty, Allen knew they were fiddling with her work. She paced up and down the hallway outside his office, muttering to herself. In some sense, if Beatty was the Lenin of *Reds*, Allen was the Emma Goldman of postproduction.

"They drove each other crazy," recalls Wenning. A source who knew Allen well explains, "The way she functions in the dynamic with the director is that she's the dutiful daughter. But Beatty would not let her be the dutiful daughter, which totally short-circuited her. At the beginning, she went out and found apartments for him, tried hard to find the perfect one, to make him happy, and he wouldn't even look at them." But the apartment hunting, eventually delegated to others, went on throughout postproduction and became a way for Allen to keep him preoccupied and out of the editing rooms.

By the end of postproduction, Beatty and Allen were barely speaking. Says Kaplan, "It was terrible. She was just coming apart. There were days when she just sat down on the floor and put her head in her hands." Occasionally, he even reduced her to tears. Says Hirson, "There was a lot of anger and bitterness and unhappiness on both their parts. It was like when your parents were fighting. It was a dysfunctional marriage. But however much they fought, for Dede, whatever Warren wanted, Warren got." Adds Kaplan, "She would eat herself up inside, but she would never say anything because that would be disloyal to the film and the director."

LIKE HIS relationships with Christie and Phillips, Beatty's with Keaton flickered on like a guttering candle. To torture a memorable quote from *The Godfather*, Beatty kept his friends close and his ex-girlfriends closer. Says Bo Goldman, "Diane loved him desperately. Yes, there'd been a falling out, but then there was a rapprochement. She'd seen an assembly of *Reds*, and she said, 'Well, this guy, he had this insane notion to make this movie about Reds, and you know something? There's a movie there. Who would have believed it?' Her admiration for him was rekindled. Like he'd pulled the rabbit out of the hat, when she thought that there was no rabbit and no hat. Even after her horrible experiences with him, romantically and sexually, whatever, she respected him."

Still, Beatty drove her crazy by making dates and either breaking them or being unconscionably late or casually neglectful. On her thirty-fourth birthday, January 5, 1980, he was interviewing Judith Evans for a job, happily chatting away, oblivious to the time. Keaton kept calling, saying, plaintively, "Where are you? You're supposed to be here. We're going out. It's my birthday!"

It didn't help that Beatty was seeing other women, plenty of them: Charlene Gehm of the Joffrey Ballet, as well as models Bitten Knudsen and Janice Dickinson, not to mention Mary Tyler Moore. Dickinson first met Beatty at a party thrown by photographer Ara Gallant in New York. He was with Knudsen. She invited the two of them back to her place, where the women drank Cognac and did blow while Beatty fell asleep. On another occasion, she was in his suite when he was on the phone with Keaton. "I could imagine Diane on the other end, feeling deeply loved," Dickinson recalled. "Then the second line rang and he had to ask her to hold and it was the *other* woman in his life, Mary Tyler Moore. He made *her* feel deeply loved, too." He hung up, and "rubbed his hands together like a man about to sit down to a good meal." But Dickinson didn't sleep with him that night either. By the time she went to the Caribbean on a photo shoot for *Elle,* she still hadn't had sex with him, but she said she "spent the entire shoot thinking about him." When she returned, she called him from the airport.

"Where are you?" he asked.

"At JFK," she said. "You sure nobody's there? You're not juggling calls again, are you?"

"Why don't you come over?"

"Bitten's not there? Can it really be—Warren is all alone?"

"I won't be if you come over."

She made a beeline to the Carlyle. What followed was right out of the Warren Beatty playbook: "He sat down and played the piano for me—what a delight—then ordered room service. We ate by candlelight. He asked me about me. Hung on my every word. Made me feel like the center of the universe. Of course I slept with him. He knew where everything was and what to do with it. But of course he'd had lots of practice. I tried not to think about just how much.

"I woke up a few hours later, at around three in the morning. Warren wasn't in bed. I looked across the room and found him admiring himself in the mirror. 'What are you doing?' I asked in a sleepy voice. 'Nothing,' he said. But he couldn't take his eyes off himself. He ran his hands through his hair, staring at his reflection in the mirror. I went back to sleep. In the morning, when I woke up, he was standing there again, playing with his hair, mussing it; trying to get it just right—going for that just-been-fucked look. . . . I saw Warren for the next eight months. He made me feel loved and important. I knew he was making half a dozen other women feel the same way at the same time—sometimes on the same day, even—but it didn't matter. I needed lots of nurturing, and I was getting it from Warren Beatty."

Mary Tyler Moore was in the process of divorcing Grant Tinker. She was up for an Oscar—always catnip to Beatty—for *Ordinary People* (1980), which she lost to Sissy Spacek the following April. At

Christmas of that year, she reportedly gave him a piano. Keaton had bought the twenty-fourth floor in one of the twin towers of the San Remo, a landmark building on Central Park West and 74th Street. She turned it into a big white-on-white loft. The chairs were white, the sofa was white, everything was white, including a long white table surrounded by a dozen or so white oak school chairs that swiveled. She had an extensive art collection, but very little of it was on the walls. Nor did she display her photography. Just a few floors below her, in the other tower, lived Moore, who always left the blinds up. Keaton could see into her apartment, and would point it out to friends, hissing, "Look, that bitch lives over there. You don't even need binoculars. He was due here, he was late, I saw him over there! And all he could come up with was some lame excuse: 'I'm sorry, honey, I was busy.'"

Keaton had a close friend named Robert Younger, who was a gifted graphic designer—record albums, posters, and the like. He accompanied her to gallery openings, movies, concerts, the zoo, everywhere Beatty couldn't or wouldn't go with her. Through her, he and Beatty became somewhat friendly, and the star impressed him by helping him out with a medical problem and paying his bills. One day, Beatty invited him to the editing room. Over Chinese take-out, Beatty praised Keaton extravagantly: "She's a peach, Diane can do anything, comedy, drama, anything." Younger had the feeling Beatty knew he would report back to Keaton, and that he was being used as a go-between. Then, out of the blue, Beatty said, "Diane says you have a great eye. I have all these stills, I can't find one that's right for the poster. I've had Milton Glaser looking, Dick Sylbert, nobody's been able to find one. Do me a favor, look through them for me? It needs to be of me and Diane, and it needs to say 'love story.'" Beatty never offered to pay him, and the designer didn't ask. There were a dozen or so looseleaf books stuffed with proof sheets. After days of culling the stills, Younger found one of Reed and Bryant embracing at the train station after he returned from Baku. Younger circled it in red with a wax pencil. He showed it to Beatty, saying, "Warren, look at this. This is the one."

"I missed that one. Let me think about it, show it to some people." Emboldened, Younger explained that he'd had a lot of experience designing album covers, and asked to be considered for the poster. Beatty didn't say yes, didn't say no. Paramount was involved, he'd think about it, be in touch, etc., etc. Says Younger, "That was the last time we spoke."

Cut to a month or so later, Younger and Keaton had just come out of a movie, and were walking across 57th Street toward Central Park West. As he recalls, he asked his companion, "What's up with the poster?"

"Oh, gee, Warren found the most beautiful shot for the poster, to die for. He's got such a great eye."

"Di, can you describe it to me?" She did so.

"Did you notice that it was circled in red?"

"Yeah, that's the one."

"That was my select. That's my circle!"

"That cocksucker. That cheat . . ."

Younger could sense she was spoiling for a fight. She had the bit in her mouth, and ran with it.

"He's not going to get away with this. I hope he paid you well."

"As a matter of fact, he didn't pay me at all."

"That filthy motherfucker, stealing from you . . ."

"Diane, there's no sense getting into a huff, because we didn't discuss money. I didn't ask him for any."

"Well, you should have. And what about him grabbing credit for it? He always does that shit."

"It's all right. He's an auteur. He's allowed to do what he wants. Calm down."

"I'm going to call him right now!"

"No, Diane, there's no issue here. Don't make one where there isn't one. Did you see the poster?"

"There is no poster. You're damn well gonna do that poster, I can tell you that right now. You're hearing that from me. You're gonna do that poster."

Younger had to make the train to Philadelphia, where he lived. The next night, about 1:30 in the morning, his phone rang. It was Beatty. Younger recalls that he was in "panic mode."

"Robert, you have to do me a favor."

"What is it?"

"Robert, Robert, Robert, did we ever talk about money? When I had you look at those proofs? Did we?"

"No, Warren, actually we didn't. No."

"So get on the phone with Diane and get the bitch off my back. She's killing me. I've got too much to do, she's losing her mind. Just tell her that we had no money discussions whatsoever. You live in Philadelphia, get her out of town. Invite her to a swap meet or something."

"I don't want to invite her to a swap meet."

"She's acting like a big baby. She was awful on the set, bitching and moaning. She wouldn't speak to me. She cried all the time. I couldn't talk to the actors, I couldn't focus on my performance. She always feels slighted. She gets pouty, loves to go stalking off. She's a pain in the ass, mainly."

"This is between you and her. I don't feel comfortable calling Diane. Besides, it's two in the morning, she doesn't take calls after eleven o'clock."

"She's there and she's up, I just talked to her. Tell her to back off."

Younger called Keaton, who did pick up, and unleashed another fusillade in her proxy war with Beatty.

"You deserve to do that poster, he's really a shit. He can't get away with this kind of thing."

"Di, that's absolutely ridiculous. It's over. Let it go."

"I won't let it go. I insist. You have to insist. And I want to be there when he apologizes to you, and I want to be there when you sign the contract for the poster." Younger's call waiting began to beep. An hour had passed, he was tired, clammy with sweat. He told Keaton, "Hold on a minute, that's probably Warren. I gotta go."

"Oh, it's your new friend?"

He picked up. Beatty said, "That was her, right?"

"Yeah, that was her."

"Can you at least tell her that I'm clean here?"

"She knows that we didn't talk money, but what I really don't like is your bringing me into this. It's a private argument. You're acting like children. I feel targeted."

"But it's all about you, Robert. It involves you. She thinks that I'm cheating you, in not giving you the poster job. You understand I can't give you the poster job. It's Paramount, it's Paramount, they're doing the poster." Younger thought, but didn't say, I'm sure if I was Milton Glaser, Paramount might not be the issue. He also didn't say, "Why did you go around saying you selected the image?"

Beatty suddenly dropped the subject and veered off onto *True Con-*

fessions, a movie with Robert De Niro and Robert Duvall that had just been released. Suddenly Younger's call waiting began to ring again. But Beatty wouldn't let him get off. Younger found it impossible to break the connection. He was drawn in, uh, seduced. There was that feeling of intimacy, warmth, well-being. Beatty took another call, and put Younger on hold, came back, told him who the other call was from, and recounted the conversation. Younger's call waiting rang again, stopped, then started. Younger said, "I'd better get this."

It was now 3:30, 4:00 A.M. Keaton was angry. She said, "Oh, so you and your new buddy Warren, you've been having a nice conversation? I've been ringing and ringing, you must have been enjoying yourself. I've been calling for over a half hour."

"I didn't keep track of the time. Should I have?"

"You're making a mistake if you consider him a friend. He'll just use you and spit you out. What did he tell you to tell me?"

"He didn't tell me anything to tell you."

"Robert, why don't you just stand up to him? What are you afraid of, losing your Warren Beatty connection? Damn!" She slammed the phone down. Younger had plenty of time to think about that night, because he didn't hear from Keaton for six months. Whatever had happened had damaged and nearly ended his relationship with her. He started to suspect Beatty had involved him for that purpose. "He knew I was no competition, but he also knew that Diane was very fond of me. Warren has learned some very interesting tricks." He explains. "Dispatching any kind of male friend—even if not a threat—is part of a skill of being a lover. He's really clever. I guess it's called manipulation."

Younger always wondered why Keaton hung in so long. "He did ask her to marry him a couple of times. But by that time, she knew too much. Knew he was incorrigible. She would have liked it to be, You're mine and I'm yours. It was all about faithfulness for her, let's build a family, sharing. Diane actually believed she was going to make him monogamous, but it wasn't in the cards. Yet she was riding it because she was an extremely driven woman, and extremely—I don't want to call her opportunistic, but it's not not opportunistic. The trophy wasn't just her, it was him too. He was a Hollywood Royal, and she aspired to that."

For his part, Beatty "didn't ever think his relationship with Diane was going in the direction of marriage," says Judith Evans. He "is a very conventional person about women. He always used to say he wanted to marry a librarian."

Beatty and Keaton continued to see each other sporadically. She went on to star in Alan Parker's *Shoot the Moon* (1982), and was romantically linked to co-star Peter Weller. Although their relationship would never be the same, Keaton patched things up with Younger, and she told him to call her at home, advised him of the best times to reach her. Every time he called Keaton, Beatty was in bed next to her. In the course of one of these calls, Younger said, "I thought Warren doesn't come by much."

"Well, he's really here on this one," she replied. "Do you want to talk to him?"

"No, not really. Can I call you later? Or why don't you call me back another time."

"Sure."

"This is about Peter, right?"

"What do you think? I don't take it personally!"

8

ONE FROM THE HART

How *Reds* swept the Oscar nominations, but lost to
Chariots of Fire, after which Beatty plunged into the Hart
campaign, and gave *Ishtar* to Elaine May as a thank you for *Reds*.

"Losing the Oscar broke Warren's heart, because that was really the
first time he'd had a chance to do everything he ever dreamed of."
—*Dick Sylbert*

S 1980 WORE on, Beatty's lovers came and went, Ronald Reagan was elected president, and John Lennon was killed, but *Reds* was forever, or so it felt. Even shooting had resumed—in stutter-step fashion—in August 1980, and continued in a desultory way into winter in New York and Washington. As late as the middle of May 1981, Beatty would do five additional days on the Paramount lot.

Meanwhile, back at Trans-Audio on 54th Street, postproduction ground on. Rumors were rife that Paramount was going to shut down the New York operation and move it to L.A.

Diller called periodically, screamed at Beatty. Beatty screamed back. Among other things, the Paramount chief demanded that Beatty rein in David MacLeod, who had substantial expenses. Beatty responded by threatening to quit. He yelled into the phone, "You want to come in here and take over? You do it. I'll leave!"

Craig McKay was cutting one of Beatty's scenes, sorting through the takes for the millionth time, when he came across a close-up in which it was clear to him that Beatty was giving his best line reading. But crow's-feet were faintly visible at the corner of one eye. Recalling that Beatty had once warned him, "I'm the biggest narcissist in Hollywood," he mentioned to his assistant, "That's his best take, but he's gonna react to that."

"Yeah, he's gonna want you to cut it out, because he doesn't look too good."

"Well, I'm gonna leave it in, because we don't know if he's going to spot it or not." When McKay was ready to show him the sequence, Beatty sat down at the editing bay and folded his arms across his chest as the editor ran the scene for him. According to McKay, he said, "It's good, it works." Then he paused for a moment, and added, "You know that shot of me where I say this, this, and this?"

"Yeah," McKay replied.

"Don't you think it's got a little too much character?"

"Warren, it's your best performance."

"Well, it's good, but it's not quite the tone I want. Find something else." And he walked out of the room.

There was such a crush of footage, that every once in a while Allen brought in a "guest editor" to work on a few selected scenes, like Jerry Greenberg, who had cut the ambush in *Bonnie and Clyde*. "The tenor of that cutting room when I arrived was dour," he says. "Most of the assistants were abraded. They were working day and night. You can't just throw more people at a situation and make it happen quicker, better. It happens quicker, worse. Dede is not an easy person to work with under that kind of duress. And she was very open about how difficult Warren had become."

Among other things, Greenberg was brought in to recut the scenes between Bryant and O'Neill, particularly the bravura "seduction scene" set in Provincetown wherein he initiates their affair. According to one source, "Jack was so good that Warren and everyone else said, 'Oh my God, this scene is unbelievable. He walked away with the movie.'" But it was Greenberg's opinion that Beatty thought Nicholson's performance could use the help of a good editor, although the director would never—ever—come out and say so. According to him, Beatty said, "'You know Jack, right? Nicholson?'

"'Yes, I know Jack.'

" 'And you appreciate Jack's acting?'

" 'Yes, very much.' This was at a time when Jack was still that brash youngster, and playing Eugene O'Neill might have been a stretch for him. That was Warren's implicit [meaning], implicit in his asking me to work on Jack's scenes." But, according to actress Joyce Hyser, who would live with Beatty in the late 1980s, "Warren was a little in awe of Jack as an actor, how versatile he was. Jack really blew him away when he was doing *Reds*. Sitting behind the camera, he'd get so caught up in Jack's performance, he'd forget that he was directing."

Of course, admiration and competition are by no means mutually exclusive; the one may engender the other. Says a source, "Jerry came in and recut the scene. Nicholson was diminished in it." Adds a second person who saw Greenberg's cut, "I was shocked. The sexual tension that just kept building and building and finally culminates in that kiss, when she stands up on her toes—it was just wonderful—had dissipated. Jack had ad-libbed really wonderful, funny, sarcastic things—they were gone." The source continues, "Warren looked at the scene, half of what it used to be, turned around to Jerry and said, 'Jerry, when do you want your blow job, now or later?' " (According to assistant editor Billy Scharf, Beatty preferred his "blow job" compliment to Greenberg for his work on a different sequence.) Cynics among them concluded that Nicholson's performance was too good. As one put it, "Beatty couldn't handle it."

"The big fight was how the movie was gonna end," recalls Beatty pal Pat Caddell. When the White Army attacks the train full of Bolshevik officials returning from Baku, interrupting Reed's dispute with Zinoviev, the Red Army troops guarding them charge out of the cars to counterattack. Reed runs after them, and is shown frantically chasing a caisson. It's a reprise of a scene from the beginning of the movie showing Reed in Mexico, in the heat of battle, chasing an artillery piece, which he catches up to and clambers on. But this time he doesn't. The brief image of the caisson disappearing into the dust of battle as Reed futilely chases it is a perfect illustration of Beatty's point to Griffiths that "a bullet is worth a thousand words." But what words? For all that this image crystallizes the themes of the movie, there remains an ambiguity. On the one hand, the revolution vanishes into the distance, just beyond Reed's grasp. More was shot—Reed catches up to the caisson and gets on—but wasn't used, once Beatty decided that he wished to convey the notion that revolution is an ideal never to be realized. "For me, you will never catch it," he says. "You will always be chasing after the revolution. If he had gotten onto the cart, then where would he have gone? China? A new movie! If you're chasing the locomotive of history, you do your best, you fire your best shots, and you live and learn, and then you die. It would be great if you had some fun, and it would be really great if you had some kids."

But the White Army attacks soon after Goldman's argument with Reed in which she forcefully asserts that the Bolsheviks have betrayed their principles, and immediately after Reed's argument with Zinoviev, suggesting that instead of running to join the Red Army in battle, Reed is trying to escape the Bolsheviks. Beatty was happy to have the scene read either way, or both, leaving the issue of Reed's disaffection unresolved.

After the picture editing is finished and the movie is locked, the sound mixing begins, wherein—to oversimplify—dialogue, sound effects, and music are blended together. At the time, a mix for a standard picture might have lasted five or six weeks. The mix for a long film like this one might have stretched to eight weeks. *Reds* took four months to mix, through the summer of 1981, for the simple reason that *Reds* was never locked. Says Dede Allen's son Tom Fleischman, a sound mixer, "While we were mixing, he was recutting the movie. Rewriting the movie! Dede was upstairs trying to keep Elaine away from the Moviola. She had gone in and wanted to do something, and Dede said, 'No, there's no time. We can't do any more.'"

But Beatty's faith in May's instincts remained undiminished. There is an important scene at the end of Part 1—*Reds* was one of the last movies released with an intermission—that takes place in a St. Petersburg factory. The workers are debating whether or not to strike, a first step toward fulfilling the Bolsheviks' pledge to take Russia out of World War I, which they regarded as a capitalists' war. Reed is asked to speak, and does so, unwillingly at first, then with increasing passion, as the crowd sings the "Internationale." The scene is a prelude to the actual outbreak of revolution, and is gradually transformed into a montage featuring stunning night shots of backlit marchers emerging from the murky darkness waving blood-red flags and banners, cutting to triumphant workers pouring through the Winter Palace, and ending with Reed and Bryant in a passionate embrace. The factory scene was shot in Finland, and neither the actors nor the extras spoke Russian. "They were just speaking nonsense, counting, and stuff like that, so we did this quick-and-dirty temp mix with a loop of crowd effects and music," recalls Fleischman. "When it came time to actually mix the film, Warren wanted to write real speeches for the actors, hire Russians to voice them in their native tongue, and then hire Russian speakers for the crowd to respond to the speeches, so that if you were a Russian watching that scene, it would all make sense." Beatty hired Zina Voynow, Sergei Eisenstein's sister-in-law, to corral all the great Russian actors in New York, most of whom could not find employment. Scharf went to Cleveland and taped the Cleveland Choir singing the "Internationale." Maurice Schell, one of the sound editors, laboriously recorded the results. It took days to mix all the elements. Beatty looked at it and loved it. It was exactly what he had asked for. Then he screened it for May. She said something like, "I hated that."

"You hated what?"

"I hated the way—something's changed. And not for the better."

"What?"

"I don't know, the sound, the whole thing with the revolution . . ." Says a source, "You could see the people who did the work, melting like—'Oh my God, can someone put tape over her mouth?' 'Shut up Elaine, you're ruining everything I did. You don't know anything about sound.' They tried to tweak the mix to make her happy. After a few weeks of work, they screened the reel for her again. She said, 'Yeah, it's better, but it's still not quite like it was.'" Says Fleischman, "Poor Maurice had done so much work, he was ready to slit his wrists. We didn't know what else to do, and Warren would not let go of this. It just bothered him. There was something in him that was saying she's right, and he would not just say to her, 'No, no, we can't get that back,' because there was no way for us to reproduce what was in that temp mix that was thrown together six months before. Finally, Warren said, 'Well, we have to use the temp mix.' He scrapped the whole idea of Russian actors, and we actually took the one copy of the temp mix that existed for that scene and transferred it into the master."

Schell and Voynow were furious, considered taking their names off the picture. Says Scharf, "It was extraordinarily discouraging to those people, but Elaine was right. Because she had the perspective of standing back, and he knew to trust not the people who spent hours of their lives creating it, but somebody who had no stake in it."

With the endless cutting and recutting, "they made the film many many times," as sound apprentice Susan Lazarus puts it. Some of the editors thought it was getting worse, not better. At three hours and twenty minutes, McKay and Allen cut a three-hour version, which they both liked, but Beatty insisted on restoring the footage. Recalls Cindy Kaplan, "It was frustrating for Dede, because you couldn't talk any kind of sense into him." To this day, the star insists that he wouldn't change a frame.

As the picture inched toward completion, Bluhdorn began pressuring Beatty to show it to him. He resisted. "I never liked to show people pictures early. He thought if the film worked, I would have showed it to him already, so he assumed it didn't work. He thought I wasn't showing it to him because he was going to be embarrassed and humiliated, since *Reds* was a Communist picture. He was so miffed he went out and bought *Ragtime*. Which was also a period movie, and also expensive." Beatty suspected that Bluhdorn may even have contemplated shelving *Reds* and giving its slot to *Ragtime*, which made him crazy. According to Pikser, Beatty treated Bluhdorn and the studio as the enemy. Art director Simon Holland remembers him saying, "One of the things that gives me the biggest kick about making this movie about an American Communist is that I got the money to do it from one of the most right-wing fascist people in Hollywood, Charlie Bluhdorn!" But the bottom line was that Paramount made the picture, and no matter what Beatty said in private, publicly he was careful to heap praise on the studio.

When he finally did screen *Reds*, he did so first for Diller, then for Bluhdorn. There was a protocol for these screenings: The guest of honor was never on time. How late he was depended on where he stood in the pecking order. If, say, a screening was scheduled for Beatty at eight in the evening, he might show up at any time after that, but never at eight. When he screened the film for Diller, Beatty would arrive punctually at eight, but Diller was late. (Nicholson was at that screening, and he drawled, in his Nicholson voice, "Hey, Dil, hy'a doin' Dil?") When Beatty showed the picture to Bluhdorn at the screening room on the thirtieth floor of the Gulf + Western Building on Columbus Circle in New York, he and Diller were on time, but Bluhdorn was late. (He was accompanied by bodyguards, who locked the doors of the room.) During the intermission, picking food off silver trays, Bluhdorn said something like, "Vahrren, yoo haf made a vonderful movie, iz fantaztic, I luff yoo in dis, ezpecially, but I haf vun question."

"What is that Mr. Bluhdorn?"

"Vill it zell in Indiana?"

The answer was, "No, of course not."

As postproduction was winding down, the sticky question of writing credits arose. Beatty was anxious for Griffiths to share the credit, probably because otherwise he'd have to say he'd written it himself, and no one would have believed him. Beatty persuaded him to watch the movie before he made up his mind. He was impressed by *Reds.* "John Reed definitely left a mark in the sand," he says. "Unfortunately, the American tide came in and wiped it out. It's to Warren Beatty's eternal credit that he produced a movie that again gave Reed some kind of visibility." Griffiths agreed to take the co-writing credit.

Powerful directors and producers collect writing credits like butterflies, which is why the Writers Guild raises the bar for them, but a determined director or producer (in this case Beatty was both) can often get his way. Did Beatty deserve his credit? In a lengthy and close collaboration like this one, it is often impossible to untangle the who-did-what knot. Beatty was not a facile writer, but by the time he started on *Reds,* he had spent plenty of time doing it. As Griffiths admitted, "He's written thousands of lines of dialogue." Indeed, much of the dialogue in *Reds,* even that spoken by characters other than Reed—rings with the cadence of Beatty's voice. To hear him tell it, he continually rewrote on the set. Says Pikser, choosing his words carefully, "Warren made some contributions in terms of actually moving a pencil across a yellow pad. The scene on the train with Zinoviev, where Reed says, 'The revolution is dissent,' that's Warren." Structure, character development, ideas? "I don't think he does much of that," Pikser continues. "But every line that anybody writes has to be processed through the filter of Warren's sensibility. A lot of the time, writing with Warren is like channeling him. You're gonna write jokes that are his jokes. He may not write them, but neither would you were you not writing a Warren Beatty script."

The rewriting, rerecording, and remixing went right down to the wire. With the premiere—to the editors, it was like the Second

Big sister Shirley MacLaine and young Warren Beatty with mother, Kathlyn, and grandmother, c. 1940–41. *(Photofest)*

Beatty, front, with cigar, in a variety show at Northwestern University, c. 1955.

Beatty with Joan Collins, c. 1959. She said, "He was just *desperate* to become famous." *(Photofest)*

Elia Kazan welcomed, even solicited Beatty's suggestions on the set of *Splendor in the Grass* (1961). *(Time Life Pictures/Pix Inc./ Getty Images)*

Kazan with Natalie Wood. He believed she and Beatty had begun an affair during the production, but most others deny it. *(Sam Falk/ New York Times/ Redux)*

Playwright William Inge, with Beatty on the set of *All Fall Down* (1962), was the architect of Beatty's early career. *(Photofest)*

Agent and producer Charlie Feldman, one of Beatty's early mentors. They quarreled over *What's New Pussycat?* (1965), but the star admired Feldman's style. *(Jean Howard Papers, American Heritage Center, University of Wyoming)*

Beatty got more than he bargained for with Leslie Caron, including a raft of bad press and legal entanglements. *(Photofest)*

A premonition of things to come, as Alexandra Stewart, whom director Arthur Penn said "had no inner fire," rehearses the embarrassing *Mickey One* (1965), with Penn and Beatty. *(Sam Falk/ New York Times/Redux)*

Beatty's first glimpse of Julie Christie, shaking the hand of Queen Elizabeth II at the premiere of *Born Free* (1966), as Leslie Caron watches, joined by Bill Travers, Catherine Deneuve, Christopher Lee, Ursula Andress, and Raquel Welch. *(Photofest)*

Beatty and Faye Dunaway were barely speaking during *Bonnie and Clyde* (1967), a film that turned Hollywood on its head.

Beatty, who produced as well as starred, takes a sorely needed nap on the set of *Bonnie and Clyde*. *(Photofest)*

In the wake of the assassination of Bobby Kennedy in 1968, Beatty, who campaigned on his behalf, speaks out for gun control at a Giants game in San Francisco to a mixture of cheers and boos. *(AP Photo)*

Beatty learned to write on *McCabe and Mrs. Miller* (1971). Here with director Robert Altman. The two were like oil and water. Altman hated big stars, and Beatty hated his slap-dash directorial style. *(Courtesy of the Everett Collection)*

Anti-star Julie Christie dressing down in bib overalls on the set of *Shampoo* in March 1974. Although she and Beatty had already broken up, they continued to be involved. *(Ron Galella)*

Writer Robert Towne was so close to Beatty he was like his "shadow," says Buck Henry. Here, the two converse with *Shampoo* (1975) director Hal Ashby, left. *(© Steve Schapiro)*

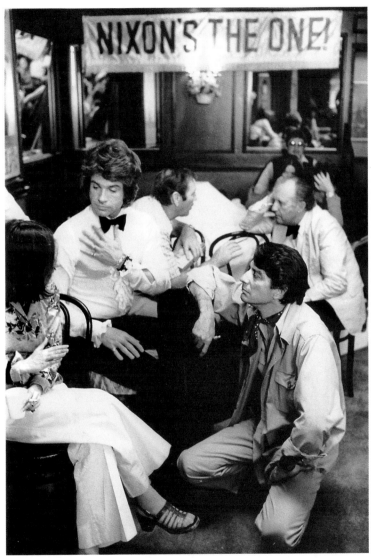

Beatty and the acid-tongued Dick Sylbert, a close friend and collaborator who designed the production, on the set of *Shampoo*. *(© Peter Sorel/ Courtesy of the Academy of Motion Pictures Arts and Sciences)*

Beatty segued from Christie to former Mamas and the Papas beauty Michelle Phillips, replacing Jack Nicholson. Here with daughter Chynna Phillips at the Broadway opening of *Man on the Moon* on January 29, 1975. *(Ron Galella/WireImage/Getty Images)*

Beatty, agent Sue Mengers, and Jack Nicholson, along with former Paramount production head Robert Evans (far right) at the premiere of *Black Sunday* (1977). Evans worshipped Beatty, offered him almost every picture that came along. *(Alan Berliner © Berliner Studio/BEImages)*

Beatty and Buck Henry "co-directed" the 1978 hit *Heaven Can Wait,* but when the star realized he could do it himself, he did so without hesitation, elbowing Henry aside. The film became the first he directed. *(Photofest)*

Beatty with then Paramount head Barry Diller. The two men were fast friends but fought like tomcats over *Reds* (1981), then patched up their differences. *(Ron Galella/ WireImage/Getty Images)*

On location in Spain, in the shadow of Karl Marx, shooting *Reds*. Beatty was no Communist but empathized with the idealism of the American left, and the film, his masterpiece, reflects his ambivalence. *(David Appleby)*

The *Reds* brigade: Beatty behind the camera, director of photography Vittorio Storaro to the right of Beatty, Zelda Barron, script supervisor, far left; associate producer/1st assistant director Simon Relph behind Beatty, editor Dede Allen behind Relph. *(David Appleby)*

On the beach with Beatty and Diane Keaton. The two fell out during the course of the production, but Beatty insisted he would not have made *Reds* if she hadn't agreed to play Louise Bryant, a role originally slated for Julie Christie. *(David Appleby)*

Elaine May on the set of *A New Leaf* (1971). Beatty gave her *Ishtar* out of gratitude for her contribution to *Reds*. *(Photofest)*

Isabelle Adjani on the set of *Ishtar*. About her relationship with Beatty, Dustin Hoffman says, "There wasn't two sentences between them. It was awful." *(© Columbia Pictures/ Courtesy of the Everett Collection)*

Beatty's cousin and right hand man David MacLeod being hustled from the 83rd Precinct to central booking, December, 8, 1989. *(Ken Murray/The Daily News)*

Beatty and Madonna at the *Dick Tracy* premiere in Washington, 1990. The affair ended when the shooting stopped. *(Mark Reistein/IPOL/Globe Photos)*

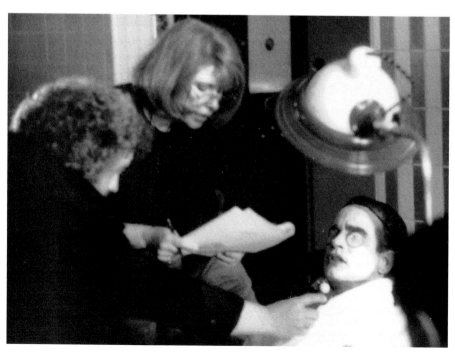

Beatty, who was afflicted with puffiness around the eyes, taking the cucumber cure on the set of *Bugsy* (1991). *(© Peter Sorel/Courtesy of the Academy of Motion Pictures Arts and Sciences)*

Few knew about Annette Bening's relationship with Beatty during the *Bugsy* shoot, let alone her pregnancy. Director Barry Levinson, left, observes the chemistry between the two. *(Peter Sorel/Courtesy of the Academy of Motion Pictures Arts and Sciences)*

Bugsy writer Jim Toback takes a stroll in the desert with the star. Toback was nominated for an Oscar. *(Columbia/Courtesy of the Neal Peters Collection)*

Beatty cutting loose with Halle Berry in *Bulworth*. A razor-sharp commentary on contemporary American politics, it was one of his best pictures, but it never got the business nor recognition it deserves. *(Photofest)*

Nastassja Kinski playing the cello in the nude while Beatty watches, transfixed. He feared this opening of *Town & Country* would make his character unsympathetic, and he was right. *(Photofest)*

Coming—scheduled for December 3, 1981, Beatty and company were still working feverishly into the final days of November. Recalls Fleischman, "The last night that we mixed, we had to have a track negative finished and on the plane at seven o'clock in the morning so they could get the film to Technicolor in Rome, where they were printing it. But that night, Elaine and Warren were writing lines of dialogue! We were just waiting there, 7:30, eight o'clock at night, while they were recording it. They didn't get it to us till midnight. We mixed it in a couple of hours, and delivered it to the guy who had to shoot the negative—he kept his lab open—at two in the morning, then it went to the plane."

Playwright Herb Gardner once said, "Films are never finished, they're abandoned." This was certainly true of Beatty's. But not everyone likes to work that way. McKay says he would never work with Beatty again: "We were going crazy. The process of *Reds* was trying stuff and trying stuff and trying stuff. Then all of a sudden, you're over the cliff. We just ran out of time. Wherever we ended, that was the movie. It wasn't a process that made it possible to work it into a shape. There were parts towards the end that just got left in that should never have been left in. It could have been more refined. And then he still wasn't willing to let go, and say, 'This is it, my movie.' I didn't like working that way. But I have to say, I'm proud of that film. We did a lot of really good work on it. This is a guy who had a passion, and followed his passion, you gotta say that for him."

MARKETING *REDS* was going to be no picnic. The film was long, complex, and the subject matter was alien if not distasteful to a large segment of the American audience, which had just elected Reagan president. Moreover, the Paramount marketing team was not used to selling films like *Reds*. The exhibitor screenings raised a red flag, so to speak. Theater owners complained about the length and the subject matter, said things like, "Oh my God, Communism—I know it's a part of our history, but do we have to have a movie about it?"

Beatty was used to controlling every aspect of the production; marketing, generally the province of the studio, was going to be no different. Nothing Paramount did was right. Beatty hated the trailer, so much so that when the trailer guys came in to show him what they'd done, he was so hard on them they started popping Maalox tablets like M&Ms. But Paramount was not about to roll over and play dead; Beatty would have a fight on his hands. In the same way that he brought Elaine May and others into the editing room, he injected Pat Caddell into the marketing process, armed with his expertise at surveys and polling. Alluding to Francis Coppola's way-over-budget *Apocalypse Now,* Caddell says, "Everyone was telling him this was the greatest disaster since—I used to call it *Apocalypse Again.*" Marketing and distribution were headed by Frank Mancuso, who would later become head of the studio. "Frank was not a big fan of it," Caddell recalls. "He thought this thing was death. Except for Bluhdorn and Diller, the suits, down the line, just wished it would go away. They were terrified. The marketing of this movie was undermined the whole way through."

Neither age nor experience had dulled Caddell's edge. He wasted no time telling the studio people they didn't know what they were doing. "Of course nobody in the movie industry had done any real surveys, except for those yo-yo things they did," he says. "They knew nothing about their audience in those days." But the Paramount executives didn't like to be told their business by an outsider who was Beatty's creature, and arrogant to boot. Caddell was the match that ignited an explosion. "Warren just ripped the shit out of them. He was just angry because of the way they were treating me, because he read that as treating him [badly]. He just took apart the whole place. He and Barry would just knock the living hell out of each other. Warren would drive Barry wild, and Barry would not put up with it. He reamed Warren out because he was bullying and browbeating everyone at Paramount, while they were all breaking their asses trying to help him, and would he please stop this before he destroyed the place! Sometimes Barry would say, 'Fuck it,' and just get up and leave.

"Frank [Mancuso] used to say of himself, 'I think I'm the only adult around here.' Warren at that time was operating on the *Reds* campaign schedule, as we called it, where meetings didn't start till two in the morning, if you were lucky. It would just drive Frank nuts. This was not the only project Paramount had. He and the rest of them had their day job, with other movies. But it was gobbling up 90 percent of their time. With Warren, there's only one film, his. And he's got the strength of personality to impose his will. Warren is a really manipulative person. He would have been an unbelievable politician. He'd put Lyndon Johnson to shame."

Paramount was frightened that Beatty and his film would be red-baited by the Reagan right. Caddell dismissed this as a "paper tiger." There were a few predictably hostile editorials in *The Wall Street Journal, Barron's,* and other corporate mouthpieces, of which Beatty observed, they attacked Bluhdorn "for having financed the movie—fearful, underneath, that Khrushchev was right, that when he banged his shoe and said, 'We will bury you,' that, yeah . . . we were going to get buried by Communism eventually. Well, all you had to do was go there to know that you weren't going to get buried."

Beyond that, the red baiting never materialized, perhaps because Beatty cleverly headed it off by screening the picture at the White House for Barbara Bush (her husband was the vice president), Nancy Reagan, and the president himself. Beatty was first exposed to the idea of Reagan as the great white hope of the right wing by Jules Stein, who founded MCA in 1924. Stein told Beatty, " 'I was talking to Walt [Disney], and we got a guy who we think would make a hell of a president.'

" 'Who's that?'

" 'Ronnie. Ronnie Reagan.' " Beatty recalls, "I thought, Jules is senile. He's gone." He continues, "I met Ronnie at this poolside party at Jules Stein's house when I first came to Hollywood. I was about twenty. He was a very friendly, very affable, very loquacious and cheerful man. And we developed a kind of running banter through the years, with me expressing my sadness about his inability to see the wisdom of my political ways."

By 1980, Beatty had changed his mind about Reagan. "We used to laugh at Warren, because he argued that Reagan would take the presidency," says Caddell. "He smelled some very bad things, so he dropped out to do *Reds,* was out of the country for a whole year." Beatty continues, "Ronnie was not someone that had any particular interest in a left-wing hero. He was very complimentary, but he said he was kind of hoping for a happy ending. Which I think he thought he got in 1989, when the Soviet Union disintegrated."

The damaging buzz about *Reds* came from elsewhere. Well before postproduction ended, the press began sniping about the cost of the picture. Says Dick Sylbert, "We shot in studios all over Europe, we shot in every fucking country in the world, we came back and filled the studios in L.A., we were in New York, we were in Washington. You couldn't pay for that picture today." (Beatty shot in sixteen cities in six countries.) The figure Paramount was giving out was $33.5 million. Beatty says he's not sure, maybe $34 million. The figures in the press, which weren't really based on anything but one another, gradually crept up into the $40s. But Aaron Latham in *Rolling Stone* quoted an unnamed Paramount source who put the figure at near $50 million. And according to Caddell, the budget was over $50 million—"no one would ever say the right number"—which would be equivalent to about $250 million in today's dollars. (For comparison's sake, the budget of *Heaven's Gate* was estimated to be $44 million.) Says Bob Evans, "I don't know how much *Reds* was in the red, it never came out, but you and I for the rest of our lives, should make what that film lost. No one will ever know. When it came to fixing the books, Bluhdorn was a genius."

To make matters worse, British producer David Puttnam, shortly to become chairman of Columbia Pictures, harshly and publicly attacked Beatty for overspending, calling *Reds* "lunacy" and "despicable." He even said that Beatty should be "spanked."

(It didn't escape the notice of Oscar watchers that this was probably the first shot in his campaign for his own picture, *Chariots of Fire*, which could be expected to go up against *Reds*. There were already hard feelings between the two productions. When *Chariots*'s Milena Canonero tried to find costumes for her film, she discovered that *Reds* had hoovered up everything in England from caps to socks for the same period, and had to have hers handmade in Italy.)

Beatty flummoxed the studio by declining to do press, making a difficult marketing job nearly impossible. His thinking, which he now calls "quaint," is that he would have inevitably oversimplified or caricatured the film by speaking about it. He refused to screen it for *Life* magazine, which was prepared to do a major spread. Ditto *Newsweek* and *The New York Times*. "He had his own psychology about being a recluse and all that," observes Caddell. "Of not being worn out by TV, the small box that tends to diminish stars if they're on too much." Adds Pikser, "His whole approach is constantly rope-a-dope. 'I'm going to do everything I possibly can to lose, and see if I can somehow win.' That's Warren."

But that didn't mean that he didn't care about press. When he screened the picture for the *Times*'s Vincent Canby, he sent Cindy Kaplan with it, to keep an eye on the film cans and assess the reviewer's reaction. "Warren grilled me about every little eyebrow movement, every flicker of his eye. Did he like it? I couldn't tell."

When *Reds* was screened for the cast and crew, the audience—mostly the crew—was so disgruntled that they actually booed when Beatty's name flashed on the screen.

Reds OPENED on December 4, 1981, in 389 theaters, a relatively modest number, and took the weekend with a $2,411,083 gross. (*On Golden Pond* opened the same time.) *Reds* was so long that it could only play once on weeknights, and three times a day on weekends, reducing the box office, which was good, but not great. In its first run, it grossed $30 million. Theater owners complained that had Beatty promoted it, it would have brought in an additional $25 million. Caddell says Paramount considered it a disaster, although the studio had tax-sheltered *Reds* with Barclays Bank, easing the pain with a sale-leaseback agreement, and put together a currency deal hedging pounds against dollars that went the studio's way. "That was just a piece of bird-brained luck that took any sting from *Reds*," Diller says. "By the time the picture was finished, we were in profit!" Beatty too says the picture eventually made its way into the black.

As it turned out, Canby, like most other critics, loved it. He called it "an extraordinary film, a big romantic adventure movie, the best since David Lean's *Lawrence of Arabia*," high praise indeed. Comparing *Reds* to *Doctor Zhivago* and *Citizen Kane*, Richard Corliss wrote in *Time*, "*Reds* is a big, smart movie, vastly ambitious and entertaining, full of belief in Reed and the ability of a popular audience to respond to him." Ironically, Pauline Kael, who arguably might have recused herself on the basis of her personal involvement with Beatty, panned it. "It isn't really very good," she wrote. "The movie keeps backing away from its subject. It's possible that Beatty . . . got so far into the material and changed his thinking so many times that he lost the clarity needed to dramatize it. . . . The film is tentative, full of doubts and second thoughts and fifteenth thoughts." She added that "Beatty could have been reciting from a manual, and Keaton might be dubbed—the words don't seem related to anything going on in her head," which was total nonsense in view of the across-the-board electric performances to which she was oblivious.

Kael was so far off base that it's hard to avoid the conclusion that her spleen was showing. Says Toback, "I was the reason she left Paramount, and yet for reasons I will never understand, she harbored resentment towards Warren, which is reflected in her review of *Reds,* which I think was personally vicious, intended to wound him. She must have thought to herself, What can I say that will hurt him the most. And what would that be other than he didn't direct Diane Keaton well. This was his girlfriend, this was the female lead, and he's supposed to know more about women than anybody, and he failed with her." Paul Sylbert adds, "Warren betrayed Pauline. She was a woman who was small and not particularly attractive. But make no mistake: she had a real ego too. Every movie she viewed, she went in there like it was a date. I said to her once, 'At the age of twelve, you sat in a movie with one hand in the popcorn and the other hand on your crotch, having yourself off.' Look at the titles. *Kiss Kiss Bang Bang. I Lost It at the Movies.* That's the reason she turned against these people. It was like a bad fuck." Said Beatty, in the mid-1990s, "I haven't spoken to her in ten years. And do you know what's worse? She doesn't know it! The vituperative bitch."

Critics of the film have said that Keaton was miscast, and it's true that she doesn't convey the sexual heat that would have made Bryant a "heartbreaker" as Nicholson's O'Neill calls her. She's too fragile, too brittle. But there is an undeniable intensity to the relationship between Reed and Bryant, and the film comes to life more in conflict than in passion—their screaming matches appear to be so authentic they're scary—a testimony to Beatty's success in tapping into the combustibility of their off-screen relationship with endless retakes. Whether the inspiration for their performances lies in anger or affection, in the actors or the characters, or in all of the above, they work, as do all the other performances with which this movie is packed. We care about them. And in that sense Beatty's gamble casting his lover paid off: he never spilled the consommé.

Bryant repeatedly asks, "What as?" querying the different roles she is asked to play in her life, so much so that it becomes a refrain, and we have to ask, Just what are these two to each other? Ultimately, they are "comrades," the title of Griffiths's first draft, and the word Reed whispers in Bryant's ear on his deathbed. More than just lovers, more than just revolutionaries, they have made political lives, lived their politics. If nothing else, *Reds* is a tribute to that kind of high political seriousness.

But it was not like Beatty to explore one half of a dialectic without the other, so at the same time, *Reds* dramatizes the high costs of the political life, the sacrifice of the personal, which, among other things, gives the film its complexity. The puppy that Reed gives Bryant, which Kael makes fun of and many took to be no more than a sop to the audience intended to sugarcoat the political pill, for Beatty also stood for the child the couple never had. He underlines this by letting his camera linger on a boy Bryant encounters as she tends to Reed dying in the hospital. Reed has to learn to stop running away from himself and his relationship with Bryant. Ultimately, of course, he chooses political commitment over personal commitment, and is punished by death, the ultimate disincentive.

Problematical as Kael's review was, she did zero in on some of the picture's weaknesses, mostly having to do with its sexual politics, like the emergence of the hoary double standard. We learn from conversation between Reed and Bryant that he has apparently had numerous flings, but they're never dramatized because, as he argues, they don't mean anything, while her one transgression with O'Neill is all important. Reed is invariably portrayed bringing Bryant armfuls of white lilies—her favorite flower—when he returns from his various trips, only to find her in a snit over something or other, or worse, in O'Neill's arms. In other words, Reed is the victim in love, much as Beatty liked to portray himself in life.

In the first half of the picture, Bryant is fiercely independent and ambitious, but as the plot unfolds, she devolves into a dutiful wife, ending up, finally, in that most traditional of female roles: a nurse. She has to learn not to be such a fierce feminist, competitive and careerist. The public life that exercises such sway over her husband is not supposed to be for her.

On February 11, 1982, the Motion Picture Academy announced that *Reds* had scooped up twelve nominations, two more than its nearest competitor, *On Golden Pond*, three more than *Heaven Can Wait*, and the most any picture could boast of since *A Man for All Seasons* in 1966. Beatty's four personal nominations matched his four for *Heaven Can Wait*, setting the bar so high that it has never been matched. (Welles was nominated in this quartet of categories only once.) Also nominated for Best Picture that year were *Raiders of the Lost Ark*, *Atlantic City*, and, in what seemed like a footnote, *Chariots of Fire*.

As it turned out, it was a tough year, with both Beatty and Keaton drowned by a wave of nostalgia for Henry Fonda and Katharine Hepburn, who won Best Actor and Actress for *On Golden Pond* on March 29. Dick Sylbert lost to *Raiders of the Lost Ark,* to a big rolling stone, as he put it.

In the end, *Reds* won only three Oscars: Storaro for cinematography, Stapleton for supporting actress, and Beatty for directing. In an otherwise generous speech Beatty thanked almost everyone—except the editors, reopening the wounds of postproduction. Recalls Craig McKay, "Dede was in shock, she was furious." Later at the Governor's Ball, she lit into Beatty, said something like, "You're ungrateful. With all we did for you, the least you could do is recognize us." Beatty made an excuse, saying that he was so sure that he was going to win Best Picture that rather than repeat himself, he intended to acknowledge her then. But he never did anything without forethought, and those who knew recalled the bad blood between the two and rolled their eyes. Says McKay, "I saw a friend of mine out in the hall, he turned to me, and he said, 'Man, what a slap in the face.'"

If indeed it was Beatty's intention to thank Allen and the rest on his second trip to the stage, it was thwarted. As Loretta Young tore open the envelope, Spielberg, who knew *Raiders* didn't have a chance, squeezed Puttnam's shoulder, saying, "It's going to be you—I know it's going to be you." Indeed, it was. *Reds* lost Best Picture to Puttnam's feel-good soufflé, *Chariots of Fire.* It was 1978 all over again, only worse. Beatty suspected that *Reds* might have been a victim of endemic anti-Communist sentiment in the Academy. "The character who had the clearest anti-Communist message in it was Emma Goldman, and Maureen won the Academy Award," he says. "It also won cinematography and direction, because those things were separable from thinking, Well, Jesus, we're endorsing a Communist movie." (Of course, by this argument, Nicholson, whose O'Neill sneered at his friends' politics, should have won for Best Supporting Actor, instead of John Gielgud, for *Arthur*—another vote against death.) A more likely explanation is that Puttnam's attempt to portray *Chariots* vs. *Reds* as a David and Goliath contest had worked. "I went out of my way to get it seen in those terms," he admitted. "I played up the cost of *Reds,* which at the time Beatty and Diller were desperately trying to play down. I crazed both of them." Beatty and Puttnam "hated each other," says

Dick Sylbert. And, of course, as one source puts it, "A lot of people in Hollywood did not want to see Warren succeed. He just had too many fingers in too many pies. Actor, producer, director, writer—they were out for him."

But there were consolations. Beatty screened the picture for Lillian Hellman, who by that time was nearly blind. She didn't see it, she heard it, but she liked it enough to sit through it. (Hellman would die at the age of seventy-nine on June 30, 1984.) He also showed it to Elia Kazan. Kazan had not, apparently, liked *Shampoo*, and had told Beatty at the time, "You know, Warren, you should have talked to me before you made that movie." But after *Reds*, he called Beatty and said, "You really are a good director."

Despite the film's failure to win Best Picture, *Reds* put to rest precisely that question: How good a director was Beatty? One day, by the pool, during the *Heaven Can Wait* shoot, Julie Christie confided to a friend, "Warren doesn't have an aesthetic bone in his body." Paul Sylbert, for one, disagrees, but he understood what she meant. "I sent him some sketches, and he called me up and said, 'Paul, they brought tears to my eyes.' He was dead serious. Elements of his responses are genuine, but they're not aesthetic. Warren may be in some sense what Mervyn LeRoy was—he said it himself—'I'm not a director, I'm a selector'—which means you let the camera run a lot, get a bunch of stuff, sit with the editor, and you pick the best stuff and figure out how to work it. He takes in information endlessly, processes it, sifts it, and something finally pops out, and it pops out for a lot of reasons that he's calculated. But artists do not calculate. They work from other sources. He does calculate. He's a processor."

But of course, there is more than one kind of artist, and if Beatty was indeed a "selector," or a "processor," as opposed to an intuitive artist, that didn't necessarily make him any less an artist. Raised on the films of the postwar Italian neorealists, studio directors like Stevens and Wyler, the naturalistic theater of the '30s, '40s, and '50s via Inge, Williams, and Kazan, and even the improvisational looseness of Altman, Beatty tried to leave few fingerprints on his work. He effaced himself stylistically in the same way that he did as a writer, as Buck Henry points out, and as an actor, playing against his image. Distinguishing himself from the activist directors, Beatty always compared himself to the "passive" ones, like Hal Ashby. Dick Sylbert puts it this way: "Film schools gave us guys—Spielberg, Lucas, Coppola, Scorsese—who were much more interested in moving the equipment than in moving the audience. They loved the mechanics. On *Cotton Club,* Coppola said to me, 'This is going to be the Kurosawa shot.' I had never heard anybody say that in my life. All their references were to other movies. Nobody I ever worked with would ever have thought of doing that. They came from the theater, and their references were to real life. Behavioral. Emotional. The Fords and the Hawkses and the Wylers, and the Stevenses, that whole generation, as well as the Kazans and the Rittses and the Lumets—they all wanted to disappear so you could watch the movie."

Unlike most of the New Hollywood filmmakers of the 1970s, Beatty did not aspire to be an auteur in the European sense; his headliner's regard for commercial success saved him from that trap. (He would say things to novice screenwriters like, "Get rid of all that Antonioni crap.") Deriding the auteur theory, Beatty strove for directorial transparency, avoiding the flashy flourishes that called attention to themselves, the jittery camera and long tracking shots that Scorsese favored, or the signature 360 degree tail-swallowing pans so dear to Brian De Palma. Like Kazan he was an actor's director, and the heart of his films lies in casting and performance. He discovers his films as he goes along, which is one of the reasons he does so many takes, excessive as that may seem. And yes, in the editing room, he combs through those takes looking for the sparks, the happy accidents, the flashes of inspiration. Beatty is at the opposite end of the spectrum from painterly or pictorial directors for whom the look of the film is all important, and who keep their shooting ratios down by storyboarding every shot. He is at the opposite end of the spectrum from the visionaries like Scorsese, who carry their films in their heads. His movies are less aesthetic objects in themselves than windows on the world. But he is no less an artist or auteur for that. It's the difference, to borrow from Isaiah Berlin, between the hedgehog and the fox. If Scorsese is the hedgehog, exploring a singular vision, Beatty is the fox, who allows the material to dictate the aesthetic of the movie. It's the difference between regarding the world through one lens, and looking at it through a kaleidoscope. The logical extreme of his kind of naturalism is documentary. Beatty tiptoed up to the edge in *Shampoo,* with his use of TV news clips as source music, as it were, and went even further in *Reds*, with his use of the Witnesses and nonactors like Kosinski and Plimpton, but he always pulled back—saved, again, by his commercial instincts.

The star's aesthetic conservatism—his belief in transparency, in naturalism, in letting script and acting inform the film—makes it difficult to identify a Beatty style, a Beatty film, except in the negative: his refusal to move the camera, his reluctance to break up performances with quick cuts. But what can be said of Jean Renoir's signature? Or Coppola's? No one would deny the auteur label to either of these filmmakers. If one key element of film artistry is the amount of control exercised over what is essentially a complex industrial process, as a quadruple hyphenate Beatty's sensibility permeates his movies as fully as any of the more readily acknowledged auteurs of his era.

Oddly, *Reds* might have done better had it come out earlier or later. Earlier, because the dumbing down of the smart, early 1970s movie audiences brought up on European films and the likes of Nichols, Altman, Scorsese and so on was already in full swing, and later, because *Reds* was eerily prescient. It's a picture that almost has to be read backward, in the light of events that occurred subsequent to its release. It anticipated both the breakup of the Soviet Union and the rise of Muslim fundamentalism. Beatty adds, more in sorrow than in anger, "In the subject matter and the willingness to gamble, *Reds* marked the end of something. What moved the late '60s and '70s was politics. *Reds* is a political movie. It begins with politics and it ends with politics. It was in some sense a reverie about that way of thinking in American life, one that went back to 1915." But it was also, he says, a reverie about the two decades just past, about Beatty's own generation. "We were those old lefties that were narrating this movie," he continues. "We, me, the people who were interested in politics. *Reds* was a death rattle."

AFTER LOSING Best Picture to *Chariots of Fire*, Beatty was burned out and exhausted. He talked openly about quitting pictures. "I think there was something in me that quit after *Reds*," he says. If anything, his fascination with politics had been heightened by his immersion in *Reds* and the parlous times in which he found himself when he emerged from the Russian Revolution to contemplate the brave new right-wing world of Reagan's America. Like a dog coming in out of the rain, Reagan tried to shake off the damp residue of defeat left by the Vietnam War by militarizing his foreign policy. He picked safe targets—bombed Libya, and overran Grenada. Domestically, he made a shambles of government, staffing agencies with corporate lobbyists from the very companies they were intended to regulate. "It was said that government doesn't solve problems, government is the problem," Beatty recalls, paraphrasing one of the president's slogans. "So you wind up with no government. And so what happens? You're governed by the rich, you're governed by money, you're governed by advertising."

Congenitally upbeat, Beatty barely paused to mourn Jimmy Carter, for whom he had no use, saying, "You can mark the end of the politics of the '70s with the election of Carter. There's nothing that can destroy the Democratic Party like a Democrat." In fact, he regarded the electorate's repudiation of Carter and romance with Reagan as an opportunity to revitalize the Democratic Party at a time when the old-guard New Deal, Great Society Democrats—think Ted Kennedy—were bloodied and bowed. Enter the New Democrats, the generation of younger politicians that included the likes of Bruce Babbitt, Dick Gephardt, Joe Biden Jr., and Chuck Robb, who would soon find happiness in the embrace of the Democratic Leadership Council, which would be founded by Al From and fellow travelers in 1985 in response to Reagan's burial of Walter "Fritz" Mondale in the previous year's presidential race. The DLC's strategy—later implemented by Bill Clinton—was to co-opt the Republican program, that is, dump Lyndon Johnson's Great Society in favor of free market economics, deregulation, and small government.

Prominent among these born-again Democrats was Beatty's old friend Gary Hart, now a Colorado senator. Hart liked to say that the contest wasn't between left and right, Democrats and Republicans, but between the past and the future, with himself, of course, incarnating the future, while he tarred Mondale with his old-fashioned Midwest and Eastern industrial base as a backward-looking "soot and smokestack" Democrat. Hart voters were the big chillers—baby boomer yuppies, the hind end of the Vietnam generation about to become dot-com millionaires, the "Atari Democrats" or "Quiche Corps" as his staff liked to call them with not a little contempt. Hart cast himself as a nonideological technocrat intent on steering the Democratic Party away from traditional "interest group" liberalism. He advocated creating jobs by growing the technology sector. That having been said, however, Hart had one of the most liberal voting records in the Senate.

It was no secret that Hart had designs on the presidency, which made it almost inevitable that he would turn to Hollywood for cash. Reagan's success had dispelled much of the stigma that clung to Tinseltown activism since the blacklist, and it seemed that what worked for Reagan might work for Hart as well. In no time at all, Hart became the darling of the Hollywood left, people like Jane Fonda and Tom Hayden, Danny Goldberg, Lorne Michaels, to whom he seemed like a breath of fresh air compared to the stiff, standoffish Democrats they were used to. Hart was more than ready to return the favor. He "was excited by being with celebrities, that gave him a thrill, a kick, and he wanted to emulate their lifestyle as far as drinking and nightlife and women and all the rest," said former Kennedy staffer Ted Sorensen. But it was, as Ron Brownstein calls, a "fatal attraction."

Political consultant Bill Bradley met Beatty for the first time in November 1982 at a planning meeting that preceded a Hart fund-raiser on the studio lot thrown by Fox owner Marvin Davis. Beatty headlined the $5,000-a-plate event, which raised $100,000 for his friend. Bradley started in politics in the late 1970s working with Hayden and Fonda's Campaign for Economic Democracy. He would become Hart's Northern California coordinator, as well as a close friend of the actor's. He says, "Maybe if *Reds* had been a huge hit, which it was not, maybe if it had won Best Picture, Warren would have acted differently, but he was pooh-poohing movies: 'I've done movies, this is more important, we can make history here.'"

Remaining aloof from Hart's network of entertainment industry supporters, Beatty operated behind the scenes. He monitored the campaign by phone. Said Hart press secretary Kathy Bushkin, "He was disruptive to my sleep. He was the kind of person who called you at three in the morning and just wanted to know what was going on." He intervened directly only when he believed it couldn't be helped. More a traditional Democrat than his friend, the star kept Hart from going too far down the neoliberal road. Beatty was the only person who could calm Hart down, focus him. He was often the last man to leave the room before a debate. Hart would take criticism from Beatty that he would not take from his staffers because he feared they might be trying to forward their own careers at the expense of his own. "Warren has that manner that makes you feel very confident about things," says Bradley. "You can get off the phone with him and think, Well, if Warren believes that, then of course. He's very good with politicians, and he's very good with actresses, and there are similarities between the two." But according to Brownstein, Hart believed that Beatty could never quite accept the fact that he wasn't running for president himself. Still, Hart's candidacy was the next best thing, maybe even better. Had Hart won, Beatty would have been the power behind the throne, in the role he liked best: the "phantom."

Hart, then forty-five, announced in February of 1983. Like McGovern, he was an underdog from the outset, and initially stumbled badly. He made a poor showing in the straw polls that ranked the Democratic hopefuls, barely breaking 1 percent against a field that included heavy-hitters like Mondale, Ohio senator and former astronaut John Glenn, and California senator Alan Cranston. Too often Hart seemed like he was doing little more than channeling JFK. When he orated, he chopped the air with his forefinger like his sainted predecessor, while borrowing his rhetorical flourishes. But they served him poorly, calling attention instead to the dissimilarities between himself and Kennedy. Rather than inspiring, his speeches were soporific. Dishing out policy wonk rhetoric in a monotone, he sounded as if he were addressing the Council on Foreign Relations. He rarely smiled, and consequently came off as aloof and distant, John Kerry before John Kerry.

Beatty urged Hart to rid himself of the inside-the-Beltway locutions. "If Gary was using language in a speech or a debate that was too lawyerlike or Washington-oriented, Warren could remind him that [that] couldn't sell," explained Bushkin. "He was trying to get Gary [centered] on . . . making his points in graphic, effective ways."

But more problematic than Hart's style was his message, which was vague and unfocused. First he was the environmental candidate. Toward the end of the year, Hart's advisers abruptly announced that Hart would be the candidate of women. What they meant was that he would promote women's rights, but those who were close to the candidate snickered, because even in those days rumors of his infidelities were rife. When he was running the McGovern campaign in 1972, he had a life-sized cutout of Candice Bergen in his office, and he liked to play a game called, "Who's Attractive?" "Certain campaigns have a buzz about them, a sexual charge," explains Bradley. "They attract a lot of women who are very open to suggestion and often make the suggestion themselves. There's a lot of availability."

When Hart's campaign hoisted the "candidate of women" flag, Beatty's attitude was, "You're floundering—'the candidate of women'— give me a break! We need strategic direction. You've got to bring Pat back in." Bradley continues, "Pat Caddell and Gary had always had a prickly relationship. Gary thought that Pat was a difficult guy. Pat thought he was bigger than Gary, even though Gary was a senator running for president. A fair amount of what Warren did in the Hart campaign was patch up things between them."

Beatty brokered a fragile truce between the two men, perhaps facilitated by the fact that Mondale had been quoted in the *Boston Globe* calling Caddell "crazy," which infuriated the pollster. Caddell became Hart's chief strategist and "message doctor," as *Newsweek* called him.

BEATTY WAS looking for a project to do with Elaine May, who would write and direct while he would produce. "He owed her for *Reds,*" says Peter Feibleman. "And for *Heaven Can Wait*. He did it out of gratitude." Beatty had not been able to shake the idea for a film about a director who goes to Latin America to make a picture about a revolution, during which a revolution actually breaks out. The more he thought about it, the more it appealed to him. He thought maybe this was the picture for May. "I wanted the director to be played by Orson Welles," he recalls. Beatty knew Welles the way he knew everyone. He occasionally used to join him and filmmaker Henry Jaglom at their weekly lunches at Ma Maison on Melrose. Like others of his generation, he shared Jaglom's veneration for the orotund auteur of *Citizen Kane*.

But by the early 1980s, Welles was virtually unemployable. "Orson couldn't get a movie done," Jaglom remembers. "So I said, 'Orson, there's nothing to be done except for you to write a new script. Tell me some stories.'

" 'I can't write anymore, I'm no longer capable of doing it.'

" 'That's bullshit. Just tell me the stuff.'

" 'I can't, I know what I can do, I know what I can't do.'

"After a series of lunches. he told me one story about this old Roosevelt-type guy and his protégé, a young senator, a Kennedyesque character. Three weeks later, I got called at four in the morning. 'I don't know what the fuck you're making me do this for, I can't sleep, but I've written three pages.'

" 'Read them to me.'

" 'They're terrible.'

" 'Read them to me anyway.'

"Of course they were great. I got him to write this entire script called *The Big Brass Ring,* about America at the end of the century, the way Kane was America at the beginning of the century." Jaglom was thrilled. "I couldn't fuckin' believe it—I've got the bookend to *Citizen Kane*!" He continues, "But I couldn't get anyone to do it. Then Arnon Milchan agreed to $8 million if I got one of eight stars. We opened a big bottle of Cristal, because Orson always thought that actors would never betray him. One by one these actors came up with reasons—including my two friends, Jack and Warren. But Warren behaved better than anybody. He was very honorable, and Orson never blamed him. He had just come off of *Reds,* and he said to me, 'Oh, God, tell Orson it's like coming out of a whorehouse into the sunshine after being up all night fucking, I'm exhausted, and there's Marilyn Monroe with her arms flung out, ready to embrace me, I look at her and I say, "I would love to, but I can't," and that's the way I feel about this movie. I would love to do it, but I can't.' "

In April 1983, looking for places where revolutions were in fact breaking out, Beatty, along with May and Feibleman, took off to Central America, where they had many strange and wonderful adventures that don't concern us here. But, Beatty continues, "Elaine wasn't interested in Central America, she was interested in the Middle East. Besides, she doesn't like to be given an idea and then go do it. She decided, I'm going to do my own thing."

That fall Beatty was honored by the Toronto International Film Festival, then trying to put itself on the map by showcasing Hollywood stars. David MacLeod, a Toronto native, was known to the organizers of the festival as "their man in Hollywood," friend to Beatty, Nicholson, and Christie, all of whom he promised to deliver to the festival. But it was easier said than done. The festival organizers were not novices at managing celebrities; they had already staged tributes for Martin

Scorsese, Robert De Niro, and Robert Duvall. But, as Brian D. Johnson wrote in his history of the event, "In Warren Beatty, the festival met its match. After the tributes to Scorsese and Duvall, honoring Beatty in a manner that would make him feel comfortable required an entirely different order of diplomacy. Scorsese was a great director, Duvall was a great actor and Beatty was a bit of both. But he had something that was beyond their reach: the glamour and power of Hollywood royalty." Said theater manager John Allen, "There was a feeling that we were doing God's work here. There was the Normandy invasion, and then there was putting on the tribute."

MacLeod, who micromanaged the Beatty event, had plenty of friends in Toronto. "We got high together," says the festival's David Gilmour. "We did Mandrax and went skydiving—he and one of his little Indian boys, Ronnie, a real pretty-boy Indian. . . . [Mandrax is] a major tranquillizer with a kick to it. David was a serious pill boy."

As is customary on these occasions, the festival prepared a montage of clips drawn from Beatty's films, all of which had to be approved by the star. "They wanted to control the images," said Bill House, who produced the tribute. "They made us cut a scene from *Splendor in the Grass,* the scene near the end of the movie with Natalie Wood against the lockers, the prelude to a kiss. They didn't want that because of whatever notions there were about Beatty and women.

"We had plainclothes cops all through the venue. I couldn't quite figure out why that had to be. I was thinking, this is Toronto, what are you guys talking about? Then when I met him, there was this sense of fear, as if there were people who hated him because he slept with a lot of women, because his politics were left, because he was so good-looking—whatever. It was like you were guarding against some kind of attack or assassination. And I don't think I'm being dramatic."

The afternoon of the tribute, they did a run-through at the University Theatre. Preoccupied with how he was going to extract himself from the premises at the end of the ceremony, Beatty was leaving nothing to chance and bombarded theater manager Allen with questions about the exit route. "We'll take you down these stairs, and then we can go down the alley to your limousine in the back," said Allen.

"How far is it?" Beatty asked.

"I don't know. About 30 or 40 feet."

"Let's find out." Beatty hopped off the stage, and placing one foot before the other, paced off the distance to his limo. Returning, he informed Allen, "It's 47 of my feet. But I think my foot is not quite a foot. Let's call it 40 feet. How long do you think that will take me?"

"Will you be with other people?"

"Let's do it two ways, one with me walking by myself, and one with other people." He retraced his steps while Allen timed him. Then he did it again accompanied by several other people, determining that indeed it took more time.

Beatty was a reluctant participant. He sat in the audience next to MacLeod and Diane Keaton. Even at that late hour, the organizers of the event weren't sure if Beatty intended to go up on stage and deliver a speech. Much to their relief, he did. Johnson thought, This must be the Big Time. Finally, the festival had made it. We could all relax, because this was as good as it gets. Warren and Jack—Hollywood's Mick and Keith—made the dream come true.

Before he left Toronto, Beatty paused for a few moments to make out with Sandra Bernhard in front of the elevator bank of their hotel. "I didn't know if I should have taken that as an insult or a compliment—but it was fun kissing him," she says. "He used to call me late at night, and be kind of sexy, say, 'It's Uncle Warren. What are you doing? What are you wearing right now? What's going on?'

" 'Well, I'm laying in bed, I'm wearing my flannel pajamas, nothing too sexy. Kind'a cozy.' It was like he was going through his phone book and said, 'I'll give Sandy Bernhard a call.' It was just a shtick. That's as far as it ever went. But I have a lot of affection for him. He's an amazing man."

Diverting as the Toronto tribute may have been, there was still the issue of May's picture. One night, Beatty was having dinner in New York with her and attorney Bert Fields, who represented both of them. During a lively discussion about who would play opposite Beatty, Dustin Hoffman's name came up. Beatty and Hoffman didn't really know each other, despite arriving in New York around the same time, but Fields represented Hoffman as well, and had brought May into *Tootsie* three years earlier to replace writer Larry Gelbart. Hoffman had loved her work. At the end of the dinner, Beatty and Fields walked May home along Central Park West. The story goes that they were having a good laugh at the idea of May directing the two stars. How better to bust a studio?

May began making up scenes. The idea was to riff on the string of Bob Hope and Bing Crosby "Road" movies that were big in the 1940s. Beatty and Hoffman would play two schlemiels, a pair of hopelessly bad, sub–Simon and Garfunkels a decade and a half late, staggering from one tacky venue to another. Unable to make a cent in the U.S., the two get a gig in Morocco, where they stumble into the crossfire between left-wing guerrillas and the CIA. May had the bright idea of scrambling the casting, which struck her as funny: Hoffman would play the Crosby role, the suave ladies' man, while Beatty would assay Hope's, the klutz.

Beatty took the story idea to his old friend Guy McElwaine, then chairman of Columbia Pictures, which had been purchased by Coca-Cola in 1982. The star's high opinion of May was evident in the marching orders he gave his attorney: "Bert, anything she wants. Period. That's my negotiating position." It was submitted as a Beatty-May collaboration, with the possibility of Hoffman coming aboard. But McElwaine was wary. May had not directed a movie since *Mikey and Nicky*, in 1973, and her reputation preceded her, as did Beatty's and Hoffman's, perfectionists all, for whom nothing was ever good enough. In Beatty, Hoffman, and May, the project featured three people who loved to argue. That may have been just the thing to stave off Alzheimer's by burnishing the gray matter, but it wasn't good for the budget. With the exception of Stanley Kubrick, May was the only director who shot as much film as Beatty. Columbia's "nightmare was having a trio of Hollywood's most uncompromising talents working on the same project somewhere in the Sahara Desert," says a source close to the film, who adds that the studio wanted the desert sequences shot in California or Arizona, not Morocco, where they finally ended up. (Coca-Cola went along with Morocco, because the company had frozen assets there that could only be spent within the country.) "Months before we started shooting, people were willing to lay down substantial amounts of money that there would never be a first day of shooting, let alone a last day. Columbia's other nightmare, however, was passing on a project that included Warren, Dustin, and Elaine, having it go to Fox or Universal, and watching it be a huge hit."

"You have to be very careful if you're going to say no to something of Warren's, because his record as a producer," McElwaine explained at the time, "is 1,000 percent in terms of just recouping on a per-picture basis, cash." The executive knew full well that *Shampoo* had brought Columbia $24 million in film rentals and four Oscar nominations, while *Heaven Can Wait* had earned nearly $50 million in rentals for Paramount, not to mention nine Oscar nominations, and *Reds* had scored 12 nominations. He also knew that Hoffman had made two of Columbia's biggest hits, *Kramer vs. Kramer* in 1979, and *Tootsie* in 1982. Nor was the studio afraid to spend money, witness its then recent comedies: *Ghostbusters* at $33 million and *Tootsie* at $35 million, both of which made their money back and more—much more. Said McElwaine, "I spent a lot of time with Elaine, talking about this project. And she assured me she was not going to misbehave." But this was like asking Amy Winehouse to go into rehab. Still, on the basis of Beatty's persuasiveness and May's assurances, McElwaine committed without a script.

But Beatty did not intend this to be his next picture. As always, he had other irons in the fire, and he couldn't decide which to do next. As he puts it, "What happens sometimes when you have too many choices, you can't make any." He continues, "Kazan asked me if I would star in a remake of *A Face in the Crowd*. I told him I didn't think that he should be remaking his own movies. But if he remade it, that I would do it."

At the same time, Beatty announced that he would appear in Towne's *Tequila Sunrise*. Towne was also working on a script called *Mermaid*, in which Beatty was to star, with Arthur Penn directing. But Beatty and Towne were so dilatory, it was rendered redundant by *Splash*. Paul Mazursky offered him the part of the filthy, unshaven, homeless bum in *Down and Out in Beverly Hills*, which would become a hit for Disney in 1986. "I originally went to Jack Nicholson," he recalls. "Jack wanted to play the part. But there was one little problem: 'I owe a favor to Bobby. Bobby Evans. Gotta do *Two Jakes*.'

" 'I don't want to wait.' "

So Mazursky went to the next guy, Beatty, who was also interested. Mazursky knew that Beatty always said he was interested, but he waited by the phone anyway. Having been down this road before, the director gave himself a deadline: three days. Three days came and went, and no call. He gave him another three days. That brought him into the weekend, a few more days. Still no call. Another four days passed. Finally the phone rang: "What's your address," a soft voice whispered. Shortly thereafter, the doorbell rang. Mazursky's two teenage girls were there with their fourteen-year-old friends. They were extremely striking, and the director well knew that teenage girls "made Warren tremble." They shrieked with delight when Mazursky told them who was at the door. Somewhere in the back of his mind he was uncomfortably aware that he was pimping his own girls in exchange for a commitment to the picture. Idly examining a framed photograph of Mazursky with his pal Federico Fellini, Beatty smiled and murmured, "You want Jack. I know you do."

"He's perfect for the part. But he can't do it. He has to do *The Two Jakes* first. But that doesn't mean you aren't."

"Yeah, but you want Jack."

"Just think of a dirty, filthy Warren Beatty, lying in the gutter, who gets all cleaned up and gives it to Bette Midler. It can't miss! It cannot miss!"

Beatty said, "I'll call you," and left.

After waiting a month or so for Beatty's call, Mazursky went to Nick Nolte. "I got him," he says, "and it turned out great."

In addition to sniffing the picks of the current litter, Beatty had his own pet projects lined up. He had promised Jim Toback that if he did not produce, he would at least launch his next film, *The Pick-up Artist*. He was also noodling a remake of *An Affair to Remember*. The press reported that that Beatty's next project would be *Howard Hughes*. Then there was *Bugsy*, the true-life tale of Benjamin Siegel, the gangster who charmed Hollywood and built the Flamingo Hotel in Las Vegas. Beatty had hired Toback, who seemed to be ideally suited to the subject, to write the script. He paid him an advance of $150,000, against $350,000, or $500,000 if the movie went into production.

But first on the runway waiting for takeoff was *Dick Tracy*. Beatty had grown up on Chester Gould's comic strip, which had first appeared in the *Detroit Mirror* in 1931. He explained that his father had read it to him, and then, at the age of four, he learned to read it himself by parsing his way through the speech balloons. From the outset, it was distinguished by Gould's idiosyncratic style, infected by Weegee and Samuel Fuller. Colored by tabloid yellow journalism, it was characterized by its brutal primitivism and populated by sideshow grotesques with names like Flattop, Itchy, the Blank, the Brow, Pruneface, Rodent, and Shoulders.

Beatty had been noodling the idea of making a Tracy movie for

many years. But he was beaten to the punch by producer Art Linson
(*The Untouchables*) and director Floyd Mutrux (*American Hot Wax*),
who had acquired the rights from the Tribune Syndicate in 1977. They
brought it to Michael Eisner and Jeffrey Katzenberg at Paramount. In
the days before *Star Trek* and *Superman,* there were virtually no tent-
poles, and the two men pitched it as the studio's answer to James Bond,
"a series—a Dick Tracy every summer," recalls Mutrux. According to
him, Eisner, virtually jumping up and down, got so excited he said,
"Shut the door. Close the deal right now. It's an annuity!"

The project went through many permutations, and by 1985, Linson
and Mutrux were out, and Beatty took control of the project. Mutrux
was bitter. "Warren has a reputation for using people," he says. " 'Yes's'
turned into 'maybes' which turned into phone calls going unreturned.
Warren kills projects. Movies die at his feet. We're talking an epidemic
jerk-off here—you're playing with other people's dreams. Warren is the
most flagrant violator. How come I decided on him? I guess my brain
was damaged."

Meanwhile, in late 1984, early 1985, Beatty put in a series of
3:00 A.M. calls to G. Mac Brown, a young unit production manager, telling him, "I'm tired of Hollywood, I want to work here in New York,
maybe you can help." He said he was planning to do a slew of movies
there, and that he was looking for a production person. Brown was
excited at the prospect of working with Beatty; he had married Sherri
Taffel, the postproduction coordinator on *Reds,* who revered the star.
"The people I knew loved him, adored him, thought he was a genius,"
Brown says. He met Beatty at his suite in the Ritz-Carlton. It was four
o'clock in the afternoon; he was wearing a bathrobe as if he had just
gotten up. "For the first thirty minutes he didn't say a word," Brown
recalls. "He just wouldn't talk. A sentence would be three words. He
was very mysterious, so I never knew what movies he was talking
about." Finally, the star said, "Thanks for coming," and dismissed him.
Then MacLeod called him, saying, "You've got the job." Brown found
production offices at 110 West 57th Street, the Directors Guild building. He had the impression he was prepping *The Pick-up Artist,* but he
wasn't sure. "It was the most secretive group of people I've ever been
around," he recalls. "Doors were always shut and locked, filing cabinets
locked, everything kind of in code. I liked MacLeod. He was clever, and
always very fair with me. But you could work with him day in and day

out and have conversation after conversation, and he would never give you any information." Abruptly, *The Pick-up Artist* turned into *Ishtar*, then known as "Two Star Movie," that is, untitled, with the two stars being Beatty and Hoffman. Three months after McElwaine gave Beatty the green light, May came up with a script entitled, *Blind Camel.* The picture was slated for a Thanksgiving 1986 release.

BEATTY AND Hoffman were an odd couple, occupying parallel universes. Where Beatty was tall, powerfully built and WASPy, Hoffman was short and Jewish with, he was fond of saying, "acne so bad my face looked like a rifle range." But they had things in common besides arriving in New York around the same time—Beatty from Virginia and Hoffman from L.A., where he was raised. They were the same age (Hoffman was also born in 1937), both played the piano (at one point Hoffman wanted to be a singer), and each dropped out of college after a year to pursue acting. Both were nominated for Best Actor Oscars in 1967, for *Bonnie and Clyde* and *The Graduate*, respectively. They were nominated for Best Actor in succession in 1981 and 1982, for *Reds* and *Tootsie.* And neither had made a picture since, although Hoffman had enjoyed success on Broadway playing Willy Loman in *Death of a Salesman.*

Hoffman first met Beatty in an ice cream parlor in Beverly Hills shortly after *The Graduate* and *Bonnie and Clyde* had made them both supernovas in the celebrity firmament. Beatty was with Julie Christie. "I was sort of self-conscious about being a new movie star, and he looked very comfortable with the role," Hoffman remembers. "He was wearing sunglasses, sitting on a bench. He made some kind of sexual double entendre, something about sixty-nine flavors, and I just kind'a looked at him. He said, 'You don't like that flavor, huh?' I told him later I thought he was hostile."

Although Hoffman couldn't know it, this was vintage Beatty, catching the contradiction in the man. By exploiting his boyishness, Beatty would make a career playing naïfs, innocents, all variations on small-town Bud in *Splendor in the Grass.* For this version of himself, ice cream was his best prop; he loved to eat it, and wherever ice cream could be found, so could he, licking a cone like Archie Andrews. But the double entendre hinted at another Beatty, and suggested a coarseness that qualified the innocence, both complemented and contradicted it. The two together comprised the whole package. Forget the "ghost in the machine"; it was the satyr in the creamery, cavorting among the dairy maids.

The next time Hoffman ran into Beatty was at Aware Inn on Sunset. Hoffman was eating a salad at an outside table when Beatty sat down. Hoffman recalls. "He kind'a leaned forward, saying, 'You and I should work together. I just want you to know, if you come upon anything—I thought he was gonna say, 'I'll be in it with you.' But he didn't, he said, 'I'll direct it.' Then he left. He hadn't done any directing then, and I said to whoever I was with, 'Can you believe that fucking guy? Like he's telling me something I want to hear? The conceit! Oh yeah, like, I'm going to go to Warren Beatty? He's my first choice to direct?' And then he turned out to be a brilliant director. We're friends now and I can't get him to direct anything. I always say, 'You should be directing, Warren, there's nobody better than you.' He always answers, 'No.' I say, 'Why?' And he says, 'I gotta be in it, I gotta star in it.' I say, 'Why?' He says, 'Because I can't make enough money just directing.'"

Beatty gave Hoffman May's script, now entitled *Ishtar*. "When I read it, I had misgivings about it," he continues. "I turned it down." Beatty persisted, requested a meeting. Hoffman recalls, "It was a hotel room in New York, and he had a toaster oven, and he was toasting some kind of German pumpernickel bread. I said, 'What're you doing?'

" 'Are you allergic to wheat?'

" 'I don't know . . .'

" 'If you get tired, you may be allergic to wheat.' He started in by being a Jewish mother." Indeed, as was his custom, Beatty wooed Hoffman, deployed his considerable powers of seduction. One day, he dropped in on him and his wife, Lisa, at their apartment. "He said to my daughter, who was two years old—she'd never met him before— 'C'mere, gimme a kiss.' He was sitting on an ottoman. She walked up to him, and put her arms around him, and kissed him on the lips, and didn't stop. And it went on and on and on. It was an astounding moment. She had never done something like that before. Even he was a little taken aback. There was something about Warren—he gives off something."

In those days, Hoffman rarely made a creative decision without consulting his guru, playwright Murray Schisgal. Excited, Schisgal told him, "You gotta meet with Elaine. Elaine's a great director." The two of them got together with May and Beatty. Both Hoffman and Schisgal still felt that the action plot—the intrigue, the chases, the explosions—overwhelmed the smaller, more delicate story at the heart of the drama. "We felt that the movie should not have left New York," Hoffman recalls. "That whole Hope and Crosby thing in Morocco, was [a distraction]. Just stay with these guys who think they're Simon and Garfunkel, and play that out. They disagreed." Hoffman was also uncomfortable with the idea that "I was the guy who gets all the women, while Warren had to pretend that he couldn't get girls. It was a conceit that did not ultimately work. And you didn't need it. But Warren deferred, deferred, deferred to Elaine."

Hoffman could see that May was proprietary and inflexible, foibles with which he was all too familiar. "I couldn't get any movement on the things I didn't think worked," he continues. "Murray said to me, 'They're not going to change anything.' I replied, 'That's my feeling. They as much as said it.'" May just wanted to shoot her script. But Beatty took Hoffman aside and told him, "You saw those movies that Elaine did. You know she's never had a good producer? You know that they never surrounded her with the right people? I've got Fellini's guy, Giuseppe Rotunno as the DP, I've got Tony Powell, the costume designer, he won an Oscar, and I'm going to be there, and I'm going to make sure that she has the room to do her best work." Hoffman continues, "He was saying, 'Don't worry about the script, go with her talent, go with us'—he wasn't wrong, you do go with the talent, and you do go with the synergy of what's gonna take place. What he didn't predict—what no one predicted—was that he and Elaine were going to clash. And Elaine was gonna clash with Vittorio Storaro," who would be hired to replace Rotunno.

Like Beatty, Hoffman was far more inclined to say no than yes. But that meant there were long stretches where he didn't work, at least in movies. He thought to himself, God, I can't wait another three years before I make a movie, I'm getting too old. Either I say no, like I always do, or I decide to work and just be a color on her palette. As he and Schisgal were walking out, Schisgal turned to his friend and asked, "What are you going to do?"

"I'm probably gonna take it."

"Why?"

"Partly as a favor to Elaine, and also because Warren is so persuasive. I've had good success with *Tootsie*, with *Salesman*, I deserve a flop!" He explains, "Because my resistance was so fundamental, in terms of keeping it in New York, that once they disagreed with that—it was, let 'em have their vision and let's hope for the best. I'm just going where they want to take this."

Beatty and Hoffman got about $5.5 million each for acting in the picture. Beatty got an additional $500,000 for producing, and May $1 million for her original script, plus directing, which adds up to a good chunk, $12.5 million above the line before a single frame of film went through the gate. In addition, Beatty and Hoffman were each rumored to be getting 5 percent of first-dollar gross.

Nailing down the budget is more difficult. There were several. According to Beatty, the original below-the-line budget was a spare $26 million. The *Los Angeles Times* reported that according to Columbia, *Ishtar* "could perhaps be made for $34 million." With above-the-line and p&a added on, the total price tag could well have been at least $65 million, which meant that the picture would have to gross well over $130 million for the studio to see any profit.

There was nothing unusual about the size of Beatty's and Hoffman's salaries, approximately equivalent to what Tom Cruise or Leonardo DiCaprio would get in today's dollars. At the time, they were the two brightest stars in Hollywood, and as McElwaine pointed out, at that point Beatty had never stumbled on a picture that he produced. "I was always aware of the fact that our salaries were hefty salaries," said Hoffman. "I knew that could not help us—it could only hurt us. I remember saying, 'Why take all that money?'" The three principals offered to defer their salaries, but the studio declined. (According to Fields, Columbia had a deal with HBO that covered a chunk of the budget. The more it paid out, the more it got back.) What was unusual was putting two such highly paid actors in the same picture. And what was even more unusual, although Beatty denies it, was that he, Hoffman, and May apparently had the equivalent of final cut! McElwaine was blithely sailing his ship into a perfect storm.

THE FACT that Beatty had no use for Jimmy Carter and was personally friendly with Reagan may have taken some of the sting out of the new right-wing hegemony, but he nevertheless threw himself into Hart's campaign, albeit still operating in the shadows.

When the primary campaign finally got going, Hart began racking up impressive numbers. On February 20, 1984, he came in a strong second to Mondale in the Iowa caucus, with 16 percent of the votes. Eight days later, in a stunning upset, he bested Mondale by ten points in New Hampshire. The Colorado senator went on to trounce Mondale in Maine and Vermont. According to a Gallup poll completed in the third week of March, Hart led Reagan by 52 percent to 43 percent.

But the relationship between Hart and Caddell started to unravel, beginning with the candidate's loss to Mondale in Illinois on March 20. Hart blamed Caddell; Caddell blamed Hart. "Warren knew there was real trouble," says Caddell. "That's when he told me that he was there to put Gary and I back together again." Caddell told Beatty, "You gotta be kidding! Warren, even you cannot do this."

"Oh yes I can. You have to come with me to New York, and I'm going to intercede for you with Gary."

Caddell continues, "They considered him God. Gary was now only speaking to Warren. They were having dinner every night. It was very strange."

Beatty and Caddell stayed at the Ritz-Carlton in New York for two weeks. Every night Beatty came down to Caddell's suite, and the two men talked into the wee hours about Caddell's relationship to Hart. "Warren was trying to make me understand what kind of pressure Gary was under," Caddell recalls. "Which I sort of understood, but I can't say I was that sympathetic to. The first thing that Warren always wants to do is understand [the issues]. He puts you right to the fire. He would grill me upside and down for hours about my strategy, why it was gonna work, why this, why that, every painful inch of it. He did what he should do—he went in there with the idea of, 'Prove it!' Which I could do. But it was still a problem convincing Gary. Gary would immediately contradict me, and I would think, I don't wanna be here! I was there because Warren made me be there. It was very frustrating."

Rumors about Hart's extracurricular activities, hitherto confined to his staff, had begun to circulate beyond it. Debra Winger had a "provocative encounter" with Hart during the 1984 campaign that made its way into the pages of *People* magazine, which described the actress as disappearing into Hart's room one night at 10:00 P.M. and emerging the next morning at 3:45. It was also widely known that he had an affair with at least one woman who worked in the campaign. As reported in *Newsweek,* "An airport-limousine driver, noticing the Hart button on the lapel of a fund-raiser in from California, said, 'Oh, I know Senator Hart. I took him to his girlfriend's house last night.' To convince doubters, the chauffeur had kept the woman's name and address."

In those days, which seem oh so long ago, the press considered the sexual peccadilloes of politicians off limits. "We were still in that post-JFK thing, where you had to be dead before this stuff would come out," adviser Bill Bradley explains. "Still, we were concerned that might change, because there were rumblings. We were aware that there was a potential critical mass of stories about Gary with women who were not his wife. People in the media warned us. Gary started getting questions about it. And little things would start finding their way into the tail end of the story, like, 'Gary Hart, who was named by *Playgirl* as one of the sexiest men in America' ... 'Friends with Warren Beatty' ... It was, 'Oh, this is not good.'" Added John McEvoy, a key adviser in the 1984 campaign, "He [was] always in jeopardy of having the sex issue raised if he [couldn't] keep his pants on."

Recalls Caddell, "[I had] my problems with the weirdos, the Indian dancer who I used to call Princess Winter-Spring-Summer-Fall." Bradley was detailed to "manage" her, told, "You're in charge of this woman," a Native American named Marilyn Young-bird who, according to Gail Sheehy, writing in *Vanity Fair,* styled herself Hart's soulmate. Says Bradley, "Gary bonded with her in a tent in Colorado. She was a spiritual healer. When Sheehy got wind that Gary had a friendship with this woman, she tracked her down, and got her to say all these things about Gary having to do with rocks and trees. Stupid things. And when she mentioned her to Gary, his face lit up." Hart called her his "spiritual adviser." Described as a "radiant divorcee," she told Hart that the "Great Spirit" had chosen him to "save nature from destruction." She suggested that he "hug a tree," but worse, during one of several separations from his wife, Lee, she persuaded him to attend a "sunrise ceremony," which she described as "so romantic": "They brushed the front and back of our bodies with eagle feathers. It was sensual, oh yes."

Still, there were people in Hart's camp who were leery of the candidate's friendship with Beatty; they thought it a mistake for him to stay at the actor's Mulholland Drive home when he went to L.A., drive his Mercedes, and so on. Caddell dismissed the concern about Beatty as a nonissue: "It was bullshit," he says. "Gary didn't give a shit what people said. And I knew Warren was important to him." But it wouldn't go away, and it colored everything, even the theme music for the campaign. Initially, it was Willie Nelson's "On the Road Again." But that made some of Hart's staffers uneasy. They said, "You know, people might say that maybe he likes to be out on the road for other reasons, so maybe you should use a different song." It was replaced by the theme of *The Magnificent Seven*, one of Hart's favorite movies. That made some sense; the picture is about helping people help themselves. It had the added virtue of being a western, underlining the candidate's regional appeal. But after he broke out, his advisers started to worry that it was too regional, and they adopted the theme song from *Chariots of Fire*, which was played over and over at Hart's rallies. It is not hard to imagine what went through Beatty's mind when he heard it, and indeed it wasn't long before *Chariots of Fire* was gone, and *The Magnificent Seven* was back.

In any event, Beatty succeeded in convincing Caddell to remain with the Hart campaign. After Mondale beat him in Illinois, the New York primary became very important. Mondale had countered Hart's "new ideas" mantra with an all too effective riposte of his own: "Where's the beef?" a slogan borrowed from a popular Wendy's hamburger commercial. The clear implication was that Hart was all style, no substance.

Mondale beat Hart again, in New York, another stunning defeat. Again, Caddell blamed Hart. Hart blamed Caddell. Hart called a meeting of his principal advisers, saying he wanted a consensus on the direction of the campaign by the next morning. Says Caddell, "I didn't want to be there, I was so furious. I didn't give a shit. I was out the door. Warren was the person who ramrodded this meeting. I didn't say a word. So Warren took me outside, and said, 'You're not saying anything.'

" 'I have nothing to say.'

"Warren was annoyed as hell. He knew I was sitting back and letting the thing fall apart, and he kicked my ass to go in and say what I believed. So I somehow managed to swing everyone around, which was the one thing Gary never expected. Warren was doing his best to bring it together, and that night I think he thought he had. Gary said he would do whatever we came up with, and of course he didn't." To no one's surprise, Caddell and Hart quarreled again. Says Bradley, "Even

Warren couldn't pull it off." Caddell walked out, taking a final shot at Beatty: "It's your campaign, you take care of it."

Says Bradley, "Warren, to his discredit, by constantly encouraging and patching up the Hart-Caddell relationship, contributed to some of the craziness of the campaign. Caddell was enabled or empowered by people like Warren to continue this disruptive behavior, because he was a super-hot political consultant. Everyone agreed that Caddell had gotten out of control. He had that ability to create havoc in the campaign."

In the aftermath of the disastrous New York primary on through the Pennsylvania primary, Beatty was the strong presence in the Hart campaign, according to Brownstein. He understood the Hart effort was in shambles. But after Beatty recruited John McEvoy, a seasoned politico, to run Hart's campaign, he evaporated, reverted to speaking to Hart on the phone. McEvoy brought order to the campaign, but it was too late. The Democratic convention in San Francisco nominated Mondale in mid-July. Caddell believed that Hart was not temperamentally suited to run for president. "Gary was a lot better behind than as a front-runner. Every time we were ahead, he would do something to destroy himself. He had a death wish. Warren thought it could have been strategic, that Gary thought it was better not to win. He didn't really want to beat Mondale because he never thought he could beat Reagan. He preferred to be a strong second, and the odds-on nominee in '88. Warren would voice those speculations—without ever articulating them quite that way, or attributing them to Gary."

Some of Hart's advisers believed that there was a chance that Hart might find his way onto the ticket as Mondale's running mate. But such belief was short-lived. Recalls Caddell, Democratic Party activist Miles Rubin handed him Gail Sheehy's piece about Marilyn Young-bird on the shuttle going to New York at seven in the morning. "He said, 'I want you to read this as if you were Walter Mondale and thinking about picking Gary for vice president.' That's when I knew there wasn't a prayer that Gary would be vice president."

IN FEBRUARY 1984, Beatty met Isabelle Adjani in Paris, a stunning, dark-haired French Algerian actress with full, sensual lips. In 1976, at the tender age of twenty-one, she had been nominated for a Best Actress Oscar for François Truffaut's *The Story of Adele H* (1975). By the time she met Beatty, she was twenty-nine, he was just about to turn forty-seven. Despite their disparate backgrounds, they shared some common ground. Both were on the political left. And like Beatty, she had a "dark and depressive" father.

Beatty put her in *Ishtar*, where she played a fiery revolutionary. Charles Grodin, who had appeared in *Heaven Can Wait* and was an old friend of May's, played a CIA agent. Paul Sylbert designed the production. Composer Paul Williams had the unenviable job of writing bad—but not so bad that audiences would run for the exits—songs for the luckless performers, Lyle Rogers (Beatty) and Chuck Clarke (Hoffman). "I began meeting with Warren and Elaine at his place in L.A., and I couldn't get him to commit that I had the job," said Williams. "For the longest time, he was trying to get Elaine to say what she wanted. I'd write songs, and she would kind of go, 'I don't know.'"

Beatty's romance with the French Algerian beauty by no means put a crimp in his social life. Fran Drescher, star of TV's *The Nanny* (1993), was blessed with a world-class body and a winning smile. She read for a small part as the wife Clarke leaves behind when he goes off to Morocco. At the audition, Beatty read with her. Her "heart was fibrillating with excitement," especially when he walked her to the elevator, told her, "I think you're a tremendous talent," and invited her and her husband to dinner. She was convinced they'd made a "cosmic connection." When he saw her next, he said, "I haven't stopped thinking about you." She observed that "Warren was the most powerful and openly aggressive man I'd ever met." Then he offered to introduce her to Adjani, saying, "We were both talking about you while lying in bed last night." Adjani told her, "You are very beautiful." But it wasn't until Beatty added, "We were both hoping you would like to join us for dinner this evening, just the three of us," that the flashbulb went off: "I sure as hell knew a ménage à troiserino when I saw one," she thought. Drescher declined. Eventually, her part was cut, and she didn't see or hear from Beatty for many years. One day, a friend of hers who happened to sit next to him and Annette Bening at a fund-raiser and dropped her name, told her he said, "We love her, she's so funny on *The Nanny*. We lie in bed and watch her all the time." Drescher reflected, "Annette and Warren lying in bed, speaking of me. . . . Boy, sometimes things sure do come full circle."

DeLauné Michel was a slender, leggy eighteen-year-old with the bone structure of a model who was working at the Four Seasons restaurant in New York, and indeed doing some modeling. (Michel would later become a novelist.) "She was the hatcheck girl," Beatty recalls. "Beautiful." On a Saturday night in late August 1985, subbing for the hostess and wearing a polyester green Nehru jacket, she brought a telephone over to his table, which he was sharing with Adjani and another woman, also striking. Michel recognized him right away, having seen *Heaven Can Wait* with her grandmother in grade school. On her way back to her post, she imagined he had given her a look, but then thought to herself, Oh, good lord, come on, he's with Isabelle Adjani, for God's sake, she was on the cover of *Time*, and I'm wearing this horrible restaurant uniform. No one is looking at you. But she was wrong. The following Saturday, on cloakroom duty, she was whiling away the time reading *The New Yorker* when he appeared before her and introduced himself. Having already done his homework, interrogating the maître d' about her, he asked, "Is your name DeLauné?"

"Yes."

"Are you an actress?"

"No."

"What are you then, besides beautiful?"

"A model, or trying to be."

"You're from Louisiana?"

"Yes."

"I'd like to help you. Call me. I'm at the Ritz-Carlton. On Central Park South."

"What's your room number?"

"Just say my name. They'll be able to find me."

He turned and walked into the men's room. He didn't really have to go, was just nervous, and he thought to himself, Fuck, now what do I do? He washed his hands and gave the attendant a dollar. On his way out, he regretted not getting her number, wondered if she would call him.

But she did, and a few days later, Michel found herself in his suite. Dressed casually in jeans, a T-shirt, and sneakers, he grilled her about her background, ascertained that she came from a literary family in New Orleans. Andre Dubus was her uncle, and James Lee Burke is her cousin. Her father, whom she worshipped, had abandoned her and her sister after he divorced their mother some years earlier. Enclosing her in the bubble of his attention, Beatty said, "Do you know how many beautiful women I've seen? You are—purrfect." Then, changing gears, he added, "You're the daughter I never had." She recalls, "This was right before we had sex for two hours. I did not find it odd that he would say that. That was the basis of our relationship. It was a father-daughter relationship. To me that was how he expressed his love, and he wasn't literally my father, so it wasn't really incest, but what he was clearly saying was, he didn't have a daughter. I at that moment did not for all intents and purposes have a father, and I needed one. He just gave me a level of security that I did not have. I found someone incredibly powerful, incredibly intelligent, incredibly gifted, and to me, nothing but supportive and kind. He steered me through very difficult years. Warren never made a promise to me that he didn't keep. He was an absolute rock."

In the course of their lovemaking, he muttered, "I love you." She recalls, "He was very uncomfortable saying 'I love you.' He literally had a hard time getting the words out. He kind of coughed through it. But he said it immediately when I met him, which made sense to me because I did feel a connection with him that was not like one that I've had with other people. I felt like he had a piece that fit perfectly into the part of the puzzle that I had, and vice versa. Not sexually, but psychically. He did have all those women in his life, and yet for some reason none of them fitted that shape, and for some reason, I did. Maybe part of it was my extreme naïveté, a kind of innocence which he saw, and a common Southern background."

AIDS was in the air, but for heterosexuals, it wasn't yet a reality, and Beatty didn't use condoms. Or at least not always. He had been at a New Year's Eve party the year before. When the clock struck midnight, suddenly his voice was heard above the general merriment—the smooching and carousing—saying, "How do we know AIDS is a homosexual disease? Do you know any other homosexual diseases?" Everyone just froze.

After that first time, Beatty declined to have sex with her again. She understood that somehow her relationship with him wasn't about that. They talked and talked, sometimes in person, often on the phone. She learned to call him in the morning and late at night, when he seemed softer to her, more vulnerable. She had the impression that as the day progressed, he became tougher, more guarded. She also understood that it was a clandestine relationship. She never met any of his friends with the exception of Jack Nicholson. Beatty always gave her a $100 bill to cover her cab fare home. So far as her modeling career was concerned, he promised to help her, and was as good as his word. She says he introduced her to Frances Grill, who ran a modeling agency called Click, walking her pictures down to the Click office in the Carnegie Hall building. She went to Milan to work. When he talked to her long-distance, his preternaturally alert phone antennae sensed that she had picked up some bad habits. He asked her repeatedly, "Have you been smoking?" "Have you been doing drugs?" She recalls, "He would always say to me at the end of every phone call, 'Don't do drugs. Read books.'" (Beatty has no recollection of her modeling, says she was an actress.)

There was a proprietary element to the relationship, the way he would say, "Get over here!" or demand to know if she loved him, or promise her that "I'm going to be in your life for a very long time." Later he would encourage her to see other men, but when she did, he made fun of them and wanted to know all about the particulars of the sex they were having, or asked, "Do you love me more than him?" It was all on his terms, which they both knew, even if it was hard for her to accept. She knew he was seeing many other women, but tried not to think about it.

One day she was in his suite looking at glossies of *Ishtar*'s Moroccan locations when the phone rang and a young girl came up. She was pretty, of course. Wondering why the other girl was there, intruding on their idyll, she comforted herself with the thought, He loves *me*. Some time passed, and then he got up and said, "Honey—" She thought, Thank God, he's finally making her leave. Instead, he took Michel's hand, saying, "I'll walk you down." Waiting for the elevator, he covered her face and hands with kisses, but she shoved him away, snapping, "Stop it."

"Are you mad at me?" he asked, trying to kiss her again.

"Quit it. What is your problem? Haven't I told you no?" The elevator descended to the lobby. They found themselves amidst a corps of soberly uniformed attendants, the Ritz-Carlton's finest. "I thought you loved me!" she shrieked.

"Come on. We're getting you a cab," was his only reply, his face reddening. She pummeled him with her fists, until he got her into a taxi. As it whisked her off, he said, "I'll call you in the morning."

Michel got over it. She realized that although he was not hers exclusively, although they weren't even having sex, he gave her his most important gift: phone access, night or day, New York, L.A., wherever. "I could call him, would call him, did call him every day, anytime, and he always took my phone calls. He never did not come to the phone. He would immediately say, 'Where are you? How are you?'" But one day, when she got him on the phone, he told her he was leaving for Morocco, where long-distance phone service was dubious at best.

9

FATAL ATTRACTION

How Elaine May taught Beatty that no good deed
goes unpunished, while he watched Gary Hart end up
a footnote to history instead of president.

"Warren and Elaine—you couldn't get closer than those two—
suddenly it was like *Who's Afraid of Virginia Woolf?* But no shouting. It was worse than shouting. They stopped talking to each
other. Ice."

—*Dustin Hoffman*

A T THE TIME *Ishtar* began shooting toward the end of October 1985, Morocco was not the most hospitable location
for a major Hollywood production, especially one that featured a rich Jewish movie star. On October 1, Israeli war planes had
bombed the headquarters of the Palestine Liberation Front in nearby
Tunis. A week later, most likely in reprisal, six PLF hijackers seized a
cruise ship, the *Achille Lauro*, and dumped Leon Klinghoffer, a Jewish
wheelchair-bound passenger, overboard into the warm waters of the
Mediterranean. To make matters worse, the Moroccan government
was involved in a protracted struggle with guerrillas of the Polisario
Front on its southwestern border with Mauritania. According to one
source, "We had been out looking for locations when this extremely
agitated Moroccan general came rushing up. 'You have to wait for

the minesweeper!' he shouted. 'There are mines all around here. You could lose a leg.' We had been walking for three days. Everyone went white."

The air was alive with frightening rumors. "We heard there were armed Palestinians headed our way," recalls Paul Sylbert. "There we were with Dustin, who sort of stuck out." Hoffman feared that he and his family were prime kidnap targets. Says associate producer Nigel Wooll, who had worked on *Reds,* "Dustin was very nervous, very, very nervous. He agreed, I think, to come over because the King of Morocco gave him his own personal bodyguard." (Each of the principals, Hoffman, Beatty, and May, were assigned bodyguards.)

Associate editor Billy Scharf, who had also worked on *Reds,* flew into Casablanca on his way down to the location near Laayoune on the Atlantic ocean in southwestern Morocco, close to the site of the fighting. The entire area was a military zone, and the atmosphere was tense. He had to board a small turboprop for the flight south and bring with him some baggage destined for the production, namely, large, sealed wooden crates marked "Warren Beatty" and "Dustin Hoffman." Recalls Scharf, "I was standing on the tarmac, [surrounded by] police with machine guns, going 'They have to be opened, they have to be opened, you can't leave.' I was scared—praying to their God and my God. I didn't want to have to show if I was circumcised or not. I wanted to take a dump in my pants."

The stars, along with the rest of the above-the-line talent, were staying at the nice hotel in Laayoune. Continues Scharf, "There was a swimming pool in the back, Dustin was there with his snorkel, complaining, 'The snorkel doesn't fit,' like a little kid. I took the opportunity to introduce myself, 'Hi, I'm Billy Scharf, we haven't met, but I have to ask you, I just flew in with these crates for you, I hope there was something important in them, because I had machine guns pointed at me. Can I ask you what was in them?' 'Yeah, my matzoh!'"

Shooting in Morocco presented a raft of problems. Reports another source, "The Moroccans were extremely cooperative. But they were not set up to do a movie. It's a very poor country. When we had a casting call for two hundred extras, eight thousand people showed up. When we would say, 'I've got to have thirty camels at seven o'clock tomorrow morning,' they would say, 'No problem. You can have three hundred.' Then comes seven o'clock the next morning and there are no camels."

Ah, the camels. One saga instantly became the stuff of Hollywood legend: the hunt for the blind camel—actually, a blue-eyed camel that registered blind on film. Or blue-eyed "camels"—they figured they needed four, in case one or more broke a leg. The first stop was Marrakech, the camel market, where the animal trainer, Corky Randall, and his assistant found just the right camel, for about $700. But being shrewd traders, they didn't want to buy the first camel they laid eyes on; they thought they could do better. Also, they had to show a photo of the camel to May, who needed choices, lest she make up her mind too easily. So they told the camel trader, "Thanks a lot, we'll get back to you." But, as it turned out, blue-eyed camels were a rarity. Search as they might, none of the subsequent camels they came across measured up to the first. As David Blum put it in *New York* magazine, "The humps would be too large or too small. The facial hair would be beige or brown. It was always something." Finally, they gave up, went back to the first dealership to buy the perfect camel. "Remember us? We'd like to buy that camel of yours that we looked at the other day."

"Sorry," the dealer replied. "We ate it."

Even before production was slated to begin in Morocco, tensions developed between Beatty and May. "In New York, before we left, we were scouting nightclubs," remembers Sylbert. "She didn't know that world, hadn't been to a lot of these places. But she pretended she had. She went, 'Oh, I remember that, blah, blah . . . ' and said something that revealed she had never been there. She was faking it. Warren was both half amused and shocked. He turned around to me, and he said, 'She's a fraud!' It was a striking remark, coming from him. He never says anything like that." Sylbert got the impression that she was afraid that she was in over her head.

In the Sahara desert, May was very much a fish out of water. She must have looked around her and, like Dorothy in *The Wizard of Oz*, thought, "We're not in Kansas anymore," or, in her case, Manhattan. As things would turn out, the blind camel, armed Palestinians, and the Polisario Front would be the least of her problems. May would be her own worst enemy. She wasn't cut out for the role of Lawrence of Arabia. Like Pauline Kael, she was allergic to the sun, swathed herself head to foot in gauzy veils, wore big hats and sunglasses, protected herself with parasols, and took shelter under tents whenever possible. She suffered from toothaches throughout much of the shoot, but refused to use a Moroccan dentist on principle, as if only a New York dentist would do.

From the first, dunes were a problem. Sylbert was the designated dune guy. He says, "I listened to nothing but talk about dunes." Before they left for Morocco, he looked at dunes in Southern California and Idaho. None of them would do. "It was hopeless," he recalls. "Nobody was satisfied. They kept talking about Morocco."

Once they set foot in Morocco, Sylbert embarked on a tour of the country looking for the perfect dunes. He finally found them—he thought—near Laayoune. "There were these great coastal deserts," he recalls. "Perfect. But Elaine was not prepared to use them. With all the talk of dunes, her idea of the desert was Brighton Beach. Whenever she was faced with a decision and she didn't know what to do, she would stall, and I could see that she was stalling now. There's a story about a costume designer, Edith Head or Diana Vreeland, working with a famous actress, and saying to the actress, 'You'd look wonderful in yellow,' and the actress said, 'I hate yellow,' whereupon Head or Vreeland replied, 'Who said anything about yellow?' On the drive back from seeing the fabulous dunes—me, Warren, and some others, we knew we had found our location—she suddenly said, 'Dunes? Who said anything about dunes?' All flushed, puffed up like an infant who's about to wail, 'What's all this about dunes? I want flat!' "

Sylbert took eleven bulldozers off a construction site about twenty-five minutes from Laayoune and leveled a square mile of sand. He says, "That cost them a few bucks, and more time." But according to artistic consultant Phillip Schopper, "None of that happened. If they're crawling across the desert, it has to look like the Sahara, but the land was hard-packed, so we trucked in a lot of sand. But we didn't take any dunes down. Paul Sylbert and Elaine were hostile to each other. He will say nothing but horrible things about her. Paul is out of the side of his mouth nasty." Several other crew agree that there was no bulldozing. "Elaine was nobody's fool, and she was too smart to do stupid things like that," says Scharf. "Sylbert hated her."

But others concur with Sylbert's assessment of May. Says Wooll, "She would change her mind about anything—anything and everything: setups, locations, costumes. If you'd ask her, 'Black or white?'

she'd say, 'Yes!' Nothing suited Elaine. *Ishtar* was a really difficult film. They went crazy in Morocco." May's indecision may in part have been strategic. As one crew member put it, "Directors control in different ways, and she controlled by creating mass confusion."

There was a "what planet are you from" aura about May. Once, while she was engaged in an intense discussion about a shot, she was peeling an orange and making a neat pyramid with the pieces of peel. She separated the sections, methodically laying them out in a straight line. Then she proceeded to leave the sections and eat the peels.

If it was Beatty's purpose to enable May by surrounding her with the best of the best, he succeeded all too well. Be careful what you wish for. Storaro had four camera operators, one of whom was named Enrico. She called them all "Enrico." "She completely neutralized Storaro," says Sylbert. According to Wooll, "One problem was that she had no idea where to put the camera. She relied totally on Storaro. But if Storaro said, 'Why don't you put the camera here,' she wouldn't listen." Storaro, who instantly located the finest Italian restaurant in Morocco and managed to be the best-dressed human being in the Sahara desert, wearing gossamer-thin cashmere sweaters when everyone else wore T-shirts and jeans, would constantly complain about her. According to Hoffman, he said, "Elaine, I love her, but she drive me crazy." He loved to tell the story of how he outsmarted her. He would arrive at the location having to match a shot from the day before, meaning the light would have to be the same. He'd say something like, "Elaine, I'm going to put the camera over here today, and they come over that dune."

"Vittorio, no, I'd like the camera on the opposite side, 180 degrees, over there. And they'll come over *that* dune."

"Every day, the desert, she look the same. Every direction, dunes, dunes, dunes. Elaine, there no good reason for this, the sun will be—"

"No, Vittorio, trust me!"

"Elaine, is no going to match. We get the shot off, the sun, it will be coming from front of them, when yesterday was behind them. The dune, she looks like the same dune."

"No, no, Vittorio, that was the dune they were coming over." She waved her hand vaguely at the horizon.

"But nobody know the dune, they know the sun." This would go on for days. She would always say the same thing and he'd reply, "But Elaine . . ." and get more upset. Eventually, he thought to himself,

Today I put the camera where I no want the camera. She say, No. I move the camera opposite, where I want it. Which is what he did. As Sylbert puts it, "We all figured out ways to work these people. If you can't intimidate them, which you do if you can, manipulation is the name of the game. You stack the cards. If you don't, they'll fuck up your work, there's no question about it."

May relied on Schopper in her fights with Storaro. "The notion of her eccentricity is greatly exaggerated," he says. "Eccentricity is in the eye of the beholder." From May's point of view, Storaro was designing shots with an eye to their composition, their beauty, whereas she was composing for comic effect. In the beginning, Storaro looked to Beatty to take his side. But respectful of his director, Beatty was not about to intervene. Recalls Nicola Pecorini, Storaro's steadicam operator, "Warren never pushed her to make a decision. We spent days and days doing nothing. Vittorio took the job very seriously, but after a week or two, we just worked on our suntans. Vittorio sat in his chair and pulled out a book. That's when he discovered Rudolph Arnheim. He was always sorry that he'd taken the job."

Risible as they may have been, there was nothing funny about May's clashes with Storaro. They exacerbated the tensions on the set and probably worsened May's estrangement from Beatty. Despite Beatty's hesitancy, recalls Hoffman, he would eventually agree with Storaro, "one of the great DPs of the world, about the placement of the camera. She probably felt ganged up on by the two of them. Elaine became suspicious, and less collaborative. She wanted to make *her* movie." Hoffman thought it was ironic that when he had reservations about the script, Beatty brushed them aside and persuaded him to put himself in May's hands, but once they got to Morocco, it was Beatty who had the problems. "Paralysis descended on the set," Hoffman continues. "When the tension started, I didn't want to be in there at all. I just wanted to do my shit and go back to the hotel." Neither Beatty nor May would give Hoffman any direction. May, who probably didn't know what to tell him, said nothing. Beatty, who probably did know what to tell him but didn't want to usurp May's prerogatives, also said nothing. Recalls Hoffman, "I would have to ask, 'Elaine, what do you want me to say?' I'd go to Warren, 'What do you want me to say?' There were times there when I was the go-between. Me, of all people!—who had my own reputation—was going back and forth, saying 'C'mon, guys!'"

As if things weren't bad enough, Adjani wasn't happy either. She didn't seem to get along with May, appeared to feel that May didn't like her. Her character was disguised as a boy throughout most of the movie. "Isabelle's greatest attribute are her lips, and they were covered up by a shmatta," observes one crew member. "I'm sure she wasn't thrilled. Elaine kibitzed with Dustin, a New York kind of thing, and she had her relationship with Warren, but she didn't have one with Isabelle, who was an equal star. She didn't give her the attention that Isabelle was entitled to from the director. Elaine should have related to Isabelle directly, but she let Warren [handle it], and Isabelle probably thought Warren would go to Elaine on her behalf, but who knows if he ever did."

With little else to do except watch the director hither and dither, people speculated about the reasons she shunted Adjani aside. Says Sylbert, "You know why *Mikey and Nicky* went on for as long as it did? Because Elaine was the meat in a sandwich between two men she was crazy about, Peter Falk and John Cassavetes. She went on the longest double date in history. And you had the same situation on *Ishtar*. But there was no other woman in *Mikey and Nicky*. When there was another woman, she paid for it. Elaine buried Isabelle, because her whole thing was what she got by being between these two guys. It was a sex fantasy."

According to Hoffman, the relationship between Beatty and Adjani was strained to the breaking point. "There wasn't a lot of speaking there either," he says. "I think that it was painful, God knows, for Warren. Because on the one hand he's having trouble with one of his closest friends and colleagues, and on the other hand he's got a girlfriend who's [unhappy]. He was holed up in his suite. He would not come out—I was in the pool with my kids, but I never saw him out there. I'd call him up sometimes, 'C'mon, Warren, why don't you come swimming?' He was kind of in seclusion. Then he'd say, 'Let's have dinner.' Lisa and I would go to dinner with them at the Mamoonia, in Marrakech, and there wasn't two sentences between them, they would be looking in opposite directions. It was awful."

"He was very cold [to Adjani], at least in public," says Pecorini. "He had to feel free to go after other women. For Isabelle, it was her first, or one of her first American productions. She made it as a choice to fuck Warren, and therefore she would take anything as long as it was getting her somewhere."

Pecorini's girlfriend was visiting the set. He continues, "Warren was turning to her between set-ups, flattering her, charming her. I was just a minion. He couldn't have cared less [about me.] But she dismissed him, rudely. That pissed him off." As if following the script of the movie, "she fancied Dustin," he continues. "Warren couldn't believe it, as if Dustin shouldn't even be in competition. She told him, 'He's funny.' Warren couldn't understand that a woman would go for fun, not for beauty. He was furious! He was like a kid, kicking the sand."

Storaro wasn't the only one flummoxed by May. So were the editors. They grasped at anything that might give them a clue to her intentions. Usually, when a director watches dailies with an editor, he or she will whisper something approximating, "I like take 3 and take 5," while the editor takes notes. May didn't do that. She took notes herself and wandered away with her pad, instead of sharing what she'd written with them. There was no Staples in Laayoune; pads and pencils were in short supply, and it wasn't long before they started to run out. Thinking he was being clever, one of the assistants tied May's pencil to her clipboard and the clipboard to the chair she was sitting on. At the end of one screening, she ran off after Storaro, clipboard in hand, yelling, "Vittorio, Vittorio," dragging the chair with her. Even she noticed the impediment to her forward motion. She cried, "Why is this chair coming after me?"

Often, neither Beatty nor May would show up to watch the dailies. It was forbidden to start without them, so Pecorini and the others killed time by playing charades. "Then we said, 'Okay, let's go and have a drink.' It was a bit of a joke, because we were working such light hours. The more Coca-Cola was spending, the happier they were. We would do 15 hours overtime, and they would pay us for 25. We went to Nigel Wooll, one of the stingiest guys on the planet, and said, 'There must be some mistake.' He'd say, 'There's no mistake. You want to give it back?' It was the best money I ever made."

There were extravagances great and small, including, reportedly, two 727s to fly the crew to Marrakech when only one was needed, because Hoffman insisted on his own. He thought Beatty had one of his own. The other end of the spectrum included Evian water and toilet paper Fedexed from Los Angeles to Morocco.

Like Beatty, May did a great many takes. For one scene, she did something like fifty, employing three cameras. It is said, doubtless in jest, that a snake charmer walked into the production office in Marrakech one day with a limp cobra draped over his arm. He burst into tears, claiming the cobra had endured so many takes it had had a heart attack and died. He wanted $2,500, but settled for $150.

Beatty and Hoffman worked differently. According to Pecorini, "They were always out of sync, never at their best on the same take. Warren needed forty-five takes to warm up, and Dustin had given his all by take five. He would get bored, and drag his feet. There was not much sympathy between them. Each was making the other nervous."

Hoffman complained, "Warren would never learn his lines. He would be getting warmed up by the time I was running out of gas. We'd be shooting—forty takes—it was brutally hot, and he'd be learning the script on camera. Which would have been fine if I wasn't there too. It was hard, but there was nothing I could do about it. I've had other actors be the same way. Brando was a brilliant actor and could have his lines written on the ceiling. You can't argue with them, because you can't say, 'You're supposed to know your lines.' There's a spontaneity that's the most important thing in making a movie, so when they're searching for their lines, many times it looks like really good acting. 'Cause they're really thinking. It is harder to be fresh and spontaneous over and over and over again if you know the lines cold. [But]—and I'm guessing—Warren was not coming from a good place. I was coming from a hotel where my marriage was, but he was ending a relationship. It hangs on, both parties know it's over, but they're still together. It's always the worst that way. It must have been hard for him to concentrate."

May was feeling the pressure. Coca-Cola's money or no, there were tens of thousands of dollars at stake with every passing minute. According to Sylbert, one day "she leaned against me, and she said, 'Oh, I'm making so many mistakes.' It was really sad and touching. That pitiful utterance was just this little crack that appeared with me, because I'd worked with her before, but she didn't want the world to know."

The simmering tensions came to a head when it was time for May to shoot the battle sequences. "Warren put himself in a tough spot, where he couldn't do much with Elaine once things started to go down the sewer," says Sylbert. "Then he had a moral choice to make. The day he made it was the day the biggest showdown came, when she would not shoot the battle scene. She knew nothing about action sequences. A battle scene for this woman who had done everything by improvisation? You can't improvise a battle scene.

"One night, I got a call from Warren, and he said, 'Listen, all she wants to do is do pickups on the stuff she's already done.' She wanted to go backwards. Money was just pouring out at this point. She knew he couldn't let her do that. She was afraid. He told me, 'Do me a favor, do some sketches so we can show her how to do it.' I made the sketches, brought them to a meeting in Warren's trailer. We tried to show her, get her started. She was fighting us. She was in the same state she was in with 'Who said anything about dunes?' This was 'Who said anything about battle scenes?' I said, 'Look, you can put the camera here, put the camera there, you can bring them in from here'—she wouldn't move. She fucked up everybody, neutralized everybody with her fears. There was always some little thing she would put in your way that made you just grind to a halt. She could have said to him, 'I've never shot a battle scene before, could we discuss it, could you give me some help with this?' But Elaine wouldn't ask for help. She was paranoid. She was locked up, stubborn. Nobody could get anything out of her. She was like a black hole. Swallowed everything, nothing escaped. Except her fears. And that little utterance, 'I'm making so many mistakes.'

"You could see Warren was getting very angry and frustrated, but he never blew up. But he finally challenged her: 'Something's got to be done,' blah, blah . . . She said, 'You want it done? You shoot it!' He was stunned. At that moment, he had to make a decision. He knew he had no move on the chessboard. If he stepped in then, he would have had to take over the movie." Beatty had not hesitated to nudge Hal Ashby aside on *Shampoo*, nor Buck Henry on *Heaven Can Wait*. But it would have embarrassed him to step in for May, when the whole point of *Ishtar*, so far as he was concerned, was to empower her. As Sylbert puts it, "His instincts saved him: 'I'm the one who brought her into this, so I'm the one who has to live with it. I gotta take the responsibility.' He couldn't become one of those producers who fired the director. Although he was right on the edge. But it was too late. It wouldn't have saved the movie to do it at that point anyway."

Moreover, Beatty's instinct for self-preservation was up there with his libido, and he was nothing if not shrewd about his limitations and options. He was looking ahead at what remained to be shot. Ninety percent of the Morocco portion had been finished. He hadn't done any prep work for the upcoming New York shoot. The city was May's hometown; she would be more comfortable working there than he would. Especially since he had his acting and producing to worry about. "It was just too hard," explains Sylbert. "He would have been walking into a real shitpot full of trouble. His energy was dying. I don't think he wanted to take the risk. I think he was depressed, in a quandary. We saw rushes, and they weren't funny. They were confusing. But people in this business—they pump themselves up to get going the next day. They put their heads down and just go. Here's a guy who has nothing to do with velocity. If you watch him run with the football in *Heaven Can Wait*, you realize, this guy is no Jesse Owens. This is a guy who is all about momentum. He's like a locomotive. It takes a world of energy to get him started, but he ain't easy to stop once he gets going. He had to support her, but it cost him a bad movie."

Beatty knew he had no choice but to let her alone. Says Pecorini, "In any other circumstances she would have been fired." Sylbert continues, "She solved the problem of the battle sequences by getting rid of them, the same way that she solved the problem with dunes by getting rid of them. The jeep pulls up, they get behind it, take out the weapons, go bang, bang, bang, and the helicopter turns around and leaves! What the hell is that!"

Beatty had put together an extraordinary cast and crew for *Reds*, a vast undertaking. He was very shrewd about talent and people with talent, particularly May, whom he knew as well as he knew anyone. How could he have misjudged her so badly? How could he have made, in effect, a $40, $50 million blunder? "Warren did not have an easy time on *Reds* because of Keaton," says Peter Feibleman. "Elaine was always there when he wanted her and needed her. She so directed his hand in terms of story line and structure—she corrected him constantly—he would have had to be Solomon to guess that she would not know how to do it herself. Warren and Elaine were locked into a kind of dance of death." Adds Sylbert, "Great composers are not very good conducting their own music, like Stravinsky. I once said to Elaine, 'How are we going to do this scene?' She said, 'I don't know, I just typewrite.' When she said, 'I typewrite,' it meant that everything is her ear. You're listening to the radio. Small movies that depend largely on talk. She's not visual at all. She really cannot see. And they gave her the Sistine Chapel. It was just much too big for her."

Despite his extraordinary difficulties with May, Beatty never complained about her—except once. He and Hoffman were in the desert, along with 150 odd extras. He took his co-star aside and started venting. "Warren was going off about how painful it was to make this movie with Elaine," Hoffman recalls. "He said, 'I was going to give this gift to Elaine, and it turned out to be the opposite. I tried this and I tried that . . . ' He was so passionate, but in the middle of it—it's like he had eyes in the back of his head—because there was some girl walking by, maybe fifty yards away, in a jallaba. He turned and froze, just watched her. I mean, this was while he was producing, and everything was going in the toilet. But he couldn't help it. Finally, he turned back, said, 'Where was I?'

" 'Warren lemme ask you something. Here everything is going wrong on this movie that you planned out to be a perfect experience for her, you got her this person and that person, you got her the budget she wanted, blah, blah, and here's a girl that you can't even see a quarter of her face because of the jallaba—what is that about?'

" 'I don't know.'

" 'Lemme ask you something else.' He's much taller than me, so I was always looking up, I said, 'Theoretically, is there any woman on the planet that you would not fuck? If you had the chance?'

" 'That's an interesting question: Is there any woman on the planet'— he looked up at the sky—'that I wouldn't fuck . . . Any . . . woman at all?' He repeated the question. 'Cause he took it very seriously. This problem with the production was now on the back burner, and it was like he was on *Charlie Rose.*

" 'Yes, any woman.'

" 'That I wouldn't . . . fuck. No, there isn't.'

" 'Theoretically, you would fuck any and every woman . . .'

" 'Yes.'

" 'You're serious.'

" 'Yes.'

" 'Why?'

" 'Why?' He was thinking. He was searching for the right words. 'Because . . . you never know.' I thought that was the most romantic thing I'd ever heard a man say, because he was talking about spirits uniting. He was not talking about the cover of the book. 'Because you never know.' And then it was, 'Where was I? I just don't know what to do about Elaine . . . ' But this took precedence."

Hoffman was right. Beatty was searching for perfection. It was the same passion that fueled his prodigious appetite for takes: ". . . because you never know." Unlike Jim Toback, he was not a gambler; he was not going to risk everything on one throw of the dice. Were he to gamble, he'd be a card counter. Beatty was an empiricist. There was safety—or at least opportunity—in numbers.

Ishtar was originally scheduled for about ten weeks in Morocco, but the studio was so concerned about the runaway production that it was willing to trade economy for control. "They really hate it when you're too far away from them," Sylbert explains. "Warren has got to be held responsible to some degree for the scheduling. The glacial part of *Ishtar* is probably as much his responsibility as hers." The cast and crew arrived back in New York just before Christmas, on December 23, 1985.

Fay Vincent, later the commissioner of baseball, was then executive vice president of Coca-Cola and chairman of Columbia Pictures. Vincent recalled, "Halfway through the movie, Warren came to me and said, 'We have a big problem. Actually, you have a big problem. Elaine can't direct.'

" 'You're the producer. Fire her.'

" 'I can't. I'm a liberal Democrat, a progressive on women's issues. I can't fire her. But she can't direct at all.'

" 'Well, then, I'll fire her.'

" 'Then Dustin and I will walk off the picture.' "

Vincent said that Beatty proposed that they shoot dual versions of every scene—his and May's. When they got into the editing room, where Beatty could exercise more control, he would simply consign May's footage to the cutting room floor. Vincent, his eye as always on the bottom line, replied, "So we're paying for two movies and only getting one?" Beatty nodded.

Sets for the unfinished sequences in Morocco were built at Astoria Studios in Queens, New York, where Woody Allen was shooting *Radio Days.* Production resumed in the third week of January, after a one-month break. Production manager Mac Brown had not been in Morocco and had never been on a Beatty set. MacLeod warned him, in his words, that when the star was "acting, I had to be very careful when I talked to him about problems, because acting was hard for him, he took it very seriously, and he got tense and nervous, even though he never wanted to show it." Brown quickly formed the same opinion of May as everyone else. He realized that he had his hands full. He recalls, "It was the big movie stars who did what they wanted and Elaine, who was just nutty."

But out of the blazing sun in the safety of darkness—the interiors of Manhattan clubs—May did seem energized while the others were just drained. "By the time they got to New York, they just wanted it done," Brown continues. "Storaro had given into the insanity of it. It was easier to say, 'We'll do it your way, Elaine.' Warren would say, 'Oh, she's a fuckin' pain in the ass, she's just impossible, what the hell is she going to do next? If she wasn't so goddamned brilliant, I'd . . .'"

By February 28, May was directing Beatty and Hoffman on the premises of the defunct, dungeonlike Upper West Side club Trax, re-named the Song Mart, where Rogers and Clarke, were premiering their first song together on an open mike night. May was nervous. She was trying to give up smoking (for the nth time), and constantly pacing the floor, munching on rice cakes, or ferociously chewing gum. "Do what you do in a place like this," she instructed the audience of extras, "which is to kill yourself trying to get a waitress's attention."

With their spiked do's, Day-Glo mohawks, and studs-'n'-leather accessories, the extras looked like refugees from the set of *The Road Warrior.* An effects man torched a spectracookie, which is used to make smoke, with a Bic lighter, and indeed, smoke filled the room. Spectra-cookie smoke is vile; the Screen Actors Guild contract called for a bonus of $14 a day for extras when it is used in a scene. "Dustin and Warren are on their way," announced a PA importantly, while three cameras were rolled into position. Beatty glided onto the set so smoothly he looked like he was on Rollerblades. He paused briefly to confer a few friendly kisses on available female lips. After fourteen takes and at least twice as many rehearsals, May wanted more. She was still refusing to turn the camera off, routinely shooting thirty thousand feet a day. (At that time, a director would shoot three thousand to five thousand feet a day on an average picture.) Although Beatty was preternaturally patient with May, he was all too familiar with her buttons, and sometimes he'd play head games with her. For example, it was sometimes difficult just getting her to say the words that made it possible for the cameras to roll. In a scene where he's asleep, and wakes up to see Adjani for the first time, believing her to be a boy, he needed May to cue him to open his eyes. He asked, "So what are you going to say?" She replied, "I'll say, 'Wake up.'" Instead, on the first take, she said, "Awake!" Beatty knew perfectly well that that was his cue, but he refused to open his eyes. She said it again: "Awake!"

"You said you were going to say, 'Wake up.' We just had that conversation. Thirty seconds ago. And now you say 'Awake'?"

The production moved into an Upper East Side club renamed the Ad Lib Club, aka the Comic Strip. The shooting continued to be exhausting—twelve-hour days. It would be hard to mistake a spectra-cookie for a real cookie—they're metallic-looking, flat, with regular edges, like a silver dollar, charcoal-colored—but May found a way. "She picked up one of the smoke cookies and ate it," Sylbert recalls. "I was right there. Nobody in their right mind would put one in their mouth."

May shot for just under two and a half months in New York and wrapped on March 30, 1986, which also happened to be Beatty's forty-ninth birthday. The production was originally scheduled for ninety-four days, but it lasted about five months. In April, *Ishtar* claimed another casualty. If Beatty couldn't bring himself to fire May, Fay Vincent had few compunctions about firing Guy McElwaine. He replaced him with David Puttnam, who had endeared himself to Coca-Cola with his highly publicized crusade against the financial sins of the industry. As the *L.A. Times* put it, he "oozed integrity." But placing Puttnam at the head of a studio was like making Jerry Falwell the mayor of San Francisco.

Puttnam was a magnet for the press, which, in the go-go business climate of those years, was increasingly eager to heroize executives and cover the business end of the movies. He had a history with Hoffman as checkered, if not more so, as his with Beatty. The two had had a bitter falling out over *Agatha* (1979). Neither Hoffman nor Puttnam had forgotten. Hoffman recalls. "After he went to Columbia, I looked at the front page of the Calendar section of the *Los Angeles Times,* and he was quoted as saying, "'Dustin Hoffman is the most malevolent person I've ever worked with.' Being the intellectual that I am I had to look the word up."

Needless to say, neither of *Ishtar*'s two stars welcomed Puttnam's

arrival. Says DeLauné Michel, who would shortly resume her relationship with Beatty, "Puttnam was on his most hated list, and he went into
long rants about him." Beatty told Columbia, "I don't want to deal
with him. He's going to torpedo my picture." In an attempt to head off
controversy before it started, the studio announced that because of his
prior history with the two stars, Puttnam would recuse himself from
personal involvement with *Ishtar*. But that just made things worse. He
gave the impression that he was hands off *Ishtar* because it was radioactive, which just angered the stars more.

The editing began in earnest in the spring of 1986, at 1619 Broadway, with Steve Rotter (*The Right Stuff*), Bill Reynolds (*The Godfather*), and Richie Cirincione (*Reds*) wading through at least 2.6 million
feet of film, 108 hours or four and a half days' worth, according to *The
Hollywood Reporter*. (At that time, an average director shot 200,000
feet for a 10,000 foot release print for a shooting ratio of film shot to
film used of 20 to 1. May arrived at a shooting ratio of 2600 to 1.)

The strains among the principals, already battered and bruised, continued into post. May, who was supposed to direct the actors when
they looped their dialogue, often didn't show up at all, leaving Beatty
or Rotter to do the honors, especially with Adjani. "If your director's
not there at a looping session, that's horrible," says a source. Whatever
the reason, it was interpreted as a snub. Rotter muttered, "God, is this
gonna be frosty." Since Adjani was disguised as a boy, she was always
being told to drop the register of her voice to make the ruse convincing,
especially in a scene where she's being tackled. Beatty said, "Lower your
voice, like you're being squeezed," and proceeded to demonstrate. She
snapped, "I've been squeezed enough on this film already so remove
your hands now!" Adds Schopper, "Towards the end of the shooting,
they weren't talking to each other. Isabelle was tired of Warren and his
shenanigans. You felt her attitude was, I'm not putting up with this stuff
anymore. It was the same as it was with Diane at the end of *Reds*."

Beatty was staying at the Ritz-Carlton. Across the hall from his
suite was the lair of notorious, abrasive former cokehead Julia You'll-
Never-Eat-Lunch-in-This-Town-Again Phillips, in New York producing her comeback indie, *The Beat*. She would run into him here and
there, most often at Columbus, the hot Hollywood hangout on the
Upper West Side, where she saw him with young Molly Ringwald and
wondered, "How does this guy avoid jail?" One day she spotted him at

the Jockey Club discussing PR for *Ishtar* with publicist Lois Smith. As she told it, he asked, " 'So tell me, Julia, don't you ever have an inclination to knock on my door late at night?'

" 'Not in the least. Not ever.'

" 'Well, what would you do if I knocked on your door?'

" 'I'd send you away . . . ' Lois asks how Kate is.

" 'Oh, you have a daughter?'

" 'Yes, she's just about 14 . . .'

" 'Well, what about you and me and your daughter . . . ' "

DURING THE Morocco shoot, Beatty walked into Sylbert's trailer one day and said, "You gotta do me a favor."

"Yeah?"

"Will you do a picture for me? A small one. It's not a big picture."

"Sure, what is it?"

"*The Pick-up Artist.*"

The story focused on a man named Jack Jericho, who hits on every girl he runs across, until he falls in love with Randy Jensen, a museum tour guide whose boozy father is up to his neck in debt to the mob. Jericho becomes her devoted slave. This was a story line that obviously had some appeal to Beatty, as the future would prove. The film stars Robert Downey Jr. and Molly Ringwald. Just eighteen, with curly red hair and a fresh, insouciant look, Ringwald was the flavor of the moment, having starred in two John Hughes teen hits, *Sixteen Candles* and *The Breakfast Club*. She was shooting another that he'd scripted, *Pretty in Pink*. According to Toback, Ringwald was not his first choice. She had come across the script among a pile on the coffee table in Beatty's living room. She wanted to do it, and so it was. Rumor had it that Ringwald had told some PAs on *The Pick-up Artist*, "You think he wasn't fucking me?" But, says Mac Brown, who was the unit production manager on the picture, "If they were having an affair during *Pick-up Artist*, it never showed."

MacLeod was to produce, his first film out from under Beatty's shadow, while the star was undecided about whether he would take a producer's credit as well. According to Toback, MacLeod was a terrific producer. "In terms of preparing the movie, he was almost fanatic about detail," he recalls. "At the end of every day he would say, 'What else? What haven't we done? What haven't we covered? What are we missing?'" In addition to Sylbert and Brown, Beatty brought on Gordon Willis, who had shot *Parallax View,* as the DP.

The day before production was slated to begin, a bombshell exploded. MacLeod was arrested in front of the Fox production office on 57th Street for soliciting three runaway boys in Times Square. Beatty called Toback, said, "I had some bad news about MacLeod."

"What?"

"The worst."

MacLeod "was like a brother" to Beatty, says Toback. "Warren was devastated." He added, "MacLeod basically ran his life for 20 years. The only person who knew exactly what was going on with Beatty was him." Losing his cousin left him with "a sense of tremendous frustration. Beatty does not like failure. Not that it's his failure. It's just that the whole thing was a disaster."

Beatty circled the wagons. He phoned Brown, told him, "You're gonna get called by the press, 'cause he was arrested right in front of the office. [You should say,] 'It would be inappropriate to comment on a matter that was still before the courts.'" According to Sylbert, "We all got called to send letters to the judge. Character things." Television news crews captured Beatty and Hoffman visiting MacLeod in jail.

Of course, the questions of the moment were what did Beatty know and when did he know it. According to Sylbert, "Morocco was where all the boys are. That's what he loved about it. Look at movie sets. Somebody always has a dame on their arm. Never with David. That was very unusual. But no one ever gave it a second thought. He always kept his room locked in Morocco. There was always a sign on the door, 'Do Not Disturb.' David fooled us all. Including Warren."

Toback agrees. "We were in constant contact," he says. "David never once admitted to me that any of it was true. On the surface, it appears to have been, and he never said it wasn't, he just never talked about it. He was immensely secretive. He could keep things to himself in a way that very few people can—like Warren. And I'm sure he didn't tell Warren."

But some people had noticed MacLeod's fondness for young boys at least as far back as *Reds.* Little David, probably in his early twenties by 1986, MacLeod's favorite then, was still with him on *Ishtar.* Says Toback, "There was no ostentatious, or even vaguely conspicuous display of anything" between the two Davids, and Little David always denied that there was anything of a physical nature between them.

"I spent two years with this guy, and I never put it together," recalls Dick Sylbert. "Warren had him for four years. He was closest to him, in terms of the secrets; he was family. He must have known. Warren will never speak his name."

Says Sherri Taffel, who was friendly with both Davids, "Warren really loved David MacLeod. It's really hard to see people you love clearly. Something did feel not right, but I never let myself go there because I liked them so much. You protect people you like. I think Warren did know. But even if he did know, it was tragic. David was a good guy, with an illness, I don't know what else to call it. His life was undone by it and yet he continued [to do it]. If you know something like that about somebody you love? I don't know what you do."

Regardless of what Toback and Paul Sylbert say, it seems virtually impossible that MacLeod, who was Beatty's shadow, lived in his pants, managed to fool his cousin, a man who noticed everything. Perhaps Beatty just looked the other way for the aforesaid reasons, or because his cousin was a sexual outlaw, a species with which he was all too familiar, and not unsympathetic. If Julia Phillips is to be believed, not to mention Cher, Beatty had had his own encounters with teenagers, albeit of the opposite sex.

In any event, MacLeod was out of the picture, pending the resolution of his case. According to Brown, who was unit production manager, Beatty, who had his hands full, what with the postproduction of *Ishtar*, was uneasy in the producer's role and "he distanced himself from [*The Pick-up Artist*] completely. When David got arrested, he made it very clear, 'I am not the producer.'

" 'Who's gonna produce the movie?'

" 'Tell them you are.' "

On the other hand, Toback says, "Warren was basically in effect the unnamed producer. He was on the set every day, and intimately involved." So intimately that he directed Ringwald while Toback directed Robert Downey.

Eventually, MacLeod plea-bargained his way onto probation—he admitted to one charge of reckless endangerment of a minor, referred to in the press as "sodomy"—and returned to the production. Ultimately, MacLeod got a producer's credit, and Beatty took executive producer.

The star remained close to Toback, but Brown felt that others who worked on that production were forever stigmatized in Beatty's mind by the unhappy events with which it was associated. "I had hoped to work with Warren again, but he left town," Brown says. "It seemed to leave a bad taste in his mouth." He appeared to abandon his plans to make pictures in New York, if he ever had any in the first place.

INITIALLY, BEATTY allotted six and a half months for the postproduction of *Ishtar*, aiming for a release date of Thanksgiving, possibly Christmas 1986, but it was ten months before it was locked. As long as McElwaine was still in place, Beatty did his best to satisfy Columbia. Once Beatty's friend was replaced by his enemy, Beatty was not about to miss an opportunity to punish Puttnam for his attacks on *Reds*. "Warren's feeling was that since we no longer have the pressure to do it for Guy, let's let her [May] do it the way she wants," Fields continued. Letting May out of the bottle had the added advantage of running up postproduction costs and interest on the loans Columbia had undertaken to finance the picture, each of which would put the new chairman in the hole.

Puttnam believed that once production had ended, the bleeding would stop. "I was staggered by the postproduction costs that kept coming in," he said. Beatty reportedly told one Columbia executive, "Who gives a shit what Puttnam thinks. I certainly don't. Just tell the asshole to keep paying the bills."

Ishtar missed its Christmas release date. Beatty's father had been diagnosed with leukemia. The star flew back and forth between New York and Virginia to see him. His relationship with him had always been strained. MacLaine describes both parents as withholding and distant, to one degree or another, and she felt starved for emotional connections. To her, Ira Beaty was "a stern man with light blue eyes full of suspicion, the censor of all he surveyed. . . . He sat in judgment on our actions and behavior. . . . the fear of his own feelings was sometimes too painful to witness." She added, "My dad internalized most of his tumultuous emotions and suppressed them with liquor."

Most of the important things between Beatty and his father remained unsaid, which gave added poignancy to the small things. Toward the end, his father told him, "Shaving gel works better than shaving cream."

"What?"

"Shaving gel. You don't get as many nicks."

Later, the actor recalled, "He was right. I use shaving gel, and every time I use it, I think of my father."

Still, some things came out. The old man was concerned about the spiritual void he observed in his son, but Shirley MacLaine's New Age chatter bothered him as well. Beatty recalled, "I remember my father sitting on the side of the bed, his feet were kind of dangling, and he said to me, 'Warren, what do you think about these ideas of Shirley's?' I said, 'I don't know what to think of them.' He said, 'I just don't think I want to do what I have to do to find out.' "

MacLaine recalled, "Before my father died, I talked to him a lot about his own feelings of failure, and asked if he could accept that Warren's success and mine were also his. In the end, I think he did see things that way, that maybe he had come into the world to help us and not himself."

The actor was at his bedside when Ira Owens Beaty died at Johns Hopkins Medical Center on January 15, 1987, four days shy of his eighty-seventh birthday. Beatty complained that Adjani couldn't understand why he was so upset. She behaved, he said, as if the Chinese food hadn't been delivered. The funeral was held in Arlington on January 19. Afterward, the actor drove back to New York. On the way he stopped in Philadelphia to pick up Joyce Hyser, with whom he would have a year-and-a-half relationship. Then twenty-nine, Hyser was smart and articulate, very much her own person, and a political junkie like him. She was a struggling actress who had been with Bruce Springsteen for five years, and then David Geffen. She was also close to Jack Nicholson. With dark brown hair, hazel eyes, chiseled features, and an athletic, perfectly proportioned body, she looked a little like Natalie Wood, which apparently struck a chord with Beatty. He had been pursuing her for some time, pestering her girlfriends, most of whom he had gone out with, to introduce her to him. One of them finally did. Initially, Hyser was cold to Beatty, who was then nearly twenty years older than she was. "I had zero interest in him," she recalls. "To be honest, it was a joke. I made fun of him. At one point, I had a girlfriend over, and I put him on the speaker phone. I was really nasty, but the idea that I was not falling at his feet just intrigued him more."

When he arrived in Philadelphia, Hyser was visiting her parents. He took the entire family out to dinner. They were nonplussed. "He was

Warren Beatty!" she explains. "It felt weird. His father had just died. He seemed really sad. But he could not have been more charming. He was open, talking about his dad to these people who were strangers. He had just spent a lot of time with Dustin and his family. He was forty-nine, and starting to get that sense that it was time for him to settle down. The reason he hadn't gotten married was, he grew up in a Southern, conservative family, and to him getting married meant, that's it, you never sleep with anyone else again but your wife. In his head, he had to know that that was going to be okay. It was on that night that I saw him in a more positive light. He became someone entirely different, not this crazy dude who had been chasing me for a year. His attraction to me was that I had a strong sense of family myself, and I had a difficult relationship with my father. We had that in common."

Driving through the dark up to New York, Beatty talked about him nonstop. "Parents help to create who we are, either through what they give us or what they don't give us, and in his case it was more about what he didn't give him," Hyser continues. "I don't think he knew what to do with his feelings. He seemed totally lost. Warren admired his dad. But I had the sense that his father did not approve of him." MacLaine recalls her mother saying her father had "visited" her soon after his death. "It wasn't entirely comforting, she said, because she wanted to be free of him and felt that even after death he was observing her." Hyser continues, "It was hard for him to please his dad, he never felt that [his dad] was proud of him or even knew him. Warren would never say he felt inadequate, but there was something unattainable there, a distance, a disconnect, a gap that he was trying to fill. He tried to make up for it in his work, which is why I believe he's such a perfectionist."

When they got back to the Ritz-Carlton in New York, he invited her up, asked if she would stay over. She declined, said, "I'm really enjoying getting to know you, but I just broke up with somebody, and I'm not going to suddenly go from him to you." He persisted, and again she declined, saying, "I told you, No. This is boring."

"Really?"

"Really." She recalls, "He was stunned."

When Hyser returned to L.A., Beatty followed. She moved out of her boyfriend's house and in with a girlfriend who was in the middle of a decade-and-a-half-long relationship with Bob Dylan. Dylan lived near Beatty, off Mulholland. Wooing Hyser, Beatty was a frequent visitor. He loved Dylan, said he made him feel "normal." Beatty was so secretive that Dylan thought he was a Mason.

Hyser, on the other hand, did get Beatty, and fell in love. Up to that point, she was the only woman with whom he would have a lengthy relationship who hadn't won an Oscar or wasn't otherwise famous in her own right. Indeed, she wasn't quite sure why he was with her. But she understood that "compared to his other girlfriends, he would say, I was 'a day at the beach.' Everyone else is nuts." But days at the beach can get boring, and he asked her to do a threesome. "He said to me, 'I bet you're a woman who never slept with another woman, because you love your mother.' I said, 'Yeah, and I'm not going to be that person.' He wasn't trying to force me into it, and he didn't pursue it."

Hyser too recognized that he found trust and openness difficult. "Warren is a contained individual," she says. "He's got this other self standing over him saying, 'It's okay to do this, it's not okay to do that.' He judges himself 24/7. His relationship with women is a place where he lets go and doesn't judge himself, especially with women he's not that close to, which is one of the reasons he finds relationships where he is intimate more difficult. He's pretty cynical." If he were asked, "What makes you happy?" he'd be likely to parry the question with another question: "What is happiness?" Perhaps, she continues, he finds "happiness when he can reach a place of true intimacy with somebody — not necessarily sexually — when he feels like he can be himself, which I don't think happens a lot for him."

Beatty wouldn't do anything for his fiftieth birthday "except get upset about people who didn't call him," Hyser remembers. "Like Diane would never call him for his birthday. He was hurt." (He did, however, make a dramatic entrance to someone's else's birthday party, around the same time as his, exclaiming, "I'm here for my birthday boff!") He and Hyser went out to dinner with his attorney, Bert Fields, one of the few people Beatty admired for his mind and acumen. Hyser gave him a German shepherd puppy.

Hyser was Jewish. She continues, "He loved that I was Jewish, and that I wasn't a self-loathing Jew, because he said that all the Jews he knew in Hollywood were self-loathing Jews." Beatty prided himself on his command of Yiddish, especially gross, politically incorrect sexual and racial slurs that he used to shock his Jewish friends. Speaking of an actress who wasn't right for a role, he'd say, "She's too pretty, I want her to be more of a *mieskeit*," that is, homely. Hyser goes on, "He acted more Jewish than I did. He's not a whiner, but he's got the guilt, real Jewish guilt. I don't know where that comes from." She tried to make him more hip, bought his clothes for him and convinced him not to wear his pants so high.

When Beatty introduced her to his friends, he often referred to her as "Springsteen's former girlfriend." He seemed inordinately proud of her. He'd say, "Look at her, isn't she just the greatest?" Hyser recalls, "He seemed genuinely taken with everything I said or did. I had this guy who was worshipping the ground I walked on, and it was Warren Beatty. It was really great—for a while."

FOR THE most part, Beatty and Hoffman stayed away from the editing room, letting May have her way with the footage. They seemed unaware that the new release date, late spring 1987, was bearing down on them. Somewhat belatedly, they appeared to remember that each of them had say over the final cut, and that if they wished to exercise this right, they needed to get started on their own versions of the film, since May was well advanced with hers, nearly ready to mix her sound. Finally, the day of reckoning came when Hoffman was informed that, apropos a particular scene, "If you don't get this in today, it won't be in the cut anyway."

"Whaddya tawkin' about?"

"Dustin, the negative's being cut next week."

"What? I'm going down the hall, I'm tawkin' to Warren!" Hoffman grabbed Beatty, cried, "Waaarren, they've been bullshittin' us, man, they've been flimflammin' us."

"What do you mean?" Beatty asked him. Hoffman told him, and he became extremely agitated. Beatty has large hands, with long fingers. When he wants to make a point with particular emphasis, as he did then with May, reading her the riot act in a loud voice, he stuck his finger right in her face, almost touching her nose. Without speaking a syllable, May encircled his finger with her thumb and forefinger, moving them rapidly back and forth over his finger, as if to masturbate him. His face turned deep red, and he started to laugh. Says someone who was there, "Elaine's so smart. She knew just how to get to him. Which allowed her to disregard what he said."

May was working with Rotter; Beatty and Hoffman began to edit with Scharf, Hoffman during the day, Beatty at night. Every morning, Hoffman would ask, "What did Warren do to my scene last night?" Every night, Beatty would say, "Lemme see what Dustin did to my scene today." According to the *L.A. Times*, there were three separate teams of editors working around the clock and being paid double time, and the even more expensive golden time (two-and-a-half time). The differences between the cuts weren't dramatic; they essentially boiled down to the distribution of close-ups, like, Is the camera on Dustin's hands playing the piano, or on Warren's face as he grabs the mike?

A few of the alternative versions were tested with audiences. But there came a day when Hoffman learned that one of his cuts would not be tested. "The idea was there was going to be a screening where all three of them were played for an audience, one after another, to see which one got the best response," recalls sound mixer Tom Fleischman. "I was there on a Saturday mixing Dustin's version of the scene, when he got the word that it wasn't going to be shown at the screening. Somehow, Elaine weaseled out of it. Dustin flipped out, just walked out of the mix. Basically walked away from the whole thing. His assistant was trying to stop him from going down in the elevator, and he was so furious he pushed her aside and left her in tears."

The atmosphere in the editing room was tense. "Warren and Elaine had a huge fight," Hyser recalls. "He felt that she screwed him." Finally, according to one source, Bert Fields was invited into the cutting room to mediate among his three final cut clients in an all-night meeting. "Bert Fields had final cut," he says. "It's a fact." Along with the editors, the principals gathered in front of the KEM editing console. Fields chaired the meeting, switching back and forth among cuts. An assistant would put up one version, usually May's, and then Fields would ask, "Anybody have a problem with this scene? We'll run it until somebody has a problem." Eventually, one of the three players would say something like, "That's not the version I want to show." Fields would reply, "Let's see yours." One of the assistants took notes that read like, "We'll use Dustin's version of this scene, we'll use Warren's version of that scene . . ." (According to Beatty, this account is "bullshit." He says he doesn't remember Fields ever in the editing room.)

Some of the notes were not honored in practice. According to the source, when Beatty asked what one of the notes said, claiming he couldn't read the handwriting, he was told, "It says, 'Use Dustin's close-up version.'" But he still insisted, "I can't read that! I don't see that," meaning he didn't want to see it, so that he was free to do what he wanted.

According to Phillip Schopper, "Warren kept trying to do things mostly with Isabelle's scenes, because she was his girlfriend. Since the relationship had become a bad one, Warren was trying to be as generous to her as could be. He was overcompensating. They fought and they fought, Warren and Elaine, things being thrown up to Bert—it was like a bake-off—and Bert going with Warren."

But the principals knew they had to make the process work, no matter how tense the relationships had been on the set. They were elaborately polite with one another. It was as if they all knew there was too little time left to whack away at one another. The goal was not necessarily coming up with the best cut, but rather the best cut they could all agree on.

From their point of view, the process was working. At one point, Hoffman called his wife, Lisa, and spritzed, "We're doing great work here!" Beatty says the cut at which they arrived was basically May's. According to Schopper, "Elaine finally said, 'You have to lose some of the battles to maintain the whole,' but she won her way for the most part." When the sun came up, Fields said something like, "We have a movie!" But the editors were scandalized. Rotter was a quiet man, not given to emotional outbursts, but he exploded, yelling, "We don't have anything. All we have is a lot of paper. How do you know any of this stuff works?" (Rotter refused to comment.) Says the source who has knowledge of what went on in the room, "It was sad. We were just dumbfounded that these intelligent people could have ever let this occur. This was not the way you make movies. Each change affects everything else. The movie has to be screened in its totality several times."

The editors derisively referred to the final version as the "Bert Fields cut."

AT THE same time that postproduction on *Ishtar* was winding down, Beatty had a second drama on his hands, considerably more riveting. Like *Ishtar*, it played out as a farce, although it would have grave implications for the direction of the country. On April 13, 1987, five weeks before *Ishtar* was due to be released, Senator Gary Hart announced at a press conference in Denver that he would run for president in 1988. This time around, he had none of the encumbrances he had struggled to overcome in 1984. True, he had lost to Mondale, but not by much. He enjoyed the name recognition he had lacked then; he had accumulated a campaign kitty of $2.1 million; and he had addressed the "Where's the beef" issue by writing a book about reforming the military. In March 1987, the ABC/*Washington Post* preference poll put Hart ahead in the contest for the Democratic nomination 46 percent to 14 percent for Jesse Jackson, his nearest competitor. No other Democratic hopeful cracked 4 percent. With Ted Kennedy out of the picture—he disavowed any intention of running in December 1985—the candidacy was Hart's for the taking. After nearly two terms of Reaganomics that left staggering trade and budget deficits, high unemployment, and the so-called Reagan recession, Hart just had to avoid mistakes of his own making. According to another national poll, he would defeat whomever the Republicans put up against him, George Bush or Bob Dole. With Hart so close to the presidency, and Beatty so close to Hart, the actor was on the verge of unprecedented access to the beating heart of the American political system. Short of winning the presidency himself, which was not in the cards, Hart was the next best thing.

But almost immediately, the rumors about Hart's extramarital affairs, which had bubbled under the surface of his last campaign, boiled over, and along with them, the issue of his relationship with Beatty. Among Hart staffers, "there was a widespread view that a little Warren Beatty went a long way," says political adviser Bill Bradley. Bradley hadn't seen any reason for Hart to shun Beatty's hospitality during the 1984 campaign, but now he changed his mind. He recalls, "There was an item in *Parade* magazine that one of my brothers-in-law saw, a doctor who gave money to Hart—one paragraph, but read by millions of people. He called me up, and asked, 'What's he doing there at that house with Warren Beatty?' Because Warren had created this whole mystique about himself, that he had hot and cold running starlets and centerfolds in his Jacuzzi on Mulholland Drive. If you put the front-runner for president of the United States, who's an attractive guy known to have a roving eye, in that Jacuzzi, the imagination runs wild."

Hart always denied that anything outré occurred while he was at the house. He was probably telling the truth; Beatty, if not the candidate, was too smart to jeopardize the campaign with hanky-panky. Still, the star had introduced Hart to Jennifer Lee way back in January of 1973. She didn't like him, noticed that he "laughed and laughed at everything Warren says," and described him as "a poor man's version of Warren. He flirts, and not well. He's too eager and too goofy, and what an ego. He acts as if he's arrived at a party given in his honor, smiling at every woman, every waitress, *anybody* whose eyes he might possibly catch." He called her subsequently on several occasions, but she ducked him. Still, if Beatty introduced Hart to Lee, it beggars the imagination that over the years Beatty never introduced him to any of his other female friends. On the other hand, whether Beatty did or not didn't really matter. As Bradley puts it, "A lot of the time when people imagined that they were entertaining themselves with *Penthouse* centerfolds, they could have been reading Thomas Jefferson together, but the perception becomes the reality." Many Hollywood liberals opened their homes to Hart; in fact, they competed for his company. "But nooo," continues Bradley, "Gary had to stay at Warren's. That drove me nuts."

Bill Dixon had become Hart's chief of staff. Dixon had worked on the 1972 McGovern campaign and was a close friend of Hunter Thompson's. But he had also run the Senate Banking Committee for Wisconsin senator William Proxmire, served on the board of the World Bank, and been the Wisconsin State Banking Commissioner, and as such he brought formidable credentials to the position. One of Dixon's jobs was to manage the Beatty "account." Sometimes he would intercept Beatty's calls. "It wasn't so much that Bill was trying to block Warren from talking to Gary, but he was attempting to make sure that Warren was very aware that if there were centerfolds or supermodels or starlets in the Jacuzzi with him and Gary, it was something that they should cut back or be very discreet about," Bradley explains. Eventually, Hart began to pull away from Beatty, just enough so that it was apparent the candidate was taking his staff's anxieties seriously.

Hart flat-out denied the rumors in an admiring *New York Times Magazine* profile by E. J. Dionne published on May 3, 1987, but sank himself by famously saying, "If anybody wants to put a tail on me, go ahead. They'd be very bored." Little did he know that reporters from the *Miami Herald* were already following him around and, as things turned out, they were not so bored as he might have wished. Hart was involved with a woman named Donna Rice. He had met her, a twenty-nine-year-old AMW ("actress, model, whatever") at a New Year's Day party at the home of Don Henley, former lead singer for the Eagles, in Aspen, Colorado, which he had attended as a guest of the former agent, now Orion executive, Mike Medavoy and his wife, Patricia Duff. A striking blonde, Rice had briefly dated Henley and posed for a picture in a redneck bar with one breast bared, draped in the Confederate flag. Hart began calling her from the road, usually from pay phones. He had long soulful conversations with her wherein he asked her questions like, "What do people your age think about America?" As Bradley puts it, "Partly he was conning her, partly he was conning himself, and partly he was being sincere, courting her."

Meanwhile, Hart had incautiously struck up a friendship with William C. "Billy" Broadhurst, a lobbyist, fund-raiser, and political fixer from Louisiana. Broadhurst liked to have fun, and he and Hart partied together. Several Hart staffers thought there was something squirrelly about Broadhurst, and warned the candidate. They also learned that news organizations were considering surveillance of Hart's house, and they warned Dixon. "We knew there was going to be a stakeout," one staffer said, "and still nothing was done."

In late April, Hart and Rice found themselves headed for Bimini together aboard an eighty-three-foot yacht chartered by Broadhurst and aptly named *Monkey Business*. On board as well was Broadhurst's companion, Lynn Armandt, a foxy brunette, also twenty-nine and also Rice's friend. Hart had a theory that media scrutiny came in waves: very intense periods alternated with slack periods, during which he would be virtually ignored. Since he believed he had just come out the other side of the media blitz ignited by his announcement that he was going to run for president, he somehow thought he would be invisible and allowed Armandt to take some snapshots of Rice sitting on his lap. When Armandt offered to take the roll to be developed, he said, "Sure." Meanwhile, Tom Fiedler, executive editor of the *Miami Herald*, had gotten an anonymous tip from a woman who told them that Rice would be flying to Washington's National Airport on Friday, May 1. He asked investigative reporter Jim McGee to take Rice's flight, but McGee lost her in the airport. Staking out Hart's townhouse on Capitol Hill, however, a team from the *Herald* saw Hart and a woman entering and leaving.

The *Herald* published its story on Sunday, May 3, the very day that Hart's dismissal of rumors of marital infidelity appeared in *The*

New York Times. As *Time* magazine put it, "For Gary Hart, the end came with breathtaking speed. As the week began, he was the overwhelming front runner for the Democratic presidential nomination, a Gulliver surrounded by political Lilliputians. But then came the most harrowing public ordeal ever endured by a modern presidential contender. . . . Like Hester Prynne, Hart stood in the public dock accused of adultery." Hart reluctantly decided to abandon the race. Early in the morning of Thursday, May 7, Hart told his staff, "Let's go home," and flew to Denver on a chartered flight. He sat by himself and read a novel by Tolstoy, *Resurrection.*

Like everyone else, Beatty was stunned. But whereas Hart's other Hollywood supporters fled, as if he had the plague, Beatty remained constant, directing his anger—he was "angry at everything" said one friend—not at Hart but at the news media and, for a moment, at Pat Caddell, whom the gossip mill had implicated in a plot to set Hart up. (Caddell was then working for Maryland senator Joe Biden, one of Hart's rivals for the nomination.) When Caddell called Beatty that Thursday night, the actor said something like, "If I ever find out it was you, I'll kill you," and advised him to "look for cover."

"It amazed me because Warren knew it wasn't true," recalls Caddell. "If I had wanted to take Gary Hart out with personal information, I would have had him out long before the race started. That's not the way I do business."

Beatty quickly came to his senses and insisted that Caddell come up to his house immediately. Caddell did so and found Beatty with Joyce Hyser and Sean Penn. Beatty was on the phone with Hart. Penn disappeared, and Caddell went to dinner with Hyser in Beverly Hills, where the actor finally joined them after they'd finished. Beatty asked Caddell for his thoughts. "Everyone is telling him to get out of the race," Caddell responded. "I wouldn't get out of the race." He explained that to do so would enshrine him forever as "Donna Rice's playmate." Rather, Caddell continued, he should hold a press conference and say, "You're not going to drive me out of the race. Let he who is without sin cast the first stone."

Beatty got it right away. As Caddell put it, "That was his great political gift; he understood drama." The two men left the restaurant and raced up Benedict Canyon to Beatty's home, where the actor again got on the phone to Hart, who was preparing his withdrawal speech. Beatty urged him to stay in the race. "You're crazy," Beatty told him. "Don't get out. There are a lot of people who think you have been wronged. You should tell them, 'Hell no!'"

Hart replied, "Thanks, Warren," and he began to draft a hell-no speech.

At 5:00 A.M. the next day, Beatty urged Hart to admit he was an adulterer and then refuse to answer any more questions about his personal life. He thought the flap would blow over.

Deputy campaign manager John Emerson said, "Warren, it's raining concrete."

Recalls Hart, "Warren told me not to withdraw, just drop off the campaign trail and see if sanity would reassert itself. But there were five hundred reporters camped out at my front gate. I was not inclined to wait it out." He withdrew.

Says Caddell, "The candidate had a deep need not to win."

Later that morning, on Friday, May 8, a blindingly brief twenty-five days after he had announced his candidacy, Hart held his press conference at Denver's Executive Tower Inn. "Under the present circumstances, this campaign cannot go on," he said. His tone was harsh, relentless, and totally unapologetic: "I refuse to submit my family and my friends and innocent people and myself to further rumors and gossip. It's simply an intolerable situation."

Beatty slept through it, knowing the outcome. From his point of view, it was an assassination by the press. "I don't think there is anything to be admired in lying and cheating, or philandering," he said. "But there might be something to be admired in not burning people at the stake because they have these weaknesses."

Says Hyser, "Warren was right there with him, as close as you could be to the next president of the United States. I don't think he realized that Gary was a ticking time bomb. He was devastated. Incensed. Gary is totally self-destructive. How can you run for president and have a picture taken of a girl on your lap? How could you be so stupid? Warren felt that if Gary (or later Clinton) had just said, 'It's none of your business,' we could be looking at a different world today.

"I believe Warren and Gary are very similar. To them, there's something about the chase, the getting there, the possibilities of something happening, whether it be in a relationship or a career or a film project, that's more exciting than the end result. Running for president is much more exciting than the reality of being president. We always used to joke that Warren wanted Gary's life, and Gary wanted Warren's life. But Gary was no Warren Beatty. That wouldn't have happened to Warren. There's nobody better at having a clandestine relationship than he is."

Despite the candidate's evident willingness to set the match to a spectacular auto-da-fé, some on Hart's staff suspected that the candidate had been set up. In the mid-1970s, as senator, Hart had been a member of the Church Committee that had investigated CIA plots against the lives of foreign leaders and aired a lot of dirty CIA laundry. He also issued the highly critical Schweiker-Hart report, which concluded that the Warren Commission's examination of the Kennedy assassination had been hobbled by the refusal of the CIA and the FBI to divulge crucial information. Hart not only favored reform of both agencies, he had called for reopening of the Kennedy investigation, thereby making enemies for himself within the intelligence community. As Bradley puts it, "He had poked his nose into a lot of places where powerful people don't want noses poked." Beatty had lived through one of the most violent passages in American history. While too sensible to be a conspiracy buff, he had nevertheless made *The Parallax View*, and was fascinated by the so-called secret history of the United States. Bradley continues, "He felt that Hart should have assumed right from the start that a lot heavier people than the *Miami Herald* would be following him around, like the CIA, especially since Bush, the Republican candidate, had been its director. He felt that Gary should have been much more cautious and not have assumed that there were moments when it was safe for him to indulge himself in ways that were not totally discreet." As Beatty puts it, "I've assumed since 1961 that my phones may have been tapped."

Caddell thinks watching what happened to Hart soured Beatty on running for office. "Not the Donna Rice part," he says. "Warren doesn't have anything to hide. He's never cheated on his wife, he's never been divorced, but it was watching Gary compromise. Warren's not very good at compromising what he thinks is the truth. It's not going to happen." Says Beatty, "By the time it got around to '88, what with the media frenzy combined with the financial necessities of running for office, it just seemed that I didn't have the level of altruism required," he says. "With the negative campaigning, more and more the honor was being sucked from the profession. The people who held public office were held up to ridicule and scandalized. And with the increasing sophistication of public opinion polling and the pursuit of money, anyone who was still trying his level best to contribute felt more and more prostituted in raising money and would get out."

Ironically, minimizing Beatty's role in the campaign may have backfired. "If Gary was going to be running around with other women, there probably wouldn't have been any better running mate than Warren, because Billy Broadhurst turned out to be a complete idiot in handling the situation," says Bradley. "Warren would have sussed it out in an instant. 'Cause he gets that stuff immediately."

If he was disappointed in Hart, Beatty never expressed it publicly. Albeit not yet married, the behavior for which Hart was pilloried was too close to his own for him to throw stones. Jack Nicholson summed up the despair of many on the left when he said, "It was a catastrophe for all of us—like *Ishtar*. The disqualification of an inspired public servant. It made you embarrassed to be an American. Everyone was back on TV talking about God. I like Gary because he fucks."

Dustin Hoffman saw Beatty almost every day and was as close to him as anyone during that period. He says, "I didn't even know about Gary Hart. He never mentioned him."

MISSING A release date is like raising a red flag on which is inscribed in bold letters "Film In Trouble." And indeed, after *Ishtar* failed to make its Christmas 1986 opening, the press, already alerted to budget overruns, smelled blood in the water. It was too expensive, it was going to be a bomb, etc. *Time* magazine wondered whether Beatty could "turn movie production into a form of seduction, in which large, supposedly rational corporations are encouraged to spend bloated sums of money for unlikely enterprises." The answer was yes, but in the case of *Reds*, that was a good thing. In the case of *Ishtar*, it wasn't such a good thing. Beatty had narrowly dodged a bullet with *Reds*, but *Ishtar* became the new poster boy for over-budget movies. The *Los Angeles Times* tarred it as "the most expensive comedy ever made," and started referring to it as "Warrensgate," an allusion to the legendary flop *Heaven's Gate*. Noted Dustin Hoffman, "The word went out that we're perfectionists—which made it sound as if we had some disease."

Hyser recalls, "Warren started to take it personally. It was all about him and his indecision."

Ishtar was being distributed by an unfriendly studio that Beatty suspected was sabotaging its own picture. He fought bitterly with Diller, who was in his camp, over the marketing of *Reds*. It can only be imagined how he dealt with Columbia. He reportedly rejected one studio marketing veteran assigned to *Ishtar,* saying, "I can't use you. You're a Puttnam man, and I think you'll always be loyal to David and not to me." According to another Columbia executive, "Everybody worked for Puttnam, and Puttnam was against the picture, so every decision that came from the studio he saw Puttnam influencing or controlling. I think in some respects he was right."

The hostile press put *Ishtar*'s publicity campaign under a microscope. It was discovered that Beatty hired "Warren's friend," in Hoffman's words, DP Bill Fraker, to shoot his TV interviews on 35 millimeter film instead of videotape. The day before *Ishtar* was released, Tom Shales, writing in the *Washington Post,* quoted several TV producers speculating that Beatty required 35 millimeter because people look better on film—read, younger—than on tape. He also revealed that a "five-part 'GMA' [*Good Morning America*] interview had never aired because Beatty additionally withheld some of the material shot, refusing to release it to the program." *The New York Times* reported that "Mr. Beatty edited his interview with that program while transferring it from film to tape."

Beatty's reluctance to do press for his pictures was well known. "I'd rather ride down the street on a camel than give what is sometimes called an in-depth interview," he said. "I'd rather ride down the street on a camel, nude . . . in a snowstorm . . . backwards." But he realized that his refusal to speak to journalists hurt *Reds,* and in this case, the need for damage control was so great as to make riding a camel in a snowstorm nude and backwards the greater of two evils. He waged a vigorous, but ultimately fruitless, battle to deflect attention from the picture's finances. He deplored, and rightly so, the growing obsession with box office, which began after Reagan was elected, when the patina of corporate America was buffed to a high gloss and money became the measure of all things. In practical terms, it meant that the list of top weekend grossers moved out of the trades and into the daily press, and worse, from the business section to the arts pages, which suggested that a movie's bottom line was becoming the new standard of taste. And worst of all, this information migrated to TV, where grosses became a staple of new celebrity shows like *Entertainment Tonight*, reported with the avidity that the business press reserved for the Dow.

But the good news was that *Ishtar* had three successful previews. Beatty said of the one in Toronto, "I have never had a more successful preview," so much so that the studio and the principals discussed striking more prints and taking more theaters. May was apparently under the impression that it was going to be a big hit and went off to Tahiti on vacation.

But on Friday, May 22, 1987, it all came crashing down. *Ishtar* was released on 1,390 screens. It was number one that weekend, grossing $4.3 million, but was almost edged out by a horror movie called *The Gate*, with no stars, a $4 million budget, and a gross of $4.2 million on the same number of screens. (Also by way of comparison, on the following Memorial Day weekend, *Beverly Hills Cop II* opened to a $26.3 million gross.)

Marylouise Oates, who was married to Beatty's friend Democratic campaign consultant Bob Shrum, was covering the opening night for the *L.A. Times*. She had her young son Michael, twelve, in tow. They were standing outside, watching the crowd emerge from the theater. Beatty didn't want to talk about *Ishtar*; he wanted to talk about Gary Hart. He explained to Michael, "The movie's not important. Politics is important." While he was delivering this message, he was idly snapping Oates's bra strap. Michael said to him, "Stop, that's my mommy's." He replied, "Oh, sorry, I just do it out of habit. It's nothing personal."

Ishtar got mixed reviews. Janet Maslin, writing in *The New York Times*, was most generous: "It's a likable, good-humored hybrid, a mixture of small, funny moments and the pointless, oversized spectacle that these days is sine qua non for any hot-weather hit." Considerably less generous, David Denby called it a "vanity production . . . [a] gigantic party joke," in *New York* magazine, and tossed in a few more choice epithets like "crazy," "greed," "folly," and "obsession."

Like many of Beatty's movies, *Ishtar* has a political subtext having to do with oil, poverty, and power. One of the picture's revolutionaries says, "The dome of the emir's palace is gold, and the people of Ishtar have never seen a refrigerator." But you'd never know it from watching the movie. Beatty had generally worked within the genres, using them as protective coloration to cloak his more serious concerns. When the films worked, he successfully pressed the genre conventions into the service of his ideas, the way he did in *Bonnie and Clyde, Reds,* and later *Bugsy.* When they worked fitfully or not at all, the conventions smothered the life of the movies, as in *Ishtar*—and later, to some degree, *Bulworth.*

Paul Sylbert's acerbic critique of the movie is unforgiving, but essentially on target. "When you make a movie like *Ishtar,* the audience's expectations can be exceeded, but they can't be disappointed. This one disappoints all around. First of all, you have to have romance where, according to convention, one of the two guys who were vying for her has to get her. But in *Ishtar,* nobody gets her. You can't keep asking people to keep listening to songs that are bad but not funny. It was a funny script, but Elaine wasn't able to execute it. Even the performances are not much to talk about. She flattened everybody out. I cannot imagine that anybody who worked on that movie left it feeling that they did their best work. I didn't. Nobody did."

Beatty's relationship with May was never the same. "Elaine was blaming him," Joyce Hyser recalls. May felt that he didn't do enough press, and that the press that he did do was compromised by his excessive attempts to control it, which just antagonized everyone. Nor did she appreciate what she considered Beatty's backhand compliments, like, "Who can control Elaine? She's such a genius." For a year or two after *Ishtar* came out, they were barely speaking. Although they warmed up some after that, the whole experience left a sour taste. Buck Henry adds, "Whenever I see Elaine, she has a wisecrack about Warren. It's compulsive. And slightly mean. The sense of it is, 'Are we having a good time in life, or are we working with Warren?' "

Beatty fell victim to his own success. "The great producer—how did this happen to him?" Sylbert says. "*Shampoo* was on the money in every way. So was *Heaven Can Wait.* If he said 'She's a fraud' early on in the movie and didn't do anything about it, I can't account for it. You can get pretty puffed up in this business if you have the kind of successes Warren's had, and even when the movie's not a big hit, the fact that he got it made, in the case of *Reds,* and got the Oscar, can certainly affect your judgment." He adds, "If he hadn't gotten so good at keeping the studio away, and getting his way with things, and taking the time he wanted to take, he might have examined what he was making."

For his part, Beatty most likely regarded the entire episode as a specimen of no good deed goes unpunished, but he continues to defend the picture to this day, although he allows, "We probably shouldn't have gone to Morocco." Even Hoffman, who didn't much like the script in the first place, defends it, albeit without enthusiasm. He says, "*Ishtar* was a B minus, C plus comedy." But, he adds, "given its flaws, there was something aside from Warren's seductive powers that made me do it. There's a spine to it: isn't it better to spend a lifetime being second rate at what you're passionate about, what you love, than be first rate without a soul. That's magnificent, and that's what she was after. I'd do it again. I just wish it had worked out better."

When its run ended, *Ishtar* grossed only $12.7 million. As with *Reds,* the real cost of the picture may never be known. According to *The New York Times,* sources put the final cost, including overhead and financing charges but excluding prints and ads, at $51 million. According to Mac Brown, "We were wildly high on a budget, but it wasn't that we went over, it was that there was no budget, at least none that we submitted, where we said, 'This is what it's gonna cost,' and signed off on it. But they went ahead and started the movie anyway. I think we ended up around $50 or $51 million. It shouldn't have cost what it cost." (The average production budget in 1987 was $17 million.) The *L.A. Times,* citing *Variety*'s numbers guru Art Murphy, reported that the outlay for prints and advertising (P&A) could have reached another $20 million, which would have put the total budget, including P&A, up around $70 million.

According to Fay Vincent, *Ishtar* lost about $40 million, becoming the flop the press predicted it would, which Beatty regarded as a self-fulfilling prophecy. He blamed the press for embalming the picture before it even hit the theaters. And he blamed David Puttnam for launching a whispering campaign against the film. "The man didn't see the movie," Beatty charged at the time. "He never called me, wrote me a letter, sent me a note, asked me a question. And didn't with Dustin or Elaine May either. There was absolutely no communication with any of us from the man who was running the company. Usually you would expect negative gossip to emanate from other sources. When it emanates from your own studio, it tends to make you want to go to Barbados."

"In some respects, Warren was right," said Vincent. Puttnam "never even saw it." Puttnam's attitude was probably captured best by an anonymous Columbia marketing executive who wondered, rhetorically, at the time, "Could David have gotten involved and tried to make peace with the two of them? I guess he could have tried, but honestly I don't think he gives a shit. It's possible to live a fairly complete life without Warren or Dustin."

The fallout from *Ishtar* was substantial. "It hurt me," said Vincent. Referring to the producer who was a power at the studio, he added, "Ray Stark went after me, and the people at Coke went after me politically." Puttnam, who had been hired to rein in star salaries, curb the power of the agents, and contain production costs—in short, to prevent future *Ishtars*—was fired in October 1988, having learned a harsh lesson: stars are forever, while suits—especially those cut from foreign cloth—have a brief shelf life. As composer Paul Williams put it, "You must remember one thing about Hollywood. Even if 'Ishtar' is a big bomb, Warren, Dustin, Elaine and I will all work again . . . only next time at a higher fee!"

But Williams was only partly right. Beatty and Hoffman worked again, but May never directed another movie. Nor was the studio itself immune. Said Lisbeth Barron, an analyst at the Wall Street firm Balis Zorn Gerard Inc., "With the negative publicity surrounding *Ishtar,* Coke management said, 'What are we doing in this business?'" Just as Transamerica sold United Artists after *Heavens' Gate* in 1981, Coca-Cola sold Columbia to Sony in 1989.

Although Puttnam lost the battle, setting back the attempts to rein in costs for nearly a decade, the war would continue. Beatty may have resisted, but he saw, as clearly as anyone, where things were going. "A big problem," Beatty said, "is that the cost of production, distribution and promotion of films has become so great that you have to open your movie in more than 1,000 theaters at once. As a result, you have people making films that are designed to appeal to the broadest possible audience. . . . Things are in pretty bad shape right now." Ironically, Beatty would play a major role in the next skirmish as well, targeted by Disney chairman Jeffrey Katzenberg in his notorious 1991 memo after his studio produced and released *Dick Tracy.*

Nineteen eighty-six and 1987 had not been kind to Beatty. Cousin David MacLeod had been arrested and charged with sodomy; his father had died; *Ishtar* had flopped; his friendship with Elaine May had dissolved in acrimony; his romance with Isabelle Adjani had ended; and with Gary Hart retired to Troublesome Gulch, his hopes for being the power behind the president lay in ruins, the big brass ring snatched from his grasp. Beatty was depressed. He confessed to a model he had been calling every night for a lengthy period of time, "I think I'm becoming slightly reclusive myself because I realize I haven't left my house for weeks." It had to get better. As the holidays approached, Beatty put all that behind him. He had moved Hyser into his house, and the two of them celebrated Christmas 1987 in Washington, D.C., with a dinner attended by his mother, MacLaine, Bella Abzug, and four or five others. They got into a conversation about the meaning of Christmas that segued to the subject of the Resurrection, Jesus, and how it really happened. The chatter went on and on, until it was brought to an abrupt halt when MacLaine suddenly threw her silverware down on the plate with a deafening clatter, and announced, "I know because I was there!" Hyser, who had a mouthful of food, launched it, projectile-style, across the table. MacLaine burst into laughter. Turning to Hyser, she said, "When you get to know me a lot better, these things won't surprise you." Beatty didn't think it was funny. Hyser recalls, "Warren was completely horrified by it. He's not a spiritual man by any stretch of the imagination. The concept of God is totally abhorrent to him. You have to be able to reason everything out. He totally adores her, but he doesn't get her, there's a complete disconnect there. She is pretty wacky, but she's fabulous."

10

MATERIAL BOY

How Beatty had a demographic romance with Madonna,
created a wholly original comic strip movie, *Dick Tracy,*
and lost or gave up *Howard Hughes.*

"Warren told me that *Ishtar* had dimmed his star, and he needed
a big, fat commercial hit. He felt *Tracy* was his ka-ching, that it
would make a lot of money."

— *Bo Goldman*

BACK IN THE mid-1970s, Beatty had signed a contract with Warners that obligated him to do *Howard Hughes* before *Heaven
Can Wait.* But contracts were made to be broken, he was a star,
and used to having his way with the studios. If *Hughes* wasn't ready,
it wasn't ready. He was not about to be rushed. Eventually, Warners
accepted the fact that *Heaven* was going to happen first, but insisted
that *Hughes* be up next. Still, after *Heaven Can Wait* he did *Reds,* and
then *Ishtar.* Warners was again insisting that *Hughes* be his next picture. And indeed, at one time, he said that would be the case, but the
catastrophic crash of *Ishtar* had made him reconsider.

Never one readily to admit mistakes, and still blaming the studio
and the press for the failure of that picture, when the subject came
up he shrugged it off, made a joke. But it was no laughing matter.
Beatty was frustrated and puzzled by *Ishtar*'s poor box office. Ac-

cording to Pat Caddell, "You think you've made a good movie, and everybody's saying it's terrible." Beatty had seen too many directors of his generation—Billy Friedkin, Peter Bogdanovich, even Francis Coppola—successfully fingering the pulse of the public one moment, only to discover the patient comatose the next. The relationship between director and audience has always been shrouded in mystery, and when the director is churning out hits, like a batter in the "zone," better left unexamined. But Beatty approached the failure of *Ishtar* with his customary pragmatism. It was a problem to be analyzed and solved. Fearing that the culture, always a capricious mistress, had withdrawn her favors, he looked at everything that came out, sometimes two movies a day, trying to figure out if, in Caddell's words, he'd "missed something."

And now, thinking about *Hughes,* he was having second thoughts, despite the fact that he still owed Warners the picture. According to Mab Goldman, wife of Bo Goldman, whom Beatty would hire to do a page one rewrite of *Tracy,* Beatty expected "he could get *Tracy* done quickly, and that they'd put up with it. That was why he was willing to endanger his relationship with Warners."

Several of his friends advised him against it, wanted him to do a romantic comedy of the kind he'd had so much success with in the past. "Dick Tracy has no 'hooks,'" said Dick Sylbert in 1989. "It offers you nothing. The guy is no Sherlock Holmes, he doesn't have superpowers, there are no big action scenes. The highlight of his career is 'Stick 'em up,' right?" Besides, no one under forty-five had ever heard of Dick Tracy. Many of them hadn't even heard of Beatty. As Sylbert put it, "The kids already say, 'Warren who?' They even say, 'Jack who?'" But the actor, whose trust in his instincts had most often paid off in the face of the conventional wisdom arrayed against him, or the advice of his friends, which all too often turned out to be the same thing, plowed ahead. He decided that *Tracy,* not *Hughes,* would be his next movie.

Beatty had acquired the rights to *Tracy* in 1985, and now he took it to Disney, where two of the refugees from Paramount ended up, Michael Eisner, who was CEO of the company, and Jeffrey Katzenberg, who ran production. Again, as Bob Evans pointed out, he targeted a studio that had a new regime. When he was still at Paramount, Eisner had written a memo arguing that the studio's films were too expensive, using *Reds* as a case in point. But at Disney, while charting a penurious but profitable course for themselves, the two men had watched enviously as the other companies put their eggs in the blockbuster basket and saw their profits grow. By the late 1980s, Paramount was doing the third *Indiana Jones,* Fox the second *Die Hard*, Warners the second *Lethal Weapon*, and Universal the second and third *Back to the Future*. Deploying a dazzling mix of charm and financial acumen, Beatty seduced Eisner and Katzenberg, who for the second time saw an opportunity for their own tent pole. Of course, as soon as they bit, he turned around and made them sell it to him.

Beatty never thought he was right for any role, possibly a reflection of his lack of confidence in his range as an actor. The same was true of Tracy. He didn't think he looked like the hatchet-jawed detective, meaning his features were too soft for a character that called for an action hero, a tough guy with a hard-edged, flinty look, like Clint Eastwood, who had been interested in the role at one time. And in this case there was also the question of how to deliver comic strip dialogue without it sounding like comic strip dialogue, which would have been embarrassing.

Nor was Beatty his own first choice to direct. But he was having trouble finding someone to do it. On April 8, 1985, *Variety* reported that Martin Scorsese would direct a script written by Elaine May and Herb Gardner. But that was before *Ishtar*. Then Scorsese withdrew, complaining later that Beatty would not give him final cut. Bob Fosse turned down the job as well. So did Brian De Palma, so did the Coen brothers, Sam Raimi, and Hal Ashby. During the course of Beatty's conversations with Ashby, the director complained about what he thought was a bite on his leg. And on the other leg as well. It struck Beatty that what resembled a bite was what he had always imagined phlebitis would look like. He said, "I don't like that." He called a doctor he knew at Johns Hopkins, and asked him, "Is there such a thing as phlebitis on both legs?" The doctor replied, "There is a migratory phlebitis which comes as a result of pancreatic cancer." Beatty recalls, "That scared the hell out of me. We had some CAT scans done of the liver and the pancreas, and of course he did have malignancies in the pancreas and the liver, so we took him to Hopkins." Ashby hated doctors and refused to have surgery, but Beatty kept at him. "You ask Warren to do something, he's gonna do it whether you like it or not," says Dick Sylbert. "He knows more about cancer than the oncologists do." Ashby gave in, had the surgery, and as a result lost part of his liver. He had chemotherapy as well. He lived out the last weeks of his life in excruciating pain, for which he blamed Beatty, and wouldn't let him visit. Ashby died on December 27, 1988.

Despite his fears that he didn't look enough like Tracy to play him, he realized that nobody else did either, so, why not him? He also decided to direct it himself, as well as produce. Beatty rounded up the usual suspects, reconstituting, with some exceptions, the Beatty Bunch: Dick Sylbert to design the production, Vittorio Storaro behind the camera, and Stephen Sondheim to write the music. He added Milena Canonero to design the costumes.

So far as the actors went, Beatty drew on his friends, as well as people he had worked with in the past. Dustin Hoffman played Mumbles, Paul Sorvino played Lips Manlis, Michael J. Pollard played Bug Bailey, Estelle Parsons played Tess's mother. He also gathered a rogues' gallery of offbeat character actors, like Ian Wolfe, R. G. Armstrong, Mary Woronov, Seymour Cassel, Allen Garfield, Kathy Bates, Mandy Patinkin, and so on. Every once in a while, he struck out. He wanted Gene Hackman to play Big Boy Caprice, a villain invented expressly for the movie, but with the memory of Beatty demanding that he do serial takes on *Reds* still fresh in his mind, Hackman declined, saying, "I love you Warren, but I just can't do it."

One night, Beatty ran into Al Pacino in a restaurant in L.A. and asked him for a suggestion. He refused to name names, as per usual, but likely referring to Hackman, he said "[Gene] is giving me a terrible time, I want to punch him."

"Let me think about it." Beatty went home to work out. Pacino called, said, "Were you serious?"

"What do you mean?"

"About me playing this character?" Beatty claims that that had not occurred to him, but he immediately replied, "I certainly am," recalling that Pacino had done Brecht's eponymous gangster cum Hitler in *The Resistible Rise of Arturo Ui* off-Broadway. He told Pacino, "Nobody's ever seen it. I want you to take that character and just bring it to *Dick Tracy*." Which is what he did.

But there remained the two main female roles: Tess Trueheart, his

long-suffering girlfriend whom he can't bring himself to either marry
or leave, and Breathless Mahoney, the strip's slinky femme fatale, who
tries her best to get Tracy into bed. For Tess, Beatty's interest had been
piqued by Annette Bening, who at the time had done little more than an
indifferent John Candy comedy, *The Great Outdoors,* although she had
made a splash on the stage in *Coastal Disturbances* in 1987. They made
arrangements to meet, but she bowed out. He settled on Sean Young,
even though her name was synonymous with trouble. She was reputed
to be temperamental and had been involved in an ugly, protracted, and
highly publicized feud with James Woods, in the course of which she
was accused of leaving a disfigured doll at his front door. (Woods accused her of conducting a "jihad of terror" against him. But both he and
she denied that she superglued his penis to his leg, a story making the
rounds at the time.) Everyone advised Beatty against hiring her, but he
ignored them and did so anyway.

Beatty asked Isabelle Adjani to do Breathless, but she passed. He
offered it to Faye Dunaway, but she also declined. After months of
noodling, Beatty still did not have his Breathless.

NOT ONLY was Beatty now producing, directing, and starring in *Dick
Tracy,* he was trying to write—or rewrite—it himself, possibly working off the original script by Jim Cash and Jack Epps, possibly a later
draft by someone else. Beatty's MO had always been to find a writer to
work with. But his relationship with writers was prickly. They resented
his claims to co-writing credit. And by this time he had used up several
of the best ones. Bo Goldman suspected that Robert Towne, who was
writing and directing *Tequila Sunrise,* turned the actor down. Buck
Henry didn't appear eager to work with him again, and his relationship
with Elaine May was tense.

Around Thanksgiving 1987, Goldman got a call from his agent, Jeff
Berg, head of International Creative Management (ICM). Goldman
had started his career writing for the theater, without much to show
for it, but he had had considerably better luck in Hollywood, where
he started with a bang, winning an Oscar for his first script, *One Flew
Over the Cuckoo's Nest* (1975), and had gone on to make a glittering
name for himself with a series of literate and compelling scripts: *The
Rose* (1979), *Melvin and Howard* (1980), and *Shoot the Moon* (1982),

which starred Diane Keaton. He won another Oscar for *Melvin and Howard,* and in the future would be nominated again for *Scent of a Woman* (1992). He had also worked for Robert Redford.

Now Goldman was trying to find financing for his adaptation of Susan Minot's novel *Monkeys,* which he intended to direct, but was getting nowhere. Berg told him, "Warren Beatty is up there at his house, doodling around, trying to do this script of *Dick Tracy* on his own, he's having some problems, so why don't you call him." Goldman had brought a touch of East Coast snobbery with him when he arrived in L.A. in the early 1970s, and prided himself on being unimpressed by movie stars. He didn't really know Beatty. He recalled once going to the movies with actor George Furth and a very young Carrie Fisher, who dropped Beatty's name. Goldman asked, "Warren who?" They replied, in one voice, something like, "Warren Beatty, 'the Pro.'" He recalls, "I suddenly realized he was some sort of high priest. His name was spoken in whispers."

Goldman had actually met Beatty only once, on a lovely spring day in 1981 in New York, and hadn't particularly liked him. *Shoot the Moon* was in post, and the writer had met Keaton for lunch. Afterward, Keaton cabbed over to the Carlyle to meet Beatty, and Goldman accompanied her. Goldman was most impressed by Beatty's hygiene. He looked like he'd just emerged from the shower, pink and well scrubbed. The star was well into editing *Reds* and complained, "All I do is sit in the cutting room and eat pastrami sandwiches. I'm sick of New York." But, Goldman continues, "He was chilly and distant with me, I thought because Diane was fond of me. I got the feeling he was thinking, What's so great about this guy?"

Subsequently, Goldman blamed Beatty for ruining the prospects of *Shoot the Moon.* "It was ready for release in October of 1981," he continues. "But Keaton was contractually prohibited from releasing another movie in the same calendar year as *Reds.* So we had to release *Shoot the Moon* in January 1982, right after New Year's, the worst possible time for a tough movie like this. The Alans—director Alan Parker and producer Alan Marshall—begged Beatty to release her from the obligation. His answer was, 'Nope, nope, nope.' It died as a result of the release date he had screwed us on."

So when Berg made his suggestion, Goldman demurred, thought

to himself, I've never liked funnies, I don't know from *Dick Tracy*. He talked it over with his friends. "Everybody warned me," he continues. "Warren at that time was kind of an aging glamour boy. People would say to me, 'How the fuck could you work for him?' He had a reputation for being controlling, making people jump through hoops. They said, 'He's not for you, Bo.'" But Berg pressed him. The writer reflected on his life: his six children, his stalled attempt to launch *Monkeys*, and his cramped one-bedroom apartment in a funky part of Hollywood he rented while he was there working. The fact was, he needed the money. Goldman drove up to the house on Bad Boy Drive for a meeting.

"Warren was sitting up there in his home with his thumb up his ass, trying to move the script ahead," he recalls. It was a crisp fall day, a chill was in the air, and Goldman marveled at the view of the Valley out the big picture window in the living room. Beatty took him for a stroll around the grounds. When the subject of Keaton came up, he said, "Let me show you what I built." Walking toward Mulholland, they crossed the lawn. Pointing to a Jacuzzi half hidden by a hedge, Beatty said, "I built this for Diane. She's shy. I wanted her to be able to bathe without embarrassment." Goldman was impressed, thought to himself, This is a guy capable of very deep feeling.

Beatty worked in the kitchen perched on an uncomfortable bar stool at a waist-high butcher block table picking at leftover turkey cooked by Joyce Hyser, who was still living at the house. He pitched the project. Goldman recalls, "He told me, 'I think we'll get Pacino to play Big Boy, maybe Madonna to play Breathless, I have Vittorio, I have Milena,' all these first-rank people, but there was no script. It was in shambles." Still, Goldman understood the appeal of the material for the star. "People have always told Warren that he could have been a detective. He's always asking, 'Where were you? What did you do?' There's something lonely about comic strip characters trapped in that box. Warren was a very isolated man. By his own choosing, of course. And the whole comic strip is such a control thing. First this panel, and now that panel. Warren once told me he doesn't like to travel much, because when you travel, you fall into other people's hands. The air traffic controller says, 'Okay, we're bringing you in on runway 1.' He wants that to be his decision."

At that time, Goldman was making about $1 million a picture, but

Beatty offered him half that, and he took it, as so often happened, because he wanted to work with him. The screenwriter got a modest advance, about $5,000. Goldman continues, "I couldn't get my expenses out of him, stingy fuck that he is. He hates to part with a penny. His attitude is, 'Get in line.'" The writer had to appeal to Beatty's attorney, Bert Fields, to get his per diem.

Goldman excelled at character, but the actor warned him, "I don't want to see any psychology in this fucking thing. Don't try to earn your money here. Remember, this is an entertainment." The writer may have been eager to collaborate with a director of Beatty's stature, but he got more of a collaboration than he bargained for. "I used to work very closely with Milos, but I would do the writing overnight, and then I would give it to him the next day. I said to Warren, 'I'll take this home,' and he said, 'No, no, we'll do it right here. Right here at the table. The whole thing is to demystify it.' That was where I first heard that hip word. We're going to 'demystify' writing by just sitting there and doing it in front of each other. Warren wouldn't let me go home, wouldn't let me out of the room. I'd have to write the scene right there in front of him. He wouldn't be watching me, he'd take a call or make a call, but he'd come back in five minutes." There were no names on the script—Beatty always removed the top page—and Goldman never found out who wrote it. "It felt like his writing," he recalls. "In other words, it wasn't very good."

To Hyser, Goldman was the answer to a prayer. She told him, "Thank God you showed up, he sits here for hours watching football on TV." In the aftermath of *Ishtar*, Gary Hart's implosion, and the rest of it, Beatty was frustrated, uncertain, and depressed. He seemed to have lost his way. He wasn't at all sure that *Tracy* was the right project for him. She had never heard him say, "I'm really excited about this project," and now he complained, "I don't know why I'm doing this; I'm too old." Hyser recalls, "I don't think that filmmaking makes him happy—except when he's casting the women's roles!"

She continues, "Warren loved Bo. Bo really respected him. But you can respect him, admire him, honor him, and it doesn't make it any easier to work with him. Warren was almost incapable of changing a light bulb, but if you did something he couldn't do, he didn't like how you did it. Even in his writing. They'd get stuck, Bo would say, 'Oh my God, this is it.' He'd get so excited, and Warren would say, 'No. No good.' Bo's eyes would pop out of his head. I would see him sitting at the table with this long face, tearing out whatever hair he had left. Warren would sit and ponder a sentence for hours. Everything took so much time. He could be maddening."

Goldman was fascinated by Beatty. Due to the snail's pace at which the work proceeded, he had plenty of time to think about what made him tick. "Warren is Scottish," he explains. "He's suspicious, and slow to make friendships. I believe his father was superintendent of schools in Arlington, Virginia, an academic administrator, beyond which there can be nothing worse. It's like being a customs official on the French-Italian border. My guess is, those things in Warren came down from him. I met his mother, who was a lovely woman, her own person, very impressive. She wasn't sweet at all, but I thought that whatever sweetness was down deep in Warren emanated from her."

Goldman quickly realized that Beatty loved to argue, and whatever the subject, he always wanted to win. He was impressed by Beatty's voracious appetite for the printed word. "He'd arrive with *The Wall Street Journal* and *Foreign Affairs* under his arm, all this double-domed material," the writer recalls. "How does he read these fucking things? But he did. He'd say, '*The Wall Street Journal* is the only good paper in America.'" Every Friday a uniformed nurse showed up to give him shots for his allergies. He had no sense of time. "That was the thing I learned with Redford, their time is *the* time," he continues. "The poor woman would be sitting there for hours waiting to give him his allergy injection." Beatty reminded him of Redford. "They hated each other," he recalls. "Warren was eager to hear any bad news about Bob. I've always felt that Redford didn't have half the talent that Warren did."

The writer continues, "Warren gets bored very easily. He's incredibly restless. He can't function unless he's doing two, three, four things at once." In the era when car phones were a novelty, Goldman marveled at the fact that Beatty was able to drive and use the phone at the same time. "The thing was invented for him," he continues. "Once a guy came up to his home with a suitcase full of phones. It was like that scene in *Taxi Driver* where the guy sells these guns to De Niro. Warren put this guy through his paces. The guy was pushing this phone and that phone, and Warren was poking holes in his sales pitch. Like somebody who kicks tires. He humiliated the guy. It was like he handled studio people: This guy's trying to con me. Well, nobody's gonna con me, I'll con him first."

There would always be people around to amuse him, a potpourri of the current flavors, like Sean Penn or Bob Downey Jr. Sometimes old girlfriends would turn up. "Julie Christie surfaced there once," Goldman recalls. "Her career had disappeared, and she didn't look well, seemed like some daughter of a college roommate, or a distant cousin's niece, a poor relation. I felt sad for her. I had the feeling he was kind to all his old girlfriends."

One day the two of them had lunch with Bob Towne. Towne was on his way to the airport headed for London to score *Tequila Sunrise.* "Warren wanted whatever crumbs he might get from Towne," says Goldman. "Nothing goes wasted with him. We were listening to the Sage, but Warren treated him strangely, like a child who'd left the nest. He was real pissed off that Towne had one foot out the door. Here was Towne, who was like his waterboy, and now his star was up while Warren's was down after *Ishtar.* He felt that he had big-shotted him, that he couldn't control him. It was like professional athletes who were suddenly on opposing teams and hated each other."

Beatty was always on the phone, making or receiving calls. His assistant would pad silently across the room and hand him a note with a name and a phone number, in the unlikely eventuality that he didn't already know the number. Goldman would remonstrate, say, "No interruptions today, please." Beatty would reply, "Okay." He'd tell his assistant, "No phone calls today. Just interrupt me if Katzenberg calls." Gradually, the list got longer and longer.

Sometimes the call would be blowback from an old girlfriend who wanted something—a loan, a job, just reassurance that he'd still take her call. He'd glance at the scrap of paper his assistant shoved in front of his nose, and grunt, "Uh huh, I gotta take this call." He'd put the receiver to his ear and say, "Really, really." And then, "You know something? You're a very, very disturbed person." And hang up. "Can you imagine?" Beatty explained. "She wanted me to buy her a piano."

But most intrusive were the calls from his myriad friends in politics. Hyser explains, "There's nothing more important in the world to Warren than politics. Having Gary, Jesse, Joe Biden on the phone asking him for advice makes him happy. Politics makes him happy. If one of them called, he would talk for an hour in the middle of writing while Bo was sitting there waiting for him. I would yell at him about Bo, 'He's gonna get up and walk out on you too.' It's amazing that Warren has been able to retain a relationship with anybody he's ever written with."

Every so often Goldman was caught up short, when the other Warren Beatty raised his head. The writer recalls, "Once, a girl's name came up, he said, 'Well, I fucked her.' That was the only time he'd ever said anything like that, been crude, but I said to myself, I'm never gonna work with this guy again, I was revolted by his manner. It was like he was trying to live up to some press clipping."

In many respects, Beatty and Goldman were a good match. Each was among the best in their respective fields, each respected the other, each was a hard worker. But Beatty was a director who fancied himself a writer. Goldman was a writer who was a wannabe director. That spelled trouble. It was, as Goldman put it, "a marriage made in hell."

WITHOUT GARY HART, the race for the Democratic candidate for president devolved into a game of dodge ball among the remaining contenders, who were disparagingly dubbed the Seven Dwarfs: Michael Dukakis, Jesse Jackson, Joe Biden et al. Beatty made it his business to meet and grill every one of these contenders, and found them all lacking. Susan Estrich, Dukakis's campaign manager, invited the candidate and his wife, Kitty, to a dinner heavy with Hollywood liberals. Kitty sat next to Beatty. She regarded him with a blank look, and asked, "What do you do?" Returning it in kind, he said, "I'm Warren Beatty, the actor."

Beatty continued to believe that Hart should have toughed it out. He was offended by the idea that a candidate's private life could disqualify him from doing important things in America. The actor began urging Hart to reenter the race. He thought that if it were done right, it could be a moment of high drama, and the senator might get away with it. After all, polls had shown that nearly two thirds (64 percent) of respondents surveyed thought the media treatment of Hart was "unfair." During the summer of 1987, Beatty told Hart, "If you think you can contribute to public life . . . you have an absolute obligation to run despite it being painful." Shrewd as Beatty was, he seemed to be in denial, ignoring the tremors that lingered well after the Donna Rice earthquake. Perhaps he couldn't help but see himself in Hart's shoes, and so wanted to believe that his own peccadilloes would be ignored or forgiven were he ever to run for office. He desperately wanted The Gary Hart Story to have a happy ending.

In December 1987, at Beatty's urging, seconded by Jesse Jackson and a handful of others, Hart returned to the campaign. It was indeed a dramatic moment when he strode to the steps of the state capitol in Concord, New Hampshire, and announced, "I'm back in the race." His welcome, however, was chilly, particularly on the part of the press, which he had blamed for derailing his campaign in the first place. *Time* magazine, no friend to Democrats, called his comeback "self-indulgent folly." Hart staffers wryly referred to the new campaign as "88B" to distinguish it from its aborted predecessor, "88A." That aside, there just weren't enough troops on the ground to support his campaign. During the interregnum between 88A and 88B, key staffers had defected, often going to work for rival candidates. As Bill Bradley put it, "Warren is the kind of guy likes to do things out of his back pocket. He didn't take into consideration the infrastructure necessary to do a national campaign. Or even a serious statewide campaign. Gary couldn't raise any money."

Hart ran in the New Hampshire primary, but he faced repeated humiliation. At one high school where he was explaining his "new ideas," the students joked about "winning one for the zipper." Hart received only 4,888 votes, approximately 4 percent in the state that had put him on the map in 1984. In March 1988, he withdrew for the second time, returning to his home in Troublesome Gulch, augmented by 135 acres of adjacent land—to enhance his privacy—he'd bought with a $265,000 loan from Beatty.

The advice Beatty had given Hart was disastrous. It merely confirmed the impression that so far as politics was concerned, Beatty was just slumming. His fascination with it was lifelong and sincere, but unlike the professional politicians and operatives among whom he loved to swim, it was never his day job. In an important sense, he remained a political dilettante, a hobbyist, a tourist. If Hart failed, it was painful, but it wasn't his failure; he cushioned Hart's crash landing, but then he went back to making movies.

Beatty would never have behaved as incautiously as Hart did in similar circumstances, inviting the storm that broke over his friend. But there is also a dark subterranean river of self-destructiveness that runs through many of the characters he plays on screen. He may have established his reputation by resuscitating *Bonnie and Clyde,* but just as often he sabotaged himself. Beatty is as fascinated by failure as he is by success, or maybe it is the dance between the two that preoccupied him most, and perhaps it wasn't only the opportunity to become a player on the national political stage that Hart provided, but a courtside seat at his Rocky (Mountain) Horror Show, more valuable to Beatty by far than the fabled tickets to Lakers games coveted by less complex souls. It wasn't only Hart's intelligence, or his seriousness, or his presidential aspirations that drew Beatty to him; it was his weakness as well, and the wounds he inflicted on himself. This, perhaps, was the mirror that Hart held up to him. Hart was truly his doppelgänger.

BEATTY HAD still not found his Breathless Mahoney. Sean Penn had brought Madonna to Beatty's home in 1985 on their first date, a risky move, even for him. After *Desperately Seeking Susan,* a modest hit, her track record in movies (*Shanghai Surprise, Who's That Girl*) had been dismal. From the studio's point of view, if Tracy and Beatty were legends that needed dusting off, Madonna presented the opposite problem: she was incandescent, smoking hot, a virtual cultural icon then at the height of her fame. But she was not necessarily perceived as an asset for a Disney movie.

Still, everything is never enough in the entertainment business, where lack of talent is only occasionally an impediment, and she was desperate to get a foothold in pictures. "I saw the A list and I was on the Z list," she admitted. "I felt like a jerk." But if she were born to play any character, it was Breathless. "Everybody said I'd be perfect for the role," she recalls. "I waited and waited for Warren to call me. He never did. Finally, I decided to be pushy, and called him. He vibes you out. He told me I made a lot of stupid choices, which I did, out of my impatience. It took him a year to make up his mind."

Beatty took her out to eat at the Ivy. She wore a black leather jump-suit, partially unzipped to reveal her cleavage, and matching cap. She said, "I know you've heard a lot of terrible things about me, and I'm here to tell you they're all true. How about you? I've heard a lot about you." Beatty ignored her gambit. "Just as I thought," she said. "All true." But he liked her, her intelligence, directness, sense of humor. He reportedly said, as he deposited her at her door and kissed her, "Houston, we have liftoff." Ignoring his friends' dire warnings, the same way he ignored those who warned him against Sean Young, he hired her. It didn't hurt that she agreed to work for scale ($1,440 per week). But she negotiated a percentage of the gross, as well as video and merchandise sales that would put an estimated $5 million in her piggybank.

Beatty still needed to nail down his agreement with Disney. Recalls Goldman, "Warren was very proud of his ability with money. He said, 'I'm not above it, I'm not an artiste, I'm in business here. I know how to deal with these people.' He loved that side of himself." Terry Press, who would climb the ladder to VP of marketing, but was then a lowly publicity drone, understood Beatty's allure. "Jeffrey loved him. You walk in the room with Warren Beatty, it was like a switch was flipped. It's a very seductive thing."

"Warren is not impressed by executives," says Goldman. "Show him a studio head, and he'll show you a head he wants to lop off. Katzenberg would call every day," the writer continues. "Every once in a while, Beatty would give me a glimpse of the World According to Warren. By way of apologizing for interrupting our work to take these calls from Katzenberg, as he hung up one day, he said, 'Bring him in, make him feel part of the project.' He gave me this kind of Cheshire grin."

Once, in the middle of the afternoon, Beatty announced to Goldman, "We have to quit early."

"Oh, thank God."

"I gotta get my shit together. I gotta go get some money now." Goldman continues, "He was suddenly the producer. Warren came back with all the money he needed for it. I thought it was kind of wonderful." The deal was consummated in 1988 on condition that Beatty work within a $36.8 million budget, including his fee. He reportedly got $9.5 million from Disney against 10 percent (some say 15 percent) of first dollar gross and sale of merchandise, $5.5 million to act, $2.5 million to direct, $500,000 to produce, and $500,000 to write. Overages would be deducted from his share.

DICK TRACY may have been a comic strip movie, but in Beatty's hands it wasn't just any comic strip movie. He had a concept. He wanted to replicate the look of the strips in the newspapers of that era, between 1939 and 1941, which used only four or five primary colors. "I wanted to try to create a naive world, something that took me back to the emotions of when I read those comics as a five and six year old: when good was very clear to me; when bad was very clear to me. When stars twinkled," he explained. "Or the time when I first went into Times Square and I saw all of those lights and that city and I didn't yet know what all those signs were trying to sell me. I wanted to return to a world before there were Chevrolets and Fords. When there was just Car."

This nostalgia for the simplicity of his youth also dictated the color scheme of the movie. He wanted to return the audience to a time "when red was Red and incredibly beautiful, and blue was Blue, and I couldn't make up my mind which was my favorite color. . . . There were no gradations in the colors that are usually important to designers like Milena or Dick or Vittorio." (Canonero gave Beatty an eye-popping lemon yellow overcoat.) But Sylbert was a different story. Kazan had trained him in the same naturalistic tradition Beatty embraced, which dictated that films create the illusion of transparency. In abandoning this principle, Beatty was violating one of his most cherished beliefs. He says, "I knew in this movie, there had to be a little of 'I'm here, too' because that's just the style of the old strips, of Chester Gould. The artist is very much there."

Gould's strip is first and foremost devoted to Tracy's crusade against crime. But, referring to his film, Beatty insisted, "This is not some cockamamie detective story. . . . My film is about a guy torn between love and duty. My Dick Tracy is human." The crime stopper is pulled between Tess and Breathless, the mother and the whore, family and sex. Or, as Beatty put it, "It's about the temptation of Dick Tracy's love life." He even considered using the title *The Temptation of Dick Tracy*.

But Goldman takes credit for pushing Tracy's personal life into the foreground. "I gave him some kind of route into the movie," he recalls. "What could make the thing work was a sense of family. Tracy, very much like Warren, is a man who keeps women at a distance. But he and Tess and the boy could become a family. That was something he hadn't considered. It suited him very well." As Beatty said later, "The movie, for me, was all about the fatigue that I felt with bachelorhood. It was all about wanting to have a family."

Still, at the time, in his dealings with Goldman, as with Trevor Griffiths on *Reds*, Beatty regarded the family as an impediment that prevented the writer from giving the script his full attention. Beatty appeared to devote every waking moment to the script, and expected the same of his writer. They started at noon and went into the wee hours of the morning, seven days a week, with no time off on weekends. "He's obsessed by work," Goldman recalls. "It's like Sisyphus. He was rolling back that rock all the time. He woke up in the morning, the rock's still there. He hated praise. Nothing made him happier than to hear, 'This is a piece of shit, you have to start over.' It made his day. He can never get a rest from the demands he makes on himself. That's a torment, and a torment to the people around him. One director called it masochism."

In Goldman, who was by this time renting a home for his family near Malibu, Beatty saw his mirror image. With his six children, the writer was the quintessential family man, what Beatty would become, but hadn't yet. He resented the family obligations that beckoned the writer home for dinner at six o'clock the same way, according to Griffiths, he tried to prevent the writer from returning to England and his motherless children. "His lip would curl if I said I had to get home to my baby," Goldman recalls. "It was hard for him to understand. He'd be derogatory about family. He used to say I used my family to make a power point." Beatty's assistants were mostly young gay men, who never had to change a diaper. They were unburdened by families, and therefore always at his disposal. And since he saw most things politically, he gave it an ideological inflection. Goldman continues, "He'd say, 'Enough with family, that's just a big right-wing thing.'" In short, he was as conflicted about love as he was about work, about, in fact, most things.

Goldman continued to find the daily writing sessions punishing. As the writer describes the process, "At first he'd say, 'This is beautiful.' And then the tinkering would begin. He'd start picking here, and he'd start picking there, and I wouldn't even be aware of it. We'd sit at opposite sides of the table writing the same scene. It would be like a contest. Then he would approach me from the actor's point of view—'This is what would make the scene more actorable'—which would allow him to manipulate me into changing it. I'd come in with a new thing, and he'd say, 'No, let's go back to this.' So we'd go back and forth and back and forth, and then after three days there's nothing left of the scene."

The writer continues, "The indecision was the famous thing, where everybody in the business would say, 'How can you stand Warren Beatty, he can never make up his mind.' As a writer, ultimately what we have to trust is that first impulse, but what happens is that impulse gets lost in the indecision of trying to make it better. That was the problem, this desire to kill the instinct."

Goldman ran into Buck Henry months later, and the two compared notes. It was like a two-man twelve-step program for former Beatty writers, War-Anon. Henry talked about his own experience, how Beatty "tormented the material to death." Goldman continues, "And never mind the material, he does that in life, he does that with women, everything. He gets obsessive, and he takes the fucking life out of you. He can't leave anything alone. Then somehow you find that you are always arranging your life to suit his. You'd get there and you'd have to wait an hour and a half for him to get off some phone call. What would get me crazy was this feeling of being controlled—and not in a nasty way, in a very charming way—but it was still control. Even his indecision was a tool of control. If you constantly keep everything up in the air, you're the king. But once you've made the decision, once you've said yes to something or no to something, then you've lost control. And the control is the result of fear, fear of life, fear of everything. He's fearful of this going wrong, or that going wrong.

"Finally he exhausted me completely, and I just went crazy. I called Jeff Berg, and I said, 'I can't take this guy anymore.' He came up to the house, and I blew up. Of course, Warren was as cool as a cucumber. I could tell he was very angry but it would be an ice storm. He'd get very articulate, and cut you to death coldly. I was shouting, and he said, 'Okay, you want to raise your voice? I can raise my voice too!' Jeff just stood by like a referee. Next thing I know, I said, 'You know how he makes me feel?' I put my hands around his neck. Jeff jumped to his feet, and I said, 'It's like he's choking me.' To Berg's credit, it got sorted out, and it was over."

Miraculously, the collaboration worked. Despite the fireworks, Goldman found a lot in Beatty to admire. When things were going well, Goldman looked at the glass and saw it was half—perhaps even three quarters—full. He said, "Maybe it's true that he punishes the material to a fault, but I think it's really a gifted artist's intensity in a field where art itself has no meaning."

JOYCE HYSER had spent most of Christmas 1987 with her family in Philadelphia. When she returned to the Mulholland house her car, which was her pride and joy, was gone. It was a 1977 limited Champagne Edition VW, white on white. "Where's my car?" she asked Beatty.

"I got rid of it. It was too old, I'm giving you my car." He had bought a new one and had decided it was time she stepped up to his Mercedes 450. But it kept breaking down, and every time she had it fixed, it cost at least $1,000, that is, $1,000 more than she could afford. She called it the gift that kept on taking. It proved to be a metaphor for their relationship. He thought he was doing her a good turn; she wasn't so sure. They were fighting a lot, and what had been placid at first was becoming tempestuous, more like Beatty's previous relationships. After a year with him, she was unhappy.

For one thing, Beatty discouraged her from pursuing her acting career, as he had Michelle Phillips. He would grill her, asking, "Why do you want to be an actress? You're too smart for that. It's not for you." He loves actors, but he thought she had more to offer. She recalls, "He was more like family to me, like a brother or a father than a lover. He wanted more of a wife, someone who would take care of him. But I didn't really fit that bill. I was too young."

Indeed, age became as issue. "He was too old for me," she explains. "Not so much chronologically, but we were at different places in our lives. He had done everything he wanted to do. He had traveled everywhere, he knew all the famous people he wanted to know, he had been to all the best parties, he had eaten in the best restaurants, he was finished. He never wanted to go anywhere. He only saw movies in the house. He would have been happy just looking at TV and working." Producer Andy Karsch recalls being in London with him sometime later. "We made all these plans to do stuff, but what did we actually do every day? We'd sit at the Dorchester, watch CNN, and order room service, exactly as if we were on Mulholland." Hyser had the same kind of phone problems with Beatty that Goldman had. She continues, "I can't tell you how many times we said we were going out to dinner, we'd make a reservation somewhere, I'd say, 'Phone off,' and he'd get nervous. He's totally ADD. He wants to be distracted, he wants that phone call. The phone would ring, and he'd say, 'This is really important, this is one I really do have to take. I'll be right off.' An hour later, he was still talking.

" 'It's rude.'

" 'I'm sorry, it's not personal.'

"It wasn't personal. But it was one of his gigantic character flaws. It was a real bone of contention." Often, Hyser would end up walking out the door. He would question her, asking, "Where are you going? What time are you going to get there, who are you going to meet there?" Hyser would reply, "I'm going to dinner at the Ivy with my girlfriends. After dinner, I'd ask for the check and inevitably it had been taken care of. All the girls would go, 'He's so nice.' It was nice, but later I thought, Oh my God, no, he's not, he's checking up on me, he wants to make sure that I am where I am. I don't think he trusted me when I was out on my own, because he didn't trust anybody, including himself.

"He got me my first cell phone, really sweet. I said, 'Give me the bill, so I can pay it.' He wouldn't. Why? So he could see who I was calling. Once I was shopping in New York, and I bought a sweater at this store. We were staying at the Ritz, and I came back, and that very same sweater that I bought was on the bed in three different colors. I don't know how he knew. I would accuse him of following me."

Like Goldman, Hyser felt he was trying to control her. She chafed under his surveillance. "He had an idea of who I was supposed to be, how I was supposed to behave, who I was supposed to be with—there were a few of my friends he didn't like, because he was afraid that they didn't like him. That's when he would become insecure, and he was right. They didn't think he was right for me. They'd ask, 'Why are you with him? He's a legendary womanizer, who's never been faithful to anyone.'" He'd warn her, "I don't think that person has your best interests at heart. She's jealous of you." She continues, "He would always question my relationships. If he didn't like somebody he wouldn't want me to be friends with them. And with regard to those particular friends, he was incredibly perceptive."

Whereas in the beginning of their relationship, Hyser was flattered by his attentions, now she found them irritating. When he said, "Isn't she cute, look how passionate she gets, it just kills me, I love when she

gets like that," she felt, in her words, "he was being really patronizing.
I was the little girl with all those cute opinions. He valued me, my intelligence, but he always knew more than I did. That was okay, it was part
of my attraction to him, he was a lot smarter than I was, and I learned
a lot from him, but he grew up with that Madonna/whore thing, and
he puts the women he's involved with on a pedestal. That's what he did
with me. He wanted me to be something [I wasn't]. I was more an idea
than a reality."

Hyser was in therapy. Her therapist always told her that her relationship with Beatty was a mistake. He would say, "You gotta get
outta there, you gotta break it off, it's not right for you." Beatty, who
was a therapy junkie, wanted to join her: "Why don't we go see your
therapist together?"

"No, there's no point."

"C'mon. What's the worst that could happen?" Hyser gave in. She
thought, My therapist is so strong and powerful and smart, there's no
way Warren will be able to sway him. She recalls, "Within ten minutes
Warren had completely taken over the session. My therapist was saying
to me, 'Why do you feel you have to leave?'

" 'Are you fucking kidding me? I don't get this. You wanted me to
leave him!'

"My therapist was totally in love with him."

Hyser continues, "There were times when I was just so frustrated,
I'd sit with him for hours and hours, going, 'What am I doing in this
relationship, why am I here?' It wasn't that I thought he was fool-
ing around or I caught him in lies. We were together all the time, so
it would have been hard for him." It was an accumulation of factors.
"He couldn't move or he couldn't go out or he couldn't or wouldn't
do something I'd asked him to do," she explains. Hyser too thought he
was depressed. "What else is it that makes somebody unable to leave
the house? One reason it's hard for him to start something is he knows
how hard it is to finish. He could develop a movie for the rest of his life.
With *Dick Tracy*, it was never right. It was during that period of time I
understood that I had to get out of there."

Indeed, by New Year's 1988, Hyser realized that she had to make
a move. "We were supposed to spend it together, but I didn't want to
start a new year in a relationship that wasn't going anywhere. Warren
does manipulate, does create situations that are impossible for you.

[Then] he's the one who gets left. I called him and said, 'I'm not going to do this. It's time for this to end.' I'm the one who said the words. But I would never say that I left him. It had been a long time coming, and we got there together."

Beatty's serious lovers, the "heavyweights," often discovered that it was easier to bring him into their lives than to get him out, and Hyser's relationship dragged on until late July, when she finally moved out and into David Geffen's guesthouse on Rising Glen. And even then it sputtered on. Nicholson became increasingly attentive. She accompanied him to his tennis lessons at Bob Evans's house. "I'm guessing but I don't think Jack was happy when Warren started going out with Michelle," she says. "There are plenty of women out there in the world. For him to go after your former girlfriend? That may have created a little distance between them at that point. They're competitive. I got the sense that it was a little hard for Warren when Jack and I got so close. After I moved out, he was a little jealous. It's hard to trust anybody when you don't trust yourself. But we were just friends."

Beatty remained close to Hyser for some time. "He's a foul-weather friend," she says, echoing a host of others. "I went through a tough time, serious female problems. He dropped everything, completely took over. He sent me to Johns Hopkins, set me up with one of the top doctors over there. We weren't even together at that point. He's incredible that way."

Looking back on the relationship, she says, "He gave me some sage advice in my life, about my career, and he was right about so many things. I didn't have the ambition to really make it in this business. I would have learned those lessons much earlier in life if I really listened to him and didn't treat him—especially at the end of our relationship—like a very controlling person. But I was just young and stubborn and I didn't want some man telling me what I should or shouldn't be doing.

"Warren doesn't know that I just started writing now. People say, 'Why don't you take your stuff to him, he'd be so proud of you.' Part of the reason is that even if I were so lucky as to have him say, 'I want to get involved with this,' I don't want Warren anywhere involved with that, because it would never get done. That to me is one of the saddest things about him.

"The thing about him that I adore is that he never stops loving anybody. Warren is not a woman hater. I know that he'll always love me. I know that he will always love Isabelle, he will always love Diane. I know I love him. I miss his friendship."

MONTHS BEFORE the *Tracy* draft was done, Beatty entrusted Goldman with the family jewels, that is, asked him to write the *Howard Hughes* script. He told the writer that he was contractually obligated to turn in a *Hughes* script to Warner Brothers by December 31, 1990. It made perfect sense. Having written not one but two *Hughes* scripts, *Melvin and Howard*, and one called *Sonny* for Universal, never produced, Goldman knew the territory better than anyone. In Goldman's words, "I was the world's greatest living expert on Howard Hughes." Beatty must have had this in mind from the beginning. In fact, if he was the "master manipulator," as Buck Henry et al. say he was, he likely hired Goldman because of *Hughes*, used *Tracy* as a trial run. But Goldman was sick of Hughes and didn't want to write yet another script about him. Besides, he didn't want to become Beatty's in-house writer, as Towne had been. Beatty persisted, and as usual, he got his way.

By this time, Beatty's Hughes project was the stuff of myth, something he had been talking about since 1973. Says Goldman, "It was like his *Birth of a Nation*, this great thing that one day was going to come out." Adds Bill Bradley, "I was under the impression it was going to be his crowning work. You look at *Hughes*, theoretically, that could be a movie that really explains power and money in America. And the attraction-repulsion of fame."

Beatty's friends speculated about his fascination with Hughes, and it didn't take Freud to notice the affinity between the two men. They were both tangled up in movies, and used Hollywood as a sexual sandbox. "Warren Beatty *is* Howard Hughes," says Goldman. "He felt Hughes was a guy who mastered the three F's — 'the filmmaking, the flying and the fucking,' as Warren called it."

In his conversations with Goldman about Hughes, Beatty repeatedly mentioned that Hughes would never ejaculate inside a woman's vagina, but only in her mouth. "He was terrified of insemination," the actor explains. Goldman pondered the significance of this factoid, both for Hughes and to Beatty. He thought, That way he can't have children, and disease is less likely. And if you enter a woman, you're liable to end up in court with her.

Both Beatty and Hughes were students of human nature, shrewd at getting others to do what they wanted. "Hughes would never answer the phone himself," Goldman continues. "He always questioned his assistants about the timbre of the callers' voices: 'How did he sound when he said that?' He was able to interpret every little nuance. Warren did the same thing. Once he said to me, 'Let's have dinner. I'll call you as soon as'—he always had something else to do. I'd be waiting for him for nine fuckin' hours. I'd fall asleep. The phone rang for our dinner rendezvous. I picked it up, acting hyper-alert, so he wouldn't know I had been asleep. He said, 'You remember where the restaurant is? Because you're a little slow right now, you've been asleep.'"

Since he had been hearing about Beatty's Hughes project for so long, Goldman assumed there was something on paper, that Towne had written a script at one time, or May, or somebody. One day he inquired, "Okay, where's the script? The famous script." He recalls, "Warren made some excuse, like, 'Oh, you don't need to see that.' I realized there was nothing, not a page." He suspected there had never been, that the *Hughes* script was no more than a bogeyman Beatty had invented to scare off anyone who dared tread the sacred ground.

Beatty made several suggestions. "Warren was in love with the Witnesses idea from *Reds*—'it helps cover ground,' he said—and asked me to use it," the writer recalls. "It was like priming the motor. Because it had primed him for *Reds*. Knowing Warren, *Reds* might very well not have been made, it might have drifted away just like *Hughes* did, if he hadn't had this stuff in the can." Beatty also decided that he wanted to focus the script on the latter half of Hughes's life.

UNLIKE *TRACY*, where Beatty sat across the desk from him while he wrote, with the actor otherwise occupied, Goldman worked alone on *Hughes*. "It was a completely different deal," he says. "I was off on my own. He made no contribution at all, none whatsoever." (Beatty disputes this, saying they worked on the script together in the mornings, and then he went off to work on preproduction of *Tracy*, "while Bo wrote up what we discussed in the afternoons.") Goldman says he never wrote characters with Beatty in mind—neither Tracy nor Hughes—but the similarities he noted between his friend and Hughes were always in the back of his mind. In the script there's a phrase Goldman repeatedly puts in Hughes's mouth at the end scenes: "Fire him but keep him on the payroll." He explains, "That was a Hughes watchword, how he kept people close—with money, even though he didn't want to have anything to do with them. It's the sense of disposable people, and that everybody has a price. Warren was like that too. He would use people for what they were worth and then somehow find a way to keep holding on to them through either his power or his money. It's the rare Don Juan who stays in touch with ex-girlfriends and lovers—it was sometimes out of kindness, but with Warren so powerful at the time, they were always afraid to go against him. It's like being a lover of the president. The whole vision I had of Hughes was of this lonely soul who had never gotten over the infantile fear of the chaos of the world. He'd conquered that chaos, but what had he won? At that time, that's how I saw Warren."

Somewhere along the line, Beatty told Goldman that he wanted co-screenwriting credit on *Tracy*. Goldman's heart sank. Beatty's request, or demand, depending on how you want to look at it, presented a problem. The Writers Guild rules favor the original writers. Coming to the party late, Goldman had to show that he had written 50 percent of the script in order to dislodge Cash and Epps. A director who claimed a writing credit had to show he had written 67 percent of the script to dislodge the original writers. As the writing partner of the director, however, the 67 percent rule raised the bar for Goldman as well. He told Beatty, "You know, as a hyphenate, if you're gonna try to take co-writing credit, because of the 67 percent rule, I'm not going to get any credit at all." He adds, "It meant nothing to him."

How much did Beatty in fact contribute to the script? Goldman continues: "He never wrote anything. He was sitting across the table, pretending to be working. I'd show him the scene, and then he'd start marking it up. It was like doing a sitcom. He was like the show runner. He knows what the show is, and he's responsible for it. I'm not saying I wrote the whole thing, but what I had originally in many cases probably was better. He'd fuck it up. It's not that he's bad. He's not a writer. He just isn't."

In any event, Goldman and Beatty eventually finished *Tracy*. The script is spare and funny, fairly crackling with Chandleresque repartee harking back to the great Bacall-Bogart *noirs* of the 1940s, *The Big Sleep* and *To Have and Have Not*. Madonna got most of the best dialogue, glossy with double entendres. She vamps, "What I'm looking for is a driver, preferably one with some mileage." When Tracy arrests her, she cracks suggestively, "Aren't ya gonna frisk me?" And again, to Tracy: "I know how you feel. You don't know whether you want to hit me or kiss me. I get a lot of that."

Disney green-lit the script. Beatty plunged into preproduction, while Goldman worked on *Hughes*.

BEATTY WAS never long without female companionship, and Madonna was waiting in the wings. She was about Hyser's age, thirty, while Beatty was fifty-one. According to Sandra Bernhard, "Madonna and I were in the back of a limo driving to some concert in L.A., and she said, 'Sandy, did you fuck Warren Beatty?' I said, 'No.' And then a month later she started dating him. I always thought, What if I had said yes, I'd fucked him, would that have meant she wouldn't have wanted him? The deal would have been off? I guess she was just testing the waters."

Beatty began seeing Madonna in January 1990, shortly after Sean Penn famously tied her to a chair, which didn't prevent the younger man from phoning her to point out that Beatty was "old enough to be your damn father." According to a friend of his, Penn "would follow her at night and, always, they would end up at Warren's. . . . He'd sit in front of Warren's gate, waiting for her to leave. Often, she wouldn't do so until the sun rose."

As Madonna reportedly recounted to a friend, Beatty called her from the car, said, "I'm half a mile from your house. Take off your panties." A few minutes later, he called again: "I'm four blocks from your house. Take off your bra." And again, when he pulled up outside her Malibu home: "Now I want you to go downstairs and unlock the door. Then I want you to lie on your bed and wait for me to come to you and make love to you like you've never been made love to before." Apparently that wasn't good enough, because she said she didn't have an orgasm. She complained the sex was better with Penn, and wondered why she was with Beatty. But high maintenance at the best of times, she was in particular need of an island of calm. The actor supplied it. Moreover, her interest in him was piqued by rumors from the Inge-Williams days that he was bisexual.

At that time, Madonna was racking up column inches by teasing the envelope of gender ambiguity with her friendship with Bernhard, who was a lesbian and proud of it. During a dinner with Beatty at the Sushi

Cove (sushi was his food of choice), Madonna was offered a selection of vanilla or chocolate ice cream for dessert. She chose both, which got him thinking. He asked her, "You seem to like to try everything. Have you ever made it with a woman?"

"Have you ever done it with a man?"

"Do you want a woman?" he replied, ignoring her. "Because if you do, it will be my present to you. I'll get you a woman . . . if I can watch."

"All this, just from ordering two kinds of ice cream?"

Madonna called him "Old Man," but grew to appreciate his attentions in bed. "He knows a woman's body better than most women," she said. "He can pinpoint the day of your cycle. He has no restrictions. He says to me, 'If you misbehave, I'll just have to spank you.' I love that. Everything to him is living out his sexual fantasies." In *The Advocate*, when asked about the size of his member, she said, it is "a perfectly wonderful size." Madonna did complain that he didn't take enough time with her. Once he took her, creatively enough, on the piano in his living room, after dousing her with bottled water. But she said it was over so quickly it reminded her of the Minute Waltz.

The pair fought a lot, often in public, which she seemed to enjoy. The fights would go on for days, over several meals. One reportedly started at Club Nouveau, when she invited him to work out with her, after observing that he might well benefit from liposuction. He declined, suggesting that she keep her comments about his body to herself. She said, "You older guys are too sensitive. I'm just being helpful. If you want to be fat and flabby, Warren, fine with me." He was not amused. The next day the spat continued at another trendy restaurant. To the amusement of the other patrons, she was overheard to say, "Keep your stupid remarks to yourself."

"Oh, Christ, grow up."

"No. *You* grow up." She pulled a Snickers bar out of her bag and threw it at him. And the beat went on.

To cynics, it seemed like a marriage of convenience, a calculated bid on the part of each to capture a new audience—a demographic romance. "I sense that my sister isn't truly in love with him," recalls Madonna's brother, Christopher Ciccone. "She like[d] him, admire[d] him, and they ha[d] fun together, but love [didn't] come into the equation." He rarely saw them hold hands, cuddle, or kiss, even so much as touch. Adds Bernhard, who hung out with both of them, "Their relationship was very odd. One-on-one, Madonna is not the kind of person who goes super-deep or really opens up. Madonna likes hot young guys, and I'm not sure that was the reason they were together. I didn't see a lot of intimacy going on. If there was sex, it was probably sex, and boom, over. She was always complaining that Warren was a pain in the ass. It was never, 'I really love Warren Beatty' or even, 'Shaddup Warren, shaddup, you're an asshole.' She didn't really take him down, but I thought she was pretty dismissive. It was just more the way she is in general, which is the real tough chick, she's gonna be the toughest guy in the room." Instead of a mutual exchange of bodily fluids, "it could have been a mutual exchange of status," she continues. "It upped her ante as an actress, and it youthified, if that's a word, Warren, made him feel young and hip."

On the other hand, actor Marshall Bell, who is married to Milena Canonero and became quite friendly with Beatty, says, "I was there for the beginning of that. There was a lot of spark. They were having fun together. It's too easy to say that everything he does is calculated. Everything he does is not calculated. Warren is a very giving person. He's genuinely sentimental."

Jim Toback went to one of her concerts with him, in the Meadowlands, just across the Hudson River from Manhattan. "When we walked into the arena, and people saw him, they started screaming, War-ren, War-ren!," he recalls. "It was not because he was Warren Beatty, but because he was Mr. Madonna. He was sort of touched by the idea of her being alone on the stage with thirty thousand people. He was impressed at her ability to take charge."

Indeed, with regard to Madonna, Beatty adopted an attitude of bemused detachment, as if he were baby-sitting a troublesome child. "I couldn't understand the relationship," said one Disney executive. "I figured he could rationalize it as the ultimate sacrifice for the picture, that you have to sleep with her to keep her in line. 'Cause he thought there was a lot at stake if she went off. I knew the minute the picture opened, it would be over."

Three months into 1989, March 30, was Beatty's fifty-second birthday. Madonna threw him a surprise party at her home. Goldman was there, Al Pacino, and a handful of close friends. Easter was just around the corner, and unsuspecting, Beatty walked in with a chocolate bunny for her. She gave him a large portrait of a World War I flying ace in the cockpit of his plane, done in Art Deco style, saying, "Don't you think it's like you?" She saw him as an adventurer, a loner, a Charles Lindbergh, or, closer to home, a Howard Hughes. Which isn't far, after all, from how he saw himself. Dustin Hoffman walked into the party with his wife, Lisa. He noticed, as he recalls, "this guy standing with his back to the wall, next to this modern fireplace, just kind'a watching. No one was within twenty feet of him. It was Gary Hart! Here was a guy who could have been president of the United States, and it was like—scary. In this town, when your movie's a flop, people think they're gonna catch it. If they get too close, it's gonna happen to them."

It was true. Instead of *Heaven Can Wait*, The Gary Hart Story had turned out to be *Ishtar*.

PRINCIPAL PHOTOGRAPHY had begun on February 27 on the Universal lot, with scenes between Beatty and Sean Young. In the script, Tess and Tracy more or less adopt the "Kid," an orphan, which meant that the actress who played Tess had at least to pretend to have some feeling for children. According to Goldman, after reading with one of the boys trying out for the part, she turned to Beatty and said, "Oh, this kid can't do anything." He thought to himself, This is just so rude and so ugly. This woman is never going to understand this part. She hates children. Warren knew he was in for big trouble. Indeed, the dailies were terrible. Both actors were wooden. Beatty knew he needed to fire her, but he procrastinated, worried that he'd ruin her career if he dropped her. Replacing Young also meant a delay, and the overages were coming out of his pocket. A few weeks into production, he called Goldman, asked, "What do you think of Sean Young?"

"I never liked her. I think she's a creepy creature."

"I'm thinking of firing her."

"Good."

"What do you think of the dailies?"

"They're terrible. But dailies are like first drafts."

"I'll tell you who I really ought to fire."

"Who's that?"

"Myself!"

Beatty did fire Young. "It was the only time I ever heard Warren say, 'I fucked up,'" says Goldman. He replaced her with Glenne Headly. Young stated publicly that he let her go because she wouldn't sleep with him.

Beatty's close-ups were confined to a window of time during which he knew he looked best, usually between 10:00 AM and 2:00. As Marty Katz, VP of production puts it, "Warren was a genius about himself."

Reds and *Ishtar* had earned Beatty a reputation for extravagance, and he was determined to rein in costs. "Warren had to limit his normal number of takes," says Dick Sylbert. "He knew that this picture had to be done under certain financial constraints." Still, he reportedly sent Madonna flowers every day and had a masseuse on call for her. And where he needed to take time, he took time, so much so that Madonna and others voiced complaints that had a familiar ring. "Warren pisses me off by taking such a long time to make up his mind," she said in 1990. "He does lots of takes, and once he's got what's in the script, he says, 'Okay, let's fuck it up. Do anything you want.' He likes to push you, to exhaust everything in your head that you want to do." Which is the reason his method, however frustrating and exhausting for the actors, paid off, as it did on previous pictures. Mandy Patinkin says that Beatty "is a guy who spent his life learning everybody's tricks in making accidents happen. We were shooting a scene where Big Boy's banging on me, and Breathless has to defend me. There was no reason to think we hadn't gotten it. Everyone was tired, and I couldn't tell why we were doing it over again. Finally, Al started improvising. He really laced into Madonna, and all of a sudden she just broke down. It was unlike all the other takes. Warren said, 'Cut' and gave them hugs. That wouldn't have happened unless he gave it the time to happen."

"I was pissed," says Madonna, referring to the same scene. "Al kept slapping me in the stomach, being really rude. He made me cry, and Warren never really stopped him."

In May, Beatty was shooting Madonna performing onstage at the Club Ritz, singing a torch song called "I Always Get My Man." Her every move was followed by three cameras tracking her like bloodhounds. She was wearing a black gown that clung to her every curve like Saran Wrap. The decor was whorehouse deco: a glossy blood-red vinyl padded door, red rug, and milky-white ceiling. The lights bounced off her blond ringlets, blistering her lipstick. Behind her, Patinkin, his hair

slicked back and playing a character called 88 Keys, was accompanying
her on the piano. Beatty, wearing jeans and a black T-shirt and swaying
in time to the music, watched her on the video monitor. He cried, "Action!" but a second later yelled, "Cut!"

"Shit, I turned on the wrong line," said Madonna.

"Madonna, will you kiss that shoulder? Ready? Let's roll it." They
did it again. Madonna ducked her head into her shoulder, caressed it
with her cheek.

"Cut! I want to delay that move, where she kisses her shoulder. I
want an intermediate move." Madonna raised her eyebrows and gave
him a fuck-you look, but did it again anyway, following his instruc-
tions.

"War-ren, I'm losing my hard-on," she shrieked impatiently. "I'm
here Warren. I'm here now."

"I know, and we're the better for it."

"I'm going to start singing now."

"Sing." She swiveled on one heel, her back to the camera now, as she
stroked her hips with her hands like a lover.

"Cut. Great. Print that." The crew started to disperse. "Don't break
up. I want to do one more."

"Why?" She was getting upset, didn't want to do any more takes.
Beatty took her off to one side, started to put his arm around her. She
spit, "Don't touch me!"

Sighing, Beatty said, "Okay. We got it."

Dick Tracy wrapped on June 28.

Interviewed a short time later, Madonna had a lot of complaints.
"Warren wanted to pour me into my dresses. He insisted I get fatter. I
gained ten pounds. We were at Western Costume, and he'd say, 'Tighter,
tighter, cut it down lower.' I felt like a mannequin, a slab of beef. He
would walk around me like a vulture, making me feel like the ugliest
thing in the world. I was treated that way on the set—the lust factor."

Beatty's friends still failed to fathom the relationship. One day, he
was driving up Coldwater Canyon with Mike Medavoy, who started
ragging on him about her, saying, "Ya know, you and Madonna is the
worst matchup I can think of. Why don't you just get serious with
somebody?" Beatty began to rail against marriage, the boredom, waking up to the same face every morning, thinking, Oh, it's you again!

Missing the ineffable pleasure of falling in love, depriving yourself of the ultimate narcissistic delight: unfolding your petals in the warmth of a new admiring gaze. And then there was the sex, the delight of doing all those kinky things with casual partners that were impossible to do with your wife, the mother of your children. Finally, Beatty gave him his standard reply, the one he always gave when the subject came up: "Do you know anybody who's married that's really happy? Who is going to be married forever?" Medavoy thought about everybody he knew, himself included. He was stumped.

Madonna didn't trust him, was convinced he was cheating on her, but had nothing to back it up. Indeed, it was true. Beatty had resumed his relationship with DeLauné Michel, now in her early twenties, after a break, during which she had moved from New York to L.A. When she called him, he said, without missing a beat, "Get over here." The platonic affair quickly became a thing of the past. He began to have sex with her again. He explained why he had stopped: "You were such a scared little bunny. Big eyes caught in the headlights," he said. "I couldn't. You were so innocent. That was rare. I knew you weren't like all the others." Indeed, she had, in other words, seemed like a daughter to him.

Michel started going up to the home at night. No matter how still the air in the flats of Beverly Hills, a breeze, fragrant with the astringent scent of eucalyptus, rippled through the trees around his house. When she knocked on the big wooden door, he was there immediately, ushering her in. William, the German shepherd, was invariably at his side. He would sniff her, then lose interest, lie down and go to sleep. The TV was always on in the kitchen with the news. She noticed that he had thoughtfully put a bidet in the bathroom.

"Warren was just very generous, always thinking about the other person," she recalls. "That's why he's just a really great lover. He lets you come first, many times before he comes. If every man did that, the world would be a much happier place. But they don't." There were things he wanted her to do with which she was uncomfortable, still deep down a young Catholic girl from the South. She refused to do anal sex. When she demurred, he asked her, " 'So do you think I'm a sleaze-bag?' The word was shocking, such a horrible word. I said, 'No, not at all.' I think that part of him felt that way about himself, and he thought that I now viewed him that way. He also needed me to see that—You think you love me, let me show you how disgusting I am, and then you won't. But then of course I still did."

Sometimes Madonna would call while she was in bed with him. His half of the conversation consisted of, "Okay, okay, okay," punctuated by "Uh-huh, uh-huh, uh-huh." It seemed to Michel that he was constantly shoring her up. Madonna rarely spent the night with him. He would call Michel on his way to see her, and say, " 'What are you doing later? You want me to pick a fight with her so I can leave?' And that's what he would do."

With sex came circumspection. He no longer left messages on her answering machine. She imagined that he was afraid of being blackmailed. He just grunted or made a huffing sound, enough for her to know it was him. And every once in a while she was reminded of her second-class status, like the time she asked to stay the whole night, and he refused to let her, explaining, "I don't want anyone to think I've gotten married," as if, she thought, there were paparazzi camped out around his home. She realized that only the "girlfriend" spent the night.

Meanwhile, his relationship with Madonna was spiraling downward. He had accommodated her party habit when he first took up with her, but it was growing tedious. As Hyser said, he would have been happier at home watching CNN. One night, in the spring, she dragged him to Catch One, a black gay and lesbian disco on Pico near Crenshaw in South Central L.A., replete with a drag queen room. Looking uncomfortable in a three-piece Versace suit to her hoodie and shorts, Beatty as usual refused to dance, declining her invitation. Making herself heard over the music, she shouted, "Hey, Pussy Man, come on out here."

"I can't even breathe, let alone dance," he replied, giving himself a shot of nasal spray.

"Oh my God. Quit your whining, will you? I shoulda' come here with Rob Lowe."

Cinematographer Nicola Pecorini, who happened to be there, recalls, Madonna was doing her faux lesbian business, dancing with Sandra Bernhard. "I'd never seen Warren like that, sitting there, this gray man in the corner," he recalls. "He just could not keep up with Madonna and whatever games she was playing."

Says Bernhard, "We would taunt him, saying things to make him feel uncomfortable. In a loving way. He was a perfect target, because he played the befuddled old man with her: 'Wha?' 'Huh?' 'What's all this craziness?' The whole relationship was a performance."

Beatty was by no means blind to the obvious. One day he was in the car with Mike Nichols on his way up to his house. They were talking about Madonna, or Cher. Beatty said, "Women with one name, they're all pretty much alike."

"Are you nuts? What are you saying?"

"Well, think about it, it's the ultimate patricide."

Nichols thought, "Oh my God, he meant something. He can do that, startle you with a real insight and a deep observation, arrived at apparently as casually as he arrives at everything. I'm sure it wasn't that casual, but the process is hidden."

Beatty, a man who was accustomed to being worshipped by women, to being completely in control, was on dangerous ground with Madonna. Why he sat still for this kind of treatment remains a mystery. Chances are, he was taking his own advice. He would tell director Glenn Gordon Caron a few years later, "Never, ever fuck your leading lady. And if you do, don't stop until the picture's finished." He grumbled to his friends that he was too old for this. She was too volatile, too combative, too unpredictable. Nevertheless, it was reported that he bought her a six-carat diamond and sapphire ring, for which he paid $30,000, and in the middle of May asked her to marry him. Or, asked her to agree to marry him at some unspecified time in the future. She agreed to do so, after she was free of Penn.

The proposal was also reported by Madonna's brother. "One morning, when we [were] in the kitchen having coffee, she [told] me Warren has asked her to marry him." It certainly appears that Madonna believed it to be true, and who knows what darkness lurks in the minds of men.

Goldman's relationship with Beatty remained the same—"I always say about Warren, I love him and I hate him"—and just when the writer would reach his breaking point, Beatty would do something that moved him deeply. He invited Goldman to the wrap party at a big catering hall on Wilshire Boulevard. "Warren was standing around looking lonely," says the writer. "He's not a guy who's gonna dance." Suddenly, Beatty turned to him, gave him a hug, said, "You got me through it, and I want you to know that." Says Goldman now, "He would do things like that. It wasn't artificial. He could be very warm. It was touching."

Goldman handed in the *Hughes* script in the early summer of 1989, a few weeks after *Tracy* wrapped. The script was long, about 150 pages, but that didn't bother Beatty, who was used to lengthy scripts, and told him, "This is really good." He was so happy with it that during a scoring session at MGM, the actor asked him to write *Bugsy*. After six years, Toback still hadn't turned in a script. But Goldman declined. "All I knew was that I wanted to get away from him," he recalls. "There was no way I was going to go through this experience all over again."

Beatty had lined up Stephen Sondheim to write the score to *Tracy*. The writer continues, "That was the perfect thing, that he'd corraled Sondheim, who was the flavor of the century on Broadway and who doesn't do movie scores. I know this is homophobic, but he could get homosexuals to do what he wanted because he was so seductive."

It was during a scoring session that Beatty may or may not have made a strange call to Goldman's wife, Mab. "It was the most peculiar call I ever had," she remembers. "It was as though he were drunk or overdosed on something. He got on the phone and pretended to be on drugs and said the kinds of things that you could get away with saying when you were on drugs. He said that he wanted to be embraced or held by someone with wonderfully big breasts. I said, 'I don't have wonderfully big breasts. What you need to find is a nursing mother. They've really got big boobs.' I don't know why he did that, because I'm totally—I'm older than he is, I'm not a beautiful thing, but it was a sexual call. He said, 'I don't know what to do.' I said, 'Warren, just call Jack. Jack knows what to do when people have too much.' He said, 'Uhh, I don't have his number.' I said, 'Well, if you want, I'll call you right back, I'll give you the number.' Then he got off the phone.

"I spoke to him about it later, and he just denied it. I know that it was he, I'd bet my life on it. Nobody had the phone number except for our children and Warren. He'd called hundreds of times over that year, there's no way you can mistake his voice. His patterns, and everything about the way he speaks are distinctive. He has that kind of slightly halting way. It's as though he's censoring himself almost with every syllable. He's not spontaneous, he's careful. He's like a panther, a predator." Later, Goldman, who was at the scoring session with Beatty, told her, "He was just having fun. He was bored."

One day, Goldman got a call from Jeff Berg, who told him that somehow Warners had obtained the *Hughes* script. "The ax had fallen on Warren," recalls Goldman. According to him, Beatty had been having unaccustomed trouble with Terry Semel, half of the new team running Warners. Semel seemed to be one of the rare executives who was immune to Beatty's charm. The star complained, "This guy doesn't return my calls." Explains Goldman, "Warren was really bewildered by that. Because people at one time in the '70s would pray for a call from Warren Beatty." The star told Goldman that "the emanations from Warners were making him feel 'rubbery.'"

Then Goldman got another call from Berg telling him to report to work for Steven Spielberg in New York, who was now directing *Hughes*. Goldman was dumbfounded. How could such a thing happen? He told Berg, "I couldn't do that to Warren. He's going to go nuts if I go work with Spielberg."

"You have to."

"Whaddya mean I have to?"

"You're not under contract to Warren, you're under contract to Warners. You've got to work with whatever director they tell you to work with. Otherwise they'll sue the pants off you."

"Oh." Goldman called Beatty, said, "I'm going to New York."

"That's good. What are you gonna do there?"

"I'm working with Spielberg."

"Terrific. On what?"

"On *Hughes*."

"You can't be serious."

According to Goldman, Beatty "went absolutely fucking crazy, ballistic—of course, he had a right to." He felt that Goldman had betrayed him and hung up on him.

"I believe at this juncture Warren knew he was in difficulty with Warners over *Hughes*, because he had brazenly put *Tracy* first. He wasn't ready to start *Hughes*." Goldman speculates, "When Semel realized that *Dick Tracy* was green-lighted, they finally threw up their hands. Warren would not be honoring his contract. They said, 'You're out,' and took it away from him."

Meanwhile, Spielberg had somehow gotten a look at Goldman's script. According to Goldman, Beatty had never liked Spielberg. "Long before this happened, when his name would come up, he'd say something like, 'They may call me the Pro, but he's really the Pro. He plays this nerdy kid with the Super 8 camera, but he's the most vicious infighter in the business."

On May 2, 1989, it was public. Liz Smith reported that Warners wanted Spielberg to direct, with Sydney Pollack producing and Nicholson playing Hughes.

Beatty's account differs radically. He says when he was at the Directors Guild screening *Reds* in 1981, Spielberg approached him on the stage, said, "I beg of you, let me direct *Hughes*." Beatty demurred. Time passed. Then one day Spielberg showed up on the set of *Dick Tracy*, fell to his knees, and implored him to give him Hughes. According to Beatty, he said, "You did *Reds* yourself, what do you want to be the hero for?" Beatty said, "Okay."

Mab recalls that one night, Beatty, Isabelle Adjani, and she and Goldman had dinner with Spielberg and his wife, Kate Capshaw. According to her, at one point Beatty said, referring to Spielberg, "Well, should we give the kid a chance?" This would seem to indicate that Beatty was still friendly with Spielberg, and would seem to corroborate Beatty's version. On the other hand, she recalls thinking at the time, He's in danger of losing the project, so he's trying to be magnanimous.

For Beatty, as Bo Goldman puts it, *Hughes* "had been an obsession." For Spielberg, it was just another ball in the air, and eventually he lost interest, especially when Beatty reportedly asked Nicholson to turn down the role—which Beatty denies. According to him, "Spielberg and Bo didn't get along. Steven didn't get Bo. He told me, 'I'm not gonna make the movie. Do you want it back?'" Of course, Beatty answered yes. According to Berg, "There are elements of truth in both Warren's and Bo's account. I just don't remember."

Goldman got an offer from Penny Marshall to write a script about her mother, called *Time Step*. "Warren was pissed off about it," Goldman recalls, "but he had to let me go, because he wasn't paying me."

With Beatty deep into cutting *Tracy*, he apologized to Goldman, saying, "I want you in the editing room." Says Goldman, "His obsession has to become your obsession." The writer refused, thinking, Being in the editing room with Warren will be a horror. He'll drive me nuts. He recalls, "I purposefully went to Taos to write a picture, lived in the Holiday Inn, trying to get far away from him, I swear."

FROM A marketing point of view, the problem with *Dick Tracy* was that it wasn't *Batman,* which had come out almost exactly a year before, and which was going to be the yardstick by which *Tracy* would be measured, not because it was anything like *Batman*—*Dick Tracy* was already history, while *Batman* was still being published and boasted of a TV show to boot—but merely because Beatty's picture was a tent pole wannabe based on a comic strip. As Press puts it, "The question for me was, Who knows who Dick Tracy is? I had no idea except that he talked into a watch." The studio had to create awareness, make the square-jawed crime stopper a household name.

Disney did its best, pulling out all the stops. It made a huge marketing push to turn the picture into an "event." The P&A budget skyrocketed from $10 to $30 million. There were merchandising and clothing tie-ins galore, including a $300 wristwatch pager jointly developed by Motorola and Timex. McDonald's participated in the campaign, while Disneyland announced several new rides inspired by the movie. The studio published three graphic novels in hopes of introducing a new generation of kids to the cartoon detective familiar only to their fathers and their fathers' fathers. Clothing stores even stocked Day-Glow yellow raincoats.

"To Warren, on some level it represented everything awful that the movie business had become, but at the same time it was everything that he craved to make sure his movie got out," says Press. Moreover, millions of people had stayed away from *Ishtar* because of what they heard or saw about it in the media, and he realized that he could no longer afford to shun the press. Says Pat Caddell, "He could not again refuse to be part of the debate; he had to at least try to set the terms, structure the dialogue."

Adds Beatty, "I finally realized that if you don't control it, they will give you bad publicity. Our making and selling of movies is much, much too similar to a political campaign. 'On November 4, they're going to vote, so don't sodomize that giraffe until November 6.'" Instead of playing catch-up, as he had with *Ishtar,* with *Tracy* he was determined to be proactive.

As he did on *Ishtar,* he antagonized the press by trying to control it. He came to blows with *20/20* because he wanted to use his own crew, while they, of course, wanted to use theirs. Although he was on the cover of *Premiere, Newsweek,* and *Rolling Stone,* he said nothing.

There was a downside to the single-minded corporate focus on *Tracy.* It was all very well for Beatty, who was used to and expected red-carpet treatment. But *Tracy* sucked the air out of the Disney balloon, and the rest of its slate suffered. "The entire company's efforts and energies went into this movie," adds Press. "It was the first time I had ever seen what one movie can do."

As was his wont, Beatty used his charm to create allies within the various divisions who could feed him inside information and grease the studio wheels. "There were women inside Disney who fell for it hook, line, and sinker," says a Disney executive. Says another high-up Disney source, "There was this corporate executive dressed in these ass-tight blue jeans, red cowboy boots, and this white frilly blouse. You'd come into a room and these women—these ball-busters during the day— were actually sitting on his lap."

Disney was wary of Madonna and excluded her from many of their promotions, but there was no question that she was an asset to the movie. She put out two new albums (*Like a Prayer* and *I'm Breathless: Music Inspired by and from the Film* Dick Tracy) through Time Warner, and plugged the movie relentlessly on her "Blond Ambition" tour, which she kicked off in Tokyo on April 13. "I have a much bigger following than Warren does and a lot of my audience isn't even aware of who he is," she said. She was on course to make $14 million from the soundtrack.

Beatty failed to put in an appearance for the opening of the American leg of the tour in Houston on May 4. She had sent a private jet to ferry him from L.A., and held up the show for half an hour in hopes that he would materialize, but he didn't. He called afterward to explain that he was snowed under with work preparing for the release of *Tracy*, and knew she would understand. She didn't. She threw the phone down, and sequestered herself in her hotel room. He did put in an appearance when she played L.A., and she was abusive. He was backstage, trying to be invisible, when she shrieked, "Don't hide back there, Warren. Get over here. You stink, you pussy man. Can you believe I have to do this every night? Are you going to be nicer to me now, Warren?" A few weeks later, when she played New York City, she refused to let him and Nicholson into her dressing room, claiming a headache.

WHILE GOLDMAN was working with Spielberg, the decision on the credit arbitration for *Tracy* came down from the Writers Guild. Goldman lost. This was no small matter. Writers live and die by their credits. Screenwriting demands a lengthy investment of time, especially when working for Beatty. Unlike actors, who can do several movies in the course of a year, a writer is lucky to do one. Says Goldman, "And not only was it credit, quite a bit of money was taken out of my pocket, the bonus you get for credit. You probably double your fee." He was angry and bitter. "It wasn't enough for him that he was the producer, the star, and the director of the movie, he wanted a writing credit as well. Through his greed, I completely lost credit and my bonus for eighteen months' work on *Dick Tracy*."

Beatty offered him a "creative consultant" credit, but the Guild rejected it. One Saturday while Goldman was at the track, Mab, on her own, called Beatty. According to her and her husband, the conversation went like this: "You know, Warren, Bo was happy working with you. He feels a sense of accomplishment, particularly after *Hughes*. The two of you can do better work together than you can do apart. You've got to make some gesture to Bo, because this is really a terrible thing that you engineered his credit away. You ought to give him one of your points, and not your monkey points."

"So this is about money?" replied Beatty coldly. "I thought Jeff Berg was Bo's agent. You're his agent now?"

"Yes."

"You're trying to renegotiate your husband's deal. Is that what you're doing? How much do you want?"

"How's 50 cents?" Mab replied, furious, and slammed down the phone. She recalls, "I was so enraged that he couldn't get out of his own fucking way to understand that the best work that he could ever do in the future would be if he could have a relationship with Bo. I really liked Warren, a lot. He was gentlemanly, courtly, loyal. I was heartbroken."

Shortly after the conversation, Berg called her. She continues, "Warren probably called him off the tennis court, and told him, 'How can this bitch call me and say this to me? Don't you have control of your clients' wives?'" According to her, Berg said, "I just learned that Bo lost his writing credit, and I feel terrible about it. As the author of this relationship, I sometimes want to kill myself!"

Andy Karsch, who was friends with both men, was puzzled by Beatty's behavior. "Somebody of Warren's stature, you think, Why would he need to have a credit on *Dick Tracy* so badly when it's gonna cost Bo so much. It's something other writers have had a good deal of trouble with as well. Warren was so the engine of this movie, he just

knocked Bo off the train altogether. It just seemed unjust. And probably emotionally irrevocable. I'm always amazed by the kind of person
who really cares about where they sit in a restaurant. He's so of that
world."

"Why did he insist on getting writing credit when he didn't
really write?" asks Goldman rhetorically. "He wanted to be like Orson
Welles, he wanted to be the consummate filmmaker." If he had hopes
to repeat, score four nominations, as he did with *Heaven Can Wait* and
Reds, the screenwriting credit was crucial. "It's a sad memory, and I'd
never work with him again, but at the same time I'm glad I did work
with him," the writer concludes. "I'm still very fond of Warren. You
can be very fond of people and still know they're dangerous for you.
He was so much a part of my life in so many ways, and yet I've had
nothing to do with him for almost twenty years now."

Beatty too felt real affection toward the Goldmans, and over the
years made several overtures to them, but to no avail. Today, striking
a conciliatory note and parsing his words carefully, Beatty declares, "I
tried very hard to get Bo credit on *Dick Tracy*. [But] Bo might be right.
I understand his feeling about that, that I cost him . . ."—he pauses, lets
the sentence trail away to silence. "Did he not feel I had co-written that
script with him? I was very frank with Mab, and that might have been
unwise." He says he is sorry that he asked for co-screenwriting credit,
"because it knocked Bo out of the ball game."

Like her husband, Mab is ambivalent about Beatty. "He's an amazing person, full of wonderful qualities," she says. "But Hollywood
teaches you a devastating lesson, which is to play everything close to
your vest. Control is a function of fear. The sad thing is that with all
the genius that Warren has he doesn't seem to understand that until
you are fearless, you can't really live. It is removing the masks that you
put on to protect yourself that allows you to really stand naked in the
storm of life."

11

LETTING GO

How Beatty became the target of
Jeffrey Katzenberg's famous memo, said goodbye
to all that when he met Bening while casting *Bugsy*,
and turned in the best performance of his career.

"Maybe you should concentrate on mastering your own impulses,
or you're gonna spend the next twenty years of your life chasing
tail like a bobcat after a squirrel, instead of giving us another half
dozen great movies, and then finally meeting a woman who is your
equal."

—*Robert Downey Jr.*

*D*ICK TRACY OPENED on June 15, 1990. Its fiercest competition would come from Don Simpson and Jerry Bruckheimer's Tom Cruise vehicle, *Days of Thunder*, slated to be released two weeks later. Simpson sent his friend Katzenberg a fax that read, "You can't escape the Thunder!" Katzenberg replied, "You won't believe how big my Dick is." *Tracy* took the weekend, grossing $22.5 million on 2,332 screens. It led a fairly weak field, largely of sequels— *Another 48 Hrs., Gremlins 2, Back to the Future Part III*—a testimony to the depths to which the business had sunk by 1990. (*Days of Thunder* managed only $15.5 million on its first weekend.) *Tracy* made more money in ten days ($50.3 million) than any other film in Disney's history. Beatty professed to be thrilled. "The numbers are great," he said. "I really never expected anything like it. After all, *Dick Tracy* didn't have a following from a comic book or a TV series (like *Batman*)." But he had also never had a film on so many screens before either, and the per screen average was approximately $10,000, which was respectable, but not huge. It did slightly less than half *Batman*'s opening weekend gross the year before, $40.5 million, with an $18,454 per screen average. The disparity between the box office of the two films was underlined by the asymmetrical merchandising figures. If *Batman* was the gold standard, *Tracy* fell far short, with its tie-ins grossing a mere $42.7 million to that film's $500 million. Disney stock fell on the news.

On the other hand, the vast majority of reviews were favorable, not to say rapturous. In *The New York Times*, Vincent Canby wrote that Chester Gould's world "has been gloriously reinvented," and called it a "great uninterrupted grin." In *Newsweek*, David Ansen called it "a class act—simple, stylish, sophisticated, sweet."

Unquestionably, *Tracy* is great moviemaking, a feast for the eyes, a breathtaking marriage of nostalgia and violence, presenting a coldly expressionistic world that owes much to G. W. Pabst and Bertolt Brecht, but is also shot through with Dickensian and Chaplinesque sentiment. Beatty succeeded in crafting a generic world before branding, before advertising, before capitalism even, ironic in view of the massive marketing campaign that had been mobilized on his behalf. But if he did re-create the prelapsarian world of his childhood, it is no Eden, no Big Rock Candy Mountain. On the contrary, it is inhabited by a coven of infernal hobgoblins, putty-faced freaks, monsters from the id. By the time we get to *Dick Tracy*, with Reagan presiding over a me decade of rich-get-richer self-indulgence while restoring Cold War Manichaeanism with his Evil Empire rhetoric, even a liberal like Beatty was trafficking in right-wing moral fundamentalism. Evil lies within. With the storm of bad news that had broken over Beatty at decade's end, it's perhaps not surprising that his vision darkened considerably.

The dissonant minor chords that marred the chorus of hosannas greeting *Dick Tracy* sounded a note of disappointment arising from the undeniable fact that Beatty relied on design, music, and costume to carry the picture. More, the naysayers accused him of failing to connect with his character, zeroing in on the passive, even passionless way that he portrays the eponymous hero. As he did so often, the actor underplays the role. Beatty's Tracy was emphatically not Gould's tough-guy crime buster. Jules Feiffer, who can rightly lay claim to being an expert on the subject of comic book movies, thinks he miscast himself— recall that Beatty too initially thought he wasn't right for the part—that the picture needed a James Cagney–type. As Anthony Lane put it, writing in London's *Independent,* "The other actors are camouflaged by make-up, but it is the clean-cut Beatty who reveals least." Incessantly canvassing the opinions of his friends, perhaps Beatty was too much the politician to become the filmmaker he could have been. It was no accident that Caddell, the pollster, became one of his closest advisors.

It's true that Beatty was quite clear that he was not making the movie they wanted him to make, Chester Gould's *Dick Tracy.* Unlike *Shampoo,* where he was at pains to deny the obvious parallels between himself and George Roundy, in the case of family-guy Tracy, he made sure that nobody missed them, with a blizzard of comments about how much Gould's strip meant to him growing up. It was as if he were laundering his résumé with an eye to the family man he was about to become. It was out with the id, in with the superego. The Kid is a direct descendant of the nameless little boy who makes a cameo in the hospital at the end of *Reds,* as if Beatty were leaving a breadcrumb trail for those with the wit or interest to see it. He was blazing a trail for a new life.

As an advertisement for himself, for the new Beatty-to-be, *Tracy* works almost too well; it's too schematic, and therefore too bloodless to make much claim on the emotions of its audience. Perhaps he was getting ahead of himself. In real life, after all, he was still walking on the wild side, involved with Madonna, not Glenne Headly. If the star did fail to fully engage the role, perhaps it was because he wasn't quite ready to change horses. Unlike Prince Hal, he had not shown any inclination to divest himself of Toback, his Falstaff, who was at that moment writing his next movie, the dark and Dionysian *Bugsy* that Beatty had yet to get out of his system.

BY THE time *Tracy* had finished its run, it had racked up a domestic gross of just under $104 million. But the picture cost about $46.4 million, a lot of money for a film in those days, especially for the penurious Disney studio, which then tacked on a very hefty $54 million in marketing costs. (*Tracy* added about $59 million in foreign box office for a total gross of about $163 million.) Disney professed to be pleased.

The press reported that Beatty's next movie would be at the same studio: *The Doctor.* Of the $8.5 million in overages, $4.5 million were approved, $4 million disputed. Beatty told Katzenberg he would consider doing *The Doctor* if the studio forgave the $4 million. Katzenberg did, and Beatty bailed anyway.

Alas, the honeymoon would soon be over. In December 1990, Katzenberg went to Hawaii for the holidays. Disney, which had been phenomenally successful only a few years before, riding high on the profits of pictures like *Three Men and a Baby, Pretty Woman,* and *Down and Out in Beverly Hills* (which Beatty had declined), had hit a rough patch. Katzenberg's formula—low-budget pictures stuffed with bargain-basement stars who needed a hit—had ceased working. Thanks in part to his own success, as well as the growing power of Mike Ovitz at CAA to drive star salaries into the stratosphere, Disney's budgets were creeping up, cutting into its profit margins, even when its movies were successful. Katzenberg's gloomy mood was not helped by the relentless rain that confined him to the Kahala Hilton in Waikiki. Fearing that Disney had lost its way, he started putting his thoughts on paper, which eventually resulted in an 11,000-word, twenty-eight-page memo, intended for internal studio consumption only, in which he assessed the lessons of the last few years, mused on the future direction of Disney, and extrapolated his conclusions to the movie business in general.

In his own way, a newly chastened Katzenberg had arrived at the same conclusions reached by Columbia chief David Puttnam a half decade earlier. He railed against blockbusters, writing that they had a shelf life "somewhat shorter than a supermarket tomato." He seemed to feel that *Dick Tracy* had not made enough money, and was more trouble than it was worth. Katzenberg wrote that "the number of hours it required, the amount of anxiety it generated and the amount of dollars that needed to be expended were disproportionate to the amount of success it achieved." Were Beatty to pitch another $40 million project, Disney should "soberly conclude that it's not a project we should choose to get involved in." He added, "We have to avoid filmmakers like . . . Warren Beatty, talented as they may be, because their movies spin out of control." He also claimed that he'd passed on *Bugsy* for that reason.

Not everyone at Disney agreed with the memo. Says Bill Mechanic, then head of world-wide video, "You talk yourself into thinking that the movie is going to be the biggest thing ever. I don't think it fulfilled its ambitions, but it did what it should have done." Nor did anyone at Disney seem to be prepared for Beatty's reaction to the memo. Says Press, "I had to live with *Tracy* so long, I could see what Jeffrey was talking about. There was a price to be paid beyond what the movie cost. It was just common sense."

But Beatty was furious. From his point of view, he had been profligate with neither time nor money. He considered Katzenberg a good friend and felt he'd been stabbed in the back for a movie that had broken the $100 million ceiling. He responded, "Take his time? What the hell does that mean? He took *my* time, which, by contract, I didn't have to give him. It is fascinating that a man could have a picture that is as profitable as *Dick Tracy*—they got the negative cost back out of cassette sales alone—and try to put a negative spin on it because it didn't do as well as *Batman*. It never could have been *Batman*."

Katzenberg tried to mend fences. He sent Beatty an olive tree, a chocolate dart board with his own likeness in the bull's-eye, and two white doves in a gilded cage. Says a Disney source, "Warren hated all that stuff. He was hurt. I don't remember an instance when an executive had so clearly pointed to one person as being responsible for all of his mishegas."

According to Beatty, midway into postproduction Katzenberg began pestering him to do a sequel to *Tracy*, and far from turning down *Bugsy*, the Disney executive was desperate to get it. He repeatedly called Beatty and Barry Levinson, who was slated to direct, in an effort to secure the picture. Beatty says Katzenberg was annoyed, and continued to woo him through the period he was writing his memo.

"Jeffrey treated me very well," Beatty reflected. "Maybe he treated me too well. Maybe that was a problem for him. He had to put up with someone who had complete artistic control in his contract. They don't ordinarily affiliate themselves with gorillas like me. I think Jeffrey works too hard." He continued, "I'm told he tried to correct what he said about *Tracy* in that memo. But he sort of leaked this out on some fucking cable channel at 4:15 in the morning. That's like saying it on a quiet street in Fresno." Beatty didn't speak to Katzenberg for over a year.

As everyone had predicted, Beatty and Madonna had gone their separate ways. A few weeks after *Tracy* opened, it had come to her attention that he had turned down the *Newsweek* cover story because the magazine wanted to use a picture of him with Madonna. He insisted on himself alone, and that's the way the cover ran. She castigated him for excluding her from the cover shoot, as well as what she believed were his ongoing and multifarious affairs, although, according to her brother, she was cheating on him. Reportedly, he denied the affairs to her face and insisted that she only see him. She replied, "Go to hell."

On the heels of the *Newsweek* fracas, at the beginning of August, Beatty had screened a cut of Alek Keshishian's revealing documentary about her, *Truth or Dare*, in his screening room. "There's a lot of stuff with Warren that I cut out—there were phone conversations I thought were really moving and touching and revealing, but Warren didn't know we were recording. It wasn't fair," Madonna explained. "He, more than anybody, was reluctant to be filmed. Ultimately I don't think he respected what I was doing or took it seriously. He just thought I was fucking around, making a home movie."

The director recalls that Beatty was indeed unhappy with the film and that some footage wherein Madonna is talking to him on the phone may have been cut, but that "no scenes" where he is on camera "were cut at his behest."

Madonna turned thirty-two on August 16. She picked up Tony Ward, age twenty-seven, on the beach at Malibu during a party thrown for her by friends. Recalls Jeremy Pikser, who had been hired by both Beatty and Madonna to write scripts, "He tried to stay friends with her but she was mad at him." There was some backing and forthing about which script Pikser would write first. He continues, "She said I had to write hers first because she didn't want to wait on him again. She was very strong-willed and so big, she wouldn't put up with his bullshit. In those days, that's what it was all about, how much bullshit they would put up with."

BEATTY ALWAYS seemed to think he had all the time in the world, but now it was running out. At fifty-three, he was doing a good job resisting its ravages. He was doing everything in his power to maintain his youth. Marshall Bell, who had a bit part as a crooked cop in *Tracy*, had become one of his regular workout partners at the gym in his home. Bell called it "the sparring chamber," and he didn't mean physically. "I had to be really careful," Bells recalls. "He'd go, 'What do you think of so and so?'

" 'Well, I hear that she got all the way up to the top by using her dinosaur brain.'

" 'What the fuck is a dinosaur brain?'

" 'You know, dinosaurs have a brain down in the groin.'

" 'How the fuck can you talk about people like that. I won't have that!'

" 'I'm sorry.' He went upstairs. Am I supposed to leave? I thought, I shouldn't have said that. How dare I throw slanderous stuff out there about somebody behind their backs, just to sound clever. I thought he would have laughed. He probably thought that that's what I thought he was gonna do, so he [did the opposite]. Then he came back down again, and said, 'I think you were right about that person.' That's total sparring. I threw a punch, and he knocked me down, and then came back and said, 'I'm calling the fight.' "

But sometimes the sparring wasn't much fun. Bell continues, "I've been the recipient of stuff from him, where if it were cranked up about three times, which wouldn't be very hard, I could see that making somebody cry. Just a real tough character." He understood, like many of Beatty's friends, the asymmetrical nature of the relationship. "I share things with him, but there's no reciprocity," he reflects. "What you get back is, you get Warren. That sounds so sycophantic, but that's a pretty big deal. You know you're on a chessboard, somewhere, but that's okay, and fun."

Beatty's affair with Madonna had been grueling, and he was feeling a little bruised. He compensated by throwing himself into a series of affairs. Observes Bell, "When you've made your mind up you're gonna do something that's gonna change your life, sometimes you go in the opposite direction. He wanted to get that part of his life out of his system, because once *Bugsy* began, that was the end of it." Or, as Shirley MacLaine put it, "He's 50 from the neck up and 14 from the waist down." His new relationships included supermodel Elle Macpherson, as well as twenty-two-year-old Stephanie Seymour, a ravishing Victoria's Secret model then married to rock star Tommy Andrews, with whom she had a son named Dylan. Jeremy Pikser remembers seeing her at Beatty's Mulholland Drive home. "I was in his living room when he was making out like crazy with Stephanie Seymour," he recalls. "There were a few other actresses and model types there, these incredibly young, tall, beautiful creatures who, to me, were virtually another species. She was sitting on his lap. He was kissing her, totally going wild. That's how he described it, 'I'm going wild!' He had a vodka and cranberry juice. That was the only time I ever saw him drink hard liquor. I was astonished. He was trying to let go, and not be in control, which for him meant having a vodka and cranberry juice! He can never just let go. It was part of, 'Madonna's not going to make me look like an old guy' phase. 'I'm gonna get somebody younger and prettier than she is.' He was gonna let off steam, and have a good time for a while, not worry so much about who he was and where he was going. He was in a low place, emotionally, trying to amuse himself by acting like 'Warren Beatty.' Trying to have more 'fun.' What the fuck! It was clear to me that this was not his plan for a life."

Beatty was still carrying on his quiet affair with DeLauné Michel, who was a year younger than Seymour. After he and Madonna broke up, she entertained hopes that he would take them public and she would replace the singer as his numero uno girlfriend. She knew she wasn't famous like all the other significant women in his life—she didn't even know about Joyce Hyser—but she took refuge in his repeated declarations of love. Her expectations were buoyed when he invited her up to the house to watch the returns on election night, Tuesday, November 6, 1990. Most of their assignations were arranged at the last minute, sometimes when he was already in his car, on his way. This one involved more long-range planning. She felt that it was almost a coming-out party. It was a midterm contest that saw the Democrats increase—slightly—their hold over both houses of Congress. In other words, Beatty and Michel quickly found themselves in bed. While they were having sex, the phone lit up, one of his private lines, and he took the call while he was inside her. "That's when I knew it was over," she says.

Sooner than she might have wished, the doorbell rang, and fashion photographer Herb Ritts appeared with Danish supermodel Helena Christensen in tow. Beatty was on good terms with all the celebrity photographers, who not only shot him (Ritts would photograph Beatty and Bening for *Bugsy*), but would also introduce him to a steady stream of models. Christensen excused herself and went to the bathroom. When she returned, she exclaimed, "Ooo, that bathroom was sssooo cold, my pee froze midair." Michel thought she was vulgar, but when she wandered away again, Ritts turned toward Beatty, with his back to Michel, as if she didn't exist, and said, "So what do you think about her—pretty hot, huh? She'd be nice. And perfect for you." That was it for Michel. She recalls, "What more information does one need that this is the end? It was glaringly clear that he had no intention of changing our relationship. It's one thing to be secret lovers if one or both are in a relationship, but if neither is in a relationship, and it's still a clandestine thing—I wasn't going to do that." She broke it off. Michel says, "It was a double loss. It wasn't just the loss of a lover, it was the loss of a replacement father."

AFTER *DICK TRACY*, Beatty plunged into his next picture. As usual, he had several balls in the air. One was Steven Spielberg's *Schindler's List*, for which he participated in a table reading. Then there was Bugsy Siegel. Benjamin "Bugsy" Siegel was the gangster cum playboy cum visionary developer who built the Flamingo Hotel in a patch of the Nevada desert otherwise known as Las Vegas. He was a colorful character who was a close associate of Meyer Lansky, Lucky Luciano, Frank Costello, and other mob luminaries. A dapper dresser and accomplished killer, he was so prone to extravagant displays of temper that he was warily regarded even by his mob pals as a psycho with serious anger management issues, liable to lose it at the mere whisper of his nickname, "Bugsy." He was the kind of guy who, as Beatty says, "would hire a hit man to kill somebody, and then go out and do it himself. He just couldn't resist. For the fame. The glamour. I liked it when Meyer Lansky says 'Ben, for Clark Gable, famous is good. For Joe DiMaggio, famous is good. For you, it's not good.' " In other words, fame kills. *Bugsy* was *Bonnie and Clyde* all over again, Bonnie and Clyde come to Hollywood.

In 1937, Bugsy was dispatched to L.A. by the bosses back east as an advance man. Once there, he displayed a passion for movie stars, who, attracted by the frisson of danger that enveloped him like a cloud of cologne, repaid the compliment. He fell in love with Virginia Hill, a fiery mob groupie. He called her "Flamingo," after her skinny legs, and named the hotel for her. Bugsy was obsessed with Hill, even when it became clear that she might, in true *noir* fashion, destroy him. (When asked if he had ever been obsessed with a woman to a self-destructive degree, Beatty says yes, but of course refuses to say more.)

The Flamingo cost $6 million, a lot of money in the mid-1940s, and never made a dime, displeasing his underworld investors, who were further convinced that Siegel, Hill, or both were skimming off the top.

On the night of June 20, 1947, he was shot in the back of the head by a sniper as he sat reading the *Los Angeles Times* in his Beverly Hills home. The bullet exited through one of his eye sockets. The eyeball itself was later found by investigators on the floor.

Beatty, who could feel the hot breath of other Bugsy projects on the back of his neck, was anxiously awaiting Toback's script. Were he beaten to the mark, it wouldn't be the first time, and he repeatedly reminded his friend, "There's a Didion-Dunne script on Bugsy, and we're gonna end up getting screwed. You've got to finish the script."

Toback was slow and prone to depression, which made it difficult for him to work. He was desperate to direct his own scripts, thought of himself as a "master creator," which made him resent it when Beatty hired him to write scripts intended for others to direct. This in turn made it even harder for him to finish his assignments.

Like Goldman with regard to *Dick Tracy,* Toback says he didn't write with Beatty in mind. He started with the character. "I wouldn't come up with something that Warren would do, it would be something that Bugsy would do—and then I would ask myself if there were any problem imagining Warren doing the same thing. Like picking up the girl in the elevator in the beginning. Not only would there be no problem, it's something he could do with his eyes closed." But he did include a number of details that were drawn from Beatty's life, little in-jokes best appreciated by those who knew the actor. For example, Bugsy picks up a couple of beauty tips from the star, like lying in the sun with slices of cucumber plastered to his eyelids and a reflector under his chin.

When Toback finally turned in his script, six years late, Beatty responded immediately:

"I like it."

"You want to do it?"

"Right away, while I can still walk."

The writer told his friend that he hoped to direct it himself. Recalls Toback, "He just listened to me. It was left, as he often leaves things, ambiguous enough so that he can legitimately go in whatever direction he wants."

Beatty took it to TriStar, a division of Sony Pictures Entertainment, run by Peter Guber and Jon Peters. TriStar was headed by Mike Medavoy. (Medavoy had just started there, another example of Beatty targeting studio heads new to the job.) Beatty wouldn't give Medavoy the script; he had to go up to Beatty's home to read it. After skimming part of it, the executive agreed to finance the picture. By that time, Katzenberg's memo had made the rounds. "There was some caution on Guber's part, there was none for me," Medavoy recalls. "I disregarded it. It was the 'it won't happen to me' syndrome." Medavoy would live to regret it. "Life according to Warren Beatty is different from life according to anyone else in the movie business," he continued. "Somehow, he is able to make his own rules and then persuade others to follow them." Beatty received a substantial fee for acting and producing, as well as about 20 percent of first dollar gross.

Immaculately clad in a lightweight cashmere sweater under a black suit, Beatty appeared at Medavoy's home, and helpfully counseled him "to lose weight, and dress better. He told me he was going to be a nightmare for me, 'cause he was going to be all over me. All of which was good advice. He needed more handling than I was accustomed to. He warned me about all the things he would do to me, that he did do to me."

Medavoy's wife, Patricia Duff, was a stunningly beautiful blonde who a decade and a half later made the tabs when she got tangled up in a protracted and brutal custody fight with former husband Ron Perelman. She had met Beatty years before, when she was partnered with Pat Caddell in his consulting business, and was working with him on the *Reds* marketing campaign. Beatty had, of course, come on to her. "He was in love with Diane Keaton," she recalls. "He was doing some soul searching about that, why she wouldn't marry him. He was depressed about it. He was a gorgeous man and very charming, when he wanted to be. I'm sure it was genuine that he wanted to take me to bed like he did all the other women, but the rest of it, Warren making you feel like you were the only person in the room, didn't feel true. He spoke in riddles half the time, liked to be mysterious and enigmatic. He was a little scary, like a spider who was spinning a web. So I just don't get that close."

Beatty had decided he didn't want to direct *Bugsy* himself. "I'm in just about every scene of the picture," he says, "and I didn't want to have to do all that other work." Toback still had his heart set on directing the movie, so it skipped a beat when the star asked him, casually, "What do you think of Barry Levinson?" Beatty had been courting Levinson ever since his marvelous debut film, *Diner*, which opened in 1982. The writer squeezed out, "I like him," while his stomach sank as he realized where the conversation was headed. "Have you shown him the script?" Toback asked.

"I have."

"Does he like it?"

"He does."

"Does he want to do it?"

"He does."

"Did you offer it to him?"

"I did."

"Did he accept?"

"He did."

Toback was hurt and angry. He made what he calls "a pathetic threat." He said, "If that's the way you feel, I may not even help out on the movie." Beatty replied, "You don't understand. Unless you meet Barry and he likes you, you *won't* be able to help out on the movie." The writer recalls, "It was a harsh moment, because in effect what he was saying was, 'You finished the script, and now, if the director I've hired without consulting you doesn't want you around, your role in this movie is over.'"

From Beatty's point of view, it may have been ruthless, but it was just business. He was unsentimentally doing what he always did— what's best for the picture—regardless of the bruised feelings of a friend. "As a producer what you try to do is get the best from everybody you're working with," Toback continues. "He probably thought to himself, If I say to Toback now, 'Forget it, you're definitely not going to direct the movie,' I would have said, 'Fine, get another writer.' But he wanted to get me to write the best possible script. He would never overtly lie, but on the other hand, he was not going to say something that would get me so down that half of me would be angry that I was writing a good script, because I would not be directing it. If he had had to choose between the two of us, he would have chosen to keep Barry as the director. It wouldn't have been, 'I'm excluding Toback,' it would have been, 'I hired a director who's excluding Toback.'"

Levinson was a good-looking man with prematurely gray hair and a track record of fine movies, including not only *Diner,* but *Good Morning, Vietnam* and *Rain Man.* He was one of the few genuine talents to come up in that benighted decade, the 1980s, and everyone wanted a piece of him. In Beatty's eyes he was even more desirable in view of the fact that Robert Redford had long since made his Levinson movie, *The Natural* (1984), a hit. When the star gave him the script of *Bugsy*, a big, sprawling thing, 250 pages long, as thick as a phone book, he expected Levinson to dilly and dally, express his doubts, request time to chew it over, seek the opinion of friends, do another movie first, discuss it some more, pick up something he'd put down years before, behave, in fact, the way he would behave. But Levinson had always been fascinated by Las Vegas, the mob, the hookers, and the hustlers, as well as the crooners, the comics, the magicians. So, says Beatty, he "came back the next day and said, 'Okay, let's do it.' I said, 'What?' I thought, I'm afraid I got mixed up with a grown-up here who actually knows how to make movies."

Mark Johnson, on the other hand, who had been Levinson's producing partner for over a decade, had no interest in Las Vegas, nor the mob, and therefore the script failed to grab him. "It was a mess and needed a lot of structuring," he says. "I didn't immediately recognize the emotional strength that it had, that would eventually make it work. Barry was much more perceptive than I." Johnson may have been no novice, but he was not Beatty, and was aware of the star's reputation for being a hands-on, micromanaging producer. He was rightly worried about being shoved aside. He continues, "I was scared of it, and I had talked to people who had been involved in *Dick Tracy*, and knew what a control freak Warren was, and quite frankly I wasn't sure why they needed me. He reassured me that during the making of the movie he had to be an actor and was not in any way going to be a producer, which was absolutely true. He completely lived up to it."

Levinson too recognized that the script was ungainly, badly in need of cutting and shaping. He recalls, "I got this long thing, and I said, There's great stuff in here, but it's at least two or three movies." Toback met with him to discuss it. "When I first met Barry, I didn't realize how smart he is," the writer says. "As a result, for the first half hour, I felt, I'm justified in carrying out the plan I have, which is, I intend to kill him after getting friendly with him. Which would have been in the spirit of Bugsy. And then I'd be director of the movie. The only person who'd really know I did it would be Warren, who would accept it. Then Barry started to make some comments that not only made sense to me, but that actually made me see the movie structurally in a completely different way, and elevated my level of excitement. I actually started thinking maybe this is a good collaboration, maybe it's actually better that it's the three of us doing this instead of me directing."

Preproduction got underway in the fall of 1990. Medavoy agreed to pay Levinson and Johnson another 10 percent of first dollar gross. As was his practice, Beatty was reluctant to circulate the script. "Warren is very secretive," says production manager Charles Newirth. "No one got copies of the script. Whoever read it did so on a must-see basis. They had to go into a room where the script was, read it, take notes, and leave without it." Adds costume designer Albert Wolsky, "Everything was so secretive. I couldn't take the script home, I had to read it on the spot." Dennis Gassner, the production designer, gave it to someone in the art department, who shared it with someone outside the company. Recalls Newirth, "It got back, and they fired the guy."

THE CASTING of *Bugsy* has gone down in the annals of Hollywood romance for one simple reason: Beatty met Annette Bening, fell in love, and then did the unthinkable: married her. As the 1980s ended, Bening, thirty-three, had become the best-kept secret in the industry. But those whose business it was to track actresses on the verge, especially those as talented as she was, knew all about her. Beatty had already stored a few megabytes of information about Bening in the hard drive he uses for a memory bank—Milos Forman sent him her screen test for *Valmont*, and she was also the beneficiary of exceptional word of mouth. "In a way, a lot of it happened before I met her because you get opinions of certain people's opinions," says Beatty. "I heard about Annette, and we were supposed to meet on *Dick Tracy*, but she couldn't because someone she cared about was going through something. I was impressed by that." Mike Nichols had cast her in *Postcards from the Edge*, which came out in September 1990, and Stephen Frears put her in *The Grifters*, which was released in December.

Beatty asked Bening to meet him at Santo Pietro, an Italian restaurant in the Beverly Glen Center, just down from Mulholland, near his office. It was right before Thanksgiving 1990, just two weeks after De-Launé Michel walked out on him. "I think Annette's agent didn't want me to meet her," Beatty recalls. "What he said was, 'He's meeting every girl in Hollywood. This is not like some very [exclusive thing.]'" The actor adds, "He thought I was just going to make a pass at her. And it turned out he was right."

But Beatty, who plotted his moves so far in advance the other players didn't even realize they were on the board, was auditioning her for wife and mother of his children, as well as for Virginia Hill. Recalls Marshall Bell, who was still working out with Beatty at the gym in his house, "By the end of [his affair with Madonna], a shift in his thinking had taken place that made him want to settle down. Rock 'n' roll is not his bag. He would rather have been at home reading. He was in that *Truth or Dare* movie saying, I don't want to be around this. Think of listening to Art Tatum, his favorite piano player, and then "Like a Virgin." That's a big leap." One day, working out together on the Stair-Master, Beatty asked his friend, "What would you do if you were me?"

"I think I would settle down and have some kids."

"Well, why don't you have kids?"

"The question was, 'If I were you,' I would do that. But I'm not you. I'm Marshall." Bell continues, "He started to feel, I'd rather have kids. He was in his fifties, so it was, Let's get moving or this isn't going to happen. When they talk about how women have their biological clock? And they're going, 'Something's missing from my life'? I think that happened to him too."

By the time Beatty met Bening, he was primed. In his office, before the lunch, he had been muttering her name to himself: "Annette Bening," "Annette Bening," "Annette Bening." He arrived at the restaurant in a state of heightened expectation. Bening, on the other hand, was oblivious to his unstated agenda: "I didn't have any sort of realization or anything. I was an actress going to an interview." Of course, she added, "I knew all about Warren's reputation as a ladies' man. I would have to live on another planet not to have."

Beatty continues, "I was elated to meet her, and then, at the same time, I had mixed feelings, because simultaneously I began to mourn the passing of a way of life. But after five, ten minutes, I thought, Everything's going to be different. I take great credit for that. For knowing that." Bening remembers that he was exceptionally verbose. "I didn't let her talk one minute the whole time," he confirms. "I went into the peacock syndrome. I couldn't shut up, I did everything but stand up and do a soft-shoe on the table."

After lunch, the two of them walked around the cul-de-sac behind his office in the hot noonday sun, while thin women with too much face work in that year's Bimmers and Benzes cruised back and forth looking for parking spaces. "She talked about her family, her mother and her father, and her brothers and sister," he recalls. "Then I went upstairs to my office. Toback was in the cutting room placing bets. He asked me what I thought." Says the writer, "He let out this growl, like 'Grrrr!' A primordial yelp of love, lust, desire, enthusiasm, a sound that one would expect a starving man to make at the prospect of finally being able to devour a huge and delicious meal. I realized that without question the role was already now settled." Recalled Beatty, driving down Benedict Canyon later, "I had to stop the car. What had happened to me was so fully engaging that I had to pull over. I sat there for about five minutes and I thought it through. It was as if all the nines had turned over and everything made sense." But well aware of his reputation, Bening was more reserved: "I didn't fall in love with him instantly. I was wary."

Beatty called Levinson, who was in Baltimore, where he lived. The director asked, "How did it go?" Beatty replied, "She's terrific. I love her, and I'm going to marry her!" Beatty took her out to dinner. "I asked her if she wanted to go to my house for dessert," he recalled. "She rolled her eyes and said okay. So there she is, in her sensible car, following me in my mid-life crisis two-seater Benz up to my house in the hills. And when we get there, we're in my kitchen, eating ice cream, and I just say to her, 'Do you want to have kids with me?' And she says, 'Yes.' And I say, 'Are you serious?' She says, 'I'm serious if you're serious.' And I say, 'Good then.'"

Production coordinator Allegra Clegg, twenty-nine, was an attractive young woman with a fine mane of blond hair. Newirth offered her a job, "*Bugsy*, with Warren Beatty." Clegg's reaction was, "Yuchh!" She was of an independent cast of mind, a bit of a feminist, and was not impressed by his reputation. "He's such a womanizer," she added, making a face. A few weeks later, Clegg and Newirth were in bungalow R on the Culver Studios lot, when Beatty walked in. As he always did, he took stock instantly, scanning the room for attractive women. His gaze landed on Clegg. He walked over, took her hand, and wouldn't let it go, saying, "I've never seen anyone so beautiful." He locked eyes with her and turned on the charm. When he finally let go of her hand, after what seemed like hours, and walked out of the room, she said, "He's not so bad." Beatty flirted with her throughout the shoot. He was still on the lookout for a suitable ovum. She recalls that one time "he came up to me, and said, 'You should have my children.'

" 'You don't want to marry me, Warren, I'm not your type. You want the actresses, you need someone who's famous.' He wasn't aggressive, he has impeccable manners, which is unusual in Hollywood. When I had to ask him something, if he was busy he'd say so. If I went to his trailer while he was eating, he'd never be rude and eat in front of me. He'd either stop and deal with me, or he'd invite me to sit down and eat with him. He's really charming, lovely."

PRINCIPAL PHOTOGRAPHY began in January 1991. Beatty, Levinson, and Toback worked well together. It was the first, best, and last incarnation of Beatty's "hostile intelligences" theory. Beatty was always more at ease when he had people around him off whom to bounce ideas and keep him engaged. "Half of him is thinking like a producer or studio executive about budgets, because he does take this stuff very seriously," Toback observes. "He needs to have that tension and nervousness defused. He takes a nap every day, which relaxes him, and then wherever he can find some kind of fun, he'll grab it. One of the reasons his performance in *Bugsy* is so good is because the three of us had such a good time that it worked well for him as an actor."

Outside, perhaps, of Arthur Penn, and less plausibly Hal Ashby, Levinson is the only director Beatty hired—when he produced—who was able to work with him productively. Levinson's secret? Self-confidence. Says Johnson, "There isn't an ounce of insecurity in Barry. The day before we started shooting *Rain Man*, Dustin Hoffman called me in a panic, because he couldn't find Barry. He wanted to go over the next day's work, and he said, 'Where is he? Where is he?' We were in Cincinnati, and I said, 'He went to a Reds game.'

" 'What are you talking about? He went to a baseball game?'

" 'Yeah, he went to a baseball game.' Dustin just could not believe it. Most directors would have been in the bathroom vomiting. So like Dustin, Warren didn't have anything to go after, to attack. They said, 'Okay. This guy, not only does he know what he's doing, but more important, we're not going to be able to get to him anyhow, so we're just going to sit back and enjoy the ride."

Beatty researched Siegel with his customary zeal, as he did John

Reed, or Howard Hughes, for that matter. "Bugsy was a fairly articulate man," he says. "He kept himself in very good shape. Slicked his hair down a lot. He was a completely split personality. I spent time with Wendy Barrie, an actress who had had a relationship with Bugsy. And when Wendy would use four letter words at dinner, Bugsy would feign horror and say to her mother, 'I just wish she wouldn't use that kind of language. It's just so upsetting to me.' On the other hand, we had transcripts from FBI wiretaps of conversations between Bugsy and Virginia Hill in which every other word was 'fuck, cocksucker, shit' all down the line. That's definitely the way Bugsy and Virginia talked to each other. He was also absolutely a fanatically meticulous dresser. Hundreds of shirts. They all said 'Ben.' The jewelry, the rings, the jackets, the suits. And the most important thing of course, was that nobody called him Bugsy. You simply did not mention that name around him. You just didn't do it."

Bugsy may not have been an unhappy set, but it was a serious one. Says Clegg, "Barry's not a very gregarious or open person. He was quiet, never shared a lot with the crew. He didn't know anybody's name, didn't even say, 'Hello.'" By way of contrast, Beatty was a happy-go-lucky backslapper.

In the beginning, at any rate, although Toback has denied it, Newirth remembers that he and Beatty constantly talked sex, who had slept with whom, how many girls each one had had, etc., etc. The two of them grazed the extras in a scene in Union Station the first week, making, in Newirth's words, "a shopping list of attractive extras. Jimmy was using Warren to get phone numbers, he would draft off of Warren's wake." Beatty was still seeing Stephanie Seymour. She used to visit the set pushing her baby in a stroller, her body tilted forward, butt out. "The men followed her around," recalls Clegg, "going, 'Oh my God,' and staring at those long legs."

Free from the responsibility for directing, Beatty was in a reasonably good humor. "It's just more fun to not direct yourself," he says. "The difference between being directed and directing yourself is the difference between making love and masturbating. We didn't really have disagreements on this movie." Beatty and Toback enjoyed each other, did schtick, *Ishtar*-grade, sometimes better. Toback, seriously overweight, showed up one day in his friend's trailer wearing a liver-colored jacket crosshatched with zippers and dripping with braid, epaulets, tassles, all manner of pendulous things. Beatty grabbed a hank of braid, made a face, and said, "This is really tacky." A PBS documentary about U.S. intelligence agencies was flickering across the TV screen behind him. Toback glanced at it and asked, "Who was the only guy who ever headed the CIA and the FBI?" Beatty was puzzled, and puzzled that he was puzzled, because he knows stuff like this cold.

"Who?"

"William Webster. Who's the only guy who headed the KGB and the Soviet Union?"

"Andropov. Can you name each KGB head in order?"

"No, I can't," replied Toback, stumped. "Can you?"

"Yes, but you'd never know if I were right, would you . . . ?" And so it went. Beatty did the same with Marlon Brando trivia, challenged Toback to name show tunes from snatches of lyrics, as if his life were a fifty-year-long game of *Jeopardy.*

Beatty was at ease enough to say things to Toback like, the writer recalls, " 'That's a fucking moronic idea. I don't think you really mean that.' It would only be if you really kept fucking up, if you were on the wrong wavelength and were never in sync, that it would start to get unpleasant.

"Warren wanted to do a Jewish accent for Bugsy. I thought, Unless I get really cruel, he may actually do this. I knew that if I was really certain I was right, I had to be ready to go down the line with it by making a really extreme statement. I said, 'That is among the most witless ideas I've ever heard. I'm not going to sit here and have you destroy everything with this idiotic idea of a Jewish accent. Why don't you just burn the negative.' "

Beatty recalls, "Bugsy was a guy who spent a lot of time getting rid of his Brooklyn accent. So I got a thick Brooklyn accent that I was very much in love with, and thought was very charming and effective, and then I worked to get rid of it. I wanted to play a guy who had gotten rid of an accent that I didn't have. That's a strange step."

Toback kept coming over to him, saying, "Would you stop with the cockamamie accent?"

"Whaddya mean, it's good for the character."

"No, it just destroys the reality."

"Why don't you talk to the director about this, because he likes the accent."

"Why don't *you* go over and talk to him?"

Beatty went to Levinson, said, "Barry, would you tell this guy about the accent? You like it, don't you?"

"No."

"Why didn't you say something?"

"I didn't want to inhibit you."

Beatty concludes, "So I dropped the accent."

On the other hand, three intelligences is not four, and Mark Johnson was the odd man out. "I don't have a lot of recollections of great times on the set," he says. He felt that Beatty was actively sabotaging his relationship with Levinson. As one source puts it, "Warren loves to mess with people. He just liked the idea of driving a wedge between Barry and Mark. So he would literally go to Barry and say, 'Mark's not doing a good job,' and go to Mark that same afternoon and say, 'Why don't you and I form a production company?' Barry was supportive of Mark, but that was the price of doing business with Warren." Says Kathy Jones, who along with Buffy Shutt ran TriStar's marketing department, "We thought something was going on to push Mark out of the picture. When we got to a meeting, we'd say, 'Where's Mark?' They'd say, 'He's not coming.' What we found out later is that they didn't tell him."

Without seeming to, Beatty controlled the rhythm and pace of the production. Levinson was not a director who shot a lot of takes. Nevertheless, Beatty required his customary quota, and Levinson generally acquiesced with aplomb. As Clegg puts it, "Warren was insecure, always wanting more takes, and Barry tried to convince him that it was okay, but then did five more takes." Albert Wolsky, who had worked on several of Levinson's movies, says, "I'm sure it was quite frustrating for Barry. Barry was used to being the boss, totally in control. This was a project where he shared with Warren. If Warren wanted another take, they did another take."

In the most unsettling scene in a movie full of unsettling scenes, one that gets even more disquieting as it plays out, Bugsy confronts Jack Dragna (Richard Sarafian), whom he thinks is skimming money off the top. Shaking with fear and drenched by flop sweat, Dragna stands still as Bugsy strokes his face with a terrifying tenderness, saying, "Do you want to make love to me? Do you want to rape me?" Dragna shoots him a look saying, "This guy is crazy," which he very well may be. Virtually foaming at the mouth, Bugsy grabs his ear. Giving it a vicious twist, he forces him down on all fours, making him crawl across the room, barking like a dog and oinking like a pig, while Virginia Hill, ear to the door, becomes sexually aroused as she listens to the theater of cruelty on the other side. Bugsy works up an appetite of his own, and when he finishes with Dragna, he sits down to dinner, and wolfs his food, shoving it into his mouth with his fingers while a rivulet of blood trickles down his cheek. This electrifying tour de force does the Marquis de Sade proud and takes pride of place among the great scenes of cinematic sadism, like the one where Lee Marvin hurls scalding coffee in Gloria Grahame's face in *The Big Heat* (1953) or Richard Widmark in *Kiss of Death* (1947) cackles like a lunatic as he pushes elderly Mildred Dunnock, seated in a wheelchair, down a flight of stairs. As Bening once remarked, speaking of Beatty's characterization of Bugsy, "There's a kind of masculinity, there's a power, there's a force, there's an animalistic ferocity in what he does, especially afterwards when he sits down and starts eating, you don't see that in movies."

The scene was based on an actual incident in which Toback says he was involved as he was about to go into production on *Exposed* in 1983. Needless to say, he is quick to point out that he was the ringmaster, while the barker and oinker on his hands and knees was David Begelman, then head of MGM, who had agreed to produce the movie. Toback was about to leave his office when Begelman picked up the phone and called the writer's agent, Jeff Berg. He said, "We have a deal. I'll call tomorrow to confirm."

"What exactly did you mean when you said, 'I'll call tomorrow to confirm?'" Toback asked. "Why didn't you just confirm it on the phone now?"

"Suppose I call him tomorrow and say, 'I changed my mind, I'm not going to make the movie.' What would you do about it?" Recalls Toback, "We looked at each other for about thirty seconds, I stroked his face—he was very fastidious, Begelman—he didn't know what the fuck I was doing. He had huge ears, so I took one of them and I squeezed it really hard, slammed him down on the ground and stomped on his throat. Then I picked him up, and slammed him down on his desk, and I said, 'What I just did to you now is a kiss compared to what I would do to you if you tried to fuck with me like that.'

"'No problem, we're going to make the movie. By the way . . .'

"'Yeah?'

"He went into a drawer and pulled out a pistol. For a moment I had this flash of fear, I thought, This asshole's gonna shoot me.

"He said, 'Don't think you scared me by threatening me like that. You think you're not afraid to die? I'm much less afraid to die than you are. I load this pistol with a bullet and put it to my head every day, and sometimes I squeeze the trigger and sometimes I don't. You'll never be as unafraid to die as I am.'" (On August 7, 1995, Begelman would blow his brains out.)

"I said, 'I want you to crawl around the room and oink like the pig that you are, and then crawl counterclockwise like the dog you wish you were decent enough to be!' He oinked and barked with great enthusiasm. There was no humiliation with him. Or put it this way: Any humiliation with him, he relished."

Toback related this story to Beatty shortly after it happened. Beatty, who had had his own run-in with Begelman over *Shampoo,* suggested, "Why don't you write that in."

"Because you'll never do it."

"Oh yes I will."

"Oh no you won't. You're not going to do something like that on the screen. As you think about it, you're gonna start to say, 'I don't think we should take the character out that far. He's supposed to be the hero, and you're gonna lose a large part of the audience right there.'"

"Write it in and I'll do it."

Toback still didn't believe him and was so sure he wouldn't do it that he never wrote the scene. He knew, as Beatty put it, "I don't enjoy bringing myself to some sort of emotional [climax.] I can't fake it, I'm actually doing it." Time passed. The beginning of principal photography was just around the corner, and Beatty asked him, "Why didn't you write that scene?" So finally he did.

Toback continues, "It was almost an act of defiance — because not only did I not think he would do it, but when he finally did, I never believed he'd do it the way he did it, which was to take what was possible in that scene and push it to the absolute limit. I was wrong. That performance allowed him to do some things on the screen that he wanted to do for a long time, because they are on some level inside him or he understands them emotionally well enough to do them and make them believable."

Toback always thought, or pretended to think, that Beatty is, as he puts it, "a closet psychopath," by which he means "someone who behaves outside the boundaries of the law, of decorum, of what's acceptable, who inhabits his own universe of behavior, but has subjected himself to the acceptable so that he can pass in the straight world for being completely normal, but I would doubt that there's a single act that hasn't crossed his mind at one time or another. His imaginative energy has gone way in excess of what he's allowed himself to do."

Toback is exaggerating for effect, but there's some truth in this. If Beatty's films are a window on his imagination, it's clear that much of his work spins on the axis of outlawry and convention. He (and his sister) have always been attracted to the dark side, to those with secret, taboo lives, like his cousin David MacLeod, or wild, larger-than-life figures who walk the edge: Toback himself, self-confessed compulsive gambler and sexual desperado, and so on. Beatty regularly scandalized propriety with his sexual escapades, and was officially, if briefly, an outlaw himself, when he was cited by Peter Hall as an adulterer.

As Shirley MacLaine, who hung out with Sinatra's Rat Pack in Las Vegas, put it, as if speaking for Beatty, "I admit to an interest in gangsters—almost like a child watching a car wreck with my hands over one eye. I couldn't stop gaping. . . . Of course my own proper upbringing in Virginia had nurtured in me an attraction to unruly, unseemly, rebellious behavior, because I always sensed that same repressed rebelliousness simmering under my own parents' surface."

Yet through it all in both his personal life and his screen persona, Beatty did manage to preserve that kernel of innocence, even boyishness. Who could have been more conventional than he, shunning alcohol and drugs, helping old ladies across the street, especially if they were named Lillian Hellman or Vivien Leigh or Kitty Carlisle Hart, *persona grata* in any Bel Air home, friend of Lew Wasserman as well as each and every studio head, even becoming a peacemaker, a go-between in industry disputes. But for Toback, it was just protective coloration, the chameleon taking on the aspects of the twig to which it clings. "I believe he's a closet addict," he goes on. "That's why he doesn't drink, why he doesn't take drugs, why he doesn't gamble, why he has disciplined himself in very strict ways to prevent himself from crossing the lines that he knew he shouldn't cross." From his point of view, in *Bugsy,* Beatty just typecast himself. Toback wondered, rhetorically, "What other actor . . . is elegant and handsome, graceful and articulate, and glib and ferociously violent under wraps, and sexually obsessed?" He once asked Beatty, "Do you act in order to avoid living out what you might otherwise had to have lived out?" Smiling, the actor replied, simply, no.

But notwithstanding the power of the performance and Toback's theories about his character, Beatty isn't Jewish, isn't a gangster, isn't psychotic; there was considerable skill involved. Always an actor who mistrusted acting, who customarily reined himself in, in *Bugsy* he let himself go for the first time in his career. Said Bening, "His performance [in Bugsy] was so different from anything he'd ever done, the way he sounds, and the eccentricities of the character are so seductive and repellent at the same time. But he touched on something true." That performance constituted, perhaps, the greatest compliment Beatty ever paid to a director.

Years before, the first thing Beatty said to Toback, after seeing *Fingers,* was, "How did you get Harvey Keitel to do that?" In a sense, *Bugsy* was his *Fingers,* and the same question he asked Toback might well be asked of him: How did Levinson and Toback get him to do all that stuff? Says Clegg, "Barry gained his trust, and then Warren let go for Barry."

As always, Beatty considered all the angles. Tongue somewhat in cheek, he looked at each of his pictures with an eye to how they might affect his political career, even though it amounted to no more than a chimera with which he beguiled himself and others. *Bugsy* was no exception. "*Dick Tracy,* with its innocence and purity, was virtually a campaign vehicle," he says. "But with *Bugsy,* every time we would get to a scene that was particularly sick, or particularly bizarre, we'd say, 'There goes New Hampshire, there goes Iowa.' There's the scene where Joey Adonis says, 'Why don't you suck your apology out of my dick?' and I say, 'Pull it out'—we said, 'There goes California. The campaign was decimated.'"

Beatty's infatuation with his own appearance suited the character he was playing. Wolsky, who dressed him, appreciated him for the very reasons others mocked him: "I've worked with so many actors who don't give you the time, feel it's an imposition," he says. "An actor who doesn't care is very hard to dress. Warren cares a great deal how he looks."

Beatty still suffered from puffiness around the eyes. "He felt he

looked better later in the day, after one, two o'clock, less puffy,"
Wolsky continues. "It's all about the close-up, so the close-ups were
held for the afternoon when the swelling went down." Said director of
photography Allen Daviau, "I hope I get to do a movie with Annette
after this, because I spent all my time lighting Warren!"

Special effects whiz Rob Bottin made a full body cast of Beatty
to produce an eerily real looking dummy for the scene in which he
is shot through the eye. "I don't think Warren had ever seen a three-
dimensional replication of himself," says Newirth. "He was fascinated,
examined his face from every possible angle, and spent fifteen minutes
questioning Rob."

On February 18, *Dick Tracy* was nominated for seven Academy
Awards, including Al Pacino for Best Supporting Actor, and a handful
of people in technical categories, including Vittorio Storaro for cinematography, Dick Sylbert for production design, Stephen Sondheim for
Best Song, and Milena Canonero for costume design. Save for Pacino,
the movie was shut out of the major categories, like Best Picture, where
the nominations went to *Awakenings, Dances with Wolves, Ghost, The
Godfather Part III,* and finally *Goodfellas,* the only film in this group
that deserved the distinction. Bening was nominated for Best Supporting Actress for *The Grifters.*

Five weeks later, on March 25, the Academy Awards were held at
the Shrine Auditorium. *Dick Tracy* won three Oscars, including one for
Dick Sylbert. Bening, who attended with Ed Begley Jr. whom she had
been seeing, came away empty-handed, but later that spring she was
offered the role of Catwoman in *Batman Returns* (1992).

A few days later, while they were shooting the scene in which Hill
tells Bugsy, "Why don't you run along and jerk me a soda," Beatty declared his feelings. Impressed as he was by Bening's evident talent, he
wasn't indifferent to her equally abundant charms, and couldn't help
thinking about having sex with her, although he thought it prudent
to take the high road, and kept his libido in his pants. "That was way
down the line," he says. "I wanted to do what we've since done, but I
said, 'As much as I am inclined to make such a vulgar move upon you,
I will refrain from doing so because I think it is terrible to have that
pressure when people have to work together, so I won't be troubling
you with that.' She was very gracious and laughed."

Beatty and Bening kept their budding romance under wraps. Few, if anyone, working on the picture realized they were involved. "Barry, Warren, and I would eat lunch every day in Warren's camper," Toback remembers. "Annette would almost always join us. Warren and Annette didn't hold hands, nothing. I just got the feeling that they got along very well, and he was very helpful to her in her performance."

Toback continues, "I used to stay very late rewriting, often till one or two in the morning, and late one night I was driving off the lot in my rented Mustang convertible thinking that the only person still around was the security guard, and there were Warren and Annette walking together. They weren't doing anything, just walking. But it was startling to see them."

Says Newirth, "They were falling in love on that film, and you can feel it on the screen." Indeed, the connection between Bugsy and Hill fairly crackles with sexual electricity, so just saying no might have helped their performances, but it couldn't last forever.

Meanwhile, Beatty was doing his genetic homework. With children in mind, and gene sequencing not even on the horizon, that meant checking out Bening's DNA the old-fashioned way, looking for the fugitive cleft lip or club foot, the tic or twitch that might indicate incipient schizophrenia, diabetes, epilepsy, whatever, anything that might mar their children. (It was the same Darwinian instinct that led him to grab Carole Eastman two decades earlier, so that he could have smart children.) There was no recourse but to meet the parents, who were straighter than straight. Her mother, Shirley, was a soloist in the church choir. Her father, Grant, was a San Diego insurance salesman who gave Dale Carnegie motivational sales seminars. Said Bening, "You ask my dad how he is, and he says, 'Good and getting better.'" She adds, "My parents are really good moral people, good Republicans." Growing up, Bening was a high achiever, focused, determined, and ambitious.

Recalls Beatty, "It got to be late in the movie, and her mother and father came to visit on the set. I invited them all to come into my trailer for lunch. I thought, Oh, what nice people. This is an actress who's human, whose mother and father seem to be very compatible and of good humor, and had [gotten] along together and been married for some forty years at that point." He was so impressed that as they were leaving, he took Annette aside, and said, "May I amend something that I said to you?"

"What's that?"

"It's about fucking."

"Yeah?"

"I'm not making a pass at you, but if I were to be so lucky as to have that occurrence, that I would probably . . . I would try to make you pregnant immediately." And, Beatty adds, "We did."

Explained Bening, "When I met Warren I was thirty-two and the biological clock was ticking. . . . If he hadn't wanted to have children, it wouldn't have worked."

Adds Clegg, Annette would say, "I want to have five kids."

Bening got pregnant "very quickly," Beatty says, "because we were trying. There was never a moment, in effect, of not being married to Annette." He continues, "It was a wonderful thing. Most people have a period in a romance that's kind of lighthearted, you play around. With us, it was this weird thing, we just never did that. And that's a nice thing for our kids to know. It's very unusual. But it's the truth."

But romantic as Beatty was, he was not a believer in destiny. He once told DeLauné Michel, "I think back sometimes on a few of the women who were in my life before, the ones my mind naturally wanders to, the heavyweights, like you. I could have married any one of you and been happy. There isn't just one true love for anyone; timing is everything."

As hard as they tried to keep their relationship under wraps, there are few secrets on a movie set. The Teamsters, along with Hair and Makeup, are always the first to know. "The Teamsters told us, the first night they were together," says Mark Johnson. "If you have a trailer, even on a studio lot, the driver assigned to it can't leave until whoever's trailer it is leaves. So some driver told the transportation coordinator that when Warren and Annette were going over lines, they were there for a long, long time, and the rumor came back the next day that something significant had happened. What neither Barry nor I knew was that Annette was pregnant." No one else knew either. Says Albert Wolsky, "I didn't know, and I made a terrible gaffe. The very last scene she does, she was in a very unforgiving dress because it was all bias. I said something about, 'You see a little bulge in her stomach?' to the girl who was dressing her. Annette overheard, and she said, 'We'll have to live with that.'"

Beatty and Bening announced the news to the world in a press release. But before they did so, they called their respective parents.

Beatty had brought his mother, Kathlyn, who had suffered several small strokes, to Los Angeles the year before. "She was really in decline," he says. "So I said to her, 'Mother, Annette and I are going to have a baby.' She was in and out of compos-mentis-dom, but she said, 'Oh, that's wonderful.' I said, 'And I think it's probably better that you don't tell anybody because we haven't told anyone.' But, of course, I figured she would not know it in another five minutes. About a week after that, I talked to the lady who was taking care of her, and I said, 'How's my mother today?'

" 'Well, she's not in very good shape.'

" 'Why?'

" 'Well, she thinks you're having a baby.' "

On July 16, 1991, they announced the news to the world. The cynics' view, of course, was that having kids would keep Bening busy, in the nursery and off the screen. Says Dick Sylbert, "He had no intention of living out *A Star Is Born.*" Indeed, Bening dropped out of *Batman Returns.*

Two months later, in September, Toback found himself at the Toronto Film Festival, where he ran into David MacLeod, who had been on the lam for more than a year and a half, in the lobby of his hotel. Back on December 8, 1989, acting on a tip that a man had set up a meeting with two boys, twelve and thirteen, in the Bushwick section of Brooklyn, the police staked out a supermarket. MacLeod spotted them and sped away in a rental car. After a fifteen-block chase, he got mired in traffic and was arrested. He told them he worked for Beatty, and gave Paramount as his address, the home of his cousin's production company. He was charged with seventeen counts of endangering the welfare of a child, as well as an equal number of counts of criminal solicitation for luring a minimum of ten boys aged twelve to sixteen out of projects in Brooklyn and the Bronx to motels in New Jersey by flashing wads of money and promising them new clothes and sneakers. According to the police, he paid them $30 or $40 for the pleasure of fellating them.

At a Bronx courthouse on December 14, after learning that detectives from Queens were on hand to arrest him on like charges, MacLeod took advantage of a break in the hearing to leave the courtroom for the ostensible purpose of making a phone call. He disappeared.

Toback feels that MacLeod was penalized for behavior that is a lot more common in Hollywood than anyone cares to admit. Either those with his predilections are never detected, or they buy their way out of it. That day in Toronto, he says MacLeod "told stories as if nothing had happened. He was making references to how great Spain was, as if he'd just been traveling, which he had. But there was no context for the travel stories." Around midnight, they ended up at a Thai restaurant. Toback asked, " 'How long are you going to be in Toronto?'

" 'Just briefly, it's just in and out.' Obviously everybody was looking for him."

Nevertheless, they spent a leisurely two hours eating. "There was no sense of depression or despair," Toback continues. "No one would have known there was a problem. No one knew there was a problem originally."

But MacLeod must have seen somebody he didn't want to see, because suddenly he jumped up from the table and said, "I have to go." Toback recalls, "He vanished into the night. I never saw him again."

THE GOOD news was that *Bugsy* was slated for a Christmas 1991 release. The bad news was that so was *Hook*. From one point of view, that put TriStar in an enviable position. With two potential holiday blockbusters, it was faced with an embarrassment of riches. But, as things turned out, "embarrassment" was the operative word. Almost immediately, the *Bugsy* gang and the studio were at each other's throats. Beatty knew that Medavoy didn't have much experience with marketing, and he also knew that it is difficult, if not impossible, for a studio to release two big pictures at the same time. Inevitably, they end up competing for the same resources. Common sense told him that if TriStar had to choose between *Hook*, the $100 million family-friendly, feel-good Spielberg fantasy based on a children's classic that was tailor-made for the holiday season, and *Bugsy*, a $40 million dark, nasty, violent gangster picture, it would favor *Hook*.

Ironically, the co-heads of TriStar's marketing division, Buffy Shutt and Kathy Jones, had a long history—much of it not good—with Beatty that went all the way back to his Paramount productions, *Heaven Can Wait* and *Reds*. Shutt and Jones were tough; they had to be to have thrived in what was essentially a male world. Jones denies that *Hook* got special treatment. "I know Warren felt that," she says. "But *Hook* was pretty straightforward. We didn't do anything extraordinary. We always had *Bugsy* in mind for the Oscars." Toback simply brushes this off: "Despite protestations to the contrary, it's absurd for you to claim that you have two equally important Christmas movies that you're trying to push against the other studios' Christmas movies. The question becomes, Which was *the* Christmas movie? *Hook!*"

The principals—Beatty, Levinson, and Toback—were convinced, with good reason, that they were working on something special, with a stellar script and remarkable performances from Beatty and Bening, as well as an array of fine character actors in supporting roles. "That movie was everything for Warren," says Johnson. "He felt he had a lot on the line. Obviously *Dick Tracy* informed a lot of that. He was driven to make *Bugsy* a success." Adds one participant, "We were dealing with two guys—Warren and Barry—who were obsessed by Oscars. There was a lot of talk about the nominations—'Are we gonna get this one, are we gonna get that one.' This wasn't, 'This is just a movie, let's see how it does'; this was a movie that had to win Best Picture. That was driving many of our decisions. So that just added to the pressure."

Medavoy made no bones about the fact that he thought *Bugsy* was a hard sell, which just fueled the paranoia. As far as he was concerned, Beatty was no longer a big enough star—on the order of Harrison Ford or Mel Gibson—to open a movie on the basis of his name alone. Worse, *Billy Bathgate,* also a gangster movie, this one starring Hoffman, who was Beatty's age, had opened in November and lost a bundle for Disney. Worried, Medavoy wanted to downplay the mob element and sell the picture as a romance, like *The Great Gatsby*—also, incidentally, a flop.

Neither Beatty nor Levinson was shy about pressing his case with the studio. Beatty in particular went into high gear. He had fought this battle in the past and knew all the tricks. In his memoir, *You're Only as Good as Your Next One,* Medavoy wrote, "He called me constantly over the smallest things. If a story about holiday movies appeared in the trades or the *Los Angeles Times* and *Bugsy* was not prominently displayed as an important entry, Warren would call and read me the riot act." The star didn't hesitate to berate Medavoy in front of his staff, and once interrupted him in the midst of a marketing meeting at his home on a Sunday to discuss an article tangential to *Bugsy* that had appeared in *Variety.* When Medavoy confessed that he hadn't yet read it, Beatty chided him, snapping, "How can you be in the business? You are lazy." Medavoy adds, "He cussed me. It was painful." Says Jones with a sigh,

"Would he pick up the phone about the smallest thing and try to push that in Mike's face? Sure. And practically speaking, could Mike have read everything that was in the papers? No. Finally, instead of arguing, you just said, okay."

Medavoy says Beatty was involved in every decision, down to the size of the fonts on the posters. He continued, "Warren obsessed over every detail. He spent hours trying to figure out which quotes from the reviews to use and in which order they should be listed. Every photograph, every still, and every trailer had to be perfect, or Warren would order it redone—no matter the cost."

According to Jones, "The studio spent way over $1 million" just on photo shoots for the publicity materials. "Name any important photographer, and we went to him or her to shoot Warren, and Warren and Annette." They used Herb Ritts, and even the legendary George Hurrell, who was well into his eighties, and in poor health. (Hurrell died shortly thereafter, and the "joke" going around the studio was that Beatty had killed him.) Photo shoots at that time cost about at least $300,000 a session, and included fees for the photographer, hair and makeup, wardrobe, catering, and even rentals of architecturally distinguished homes where the photo sessions took place. Occasionally, Beatty would kill an entire shoot. "There were lots of good ones that we probably could have gone with, but it just went on and on and on," says Johnson, who was alternately impressed by Beatty's attention to detail and dismayed by his perfectionism. "He would take a simple photograph—not that I was inclined to say, 'Oh it's fine, let's go with it'—and he would find things in it and make changes and changes and changes, to the point where we were just defeated by it. There was a sense that, We can't do anything good enough for him."

Bugsy was not testing well, which surprised no one and alarmed everyone. It was one of those movies that caught it coming and going. Either audiences were totally repelled by the characters, or, reflects Jones, "Even if you fell in love with Bugsy and Virginia, and bought who they were as a couple, to have one of them die was difficult for an audience. Would you recommend it? That was a marketing challenge." The data indicated that *Bugsy*, like *Billy Bathgate,* skewed old. Beatty would say, "But when the kids come to see it, they like it." Marketing would retort, "Great, but they've come to a free screening. Are they leaving their homes to see it? Probably not."

Beatty was unhappy with almost every aspect of the campaign. Says Toback, "We had total control over the making of the movie, and we ended up getting it just the way we wanted, but then came marketing and distribution, where it was one fiasco after another. The trailer was atrocious. It was a trailer that made you say, 'That's the movie I know I'm *not* gonna see.' I kept saying to Warren, 'We're really in trouble, people are literally nauseous at this trailer. We've got to get rid of it.' Finally, Barry cut a trailer that was terrific. The bad one had already been attached to three thousand *Terminator* prints. We were gonna get all these trailers back and put the new one on them. But that didn't happen."

Beatty had an adversarial, accusatory style. He was a blamer, a finger pointer. "He can be a bully," says Jones. He grilled Shutt about the trailers. The conversation went something like this: Beatty said, "I saw the wrong trailer in a theater in Las Vegas."

"I guess they didn't take that trailer down. We sent another one to replace it."

"So you knew there was a wrong trailer up?"

"Yeah, we told you it would take a while to replace them."

"So, are you saying someone in the trailer department isn't doing their job? Who is it?"

"Am I on the witness stand? Am I the enemy, suddenly? Okay, it's my fault." Shutt was so angry and frustrated, she burst into tears. In her long career, he was the only man who ever made her cry. Even Beatty was shocked and backed off. "It wasn't personal," says Jones. "He has tremendous affection for Buffy, but when he's grilling, he's grilling."

Once the shooting ended, and Beatty resumed the role of producer, Johnson's position became tenuous. Says Medavoy, "Warren wouldn't talk to him. He thought he was useless." According to Johnson himself, Beatty repeatedly questioned his loyalty to the production. "It bothered me a great deal, especially when he would do it in front of Barry," he recalls. "If I would say, 'Gosh, I wish so and so's part had been a little bit stronger,' he would spin it in such a way that it sounded like I was fundamentally critical of the movie. He was so clever, he was able to twist words and make them sound like they meant something I would never have intended. It was very hard to defend against it. I found myself on guard the whole time. There was a lot of worrying about what Warren was going to think, how do I keep this from becoming an issue with Warren." To Johnson it seemed as if the pressure to succeed was so great that Beatty was dueling with phantoms. "Part of it was his flailing out," he says. "Everybody was really anxious. It was not, 'Let's see if I can screw with Mark.' Whatever it was, he really believed it. It was one of those situations where you wanted to say, 'Let's deal with something that's relevant,' but he was dealing with everything, he was consumed with the movie."

Bugsy opened on December 13. For the most part, it got rave reviews. Janet Maslin, writing in *The New York Times,* said, "Warren Beatty . . . has found the role of his career." She called Toback's script "one of the film's happiest surprises," and praised Bening for "sauntering through her role with a sexy abandon that greatly enhances the film's allure." Maslin was right. Bugsy is a version of Beatty in extremis, a narcissistic and vain man who entertains a dream of some grandeur and originality, but micromanages it to death (he insists the already completed pool at the Flamingo be ripped out and repositioned, the same way Beatty moved his own pool at the Mulholland Drive house), recklessly incurring vast cost overruns that cost him his life.

If every movie is self-reflexive, a metaphor for its own production, *Bugsy* is about a director-producer who courts his own ruination, by brazenly disregarding the budget—Coppola on *Apocalypse Now,* Cimino on *Heaven's Gate*—or Beatty himself on *Ishtar.* The star was hardly oblivious to the resemblances between Hollywood folk and mobsters. In fact, it was one of the reasons he was attracted to the material. "I liked the idea of this relationship between gangster movies and Hollywood, and the psychosis underneath, and Bugsy's wanting to be on the screen." Beatty points out that "some of the studio heads patterned their mannerisms after these guys." There's one scene where Bugsy hangs up the phone and turns to Mickey Cohen (Harvey Keitel) in disgust. Referring to his mobbed-up investors, he says words that might easily have spilled from the mouth of any director: "I'm dealing with a bunch of bloodless bureaucrats. . . . You ask Shakespeare what it cost to write *Macbeth*? Would they ask Michelangelo what it cost to paint the Sistine Chapel?"

The first weekend's grosses were $140,358 (on four screens), and then, after it went wide in 1,253 theaters the next weekend, $4.6 million. It quickly became evident that *Bugsy* was not performing up to expectations. Beatty responded by turning up the heat under TriStar. He scheduled a meeting with Shutt and Jones and their marketing department on Christmas Eve, and another one on New Year's Eve day. Shutt attended the former, Jones the latter. They concluded that he was punishing them by tying them up on holidays. Jones recalls Beatty asking, "Can we do two o'clock?" She replied, " 'Yeah, if it really will be two,' because he has a little issue with time management. I started calling him at three o'clock. It was, 'Yeah, yeah, yeah, yeah, I'm comin', I'm comin', I'm comin'.' Finally, around 4:30 I called and said, 'Okay, I'll wait, but I'm letting the staff go, because they have New Year's Eve plans.' He has no concept about other people's lives. He showed up around 5:30. And of course it was the same meeting we'd had a million times, nothing much got resolved at it, but it was about him wanting attention."

If true, attention was precisely what Beatty didn't get from Medavoy, who inopportunely seized on the week *Bugsy* went wide to take a cruise down the Nile with Patricia Duff. He told people he had no choice; it was important to his wife. People speculated that Duff pressured her husband into booking the cruise by threatening to leave him if he refused. (The couple divorced in 1994.) Medavoy denies this. "I know that Warren always felt that I was being forced," he says. "But he's crazy. I swear on everybody's life, my father's life, my mother's life, my child's life, it is absolutely bullshit." Reading between the lines, it's clear that one reason he left was to put 7,600 miles between himself and Beatty. Says Duff, "That was one place he could get away from Warren. Warren needed a lot of handholding, and he was relentless. Brutal. He's a true narcissist." Medavoy adds, "Frankly I'd had enough. I'd had enough of all the junk that went along with trying to keep the movie going, and not getting thanked for doing as good a job as we knew how to do."

Beatty reportedly urged him not to go and to pay more attention to his work. When he went anyway, the *Bugsy* gang went ballistic. "It wasn't that Mike was just away," Jones admits. "He was literally unreachable. It might not have been the best choice of a place to go." Asked Toback, rhetorically, "What studio head is on the fucking Nile the week that a movie like *Bugsy* that was getting sensational reviews, opens?" Beatty wondered, "I don't know whether it's his heart condition or his wife, or his being bored with the business or frozen with uncertainty about how to proceed, but it's literally like not having anybody home. Nothing is going to get done if I deal with him." Medavoy responds, "Warren flipped out because I'd left after the picture opened, but there was nothing else that could have been done. And there was nothing I couldn't do on the phone. You can look at that as an excuse or you can look at it as a dereliction of duty or whatever the fuck it is. What was I supposed to do, sell more tickets?"

A former client from Medavoy's days as an agent, Toback was particularly harsh. "I don't think he liked *Bugsy* as much as other people did," he says. "He had one response when he saw the first cut of the movie: too long. He was involved in Spielberg's career from the first, I don't think he was prepared for the movie to be received as well as it was."

Toback urged Beatty to go over Medavoy's head to his boss, Peter Guber. But Beatty was reluctant. "Warren's inclination would have been not to do it, except that Mike was literally missing in action," says the writer. In the second week, when the numbers started to fall off, Beatty began calling the Sony Pictures CEO on holiday in Aspen several times a day, complaining that Medavoy wasn't available to help. "Peter got upset," Medavoy recalls, "over the fact that I was gone, because he had to take the calls. A lot of them. Frankly, he meddled anyway, but he liked doing it in the background. It was great to hide behind me, but the truth of the matter was, at that point I was sick and tired of taking the calls."

When Beatty called, Guber was responsive. Toback continues, "It isn't as if Guber would say to Warren, 'You really should be dealing with Mike.' He just stepped on Medavoy's head and that was it. I don't think he said no to Warren about anything." Explains Jones, "Nobody wanted to be in the position of saying no to Mr. Mike Ovitz, who was Warren's agent. Nobody was more powerful than he was at the time. So between him and Warren—that was quite a whirlpool to be in. I know Guber didn't want to be involved, nobody really wants to be on those calls."

Johnson feels that the studio did as much as it could do. "Too much was made of the fact that Mike was taking this trip. I'm not so sure what we needed him for at that time. The movie was out, and whatever changes we needed to make, we could make them. It's not like anybody ever said, 'Okay, that's it, we're not spending any more money.'"

But it's hard to avoid the conclusion that the marketing staff wouldn't have been so exhausted if they weren't releasing *Hook* as well as *Bugsy*. And if they hadn't allowed a substantial chunk of their staff to take vacations while they had two big holiday films in release. The *Bugsy* gang were having none of Medavoy's excuses. Replies Toback,

"Mike's response was, What could he have done that he wasn't already doing? I don't know. Maybe the answer was nothing, because he wasn't doing anything."

In January 1992, the L.A. critics awarded *Bugsy* Best Picture, Best Director, and Best Screenplay, while the National Board of Review singled out Beatty for Best Actor. But after getting eight Golden Globe nominations, *Bugsy* won only one, Best Motion Picture Drama. The other drama awards were spread out over several pictures, so the Globes failed to send a clear signal. It was a significant setback, but, on the other hand, the winner of that category had won the Best Picture Oscar for the previous eight years.

With its strong reviews, TriStar recognized that *Bugsy* was a powerful Oscar candidate, and pushed it for nominations. But by January 20, the Martin Luther King holiday, the occasion for another marketing meeting, the feeling was, according to Jones, "All you wanted was for it to be over. What do I have to do to get out of this room? A couple more full-page Academy ads? Done!"

When the Academy Award nominations were announced on February 20, *Bugsy* received ten, including Best Picture and Best Director, a vote of confidence in the beleaguered movie, which immediately became the front-runner. Toback was nominated for Best Original Screenplay, and both Harvey Keitel and Ben Kingsley for Best Supporting Actor. The other Best Picture nominees that year were *JFK, The Silence of the Lambs, The Prince of Tides*, and Disney's animated feature *Beauty and the Beast*. In the Best Actor category, Beatty was up against Robert De Niro for *Cape Fear*, Anthony Hopkins for *The Silence of the Lambs*, Nick Nolte for *The Prince of Tides*, and Robin Williams for *The Fisher King*.

Guber continued to pour money into the Oscar campaign for *Bugsy*. "*Bugsy* really was the movie that everybody had their eye on for awards," says Jones. "We certainly chased it in every possible way. People teased us that we held the record that year for the number of full-page ads."

When the envelopes were opened on March 30, *Silence of the Lambs* swept the major categories, including Best Picture and Best Actor. Keitel and Kingsley canceled each other out for Best Supporting Actor, which went to Jack Palance in *City Slickers*. Callie Khouri (*Thelma &*

Louise) beat Toback for Best Original Screenplay. *Bugsy* won just two Oscars, Dennis Gassner for production design, and Albert Wolsky for costumes.

Bugsy was far and away the best picture that year, and Beatty's was the best performance. An injustice had been done, but what else was new? After all, the Academy was less the Roman Senate than the Parliament of Fowls.

According to Medavoy, TriStar lost just shy of $30 million on *Bugsy*. The film cost about $43 million, with an additional $15 million to open it, plus an additional $10 million for the Academy campaign. It grossed only $49.1 million, domestic, returning just $21 million to the studio in rentals.

Like *Ishtar*, *Bugsy* left a trail of devastation in its wake, although it took a few years for the other shoes to drop. Shutt and Jones left TriStar in 1994 and went to Universal, where they became co-presidents of marketing. The Levinson-Johnson partnership survived for another two productions, but subsequently the two split up. The seeds of their eventual parting of the ways were sown during *Bugsy*. "Up to then, Barry and I had had a lot of fun making films together," says Johnson. "*Bugsy* soured a lot of things for us. It may have been me, in that I never connected to the movie as deeply as the three of them did. Who knows, perhaps that's what Warren sensed. He is so smart." Medavoy blames Beatty for poisoning his relationship with Guber, although the two men did not get along anyway. He wrote, "I had to go through a public crucifixion over [*Bugsy*], one that would shadow me for the rest of my time at TriStar." That, along with *Hook*'s lackluster performance at the box office, paved the way for Medavoy's departure in early 1994, and TriStar ceased to exist as a semiautonomous, independent entity.

Still, despite his difficulties on *Bugsy*, Johnson says he learned a lot from Beatty. "You go to dailies, and it's very easy to say, 'Gee, that's great, that really works well, that's great, terrific performance . . .' You need to be that cheerleader, but your real job is to find out what's not working so you can address it and fix it. I like to think that's what I do, but Warren does it to a degree that even I didn't. He just stays on everything, and never lets go. He watched every single number that came out. It was literally, Why don't we add another eleven theaters in Omaha?' or, 'I spoke to somebody in Santa Fe who says we're playing on the wrong screen.' He will read the press release, reread it, and change this and question that. Some of it is absurd, but some of it, I'll be damned if he wasn't right." Adds Jones, "Is he focused on the kind of details where you want to run out of the room screaming about? Yes. Would I want to do it again tomorrow? I don't know. But when he's making a movie, he's really making the movie. This will sound weird, but I think he is kind of a genius. When it was all over, we both consider ourselves extremely lucky to be able to say we worked on those pictures."

WHILE *BUGSY* struggled at the box office, Beatty and Bening's first child was born on January 8, 1992, a daughter, named after his mother, Kathlyn, who died a little more than a year later, on February 26, 1993, at the age of ninety. "He was as close to his mother as mother and son can be," recalls Toback. "But when she died, he called me up, and we talked for about twenty minutes. Then he said, 'You know, I haven't even mentioned to you my mother died yesterday.' That's that cultural, religious background where you don't sob. It's all restrained."

Beatty and Bening married on March 12. Beatty was turning the page with a vengeance, which is not to say that he was never haunted by echoes from previous chapters. One of the weirdest was an outburst delivered from the stage of a Guns N' Roses concert in Paris that year by Axl Rose. It appeared that while Stephanie Seymour was seeing Beatty, she appeared in Rose's video *November Rain*. On their first date, she took him to the *Bugsy* set, built in an airplane hangar in the Valley, after which she ditched Beatty. According to a self-proclaimed "knowledgeable" blogger, Rose worried that she was cheating on him with Beatty. Dressed in red bathing trunks, a blue smoking jacket with red lapels, with a matching bandanna wrapped around his head, Rose cut loose with a profane diatribe directed at the movie star: "I'd like to dedicate this next song," he exclaimed, to "a man who is so empty that all he can do is play fucking games. A man who is a parasite. A man who lives his life on sucking other people's life forces, their energy. An old man who likes to live vicariously through young people, suck up all their life because he has none of his own. I'd like to dedicate this song to a cheap punk named Warren Beatty."

Predictably, Beatty's dual announcements—baby, marriage—were greeted by the media with a blizzard of "end of an era" items, as the avatar of 1960s hedonism, the symbol of the sexual revolution and the death of the family, finally bowed, it seemed, to the realities of advancing age and the pressure of convention. With Nicholson growing a paunch and losing his hair, Evans (however briefly) in a mental institution, and now Beatty tangled up in apron strings, it seemed as if it were only a matter of time before Hugh Hefner traded in *Playboy* for *Redbook*. No one quite knew what to make of it. Johnny Carson quipped, "Warren wanted a baby so he could meet baby-sitters."

Many of those who knew Beatty best were stunned, convinced that it wouldn't last. Several people who know him were of the opinion that it all had to do with the D-word. Shirley MacLaine's daughter, Sachi, was quoted as saying, "He's very frightened of the age thing so he'll marry and have kids." One anonymous friend agreed, saying, "Everything he's done all his life has been an attempt to fight off mortality. The movie *Shampoo* declared you could fuck your way to life eternal.... Now he's discovered there's an obvious way he's ignored all these years—just have a kid."

But many of his friends took it in stride. "In a weird way, the guy that he became, and is today, is who I believe Warren always was," says former Disney publicist Terry Press. Added a friend, "The only thing anyone talked about was not Warren's movies or his acting but his sexual exploits. It took him a while to understand that." Continuing the thought, Dick Sylbert observed, "Warren has always been obsessed with not being taken seriously. He couldn't get past the playboy stuff. That's what drove him to take his life in his own hands. Even the marriage is part of that."

Says Pikser, "I don't think there was a great sea change in Warren, other than it was time. He never gave up the idea of having a family, and being a movie star he was able to delay that much longer than a normal person could. If somebody said to me, 'You can fuck as many beautiful women you want until the age of fifty, and then you can get a beautiful thirty-year-old woman to marry you, and have children with you'— who's gonna turn that down? Annette was the perfect person, with a strong family background of her own, who was relatively stable, not a nut job, and a good actress. In terms of presenting her to the world, this is not a bimbo—it's a no-brainer."

12

MR. BEATTY GOES
TO WASHINGTON

How Beatty spilled tears over *Love Affair*,

tore the wings off the director, virtually kidnapped

Katharine Hepburn, but redeemed himself with *Bulworth*.

Bulworth is "the only truly political film to come out of mainstream Hollywood."

—*Jules Feiffer*

BEATTY HAD LONG nursed a sentimental affection for Leo
McCarey's *Love Affair*, released in 1939, with Charles Boyer
and Irene Dunne, as well as the same director's treacly remake,
An Affair to Remember (1957), with Cary Grant and Deborah Kerr.
He recalled them both fondly, especially the latter, apparently oblivi-
ous to the candied dialogue and overripe smell of the 1950s that make
it virtually unwatchable today. With *Love Affair* he could kill two birds
with one stone. First, it allowed him to play opposite Annette Bening,
which he was determined to do, as he did with Caron, Christie, and
Keaton. Said one friend, "He's never going to let her out of his sight.
He's got a beautiful albatross around his neck." Second, he admired
Charles Boyer when he was growing up, and now he could play debo-

nair Cary Grant in *Love Affair 3*. As the years wore on, Grant became a role model for Beatty, a better fit than Brando and Dean, especially when Beatty demonstrated a flair for comedy. Years earlier, in the sixties, Grant found himself a Hollywood party and couldn't help noticing that all the stunning young actresses were drawn to Beatty. "See that guy?" Grant reportedly said to a companion, "that used to be me." Now, Beatty was returning the compliment, if compliment it was. Warners head Steve Ross, also a fan of the McCarey pictures, urged Beatty to do another one, a quickie that would mint money for everyone. So of all the films he could have made, Beatty settled on *Love Affair*, a soapy remake of a soapy remake.

Beatty had asked Robert Towne to write and direct the movie, which was set up at Warners. Beatty took home $9 million up front. He announced the film in January 1993. Towne agreed, despite their frayed friendship. Observed Dick Sylbert, "This was a vaguely sick relationship that had been going on for a very long time. Bob was always broke." Towne, who had not repaid the loans Beatty had made him over the years, asked for an advance of $500,000 against his share of the film. Beatty wondered how he had been able to afford his lavish house in the Pacific Palisades, given his poor-mouthing. But he acquiesced, on the condition that Towne retire the loans, approximately $800,000, with his next paychecks, from *Love Affair* or elsewhere. (A few years earlier, the writer had taken his second wife-to-be on a first date to a screening at Beatty's, which Dick Sylbert, Marshall Bell, and others also attended. The star stood up and humiliated Towne by asking, "Are you still doing drugs? You've stopped that, haven't you?")

Towne tried to update the material and spike the syrupy goo with pins and needles: "I opened it up with Warren as a former football player getting a prostate examination. Then I put him on a fat farm," he explained. "He thought it was too funny and unglamorous." It took Towne a year to do the first draft, and Beatty sent him back to the typewriter. After several more drafts, Beatty finally approved one.

With Towne angry and out of the picture, the star recruited Glenn Gordon Caron the way he had Barry Levinson. He first called him in 1988, six or so weeks after the release of his first feature, *Clean and Sober*, with Michael Keaton. Then in his early thirties, Caron was a large man, a shade under six feet, heavy, around two hundred pounds, maybe more, with thinning, light brown hair and preppie taste in clothes—golf shirts, sweaters, khakis. He was of an age to have grown up with *Sham-poo* and the others. In other words, he was starstruck.

Caron was best known for his work in television. He had written and produced *Moonlighting,* which became a surprise hit in the late 1980s. The show featured relative newbie Bruce Willis opposite Cybill Shepherd playing a hip detective team whose clashing personalities created enough sparks to conjure up memories of the screwball comedies of the 1930s, like Howard Hawks's *Bringing Up Baby.* Caron was hot, and like every other TV producer, he dreamed of making features. After *Clean and Sober,* he began developing *Evita* for Madonna under the watchful eye of Jeffrey Katzenberg, who gave him a deal at Disney. It was through Madonna that he first met Beatty, who was then working on *Dick Tracy.* As no one could do better than he, Beatty wooed him with shameless flattery. "Gosh," he exclaimed, "we should do something together. If I had known you before, I wouldn't be directing *Dick Tracy,* you would." Recalls Caron, "I was thrilled."

Caron, who had turned Willis and Shepherd into the Tracy and Hepburn of the small screen, must have seemed like the perfect choice to set fire to the lachrymose dialogue of McCarey's weepie. Beatty asked Willis whether he thought Caron would be up to directing *Love Affair,* and got an equivocal response. He shrugged it off, and called Caron, asking, "Would you ever consider making a movie quickly, just for fun? Is there anything wrong with just singing 'Danny Boy'?" Caron should have seen the red flags. There has never been a quickie Warren Beatty movie, and he had no idea who or what "Danny Boy" was. Nevertheless he understood what Beatty was saying: "How 'bout doing something right down the middle?" Still, when the star said, "What I'd really like to do is a remake of *Love Affair,*" he was puzzled. He thought, I never saw either of the *Love Affairs,* I'm not interested in remakes. It didn't make any sense to him.

Caron was right to hesitate. As time wore on, Beatty was becoming disenchanted with his theory of hostile intelligences, regardless of how well it worked on *Bugsy.* He had once spoken, years earlier, words that would prove prophetic: "Basically, success breeds intolerance to the simple fatigue that comes out of a difference of opinion. Someone comes in and says, 'I hate to tell you, but this room we're sitting in is supposed to look like 1933 and it looks like 1945.' You say, 'All right, move these couches out and get rid of that desk. Change the curtains.' At a certain stage in life, at a certain point on the ladder of success, it's goddamn tiring to have a difference of opinion. It is easier to say, 'Look, I think it looks fine. Get the hell out of here. We are going to shoot it the way it is.' That's why certain directors and actors eventually become old-fashioned. They cease to be willing to undertake the fatigue that's involved when there is a difference of opinion." Would that he had listened to his own advice.

Meanwhile, Caron's new movie, *Wilder Napalm*, produced in 1993 by Barry Levinson and Mark Johnson's company, Baltimore Pictures, flopped badly. Caron recalled, "Frankly I became scared and I wondered, Am I ever going to work again?" He remembers, "Warren really wanted me to write a screenplay. So we talked and talked and talked, and then I began to write." That was the honeymoon period, the fall of 1993. Caron recalls, "We spent a lot of time together, we genuinely enjoyed each other." According to him, Debra Winger, among others, warned him off.

"She said, 'Oh, Glenn, don't do it.'

" 'Oh, no, no, no, it's gonna be great, blah blah.'

" 'That's what you think. He'll ask you to do it for all the right reasons, and then forget them the second you say yes.' "

Her words made no impression. Caron goes on, "I loved him as a filmmaker, I liked the things he stood for. As a director, to have him come to me and say, 'Direct me'—how can you not be flattered? It wouldn't have mattered what anybody said." He agreed. But when he looked up at the sunny skies overhead, he couldn't help but notice clouds gathering on the horizon.

Beatty had begun to staff up. As usual, he surrounded himself with the best in the business. He hired Nando Scarfiotti to design the production, Milena Canonero for the costumes, Ennio Morricone, who had scored *Bugsy*, and Bob Jones, who had edited *Shampoo* and *Heaven Can Wait*. "I had never done a production where I didn't pick the key personnel," Caron says. "When I came on board [as the director], Warren indicated that I'd be able to do that, but there were already people in place, and they were great people. You'd have to be a fool to say, 'I don't want Milena Canonero.' It's very hard to say no to Nando Scarfiotti. The greatest designer in the history of motion pictures. But Nando was not there because Glenn Caron was making the movie."

Beatty called Andy Davis, a production manager who had worked on *Sid and Nancy, Tapeheads,* and *Honey, I Shrunk the Kids,* as well as several less memorable movies. He was still struggling to get a foothold. Then twenty-nine, Davis was outspoken and ambitious. He had a deal at Disney, and had heard all the *Dick Tracy* gossip from the studio's point of view. "But Warren's star was still bright, and if Warren Beatty called you, you went," he explains. Davis asked him about Caron. "Because I knew from all the stories how he treats directors," he continues. "I knew that Glenn was a show runner, and television is a different world. I was interested in how it was gonna work between the two of them. Warren said all the right things: 'I want to be directed, I want somebody strong, I think this guy has the chops, he understands character,' all that stuff." Beatty charmed and fascinated Davis. Maneuvering his car out of the driveway onto Mulholland, he thought to himself, Oh, I get it, he's Satan! "Because," he goes on, "it was the most seductive experience I'd ever had in my life."

Like Caron, Davis was excited to be working on a Beatty picture. "There are certain directors who won't surround themselves with people they perceive as more talented than they are," he continues. "Warren was the opposite. He actually said to me once, 'I'd rather have a guy who's more talented and an asshole than a nice guy who's not quite as talented.' And this is a guy who never ever says, 'It's good enough.' "

And speaking of a talented guy who was prickly, Beatty also wanted Conrad Hall as his DP, an increasingly sensitive job now that Beatty, fifty-six, was still playing romantic leads. As Dick Sylbert put it, "Warren will make it last as long as he can. He'll treat himself like Cary Grant did." To do that, he needed the right light, the right lenses, the right angles—in other words, the right DP.

Hall, who was sixty-seven, was a crusty veteran who had shot *Butch Cassidy and the Sundance Kid,* as well as *Marathon Man, Fat City,* and many other important pictures. Like Gordon Willis and countless other cinematographers, he had little good to say about directors and firmly believed he could do it better.

Caron was dead set against hiring Hall. "I felt he was about the wrongest guy in the world for this particular movie," he says. "Warren was concerned about how he would look. I told him, 'Connie Hall doesn't give a shit about your face. He's interested in architecture, geometry. I wanted to use Allen Daviau, because it was clear from *Bugsy* that he knew how to shoot Warren. 'No, no, no, Connie Hall, Connie Hall, Connie Hall!' He was there because Warren had said, 'I'm gonna do this movie, this kid's gonna direct it, and you'll help him out.' Connie wanted none of that." Caron may have been right about Hall. He was more comfortable with male dramas than weepies; his lighting was dark and dramatic. Jones agrees with Caron: "I'm not sure Connie was the right person for *Love Affair.*"

In any event, the honeymoon between Caron and Beatty quickly came to an end, beginning with the writing. Like Bo Goldman before him, Caron was not happy with Beatty's style of working. "He wanted to be in the same room with me while I was writing. But I couldn't write in the same room with him. He was infuriated by the idea that I would work independently.

"Warren fancies himself a writer. My sense is he's less a writer than he is an editor. My pages would come back referencing things that had been in the previous draft. Or I would write a scene, and he would throw it away and say, 'Let's use the Towne draft,' and he'd insert something from that. Sometimes he'd go back to things that were in the original movie. I don't remember any moments of inspiration on his part involving new material."

The script that Beatty and Caron came up with stuck pretty close to the 1957 version, although former football star Mike Gambril (Beatty) and schoolteacher Terry McKay (Bening), both encumbered by significant others, meet on a flight to Sydney, Australia, instead of an ocean liner. Engine trouble brings the plane down on an island in the South Pacific, where they are transferred to a Russian love boat, the site of their budding romance. Each of them has been around the block; the script alludes to Beatty's own storied career as a lady-killer. He confesses to McKay, "You know I've never been faithful to anyone in my whole life." She replies, "I'm shocked and amazed!" She's willing to take him on anyway. They make a pit stop at Tahiti to visit Gambril's sainted aunt, then decide to test their love by separating and rendez-vousing three months later on the observation deck of the Empire State Building. He shows up, she doesn't. He concludes she has changed her mind. The two make a go of it by themselves, but he discovers subsequently that she had been hit by a taxicab on her way to meet him and is now an invalid, unable to walk. Eventually, the lovers are reunited, both better people, more mature, more serious (and more boring) for their tribulations.

THE FIRST role cast was that of Gambril's agent. "I used to call it the Charles Grodin role," Caron recalls. "I wanted Kevin Pollack, and cast him immediately." Then one day, the director made a suggestion, said, "You know who also would have been a great choice?"

"Who?"

"Garry Shandling."

Beatty looked at him blankly. "Who's Garry Shandling?"

"You gotta see *The Larry Sanders Show.*" Caron brought him some tapes. He watched them and became enthralled with the idea of Shandling.

Caron expostulated. "Yeah," he said, "it's a great idea, but we have Kevin, and Kevin's brilliant."

"I want Garry."

Caron recalls, "It put me in a horrible position with Kevin, but that's the way Warren was. I thought we had taken care of that piece of business, now let's move on to the next piece of business, but wait—if he saw something better, he had no compunctions about throwing somebody overboard for the other thing. That was new to me. Ruthless is probably the wrong word, but it was the drive to constantly perfect things."

Like Paul Schrader, Caron discovered that in Beatty's world, nothing was ever settled. Issues that seemed to have been resolved one day would be reopened the next, as if they had never been previously raised. "That was absolutely his pathology," says Caron. It happened "over and over and over again."

Pierce Brosnan was cast as Terry McKay's fiancé. One day, Beatty and Davis were standing outside Beatty's trailer on the Warners lot. In the distance, they spied a man slowly making his way toward them down one of the streets between the soundstages. He was wearing a T-shirt, and his face was covered by a dark, scruffy beard. Neither Beatty nor Davis could take their eyes off him. Then they realized it was Brosnan. Davis said, "Oh my God! He's the most stunning man

I've ever seen in my life." Without missing a beat, Beatty replied, "I'd fuck 'im!"

The real casting drama, of course, revolved around Katharine Hepburn. "Warren very much wanted to get her," recalls Davis. "There was no one else who was acceptable." Caron, who now found himself disagreeing with Beatty more often than not, did not share this passion.

"Warren had this whole thing, 'Annette deserves her, it would be so great, the audience hasn't seen her in so long.' I said, 'Warren, she does a TV movie every year.' But he was just obsessed with having Katharine Hepburn."

But there was a problem: She didn't want to do it. She had more than enough reasons—then eighty-six, she was frail as parchment, physically and mentally. She had skin cancer on her face. She was a star, a legend, but this was a small role, and she never did cameos. She was afraid she wouldn't be able to remember her lines. Nor did she like the script; she thought it was foolish. Another sticking point was that the script required her to say "Fuck a duck." She had uttered profanity before— "shit" on stage and other epithets on film, but never "fuck," which she regarded as vulgar, a "nasty word." "Warren was fascinated," says Caron, "with this idea of getting Hepburn to say 'fuck.' He took some sort of perverse pleasure in it. It was something I thought was beneath all of us. It was clear to me that if this wasn't going to be her last film, it was going to be one of her last films. It seemed like not a terribly honorable way to be remembered." In any event, for these reasons, and probably a dozen more, Hepburn kept saying, "No!"

Meanwhile, preproduction crept slowly forward. Caron was struck by Beatty's preoccupation with his appearance. "One day—I want to say the entire day, it was hours and hours and hours, ten, twelve hours—we went to Milena Canonero to fit a pair of pants and T-shirts," he recalls. "He was very particular about the way the T-shirts were cut on the neck. He liked the T-shirt to sit high, because he was self-conscious about what he called his turkey neck. Annette was exhausted, and at a certain point I just said, 'You know, this is absurd, we have to stop.' Finally she got him to put an end to it. Everybody was ready to go. Warren went into the dressing room to change back into his street clothes, and you could just see as he was changing, he was looking in the mirror, looking at the way the T-shirt sat on his neck, and was about to reopen the conversation. Annette just went, 'Ohmygod, no, no, no!' "

Beatty still wasn't willing to give up on Hepburn. He promised her that she'd be billed above the title, just beneath himself and Bening. Still no. He mounted a campaign. She had several homes, one in New York City, one in Old Saybrook, Connecticut. He determined which one she was using and began to send her flowers every day. He found out that she liked calla lilies, and had them delivered, by the armful. Wildflowers too. Still no. The flowers kept coming, for weeks and weeks. Allegra Clegg, now production supervisor, scouted gifts for her. "Every day, it was, 'Allegra, find the best chocolate place in New York,' so it was Teuscher chocolates, as well as Famous Grouse Scotch, more flowers, whatever he found out she liked, to woo her to do the movie.

"He called her constantly," Davis remembers. "She kept saying 'No,' and 'no,' and 'no.' And 'no.' We tried to see her, and she said 'no.' We called her business manager. He wanted her to do the movie, but we still couldn't convince her. I had a list of every octogenarian actress that might do it, and every week someone died and fell off the list. He would see all these people—Ida Lupino in the Motion Picture Home—but he only wanted Hepburn. One day I told Warren, 'She is *not* going to do the picture. We need to find someone else.' He refused."

Beatty enlisted her friends to intercede on his behalf, argue his case—among them Scott Berg, her biographer. "I've always been in love with Katharine Hepburn," Beatty told Berg. "She's very sexy."

"That's what Howard Hughes thought."

"Did she ever talk to you about Hughes?"

"Kate often told me, 'What you have to remember about Howard is that he was deaf." Berg brought up the project with Hepburn. She refused agan, saying, "Please tell your friend Mr. Beatty to stop sending me flowers. It looks like a funeral parlor around here."

UNLUCKILY FOR Beatty's picture, production commenced in August 1993, just two months after the opening of Nora Ephron's $90 million grosser, *Sleepless in Seattle,* which also referenced the 1957 *Affair to Remember.* Surrounded by A-list movie stars and Oscar-winning designers of various stripes, Caron struck several people as ill at ease and unsure of himself. According to him, he ran into trouble right away.

"The first day of photography there was a scene in an airplane mock-up with Annette. We got to take 8, and I yelled, 'Print!' I assumed we'd move on, but Warren walked over, and looking at me, he said, 'May I speak with her?' Meaning Annette. I thought, Well, let's see. You're her husband, you're the producer, you're the star, you claim to be the writer, so I said, 'Sure!' We did, say, another thirty-five takes. He had her laughing, he had her crying, every possible interpretation of the scene, and I thought the way he went about it was sadistic, for want of a better word. I thought, Oh my goodness, I'm not in control of this thing. This is awful.

"The next day we went to dailies and take 8 came up, and ten or twelve other takes of that scene. We then rode back to the set. Everybody left the van but Annette. She turned to me and said, 'You were right!'

" 'Excuse me?'

" 'You were right, take 8.'

"I thought, Boy, I'm not getting in the middle of this. I said, 'Some of the other takes are interesting too.'

"She said, 'No, no, no, take 8, you were right.'

"About twenty minutes later, I was standing outside my motor home smoking when Warren came out, walked over to me and said, 'For the rest of the production, if you wish to speak with Miss Bening, you'll speak with me and I'll speak with Miss Bening.'

"And that was how we proceeded. I tried to honor that. When I spoke [directly] to Annette, she seemed uncomfortable. Once I was blocking a scene on the ship, I said, 'Annette, what if you made an entrance from over there.' She replied, 'Glenn, Glenn, Glenn, let's not say anything, let's just see what happens.' I thought, Oh, she's very cognizant that if I say, 'Come through this door,' Warren is going to say, 'No, come through that door.' "

Beatty says there's no truth whatsoever in Caron's account. "I wouldn't be stupid enough to say that," he maintains. "If I ever said to a director that he shouldn't talk to her, he should talk to me, she would not throw a custard pie in my face, she would put a hot mince pie in my face, and she would keep it in my face. Annette Bening is nothing if not strong."

Recalls Davis, who was on the set every day. "I never saw Warren tell Glenn not to talk to an actor, or anyone else." Clegg concurs: "Glenn did speak to Annette directly." But she continues, "You could see that he kept taking a step back, and another step back, and in a sense stopped directing. It wasn't that Warren said, 'Shut up.' He would never do that. But you could see how he would talk to Annette, talk to Connie, say to Glenn, 'Let's do another one.' Warren put him down that way. He was rude, but not overtly, and he wasn't nasty. At the end, Glenn wasn't trying very hard. He just gave up. Somewhere along the way Warren lost respect for him. He and Connie didn't take him seriously, didn't even talk to him. He didn't direct Warren, because Warren wouldn't pay any attention to him. Warren was all of a sudden the director."

"It's got to be incredibly difficult to be Warren Beatty, to be as talented as he is, to be directed by somebody else," says Joyce Hyser. "He's not a malleable guy. If he thinks he shouldn't be standing over here, but over there instead, that's where he's gonna stand. And he's probably right. He's a brilliant director, and it saddens me that he gets in his own way."

Part of the problem between the two men was structural, attributable to the vast difference between television and film production. The marriage of a top network show runner, used to working fast and economically, and Beatty, accustomed to the deliberate pace of motion picture production—and then some, and then some more—was problematic at best.

"Warren seemed to like to create anxiety," says Caron. "I said to him, 'I don't know how you can be funny or creative if there's anxiety on the set.' It was a really contentious situation. So I made it my business to be the anti-anxiety guy. He yelled at me a couple of times. Once, in front of the whole crew, he turned to me and asked, 'Did you direct *Reds*?' I said, 'No, but I'll find out who did, get you his name!' Anything to keep it light. It was really devastating to me because I was quite enamored of him. He was one of my heroes, and at the same time I was startled by the ferocity of his need to fuck things up. I guess it really gets down to a lack of trust. And inability to surrender. So much of what we do, especially if you're an actor, is to surrender."

Four days into the production, Caron claims he went to Beatty and said, "You need to find someone else, I can't work this way, and it's clear to me you can't work any other way." According to him, Beatty called their mutual agent, Mike Ovitz, and Ovitz told Caron that if he left, he'd never work again. Again, Beatty's version is different. "About a week before we started to shoot, he said that he thought maybe he shouldn't do the movie, and I felt that maybe he was going through something—he had not had a lot of experience—I encouraged him to not worry, and I would try to carry the ball if he needed me to. In retrospect, I would say that he was right." Beatty blames Ovitz for foisting Caron on him. "Ovitz was very, very high on him, and urged me strongly to go with him. Mike's brother [Mark] was Glenn's partner. We all made a mistake."

Caron had his difficulties with Connie Hall as well. When Hall came back from scouting locations with Caron, he reportedly told the star, "You're going to shit-can this guy in a week. He doesn't know anything about anything." Caron had prepared for the shoot by meticulously drawing up a shot sheet. He recalls, "Very early on I showed up for a meeting with some notes in my hand. I said, 'It's a shot sheet.' Connie laughed, and said, 'Did you go to boss school?' His feeling was, You show me the scene, I'll tell you where to put the camera. I had never worked that way." Adds Bob Jones, "Connie didn't want any part of that [shot sheet]. When Connie threw it out, that left Glenn without any foundation to work from every day. Glenn was the director, but Connie was a big personality, and he just said, 'I'm not going to shoot that angle, I'm going to do it right.'" Recalls Clegg, "Connie didn't respect him. It was like high school. Connie and Warren and Glenn were friends at the beginning. But Connie saw that Warren was the alpha male, so he edged out Glenn. He was rude to Glenn, cranky and irascible."

Hall was at the end of his career and he didn't really care what he said to anybody, including Beatty. The star told Hall in no uncertain terms that he and Bening had to look beautiful. "Warren is very, very arrogant about the way he looks," says Davis. "Particularly at that time, when he still wanted to be a romantic lead. None of these guys want to age. They're movie stars, that's their currency. He absolutely, 100 percent, told Connie where to put the lights. Now Connie was a frustrated director, but no cameraman likes that."

Hall took his revenge by underlighting Beatty. Says Clegg, "It was very dark, dark, too dark. Where was Warren? Connie was very ornery about it, wouldn't back down, 'No, this is right.' They argued about it." Caron adds, "From the moment we started, Connie was a problem. Every Friday, he'd get up on a ladder and scream at the top of his lungs,

'I'm off this fuckin' movie.' He'd quit. Before every setup we'd place the camera, we'd videotape the rehearsal, Warren would watch the videotape, and he didn't like the way he looked. Warren set up a monitor in his motor home so he could see where we placed the camera. He would say to me, 'Tell him to bring the key light around.' I'd say, 'That's Connie Hall. I'm not going to tell him to bring the key light around. You look fantastic for a fifty-seven-year-old man. That's character.' But he was uncomfortable with that. We'd go back and forth, and finally, I'd go over to Connie and say, 'We have a problem.'

" 'What?'

" 'He wants to bring the key light around.'

" 'He wants to look like a faggot?'

"So you'd see scenes where he'd literally just shut the light off, so you couldn't see the things that Warren found objectionable, the lines on his face, the bags under his eyes. Warren was either in the dark or we were blasting him with light. Connie was not one to sculpt a face. That's not what he's interested in. It was a real wrestling match."

As was his wont, Beatty remained Eastman Kodak's best friend, insisting on take after take. Says Caron, "We would do endless takes on Warren. Endless." Davis adds, "There's the scene at the end of the movie when he sees Annette for the first time on the couch, and realizes she's crippled—Warren walking into the room, no dialogue—ninety-five takes! A day and a half of shooting. One time I was walking by him, and I looked at my watch, he said, 'Are you rushing us?'

" 'No, why?'

" ' 'Cause you looked at your watch.'

" 'I looked at my watch to see what time it was.'

" 'Don't fucking rush us. Get the hell off the set!'

"By the next day, he'd forgotten about it."

Clegg recalls the same scene: "A hundred forty takes. There was no dialogue. I had a wedding to go to, left on a Thursday night, came back Monday, and we were still shooting. There was no difference between take 1 and take 140." She concluded that he was deliberately holding up the production. "He still wanted Hepburn," she explains. "He's a smart guy, and he figured out a way to stop the locomotive. There's something about him that slows the whole process down. There were many days when he was in the trailer writing or whatever, and you'd just sit and wait. There was nothing going on. It was like we were all prisoners. He took my assistant to type stuff for him. It was like she was caught in a Venus flytrap. And when he was going after Hepburn, I laid off the crew twice while he tried to get her, for a week, and then another week to wait for her. If he doesn't have what he wants, or he doesn't feel comfortable, he creates a delay. He does 150 takes." Says Buck Henry, "I have a friend who visited the set, and noticed the clapper board, which said, take 102. He said to Connie, 'What's going on? Is that a mistake?' Connie said, 'No, no, we've been shooting it all day. Fortunately, there's no dialogue in the scene.' Maybe there's a piece of Warhol in Warren."

(There was apparently a legitimate reason, of sorts, for the great number of takes of this scene: a fluke of lighting created a shape that looked like a goiter on Beatty's neck, so the first sixty odd takes had to be discarded, and another sixty shot.)

Hall made merciless fun of Beatty for his penchant for endless takes. Paul Mazursky had a bit part. He recalls, "I was sitting in the mock airplane, and Connie was shooting a close-up of Warren. They were up to about take thirty-five or forty takes, and after each take, they'd go look at the damn monitor. And Warren would say to Connie, 'Let's do just one more.' I was half asleep, but I could see Connie's neck getting redder and redder. Finally, they get to about take 48, and Warren said, 'Okay, that's it! Which one do you think was the best, Connie?'

" 'One and 2.'

"Warren flipped. He lost his temper, [snapped], 'Connie, that's not funny!' "

Echoing Paul Sylbert, when he insists that Beatty, like Mervyn LeRoy, is more a selector than a director, Caron says of Beatty, "Most directors come into a project with a point of view. You don't sense with Warren that there's some burning vision in his head that he's gonna go out and get. Annette once said to me, 'You're more like Milos Forman. Milos has the whole movie in his head. He can act every part. He knows where the music cues go.'

"I said, 'Yes, of course.'

"Warren was appalled: 'How could you presume to know those things? The best we can do is build a set, try to capture it from as many points of view as possible, and then select the best takes.'

"That was anathema to me. I think Scorsese had a pretty good idea of what *Taxi Driver* was going to be like before he started making it.

The joke about *Reds* used to be, It's the best movie money could buy. He shot it and shot it and shot it until he got it right. I'm not saying that's invalid, but is that what you think of as directing?"

What motivated Beatty to direct? Anger? Power? Ambition? "Narcissism!" says Davis. "It's a combination of wanting to completely control his image, which he's very concerned about, and he also thinks he's the smartest guy in the room. And when you think you're the smartest guy in the room, you don't think anyone can do it better than you can."

Davis blames the dysfunctional relationship on Caron, not Beatty, although he does acknowledge that despite never seeing him "yell at Glenn, he was nasty. He would get very personal. But if you're going to open the door and walk into the world of Warren Beatty, you should know what you're walking into. You shouldn't be surprised. I wasn't surprised. The door was open for Glenn. But he never stood up to Warren. One night, very late, Warren, Glenn, and I were standing outside the stage talking about their relationship. Glenn said to Warren, 'The problem is that I've idolized you my whole life.' The moment he said that, he gave up any power that he might have had. The guy had an opportunity, and he didn't know what to do with it. It was Glenn."

Caron believed at least part of his difficulty with Beatty stemmed from the fact that the actor was working with his wife. "This was the first film he had done married," Caron says. "I don't think you can underestimate that, because a lot of the films he did, one of the ways he propelled himself through them was by romancing someone. The act of wooing provided some sort of creative fuel. He didn't have that here. There was no one to impress, to show off for." After all, Beatty did tell Norman Mailer, "It sometimes seemed that I had very little interest in making a movie until I was romantically motivated." Caron goes on, "Whenever there was a scene with a lot of women, he would be at his most difficult for me to deal with. He would want to assert himself." Adds Clegg, "He was flirting with everybody, but there was nothing extracurricular that I saw." The couple behaved like "two people totally in love," says Davis. "She knows who he is, and is not afraid to give him shit. She would tease him."

The Hepburn episode (without Hepburn) was supposed to transpire in Tahiti. Needless to say, Warners was not happy about it, wanted them to shoot in Hawaii. They went to Tahiti anyway and shot exteriors. One day, in the middle of the Tahiti shoot, Caron looked up to see Jim Toback standing behind a palm tree. He exclaimed, "My God, Jimmy, what are you doing here?"

"Warren brought me in to rewrite."

Recalls Caron, "I was surprised, because I was the writer, and I was the director, and I hadn't been consulted." He thought, If you're looking around for someone to rewrite a romantic comedy, Jimmy Toback wouldn't be the first person you thought of. I'm not inherently scatological. But there's part of Warren that is. He needed a guy to be able to say all this stuff to."

Again, Davis considers Caron naive. "Why would you be surprised that Toback showed up in Tahiti?" he wonders. "Jimmy was around all the time. One of the great two hours of my life was having lunch at the Essex House with Warren, Toback, and Norman Mailer. When I got to the table, they'd already been talking for at least five minutes about their bowel movements, and continued for another ten minutes after I sat down."

Since Beatty's wooing of Hepburn went down to the wire, her scenes were shot last. "By that time, my assistant had developed a relationship with her caretaker," Davis recalls. "We conspired with the business manager and the caretaker. We just showed up at her apartment, and said, 'C'mon, you're coming to L.A. to do the movie.' We put her on the Warner jet. It was with the complicity of her people, but we basically kidnapped her."

Beatty and Scott Berg accompanied her. Hepburn slept on one side of her face, and when she awoke, the lesions were inflamed. Beatty was visibly upset. As soon as he was alone with Berg, he observed, "My God, her face looks like a fruitcake." He instantly referred her to a doctor.

"At the airport in Los Angeles, Beatty ran around like a little boy, chasing after her: 'Is this okay?' 'Is this okay?'" Clegg recalls. "She was cranky, she didn't want to be there even then." She refused to stay at a hotel, so he rented her a house off Mulholland, near his own. "The house had to be only one story, and not too big, because she'd freak out if there was too much space," Clegg continues. "She walked in, and said, 'Too many flowers.' Warren picked up the flowers and ran out of the room with them. He did it himself. He was in awe that she was there at all, and he wanted to make it as nice for her as possible."

Hepburn's mood did not improve. According to Berg, Beatty

couldn't understand why she didn't appreciate her "opportunity." "She'll be working with the greatest living director in the world," said Beatty. Berg, who knew that the star planned to direct Hepburn himself, says the conversation continued this way:

"I'm sorry? Well, it's true, Cukor and Huston and Ford are all dead." Berg labored on. "But what about Billy Wilder and Kurosawa and David Lean?"

"I mean guys who are still working."

"How about Stanley Kubrick," Berg countered.

"Yeah, but he hasn't made a picture in years." Berg searched Beatty's face in vain for a sign of irony—a smile, a wink, something, but finally gave up. If Beatty was putting him on, he did a good job.

Berg too disliked the idea of Hepburn saying "Fuck a duck." He felt it was tasteless, and her fans wouldn't like it. He wondered, "Why upset some of the people who would be coming to the movie to see her?" He was taken aback when Beatty replied, "Nobody's coming to this movie to see her."

"I'm sorry?" Berg blurted out, thinking he'd misheard.

"I said nobody's coming to this movie to see Hepburn." Berg wrote, "Suddenly I understood that this entire casting expedition had been little more than an exercise in vanity." In the event, she did say it, quickly, so it's almost inaudible.

Hepburn's scenes were shot over the course of about four days, short days, about four hours of shooting time each, on the back lot at Warners. Beatty made every effort to minimize down time. Her scenes were prepped before she arrived so that when she stepped onto the set, everyone was ready to go. But the accounts of the shoot differ dramatically. Rumor has it that Beatty forbade Caron to speak to her. According to William J. Mann's biography *Kate*, the actress was subjected to torture by retake. He quotes Hepburn's longtime friend John Dayton saying, "I told Warren that Kate's first take was always her best take. . . . Unless something happened, there was no reason to do it beyond the second take." In one scene, where Hepburn was seated on a low couch, the script called for her to stand up, say a line, and walk out of frame. Beatty rehearsed her. According to Mann, she did it perfectly. He shot it—and asked her to do it again. "Dead silence fell over the set." Dayton recalls, "Kate looked at me and gave me this evil eye. So she did it again. She had done the rehearsal, then the first take, now the second take. She had gotten up off that couch *three times*." Beatty said, "Please do it again." Hepburn shot him a look that could kill, shuffled over to Dayton, and said, "You take me home right now," and the two of them walked off the set. According to him, all hell broke loose. He recalled, "Warren was chasing us." But it was for naught. Hepburn's scenes were over.

According to Davis, Beatty did not do multiple takes with her. He says, "Warren was too respectful." But Clegg says, "She definitely got cranky with him about the number of takes. She talked back to him, gave him flak: 'That's enough.' He'd say, 'Oh, right, right. I'm only supposed to do a certain number of takes.'" Berg, too, was under the impression that Caron was "not allowed on the set," but Caron insists that he directed her. "We certainly weren't limited in the number of takes we could do." He does not recall her stalking off the set, nor Beatty chasing her.

When it was over, Beatty told Hepburn, "If I had only met you thirty years ago." As soon as he was out of earshot, she turned to Berg and asked, "Was that supposed to be a compliment?"

That fall, when Dominick Dunne wrote on Beatty for *Vanity Fair*, Berg couldn't help noticing that when the star touched on Howard Hughes, he said, "What you must always remember about Howard is that he was deaf."

One day before the wrap was scheduled, Martin Luther King Day, January 17, 1994, at 4:31 in the morning, an earthquake centered in Northridge, just north of the city, jarred Los Angeles. Hepburn's rental home was badly damaged. Had she not left a day earlier, Beatty says, she might easily have been killed. His home was destroyed. Davis went up to the house later that day: "All the glass had blown out, the walls had caved in, it was an ugly mess. He was wandering around like a zombie. He had just experienced a tremendous loss and hadn't quite processed it. Losing the house was heartbreaking."

When production finally ended after a delay of a week or so during which the damaged sets were rebuilt, Caron practically kissed the ground. He had lost about fifty pounds. "I just kept looking over the bow, waiting to see land," he says. He says he has no idea what the budget was or how much the picture went over. But he was impressed by the lavishness of the production. Still, according to Davis, the film wasn't over budget by much. The picture cost about $45 million. (Other sources put the budget at about $60 million.) "We were four days over schedule. Warren's deal with Warners was, he was on the hook if we went a certain amount over budget. He was very worried that he was going to be out of pocket. Once, when we were two thirds of the way done with the movie, he asked me, 'How're we doin'? Is this gonna cost me any money?'

" 'You're okay.'

" 'How'd you pull it off?'

" 'We played some tricks, you're gonna be fine.' He got this giant grin on his face like a little boy, and he grabbed my face and kissed me on the lips."

"I SHOT Love Affair with the idea that as long as I have what I need, I'll do the things that he wants, the ninety-six takes of him walking into a room and looking at a picture," says Caron. "Films are made in the cutting room. That's where you attenuate performances, that's where you emphasize them. You figure out how to take an audience through the experience. The cutting room was the place where I really wanted to impress him. But I wasn't given a chance to do that."

Caron's mother was dying. She lived in New York City, and he asked Beatty, "May I cut the movie in New York?" According to him, Beatty said no. As Caron tells it, "My family moved back to New York, I flew to California, and I spent eight weeks in the cutting room with Bob Jones, who was not my cutter, he was Warren's cutter. And Jones's first allegiance was to him. I would have preferred someone who I knew better. The editing room is a place where you really want to feel free to try anything, but I really felt panicked there."

It's true that Jones and Beatty had an easy familiarity, based on months of working together. Jones knew there was no love lost between Beatty and Redford. He once worked for a couple of weeks on Redford's Indecent Proposal. He mentioned it to Beatty, who promptly asked, "How's his skin look?"

According to Jones, a few days after they wrapped, he had a rough assemblage ready to show them. Dede Allen, who by that time was a postproduction executive at Warners, looked at that cut, as well as subsequent ones and, Jones says, liked it best. But Caron didn't agree. He observes, "It was admittedly a sentimental experience, but how much sugar do you offer them?"

Jones recalls that in one sequence, on the airplane, "Glenn changed all the takes of Warren that I selected. I picked takes where he was lighter, more vulnerable. He made Warren's character a lot darker. He was deadly serious, sullen. Instead of being a playful flirt, he was almost sinister." In other words, his character was closer to the way Caron himself experienced Beatty. Jones continues, "When we were running Glenn's cut for Warren, he jumped up and said, 'What the fuck happened? What did you do to me, Bob? I hate it!'"

One day, while Caron was working on his cut, he claims that Beatty came to him and said, "We can save some money, because Ennio Morricone is coming to America, and rather than having to fly to Italy and show him the film, we can show it to him when he's here if you would be willing to show it somewhat sooner than you are contractually obligated to."

"I have no trouble showing it to anyone else. He doesn't make me nervous, you do!"

"Oh, no, no, no, you don't need to worry. I'm a director, I understand the process." Caron continues, "We had a screening, Ennio cried, I thought everything was wonderful, the lights went up, and sitting in the back of the room was a stone-faced Warren Beatty." The star had final cut, and according to Caron, said, "'I want to do a bunch of things.' And that was pretty much the last I had to do with the film."

Jones recalls that Caron had the ten weeks stipulated by the Directors Guild to finish his cut—"He had his time," he says—and that the problem was not that he didn't have the opportunity to finish it, but that it reflected an altogether different concept of the picture from Beatty's. "So Warren came in," he continues. "On one side of me I had Glenn, on the other side of me I had Warren. It was tense. Glenn was very silent, and then gradually, he moved further and further back. Warren was still by my side, but Glenn was up against the wall, and then he disappeared. He felt intimidated, or felt it was a lost cause. Warren included him in the recut, but Glenn backed away from it."

Adds Davis, "Glenn just abdicated. And after his ten weeks he quit the movie. He just left, literally disappeared."

Caron says he tried to work with Beatty once he took over: "I certainly didn't abandon it. One day I turned around and I was no longer in the editing room. Whoa! How'd that happen? Every day I'd call and say, 'May I see it today? May I see it today? Can I see what you've done? Can I give you my notes? Can I have some input?' I would never get calls back. I didn't know how to fight it. I'd fly out there, but I was never allowed back into the editing room. I was really fucked."

Jones hadn't worked with Beatty since *Heaven Can Wait*. "The editing on that film was about making it work better," he explains. "*Love Affair* was just trying to make it work, period. Individual scenes worked okay, but the overall film didn't. The script relied too much on twenty- or thirty-year-old dialogue. They were too loyal to the old film. We [never] believed in the Warren-Annette relationship. The scene where Warren comes back, goes to her apartment—that goes on forever and ever and ever, and is very sentimental. Warren kept saying, 'It's a great yarn.' But he also said he didn't know where the picture was going, he felt lost at sea."

WARNER BROTHERS finally invited Caron to a test screening somewhere in California. "I know Warren felt very strenuously that it was going to be a huge hit, and was very aggressive about it," the director says. "I was appalled by his lack of objectivity. My recollection is it scored a 69. I thought, This is the biggest piece of garbage. We shot a much better film than this. I flew back on the jet with [Warners Chairman] Bob Daly, and I said, 'Bob, I can really help this movie,' and he said, 'Glenn, you don't understand,' and he pointed across the aisle at Warren. He said, 'I need him. I need him to do *Oprah*, I need him to do—' and he rattled off a bunch of names like that. He said to me in the nicest way possible, basically, 'You're never getting your hands on this movie again!'"

Benjamin MacLean Beatty, named after his mother's family and Bening's father, was born on August 23, 1994. When Toback visited the Beattys in Malibu, he decided the baby was really named after Ben Siegel, "the progenitor of Warren's inner self," and the occasion for his introduction to Bening. Toback looked upon Beatty's wedded bliss with some skepticism, like others who had known the star in his salad days, but he had to admit that married life seemed to agree with him. Beatty told everyone within earshot that he was totally devoted to his family, and it appeared to be true.

Kathy Wenning, the Witnesses editor on *Reds*, recalls running into Beatty in New York. "I saw this familiar-looking person, walking down Madison," she says. "He stopped, and yelled, 'KATHY!'" She says that he told her, "'You know, I'm a changed man! I've finally met the love of my life.' It was very sweet."

Beatty rhapsodized about marriage with all the zeal of a recent convert, and with much the same enthusiasm as he had railed against it only a few years earlier. The middle-of-the-night calls became fewer and fewer, and he began to arise at a normal hour. To paraphrase Michelle Phillips, "Children-izing replaced womanizing." Says Dick Sylbert, "He won't let the marriage fail. I don't know how he could face himself. He just won't do it. He has a wife, a new image, new points in the community. She may be dead, he's gonna stuff her and sit her up in a chair. I don't think anybody knows the compulsive nature of this guy."

Michael Childers ran into Julie Christie one day and asked her if she'd seen Beatty. According to him, she explained, "I only call him when I need something from him." Of Bening, she said, "She made him a decent human being, which he never was. I'm proud of Annette, I don't know how she put up with it all." Perhaps in a better mood, or speaking for publication, Christie later reflected, "In the Sixties you did not know you were going to get older. But you do and you are. People become much dearer. When I see someone like Warren, with his four kids, there is that wonderful recognition of the life we have led. And a terrific sense of mortality, which is like a blessing almost: you suddenly realize what life is about."

Love Affair opened on October 21, 1994, in 1,585 theaters and grossed a weak $5,438,758 for a per screen average of $3,431. As one wag put it, "*Love Affair* fell off the screen. Beatty would have gotten better reception on his cell phone in the Holland Tunnel."

Outside of Roger Ebert, alone in his admiration for the movie ("This is one of the few Idiot Plots that works"), the reviews were uniformly unforgiving. In *The New York Times,* Janet Maslin called the script "tongue-tied," and Beatty's role one that brings him "to the brink of self-parody." The film itself she called "schmaltzy," while Katharine Hepburn was "ill-served" and appeared "uncomfortable."

No one can run away from a bomb fast enough, certainly not Towne, who always dissociated himself from flops he had written or directed, according to Beatty. He was embarrassed by the credit and publicly made fun of the movie.

But Beatty was not one to wallow in self-pity. As Toback put it, he "will refuse to acknowledge that there is a problem for which pity, or even concern, would be called for." As he blamed Columbia when *Ishtar* tanked, TriStar when *Bugsy* underperformed, so Beatty blamed the Warner Brothers marketing department when *Love Affair* barely opened. "The campaign was not going well," recalls Davis. "I had been saying, 'We shouldn't be doing it this way.' The second week the movie was in theaters, he called me at six o'clock in the morning, which means he hadn't slept, and yelled at me: 'This ad campaign is awful. I can't believe we're doing this.'

" 'Warren, I told you at least seven times I thought this was a bad idea.'

" 'If I didn't hear you, you didn't tell me!' We changed the ad campaign."

But the new ad campaign made no difference because that was not the problem. That Beatty was madly in love with Bening may have made for a successful marriage, but not necessarily a successful movie. The picture had all the freshness of moldy cheese, especially after the cleverness of *Sleepless in Seattle.* It's ripe with romantic clichés— star-crossed lovers, incapacitating accidents, improbable coincidences— not to mention smothered by mawkish Christmas cheer. Despite the flattering tricks a camera can play, Hepburn looked like she had long since passed on—dead star walking—and Beatty was not doing her any favors putting her in front of a camera. Dick Sylbert used to scornfully refer to *Love Affair* as *The Crying Game.*

By the time *Love Affair* finally limped out of theaters in the first week of January 1995, it had grossed a mere $18,250,211 domestically, a fraction of its budget, forgetting additional P&A costs. Nobody came out looking good. Delicious—or malicious, depending on your point of view—gossip, some true, some not, ping-ponged from Burbank to Malibu and back. Sample, from an anonymous source: "I ran into Connie Hall on the street in New York. His hair had turned white and was hanging down limply on either side of his head, like Nick Nolte in *Down and Out in Beverly Hills.* I said, 'What happened to you?' 'Love Affair!' " (In truth, Hall's hair had gone white before the beginning of the production.)

For his part, Caron believes Beatty blackballed him. "I was in movie jail for a very long time," he claims. "The movie performed horribly and he needed an excuse. I was the reason. People said things like, 'Your friend Warren Beatty isn't doing you any favors.' I knew I was unemployable." Eventually, he returned to episodic television.

Looking back on the experience from the perspective that the passage of time affords, he says, "I used to joke that, 'The good news about this business is that you get to know all the people you admired as a kid, but the bad news is that you get to know all the people you admired as a kid.' Moviemaking is this weird marriage of art, technology, and the management of a manufacturing process. When you do it with Warren Beatty, all the understandings that you have about how it works go out the window. It's as if it's never been done before, and you're doing it for the first time. And I can't quite explain the why of that. All I know is that it was the worst experience of my life. I was shell-shocked for a long time."

Unlike Caron, Davis enjoyed the production. "Warren and I had a great relationship; I felt like he and I were making the movie. In spite of Glenn." Nevertheless, when Beatty asked him to do *Bulworth*, his next picture, after some backing and forthing, he regretfully declined. Several years older and wiser, he didn't want to give up his life again. "Warren would call at eleven o'clock at night: 'Can you come up to the house?' There were literally Sundays where my phone would ring every ten minutes. I'd stop answering it."

So far as Beatty was concerned, the stories emanating from the set, partly true, partly apocryphal, were no laughing matter. No matter how big a star he had been, he was no longer. He was again and forever tarred with the reputation for being a director killer. Rightly or wrongly, *Love Affair* became a cautionary tale, a warning to directors to stay away from him and his projects. Increasingly, he couldn't find a director to take him on. More and more, Beatty would have to direct himself, work solely as an actor, or not at all. He often chose the latter.

Echoing the question Dustin Hoffman put to him many years before, Davis once asked him, "You're a great director. Why don't you direct a movie you're not in?" Again Beatty replied, "I can't afford to. I can't make enough money." Davis continues, "That's one of the reasons he makes so few movies. He will only do one when he feels like he can control the situation. I asked him why he didn't direct *Love Affair* himself. He said, 'I need someone to give me perspective. I want someone to stand there and say, 'This doesn't work.' But there are not that many people willing to take it on." To Beatty, "You're a great director" meant, at this point in his life, "You're too old to be a leading man." But even his friend David Geffen said, "He just can't give up the movie star." He had stayed too long at the party.

BEATTY WAS apt to take time off after a hit, but a flop energized him, propelled him into his next project. He was thinking of playing the lead in *The American President* (1995), directed by Rob Reiner from a script by Aaron Sorkin. Sorkin was a facile writer, adept at massaging genre conventions in the service of issue movies like *A Few Good Men* that played the game of provoking thought without, in fact, provoking thought. Bening liked him, though, and when Beatty decided against it, as he most often did, she took the female lead and became the cement that solidified Sorkin's relationship with Beatty. Beatty hired Sorkin to work on *Ocean of Storms*, an astronaut picture originally written by Tony Bill. At the same time, P. T. Anderson offered him the role Burt Reynolds ended up playing in *Boogie Nights*, but Beatty reportedly wanted the much younger Mark Wahlberg role.

And then there was *Town & Country*, by writer Michael Laughlin, which was, in his words, "a comedy about people on the Upper East Side of New York." Beatty couldn't decide whether to do the movie or not, and asked his friends. Jeremy Pikser told him, "This sounds like a terrible idea, and I don't think you should do it." But, also as usual, he ignored their opinions, and committed to it as his next movie. Says Paul Mazursky, "What attracted him to it was all the gals." Still, he was unsure—in this instance of whether he wanted to direct it or just star in it.

At the same time, Beatty had been mulling over the idea of a film with a political thrust. Lifelong Democrat that he was, he had fallen out of love with his party, then in the full flowering of the centrist philosophy of the Democratic Leadership Council (DLC), embodied by Bill Clinton. By the second half of the 1990s, the administration's Democratic Party-lite politics had made Clinton's name mud among Los Angeles's so-called Westside liberals. In Beatty's view, the Democrats had been running away from George McGovern since 1972. The retreat proceeded through the disappointing Carter years, when the party's candidates convinced themselves that they had to run as Reagan Democrats to win elections.

"Liberal" had become a dirty word. Beatty would tell *Newsweek* "I know what it feels like to be a suicidally depressed Democrat." Expanding elsewhere, he asked, rhetorically, "Where's the party of protest? Where's the party Bobby Kennedy was in?" Bening would attack the Clintons in 1999 for "doing what's politically expedient in the most transparent way. You feel like there's prevaricating, there's lying. You just don't trust them."

Beatty had lived too long, seen too much: "I have witnessed too many assassinations of people who were saying the right things, whether those assassinations were by bullet or tabloid scandal." With the riots that had scorched South Central L.A. like a wildfire in 1992 never far from his mind, he felt an obligation to speak out for the poor. "The underbelly of this country isn't being heard. How could they?" he asked rhetorically. "They don't have the means of being heard. It takes money to be heard. Even though I am a pampered, rich Hollywood cultural plutocrat, my leanings are to try to articulate something on behalf of those people. As the disparity of wealth increases, there are an incredibly large number of them."

Beatty wanted to make a picture that expressed his disgust with the last two decades of Democratic politics. He called it a "campaign finance reform comedy," and went on to explain, "If I'd done it straight it would have been C-SPAN. And everyone would be asleep.... I chose the name Bulworth because it reminded me of the Bull Moose Republican from that era."

While he was still in New York shooting *Love Affair*, in the fall of 1993, Beatty had approached Jeremy Pikser with a proposition. He told him he had an idea, but initially refused to tell him what it was. "He gets off on the control, and nobody knowing what's going on except him," says Pikser. In this case, all he said was, "I think I have something that you might be able to help me with. I don't know who I'm going to get to write it—I could get anybody—and I know I want to be the first credited writer, and I don't know if I really want the other writer to be you, but maybe."

"What's the idea?" Pikser asked.

"A depressed liberal senator who's sold out his ideals, become conservative, takes out a hit on his life, meets a black girl, falls in love with her, changes his mind, goes into the ghetto with her in order to hide from the people who are trying to kill him, and then—"

"Rediscovers his liberal roots! Great, love it, let's do it."

Despite Pikser's enthusiasm, he was still relatively inexperienced (among others, he had written two scripts for Beatty that had gone nowhere), and the star began looking elsewhere for a writer. He made a list. As he pointed out, he could have anyone. Or almost anyone. The blowback from *Love Affair* had put a deep chill on the relationship between him and Towne, not to mention Towne's lingering resentment over the *Shampoo* payout, and Beatty's irritation at the dilatory pace at which the writer was repaying the loans he had made him. His relationship with Elaine May was still strained, and the star didn't seem particularly interested in her anyway. He had conversations with playwright Tony Kushner, who was hot off *Angels in America*. Pikser pushed Larry Gelbart, who had written *Tootsie*, among other things.

Finally, Beatty came back to Jim Toback. He was a known entity to whom Beatty didn't have to explain himself, didn't have to worry about offending. He even had credentials, of a sort, his friendship with and book about Jim Brown. But given Toback's track record of procrastination, Beatty kept him on a short leash, paying him by the week. There was no disappearing for months at a time. Every day it was, "Where are the pages?"

Pikser, meanwhile, who needed money, asked Beatty for work. The star hired him in the spring of 1995 as a development person. In March and April, he worked on *Howard Hughes*, which was still set up at Warners. He was having story meetings with Beatty about it, and pinning cards on walls. He saw a script, but he didn't know who wrote it. Marshall Bell was at his home one night, talking to Pikser about Hughes. "Warren was in the next room," Bell recalls. "He came in, said, 'What are you gonna do, tell fuckin' Marshall about everything?'" Bell understood that part of the deal with being friends with Beatty is, as he puts it, "to dance around information that doesn't pertain to me. I was talking to Pikser about Hughes himself. I'm trained, I would never have asked, 'How's the script going?' God forbid I should have known there was a script being written. But I haven't brought up Howard Hughes since."

One day, Beatty told Pikser, "We're having a contract hiccup on *Hughes*, I'm putting it on the back burner." And *Bulworth*, not *Town &*

Country, moved to the head of the line. Beatty took the project to Fox, which had committed to *Dick Tracy* in 1987 and backed out. The star had threatened to sue, but instead, he worked out a deal whereby the studio would do another film in its place, so long as it fell within specified budget parameters, about $35 million. Beatty wanted the picture, topical, timely, to be finished quickly, out by October 1996, in time to impact the presidential elections the following month. He didn't mind if six months after the film was released it was stale. Fox, now owned by Rupert Murdoch, wasn't wild about the idea, to say the least. Bill Mechanic, who had just been made head of production there, says his boss, Peter Chernin, "was trying to find a way not to make the movie, with budgetary restrictions and time restrictions. But Warren was the wrong person to play those kinds of games with, since he's smarter than most of the people he deals with. So instead of getting him not to do it, Chernin just managed to get it pushed forward before we had a script that worked."

Beatty put Pikser to work on *Bulworth*, and hired Pat Caddell, both of whom had more interest in the subject than Toback presumably did. Pikser didn't know whether a prior script existed. "The impression I had is that we were working from scratch." Later, to his surprise, he stumbled across a 1965 Philippe de Broca film called *Tribulations of a Chinaman in China*, which Beatty had somehow neglected to mention. It was loosely based on a Jules Verne story of the same name. Jean-Paul Belmondo plays a millionaire who discovers, as the film opens, that he has lost his fortune. He resolves to kill himself, but his Chinese counselor says something like, "Don't kill yourself, we'll take out an insurance policy on your life, I will arrange for you to be killed, and then you can leave the money to your fiancée." He agrees, but then goes to a strip club, falls in love with one of the girls (Ursula Andress), and decides he wants to live. But his Chinese adviser has disappeared, and the remainder of the picture is devoted to Belmondo and Andress on the run from the thugs he has hired to kill him.

Beatty's inspiration was to take this plot and politicize it. Jay Billington Bulworth is the incumbent Democratic senator from California in the middle of the 1996 primary. He was once a Camelot-era idealist with lofty aspirations to change the world. We know this because his office is filled with photographs of the Kennedys, as well as Martin Luther King and a veritable pantheon of 1960s icons like Malcolm X and Huey Newton. As Toback points out, "Depression is the driving motivation behind Bulworth." Bulworth indeed hates himself for the hack he has become. Plus, his wife openly flaunts her infidelity. In one of many funny moments, she stalks out of a photo op on the steps of the Capitol when he's in the middle of a sentence. Bulworth, like Beatty, or at least as Beatty preferred to perceive himself or be perceived, is the slighted party.

In extremis, Bulworth trades his vote on an issue dear to the hearts of the insurance industry for a $10 million policy to be paid out to his daughter in the event of his death, and proceeds to arrange a hit on himself. He then has something of a nervous breakdown, freeing him to reclaim his old self. He becomes a version of Dostoevsky's holy idiot or Shakespeare's fool. Like a condemned man with nothing to lose, and no longer obliged to pander to venal special interests to win an election, he becomes a truth teller. He ends up in a hip-hop club dancing with Nina, a stunning black girl from the inner city half his age. Bulworth is energized and redeemed by meeting Nina, who becomes his muse. Lighting up a blunt, he delivers his message in doggerel, his honky version of rap. Now in love, he tries to call off the hit, but finds that that is easier wished for than done.

Beatty later said that the origins of *Bulworth* went all the way back to *Shampoo,* when he briefly considered having George Roundy open a beauty parlor with Richard Pryor in a black neighborhood. More to the point were the similarities with *Heaven Can Wait.* As in that picture, the comedy is ignited by the dissonance, the incongruity created by new wine in old bottles, in this case the reborn Bulworth in the old Bulworth's body. Nina is another incarnation of Julie Christie's Betty Logan.

Bulworth was the first and only picture Beatty ever made that focused on African-Americans. He was on good terms with black politicians like Jesse Jackson, and having grown up in the South, there was no way he could have been oblivious to racism. "I do remember the signs 'Colored' and 'White,'" he said. "I went to the largest school south of the Mason-Dixon line but there wasn't one black kid there. We thought Catholics were odd." Beatty recalled for the press that his namesake, his great-great-grandfather, had been a spy for the Confederate army during the Civil War, and that his great-aunts, Maggie and Bertie, referred to it as the "war between the states." He added, "They would never admit the war was about slavery." But, he continued, "My parents would have been appalled if anyone had accused them of being racist."

Both his parents loved Franklin Roosevelt. Shirley MacLaine remembers as a child returning from the movies, climbing the steps to the back porch of their house, and being met by their mother. She was "ashen and crying. 'President Roosevelt just died,' she cried. 'Oh, what will happen to us now?'" But, she goes on, father would "curse at the communists and bemoan the 'niggers' who ruined his lawn and often I'd see him reduced to tears in front of the television set at two o'clock in the morning while they played 'The Star Spangled Banner.'"

Still, Beatty rarely talked about race. In private, he delighted in shocking his liberal friends by using the Yiddish *schvartzes* to refer to blacks. "Warren is from fuckin' Virginia," says a friend. "I don't think he has thought very carefully, or seriously or empathetically, about the black experience in the U.S." Says Pikser, "I don't think he set out to do a film about race. It was more of a political thing than a racial thing." In the 1970s, especially after the *Swann* school desegregation decision in 1971 that cleared the way for busing, the Democrats came to believe that white voters were deserting the party over race. This was the issue they had really sold out over, the issue they were going to have to face if they were going to come out from under the shadow of the Republicans.

Starting in June 1995, Beatty, Toback, Pikser, and Caddell spitballed ideas. They pillaged the headlines of that summer and fall, when Bob Dole was attacking Hollywood for its lack of moral fiber, and Louis Farrakhan's march was swamping Washington with a million black men. Caddell more or less withdrew after the first couple of weeks.

As usual, Beatty savaged the writers with a blizzard of withering scorn. Toback may have been nominated for an Oscar for his script for *Bugsy,* but that was then and this was now. "Jimmy took the worst abuse I ever saw," Pikser continues. "Warren was really battering him for the stuff he had written, really being insulting. He would say, 'What were you high on when you wrote it? Is that why you think it's funny? Let me tell you it's not—can I suggest something to you? The next script you write, don't make it a comedy, okay? Because I don't think you really have any idea what funny is."

One day, Toback, Pikser, and Beatty had a meal at E.A.T. on Madison Avenue in New York, just up from the Carlyle, where Beatty was staying. Pikser continues, "Warren was just laying into Toback, it was just unspeakable: 'This is shit, this is garbage!' When Warren went to the toilet, I asked Jimmy, 'How can you take it?' He said, 'It's not personal. It's just that I'm sitting in this seat. If you were sitting in this seat you'd be getting it.' Then one day Jimmy wasn't there anymore. The way Warren has portrayed him to me, it would not be out of character for him to say, 'I'm not interested in this anymore,' and go home without even calling." But before he disappeared, he made significant contributions, especially to the opening Washington section.

When Toback left, Pikser became the sole writer. He asked himself, Why me? In this opinion, it was the same reason Beatty didn't hire May, Kushner, or Gelbart. "Warren takes a script credit on everything he's directed," Pikser says now. "He didn't want anybody to take the limelight away from him saying, 'This is not Warren Beatty's film.' I was the least threat. Nobody would say, He got all these ideas from Jeremy Pikser, like they would with Elaine. I would fight with him about stuff all the time. But there was no question about what we were fighting about: the best way to make a Warren Beatty film, not a Jeremy Pikser film."

Pikser was thrilled, but to some degree it was a case of, Be careful what you wish for. "My ability to get through *Bulworth* without killing myself or Warren proved that I had a core of mental health, because it was very difficult," he says. As Toback had predicted, once he was on the hot seat, he found himself the target of abuse. Beatty may have been passive-aggressive in other areas of his life but, Pikser adds, here "he was just aggressive." The writer continues. "He doesn't whine, he doesn't fight you through indirection. Giving writers breathing space to be creative is not much of an issue for him. I think he feels all you need to do is kick 'em in the ass. And it's not just writers. I think he feels this about the industry in general: the main enemy of good art is people not wanting to work hard. Whenever Warren was yelling at me, was mad about something in the script, he'd say, 'You have to take responsibility because you are the writer.' The rest of the time 'we' were the writers."

Pikser wasn't even sure he was the only writer. The days when Beatty would put all his eggs in one writer's basket were over, if they had ever really existed, and he had become more and more promiscuous, something that came naturally, or something that he may have learned from Charlie Feldman. The Beatty version was, as Pikser puts it, "serial monogamy in terms of writers," as well as a couple of flirtations and dalliances that happened sub rosa.

As usual, Beatty was consulting his political fellow travelers. "He was always coming in with new ideas, and I never knew where they came from," Pikser recalls. In the fall of 1995, the star asked May and Peter Feibleman to read a draft of the script. Pikser was surprised, given Beatty's and May's ups and downs, and realized that he had lost track of where they stood: "They don't speak and then they do speak. They stick knives in each other and then it's all lovey-dovey. Hollywood is like that." But their reaction made it clear. Pikser continues, "They did not think it was any good. We talked for three days, and the thing that was really devastating was that on the third day she said, 'Wait a minute, this is supposed to be a comedy? I had no idea!' She was pretending she didn't realize it was supposed to be funny. That was pretty fuckin' vicious. I'm such an Elaine idolator, I walked out of there devastated." May remarked to Feibleman, "That Jeremy's such a nice guy, what's he doing working for Warren?" For his part, Beatty was bitter about her take on the script, thought it was in bad faith, thought she was trying to hurt them. She was working on *Primary Colors,* based on Joe Klein's bestseller about Bill Clinton's 1992 primary campaign, and Beatty said, "She doesn't want us to make this movie."

Every day they started over on page one, even if they had reached page 70 the day before. "If something new occurred to him halfway down page one, we could spend the rest of the day arguing about it," Pikser continues. "He's very difficult to work with, but very rewarding. Occasionally I would say, 'What about this?'—something he hadn't suggested, and he'd say, 'Oh, that's great, I love it.' It's not, 'Oh, I didn't think of that, so I'm going to say, "I don't think that really works."' He really will take ideas from anyplace. For me it was a great pleasure if I can make him laugh. There was a lot of juice in that."

The script didn't take final shape until 1996, and by the time the picture came out in 1998, the second Clinton election was history.

Bulworth was as different from *Love Affair* as was possible. In fact, although he would never admit it, Beatty must have understood what an unspeakable embarrassment *Love Affair* was. Consequently, he and his team set out to be, in Pikser's words, "as brash and scabrous and shocking as we could at every turn. And to do it all as an expression of innocence." As British critic Philip French put it, "The film's hero is like a Mr. Deeds or a Mr. Smith afflicted with Tourette syndrome." Terms like "pussy" were flung about with abandon. One rap song Pikser wrote for *Bulworth* goes, "Pussy, pussy, pussy, I like it really fine, When you're a senator, you get it all the time." Originally, it was "The loose ones, the tight ones, I really like them all, When you live in Washington you hardly have to call." But, he remembers, "Warren thought that was over the line, bad taste, I had to pull that back. He went nuts for the expression 'nappy dugout,' which was ad-libbed by the actress Michele Morgan. It's a hip-hop expression for cunt, as in, nappy hair, dugout, like a canoe. Warren wanted to use the expression every time he could."

Almost more shocking in a mainstream studio movie than "pussy" and "nappy dugout," was "socialism," as in "socialized medicine." Beatty noted: "In America that's like saying cocksucker." Given how cautious he is in his public statements, many Beatty watchers were pleasantly surprised by how outspoken the picture was. "I was amazed that he'd go that far, because nobody goes that far," says Pikser. But "one thing about Warren is that he always wants to do things that he thinks nobody else has done. It was no different from making a movie about a Communist. While we were doing it, he kept saying, 'Let's go further.' He likes being bold."

The movie was an equal opportunity abuser, taking shots at Bill "Don't ask, don't tell" Clinton, Newt "Contract with America" Gingrich, single-taxer Steve Forbes, media conglomerates, the insurance and health care industries, deregulation, etc. What is unprecedented about *Bulworth* is that Beatty names names—individual politicians, specific corporations, particular lobbies—something few, if any, American movies had ever done. Films with politics on their minds usually make sweeping attacks on generic targets, like "big business" or "Washington." None of them was the smart bomb *Bulworth* proved to be, locking on to concrete targets, say, the Bank of America, or a sitting president. One example among many: "Clinton gets all weepy and Newt blames teenage moms . . ."

The script was dense with insider and not-so-insider jabs at people Beatty knew or knew of. There's a pushy reporter who asks Bulworth, who's separated from his wife, "Aren't you committing adultery?," a question journalists asked Gary Hart. Beatty wanted to stress the notion that the press's obsession with the sexual peccadilloes of politicians is equivalent to assassination by the pen, if not the bullet. Thus, the shadowy figure who haunts Bulworth throughout the movie, whom he suspects of being a hired gun, turns out to be a photographer working for the reporter who is trying to catch him in the act of adultery.

No one was safe. Bulworth's chief aide, Murphy, was loosely based on Caddell, who left Hart for Walter Mondale, whom he ostensibly hated. Murphy is portrayed as a person who could turn on a dime, could become furiously hostile toward the person he has devoted his life to serving. "I think Caddell thought he was giving us material about what those people were like from his wealth of experience," Pikser goes on. "He might have been shocked to know that Warren was thinking specifically of him as that character."

Beatty didn't stop with Caddell. He mocks Hart, as well as himself. In one scene, someone says of Bulworth, "If he didn't chase quite so much pussy, he might have been president," a line that could have applied to either of them. As Pikser explains, "There's a certain kind of politician where if you couldn't get your dick sucked by an intern, what would be the point of being a politician? Bulworth is a pussy hound, but 'quite' is the operative word, here. It's okay to chase pussy, so long as you don't do it so much that it distracts you, when it can become a problem. Warren was vehemently disgusted by Clinton's behavior as president. But the idea that this behavior is scandalous, he thought was preposterous."

Bulworth might have made Borat envious, but not everyone was fair game. At one point, Michael Eisner's name came up. He had recently gotten a lot of bad press for his bloated salary; a figure surfaced comparing how long it would take a wage slave making Mickey Mouse dolls for pennies in Haiti to earn what Eisner made in minutes, or something to that effect. The answer was: a lifetime. Beatty vetoed the suggestion, saying, "I don't want to do that."

"Why not?"

"Because Mike Eisner is a friend of mine."

The writers came up with a blizzard of bitingly funny, politically incorrect scenes. The story opens, according to a title, in March 1996, after Clinton and Dole have wrapped up the nominations of their respective parties. Bulworth, unshaven, face puffy, eyes red and teary, is reviewing the TV spots for his campaign. He can barely bring himself to mouth the neocon bromides attacking welfare and affirmative action that are required of him if he is going to outflank his Republican opponent from the right, à la Clinton and the DLC: "I believe in a hand up, not a handout." Moments later, on the campaign trail, Bulworth is in front of a black audience at Grace Church in South Central L.A., when he discards his fatuous canned speech—"We stand at the doorstep of a new millennium"—and instead tells them that the promises that were made to the black community in the wake of the South Central riots were so much hot air. When someone shouts, "You mean the Democratic Party don't care about the African-American community?" he replies, "Isn't that obvious? I mean, come on, you can have a Billion Man March. If you don't put down that malt liquor and chicken wings and get behind somebody other than a running back who stabs his wife, you're never going to get rid of somebody like me."

Bulworth moves on to a fund-raiser for Westside liberals. Hollywood being Hollywood, most of the deep pockets at the gathering are Jews, with some, like Stanley Sheinbaum, playing themselves. Bulworth tells them, "My guys are not stupid. They always put the big Jews on my schedule. . . . I'm sure Murphy put something bad about Farrakhan in here for you." He caps it all off by asking them why they make so much "crap," adding, "As long as you can pay, I'm going to do it all your way. Yes, money talks, and the people walk."

Most audacious, without a doubt, was the inspired notion of having Bulworth rap. By embedding the messages in ghetto rhythms, and making them funny, scandalous even, the audience actually heard them instead of rolling its collective eyes and tuning out, as was so often the case in message movies that simply preached. The risk was, of course, that he'd be laughed off the screen. But, as Pikser observes, "They were never supposed to be good raps." The cadences and rhymes were closer to Edward Lear than Biggie Smalls or Jay-Z. Robert Kennedy nephew Bobby Shriver introduced Beatty to Russell Simmons, head of Def Jam Records. He began hanging out with the stars of the rap world, Suge Knight, Tupac Shakur, and Dr. Dre. His reputation as a cocksman eased his way. "Warren Beatty is a mack," Simmons said, impressed. "He's been with a lot of women."

They had always had a big problem with the character of Nina. Originally, she was the hit woman. But they decided that nobody who was mature enough to be attractive to Bulworth would be stupid enough to kill a senator. And if they kept her scheme secret—they didn't want to tip off the audience—it gave her less to do, which made for a hole in their female lead. Eventually, Beatty decided her role was to lure him into a trap, that is, she became an accomplice, not the killer herself, throwing Pikser into despair. He said, "We need to rewrite everything to make that work."

"No we don't. We only need a few small changes."

"That doesn't help you, because you're still not getting enough of the character. Besides, there are too many assassins, would-be assassins, faux assassins. It's gonna confuse the audience."

"No it's not. It's really very simple."

"Are you going to be in the audience to explain it to everybody? 'Cause it may make sense, but nobody's gonna be able to get it from watching the film."

And so it went, draft after draft. Pikser was being paid by Fox for one draft, which was supposed to take about six weeks. "But the problem with Warren is that there is only one draft—one draft that gets rewritten ten thousand times until the movie is completed," he explains. "And Warren's notion of loyalty is that once you're in, you stay in. And you keep working until the film is shot and he's happy." Pikser had been writing drafts from June to September in L.A. His wife and young children were back in New York. After fourteen weeks on what was ostensibly a six-week job, he told Beatty, "The contract is over."

"We haven't finished a draft yet."

"I've written twelve drafts, and you're calling it all one draft. We're going over the same stuff again and again. We've come to an end three or four times, you've shown something to the studio, and I'm not getting paid. So my work is done. I want a contract for another draft."

"You're betraying me," Beatty replied, furious. To Pikser, it was déjà vu. He thought, Just like *Reds*. He drives you crazy, and then when you say you can't take it anymore, he says, "You're quitting on me." But this time he told Beatty:

"If you don't want to pay me, I will continue to work for free, but from home, in New York. I'll fax you pages, we'll keep talking, on the phone."

He went back to New York, sent Beatty a bill, and Fox paid it. They continued to talk, but the conversations dribbled away.

Beatty would fly in occasionally, try to persuade him to resume work. One such trip occurred in April 1996. Beatty said, "Why don't you come back and work on this. You know, I'm just going to get somebody else."

"Then get somebody else. Or, you're gonna have to pay me. Make me an offer."

"I can't make you an offer. What I would offer you would be an insult, and I won't do that."

"So, insult me."

"No, I'm not going to insult you."

"Then, I'm going to Europe. With my family, a vacation."

Pikser was as good as his word.

In August 1996, Pikser heard from Beatty for the first time in months. On the phone, the director told him, "We're gonna start shooting this thing in September," and asked, "Do you want to be part of it?"

"Are you gonna pay me?"

"Of course I'm going to pay you!"

By that time, most of the cast had been selected. Beatty met with actor Michael Lerner (*Barton Fink*) for the aide, the part that went to Oliver Platt. "He always said 'flop sweat' was the key ingredient in the character. He wanted somebody who could really do flop sweat," says Lerner. Beatty told him, "I'm not an actor, I'm a reactor. So you have to drive the scenes." Then he didn't hire him, said he was too old.

Paul Sorvino played the lobbyist. Beatty flattered him, saying, "You're one of the truly greatest actors in the world of your age."

"So how come I have no money, Warren?"

"Because you haven't learned to eat shit yet."

Beatty considered Tupac Shakur for the part of Darnell, Nina's brother, but thought he was unreliable. When he was killed in the middle of production, Beatty's comment was, "God, can you imagine?" Ice Cube was another candidate, but Don Cheadle was so impressive in *Devil in a Blue Dress* that Beatty gave him the part. Writer Amiri Baraka (formerly LeRoi Jones) was cast as Rastaman the griot, a sort of one-man Greek chorus.

The most difficult part to cast was Nina. For a long time the role was going to go to a prominent black actress, but then Beatty started talking about Halle Berry. According to Pikser, he said, "I need to play it with someone I could really fall in love with, and I believe I could really fall in love with her. And I don't so much believe I could fall in love with [the other actress].' " Why he felt as he did is unclear, although several times he said of the original actress something like, "I hear she eats a lot of pussy, more pussy [than I do!]" (If indeed Beatty found bisexuality unromantic, that did not prevent his reported interest in gay women. According to Sandra Bernhard, "Rumor had it that he liked to sleep with lesbians.")

Beatty was alive to the significance of every detail in his movies, and he not only surrounded himself with the best of the best—the Sylberts, Canoneros, and Storaros—he also considered the semiotics of the crew. On *Reds*, he had hired Zina Voynow, Eisenstein's sister-in-law. He always thought of *Bulworth* as a Frank Capra film, so he was at pains to give it the Capra imprimatur. He hired Frank Capra's grandson, Frank III, as first AD.

Pikser flew out to L.A., drove up Beverly Glen to Beatty's office, where he had been working before on a borrowed desk in a storeroom. He recalls, "I walked in, and there was Aaron Sorkin! Nobody had even told me that Aaron had been working on it, which was a violation of Guild rules. He had a whole office set up, with his own desk—it was the Aaron Sorkin suite! I had never had anything like that." Sometime in the spring of 1996, Beatty presumably put *Ocean of Storms* on the back burner and asked Sorkin to do a pass on *Bulworth*.

But Beatty and Sorkin were not a good match. According to Pikser, the star complained that Sorkin was impossible to work with. Sorkin said the same of him. "I could tell that Warren and Aaron had had a rough time together," Pikser recalls. "As far as I knew, Aaron didn't even realize that I'd ever worked on the first draft." Sorkin seemed to be as surprised to see Pikser as Pikser was surprised to see him. Pikser continues, "He was like, 'What is this guy doing here and why is he discussing the third act? I've taken a lot of abuse from you, and now you bring this guy in? Who's gonna rewrite me? In my face? Fuck it!' And then the next day, Aaron was gone."

Like Beatty, Sorkin was a Democrat, but his work presented a sunny, wish-fulfillment take on American politics that was almost comically at odds with the reality. "We threw out 90 percent of his script, even though it wasn't that different," Pikser continues. "His ending, his third act, had Bulworth back in his office in Washington. He'd come to his senses. Everything was the same, except that he had a photograph of Nina on his desk. The implication was he'd be more liberal now, because he had a black girlfriend—and somehow that constituted a happy ending. I said to Warren, 'If you do his ending, I will find you and I will kill you.' It would have been an enormous sellout and would have led to a really ugly fight if he had stayed around."

Toback, who should have known better, having had more experience than Pikser navigating the treacherous Beatty waters, was also surprised to discover that Sorkin had space in the offices. But, as he puts it, "Warren always likes to have an alternative universe." The scrum of writers threatened to make the writing credit arbitration process a nightmare. Beatty had his way with Toback, convincing him not to contest the dual Beatty-Pikser credit.

As he had made clear from the start, Beatty wanted first writing credit, with Pikser second. "Annette once said I had been a great help to Warren in writing the script to *Bulworth*," Pikser recalls. "Tell me the fucking pages that he wrote! I've got literally 1,500 different files on my computer for the *Bulworth* script. He has none." Still, he says, "Warren is the author of it to a very large degree, or at least half of it. On *Reds*, Elaine May had a million ideas, so in a lot of ways he was reacting to her ideas. With *Bulworth*, it was much more Warren saying, 'I have a vision of something like this. I want to capture this, I want to capture that.' Beyond that there was a lot of, 'This is shit, this isn't what I meant at all.' It was about what he wanted. Until you got what he wanted, you don't have it. You're writing to order, and in that sense it was his script."

13

IN HIS OWN WAY

———————

How *Godzilla* stepped on *Bulworth,*

and Beatty launched and then popped the *Bulworth* Bubble,

while *Town & Country* almost ended his career.

———————

"Warren could have done everything, but he just kept getting in his
own way. He fucked himself."

— *Bo Goldman*

$\mathbf{P}$RODUCTION BEGAN IN the fall of 1996, but Beatty realized the
script still needed work, and he took a hiatus of several months
to polish it further. (By the time the picture would be released
two years later, the second Clinton election was history.)

Pikser was afraid that *Bulworth* might embarrass both Beatty and
himself. He knew that his friend had done many bold movies in his
time, but none of them had been as dicey as this one. Allowing himself
to look bad was one thing, but a middle-class white guy rapping was
like wandering into heavy traffic wearing a blindfold. Beatty was no
Eminem, and he was just inviting derision, hanging a sign on his back
that reads, "Jerk!" Says Pikser, "*Reds* was doing something that was politically unheard of, but I don't think there was any fear that he couldn't
pull it off, or that he would be ridiculed for it. With *Bulworth*, he was
doing stuff where people might say, 'What the fuck is this?'" And sup-

pose, as May and Feibleman had said, it wasn't funny. Pikser adds, "If they were right, we were fucked. And how do you know?"

Bulworth's big moment, his rap debut, occurs in front of a crowd at the Beverly Wilshire Hotel. Beatty blew out his knee sprinting from a church to his limo. When he arrived at the location he was in serious pain, unable to walk without a bad limp. The scene had to be shot in one day, and most of the time was devoted to recording his arrival, before he starts rapping. When he finally began to perform, he was rushed and clumsy. He couldn't get more than three or four lines out in a row before he was brought up short. As they were leaving, he asked Pikser, "What do you think we got, on a scale of one to ten?" Pikser didn't know what to say. He thought, That's it, a total disaster, the picture's gonna fail. But he said, "Seven," thinking, It's a two, but what's the point of saying it? He's not going to do it over again. But somehow, editor Bob Jones made it work, splicing together bits and pieces. At least half the verses were dubbed in later, over cutaways.

Beatty was using a lot of actors he'd never used before, in important roles. With the exceptions of Sorvino and Richard Sarafian, everyone else—Christine Baranski, Don Cheadle, Oliver Platt, and Halle Berry were new to him. But he was warm and attentive, never critical, free, even effusive with his praise, and a good audience. Only Cheadle was uncomfortable, didn't like playing a drug dealer, felt it was racial stereotyping. Cheadle used to say that he felt that the real motivation of the Bulworth character is that he is a white man after dark meat. And the rest of it was "bullshit." Nicole Pecorini recalls that "Don thought that Warren was trying to make the black point of view his own, without succeeding, that it was a bit of a rape." According to Pikser, Beatty felt that Cheadle wanted to be his sexual rival for Nina and couldn't accept the fact that that wasn't going to happen, but Beatty let him rewrite his own dialogue anyway.

Like others Beatty has worked with, Pecorini was struck by his awareness of the camera. "He knows how to get the light exactly the way he wants it. There were scenes in the car where he had to look out the window, when he wouldn't move his head because he didn't want to show his bad side, his right side."

As usual, there was little love lost between Beatty and the crew. Jones was there every day. "I think he feels he gets more from the crew if they're intimidated," he says. Then about sixty years old, Jones had edited three of Beatty's pictures, and liked him. Still, he says, "He can be very cutting." One morning the editor had oral surgery, and then went to a screening of some footage in the afternoon. Beatty was out of sorts. Jones recalls, "He said, 'Look at Bob, he's so old he can't even keep up anymore.' He said this in the projection room. In front of other people. My jaw was falling apart. I thought, Too old to work! Goddammit, Warren!" On the other hand, says Pecorini, "I would always work with Warren, regardless of his foibles. He has thickness, depth. He has a lot of culture in him, reads a lot, and he's an extremely pleasant man to deal with."

The production wrapped in February 1997.

THE ENDING of the movie had been a vexing problem throughout the script stage and production, and continued to be well into post. "For the two years we were writing this script, we never had him shot," recalls Pikser. "We had all these other endings that Warren hated. They were all uplifting Capra endings. The only reason we wanted him shot was because we didn't know what to do with him at the end. How do you fix a broken world in a movie? That's the trouble with political comedy. If you really set out the problem in anything like its true dimensions, you can't solve it in the third act. You can't cure American politics, you can't make this guy president and save America, that would be ridiculous." Then producer Pieter Jan Brugge came up with the idea: he's shot. (Beatty says there were never alternative endings; Bulworth was always going to be shot.)

Still, the question remained, Does he live or does he die? As the picture stands, he lies motionless on the pavement. The intention seemed to be to indicate that he was still alive. As the film fades to black, Rastaman (Baraka) whispers, "Hold on, Bulworth, hold on," but it's so faint it's barely audible. Beatty actually filmed an additional scene in which Bulworth is shown recovering in the hospital, but it was never used. (For years Beatty clung to the notion of making a sequel, which would begin with that scene.) When that scene ended up on the cutting room floor, it seemed that the "assassination" might be reshot, with Bulworth showing some signs of life, but Beatty didn't think it was necessary. Pikser disagreed. He picked his fights carefully. "It depended on how worn down I was, how long we'd been at it, how badly I wanted to get the fuck out of the room, how important I thought the issue was." In this case, he thought the nature of the ending was important enough to go to the mat over.

"Do you want the message of this film to be, if you stand up and say what you believe in, you will get killed! That's what you may be putting out."

"It's not clear that he's dead."

Beatty wanted people to argue over whether Bulworth is dead or alive. Pikser felt that that was not the right question. He wanted Bulworth to be hovering between life and death, which would throw into relief what he thought was a more important question, namely, as Rastaman exhorts the senator, "Don't be no ghost, Bulworth! Be a spirit!" that is, an inspiration. Pikser explains, "You can be dead, and be alive, and you can be alive and be dead. At the beginning of this movie, Bulworth is the latter, a ghost. At the end of the movie, Bulworth is a spirit. And that's the meaning of the film for me." Pikser didn't think the ending was ambiguous so much as it was muddled. "But I'm fairly certain that Warren did not intend to say that if you stand up you're going to be gunned down."

According to the terms of the settlement with Fox, Beatty explained that he gained total artistic freedom, while Fox retained marketing control. Still, he was unhappy with the campaigns for his last several movies, and he was not one to stand by passively while Fox messed up this one. Fox senior executive VP Tom Sherak confessed, "If you ask, 'Will Warren phone you five times in a day,' the answer is yes." Commented Beatty, "I think that the company did not know what to make of the movie. The picture caused a strange sort of paralysis." Mechanic says, "It was difficult to sell. A white guy in a black world, so who's the audience? Certainly you're not going to go inner city and think that Warren Beatty is important to them, and then you're not going to go into the white world and say these are relevant issues, even if they should be."

Beatty campaigned for the picture on TV shows popular with black viewers, appeared on the black cable network BET, and the talk show *Vibe*. The rap soundtrack became a bestseller and hit the R&B charts. The picture was screened for a black audience in New York at Co-op City. Beatty was hoping that they would find the picture funny, and that that demographic would be the engine that drove the box office. But the surveys indicated that although most of the audience seemed to like it, they didn't love it. That's when Beatty began to suspect that he might be in trouble. The problem was compounded by the fact that Cheadle wouldn't campaign for the movie.

Bulworth opened Friday, May 15, 1998, four years after *Love Affair*, on 1,800 screens; the highly anticipated *Godzilla* was released five days later on 3,310 screens. Fox claimed that opening its picture against *Godzilla* was "creative counter-programming," but *Godzilla*, released by Sony, just squashed *Bulworth*, and Beatty regarded the peculiar timing as Fox's effort to bury it, by no means an improbable surmise given Fox owner Rupert Murdoch's tilt to the right.

The reviews, invoking Preston Sturges and *Network* were, with some exceptions, glowing. They gave Beatty high marks for risk taking, praised him for bravery for heaping ashes on his image and allowing himself to look foolish. In *The New York Times*, Janet Maslin praised the picture as "the kind of imaginative, anything-goes escapade that movie audiences, in the days before the pre-sold, pre-fab blockbuster, had the luxury of taking in stride." Doubtless referring to his last movie, she called him "a magically revitalized Warren Beatty, who has directed this political satire with jubilant wit and energy." Nor were the reviewers insensitive to the irony involved in Murdoch's studio releasing such an incendiary picture. As Joel Siegel put it on *Good Morning America*, "For Warren Beatty and 20th Century-Fox to make a movie like this is like getting Bambi to do a 30-second spot for the National Rifle Association." From a political point of view, it was *Reds* all over again, albeit on a smaller scale.

Not all the reviews were favorable, especially in the black press, where Beatty got worked over by some prominent activists and social commentators. He was a little taken aback, asked Pikser, "What should we say to these people?" but generally handled himself well. Jesse Jackson nailed him for cynicism and defeatism. Halle Berry defended the picture on the *Today* show, saying, "Spike Lee could make the same movie and they would say he's just an angry black man. I feel really proud that someone like Warren would speak for us. And, as hurtful as it might be to some people, the reality is that this is the country in which we live, and let's take a look at it, let's not sugarcoat it and pretend it's not out there, because it is."

Others took the opposite tack, arguing that the picture sentimentalizes blacks in the tradition of liberals like Norman Mailer, whose celebrated essay "The White Negro" was published in 1957. In *Bulworth*, the black underclass is the repository of sexuality, vitality, and truth, while whites are repressed and hypocritical. It's only when Bulworth is able to tap into the life force of the streets that he is able to liberate himself from the straitjacket of opportunism. For them, when Nina says, "You mah niggah, Bulworth"—later mocked in an episode of Larry David's *Curb Your Enthusiasm*—it was the last straw.

Garry Wills, writing in *The New York Review of Books*, zeroed in on the scene in which Bulworth gets some street kids to eat ice cream instead of selling drugs, and takes their side against the cops. He wrote, "This makes the dread crime lord L.D. (Cheadle) conclude that, hey, if one senator is going to be a truth-teller, then he'll change his evil ways, let Nina's brother off if he'll work for the senator, and bless the inter-racial union of Bulworth and Nina. Of course, that dream gets smashed when the sole truth-teller is shot. But it was a goofy and escapist dream all along."

Pikser admits, "We were aware that it was kind of thin ice. A lot of people were upset that Halle Berry would have been with Warren, say-ing, 'Why should our black queen be with some old white guy?' If you do a movie which is to a large extent about racism, in which the hero is a white guy, that's gotta be racist to a degree, because it's saying that the solution to the problem has to be some white guy, instead of saying, the real hero for this situation should have been Don Cheadle. But Warren Beatty is our star. That was a given.

"I also think you have to cop to the fact that the Baraka character is the magic Negro. But at the same time you could also say it's an endur-ing theme of American history that the soul of our politics has relied on black people to give it progressive force. Sure, right-wing racists call it a cliché, because they don't want to hear it. But we were turning Amos 'n' Andy on their heads. Instead of having black people being funny because they're trying to be white people, wear white clothes and say highfalutin words they don't understand, this is a white senator who's trying to sound black, and being ridiculous in the process. The real question is, Who's the joke on? In this movie, the joke is not on the black people. Ever! The joke is always on the white people. And to me that's what makes it antiracist."

Bulworth took in $10 million on the first weekend. Exit polls showed the audience was mostly men over twenty-five. Young African-American males were not showing up in sufficient numbers to make the film a hit. *Godzilla,* which grossed $44 million on its opening weekend, was doubtless siphoning off blacks (and whites) who might otherwise have gone to see it.

In truth, the picture had problems that had nothing to do with race. Beatty had followed a tried-and-true formula that other filmmakers—both left and right—had used in the past for message movies, namely, to arrange a shotgun marriage between message and genre. Beatty himself had done it before and largely gotten away with it. But in *Bulworth,* the marriage didn't quite take. The first two-thirds of the picture, in which the premise is laid out and Bulworth's character is revealed, is an achievement of the first order, as rapier-sharp a political satire as has ever been seen on American screens, with nearly every line a zinger. We watch agog, bystanders at a slow motion, multicar collision, as Bulworth crashes and burns on a pyre of straight talk. But in the last third, Beatty paid the price for his Faustian bargain with genre: the plot takes over, and the picture is held hostage to its conventions, with the clanky machinery they demand—a clutter of chases, assassins, and the like. Pikser was right: there is way too much business, too many shadowy figures lurking at the periphery atop buildings or behind parked cars, confusing the audience by smothering the sparks struck by the friction between truth and hypocrisy that fuels its fire.

Bulworth also has too many false endings, which brings us back to the issue of the "real" ending. Beatty is a subtle man working in an often unsubtle medium, at least as practiced by the studios, so it's no wonder he sometimes had difficulty ending his movies. But the problem over the ending of *Bulworth* goes deeper than that, speaks to Beatty's own ambivalence about how well or how poorly democracy is working, as well as his mixed feelings about playing a more prominent political role than he has. He may not have intended that the message of this film be that those who stand up for what they believe will invariably suffer for it, even unto death, but this is the message that emerges. (It's possible that the inverse is also true: throughout Beatty's career, he has been famous for his secretiveness, as if secretiveness, withholding himself, will protect him from death.)

Indeed, Bulworth's transformation, his truth telling, is predicated on his impending death, his suicide, in effect, as if only through death is he able to defy the powers that be. Like the 1960s icons Bulworth surrounds himself with in the opening scenes, he has to die. As history has shown, heaven can't wait. There appeared to be no place for truth speaking in the twilight of the American Century. Despite the aura of ambiguity that Beatty sought to protect, innocent heroes die too regularly in his films for it to be an accident.

At its heart, *Bulworth* is about the clash between innocence and experience, the structuring axis around which many of his films revolve. It is an iteration of a Hollywood staple, the story of a man who rediscovers his youth, who grows younger as he grows older. Children in *Bulworth* are pitted against corrupt adults of both races: whites with their money, blacks with their drugs. As he sheds the hypocrisies of the grown-up white world, and gives himself over to pleasure, Bulworth, appropriating ghetto styles, comes to look like an overgrown child, wearing a cap, baggy shorts, and sneakers, while nibbling on an ice cream cone, always the talisman, the signifier of innocence in Beatty's world. In the Rousseau-like ideology of this picture, the ghetto is no jungle, but a garden, a state of nature, a refuge where he's safe. At the very least, as someone who came to fatherhood late in life, Beatty was well aware of the magical ability of children to keep their parents young, while at the same time by their very youth, dramatizing the inevitability of their parents' deaths. Isabel Ashley Beatty was born January 11, 1997. When Ella, his youngest child, born April 8, 2000, turns eighteen, he will be eighty-one. Beatty would come to say repeatedly to those late-marrying bachelors in his circle, "Don't do as I did, don't wait as long as I waited."

Beatty and Pikser were nominated for Best Original Screenplay, *Bulworth*'s sole nomination. As it turned out, *Bulworth* was shut out. But Beatty remains proud of *Bulworth*, as he should. "Was there something this radical before that from the mainstream? I don't think so. If you go back and you examine the Capra movies, I cannot tell you where his social or economic interests lay. Nor could I tell you anyone else's, really. Very few movies about politicians make a decision to go ideologically in one direction or the other, because of the common assumption that you lose half your audience. It would be considered financially quixotic to take a position."

Still, we need to ask the question, Is Bulworth Beatty, or better, how much of Bulworth is in Beatty? It is a question that would come up subsequently, in "real" life, with semiserious consequences.

———

MICHAEL LAUGHLIN'S script for *Town & Country* began with Porter Stoddard, a successful, over-groomed architect on the wrong side of fifty, heading to France for his wedding. The hook was that we don't know which of several preternaturally lovely women he intends to marry. The film is devoted to a flashback that works its way through the twists and turns of serial infidelity back to the opening, when the audience is surprised to discover he's remarrying his former wife, Ellie, a similarly successful and well-appointed fabric designer. Porter and Ellie appear to be the perfect pair, with two perfect children, living in the perfect apartment across from the Metropolitan Museum of Art on New York's Fifth Avenue. Needless to say, it enjoys majestic views of leafy Central Park. They also summer in a grand home in the Hamptons the size of the Winter Palace—we're a long way from *Reds* here. But for Stoddard, apparently, too much is not enough. He is having an affair with a cellist, pictured early in the movie playing her instrument in the nude, the cello cradled suggestively between her thighs, while he eyes her from the bed, transfixed. One dalliance leads to another as surely as summer follows spring, and when Ellie finally discovers the awful truth, she tells him to take a hike and steps out on her own.

Laughlin, from a wealthy Illinois farm family, came out to L.A. in the early 1960s to go to law school, but the lure of Hollywood proved too much, and he ended up as a producer—of B-movies, albeit superior B-movies. Laughlin's star blinked dimly on the far periphery of the Beatty galaxy. He married Leslie Caron when she was on the rebound from the young heartthrob, and lived with her in the U.K. in the mid-1960s. Later, he married former Beatty assistant and ex-wife of Dick Sylbert, novelist Susanna Moore.

Laughlin wrote the script with Beatty in mind. "It had to do with Warren's deep tenderness towards his past girlfriends," he says. He was "someone who bounced amusingly from woman to woman. They were all morally sophisticated, adorable creatures." The writer gave his script to Beatty's office mate Fred Roos, who was producing on his own. (He had been Francis Coppola's casting director and then producer for many years.) Roos passed it along to Andy Karsch, who was partnered with Sidney Kimmel, an apparel millionaire, now making movies. Karsch took the script to Beatty's agents at CAA.

"When Warren told me he was going to do *Bulworth* before *Town & Country*, I was in total panic," recalls Karsch. "I thought *Bulworth* was the most ridiculous thing I ever heard; it's going to end his career. The stocking cap and the rapping, yadayada? You'd picture it, and think, My God, no. I desperately wanted him to direct *Town & Country*. But after *Bulworth,* he wasn't going to do it. It's just a lot of work."

At least, Karsch thought, it was a "go" movie. While Beatty was making *Bulworth,* CAA had set it up with New Line, a former independent company which by then was a mini-major owned by Warner Brothers and run by co-chairmen and co-CEOs Bob Shaye and Michael Lynne. In the light of future events, New Line's decision would appear problematic, but at the time, there was a certain logic to it. A fan of Beatty and protégé of Shaye, the division's precocious young production head Mike De Luca seemed to have a charmed life. He was a likable, gregarious man enjoying a spectacular run of cheap hits like *The Mask* (1994), *Se7en* (1995), *Blade* (1998), and *Austin Powers: The Spy Who Shagged Me* (1999), as well as cult favorites like *Boogie Nights* (1997) and *Dark City* (1998) that made him virtually untouchable. Like many young executives of that generation, he had missed the highs and lows—mostly highs—of the 1970s, and regarded the survivors of the New Hollywood with awe. (The executive did his best to hold up the banner of that storied decade; in April 1998, he made headlines by being caught getting a blow job at a William Morris party.)

De Luca was thrilled by the opportunity to do a Beatty film, particularly after failing to get the actor into *Boogie Nights.* De Luca explains, "I felt that *Town & Country* was a comedy of manners about how hard it was to maintain a marriage at that age—not having been married myself or yet at that age." More to the point, *The First Wives Club* had come out of nowhere to mint money that year (it would gross $105.5 million domestically before its run ended), and the production head thought those numbers, in his words, "showed that there was a demographic that was underserved by most Hollywood movies." The picture was budgeted at around $35 million. Beatty's cut was $10 million, a lot of money for someone at that stage of his career—he was now fifty-nine—just to act, and it doubtless influenced his decision to commit.

At first, everything proceeded swimmingly. Says Lynn Harris, the New Line executive assigned to the picture, "After *Bulworth,* I think Warren was genuinely looking forward to just being an actor." But it wasn't that simple. As a result of nearly forty years of filmmaking, his numerous hits, Oscars, Oscar nominations, and a gossip sheet more twisted than Mulholland Drive, he had become the very definition of the eight-hundred-pound gorilla. No one understood this better than Beatty himself. He knew that if an extra sneezed during a take or a gaffer fell off a ladder, he would be blamed. He knew he had to protect himself. If anything untoward happened at all, according to Karsch, "It was clear to Warren that he was going to be the fall guy."

For Beatty, it was a dilemma. "It's a tough thing when people know that you can direct and you can write and you can produce, and act in a movie," he says. "You have to be very, very careful, if you sign on as an actor for hire, because you don't want people to think that you are in there trying to do those other jobs. On the other hand, you want to participate. You have to walk a very, very fine line."

Beatty found himself some protection by securing two more sets of eyes. "One of his stipulations was that I be on the set all the time, almost like one of the Witnesses in *Reds*," Karsch says. "If I wasn't on the set, he wasn't on the set." The star also requested that Lynn Harris, as a representative of New Line, also be there every day from call to wrap for the length of the entire shoot.

The next step was to find a director. Needless to say, it wasn't easy. Recalls Karsch, "People just didn't want to take Warren on, given what had happened with Glenn Gordon Caron." As he had on previous films, Beatty had, according to Harris, "approval over the director, writers, cast, and what-not." Karsch and company came up with lists, placed phone calls, had lunches.

Then, one unlucky day, Laughlin had a brainstorm, Peter Chelsom. He says ruefully, "I feel kind of responsible." With several moderately successful lighter-than-air comedies to his credit, Chelsom wasn't an absurd choice. "We'd all seen *Funny Bones* and we'd all seen *Hear My Song*," continues Karsch. "They were great." Their comfort level was raised by the fact that Leslie Caron had been in *Funny Bones*. Laughlin continues, "Leslie spoke highly of him. I talked to Warren and put him in the best possible light." They hired him, along with his producing partner, Simon Fields. It turned out to be Leslie Caron's revenge.

Beatty populated *Town & Country* with friends and people he had worked with before and trusted. And as in the past, they were first-class actors. He went to Mazursky, asked him to take a minor part. Mazursky read the script, said, "I don't think you should do this unless it's rewritten. There's just not enough here, Warren." He recalls, "My words were harsh, and he was a little pissed. He shouldn't have done it. He's too good for that. He's the guy who made *Bonnie and Clyde*, *Reds*, *Shampoo*, *Heaven Can Wait*. What did he need that one for? He did it anyway, and it was a terrible movie."

Beatty recruited Goldie Hawn to play his best friend's wife. Andie MacDowell and Nastassia Kinski signed up to play Porter Stoddard's girlfriends. Charlton Heston came on board as MacDowell's father, a colorful gun-toting lunatic. Then Gérard Depardieu, who was to play the best friend, broke his leg in a motorcycle accident and was replaced by Garry Shandling. Shandling, who had appeared in *Love Affair*, was still close to Beatty. He was about to do *What Planet Are You From?*, which he had written for himself to star in and direct. By some accounts, one of the reasons he took the part in *Town & Country* was because it was small, requiring no more than fifteen days' work over a period of three weeks, at most a month. (Somewhere along the way, the sexual orientation of his character was reversed from straight to gay.) Beatty also saw to it that Billy Fraker, who had shot *Heaven Can Wait*, was hired.

Beatty asked Laughlin to approach Diane Keaton about playing the part of Ellie. She was puzzled. At lunch with Laughlin at Mr. Chow, she asked, "Why doesn't Warren just pick up the phone himself and call me?" It was Julie Christie redux. As Buck Henry thought when Beatty hired him to co-direct *Heaven Can Wait*, "Their relationship was so edgy, he knew he was gonna have to have somebody who could talk to her without her getting irritated." Keaton joined the cast, although she didn't seem thrilled. "Not that there was overt hostility, but certainly Diane at that time wasn't exactly on the best of terms with Warren," says Karsch. "She was very disengaged, didn't participate in the meetings. It was give her the pages, bup-a-bup. She wanted to do the part of Ellie and leave. There wasn't a lot of communication between Diane and Warren."

Keaton required a "stop date," a day when the production had to let her go, finished or not, to direct her own movie, *Hanging Up*. New Line accepted her condition. After all, the date was April 16, 1999, a long way off. There was no way they wouldn't be finished, or at least that's the way it seemed at the time. Beatty, whose own productions went on forever, knew enough never to accept stop dates. "It's a chancy thing to do," he says. But he was not the producer.

New Line was pleased. "The reason we all liked Diane and Goldie was because they gave us a *First Wives Club* feel," explains De Luca.

(Both actresses were in that movie.) "Since the movie was targeted at that demographic, we thought anything that would recall that movie and that kind of audience would be a good thing. And we also thought it was also a neat nod to *Shampoo,* and the other movies that Warren had done with either Diane or Goldie." Which is to say *Town & Country* was *Shampoo* twenty years later, as if George Roundy had married Jackie, with Keaton in the Christie role, one ex-girlfriend standing in for another.

At last, New Line breathed a sigh of relief. Explains Harris, "We felt, Warren's signed on to this script, he's signed on to this director, we're gonna go shoot this movie in forty days, or fifty days, whatever, and we'll have a great Warren Beatty movie." It was left to Beatty to sound a note of warning. Karsch recalls, "I was talking about the people we assembled, and how we'd have a great time, and Warren said, 'If it's a great time, it ain't gonna be any good.' " That proved to be a prophetic remark.

As soon as Beatty and Chelsom began working together, it was evident that they were ill matched. For one thing, the director was starstruck. Laughlin was still working on the script, coming up with new scenes. According to him, "Peter would read it, and say, 'Oh, this is great! Please, I beg of you, let me take credit for this with Warren!' Imagine being inside that person's head, the insecurities—it's terrifying." To several of the participants, it seemed evident that Chelsom was seriously overmatched by Beatty. Laughlin continues, "He was threatened by Warren. He was uncomfortable with Warren. He worried that he might be in the position of the director of *Love Affair.* Peter wanted to protect his turf."

Gradually, it became clear that the production had to begin in June 1998 or not at all. Says Karsch, "We had stop dates and pay-or-play commitments with absolutely everybody, and we couldn't push it any further. Suddenly it was pulling out of the station and Warren had to get on. But he just never focused on it because he's such a master at pushing movies back, he never thought it was going to roll when it did. So Warren said, 'But we don't have a script.' And we started having script meetings. And things started changing."

According to New Line's Harris, "Had the original Laughlin script been shot word for word, it would have been a delightful little movie. It was filled with holes, for sure, but it was sexy and daring and fun." Karsch agrees, "It wasn't that there wasn't a script. These actors committed to something for a reason. These aren't easy people to get on board, and they weren't going to sign on just because of Warren. Certainly not Diane." One source says, "It seemed as though perhaps Warren hadn't read the script all that carefully before he got involved. When he did, he got nervous. He started rejiggering."

Like many of the other writers the star worked with, Laughlin didn't want to play Beatty's game, where every word is up for grabs. He says, "I didn't want to defend anything," he recalls. "It's in such bad taste to try to put the writer in the corner and say, 'Okay, now tell us again why this is good.' Don't ask me to explain the jokes. End of conversation." But not with Beatty. He continues, "Warren is just an indecisive actor who wants to talk about everything. He has the ability to drive people to distraction. To chew on the discussion endlessly. I always tried to keep him in the world that he's in with women—you see the girl, you want her, you get her." Or, as Buck Henry puts it, "I don't think he second-guesses himself about life as he does about art."

But De Luca says that Beatty was right, there were script problems. One was fairly minor, the race of a baby that his character was supposed to have fathered. It was Asian, proving—in a jokey way—that he couldn't be the father, but according to De Luca, they agreed it was "corny and objectionable. We always knew we wanted to change that." But once the skin of the script was pricked, it started to bleed, and the trickle of blood quickly turned into a hemorrhage. Continues De Luca, "That started a series of rewrite conversations that upset the apple cart, and we were rewriting when we were into preproduction."

Beatty also didn't like the third act. In Laughlin's script, Porter, accompanied by a new girlfriend, Eugenie, who would be played by Andie MacDowell, has returned to New York from Aspen to get a divorce from Ellie. But no sooner do they arrive than Eugenie, a fast-talking type A who turns out to be a pathological liar, dumps him, leaving him devastated. (MacDowell, a slow-talking Southerner who radiates niceness, was miscast.) As his life unravels, he comes to his senses, but now has to campaign to get his wife back, because she has waded into the dating pool herself. Eventually, continues De Luca, "they come back to each other after they both have been unfaithful. They both have affairs—there's a balance." But, says Karsch, "Warren didn't want to do it, him getting Ellie back again."

In other words, Beatty's reputation for vanity was so pervasive that at least some of the principals suspected the worst. "I don't think that

Warren would ever play somebody who needs to get Diane Keaton back," says one source. "That's where he doesn't separate himself from the character. I never knew where Porter began and where Warren ended." Whatever the reason, fiddling with the ending may have been a mistake, and more, a mistake that sank the movie. Says De Luca, "One of the biggest changes, and probably the most damaging change, was that we rewrote the script so that Diane's character has no affairs, and therefore the sympathy for Warren's character goes out the window."

Speculates Laughlin, "I was in a meeting with Warren and Goldie, and they were talking about how fabulous they both looked. And maybe Warren thought Diane didn't look as wonderful as they did. And maybe at that moment, he decided—and they had a past together—I don't want to remarry her at the end of the movie. That minute, the ball game was over."

From Beatty's point of view, rather than stopping the train, he was only trying to get it on track. He would say, "I'm only trying to make the script better. It's not my fault that this is happening." Indeed, De Luca doesn't remember Beatty objecting to having to win Keaton back or remarrying her. "Warren never brought up not having the husband get back with the wife at the end of the movie. To this day I don't know what Peter Chelsom liked about the original script, and what he liked about what we turned it into with these rewrites. I never heard him say, 'No, let's not rewrite it this way, 'cause the movie's about that'—he just kind'a went with the flow. It was weird."

While *Town & Country* was being rewritten, Beatty was flirting with Mazursky and his writing partner, Leon Capetanos, about a script called *Hot Friday,* which Capetanos had written, about a tough private eye working his last job in L.A. before retiring to a fishing town in Oregon. Mazursky had the money, $22 million. "I was ready to go and excited," he says. He just needed Beatty to say yes. But Beatty would never say yes, or, as Mazursky puts it, "He wouldn't say yes to doing it, even though he had said yes." Instead, he would say, "Can't we fix this little thing, and change that little thing?" Mazursky and Capetanos went to work, and for several months they fixed this little thing and changed that little thing. "And then it started to become different than I wanted it to be," recalls Mazursky. "Leon and I both agreed that we just couldn't stand some of these changes. So I just said, 'Let's forget it, Warren.' The movie never happened. I haven't spoken to him since. He just stopped calling. The script is still around. I think, now and then, he calls Leon: 'Who's got the rights to that?' " Beatty and Mazursky were not close, but they had known each other for a long time, and it was the end of a friendship. "He's a funny bird," Mazursky concludes. "But I bear him no ill will. I like him, I admire him, and I wish I still saw him. But it's hard to deal with that."

READY OR not—and it was "not"—production on *Town & Country* began in June 1998. "This was not a happy set," says Harris, in a gross understatement. "Peter and Warren were a lethal combination. They did not see the same movie, or even the same scene, pretty much ever. Warren is very articulate and can see every side of every issue and every angle of every conversation. Peter's an extremely English public school boy, very polite, well mannered, but not so good about saying what's on his mind, so you have two people coming from an aggressively passive-aggressive place. If there is a tiny chink in the armor, Warren is incredibly adept at finding it, and he's not a person who has a great deal of tolerance for insecurity in his director."

First there was the "fairy dust" incident. In the script, the characters are described as behaving as if they were sprinkled with fairy dust. For reasons best known to himself, Chelsom apparently took this literally. "I was going through the prop list one day and I saw these canisters that were marked 'fairy dust,' " Karsch recalls. "Warren didn't even believe me. Then we discovered that he was going to blow particles of paper— 'fairy dust'—all over everything. It was Peter's sense of whimsy." Buck Henry, who would be hired to do rewrites, adds, "The keynote of Peter's work had been a kind of English whimsy. I don't think whimsy relates to anything Warren does or thinks about."

Karsch and the other producers considered replacing Chelsom, while Beatty stayed in the background. Laughlin explains, "Warren thought it would reflect badly on him." And Karsch, "Warren said it was up to me and Fred to do that. He was an actor." Comparatively speaking, Chelsom was a nobody, nothing. Even if Beatty declined to flex his muscles, Chelsom worked at his sufferance and knew it. The natural assumption—apparently shared by New Line—was that *Town & Country* was Beatty's picture.

New Line could have fired Chelsom, but at that moment the company was being loudly assailed by Tony Kaye, a British director with whom it had tussled over *American History X.* Kaye said the New Line crowd, "raped" his picture, tried to have his credit replaced by "Humpty Dumpty," and had taken double truck attack ads in the trades that had left the company shell-shocked. Says Karsch, "New Line was reluctant to make any changes, because they didn't want to be seen as a company that was director-unfriendly."

According to De Luca, "I was aware during production that the relationship was getting a little frayed, but if I called Peter [Chelsom] and Simon [Fields], and said, 'How's it going with Warren?' they'd say, 'Warren's Warren, but it's gonna be fine.' It was always like, 'It's gonna be fine.' Warren raised the red flags periodically, but once it was rolling, the thought of pulling the plug on a runaway, and eating the tens of millions of dollars—you hate to do it, although in retrospect, that would have been the right move, 100 percent. But when I was faced with those decisions, I had the hope that it might still work." Without New Line's blessing, Karsch's hands were tied. In the end, nobody did anything, while Beatty was getting increasingly frustrated.

At eight one morning in July 1998, Harris got a frantic call at home from Michael Davison, Beatty's assistant. He asked her to come to the set immediately. When she arrived at the actor's trailer, a full-scale firefight between Beatty and Chelsom was in progress: "You don't know what you're talking about, you don't know what the movie's about, there's no script," Beatty bellowed.

"Of course there's a script."

"Then what's it about, what's my character about?"

As Harris describes it, "The three stooges—Fields, Roos, and Karsch—were sitting on the couch with their fucking breakfast burritos saying nothing." Trying to be palliative, she said something innocuous, straight out of Corporate Speak 101, or maybe *Cool Hand Luke*, like "I think what's happening is that you two have very different ways of working, and right now, you're not finding a way to communicate." According to her, "Warren flipped out. He turned to me and said, 'This little girl is saying that we're two boys fighting in a sandbox, and neither one of us wants to give up our toys.' He lost his shit and stood up, and went around the room jabbing his finger in the air, and said, 'You and you and you and you and you can take this fucking movie and shove it up your fucking asses,' stormed out of the trailer, and slammed the door. So now we were sitting in his trailer with his cook and his breakfast burritos, and he's not there. We looked at each other, 'Okay, what do we do?' About forty-five minutes later he came in and apologized for losing his temper. And said, 'Let's get back to work.' I think it was a horrible moment for him—it was a very childish temper tantrum. Because he was not in control of the movie. He knew, 'If I'm in the movie and it spirals out of control, it's my fault, because I'm Warren Beatty.' Knowing that the finger was pointed at him, it gnawed at him, he felt that really deeply."

About three months into production and increasingly desperate, Beatty and Karsch approached Buck Henry to write them out of the hole they were in. He was the perfect choice, except for the fact that he didn't want to do it. Karsch recalls, "I worked and worked and worked on him, and finally he was like, 'Okay, these are the conditions . . . ' the central one being that he wouldn't do the endless meetings with Warren, the meetings on Saturday, the meetings on Sunday." Says Henry, "I've always hated the meetings, because they do nothing but make you crazy, and then when they're over, people like Warren say, 'Pay no attention to that meeting.' Which I like, but then why did we have to bother in the first place?" Karsch continues, " 'Buck, I promise you you're not going to have to meet with Warren.' It didn't hurt that New Line made Henry an offer he couldn't refuse." Henry thought, What the hell, I'll just stay home in New York and send in the pages. But he hadn't counted on Beatty, who started in on him: "You gotta come out here, you gotta come out here." Henry said, "Okay, I'll come out there, but I'm not coming to meetings." Finally, Henry said, "Okay, I'll go to meetings, but I'm not going to the set." He continues, "inch by inch," Beatty got his way. Beatty was one of those people who could burn your house down and then sell you another one. Henry even had a small role as the attorney who negotiates the terms of Porter and Ellie's putative divorce.

Henry wrote over two hundred pages, of which perhaps a third were shot. He wrote one very funny scene set in Shandling's antique shop, in which his character is trying desperately to come out of the closet to his friend Porter, but never manages to spit the words out because the two men are speaking at cross-purposes. Recalls Henry, "It was never going to be shot until one day Warren was looking at this pile of script pages he had, and he said, 'What's this? What's this?'

" 'That's the scene of yadayadayada. I wrote it a couple of months ago. Remember we read it once at the table?'

" 'Nah, I've never seen it before.' So he read it, and says, 'Oh, this is funny. Why don't we do this?' That's the way things happened on that movie. It might have been shot or not shot depending on the vagaries of the moment. Ultimately, Warren thinks he has all the money in the world, and all the time in the world to do it. The point is to get it right, or there's no point doing it. It doesn't mean a goddamn thing if it costs $2 billion and takes ten years to shoot. That's why people's hair turns white."

Karsch recalls, "As the budget was escalating, whatever the amount was at that point, De Luca still loved Warren and loved Warren's work. He said to me, 'Thirty-five million dollars for a Warren Beatty movie isn't bad.' I said, 'Big mistake. The problem? This isn't a Warren Beatty movie, it's a Peter Chelsom movie. And it's a great deal of money for that.' "

LYNN HARRIS was still doing her best to move the picture forward, but it was impossible. "I had no power at all," she says. "I literally had a bullet-less gun in my hand, I was the watchdog with no teeth, 'cause I was basically there at Warren's request, to watch what was happening. I could say 'No, no, no,' but if the person above me wasn't backing me up, there wasn't a lot I could do. And it's very difficult when you're having a conversation with an Academy Award–winning writer-producer-director-actor who is telling you that you're wrong. He does like people to disagree, and he does like to go away and think about things, process them, and come back, but we weren't in development, we were in production."

Beatty disputed his reputation for being a difficult actor. "Do you know the last time I was a hired actor?" he asked journalist Kim Masters, rhetorically, in 2000. "Nineteen seventy-five, in *The Fortune*," he went on, answering his own question. "Ask Mike Nichols if I ever held anything up, demanded anything. When I'm a hired actor, I do what I'm told." But Peter Chelsom was no Mike Nichols. And it wasn't just professional pride on Beatty's part. It was a bread-and-butter issue, even for him.

Still, Beatty made it very clear to Harris who was in charge. She says he turned to her on the set one day and said, "Make no mistake, if I decide that I don't want to shoot on Tuesdays because I don't like Tuesdays, we're not shooting on Tuesdays. And if I decide on Wednesdays everyone is going to wear blue shirts because Wednesday is blue shirt day, we'll be wearing blue shirts, because I am the eight-hundred-pound gorilla on the set."

More often than she wished, Beatty would give her "the finger," as she calls it, crook his finger and beckon her over. Her heart would sink. She thought, Oh shit! This is going to be a four-hour conversation.

One day, he motioned her over with the finger: "Come here." According to her, he said, in his quiet voice, making her lean in so she could hear him, "You know, New Line would benefit greatly if you would talk dirty to me between takes." She recalls, "It was the first time he'd said anything charming. All I ever saw was an unhappy man on set every day. We were in the middle of the Monica Lewinsky nonsense, so between takes we started playing games like, 'Who would you rather . . . ? Who would you rather . . . fuck? Bill Clinton or Al Gore? The problem was, to play the game with Warren, you had to read the papers, because if you didn't, you wouldn't know who the hell he was talking about. But then it always ended up back with him, 'Bill Clinton or me? Bob Shaye or me?' I said, 'I won't play the game that way, Warren.'

" 'Why not?'

" 'I wouldn't do it with you, obviously, so I won't play that game with you.'

" 'Okay.'

"But it was fun. One day, we were shooting in New York, he was sitting in his chair, and I got called over, the finger again, that terrible moment, 'cause we'd been shut down in the streets of New York spending God knows how much money—and he asked me, 'How many women do you know that I've slept with?' Now I was thirty-two, thirty-three?

" 'Like, know *of*? Like Madonna?'

" 'No, no, no, like, your friends.'

" 'None. None of my friends.'

"He was shocked. It didn't occur to him that I wouldn't know many women that he slept with prior to his marriage. But why would I?"

Beatty tried to flip Harris, that is, bring her over to his side. "He didn't do it in any kind of sexual or romantic way, ever," she continues. "I actually agreed with some of Warren's assessments about how New

Line was handling the movie. But I was still its representative. Emotionally I was very torn."

The combination of Beatty and Shandling, although it resulted in some high comedy, proved toxic, at least so far as the shooting schedule was concerned. Says Henry: "Garry and Warren were in each other's pockets." They enabled each other. Their neuroses meshed like the gears of a high- (or low-, depending on your point of view) performance engine. Partners in crime, the two actors were constantly picking apart the dialogue. Nothing was too insignificant to change. They rarely knew their lines, which had always been Beatty's way. The two of them would do take after take after take. There were reputedly reels and reels of exposed film that consisted solely of improvisational exercises. Beatty was working so slowly Henry thought that he had "lost faith in the movie and was consciously or unconsciously trying to deep-six it!"

Chelsom couldn't help recognizing that the playing field was tilted against him, and resented it. The fact that so many of the principals were friends of Beatty's probably added to his paranoia. As Laughlin puts it, "The movie should not have been cast with people that Warren had relationships with—Diane, Goldie, and his friend Garry, who was always up at the house. It was just a bit too incestuous."

But Beatty was having his own problems with his friends. Apparently content to frolic in the Beatty sandbox, Shandling was by some accounts far from a happy camper. According to one source, because the two men were close, and he was "Garry Shandling!" Beatty beefed up his role, thinking he was doing his friend a favor. But as his role got bigger and bigger, Shandling became frustrated, then angry, because he was anxious to start on his own movie. Still, he wouldn't admit this to Beatty, because he was his friend, and he was "Warren Beatty." Instead, he complained to everyone else. As one source, close to the production, puts it, "His role was tiny, and it grew into this huge thing. Warren kept roping him deeper and deeper into stuff, and Garry wouldn't say no to him. He was deeply unhappy, deeply unpleasant, and deeply difficult, saying things like, 'Leave me alone, stop writing me into things, I just want to get the fuck out of here.'"

Predictably, the relationship between Beatty and Keaton, never good, got worse. Explains Harris, "When you're an actor like Diane is, and you show up on time, and you go into hair and makeup on time, and an hour passes, and two hours pass, and three hours pass, and four hours pass, and sitting in the movie star's trailer across the parking lot is the director and three producers and a studio executive talking about things that will affect you—your role and your schedule—and you are not privy to those conversations, nor do you want to be, you feel incredibly powerless and angry."

According to Henry, "Diane said to me, 'I don't care what you write, but you have to have me in a chair facing away from him!' She wouldn't look at Warren. It's funny, I did two movies with him— *Heaven Can Wait* was the other—and in both cases the lead actresses didn't want to look at him." Harris continues, "I don't know why she did the film. Of all of us, she knew better from the beginning what it would be like. She felt that Warren had hijacked the movie. I think she blamed him." Even Goldie Hawn, who was always a loyal friend to him, complained to Harris saying, according to the executive, "This is completely unfair. We all read the script beforehand, this is what we signed on for, this is what we're paid for, we show up on time, we're ready to work, and then, next thing you know, four, five, six hours have passed, they're all in Warren's trailer, no one's come out, and when they do come out we're doing a completely different scene from what we've prepared, or there's no scene that day."

Charlton Heston was the only actor who managed to relax, perhaps because, as it turned out, he was in the early stages of Alzheimer's. Says Harris, "I always felt incredibly bad for Heston, because I felt like somehow the movie was poking fun at him, and he didn't understand it."

Despite her frustration, Harris liked Beatty. "He's not long in makeup," she recalls. "And he has boundless energy. Seventeen-hour days, and he was there to the bitter fuckin' end, wanting to do another take. One thing that always impressed me about Warren—as much as the other actors wanted to shoot themselves because they didn't know what the fuck was going on, and their schedules were yanked all over—he is incredibly generous to the person across from him, and he'll always stay and do his off-camera. He felt a big obligation to that, particularly with the younger actors, somebody like Josh Hartnett, who'd virtually never done a movie before."

On the set, he was punctilious in his behavior toward Chelsom. "It was Chelsom's set, and Warren was being as careful as he could not to interfere," Henry recalls. "Any arguments about procedure usually occurred way off camera." Indeed, Beatty was so paranoid about being blamed that he barely ventured an opinion unless it was in front of producers and executives who would testify that his suggestions could not be construed as meddling. De Luca had a T-shirt made with the words "I'm only an actor" emblazoned across the front. Beatty was not amused. According to Henry, "Warren was desperately determined not to take the rap."

Off the set was another matter. Beatty made no secret of his unhappiness. One day the actor apparently said something to Chelsom that caused the director to rush out of his trailer, slam the door behind him, and yell at the top of his lungs, "You cunt." For his part, Chelsom was just as adept at pushing Beatty's buttons. According to Karsch, on one occasion Beatty became so incensed that he threatened Chelsom with bodily injury and had to be restrained. "I knew every time we had a meeting that Peter was going to say something that was going to enrage Warren," says Henry. "I could hear it coming, like a distant train, rumbling up the tracks, and then suddenly it was there." One day, they were sitting at a conference table in the production office, discussing whether to build something or to hire someone, and Chelsom, feeling cornered, looked at him and said, "Well, everyone knows that you have approval—you have fart approval." Henry closed his eyes and put his head in his hands. "It took Warren a minute to build to it, 'cause he started very quietly, but within thirty seconds he was screaming. This was a humdinger. Warren was red-faced. I could see him punching him out. But I sympathized with [Beatty], because Chelsom's choice of words was really bad, patronizing and irritating at the same time. That sort of negative vulgarity that the English are very good at that Americans hate them for." But even in the extremity of his anger, Beatty, who loved an argument above all things, couldn't help but dissect the meaning of "fart approval" and whether or not it ultimately had anything to do with the making or unmaking of a film.

Karsch, whom Chelsom regarded, along with Fred Roos, as the enemy, as one of "Warren's guys," as he puts it, says, "Warren is like a rose with sharp thorns. He can be difficult, but he just wasn't in those meetings." As weeks turned into months, Chelsom became increasingly marginalized. Recalls Karsch, "Diane, Goldie, Warren, and I would be in the office, talking about this and that, and Peter would be there too, watching TV—the English comedian, Eddie Izzard. Nobody paid any attention to him. It was like he wasn't in the room. Pretty soon he started coming [to the set] at eleven o'clock, at twelve o'clock."

In October 1998, they were on day 66 of a sixty-day shoot and still going strong. "We were shooting for months and months and months and months," says Karsch. "It was ridiculous. We had so much footage you couldn't believe it, well over a million feet of film. For a romantic comedy. It was like, 'Oh, let's try this out. Let's try that out.'" Harris is more sympathetic. "Peter didn't say a whole hell of a lot to Warren," she says. "I think he felt that if he could just get out of the conversation and get the cameras rolling, he would be one day closer to getting the hell out of there." Says one New Line executive close to the movie, "I don't think that Mike De Luca ever wanted to go up against Warren. He was pretty checked out. It was arm wrestling to get him to come to set."

Town & Country wasn't the only bad news Beatty had to deal with. On December 6, 1998, David MacLeod, who had been a fugitive since 1989, was found dead at the age of fifty-four on a freeway overpass in Montreal. It took the police three weeks to identify the body. The police determined that he had died by his own hand—by swallowing lighter fluid, no less—and declared the case closed. Says Toback, "If you knew MacLeod at all, the idea of his committing suicide in that excruciatingly painful way is about as likely as his committing suicide by chopping off his left foot and eating it. He was a hedonist, not a masochist. What probably happened is that someone forced it down his throat. I would say that murder would be a 25-to-1 favorite over suicide. MacLeod was incredibly careful, but obviously he made some bad decisions in terms of guessing who was watching, and who had it in for him. He just got unlucky."

THE CLIMAX of *Town & Country* was still a problem. It transpired at the "Design Center," ostensibly located in downtown Manhattan, where Ellie receives a prestigious award and Porter makes an impromptu appearance, publicly apologizing to his wife.

But it just didn't work, and all Beatty's horses and all Beatty's men just couldn't make it work. "The struggle over that speech—he's wooing back his wife is what it was about—was agony," Henry continues. "Because Warren knew it was an important speech. There was a lot of writing going on. Warren wrote, Garry wrote, even Goldie wrote. We tortured that speech. By the time we got through rewriting and rewriting and rewriting and rewriting, whatever was in it originally was gone. Changed the verbs, changed the nouns, changed the tenses. He just worried it to death.

"Everyone was desperate by that time. They'd been shooting for six months. We had lots and lots and lots of takes. Each one of the scenes in that sequence took twice as long to shoot as it should have. They must have had all the actors on overages. There were three cameras working. Each one on a track. There were the hundred extras in the room, I'm not sure why. There were tables full of people listening to this, and a lot of eye rolling. It was just too complicated."

In the middle of all this, along came Keaton's stop date. Uncharacteristically, Beatty was unable to persuade her to stay. "The last few days were shot without Diane," continues Henry. "It's her fucking double that we're seeing, sideways. It was a nightmare. A nightmare."

The picture was now scheduled for a September 17, 1999, release. By the time it wrapped, at least 1.3 million feet of film had been shot, according to *The New York Times*. New Line tested *Town & Country* in a research screening on April 20, 1999. It went badly. "That was the day Columbine happened, which should have been an omen right there," says De Luca. "It became clear that only Europeans find infidelity funny. Americans do not find it funny. When I was watching it with regular people, even I felt uncomfortable—I don't care how guilty this guy feels, you really felt that it's still regarded as an unforgivable transgression, especially in a comedy, where you're supposed to feel good at the end. I remember walking out of the screening, and there was a group of middle-aged women, very hostile, angry faces, talking about how dare Hollywood put out a movie like this, it just goes to show they have no values. Very incensed at the idea of this character womanizing through three quarters of the movie, so I think it was a flawed concept commercially from the beginning, that I didn't recognize." In the past, the man who had everything had managed to make his characters vulnerable—even Bugsy—thereby ingratiating himself with audiences. This time he failed.

This screening touched off a frantic scramble for a new conclusion. New Line decided to reshoot and recut to make Beatty's character more sympathetic. But shooting additional footage meant that they had to wait nine months to reassemble the cast. Bening was scheduled to have another baby, in March of 2000, so the resumption of production was put off until April of that year, leaving the star with too much time on his hands.

"WARREN WOULD have liked to be president of the U.S.," says Joyce Hyser. He had of course mused from time to time about running for sundry offices, including president. He hid "Easter eggs," as Bill Bradley calls them, in his movies, allusions to his political aspirations best appreciated by his friends. (In *Bugsy*, for example, Ben Siegel says, "If we have a state, then we can elect a president," while Meyer Lansky replies, "What, are you planning to run for president?") For a millisecond in 1999, it looked like he might have his chance.

Arianna Huffington had completed her journey from right to left and was becoming an increasingly vocal spokeswoman for progressive causes, as well as something of a social magnet for a disparate group of angry, Clinton-hating liberals that included Pat Caddell, Bill Bradley, performer Harry Shearer, and *Nation* writer Marc Cooper. "There was definitely disappointment in how Clinton had compromised, and failed to use our prosperity to advance major issues," says Huffington. "He pulled back after the health care debacle on big ideas, and focused on small measures." Clinton's second term was drawing to a sorry close with the incumbent in disgrace, and the presidential primary season was fast approaching. Gore was the obvious candidate to succeed him, but the prospect of the famously wooden vice president didn't excite anybody either, indicating that he had electability problems. The conversation at Huffington's dinner table quickly turned to, "Couldn't we do better?" Recalls Cooper, "Going into 2000, we were desperate!"

Inevitably, in these couldn't-we-do-better talkathons, Beatty's name came up, most seriously at a dinner party at Huffington's home in the summer of 1999. After all, if a nincompoop like Ronald Reagan had gone from B-actor to president, why not Beatty, whose IQ must have exceeded that of his trailblazing friend by a good 100 points? He had charisma and name recognition to burn, no one could call him a political dilettante, he didn't smoke or drink, and most exciting of all, who was better suited to deflate the DLC mandarins who had sold out the core principles of the Democratic Party than—Bulworth!

Huffington floated the notion in one of her columns, entitled,

"Does Bulworth have a future in the White House?" published on August 9. "Warren knew I was doing the column, but other than that he didn't know exactly what I would be saying," she says. "It started this amazing firestorm. I was at Warren's a couple of days after that, and looked at his call log, which included every major TV and radio show, wanting him on. I don't really think either he or I were prepared for the response, both from the press and from leaders. I got literally thousands of e-mails, and I downloaded about a thousand of them and put them in a book for him."

Beatty started gathering string, calling Democrats and liberals of various stripes, picking their brains, canvassing their opinions. Should he or shouldn't he? He would list all of the why-the-hell-not reasons to run, and then all the reasons it would be a bad idea, most of which concerned privacy and the physical safety of himself and his family. At the time, he and Bening had three children under seven, to whom he was devoted, and another on the way. As he well knew, there are all sorts of nuts out there ready to kill famous people.

There was, however, the issue of his skirt-chasing past. "The question was, Would his past be such that it would block his ability to get out his message?" recalls Bradley. "I didn't think that was the case. All the stuff prior to his marriage to Annette could be explained." In short, they decided whatever surfaced would be survivable.

Beatty's temperament was a more formidable obstacle. He may be preternaturally charming one-on-one or in small groups, but he is not a presser of flesh. Public speaking was a crap shoot. Sometimes he was relaxed and eloquent, other times he seemed uncomfortable and tongue-tied. As Mike Nichols puts it, "It's hard to imagine him doing that because he is so guarded, and so relatively inarticulate when he's ad-libbing on TV. He's always had a hard time talking about himself." He doesn't like to be pinned down, and generally dislikes interviews. Bradley knew this would make him an unsuitable candidate. As he puts it, he seems like he'd make a good candidate "for about forty-five minutes." Bradley had lunch one day with Beatty and Bening at Santo Pietro at the Beverly Glen Center, where he said as much: "I think that you should not run for president, it would be too much of a dramatic change for you, to put yourself out there in that arena on a constant basis, and give yourself up to the process." The star understood; he had, after all, made a picture about that very subject. But Bradley told him, "I think you should use the exposure that you have to conduct an exploratory campaign, say a lot of important things about America that will influence the debate, and the direction of the Democratic Party as it goes into a critical post-Clinton election." He explains, "He could do that without making any radical change in his life and still be who he was. And if things caught fire, then go for it."

Not everyone was satisfied with Bradley's formulation. They wanted Beatty to go further. "What Arianna, Marc Cooper, and Pat Caddell wanted him to do was to actually run, and screw around with the Democrats," Bradley continues. "People were saying he should run as an independent, like Jesse Ventura, or he should go for the Reform Party nomination, but I knew that there was approximately the chance of a snowball in hell that he would do that. If he was going to run at all it was going to be as a liberal Democrat in the primaries." Beatty was—and is—a "yellow dog Democrat," a Texas term for a party loyalist: before backing a Republican, he would vote for a yellow dog were it running on the Democratic ticket. Beatty much preferred to bore from within. As he puts it, "We're living in an era where Mary Matalin can be married very happily to James Carville. It's more and more like one party, one happy party. So the question becomes, I think, not do we need a third party; it's that we need a second party."

Despite all the negatives, the idea of an exploratory campaign was too intriguing for Beatty to ignore, especially since the potential field of candidates was so dismal. Bening was urging him to do it, while a core group of four advisers, who naturally dubbed themselves the Gang of Four (Huffington, Caddell, Bradley, and Cooper), aided and abetted by a handful of fellow travelers, began spinning various scenarios over meals and cell phones. Recalls Cooper, a short, husky man with a sharp wit and ready opinions who was once Salvador Allende's translator, "That group of four—I think it was just us, but who knows who Warren's talking to at three in the morning, there could have been twelve groups of four like this—we suddenly became the unofficial consulting team." He continues, "It was bizarre. I didn't even know him. I'm not a political consultant; I never claimed to be. I was just one of probably ten thousand satellites orbiting around him. I was just having fun. But the conversations went very far very fast.

"We saw polls in places like California immediately after he came out as a possibility, where he was getting 10, 12 percent of the Democratic vote without even campaigning. We figured, If he does the TV circuit, writes a couple of op-ed pieces, the best-case scenario is that he could poll 18, 20 percent, enough so that Gore would have to look over his shoulder and recalibrate, just as Kerry would have to recalibrate his campaign because of pressure from the Deaniacs. He seemed kind'a on board for that." It was the Ralph Nader strategy, but unlike Nader, the actor was not willing to be a spoiler.

Bradley was encouraged, but he couldn't help noticing that "Warren would talk about his interest in it, but he would dance around it. Larry King had extended a standing invitation to appear on his show anytime he wanted to. Beatty agreed or seemed to agree to do it. So I would say, 'Let's just pick a date. How 'bout next Wednesday.' Then he'd say, 'Well, what would I be saying?'" He asked Cooper to craft him language for the Larry King show. "So I wrote on ten issues," Cooper remembers. "Warren would say, 'It's good, it's good. But can we get this down to thirty seconds, fifteen seconds?' That sounded like somebody who's skilled on camera and knows what he's doing and was getting ready to go on TV with sound bites."

But invariably, in the course of discussing what he might say, the target date slipped. Bradley recalls, "We could never quite get to the next Wednesday part, so we thought, 'Maybe we should just arrange it for him.' We presented that, and it was, 'No, no, I know Larry.' But it wasn't happening. Then it was, 'Is this the first show I should do? I'm not sure it's a serious enough show. Maybe *MacNeil/Lehrer*. I think *MacNeil/Lehrer* is much more substantive.'

" 'Well, yeah, but it's incredibly boring and I never watch the show. *Meet the Press*?'

" '*Meet the Press* is not the kind of show you jump into right off the bat. It ups the ante, and might make it appear that I'm actually running, rather than thinking about running. Maybe I should go on *Nightline*.'

"Then it was, 'Is he ready for *Nightline*? How will it work? What kinds of questions is he gonna get?' and by musing about different scenarios, he kept sliding from one thing to another without focusing and just going in. Ultimately, he didn't do any of them. Warren is a perfectionist, and for him, the perfect is the enemy of the good."

Beatty did decide to write an op-ed piece for *The New York Times*. "In the mini-world of this campaign, that *New York Times* piece was crucial," recalls Cooper. "It was *The New York* fucking *Times*! He talked me and Bill Bradley to death over that piece. When it came out, however, we went nuts. I said to Bill, 'How could this happen? We just talked to him a half hour ago, and he said, "Don't worry, I'm not going to publish it till everybody looks at it," and then it's there.' He played—I say this with affection—a shell game with us on that.

"The last two words were the worst possible thing: 'Stay tuned!' They raised expectations—there's more coming—implied that there was some plan, but there was no plan. Stay tuned for what? My reaction was, 'Yeah, we'd sort of like to know what was going on too!' At that point we became kind of protective of him: on the one hand, we were prodding him to go farther out, but on the other side saying, 'Lookit, if you don't want to do it, then don't do it, but don't fuck around in the middle like this, you're not going to do anybody any good, and you're going to fuck yourself, your own integrity and credibility.' "

Then Beatty was invited to speak before the Los Angeles chapter of the venerable Americans for Democratic Action at the Beverly Hilton on September 29, 1999, where he would be given their annual Eleanor Roosevelt Award. The Gang of Four was in the audience, applauding appreciatively along with an auditorium full of celebrities and gray-haired liberals. "He wrote every fucking word of that speech by himself, baring his heart," says Cooper. "It was wonderful and amusing and enjoyable and did no damage to anybody." But they were a little taken aback when he concluded with a peroration to a hypothetical "drum majorette" who might be thinking of running for president, whom he advised, "Look, drum majorette . . . speak up. Speak up for the people nobody speaks up for . . ." They exchanged glances and kicked one another under the table. It was, "Oh my God! The 'little drum majorette'? Who knows what a drum majorette is? A teenage girl? This is the last thing you want to come up with, Warren! Think of something else, like an ROTC officer."

But it was the politics of the speech that bothered Cooper more. He realized, for the first time, that he and Beatty were not on the same page. "That event was a reality check for me," he explains. "I realized that I may have been projecting some of my own politics onto him, that Warren's are such that he would not really want to challenge the Democrats, turn over the tables, saying, 'I'm going to be the skunk at the party so that we can get back on track,' which was the premise of all our discussions. This guy has tremendous loyalty to the Democratic

Party, lots of friends in Hollywood who are Democrats. There was too much at risk for him."

Still, as Cooper puts it, his ADA speech had "played on the ground like the Academy Awards." Or, as Huffington recalls, "It was covered as though it were a presidential address. There were banks of TV cameras." The Beatty gang was thrilled; their strategy seemed to be working. He was establishing his themes, and the most prominent among them was campaign finance reform. Says Huffington, "That was the beginning of his friendship with John McCain on that issue. McCain's stance was very much about reforming a broken political system, both in terms of how money is raised by campaigns, and how lobbying is used to buy public policy, and what that does to those without a voice and without a bank account."

Four years later, Beatty, ever the optimist, tried to persuade McCain to join the John Kerry ticket as his running mate. "McCain hates George Bush, so it was pretty intense," says a source. "It definitely went on. But at the same time, McCain sees himself as a Republican, so there was no chance he would do it. This was a kind of misapprehension of who McCain is." Adds Huffington, assessing Beatty's motives, "I think he was looking at how to stop Hillary Clinton from being the nominee [in the future]. He does not believe that Hillary represents what is best about the Democratic Party, in terms of the ideals of FDR: fairness, concern for the working people, as opposed to the Wall Street corporate culture."

Next up was the AFL-CIO convention, beginning the week of October 10, at which labor was going to endorse Al Gore. Cooper came up with a bright idea: Beatty would address the Teamsters. "The Teamsters are the biggest union in the AFL-CIO," he explains. "Jimmy Hoffa [Jr.] was a maverick. He didn't want to be taken for granted, a Democratic toady. He was flirting with Nader, with the idea of a third party. I knew ultimately [Beatty] wasn't willing to go off the reservation, but he was willing to fuck with the AFL-CIO over trade, because Gore is a big free trader." If Beatty endorsed job protection and opposed free trade—traditional Democratic policies—"the Teamsters would go nuts, and that would throw a wrench into the whole AFL-CIO process, possibly derail the very early rubber-stamping of Gore. I talked to Warren about this for a month. He was intrigued as hell by it. We were just tinkering, but Warren loves to tinker. At no time did Warren ever say to me that I'm going to do that thing. What he said to me was, 'Tell me about the Teamsters. Who should I talk to about this trade thing so I really understand it.'

"You should talk to Lori Wallach from Public Citizen." Wallach flew out to L.A. to brief him. Beatty asked Cooper to write a draft of the Teamsters speech. Cooper did. He continues, "The Teamsters had the space reserved, Warren was ready, it was all systems go. Warren had them on the hook."

At the Los Angeles Convention Center, Huffington and Bradley kept asking, "Where's Warren, where's Warren?" Cooper suspected the worst. "A few days earlier, the phone calls stopped being returned, and the process somehow went into a black hole. Which he's a master of. Of secrecy. He loves it, he thrills to it, the intrigue of that kind of Batman operation." Bradley called his home, talked to Bening, who told him that her husband had taken a shower and gone out. She didn't seem to know if he intended to address the Teamsters or not. As it turned out, he did not. When Bradley spoke to him later that evening, he said, " 'Well, I just couldn't do it.' He didn't want to be seen as hurting Gore." Adds Cooper, "In the end, he had a private meeting with Hoffa. I'm sure they had a nice dinner, and then nothing happened."

For those involved in Beatty's quixotic "exploratory campaign," it was like being in "purgatory," as a source described it. For Bradley and Cooper, it was like watching sand running through their fingers. Says Cooper, "For me, when he backed down on the Teamsters, that was the shipwreck. It was obvious that he wasn't running and that he shouldn't run. He would have been a bad candidate, not because he's a bad person, but because he just doesn't have the attributes to be a candidate. Maybe he's too thoughtful, too meditative to be a candidate. In any event, Warren never followed up his op-ed piece. We'd stayed tuned—he just evaporated. Bill and I were left, as they say in *The Godfather*, holding our dicks in our hands."

Says Bradley, "Warren is an actor. As an actor, you can try out different sides of your personality without actually being that person in real life. Bulworth was a great fantasy of what someone could do if he were free of the strictures of having to be a conventional politician. Arianna [and Marc] did not understand that Bulworth was an alter ego, was not actually Warren. In fact, Bulworth would not have won that election in real life, he would have been carted off to a loony bin, but it was a great vehicle to make some trenchant points about American politics and culture."

Making *Bulworth* prepared Beatty for his here-he-is, here-he-isn't run at the presidency, because it prepared him—someone who had always loved being an insider—to be an outsider. As he puts it, speaking of the movie, "You can't really make jokes like that unless you're willing to have your invitation to the table rescinded. And I've become more and more willing to have that invitation rescinded." But it seemed more and more as though he wasn't. In other words, he both was and was not Bulworth. The conflict between the two would paralyze him. As Cooper came to recognize, "This [campaign] was a script in development. You can have a hundred scripts in development, but ninety-nine of them aren't real. For those of us who were writing the script, we took it very seriously. For Warren, it was, 'I have another meeting now.' He's wonderfully erratic."

One night, in the autumn of 1999, Cooper was lying awake into the wee hours, tossing and turning, worrying about Beatty. He thought, I know what we do—let's do a quickie book that we'll crash out before the convention in the summer. Warren may not be running in 2000, but Jay Bulworth will. It will be a book about the Bulworth campaign, *Bulworth 2000*—that would, of course, be fiction, but will have within it all of the substance that Warren didn't say, because it will contain all the memos, written by Jay Bulworth. And Warren will go on TV to promote the book. It would be a way for him to have an impact in the 2000 race without having to stick his neck out. It's a great fuckin' idea."

Cooper pitched the book to Beatty, who got it immediately, said, "Let's have a meeting." They met, Beatty, Cooper, and Bradley. Although Beatty had misgivings—he still didn't want to hurt Gore—he was generally enthusiastic. He said, "Let's have another meeting." They met again, and this time he went for it, saying, "Let's do it. I'm greenlighting it. You guys have been so great, I don't want to make any money off it, you will make the money off it, I'll actually do a couple of TV shows."

"Terrific!" replied Cooper, getting excited.

"But—there's an issue with Fox that I have to resolve first. Just a little legal thing. Minor. Not important."

"Warren, do you have the rights to *Bulworth*?"

"That's not the issue."

"We have to have it done by January to get it out by the summer."

"Don't worry, I'll get it resolved by next week." Cooper started talking to publishers, and settled on Verso, a small but highly respected left-wing press. Weeks passed. Another meeting. Beatty said, "It's a green light, but I still have to resolve this thing with Fox."

Every day, Cooper or Bradley et al. would speak to Beatty on the phone. "What's happening?" One day, the answer was, "Oh, I think I'm going to run in Delaware!"

"Great. Fantastic!" Or, as Cooper, who had had enough by that time, thought, "Please don't. Outta the fucking blue, after the whole thing had deflated and we were on to the *Bulworth* book, at four in the morning Warren starts to talk about actually running in the Delaware primary! 'Why do you want to run in Delaware?' 'There's a big African-American community . . . ' or some babble—Apparently, Warren had spoken to somebody: 'You should run in Delaware.'"

Delaware was an early primary, February 5, 2000, just after Iowa and New Hampshire, and was not an entirely foolish idea. There *are* a lot of African-Americans in Wilmington, while Iowa and New Hampshire are both lily-white, less reflective of the Democratic Party base. But it sounded like this time it was Beatty, not his friends, who was confusing himself with Bulworth. He may have rapped like Bulworth-from-the hood on the big screen, but whether it would play in real life was doubtful. There was another problem: the Delaware primary is invisible. As Cooper puts it, "When had Delaware ever made a difference about anything? It was like a bad movie where you think the person is dead, and they wake up for a last gasp. He had defaulted on this campaign weeks before. Then he had this last-minute regret, and now a second default? We didn't even want it to come out that he had been talking about Delaware because it would have been too embarrassing. There was no way to explain it. While political insiders might know that that was a delirious idea, the public would interpret it that he was running for president, which he clearly wasn't. If you liked Warren at all, it was time to kill it! 'Cause he couldn't bring himself to do it himself. He's an equivocator, can't make up his mind. Many times we said Annette would be a better candidate, because she was more decisive, more outspoken, more willing to rock the boat, and more willing to be unpopular."

Meanwhile, *Bulworth 2000* had gone bust. Says Cooper, "Whatever this thing was with Fox, it never got resolved, and neither I nor Bill ever found out what that was. The window kept moving, January to February to March, and of course all the deadlines passed, and we never did it."

Subsequently, Beatty reverted to the role he liked best, "the phantom," kibitzing behind the scenes, talking on the phone to political figures of all ideological stripes. Before he and Beatty parted ways, Paul Mazursky remembers being in the car with him when his phone rang. "Hello, John?" To Mazursky, he whispered, "McCain—John McCain." Into the phone, he said, "Great! Wonderful speech last night—wonderful. You were very good. Yes, you did very well. Okay, we'll talk. Bye." He hung up. A few minutes later, the phone rang again. "Ralph, how are you?" He leaned over, whispered to Mazursky, "Ralph Nader!"

Looking back on the experience, neither Bradley nor Cooper regrets investing their time and effort. "We were into the Bulworth fantasy," says Cooper. "I had a great time. Who wouldn't want to be Warren's valet, let alone his political consultant. I'm flattered that he took any of my ideas seriously. Who was not going to love that?"

Being a movie star means never having to say you're sorry, and Beatty never apologized to Cooper and Bradley for wasting their time with the Bulworth bubble. Says Cooper, "At no point did he say, 'Shit, guys, I just couldn't pull this Fox thing together with *Bulworth*, we need to ditch this.' I didn't lecture him, 'You've been a bad boy, Warren.' This is the way he operates, and what difference does it make what you say? He's going to go on like this no matter what. How does he make these transitions? He doesn't. That's how he makes all his transitions, by not making them. What does he care, right?" He continues, "At some point, Bill and I said, 'Fuck this *Bulworth* thing.' We turned it into a joke because we knew Warren. To this day, Bill and I say, 'If we start now, we can get *Bulworth 2016*!' For all I know, Warren still thinks the *Bulworth* book is happening."

During the nine-month hiatus on *Town & Country*, when Beatty wasn't teasing his political supporters, he and Buck Henry et al. worked on the script. "I was at one or two of the meetings with Buck and Warren and Peter about how to rewrite and end the movie," says production head De Luca. "Those started to get depressing, not because there was a lot of acrimony in the air, although there might have been, but it started to feel like this was a sinking ship, we don't know how to fix it. It was all about creating a mea culpa on the part of Warren's character that would be so astounding that all would be forgiven, and you could believe that his wife would take him back. The burden of the mea culpa fell on Buck, but it became clear that there was nothing Warren's character could say that was gonna make an hour and a half of philandering okay with the audience."

The re- and additional shooting continued sporadically throughout the hiatus, while they were waiting for the principal actors to return. On March 31, 2000, at the premiere of *Boiler Room*, New Line studio head Shaye sought out Harris "to tell me," in her words, that "I was 'the laughing stock of Hollywood' and was 'lucky to have a job.'" Henry ran into Shaye at a party one night. "He was quite loaded, he dropped to his knees, and said, 'Can't you help end this nightmare?' Warren was at the same party, he was standing on the other side of the pool. I pointed to him."

On March 26, 2000, Bening was up for Best Actress for *American Beauty* but lost to Hilary Swank for *Boys Don't Cry*, and Beatty received the Irving Thalberg Award. For him, it was a bittersweet experience. He appreciated the recognition, but it was an honor reserved for the elder statesmen of the industry, and entering the award season of his life was an indication, if any were needed, that his career was on the wane.

During postproduction, Peter Chelsom went off to work on *Serendipity,* yet another romantic comedy about star-crossed lovers who find each other in the end, dumping *Town & Country* in Beatty's lap, not that it wasn't there already. "Postproduction was endless," says Harris. "Recutting the movie and recutting the movie and recutting the movie." At the time, Karsch told *The New York Times,* "It reminds me of a great line of Truffaut's. He said that making a movie is like taking a stagecoach across the old American West. You start out hoping for a fantastic ride and then you pray just to reach your destination." De Luca recalls, "It was just us, with Warren and [editor] Claire Simpson and anyone else who wandered into the editing room trying cut after cut, and making it worse. At that point, Peter was an absentee director. We did everything we could to stop the bleeding and finish the movie and still have something you could sell. And nothing we did worked."

Henry remembers, "Warren was really bitter about the final cut. To my way of thinking he was absolutely right. It was everything Warren was against. He wanted the story to be about a guy who accidentally becomes an adulterer. It's in keeping with his idea of himself, of the characters he plays, as basically innocent guys. Warren has always steered away from his own reputation as a lothario. Their cut suggests that he's having a big affair at the very start of the story." By opening the picture with the scene in which a nude Kinski plays the cello for Beatty, New Line merely made a bad problem worse, diminishing whatever sympathy the audience might have had for his character.

Still, the message of the movie is more mainstream than first appears. Read biographically, *Town & Country* is a cautionary tale wrapped in the trappings of a bedroom farce. As De Luca and the others took it to be, it is indeed a sequel to *Shampoo,* the final chapter in the lightly fictionalized, multi-film (auto)biography of a rake reformed, one who discovers—perhaps too late—that he is best suited to a monogamous marriage, a role Beatty apparently played with more finesse off screen than on. *Town & Country* is a comedy of middle age, a reluctant valedictory to philandering. In it, promiscuous sex equals death, or at least, emotional emptiness.

The consequence of the additional photography as well as the protracted postproduction was that the budget, already the size of the *Hindenburg,* just went up in flames. Many people, including the DP, Bill Fraker, and his crew, were still on salary, and those who weren't, in addition to the actors, collected overages when they finally returned. Says Henry, "They didn't have any idea of how much money they were spending." He was hired for ten weeks' work, and ended up working over twice that number, twenty-two weeks. "Around the twenty-first week, one of the producers came to me and said, 'Are we still paying you?' I said, 'Gee, I hope so.' He said, 'Can you give us some relief?' It was a little like the scene in *The Godfather,* 'Can you help me out?' As they're hustling him into the car to kill him.'" Says Karsch, "He will live until the day he dies on that money. It was millions." Henry won't say, but it was rumored that he bought a house in L.A. on the money he made from *Town & Country,* said to have been in the neighborhood of $3 million.

The budget overrun was not merely the customary 10 percent, or even 20 percent, but more like 150 percent or 200 percent, depending on the baseline—$30 million or $40 million—but in either case, according to De Luca, ending up at $90 million, maybe more. At the time, New Line admitted to $75 million, undoubtedly low, but several publications, most notably *Variety, Salon,* and Liz Smith's syndicated column, reported that the budget had ballooned to $120 million, probably too high. And this for a film with a small cast, few locations, and lacking expensive special effects. (The average budget for a feature at that time ran to $59 million.) According to Michael Laughlin, producer Fred Roos just shrugged. He'd worked on most of Coppola's pictures, and his attitude was, "All these movies get out of control. They just do."

As a result of the additional shooting, the release was postponed until the fall of 2000, then it was put off yet again. "Part of it was getting it away from competition, part of it was that the film had to be put somewhere where it wouldn't impact the quarter for New Line," De Luca says. "It became a business decision of where to hide it." As one principal at New Line put it, "When you move your release date several times, the picture starts to stink. Warren will tell you that the studio kept moving the release date, and that it was their fault. What he won't tell you is, he also felt the picture wasn't ready, and he had a lot to do with the studio moving the release date. What I kept saying was, 'The more time you give them, the more time they will take.' They would be recutting the movie to this day if we hadn't set a release date and stuck to it." De Luca, who presided over the train wreck, along with other money losers like *Little Nicky* with Adam Sandler, was fired in mid-January 2001, before the picture was finished.

After *Love Affair* tanked, Glenn Gordon Caron claimed that Beatty blackballed him. From the star's point of view, if true, he did no more than share his opinion of Caron with others who might have wished to employ him, a common practice in the industry, although a more pressing motive, protecting his own reputation, cannot be discounted. So far as the *Town & Country* fiasco went, Beatty blamed Chelsom. "After *Town & Country,* the talk was that this was Warren's last great *Titanic,* that he brought this shit down on De Luca's head," recalls a source close to Beatty. "His counter story was it was all because of Peter Chelsom. John Cusack was going to do *Serendipity* with Chelsom, and he asked Warren what he was like, and Warren said, 'He was a horror show on *Town & Country.*' But Cusack did it anyway. For him to work with Chelsom after that implicitly supported the story that Warren was the great disaster in *Town & Country*. He never liked John Cusack thereafter."

New Line had decided on a drop-dead March release date. When the picture finally opened a month later, it was indeed redolent with the stink of rotten eggs. *The New York Times* weighed in with an in-depth examination of the picture's travails under the headline: "Stumbling Toward a Theater Near You." Wrote Rick Lyman, "Now, almost three years later, the movie . . . is finally arriving in theaters . . . [accompanied by] a pervasive sense of doom like none that has attached itself to a major Hollywood release in a long time."

New Line finally dumped *Town & Country* onto 2,200 screens on April 27. There were few advance screenings, no glitzy premieres, no press campaign, no party. The reviews were mixed. Wrote Lisa Schwarzbaum in *Entertainment Weekly*, "The hermetically wealthy, tastefully neurotic, abalone white characters who populate Woody Allen's Manhattan-based comedies of manners are models of realism and diversity compared with the expensively dressed humanoids scuttling across sterile landscapes of privilege in *Town & Country*." More forgiving, Stephen Holden in *The New York Times* called it a "patched-together but still entertaining movie."

It is indeed a pleasure to see three sleekly skilled actors—Beatty, Keaton, and Hawn—circle the track, but it has to be admitted that the picture doesn't work. Beatty's character comes off half hapless and half predatory, a reflection, perhaps, of the actor's role in the production. His attempts at slapstick are embarrassing, and the less said of Heston's demented gun nut, the better. Ditto Andie MacDowell's daffy nympho, who is unaccountably (and unfunnily) attached to her stuffed animals. Garry Shandling seems so uncomfortable in his own skin that he's hard to watch. As the picture dashes madly along, the quirky quickly becomes the precious. *The First Wives Club* audience may have been turned off by adultery rampant and apparently unpunished, but the fact remains that a romantic comedy has to be affecting and funny, and this one is neither. Like its two unhappy predecessors, it smacks of self-regard, as if the pleasure of watching Beatty, Hawn, and Keaton put themselves through their paces were enough.

The movie was a disaster at the box office. Even in a season of horrendous flops, it was a standout. "In this commencement season, the now infamous 'Town & Country' is graduating to the record books as

Hollywood's biggest modern-day flop," reported *Variety* in the beginning of June. "New Line's Warren Beatty starrer leaves U.S. theaters this week after a month-long run that reaped about $6.7 million—a shadow of its reported $85 million production cost. That's no small distinction. 'Meet Joe Black,' 'Battlefield Earth,' 'What Planet Are You From?'—take your pick, they all topped 'Town' in terms of budget-to-gross ratio. Overseas receipts, which total $500,000 from several territories, aren't likely to salvage the film's fortunes." Even if Beatty was not to blame, once again a movie in which he was involved left a trail of wreckage in its wake, as had *Dick Tracy, Ishtar, Bugsy, Love Affair,* and *Bulworth*.

How DID it happen? Movie business decorum dictates that after a train wreck like this one, the engineer doesn't throw stones, just dusts himself off and goes home without looking back. Indeed, Beatty blithely shrugged the whole thing off, saying, "It was fun. You know, I didn't produce it, direct it, or write it. I was a hired actor on it. I had a good time with a cast that was terrific." Initially, at least, New Line too played by the rules. A piece for Inside.com was headlined, "New Line Says *Town & Country* Is Just Fine, and Don't Blame Beatty for the Awful Mess." De Luca took pains to exculpate Beatty, albeit in a somewhat backhanded way. "As things started to go wrong with the movie, there were a lot of unfair, cheap shots directed towards him, just because of what his reputation had been coming off those other movies." Uncharacteristically for a studio executive, he blamed himself.

But walking the high road was too much for New Line's Bob Shaye. He delivered a rant to Patrick Goldstein in the *Los Angeles Times*, saying that *Town & Country* was "one of the worst mistakes of my life." He accused Beatty of seducing De Luca into starting before the script was ready. Says Karsch, "Categorically untrue. New Line started the movie before Warren was ready. Shaye was never around and doesn't have any understanding about what went on with this movie." Beatty's attorney Bert Fields sent Shaye a "cease and desist" letter. According to De Luca, "Bob felt crazy that it was slipping away, and getting more and more expensive. He felt like it must be Warren pulling a Jedi mind trick on me to make this happen. Bob was more of a believer in the reputation—this must be Warren's fault. I think he distanced himself from his own responsibility. The script was green-lit by Bob and Michael Lynne. They were there every step of the way. I was not authorized to make decisions above a half million dollars. Everything that happened was New Line–approved."

According to a source, neither Shaye nor Lynne would stand up to Beatty. "They would swear up and down about how awful Warren was, what a pig, what a nightmare, and when Warren looked them in the face and said, 'Do you Bob Shaye or do you Michael Lynne believe that I am responsible for any of the problems that have occurred on this movie?' they backed down."

Karsch blamed Chelsom for pretty much everything. "I found him to have the most unpleasant personality of anyone I've worked with." For the few things for which Karsch doesn't blame Chelsom, he blames New Line. "I've never seen a company quite so passive," he says. "It never tried to rein the movie in, until the very, very end, which was precisely when it shouldn't have. It created its own Frankenstein. Had Warren directed it, it would have been one of the truly memorable American romantic comedies."

For his part, Chelsom blamed Beatty for much that went wrong. He generally refused to comment, but in a rare interview from the battle-field in 1999, he said, "It is a mess. I have never seen so much money wasted. I'm just a kid from the North of England so you go from being nervous with these big stars to being bored by their behavior." He accused Beatty of playing "mind games": "When you enter Warren's World it is more complicated than any world you will ever enter. Nothing is easy. It is so complex and so unnecessarily complex." Says Henry, "I'm sure Peter would make the case that Garry and Warren were woe-fully unprepared a lot of the time, because they thought they could do better than the script—and I'm sure in some cases they did. But would I work with Warren again? You bet! You forget the pain."

The issue of who was to blame will perhaps never be settled. It was a group effort. Says Harris, "It's an incredibly difficult question to an-swer. If you know Warren—you know all you need to. Have you ever gotten a direct answer? He can put the brakes on things, and it's all so ethereal and ever changing and contradictory, he can deflect the blame elsewhere. He is at the same time brilliant and creative and amazing, and also oddly self-destructive." Says one source, "He's brilliant enough to twist a room of not incredibly stupid people around so much that when you ask, 'Was it really Warren's fault,' and they answer, 'Yes, it really was,' and you ask 'How?'—then they can't fucking tell you how." All Harris can say is that "Mostly it was sheer torture for three years."

Midway through the production, one of Harris's friends asked her, "If Jeffrey Katzenberg was moved to write a twenty-page memo on why it's a bad idea to be in the *Dick Tracy* [i.e., the Warren Beatty] business, why on earth did any of you think you'd be any different?" Looking back on New Line's decision to finance the movie, Harris says, "We should all have reread that memo. But we thought, people change. We heard Warren was a womanizer, but I never witnessed anything during the three years we were together on this movie that indicated to me anything other than the fact that he was very devoted to his wife and to his children, and that's great. The fifteen million women who dated him before Annette didn't have that experience, but Annette did. So yes, there was the Glenn Gordon Caron experience, there was the *Dick Tracy* experience, but we were naive enough to think that if somebody looks you in the eye and says, 'I don't want to produce, I don't want to write, I don't want to direct, I just want to act'—Great! This is gonna be easy."

14

HE'S BEEN UP SO LONG IT LOOKS LIKE DOWN TO ME

How Beatty made a virtue out of a necessity when he plunged into family life after he became virtually unbankable.

"I believe that I can get any movie made. I always have felt that and I've never had a movie I couldn't get made."

— *Warren Beatty*

BEATTY'S DOWNWARD SLIDE had gradually been gaining momentum throughout the 1990s. *Town & Country* was the tipping point, or rather, the Humpty-Dumpty moment, when it all came crashing down. All his assets—his enormous intelligence, his drive, his instincts—became debits. Even his looks, now beginning to reflect his age, seemed to lock him in a leading man prison. Way back in 1995, after *Love Affair,* with *Howard Hughes* still unmade, Dick Sylbert observed, "Warren is in trouble. He no longer counts in this town. His fangs have been pulled. In fact, he pulled his own fangs, which is more than interesting."

As of this writing, Beatty has not had a hit since *Dick Tracy* in 1990. Tracy made $100 million, but Katzenberg's memo had cast a shadow over that, and some would argue that Beatty hasn't had a hit since *Heaven Can Wait* in 1978. He hasn't done anything at all, hit or miss, for over a decade, since 1998 when the bulk of *Town & Country* was shot. During that time, he entertained ideas for several projects, mostly plucked off a shelf heavy with unfinished scripts he had accumulated over the years, but also sequels to his hits, like *Shampoo 2*, or even flops, like *Bulworth 2*, and so on. It was reminiscent of Kazan's plans for a remake of *A Face in the Crowd*, which Beatty recognized as a bad idea. He recently sued the Tribune Company to secure the rights to *Dick Tracy*. But none of these projects has seen the light of day.

Such has been his exquisite timing, however, that his decline has coincided with his marriage and the birth of his four children—no accident, to be sure—so that he has been able to settle into a life of comfortable domesticity cushioned by an unassailable rationale for his slow fade to black, when other filmmakers, faced with a similar falling off, might have been driven to distraction, or at least golf or pinochle at the Hillcrest Country Club. Although his devotion to his family, oft publicly proclaimed, is undoubtedly heartfelt, it's also true that it concealed an unpalatable truth: not only was he no longer bankable, he may have become virtually unbankable. (Beatty himself used to poke fun at politicians who left politics "to spend more time with the family," and his case is suspiciously similar.) Despite the two audacious films he made in the mid-1990s, *Bugsy* and *Bulworth*, the studios have not been falling over themselves to finance his pictures. When his name comes up, whether as a director or producer or even actor, it's often met with eye rolling and groans. (He was offered a juicy part as Nixon in *Frost/Nixon* by Ron Howard, and very possibly several other roles.)

Not being able to find anyone to direct Beatty was troublesome enough. Not being able to find a studio to back a Beatty movie was disastrous. Says former Beatty "cheese man" Hal Lieberman, who was president of production at Universal from 1994 to 1996, "[My bosses] wouldn't let me work with Warren. They thought he was too difficult. They said, 'You're gonna get in over your head. And he's gonna fuckin' dump on you.'" Adds Bill Mechanic, "Warren at the point of *Bulworth* was no longer a big star. Stardom in today's world lasts a lot shorter span of time than it did in the past. If you don't stay in the news, your commerciality is not assured." The weak or virtually nonexistent box office for his last three pictures, followed by the black hole that was *Town & Country*—his fault or not—along with his reputation for perfectionism, for being one of the most difficult people to work with or for in the entire industry, as well as his notorious inability to commit and make decisions, may have finally done their work. Beatty may love his children and spend a lot of his time at Little League games and after-school sports of one sort or another, but the suspicion has been that he wasn't making pictures because he couldn't make pictures.

It is shocking to imagine a star as bright as Beatty was, as famous and powerful, and as gifted, being virtually unemployable. There's no shortage of reasons that explain why filmmakers go into decline. In America, at least, the movie business has always been a young man's game. Directing is hard, as physically and mentally demanding as any job on the planet. Filmmakers grow old and get tired like everyone else, while their audience seems to remain perennially young. Once directors become successful, they too often enter a bubble of privilege and lose whatever instincts enabled them to touch their audiences in the first place. As Billy Friedkin once put it, "When you take your first tennis lesson, your career is over."

For all Beatty has tried to be a "real" person—dispensing with an entourage, working out of an office at the Beverly Glen Center instead of hiding on a studio lot, mixing freely with shoppers and tourists—he still lives a largely cocooned life. Jim Toback recalls, "Warren used to say to me, 'What are you taking subways for?' And I'd say, 'Because you lose touch with the way people live and think, that's why. You lose your ear for the way people talk.' I don't think it's possible to stay in touch with that reality if you don't continue to live it in some way."

It's not that Beatty is a stranger to the fragility of talent. "Stella Adler said, 'Talent is the ability to preserve talent,' " he recalls. "[After the blacklist,] when Abraham Polonsky started working again, there was nothing left. It's very hard to keep productive. It's very hard to keep the level up for the game, for the big fight, for the World Series, for the Super Bowl, and still have a life. It's that game that people always want to talk about when they talk about talent. They talk about it with me. 'Why doesn't he make more pictures?' Or they talk about it with friends of mine, like Muhammad Ali. 'What would have happened if he hadn't stayed away from the ring for all that time?' Talent is very delicate. And when you put it out there in the world of insults and acrimony and envy and lividity, it has trouble surviving."

As for politics, after his 1999 presidential exploratory ended, Beatty did launch a vigorous and effective campaign against a grab bag of referenda sponsored by California's Republican governor Arnold Schwarzenegger in a special election on November 8, 2005—all of which Beatty correctly regarded as misconceived. He addressed the California Nurses Association, drew headlines trying to crash a Schwarzenegger rally, and followed the governor around the state in a Truth Squad bus countering the governor's message with his own. For his trouble, he was called a "crackpot" by one of Schwarzenegger's staff, but the referenda were soundly defeated at the polls, and Beatty was briefly talked about as a possible Democratic candidate to oppose the Republican incumbent in the next election. But he quickly reverted to his default position, kibitzing by phone. He more or less sat out the 2008 presidential race. He is still close to John McCain, even though he never would have voted for him, but he couldn't muster much enthusiasm for either Barack Obama or Hillary Clinton.

Says Buck Henry, "As it stands, there are big, big fans of all his hit films, and big, big detractors of all of the ones that weren't. I imagine if Warren had made more movies there would be a more settled and accurate notion of what kind of talent he had. What his voice was."

Bob Evans's judgment of Beatty is most severe. According to him, Beatty didn't lose it; he never had it. "You know what Warren's greatest talent is?" he asked rhetorically, in 1994. "How many pictures has Warren made in his career? Twenty-one? How many hits did he have? Three! *Bonnie and Clyde, Shampoo,* and *Heaven Can Wait.* That's batting three for twenty-one. In baseball, you're sent back to the minors for that. Not Warren. He's a major star. Every little kike producer says, 'I have Warren Beatty, I have Warren Beatty!' The only places Warren is known are Bel Air, Beverly Hills, Holmby Hills, and New York. But he's maintained that aura. He's still A-plus on every list. That is fucking talent, man. My hat's off to him. I love him for it."

Granted, Beatty is probably held to a higher standard because of the great expectations his gifts invited, as well as the power he enjoyed for two decades. By setting himself up as the new Orson Welles—not literally, of course, he would never be impolitic enough to claim that—he invited these judgments with the height and breadth of his aspiration, implied by the four credits for which he was nominated twice.

Beatty's doppelgänger, Robert Redford, will leave Sundance behind him, which, for all its faults, is an admirable institution. If it seems paradoxical to regard someone with Beatty's achievements as in some way a disappointment, it is because there has always seemed to be something broken about him, at least to some people, because this kind of assessment is made over and over again. "Warren is an underachiever," says Bo Goldman. "He could have been Orson Welles. He could have made five more wonderful movies, he could have been governor, he could have done everything, but his ego gets in the way. It's a form of narcissism. It's always about him." It's a harsh verdict. But if the lens is moved a fraction, it seems that on the contrary, Beatty did it all, made an indelible mark on his profession and still managed to embrace the breadth and variety of the experience that was available to him. It makes you wonder if that jury of movie people values films more than the fullness of life. Beatty always says that Charlie Feldman taught him "that life is short, and that movies are written on water, that you can't take them with you, and that the quality of your own life is the reality."

Perhaps it's not the last decade that makes them wonder, but the years he spent, so unproductively, chasing skirt. Perhaps it's the fact that Beatty turned down so many roles, in so many films, and missed so many opportunities to work more effectively and decisively in politics. He seemed to do so much less than someone with his gifts could have done. Perhaps it's that he always seemed so emotionally closed, so self-protective that, as Mab Goldman put it, he was unable to "stand naked in the storm of life." It is hard to avoid the conclusion that despite the many ways in which his parents, in their timidity, were a negative example for him, showed him the way *not* to conduct himself—in his extreme caution, in his behavioral conservatism, he couldn't help reflecting their influence.

A man with as much pride as Beatty has, who has achieved as much as he did, understands that if *Town & Country* proves to be his last movie, it is too much of an ugly duckling to make an appropriate swan song for such an exceptional career. But it is an instructive one. The interesting question with regard to *Town & Country* is not "how?" but "why?" The picture is a lightweight piece of fluff, at best. Why did he agree to make it? Maybe, ever the politician, he was playing it safe after *Bulworth*, just as he thought he was playing it safe making *Ishtar* after *Reds* and *Dick Tracy* after *Ishtar*. Surely, with more children on the way, a more dedicated filmmaker might have slipped in another movie before the PTA ate up what was left of his career. He still hadn't made *Hughes,*

his only remaining one-from-the-heart project, but he had always behaved as if he would live forever—to quote George Roundy—and
maybe he thought he had all the time in the world, until Scorsese beat
him to it with *The Aviator* (2004).

Beatty was impaled on the horns of a dilemma. As he said repeatedly,
he couldn't afford to just direct, because he wouldn't get his acting fee.
But, neither, as Pikser puts it, can "Warren just act in a movie he's not directing without making serious problems. He needs to be able to control
his environment. He can never let go, ever." He doesn't really trust anyone to direct him, and directors know this. Despite his good intentions,
his personality is such that he just can't help trying to "help," at the very
least, and seizing control at the very most. The good filmmakers, like
Scorsese who nearly directed *Dick Tracy,* have been smart enough to
give him a wide berth. And the not-so-good directors just brought out
the worst in him. What was the upside for them? Even if they turned
out well, as these collaborations occasionally did, witness *Bugsy,* the
director would merely be credited with a "Warren Beatty picture" and
tarred with faint praise, a reputation for being good at obeying orders.
If they didn't go well, Beatty might take the fall, but the director would
be scarred for life, or nearly so, the fate of Caron and Chelsom. It wasn't
just that no director would work with Beatty more than once; directing
Beatty could be a career ender, or at least retarder—witness those three.
(May never directed again, Caron made only one more feature, then resumed his career in television—successfully—while Chelsom struggled
until he regained his footing with *Shall We Dance* in 2004 and *Hannah
Montana* in 2009.)

But directing every picture in which he wanted to act was too much
of a burden, too emotionally and physically draining, and it precluded
him from following the path blazed by Clint Eastwood, who grace-
fully segued into directing when his leading-man days tapered off. It
couldn't have been easy for Beatty to sit in the audience at the Academy Awards, while Eastwood, a former TV cowboy, and seven years
older than he, became a regular nominee. Indifferent as he appears to
be, it was tough on him. "He hates it," says Pikser. "He's plagued with
envy."

Then too, Eastwood is a different kind of director, a man of few
takes, as he is of words, fast to commit and quick to execute. Beatty's
pictures were better, but Eastwood's were good enough, and way more

numerous. (By way of comparison, he has directed thirty-three pictures, to Beatty's four, and acted in about forty-seven, excluding his TV work, to Beatty's twenty-two, also excluding his TV work.) And perhaps most important, he has been able to keep making movies.

Beatty was sixty-four when *Town & Country* was released. He had always been a romantic leading man. Unlike Eastwood—a man's man, which is to say, an unromantic leading man—he has never been comfortable showing his age. Nor was he the kind of leading man who was essentially a character actor, like Jack Nicholson, Dustin Hoffman, Robert De Niro, or Al Pacino, which made it easy for them to slip into ensemble or even supporting roles when their starring days were over. Karsch once said to him, "Why don't you do more supporting roles?" He replied, "I'd like to. Why don't you find me one? One that will steal the picture!" Playing a supporting role was never, in other words, a real option. He momentarily contemplated one that Quentin Tarantino had more or less written for him—Bill, in *Kill Bill*. Metaphorically speaking, it was the perfect vehicle for "the phantom": the other characters spend the entire movie talking about Bill, the film's éminence gris, absent center, Wizard of Oz, whatever, who doesn't appear until the final scenes. Better still, and more in keeping with Beatty's persona, would have been had Beatty's Bill never appeared at all, which is exactly what happened when the star finally withdrew from the project. Beatty offered several explanations: it originally appealed to him because it was a small part, but Tarantino kept enhancing it until Beatty thought it would take too much of his time. He also couldn't help noticing the script was long, more than double the standard length, and way longer than could be accommodated by the shooting schedule he had been given. He was afraid it would go over and he'd be blamed for it, the way he was for *Town & Country*. (He was right about the production schedule, which did go way over.) Bill Bradley thinks it was too bloody for him, now that he had become a father.

All this having been said, it's foolish to count him out. As Dick Sylbert puts it, "He may still pull it off. Robert Rossen, when his back was against the wall—that's when he did something interesting." Beatty desperately wants to direct at least one more picture of significance, one more picture that is worthy of his gifts. Lately, he has begun to talk about *Howard Hughes* again, which would indeed be a fitting end to his career. The word on the street is that he has a good script that is focused on the latter half of Hughes's life, Hughes at the end of his days, which Beatty considers more interesting than the first half of his career. That would also serve to distinguish it from *The Aviator*. He has been talking to actors. Beatty even had a start date, March 2009, although that date has come and gone, replaced by a June or July, and at this writing, November 2009 date. Meanwhile, said Bening of her husband, "He's preparing. . . . He's always preparing."

ACKNOWLEDGMENTS

This book has been along time in the making, and many of the people who have helped me have undoubtedly forgotten about it, particularly Kim Masters and Corie Brown from the late, lamented *Premiere* magazine. I wish to thank my British researchers, Stephen Hyde and Sarah Cheverton, aided and abetted by Carl Bromley, who mined the collections at the British Film Institute National Library and the University of Portsmouth Library, assisted at the latter by Christopher Martin. Likewise, thanks to Sandra Archer, the head reference librarian at the Margaret Herrick Library of the Academy of Motion Picture Arts and Sciences, and Jim Hosney and Myriam Despujoulets at the American Film Institute, who provided invaluable aid. Thanks also to assistants at *Vanity Fair* who gladly found articles for me and tracked down sources, especially Jaqueline Gifford, John Ortved, and Louisine Frelinghuysen. Fellow writers and journalists who sent me their books and shared contacts included Sylvia Townsend, Brian D. Johnson, Nick Dawson, Nicole LaPorte, and Dennis McDougal. Thanks, too, to Howard Karren, John Clark, Wesley Brown, Ruth Reichl, Michael Singer, Richard Brick, and Ron Yerxa, who helped me in my vain efforts to find a decent title for this book. As always, I benefited beyond measure from the critical eyes of Sara Bershtel and Bruce Handy. I am grateful to Graydon Carter of *Vanity Fair* for keeping me alive while the leaves flew off the calendar and my advance from Simon & Schuster dwindled faster than the GNP. And speaking of, I commend the patience of Melissa Goldstein, my photo researcher; Bob Bender, who did a fine job editing the manuscript; his assistant, Johanna Li; copy chief Gypsy da Silva; and publisher, David Rosenthal. Kris Dahl, my agent, has always been a source of unstinting support. My wife, Elizabeth Hess, wrote and published her own book while I was writing mine, and probably could have written another one had I not been such a nuisance, while my daugher, Kate, grew up while I wasn't looking. And last but not least, I would like to thank Warren Beatty, a truly remarkable person and exceptional filmmaker. He may not like everything he sees in the mirror I have held up to him, but he has lived a life inspiring enough to write a book about, no small accomplishment.

NOTES

A NOTE ON THE RESEARCH

When thoughts are attributed to a principal, they are also derived from interviews.

WARRENOLOGY: AN INTRODUCTION

1 Epigraph: *Bonnie and Clyde*, DVD, "Making of—Documentary."

2 *"It's fundamentally destructive":* AI, 10/2/91.

2 *"In forty-five years you never opened":* AFI Life Achievement Award, 6/12/08.

2 *"If you have something to hide":* Lynn Hirschberg, "Warren Beatty Is Trying to Say Something," *The New York Times Magazine*, 5/10/98.

2 *"Warren has a theory":* Gary Younge, "Rebel with a Cause," ZA@PLAY, 6/10/99.

3 *"Even when he is saying nothing":* Lynn Hirschberg, "Film Star, Womanizer, Charmer, Man of the People. Warren Beatty for President," *The Observer* Review Page, 5/17/98.

3 *"He's one of the strangest":* Michael Sragow, "It's About How Much Craziness You Have to Accept," *Salon*, 8/19/99.

4 *"When he and I are standing":* AI, 11/19/06.

7 *"Women are like":* Confidential source.

7 *"You know that book":* Phone conversation, c. 2000.

8 *"is a game where the winner":* AI, 3/4/05.

9 *"master manipulator":* AI, 12/7/94.

10 *"How can you not hate a guy":* AI, n.d.

1. A STAR IS BORN

13 Epigraph: Fiona Macdonald Hull, "Warren's Women," *News of the World*, 9/10/78.

14 *"Hollywood was candy land":* AI, 4/14/06.

14 *"No matter how hot":* Confidential source.

14 *"My childhood was":* James Spada, *Shirley and Warren*, New York, 1984, p. 4.

15 *"That boy who's looking":* Joan Collins, *Past Imperfect*, Boston, 1978, p. 232.

15 *"I really thought I was hot shit":* AI, 10/2/91.

15 *"I thought he was gay":* AFI Life Achievement Award, 6/12/08.

15 *"Look, are you afraid"*: Jeff Cronin, "Beatty and the Two Beauties," *Photoplay*, 12/61.

15 *"Cut! Stop!"*: Ibid.

15 *"Oh my God"*: AI, 10/2/91.

16 *"nothing would stop him"*: AI, 6/7/92.

16 *"Hi, did you get"*: Collins, *Past Imperfect*, p. 236.

16 *"I can hardly wait"*: Ibid.

17 *"I'm coming up"*: Ibid., p. 238.

17 *"I don't think"*: Ibid., p. 250.

17 *"Maybe he did"*: Graham Lord, "The Fastest Lady in Hollywood," London *Daily Mail*, 8/20/07.

18 *"Warren was 21"*: Ginny Dougary, "Wicked Lady," *London Times Magazine*, 10/27/01.

18 *"When I got out here"*: AI, n.d.

18 *"He'd come home drunk"*: Shirley MacLaine, *My Lucky Stars: A Hollywood Memoir*, New York, 1996, p. 7.

18 *"Can Warren talk medicine?"*: AI, 6/7/94.

19 *"I saw you necking"*: Collins, *Past Imperfect*, p. 243.

19 *"I remember the morning"*: Shirley MacLaine, *Don't Fall Off the Mountain*, New York, 1971, p. 16.

19 *"Warren and I might have believed"*: MacLaine, *My Lucky Stars*, p. 18.

20 *"A friend of mine"*: AI, 10/2/91.

20 *"I needed money"*: Howard Smith, "Beatty Raps," *Eye*, c. 1968.

21 *"A friend of mine"*: AI, n.d.

21 *'Where ya going?'*: AI, 10/1/91.

22 *"Here comes Mr. Broadway"*: Beatty, AI, n.d.

22 *"Criticized Warren"*: Rita Gam, *Actors, A Celebration*, New York, 1988, p. 227.

22 *"Warren always wanted"*: AI, 4/6/05.

22 *"weighty," not "Wheaties"*: John Parker, *Warren Beatty: The Last Great Lover of Hollywood*, New York, 1993, p. 70.

23 *"Inge was in love" and following*: Ellis Amburn, *The Sexiest Man Alive*, New York, 2002, pp. 5, 21.

23 *"How smart of Warren"*: AI, 3/1/05.

23 *"I liked Warren"*: Jeff Young, *Kazan: The Master Director Discusses His Films*, New York, 1999, p. 255.

23 *"wanted it all"*: Elia Kazan, *A Life*, New York, 1988, p. 603.

24 *"There was this period"*: AI, 6/11/94.

24 *"They say that fighters"*: *Washington Post*, 1980.

25 *"he feels a wreath"*: Suzanne Finstad, *Warren Beatty: A Private Man*, p. 190.

25 *"I thought, I gotta"*: AI, 10/2/91.

25 *"You can't do a play"*: Spada, *Shirley and Warren*, p. 32.

26 *"Warren won't listen"*: Rex Reed, "Will the Real Warren Beatty Please Shut Up," *Esquire*, 8/67.

26 *"Warren kept me"*: "The Return of a Sexual Pioneer," *Toronto Star*, 8/26/06.

26 *"Don't go, Butterfly"*: Collins, *Past Imperfect*, p. 248.

26 *"changed lines"*: Reed, "Will the Real Warren Beatty Please Shut Up," *Esquire*, 8/67.

26 *"was written to"*: AFI seminar, moderated by Jon Avnet, 5/14/09.

26 *"In my forty-year career"*: Parker, *Warren Beatty*, p. 47.

27 *"sensual around the lips"*: Kenneth Tynan, *The New Yorker*, 12/12/59.

27 *"mercurial, sensitive, excellent"*: Spada, *Shirley and Warren*, p. 36.

27 *"There's no more"*: AI, 10/18/91.

27 *"The New York theater's"*: Spada, *Shirley and Warren*, p. 36.

27 *"I said 'Oh this is lovely'"*: Jackie Collins, quoted by Scott Haller, reported by David Wallace, "Scenes from a Sisterhood; Joan and Jackie Collins Turn Sex and Passion into a Family Plot," *People*, 11/12/84.

28 *"part of the reason"*: Victor Navasky, *Naming Names*, New York, 1980, p. 204.

28 *"Kazan was a pariah"*: AI, 6/29/05.

29 *"We were taught"*: MacLaine, *Don't Fall Off the Mountain*, pp. 1–2.

29 *"I went through"*: Younge, "Rebel with a Cause."

30 *"Her mother was"*: AI, 3/1/05.

30 *"When they were sober"*: AI, 4/6/05.

30 *"When Natalie was first suggested"*: Young, *Kazan*, pp. 258–59.

30 *"When I saw her"*: Kazan, *A Life*, p. 602.

30 *"good girl"*: Ibid., p. 603.

30 *"I saw a screen test" and following*: Beatty, AI, 10/2/91.

31 *"Pregnant?" and following*: Collins, *Past Imperfect*, p. 251.

32 *"I desperately wished"*: Hull, "Warren's Women."

32 *"Kazan said to me" and following*: AI, 4/6/05.

32 *"scared and worried"*: Howard Thompson, "Inge's Kansas Through a Kazan Kaleidoscope," *New York Times*, 5/22/60.

32 *"I suppose I have a method"*: *Cosmopolitan*, 1962.

33 *"a spectacular disappointment"*: MacLaine, *Don't Fall Off the Mountain*, pp. 9–10, 11.

33 *"didn't like good looking guys"*: Richard Schickel, *Elia Kazan*, New York, 2005, p. 376.

33 *"turkey neck"*: Glenn Gordon Caron, AI, 5/31/07.

33 *"Just shut up"*: AI, 8/25/92.

33 *"Lemme ask you something"*: Beatty, Schickel, *Elia Kazan*, p. 376.

33 *"In some patricidal attempt"*: Holly Millea, "The Revolutionary," *Premiere*, 11/06.

33 *"What did you say?"*: Schickel, *Elia Kazan*, p. 377.

33 *"the terrible effect" and following*: Millea, "The Revolutionary."

34 *"I like the title"*: AI, 10/2/91.

34 *"does not rebel" and following*: Schickel, *Elia Kazan*, p. 378.

34 *"It was never consummated" and following*: AI, 4/16/93.

34 *"Warren was a little"*: Kazan, *A Life*, p. 603.

35 *"The enemy"*: Finstad, *Warren Beatty*, p. 237.

35 *"Warren was a pain"*: Suzanne Finstad, *Natasha*, New York, 2001, p. 257.

35 *"I'm the vainest" and following*: Confidential source.

36 *"I was not about"*: Collins, *Past Imperfect*, p. 260.

36 *"Their marriage was crumbling"*: AI, 4/20/05.

36 *"It was clear to Natalie"*: Kazan, *A Life*, pp. 602, 603.

36 *"If they were kissing"*: AI, 4/20/05.

36 *"Beatty had nothing"*: Robert J. Wagner, with Scott Eyman, *Pieces of My Heart*, New York, 2008, p. 136.

37 *"I would have known"*: AI, 12/5/08.

37 *"There's a lot"*: Beatty, AI, 10/2/91.

37 *"Here comes MA"*: Finstad, *Natasha*, p. 258.

37 *"She had great disdain"*: AI, 4/20/05.

37 *"Warren wasn't coming through"*: Finstad, *Warren Beatty*, p. 239.

37 *"Absolutely beautiful" and following*: Collins, *Past Imperfect*, p. 266.

38 *"pimply, bespectacled"*: Ibid., p. 272.

38 *"I'm terribly sloppy"*: Cronin, *Photoplay*, "Beatty and the Two Beauties," 12/61.

38 *"I think [Warren] hides"*: George Christy, "Queen of the Tiny Screen: Joan Collins," *Interview*, 9/1/84, pp. 84–90.

39 *"During that time"*: Nigel Parndale, *Sunday Telegraph Magazine*, 10/17/04.

39 *"My first Hollywood party" and following*: AI, 10/1/91.

39 *"Could I talk?"*: Avnet, AFI Seminar.

39 *"So I went over"*: Ibid.

40 *"I was so stupid"*: Ibid.

40 *"He chased way more"*: AI, 4/27/05.

41 *"They spoke"*: AI, 11/9/00.

41 *"Charlie's patio was always"*: AI, n.d.

41 *"As nearly as I"*: AI, 12/11/00.

41 *"turned out to be"*: AI, 12/11/00.

41 *"Charlie taught Warren"*: AI, 5/12/93, 5/2/00.

42 *"Warren never answers"*: AI, 2/27/94.

42 *"I wanted to play"*: AI, 10/2/91.

43 *"What's going to happen" and following*: Gavin Lambert, AI, 3/4/05.

43 *"I said to myself" and following*: AI, 1/14/06.

44 *"I put on a bathrobe"*: AI, 10/2/91.

44 *"Tennessee was very"*: AI, 3/4/05.

44 *"He is so beautiful"*: Peter Evans, "So What Finally Tamed the Great Seducer?," *London Daily Mail*, 4/4/07.

44 *"He didn't say"*: AI, 3/4/05.

44 *"devastatingly handsome"*: Collins, *Past Imperfect*, p. 282.

45 *"Like most women"*: Reed, op. cit.

45 *"They were at it"*: Evans, "So What Finally Tamed the Great Seducer?"

45 *"I knew Lenya"*: AI, 3/4/05.

45 *"I don't think"*: Ibid.

45 *"It was a mess"*: Michael Wilmington and Gerald Peary, "Interview with Warren Beatty," *Velvet Light Trap*, #7, Winter, 1972/73.

45 *"It was the high tide"*: AI, n.d.

45 *"charming and intelligent" and following*: Susan Strasberg, *Bittersweet*, New York, 1980, pp. 120–21.

46 *"who could get to the mirror"*: Parndale, *Sunday Telegraph Magazine*.

46 *"It's crap"*: Collins, *Past Imperfect*, p. 289.

46 *"It was obvious"*: Finstad, *Warren Beatty*, p. 262.

47 *"silent, studious"*: Lana Wood, *Natalie: A Memoir by Her Sister*, New York, 1984, p. 64.

47 *"The way Natalie Wood":* Wagner, *Pieces of My Heart,* p. 141.

47 *"I wanted to kill":* Ibid., p. 142.

47 *"Even as a kid":* Spada, *Shirley and Warren,* p. 4.

48 *"an astonishing campaign":* John Houseman, *Unfinished Business,* New York, 1972, p. 401.

48 *"almost against [his] will":* Ibid.

48 *"Our most serious problem":* Ibid., p. 401.

48 *"I said, 'Oh?'":* AI, 4/6/05.

49 *"Our veteran cameraman" and following:* Houseman, *Unfinished Business,* p. 401.

49 *"The press has":* AI, n.d.

49 *"a frank and ferocious":* Bosley Crowther, *The New York Times,* 10/11/61.

50 *"should make the big":* Time, 10/13/61.

50 *"Andy Hardy story" and following:* Ralph F. Voss, *A Life of William Inge,* Lawrence, Kansas, 1989, p. 196.

50 *"Oh my God, you're":* Mark Harris, *Pictures at a Revolution: Five Movies and the Birth of the New Hollywood,* New York, 2008, p. 21.

50 *"I hate to bother you" and following:* Finstad, *Warren Beatty,* p. 277.

51 *"What I liked":* Michel Ciment, New York, 1974, p. 139.

51 *" 'I'd like to tell":* Ciment, *Kazan on Kazan,* p. 139.

51 *"Number One would like":* Gavin Lambert, *Natalie Wood,* New York, 2004, p. 188.

51 *"Mr. Beatty . . . is":* Spada, *Shirley and Warren,* p. 66.

52 *"It was much":* Jack Nicholson, AI, 1990.

52 *"When I was 16":* Eugenie Ross-Leming, "Playboy Interview," *Playboy,* 12/1/88.

52 *"Everyone in this story":* Reed, op. cit.

52 *"Bosley Crowther has never":* Spada, *Shirley and Warren,* p. 66.

52 *"Warren Beatty, whose":* Stanley Kaufman, *The New Republic,* 4/23/62.

52 *"preferred to play golf":* AI, 1989.

53 *"The White House had asked" and following:* AI, 6/11/94.

53 *"crap":* AI, 1989.

53 *"I was not prepared for it":* Ibid.

54 *"blended into a series":* Reed, op. cit., p. 83.

54 *"I realized that she":* AI, 10/31/97.

55 *"Society considers the person":* "Lessons Learned in Combat: Interview with Robert Rossen," *Cahiers du Cinéma in English,* #7, 1/67.

55 *"the plight":* AI, 10/2/91.

56 *"When he said," and following:* AI, 9/8/05.

2. ALL FELL DOWN

page

58 Epigraph: Roger Ebert, "Warren Beatty and Julie Christie and the Map to Presbyterian Church," *Chicago Sun Times,* 8/1/71.

58 *"Natalie would lie":* Lana Wood, *Natalie: A Memoir by Her Sister,* p. 64.

58 *"After a few hours":* Ibid., p. 63.

59 *"Natalie was a lightweight":* AI, 5/26/93.

59 *"My impression was":* AI, 3/4/05.

59 *"The morning of the day"*: AI, 4/6/05.

60 *"Natalie told me"*: AI, 3/4/05.

60 *"Warren goes through"*: Peter Evans, "So What Finally Tamed the Great Seducer?"

60 *"At the outset"*: *Cahiers du Cinéma in English*, #7, 1/67.

61 *"If the director was indecisive"*: *Time*, 7/3/78.

61 *"I hired you because"*: Finstad, *Warren Beatty*, p. 301.

61 *"Beatty was extremely difficult" and following*: AI, 5/15/05.

61 *"I was intimidated"*: Stanley Paley, "The Shooting of *Lilith*" Art Films International, 4/1/64.

61 *"Warren Beatty's behavior"*: David Richards, *Played Out: The Jean Seberg Story*, New York, 1981, p. 137.

61 *"because we all"*: AI, 7/25/09.

61 *"I've read* Crime and Punishment*"*: Paul Gardner, *The New York Times*, 7/21/63.

61 *"Warren was a man"*: AI, 8/25/92.

62 *"I don't think that anybody" and following*: AI, 5/15/05.

62 *"She got him"*: AI, 7/25/09.

62 *"Peter was running around"*: AI, 5/15/05.

62 *"psychotic"*: Wilmington and Peary, "Interview with Warren Beatty."

62 *"When he came"*: Jean Seberg, "Lilith and I," *Cahiers du Cinéma in English*, #7, 1/67.

63 *"From day one"*: AI, 5/15/05.

63 *"At the end of the filming"*: Seberg, "Lilith and I."

63 *"If I die"*: Muriel Davidson, "Public Image vs. Private Man," 1970.

63 *"Beatty probably contributed"*: AI, 5/15/05.

63 *"Warren's vision"*: AI, 4/9/93.

63 *"Hollywood was a closed club" and following*: AI, 1/12/93.

64 *"I found him"*: AI, 6/29/05.

64 *"to push American movies"*: *Time*, 10/8/65.

64 *"I don't understand" and following*: Penn, AI, 1990.

64 *"That didn't particularly fly"*: Penn, AI, 6/29/05.

64 *"It's too fucking obscure"*: Richard Porton, "An Interview with Arthur Penn," *Cineaste*, 12/93.

65 *"All the time, everywhere" and following*: AI, 4/26/94.

66 *"Warren used to"*: AI, 4/9/92.

66 *"Stanley was the"*: AI, 4/9/92.

67 *"It was like lightning" and following*: Dick Sylbert, AI, 6/7/94.

67 *"I was struck"*: George Gordon, "You Can't Beat Beatty," London *Daily Mail*, 3/14/94.

67 *"We practically did not leave"*: Aaron Latham, "Warren Beatty Seriously," *Rolling Stone*, 4/1/82.

68 *"My tiredness, her anxieties"*: Peter Hall, Shaun Usher, "Passion Plays," London *Daily Mail*, 9/6/93, from *Making an Exhibition of Myself*, London, 1993.

68 *"Mickey One 1/2"*: AI, 8/25/92.

68 *"Movies didn't have"*: AI, 6/29/05.

69 *"We had a lot of trouble"*: Wilmington and Peary, "Interview with Warren Beatty."

69 *"Nobody's going"*: Beatty and Penn, *Projections* 4, 1994, p. 125.

69 *"I felt they were pretentious"*: Wilmington and Peary, "Interview with Warren Beatty."

69 *"At that stage"*: AI, 6/29/05.

69 *"He doesn't like"*: "Penn on Penn," *Projections* 4, p. 125.

69 *"a certain flamboyance" and following*: AI, 6/29/05.

70 *"Oh, she's wonderful"*: AI, 6/29/05.

70 *"'Yes, I was having'"*: Rebecca Hardy, "My Passion for Beatty Killed My Marriage," London *Daily Mail,* 1/27/93.

70 *"I didn't blame"*: Hall and Usher, "Passion Plays."

70 *"Wonder why we hate ourselves"*: Harris, *Pictures at a Revolution,* p. 51.

71 *"In the original script"*: AI, 6/11/94.

71 *"a lovable guy"*: Harris, *Pictures at a Revolution,* p. 40.

71 *"You seem to forget"*: Charles Feldman, Feldman Collection, AFI Library.

72 *"for the past two weeks"*: Roderick Mann, "I want so much out of life, says Leslie Caron", *Los Angeles Times,* 6/14/64.

72 *"When you're falling in love"*: Quoted by Robert Younger, AI, 10/22/07.

73 *"Warren said, 'Charlie'"*: AI, 5/12/93.

73 *"I finally walked out"*: AI, 10/2/91.

73 *"I diva'ed my way"*: Harris, *Pictures at a Revolution,* pp. 86–87.

73 *"Woody was very unhappy"*: AI, 10/2/91.

74 *"a muddy performance"*: Crowther, *The New York Times,* 9/21/64.

74 *"I needed some confirmation"*: Gary Arnold, "So Much in Common; Beatty Shows 'Love Affair' Includes Kids and Friends as Well as Movie," *Washington Times,* 10/23/94.

75 *"he told me I was"*: Lana Wood, *Natalie,* p. 66.

75 *"Warren's coming over"*: Mart Crowley, AI, 4/6/05.

75 *"raised voices" and following*: Lana Wood, *Natalie,* p. 110.

76 *"It was just a miracle" and following*: AI, 4/6/05.

76 *"Nothing happened"*: Gavin Lambert, *Natalie Wood,* New York, 2004, p. 217.

76 *"I saw him about two months" and following*: AI, 4/6/05.

77 *"Maybe seeing Warren"*: AI, 3/4/05.

77 *"In ten seconds"*: Henry Jaglom, AI, 2/1/08.

78 *"It was a very upsetting period"*: Curtis Lee Hanson, "An Interview with Warren Beatty," *Cinema,* v. 3, no. 5, Summer, 1967.

78 *"He had this ability"*: AI, 6/14/94.

78 *"Bob was an extraordinarily"*: AI, 11/5/96.

78 *"He set up a meeting"*: AI, 3/3/94.

79 *"They were so intimate"*: AI, 6/14/94.

79 *"Towne was like this shadow"*: AI, 12/7/94.

79 *"He was great"*: Terry Gilliam, AI, 4/3/09.

80 *"Am I to assume"*: Harris, *Pictures at a Revolution,* p. 92.

80 *"I don't think Warren"*: AI, 12/9/92.

80 *"He seems to me"*: Luke Menand, "Paris, Texas," *The New Yorker,* 12/14–24/03.

80 *"Truffaut was utterly bored"*: Finstad, *Warren Beatty,* p. 343.

80 *"There was this funny thing"*: AI, 10/2/91.

80 *"This is Warren Beatty" and following*: Benton, "AMC Backstory," *Bonnie and Clyde,* 8/1/00.

81 *"My wife was in blue jeans"*: Benton, *Bonnie and Clyde*, DVD, "Making of—Documentary."

81 *"I want to do it" and following*: Benton, AI, 4/25/94.

81 *"He was walking around"*: AI, 3/3/94.

82 *"For me, producing means"*: Rossen, "The Face of Independence," *Films and Filming*, #11, 8/62.

82 *"Pretty boys didn't" and following*: Avnet, 5/15/08.

82 *"Up until the very last"*: Hanson, "Warren Beatty as Producer," in Wake and Hayden, eds., *Bonnie and Clyde*, pp. 179, 180.

83 *"that it was out"*: Harris, *Pictures at a Revolution*, p. 96.

83 *"affected and oddly amateurish"*: Bosley Crowther, *New York Times*, 9/9/65.

83 *"Warren and I were talking"*: AFI seminar with Robert Towne, moderated by James Powers, 1/22/75.

84 *"It was that period"*: AI, 10/2/91.

84 *"I wanted to challenge"*: Beatty, AI, 10/15/91.

84 *"It's an outlandish thought"*: Beatty, AI, 3/2/05.

84 *"That would be adding"*: Spada, *Shirley and Warren*, p. 112.

85 *"I'd love to do" and following*: Ibid., p. 110.

85 *"Some of these clowns"*: Beatty, letter to Benton and Newman, 3/14/66.

85 *"the face that launched" and following*: James Delingpole, "On the Couch with Julie Christie," *Daily Telegraph*, 7/12/95.

86 *"When Julie walked in a room"*: AI, 3/1/05.

86 *"One wanted to see"*: Pauline Kael, *For Keeps: 30 Years at the Movies*, New York, 1994, pp. 376–77.

86 *"I hate myself"*: Quoted by Oriana Fallaci, in Michael Feeney Callan, *Julie Christie*, New York, 1984, p. 107.

86 *"I was always deeply anxious"*: Tim Adams, "The Divine Miss Julie," *Observer*, 4/1/07.

86 *"Julie was the most beautiful"*: AI, 6/11/94.

86 *"Warren has an interesting psychology"*: Spada, *Shirley and Warren*, p. 133; Parker, *Warren Beatty*, p. 4.

87 *"I don't know"*: Benton, AI, 12/9/92.

87 *"There were a lot"*: AI, 12/9/92.

87 *"I thought I had"*: Bernard Weinraub, "Director Arthur Penn Takes on General Custer," *New York Times*, 12/21/69.

88 *"I don't want to do" and following*: Penn, AI, 3/2/05.

88 *"He punched every button" and following*: AI, 1/12/93.

88 *"Penn was a court"*: AI, 3/3/94.

88 *"Arthur was obviously"*: AI, 8/25/92.

88 *"We made an agreement"*: Andre Lebarthe and Jean-Louis Comolli, *Cahiers du Cinéma in English*, 12/67, in Wake and Hayden, eds., *Bonnie and Clyde,* London, 1972, p. 167.

88 *"Look, we're going"*: Wilmington and Peary, "Interview with Warren Beatty."

89 *"Beatty and I both"*: Bernard Weinraub, "Director Arthur Penn Takes on General Custer," *New York Times*, 12/21/69.

89 *"Once I said"*: AI, 1/12/93.

89 *"Being an outlaw"*: AI, 8/6/92.

89 *"part of it,"*: Penn, AI, 1/12/93.

89 *"Arthur suggested the whole notion"*: AI, 8/6/92.

90 *"the myth of Bonnie and Clyde"*: David Newman and Robert Benton, "Lightning in a Bottle," in Wake and Hayden, eds., *Bonnie and Clyde*, p. 27.

90 *"Two months in Texas"*: Lana Wood, *Natalie*, p. 123.

90 *"She had a lot"*: AI, 3/1/05.

90 *"She never understood"*: Quoted by Dick Sylbert, AI, 6/7/94.

90 *"Tell her how you say"*: Lambert, *Natalie Wood*, p. 236.

90 *"You're exquisitely beautiful"* and following: Jaglom, AI, 4/25/06.

91 *"Warren was the very definition"*: AI, 4/14/06.

91 *"You bastard"*: Millea, "The Revolutionary."

91 *"I'd watch the Warren Beatty show"*: AI, 12/7/04.

92 *"because he was great"*: Parker, *Warren Beatty*, p. 218.

92 *"He had nothing"*: AI, 9/8/93.

92 *"It just struck me"*: AI, 1/12/93.

92 *"Let me tell you"* and following: AI, 8/6/92.

92 *"Newman was skeptical"*: AI, 3/2/05.

93 *"None of us felt"*: AI, 3/3/94.

93 *"We were so excited"* and following: AI, 2/12/94.

93 *"the characters are"*: *Bonnie and Clyde*, DVD, "Making of—Documentary."

93 *"an on-again, off-again actor"*: Stefan Kanfer, quoted by Harris, *Pictures at a Revolution*, p. 192.

93 *"The lot seemed to me"*: AI, 1/12/93.

93 *"If they hadn't done that"*: AI, 6/23/92.

94 *"Warren said, 'He's'"*: AI, 2/15/94.

94 *"He always hated me"*: AI, n.d.

94 *"I used to think"* and following: AI, 4/9/92.

94 *"Colonel"* and following: Joe Hyams, AI, 4/9/92.

95 *"Probably. Possibly"*: Ebert, "Warren Beatty and Julie Christie and the Map to Presbyterian Church."

95 *"Look, just give me"*: Beatty, AI, 3/2/05.

95 *"Would I be letting you down"* and following: Penn, AI, 3/2/05.

95 *"It's too episodic"*: AI, 3/3/94.

95 *"Towne was"*: AI, 1/12/93.

95 *"When I was a kid"*: AI, 11/6/97.

96 *"Towne was Warren's buddy"* and following: AI, 8/6/92.

96 *"When Warren Beatty asked me"*: Allan Hunter, *Faye Dunaway*, New York, 1986, p. 39.

96 *"Most of the casting people"*: AI, 3/30/94.

97 *"I didn't have much"* and following: AI, 6/19/07.

97 *"I was doing a TV show"*: AI, n.d.

97 *"We're going to get"*: Beatty, AI, 11/19/99.

97 *"Warren believed in fly-fishing"*: AI, 4/25/94.

98 *"'You can't mix comedy'"*: Beatty, AI, 6/11/94.

98 *"We got turned down"*: Beatty, "AMC Backstory," *Bonnie and Clyde*, 8/1/2000.

98 *"We like this girl"* and following: Newman, AI, 2/12/94.

98 *"We were getting pretty close"*: AI, 1/12/93.

98   *"Faye was not"*: Penn, "AMC Backstory," *Bonnie and Clyde*, 8/1/2000.

99   *"When we left them"*: AI, 12/9/92.

99   *"She doesn't look"*: Harris, *Pictures at a Revolution*, p. 248.

99   *"This was the first"*: *Bonnie and Clyde*, DVD, "Making of—Documentary."

99   *"'Who wants to see'"*: Larry King interview, #1251, 10/14/94.

99   *"We're not going ahead" and following*: Beatty, AI, 3/2/05.

99   *"He answered me"*: Barbara Walters, *How to Talk with Practically Anybody About Practically Anything*, New York, 1970, p. 39.

100 *"empty of narrative substance"*: Bosley Crowther, *New York Times*, 9/23/66.

3. THEY ROBBED BANKS

page

101 Epigraph: AI, 4/8/05.

101 *"Warren said one day"*: Robert Towne, "A Trip with Bonnie and Clyde, *Cinema*, v. 3, no. 5, Summer, 1967.

102 *"Why aren't they"*: Mark Harris, *Pictures at a Revolution: Five Movies and the Birth of the New Hollywood*, New York, 2008, p. 258.

102 *"the first time"*: Howard Smith, "Beatty Raps," *Eye*, c. 1968.

102 *"they were appalled"*: Geoff Boucher, "Remembering 'Bonnie and Clyde': Warren Beatty and Arthur Penn Recall How Their Cinematic Spree Transformed Hollywood," *Los Angeles Times*, 3/23/08.

102 *"He was the producer" and following*: "Penn on Penn," *Projections* 4, p. 134.

102 *"Clyde came from the South"*: AI, 6/29/08.

102 *"It is all detail"*: Curtis Hanson, "Warren Beatty as Producer," in Wake and Hayden, eds., *Bonnie and Clyde*, pp. 179, 180.

103 *"By the time"*: Beatty, Howard Smith, "Beatty Raps."

103 *"There's no peaches" and following*: Towne, AI, 3/3/94.

103 *"There wasn't a car"*: Dede Allen, AI, 3/19/05.

103 *"Warren just wrote"*: *Bonnie and Clyde*, DVD, "Making of—Documentary."

104 *"Warren questioned everything"*: AI, 1990.

104 *"Warren would be talking"*: *Bonnie and Clyde*, DVD, "Making of—Documentary."

104 *"'Whoever gets tired'"*: Quoted by Dunaway, "Making of—Documentary."

104 *"I can be obnoxious"*: Harris, *Pictures at a Revolution*, p. 246.

104 *"For example, Arthur"*: AI, 3/3/94.

105 *"I am just beginning"*: Hanson, "Warren Beatty as Producer," p. 179.

105 *"comes in with eighteen cans"*: Ibid., p. 180.

105 *"that film is really"*: Ibid., p. 194.

105 *"No, it's just plain"*: AI, 1/12/93.

105 *"When Warren makes"*: AI, 8/25/92.

106 *"Warren was wonderful"*: AI, 1990.

106 *"You should not"*: David Thomson, *Warren Beatty and Desert Eyes*, New York, 1987, p. 373.

106 *"Even in the SMU" and following*: Philip Wuntch, "Warren's Love Affair," *Dallas Morning News*, 10/16/94.

106 *"I don't think anybody"*: AI, 1990.

107 *"[After every take]":* Towne, AI, 3/3/94.

107 *"The first days":* Penn, AI, 1/12/93.

107 *"She wouldn't ride":* Jane Summer, "Filming of *Bonnie and Clyde* a Story in Itself," *The Dallas Morning News,* 8/12/00.

107 *"Sit down" and following:* Towne, AI, 3/3/94.

107 *"We need to talk about":* Beatty, Harris, *Pictures at a Revolution,* p. 250.

107 *"Bernie fought everything":* Dede Allen, AI, 3/20/05.

107 *"I was there when":* Bonnie and Clyde, DVD, "Making of—Documentary."

108 *"I'd like you to":* MacLaine, unsourced.

108 *"The Vietnam War":* AI, 1/12/93.

108 *"There's a lot more" and following:* Richard Porton, "An Interview with Arthur Penn," *Cineaste,* 12/93, v. 20, issue 2.

109 *"How do you make":* Spada, *Shirley and Warren,* p. 125.

109 *"In the [Production] Code":* Bonnie and Clyde, DVD, "Making of—Documentary."

109 *"In those days":* Beatty, AI, 6/11/94.

110 *"The speed of some":* Penn, AI, 6/29/05.

110 *"That was one of those":* Penn, AI, 1/12/93.

110 *"I told her: 'Look'":* André Labarthe and Jean-Louis Comolli, "The Arthur Penn Interview," in Curtis Hanson, "Arthur Penn as Director," *Cinema,* v. 3, Summer 1967.

110 *"There was closer":* Penn, AI, 1/12/93.

110 *"When you're very":* AI, 12/12/05.

111 *"Have you ever":* AI, 3/20/05.

111 *"Cut it down":* Allen, AI, 3/19/05.

111 *"You had 30 seconds":* Gaylen Moore, "On the Cutting Edge of Film Editing," *New York Times,* 12/14/80.

111 *"Dede was the first":* AI, 5/4/05.

112 *"That made it":* Allen, 3/19/05.

112 *"shock cutting" and following:* Moore, "On the Cutting Edge of Film Editing."

112 *"There was a lot":* AI, 3/20/05.

112 *"The way he discarded":* Latham, "Warren Beatty Seriously."

112 *"Warren was wonderful":* Angela Levin, "Thank Heaven Gigi Still Can't Stop Herself from Falling in Love Again," London *Daily Mail,* 6/17/95.

112 *"You're sleeping!":* Gavin Lambert, *Natalie Wood,* New York, 2004, p. 179.

112 *"He could not pass":* Carinthia West, "The Trouble with Gigi," *Daily Telegraph,* 9/2/2003.

112 *"I will not tolerate":* Fiona Macdonald Hull, "Warren's Women," *News of the World,* 9/10/78.

113 *"A Hollywood movie star":* AI, 6/18/97.

113 *"I was always attracted":* James Delingpole, "On the Couch with Julie Christie," *Daily Telegraph,* 7/12/95.

113 *"I got to San Francisco":* AI, 6/18/97.

114 *"'Miz Allen,'" and following:* AI, 3/19/05.

114 *"I'll tell ya something":* Beatty, AI, 6/11/94.

114 *"Faye was wearing":* AI, 10/31/97.

115 *"Don't tell anybody":* AI, 3/19/05.

115 *"September, in those days" and following:* AI, 1/10/05.

115 *"language made Jack Warner":* Patrick Goldstein, "Blasts from the Past," *Los Angeles Times*, 8/24/97.

115 *"Dick, we've seen" and following:* Lederer, AI, 1/10/05.

116 *"Interviewing Warren":* Rex Reed, "Will the Real Warren Beatty Please Shut Up," *Esquire*, 8/67.

116 *"Well, Warren Beatty" and following:* Beatty, AI, 6/11/94.

116 *"I remembered they":* AI, 4/9/92.

116 *"What a reaction":* AI, 6/23/92.

116 *"I knew Crowther":* AI, 1/12/93.

117 *"a cheap piece":* Bosley Crowther, *New York Times*, 8/14/67.

117 *"I was scared":* AI, 6/23/92.

117 *"Look, it's just":* Benton, AI, 4/25/94.

117 *"Then Crowther":* Penn, *Cineaste*, 12/93.

118 *"Everything was different":* AI, 6/11/94.

118 "Bonnie and Clyde *is":* Pauline Kael, "Bonnie and Clyde," *The New Yorker*, 10/21/67.

118 *"something is happening here":* Bob Dylan, "Ballad of a Thin Man," *Highway 61 Revisited*.

118 *"Without her, Bonnie":* AI, 11/6/97.

118 *"Her review was":* AI, 2/12/94.

118 *"He came on very strong":* Kael, AI, 8/5/95.

119 *"It's a piece":* Lederer, AI, 6/23/92.

119 *"Let me pay you" and following:* Beatty, AI, 6/11/94.

119 *"mosquito":* Goldstein, "Blasts from the Past."

119 *"I really think this man":* AI, 6/23/92.

119 *"He was like a bulldog":* AI, 4/9/92.

119 *"Warren had the studio":* Goldstein, "Blasts from the Past."

120 *"Bessant was still":* Callan, *Julie Christie*, p. 110.

120 *"I don't think":* Anthony Hayward, *Julie Christie*, Bath, 2001, p. 135.

120 *"Sometimes I got":* Parker, *Warren Beatty*, p. 147.

120 *"closing the Christie":* Gerard Garrett, "The Melting Moment When Julie Christie Makes Warren (*Bonnie & Clyde*) Beatty," *Evening Standard*, 10/22/68.

120 *"He ran roughshod":* AI, 6/23/92.

120 *"'You're the producer'":* Tim Ewbank and Stafford Hildred, *Julie Christie: The Biography*, London, 2000, p. 164.

121 *"It helped start":* AI, n.d.

121 *"Once the word came":* AI, 1/12/93.

121 *"They were very happy" and following:* AI, 6/11/94.

121 *"I was discouraged":* Lederer, "AMC Backstory," *Bonnie and Clyde*, 8/1/00.

122 *"He said to me":* AI, 8/8/06.

122 *"the best movie of the year":* Time, 12/8/67.

122 *"Eliot, we have" and following:* Beatty, AI, 6/11/94.

123 *"The reason why":* AI, 3/19/05.

124 *"gets through women":* John Schlesinger, John Schlesinger Collection, BFI, JRS/66/6, Folder H.

124 *"But one can't":* Ibid.

124 *"very good for her future"*: Chris Hastings, "Julie Christie Was Warned Off Warren Beatty," *Telegraph*, 4/05/08.

124 *"The Julie and Warren thing" and following*: AI, 3/1/05.

124 *"Often I didn't feel" and following*: D. Lewin, "Julie Christie at 45," Brisbane *Courier-Mail*, 3/14/87.

125 *"If ever a movie star"*: AI, 11/6/97.

125 *"You get slapped"*: Beatty, AI, n.d.

125 *"Julie's smart"*: AI, 3/1/05.

126 *"by the time"*: AI, 6/11/94.

126 *"There was so much done"*: AI, 4/9/92.

126 *"I would be seated"*: Time, 7/3/78.

126 *"Beatty had no"*: Luke Menand, op. cit., *The New Yorker*, 12/14–24/03.

127 *"The idea at the time"*: AI, 6/19/07.

127 *"We were so fucking sure" and following*: Newman, AI, 7/30/92.

128 *"You know the really great thing"*: Boucher, "Remembering 'Bonnie and Clyde.'"

128 *"We're all disappointed"*: Modern Screen, n.d.

128 *"There were people"*: AI, 12/17/92.

128 *"We didn't know"*: Penn, AI, 1/12/93.

128 *"The Freudian nature"*: Hanson, "Warren Beatty as Producer," in Wake and Hayden, eds., *Bonnie and Clyde*, pp. 179, 180.

128 *"The feeling was"*: Towne, AI, 3/3/94.

129 *"The political message"*: Jay Carr, "Dick Tracy Speaks," *Boston Globe*, 6/10/90.

129 *"Warren's fundamental belief"*: AI, n.d.

131 *"Warhol was giving parties"*: AI, 7/30/92.

133 *"it was clear"*: Hunter S. Thompson, *Fear and Loathing on the Campaign Trail '72*, New York, 1973, p. 140.

133 *"It was Bonnie and Clyde"*: AI, 6/11/94.

133 *"Warren would stay" and following*: AI, 4/29/00.

134 *"I have never been"*: Finstad, *Warren Beatty*, p. 391.

134 *"thought Beatty was"*: Confidential source.

134 *"JFK was a very impressive figure"*: AI, 11/27/99.

134 *"I'm a Bobby Kennedy Democrat"*: AI, 11/19/99.

134 *"picking up the pieces" and following*: AI, 11/29/99.

134 *"I loved the way"*: Tim Adams, "The Divine Miss Julie."

135 *"One night I got"*: AI, 11/29/99.

135 *"I met Lillian"*: AI, 10/2/91.

136 *"Lillian hated actors" and following*: AI, 4/14/06.

136 *"We were taught"*: AI, 4/27/05.

136 *"I was in the park"*: AI, 6/28/94.

137 *"You couldn't believe" and following*: AI, 12/12/05.

138 *"Old women are"*: AI, 5/3/05.

139 *"If I went to someone"*: Thomas Thompson, *"Under the Gaze of the Charmer,"* Life, 4/26/68.

139 *"There's one last thing" and following*: Suzanna Moore, AI, 5/5/93.

139 *"I'm kind of exhausted"*: Howard Smith, "Beatty Raps."

139 *"People were dying"*: Ronald Brownstein, *The Power and the Glitter: The Hollywood-Washington Connection*, New York, 1990, p. 242.

140   *"There was a wish"*: AI, 6/28/94.

140   *"Warren and I"*: Joseph McBride, ed., "Robert Towne," in *Filmmakers on Film-making*, vol. 2, Los Angeles, 1983, p. 76.

140   *"Bob would love"*: Ayres, 6/14/94.

140   *"Towne could talk"*: AI, 2/27/94.

140   *"Robert had written"*: AI, 6/11/94.

141   *"He would not allow"*: AI, 11/6/97.

141   *"Look, I don't wanna"*: Beatty, AI, 6/11/94, 3/16/95.

141   *"You can't possibly" and following*: AI, 6/7/94.

142   *"give her a kick"*: John Schlesinger, John Schlesinger Collection, BFI, 3/11/68, JRS/66/8, Folder W.

142   *"I am ridiculously"*: Melvyn Bragg, *Richard Burton: A Life*, Boston, 1988, p. 262.

142   *"Wouldn't it be ironic" and following*: Parker, *Warren Beatty*, p. 162.

143   *"It was the end"*: Spada, *Shirley and Warren*, p. 165.

143   *"There I was"*: Callan, *Julie Christie*, p. 118.

143   *"Warren doesn't drink"*: Robert Ottaway, "The Unlikely Magic Between Julie Christie and Warren Beatty," *Daily Sketch*, 8/22/70.

144   *"About a year ago"*: Parker, *Warren Beatty*, p. 175.

144   *"I went up"*: AI, 3/16/95.

144   *"All over town"*: AI, 4/7/93.

144   *"Roman did a press conference"*: AI, 3/16/95.

4. EASY WRITER

page

146   Epigraph: AI, 6/28/94.

146   *"Let's find a picture" and following*: Beatty, AI, 6/28/94.

146   *"He was this bombastic rebel"*: AI, 10/17/94.

147   *"He did not wear"*: AI, 6/28/94.

147   *"It was the first time"*: AI, 10/17/94.

148   *"Julie never wanted" and following*: AI, 6/11/94.

148   *"Don't do anything"*: Tony Earnshaw interview with Mitch Brower, "It's All a Crapshoot," *Cinema Retro*, vol. 3, #7, 2007.

148   *"Assigning those three"*: Vincent Canby, *New York Times*, 3/5/70.

149   *"feel like Lassie"*: Michael Feeney Callan, *Julie Christie*, New York, 1984, p. 117.

149   *"foolishly absent" and following*: Britt Ekland, *True Britt*, Englewood Cliffs, New Jersey, 1980, pp. 131, 132, 133–34.

150   *"selling tool"*: Jacoba Atlas and Ann Guerin, "Robert Altman and Warren Beatty Make the Western Real," *Show*, vol. 2, #6, 8/19/71.

150   *"It had all the clichés"*: Walker Arts Center, 4/25/92.

150   *"and Brian [McKay] had"*: Patrick McGilligan, *Robert Altman: Jumping Off the Cliff*, New York, 1984, p. 340.

150   *"Your words brought"*: McGilligan, *Robert Altman*, p. 340.

150   *"It was pretty clear" and following*: AI, 6/28/94.

151   *"I would take these"*: AI, 6/11/94.

151   *"I worked quite a bit"*: Michael Wilmington and Gerald Peary, "Interview with Warren Beatty," *Velvet Light Trap*, #7, Winter, 1972/73.

151   *"It was good for me"*: AI, 3/16/95.

151   *"Warren was not"*: AI, 6/7/94.

151   *"Simply turned Julie's stuff"*: McGilligan, *Robert Altman*, p. 340.

151   *"I like to play schmucks,"*: Wilmington and Peary, "Interview with Warren Beatty."

151   *"shared a sort"*: AI, 6/28/94.

151   *"Let's have him"*: Margaret Walters, "Digging Up the Past," *The Listener*, April 12, 1990.

152   *"We didn't have a clue"*: Brian Case, "Fraught in the Act," *Time Out*, 2/19/97.

152   *"Bob had a talent"*: AI, 6/28/94.

152   *"One of the big problems"*: Altman, AI, 5/3/96.

152   *"It was considered"*: AI, 6/28/94.

153   *"Bob had a lot of guys"*: AI, 11/16/94.

153   *"Sam Peckinpah is a prick"*: Jim Margellos, AI, 6/28/97.

153   *"He stormed off"*: McGilligan, *Robert Altman*, p. 344.

153   *"Bob was crazy" and following*: AI, 3/1/05.

153   *"nit-picking"*: Altman, Gerard Plecki, *Robert Altman*, Boston, 1985, p. 39.

153   *"He'll chew something"*: Jack Nicholson, AI, 1990.

153   *"Warren wouldn't start rehearsing" and following*: Altman, AI, 5/3/96.

154   *"We shot it once" and following*: AI, 10/18/95.

154   *"It was like"*: AI, 6/28/97.

154   *"Finally, Bob said"*: AI, 10/18/95.

154   *"The path to success"*: AI, 10/13/95.

154   *"A lot of times"*: AI, 6/28/94.

155   *"Warren was buried"*: Margellos, AI, 6/28/97.

155   *"If we are"*: James Spada, *Shirley and Warren*, New York, 1984, p. 138.

155   *"Warren never allowed"*: AI, 10/8/97.

155   *"Infidelity destroys love" and following*: Tim Ewbank and Stafford Hildred, *Julie Christie: The Biography*, London, p. 179.

155   *"She used to sit"*: Callan, *Julie Christie*, p. 130.

156   *"It's not easy"*: Spada, *Shirley and Warren*, p. 140.

156   *"If ever we split up"*: London *Daily Mirror*, 3/3/72.

156   *"That script didn't work"*: AI, 3/6/95.

156   *"Badge can get me" and following*: Confidential source.

156   *"Warren was a terrible"*: AI, n.d.

156   *"Like so many"*: AI, 12/7/94.

157   *"Don't tell anybody"*: Confidential source.

157   *"Bob claims to have done"*: AI, 6/11/94.

157   *"You cunt"*: Confidential source.

157   *"Towne was tremendously" and following*: AI, 3/29/95.

157   *"Towne treated Jack"*: AI, 2/27/94.

158   *"Never underestimate"*: AI, 3/16/95.

158   *"one of the most conceited" and following*: Leonard Lewis and Andrew Crofts, "Leonard of Mayfair," London, 2000, extracted in London *Daily Mail*, 3/20/00.

158   *"He was very possessive"*: AI, 3/15/95.

159   *"very persuasive"*: Sheila Weller, *Girls Like Us*, New York, 2008, p. 360.

159   *"Oh, let's be honest"*: Official Carly Simon Web page.

159 *"It certainly sounds"*: *Washington Post*, 1983, quoted on Official Carly Simon Web page.
159 *"They find a new girl"*: Weller, *Girls Like Us*, p. 367.
159 *"I just got out" and following*: Jennifer Lee, *Tarnished Angel*, New York, 1991, p. 29.
160 *"ball-and-chain"*: Ibid., p. 32.
160 *"For all his reputation"*: Ibid., p. 30.
161 *"The extra person becomes"*: Ibid.
161 *"then have sex" and following*: Confidential source.
161 *"What do I care"*: Confidential source.
162 *"Where are you?"*: Confidential source.
163 *"I couldn't hear"*: AI, 6/28/94.
163 *"The soundtrack was"*: AI, 6/7/94.
163 *"Warren was infuriated"*: Bruce Williamson, *Playboy*, 8/76.
163 *"The principals thought"*: AI, 10/18/95.
163 *"It still is bad"*: McGilligan, *Robert Altman*, p. 344.
164 *"You think we"*: AI, 12/11/97.
164 *"Things had progressed"*: AI, 6/28/94.
164 *"I can hear it"*: AI, 5/3/96.
164 *"There was something wrong"*: AI, 5/3/96.
164 *"It wasn't checked"*: AI, 5/13/96.
164 *"The intentions"*: Vincent Canby, *New York Times*, 6/25/71.
164 *"a beautiful pipe dream"*: Pauline Kael, *The New Yorker*, 7/3/71.
165 *"It still hasn't grossed" and following*: AI, 5/3/96.
165 *"It prevented it" and following*: AI, 6/28/94.
166 *"I've spent"*: AI, n.d.
166 *"The McGovern campaign"*: AI, 6/28/94.
167 *"painfully earnest"*: Hunter S. Thompson, *Fear and Loathing on the Campaign Trail '72*, New York, 1973, pp. 81, 125.
167 *"Mr. Peepers"*: Chris Chase, "Warren Beatty Stars in the Great McGovern Money Hunt," *Life*, 6/23/72.
168 *"ski instructor"*: Hunter S. Thompson, *Fear and Loathing on the Campaign Trail '72*, p. 174.
168 *"The potential of women"*: AI, 9/9/04.
168 *"It was a howling"*: George McGovern, AI, 1990.
169 *"It was not only"*: Parker, *Warren Beatty*, p. 190.
169 *"I felt that"*: Brownstein, *The Power and the Glitter*, p. 241.
169 *"She's in bed" and following*: Dick Sylbert, AI, 10/8/97.
169 *"the permanent enfant terrible"*: Howard Fineman et al., "A Blood Sport," *Newsweek*, 4/6/92.
170 *"I was so young" and following*: AI, 3/4/05.
170 *"Beatty operated at"*: Brownstein, *The Power and the Glitter*, p. 243.
170 *" 'Mr. Beatty, what is' "*: Ibid., p. 242.
171 *"I won't take that"*: Pat Caddell, 3/4/05.
171 *"Warren invented"*: AI, 6/19/04.
172 *"I said, 'Is there' "*: AFI Life Achievement Award, 6/12/08.

172 *"looked at the draft":* Bob Shrum, *No Excuses: Concessions of a Serial Campaigner,* New York, 2007, p. 43.

173 *"Eagleton went out":* AI, 3/4/05.

173 *"Don't you think" and following:* Caddell, AI, 3/4/05.

174 *"would have been":* Hunter S. Thompson, *Fear and Loathing on the Campaign Trail '72,* p. 474.

174 *"represents that dark":* Ibid., p. 417.

174 *"He was one of":* McGovern, AI, 1990.

174 *"I'm real good":* Beatty, Carr, op. cit.

175 *"brought out all":* John Higgins, untitled, *New York Times,* 4/29/76.

176 *"He liked chaos":* AI, 4/26/07.

176 *"We always said":* AI, 11/16/06.

176 *"It was done sub rosa":* AI, 6/3/96.

177 *"Every morning during":* AI, 4/26/07.

177 *"call me and say" and following:* AI, 11/16/06.

177 *"Both Alan and Warren":* AI, 4/26/07.

178 *"Warren Stirs Soup":* Koch, AI, 11/16/06.

178 *"Gordon had no patience" and following:* AI, 4/26/07.

179 *"Mike Nichols wanted to do it":* AI, 1/25/08.

179 *"Medavoy is fuckin' senile":* AI, 3/6/95.

179 *"Obviously, it's very tempting":* Fiona Macdonald Hull, "Warren's Women," *News of the World,* 9/10/78.

179 *"as a charmer" and following:* AI, 4/26/07.

180 *"I'd fuck you" and following:* Confidential source.

180 *"Oh, how wonderful":* Weller, *Girls Like Us,* pp. 524–25.

180 *"This is Warren Beatty":* AI, 10/7/08.

181 *"As long as I had control":* Sue Clarke, "Beatty," *Photoplay* (U.K.), 7/75.

181 *"We talked about":* Ralph Appelbaum, "Positive Thinking," *Films and Filming,* 7/78.

182 *"Warren was a giant star":* AI, 6/20/94.

182 *"Hal and Towne" and following:* AI, 3/6/95.

182 *"He's always answering":* Karin Winner, "Warren Beatty on Movies and Politics," *W,* 5/3/74.

182 *"Everything is very secret":* Dick Sylbert and Sylvia Townsend, *Designing Movies,* Westport, Connecticut, 2006, p. 194.

183 *"Anyone who can":* AI, 6/11/94.

183 *"He exploits everybody":* AI, 6/17/94.

183 *"Warren could get anybody" and following: Designing Movies,* p. 140.

184 *"Robert's failure to deliver":* AI, 3/6/95.

184 *"Warren saw Nic":* AI, 6/7/94.

184 *"I got the picture":* AI, 2/27/94.

185 "Don't *tell* [*Towne*]": Nick Dawson, *Being Hal Ashby: Life of a Hollywood Rebel,* Lexington, Kentucky, 2009, p. 153.

185 *"I'm gonna make":* AI, 3/6/95.

185 *"Warren used his":* AI, 11/6/97.

185 *"Well what if":* Richard La Gravenese, 8/17/03.

185 *"the most creative ten days":* Dawson, *Being Hal Ashby,* p. 153.

186 *"Warren is the kind"*: Joseph McBride, ed., "Robert Towne," in *Filmmakers on Filmmaking,* vol. 2, Los Angeles, 1983.

186 *"Did Warren really write"* and following: Jeremy Larner, AI, 4/1/95.

186 *"He was so courageous"*: AI, 6/12/94.

186 *"It was very hard-hitting"*: AI, 2/25/95.

187 *"Warren knows how"* and following: AI, 6/11/94.

187 *"He turned out"*: Beatty, AI.

187 *"People thought Columbia"*: AI, 3/6/95.

187 *"Up to a week"*: AFI seminar with Robert Towne, moderated by James Powers, 10/13/76.

187 *"When Begelman reneged"* and following: AI, 3/6/95.

188 *"I had to go back"*: Beatty, AI.

188 *"it's not true"*: Beatty, AI.

188 *"Everybody hated"*: AI, 6/3/96.

188 *"I said, after reading"*: AI, 2/25/95.

188 *"I never made you"* and following: Beatty, AI, 6/28/94.

5. DON JUAN IN HELL

page

190 Epigraph: AI, 4/7/93.

191 *"Being the producer"*: Mary Murphy, "Don Juan with a Social Conscience," *Los Angeles Times,* 5/31/74.

191 *"We had a rough start"* and following: Ken Gross, "Lee Grant," *People,* 10/23/89.

191 *"I was not happy"*: Christopher Wilson, *Absolutely Goldie: The Biography,* London, 1999, pp. 105–6.

191 *"He's a multitalented"*: Peter Haining, *Goldie,* London, 1985, p. 125.

192 *"He offered to"*: *Rolling Stone,* 10/15/92.

192 *"I said, 'You're'"*: Sylbert and Townsend, *Designing Movies* (Westport, Conn.: Praeger, 2006), p. 141.

192 *"Warren treated him"*: Nick Dawson, *Being Hal Ashby: Life of a Hollywood Rebel,* Lexington, Kentucky, 2009, p. 152.

192 *"One day, Warren"* and following: Anthea Sylbert, AI, 7/22/93.

193 *"I hate even"*: Sylbert and Townsend, *Designing Movies,* 2006, p. 141.

193 *"I'll show you"*: Karin Winner, "Warren Beatty on Movies and Politics," *W,* 5/3/74.

193 *"We'd get three different"*: Suzanne Finstad, *Warren Beatty, A Private Man,* New York, 2005, p. 417.

193 *"Hal would never"*: Confidential source.

193 *"Warren just chewed"*: AI, 8/18/95.

193 *"It was tough"*: AI, 10/5/94.

194 *"'I can't take it anymore'"*: AI, 3/15/95.

194 *"not to be too harsh"*: AFI seminar with Hal Ashby, moderated by Rochelle Reed, 3/12/75.

194 *"It was very difficult"*: AFI seminar with Hal Ashby.

194 *"I'm not a hired actor"*: Tag Gallagher, "The Stud as a Thoughtful Man," *Village Voice,* 2/24/75.

195 *"usually the right thing prevails"*: Beatty, AI, n.d.

195 *"You're fucking whining" and following:* Dick Sylbert, AI, 3/3/94.

195 *"Warren was towering":* Towne, AI, 11/6/97.

195 *"The difference between":* AI, 10/5/94.

195 *"Hal understood something":* AI, 6/28/94.

196 *"what the seventies":* Sylbert and Townsend, *Designing Movies,* p. 136.

196 *"When you have a shot":* Ibid.

196 *"You get a mirror":* Ibid.

197 *"One day I'm going" and following:* Michelle Phillips, AI, 12/99.

197 *"I started seeing Warren" and following:* AI, 3/4/08.

197 *"I was concerned":* Fiona Macdonald Hull, "Warren's Women," *News of the World,* 9/10/78.

197 *"He was very cautious":* AI, 3/4/08.

197 *"You're likely to feel":* Vincent Canby, *New York Times,* 6/20/74.

198 *"It was a major film":* AI, 6/3/96.

198 *"Had I produced":* AI, 6/28/94.

198 *"Jack was always wild":* AI, 3/15/95.

199 *"Carole was born":* AI, 2/7/95.

199 *"was coughing herself":* AI, 9/26/94.

199 *"Jack had no":* AI, 3/3/94.

199 *"What is this arch":* Dick Sylbert, AI, 8/25/92.

199 *"Jack is a kingmaker":* AI, 9/26/94.

199 *"her arm so tightly" and following:* Finstad, *Warren Beatty,* p. 422.

200 *"I have theories":* Avnet, AFI seminar.

200 *"I hated the script" and following:* AI, 9/26/94.

201 *"Don is extremely honorable":* AI, 4/19/96.

201 *"I'm sure if Devlin":* AI, 2/7/95.

201 *"I was the voice":* AI, 9/26/94.

201 *"I didn't read":* AI, 6/28/94.

201 *"None of them" and following:* AI, 9/26/94.

202 *"I had no control":* AI, 3/6/95.

202 *"Part of it in truth" and following:* AI, 9/26/94.

202 *"I stayed away":* AI, 10/5/95.

202 *"There was another":* AFI seminar with Hal Ashby.

203 *"I like to leave":* Ibid.

203 *"When Warren wanted":* AI, 10/5/95.

204 *"I noticed there was":* AI, 5/31/07.

204 *"He won't show you":* AI, 9/8/93.

204 *"He really loved Chynna" and following:* AI, 3/4/08.

204 *"For a very long time":* Hull, "Warren's Women."

204 *"carrot dangling" and following:* Weller, "California Dreamgirl," *Vanity Fair,* 12/07.

205 *"never really knew":* Hull, "Warren's Women."

205 *"The legend is Carole":* AI, 2/7/95.

205 *"The script was":* AI, 12/22/93.

205 *"Mike got more" and following:* AI, 9/26/94.

205 *"She'll never fit":* Hank Moonjean, *Bring in the Peacocks: Memoirs of a Hollywood Producer,* Bloomington, Indiana, 2004, p. 317.

206 *"We're never going"*: Confidential source.

206 *"There was a tremendous"*: AI, 9/26/94.

206 *"Jack was doing"*: AI, 4/19/96.

206 *"Mike hated what"*: AI, 9/26/94.

206 *"It's insane"*: AI, 3/16/95.

206 *"Warren turned to Mike"*: AI, 9/26/94.

206 *"This was her first"*: AI, 4/19/96.

206 *"like jerks"*: Jack Kroll, *Newsweek*, 8/6/08.

206 *"Mike Nichols had to bar me"*: Weller, "California Dreamgirl."

206 *"She just ignored it"*: AI, 9/26/94.

206 *"I was madly"*: Weller, "California Dreamgirl."

207 *"$30 million"*: Confidential source.

207 *"It wasn't just a dirty moment"*: AI, 6/28/94.

207 *"The audience was"*: AI, 6/28/94.

207 *"One third of the audience"*: AI, 11/22/94.

208 *"They can't all" and following*: Beatty, AI, 6/28/94.

208 *"Sue Mengers hated it"*: AI, 2/25/95.

208 *"All of them"*: Larry Salvato and Dennis Schaefer, "Interview with Hal Ashby," *Millimeter*, 10/76.

208 *"when the Teletypes"*: AI, 9/26/94.

208 *"Hal Ashby's* Shampoo*"*: Vincent Canby, *New York Times*, 2/16/75.

208 *"Shampoo is the"*: Kael, "Beverly Hills as a Big Bed," *The New Yorker*, 2/17/75.

208 *"Warren and Bob Towne"*: AI, 3/22/06.

209 *"Everyone knew that"*: AI, 12/7/94.

209 *"There's a trick"*: AI, 3/2/07.

209 *"She'd take out"*: AI, 7/27/09.

209 *"Towne had Kael" and following*: AI, 12/7/94.

209 *"The ending is"*: Jay Cocks, *Time*, 2/24/75.

210 *"You can kill a movie"*: "Warren Beatty Says Too Much Talk Hurts Films," *Box Office*, 3/31/75.

210 *"I don't think"*: Tommy Thompson, "There's Something Peculiar About Warren Beatty These Days," *Los Angeles*, 3/75.

210 *"I know that"*: Frank Rich, "Warren Beatty Strikes Again," *Time*, 7/3/78.

211 *"I don't see it"*: Jerry Hellman, AI, 6/20/94.

211 *"There are some things"*: Corie Brown, AI, 12/19/94.

211 *"Begelman fucked us" and following*: AI, 11/6/97.

212 *"Towne talking about"*: AI, 3/6/95.

212 *"Bob thought he had"*: AI, 1/95.

212 *"Bob always said"*: AI, 4/18/96; Corie Brown, "No Love Affair," *Premiere*, 2/95.

212 *"Robert has some"*: AI, 3/6/95.

213 *"Half the audience"*: AI, 4/27/05.

213 *"Vietnam polarized the town"*: AI, 6/28/94.

213 *"Basically the upper class"*: Diane Jacobs, "Coming Home—It's Hal Ashby at His Best," *Minneapolis Star*, 5/12/78.

214 *"It's my point"*: AI, 1990.

215 *"a message [Warren] wanted"*: Finstad, *Warren Beatty*, p. 416.

216 *"Men over thirty"*: James Spada, *Shirley and Warren*, New York, 1984, p. 168.

217 *"Many times I'm called upon"*: Confidential source.

217 *"I'd love to fuck you"*: Confidential source.

217 *"has an unsublimated libido"*: Bob Thomas, *Los Angeles Herald-Examiner*, 8/31/75.

218 *"Warren, get your hand"*: People, 3/17/75.

218 *"I don't know what"*: AI, n.d.

218 *"There was a"*: Biskind, "The Crucible: An Oral History," *Premiere* Special Issue, 1994.

219 *"It's very strange"*: Hull, "Warren's Women."

219 *"I'm sorry, I'm sorry"*: Devlin, AI, 11/22/94.

219 *"Warren told me"*: AI, 8/25/92.

219 "The Fortune *is a bleak"*: Jay Cocks, *Time*, 5/26/75.

219 *"Mike was shattered"*: AI, 5/1/05.

220 *"Warren was laughing"*: AI, 11/22/94.

220 *"I heard the word"*: Frank Rich, "The Misfortune of Mike Nichols: Notes on the Making of a Bad Film," *New Times*, 7/11/75.

220 *"He felt that he was"* and *following*: AI, 12/3/91.

220 *" 'Do you want' "*: AI, 12/3/91.

221 *"Two people cannot"*: AI, 3/4/08.

221 *"Warren didn't want"*: Weller, "California Dreamgirl," *Vanity Fair*.

221 *"Warren would tell me"*: Sally Ogle Davis, "How Many Women Does It Take to Change a Lothario," *Mail on Sunday*, 5/24/92.

221 *"When I told him"*: Weller, "California Dreamgirl," *Vanity Fair*, 12/07.

221 *"I knew that"*: AI, 3/4/08.

221 *"The last year"* and *following*: Hull, "Warren's Women."

221 *"Warren is not a"*: Spada, *Shirley and Warren*, p. 170.

221 *"That is what Warren"*: Weller, "California Dreamgirl," *Vanity Fair*, 12/07.

221 *"When Barbara Walters"* and *following*: AI, 3/4/08.

222 *"The decision to end"*: Hull, "Warren's Women."

222 *"He was the best-looking"*: AI, 4/14/06.

222 *" 'One liked to watch' "*: Quoted by James Toback, AI, 7/27/05.

222 *"I was emotionally"*: Hull, "Warren's Women."

222 *"I want to marry you"* and *following*: Phillips, quoted by *People*, 10/2/78.

223 *"He loves people thinking"* and *following*: Hull, "Warren's Women."

223 *"I don't have bad memories"*: AI, 3/4/08.

223 *"Warren's gonna be"*: G. Mac Brown, AI, 8/7/08.

224 *"Listen, you can make"*: Néstor Almendros, AI, n.d.

224 *"It took me"*: AI, 12/21/05.

224 *"the playboy"*: Aaron Latham, "Warren Beatty, Seriously," *Rolling Stone*.

224 *"an inordinate desire"*: Beatty, AI, n.d.

226 *"It can be very hard"*: AI, 12/12/05.

226 *"I realized"*: 10/2/91.

226 *"Trevor felt, 'I'm' "*: AI, 6/27/05.

226 *"Warren spoke as if"*: AI, 10/11/05.

226 *"Warren saw himself"*: Latham, "Warren Beatty, Seriously."

227 *"He asked me"* and *following*: AI, 10/11/05.

227 *"Let's trade"*: Robert Rosenstone, AI, 5/1/06.

227 *"this strange kind"*: AI, 5/6/06.
228 *"It wasn't the best"*: AI, 10/11/05.

6. ORSON WELLES, C'EST MOI

page

229 Epigraph: AI, 3/22/06.
230 *"Something about the theme"*: Charles Champlin, "Warren Beatty: Two Sides to a Hollywood Story," *Los Angeles Times*, 1/28/79.
230 *"They were very different"*: AI, 8/8/06.
230 *"She knew the subtleties"*: James Sacks, Wikipedia.
230 *"Elaine May is the"*: Wikipedia.
230 *"She was very, very difficult"*: AI, 6/24/06.
231 *"It was two o'clock"*: AI, 3/20/06.
231 *"Elaine May is"*: David Blum, *"The Road to 'Ishtar,'"* *New York* magazine, 3/16/87.
231 *"There's nothing sexual"*: AI, 3/22/06.
231 *"If you were a female" and following*: AI, 4/14/06.
231 *"Ideas fly off her"*: AI, 3/22/06.
232 *"Where is Warren?"*: Michael Laughlin, AI, 10/23/06.
232 *"All directors think"*: AI, 4/14/06.
232 *"Warren wasn't happy"*: AI, 3/22/06.
232 *"Warren, who was among"*: AI, 12/11/97.
232 *"asshole"*: Confidential source.
232 *"Do you want to make"*: Confidential source.
233 *"They just kept irritating"*: AI, 3/6/95.
233 *"He's still a goalie"*: Confidential source.
233 *"I got in a big fight"*: Robert Evans, AI, 6/11/94.
233 *"I just think Warren"*: AI, 3/25/06.
234 *"Buck was into"*: Confidential source.
234 *"I knew Warren a little bit"*: AI, 8/8/06.
235 *"Warren gets me"*: Champlin, "Warren Beatty: Two Sides to a Hollywood Story."
235 *"We both knew" and following*: AI, 3/2/07.
236 *"Warren, haven't heard" and following*: AI, 11/16/06.
236 *"Warren never spends"*: AI, 3/25/06.
237 *"She was my idea" and following*: AI, 3/2/07.
237 *"We did this pretend" and following*: AI, 12/7/94.
237 *"When he finally got her"*: AI, 11/16/06.
237 *"I think he had"*: AI, 8/8/06.
238 *"I'm not going to" and following*: Hal Lieberman, AI, 4/27/07.
239 *"I think"*: Confidential source.
239 *"like a kid" and following*: AI, 11/16/06.
240 *"I never tried to block"*: AI, 3/25/06.
240 *"Warren doesn't come off"*: AI, 11/16/06.
240 *"When you take on"*: AI, 3/2/07.
240 *"He agonizes over"*: AI, 3/22/06.
241 "Heaven Can Wait *was"*: AI, 11/16/06.

241 *"I was sitting in"*: Charles Grodin, AI, Biskind, "Inside Ishtar," *American Film,* 5/87.

241 *"I had to put up with"*: AI, 11/16/06.

242 *"I had to get" and following*: AI, 11/16/06.

242 *"Certainly Warren is"*: AI, 12/7/94.

243 *"Poor Buck, what"*: Quoted by Koch, AI, 11/16/06.

243 *"It was always about"*: AI, 8/8/06.

244 *"Warren beat the shit"*: AI, 3/15/95.

244 *"Warren'll put" and following*: AI, 12/7/94.

245 *"You might not believe it" and following*: Toback, AI, 9/28/04.

246 *"Ma Barker"*: James Wolcott, *Vanity Fair,* 4/97.

246 *"Jimmy made him laugh" and following*: AI, n.d.

247 *"Proceed"*: Toback, AI, 1/24/95.

247 *"The script was Elaine's" and following*: AI, 3/22/06.

247 *"He was tough"*: AI, 3/2/07.

247 *"Warren would see" and following*: AI, 3/22/06.

248 *"The dividing line"*: AI, 3/2/07.

248 *"Cary Grant and Warren" and following*: AI, 3/22/06.

248 *"He was an unbelievably" and following*: AI, 4/27/07.

249 *"There was a lot"*: AI, 3/2/07.

249 *"Warren Beatty believed" and following*: Charles Grodin, *We're Ready for You, Mr. Grodin,* New York, 1994, pp. 296–97.

249 *"David used to bring"*: Confidential source.

249 *"walking around bare-breasted"*: Grodin, "How I Got to Be Whoever It Is I Am," New York, 2009, p. 144.

249 *"The worst battle"*: AI, 3/20/06.

249 *"I'm not sure Julie"*: AI, 3/20/06.

249 *"She didn't like"*: AI, 11/16/06.

250 *"She was crying"*: AI, 3/1/05.

250 *"Would you please"*: AI, 3/2/07.

250 *"Pleeease, don't tell" and following*: AI, 8/8/06.

252 *"Warren came up"*: AI, 11/16/06.

252 *"I vividly remember" and following*: AI, 8/8/06.

252 *"de-celebritisation" and following*: Tom Gliatto, Bryan Alexander, Jeffrey Wells, Dennis Passa, "Darling: Julie Christie, Reluctant Star of the '60s Returns in *Afterglow,*" *People,* 2/9/98.

252 *"I thought I was"*: Tim Adams, "The Divine Miss Julie," *Observer,* 4/1/2007.

253 *"Warren, where's my name?" and following*: AI, Confidential source.

253 *"I couldn't fathom"*: AI, 4/27/07.

253 *"Oh, hi" and following*: AI, Confidential source.

253 *"He was having me" and following*: AI, 4/27/07.

254 *"I remember" and following*: AI, 1/11/06.

255 *"Warren always liked"*: AI, 9/8/05.

255 *"I got a call"*: AI, 2/27/94.

255 *"Having already produced"*: Frank Rich, "Warren Beatty Strikes Again," *Time,* 7/3/78.

256 *"I was there opening night"*: AI, 11/16/06.

256   *"the star (who is also)"*: Kael, "Fear of Movies," 9/28/78, in *For Keeps: 30 Years at the Movies*, New York, 1994, pp. 774, 776–77.

256   *"There are certain actors"*: AI, 3/2/07.

257   *"He was good"*: AI, 3/22/06.

258   *"the phantom of the Southwest"*: Robert Towne, *A Trip with Bonnie and Clyde*, in Sandra Wake and Nicola Hayden, eds., *Bonnie and Clyde*, London, 1972, p. 175.

258   *"The Phantom"*: Brownstein, *The Power and the Glitter*, p. 321.

258   "Heaven Can Wait *is*": AI, 3/25/06.

258   *"that he'd fucked Jackie O" and following*: Christopher Andersen, "Jackie After Jack," New York, 1998, excerpted in London *Daily Mail*, 4/15/98.

259   *"Warren was sitting"*: AI, 11/6/07.

259   *"All the joking references"*: Charles Champlin, *Los Angeles Times*, 4/11/79.

259   *"Warren rang me up" and following*: AI, 10/11/05.

260   *"Everything you've just seen"*: AI, 5/3/05.

260   *"Warren wanted to"*: AI, 10/11/05.

260   *"Warren was huge" and following*: AI, 5/3/05.

260   *"That draft had two"*: AI, 10/4/07.

260   *"It was really painful"*: AI, 10/11/05.

261   *"It's often more hostile"*: AI, 5/3/05.

261   *"Absolutely not"*: AI, 10/11/05.

261   *"He was sweet"*: AI, 5/3/05.

261   *"It was not just in" and following*: AI, 10/11/05.

262   *"Would I do something like this?"*: AI, n.d.

262   *"Absolutely!"*: AI, 8/8/06.

262   *"Pure Warren Beatty"*: AI, 6/24/06.

262   *"The atmosphere around us" and following*: AI, 10/11/05.

263   *"That's the great thing"*: AI, 5/3/05.

263   *"It was a huge relief"*: AI, 11/8/07.

263   *"Casting is the whole"*: *Reds* screening, Lincoln Center, 10/4/06.

263   *"He was making"*: AI, 8/8/06.

263   *"It sometimes seemed"*: Norman Mailer, "The Warren Report," *Vanity Fair*, 11/91.

263   *"I didn't really believe"*: AI, 1/11/06.

264   *"I said, 'I've got'"*: AI, n.d.

264   *"worried and worried"*: AI, 10/24/05.

264   *"Jack gave up"*: AI, n.d.

264   *"Warren said to me"*: AI, 10/24/05.

264   *"did not know how"*: AI, 1/23/08.

264   *"Maureen, if you don't"*: Confidential source.

265   *"You're crazy to do this"*: Beatty, n.d.

265   *"I can't trust anybody" and following*: AI, 6/7/94.

266   *"One day Vittorio"*: AI, n.d.

266   *"We had an audience"*: AI, 5/3/05.

266   *"It's not like you think"*: AI, 11/19/99.

266   *"If exposition kills"*: AI, 5/3/05.

267   *"Miller had nothing"*: AI, 3/20/05.

267   *"You seem to be after" and following*: Pikser, AI, 5/3/05.

267   *"I have to make"*: AI, 5/3/05.

267 *"If you have"*: AI, n.d.

267 *"Warren functions creatively" and following:* AI, 5/3/05.

7. FROM RUSSIA WITH LOVE

page

269 Epigraph: AI, 6/11/94.

270 *"Talk about obsessed!":* AI, 6/7/94.

270 *"I'd been hearing":* AI, 12/29/05.

270 *"Charlie really loved":* Don Simpson, AI, 7/21/93.

270 *"How much iz diz" and following:* Beatty, AI, 12/12/05, 3/16/95, 6/28/94.

271 *"If you know":* Beatty, AI, 1997, also 12/12/05.

271 *"It was really not possible":* AI, 12/29/05.

272 *"You need a producer":* Toback, AI, 9/28/04.

272 *"You tell Fellini,"* AI, n.d.

272 *"Here was the Voice":* AI, 3/22/06.

272 *"Because of her power":* AI, 12/23/91.

272 *"The whole point":* AI, 12/7/94.

273 *"She would not":* AI, n.d.

273 *"This is terrible" and following:* Albarino, AI, 7/27/09.

273 *"This is awful" and following:* Beatty, AI, n.d.

273 *"Warren wanted to work":* AI, 7/27/05.

273 *"You're being very stupid" and following:* Toback, AI, n.d.

273 *"Toback, against":* Toback, AI, 7/27/05.

273 *"I was polite":* Toback, AI, n.d.

273 *"Let's see if we can" and following:* Toback, AI, 9/28/04.

273 *"Don Simpson had no":* AI, 8/5/95.

273 *"Hiring her":* AI, 10/18/91.

274 *"We sat in Moscow":* AI, n.d.

274 *"Everyone was in good humor":* AI, 12/12/05.

274 *"There are some movies":* AI, 12/21/05.

275 *"The budget was actually":* AI, 10/24/05.

275 *"We had to wait":* AI, 8/8/05.

275 *"Maureen Stapleton Lost at Sea":* Nina Rosenblum, AI, 1/23/08.

275 *"He was as good-looking":* AI, 7/8/08.

276 *"If I'm reincarnated":* Dan Allentuck, AI, 1/24/08.

276 *"What do you want":* James Spada, *Shirley and Warren,* New York, 1984, p. 196.

276 *"He was such a goddamned":* John Parker, *Warren Beatty: The Last Great Lover of Hollywood,* New York, 1994, p. 7.

276 *"After a while, she":* AI, 1/24/08.

276 *"wouldn't stop the camera" and following:* AI, 8/8/05.

277 *"It was a point of pride":* AI, 12/5/05.

277 *"I saw several actors" and following:* Confidential source.

277 *"Put it this way":* AI, 1/12/06.

277 *"The dialogue, the cadences":* Jeremy Pikser, AI, 5/3/05.

277 *"Warren did something like":* AI, 10/29/05.

278 *"Stop it":* James Spada, *Shirley and Warren,* New York, 1984, p. 195.

278 *"It must have been":* AI, 10/24/05.

278 *"At the same time":* AI, 1/11/06.

278 *"It was a pleasure":* AI, 12/15/05.

278 *"A lot of people":* AI, 12/4/05.

279 *"He's reasonably affable":* AI, n.d.

279 *"That may be":* AI, 1/12/06.

279 *"Within a week" and following:* AI, 12/29/05.

279 *"I think there was":* AI, 3/16/95.

280 *"Around dinnertime":* AI, 10/29/05.

281 *"This is an important film":* Confidential source.

281 *"They came storming" and following:* AI, 8/8/05.

281 *"He did not find":* AI, 10/11/05.

281 *"Warren thought I was" and following:* AI, 5/3/05.

282 *"the Beatty curtain" and following:* Jack Pitman, "Insiders Say Beatty's *Reds* Price Tag May Hit $30 Mil," *Variety,* 3/26/80.

282 *"Everyone appreciates the work":* *LA* magazine, 1/80.

283 *Grabber News:* n.d.

283 *"He was drawn" and following:* Aaron Latham, "Warren Beatty Seriously," *Rolling Stone,* 4/1/82.

284 *"He was coughing":* AI, 3/4/05.

284 *"Warren felt isolated":* AI, 5/3/05.

284 *"He's fighting off":* AI, 7/8/08.

284 *"We do have our":* AI, 10/18/91.

285 *"Directing your girlfriend":* AI, 12/24/05.

285 *"Making a movie together":* AI, 12/12/05.

285 *"Warren was always":* AI, 5/3/06.

285 *"God help me":* AI, 1/12/06.

285 *"Warren didn't have an easy":* AI, 4/14/06.

286 *"I don't think":* AI, 1/11/06.

286 *"It was sometimes hard":* AI, 12/25/05.

286 *"Diane wanted to be":* AI, 6/27/05.

287 *"I don't think he understands":* AI, 8/8/06.

287 *"I saw her as somebody":* AI, 1/11/06.

287 *"No":* AI, 12/12/05.

287 *"It was completely":* AI, 1/11/06.

288 *"It was at the time":* AI, 8/8/05.

288 *"She went to the airport":* AI, 8/8/05.

288 *"Yes, it rings a bell":* AI, 1/11/06.

288 *"It's completely not true":* AI, 12/12/05.

289 *"It was the greatest":* AI, 1/16/08.

289 *"I was overwhelmed" and following:* AI, 3/20/05.

289 *"We went through over":* AI, 8/8/05.

289 *"I had a quarter":* AI, 1/15/08.

289 *"Give me Diane" and following:* Confidential source.

290 *"She saw her role":* AI, 1/16/08.

290 " 'Are you kidding?' " and following: AI, 9/8/08.

290 "I had a gallstone attack": AI, 7/3/08.

290 "Being a woman": Kate Hirson, AI, 9/20/07.

290 "People were very angry": AI, 1/22/08.

290 "Dede was such": AI, 9/20/07.

290 "According to Dede" and following: AI, 1/15/08.

291 "When it was over": AI, 1/22/08.

291 "I was working": AI, 1/16/08.

291 "Making this film": 1/16/08.

291 "Once his mother called": Kane, AI, 9/8/08.

291 "He had that charisma": AI, 12/4/05.

291 "All the women": AI, 1/15/08.

291 "One Sunday, I was": AI, 1/15/08.

292 "You didn't have to" and following: AI, 9/8/08.

292 "Little David didn't know" and following: AI, 9/8/08.

293 "You felt there was": AI, 9/8/08.

293 "Once, when Chynna": AI, 3/4/08.

293 "Chynna was wearing" and following: AI, 9/8/08.

293 "Do you want": AI, 1/15/08.

293 "He came by my desk": AI, 9/8/08.

294 "He was very flirtatious" and following: AI, 1/16/08.

294 "Once one of the temps": AI, 9/20/07.

294 "He really loved women": AI, 1/22/08.

294 "I had a great time": AI, 1/15/08.

294 "He had this": AI, 10/23/07.

295 "What would be frustrating": AI, 1/15/08.

295 "People were pulling him": AI, 10/23/07.

295 "We'd go through": AI, 9/8/08.

295 "A lot of time was spent": AI, 10/23/07.

296 "so we can just hose it off": Confidential source.

296 "Give me back": Confidential source.

296 "Elaine is probably": AI, 2/15/08.

296 "They drove each other crazy": AI, 1/15/08.

296 "The way she functions": Confidential source.

297 "It was terrible": AI, 1/16/08.

297 "There was a lot": AI, 9/20/07.

297 "She would eat herself up": AI, 1/16/08.

297 "Diane loved him desperately": AI, 6/24/06.

297 "Where are you?": Judith Evans, AI, 10/23/07.

298 "I could imagine Diane" and following: Janice Dickinson, No Life Guard on Duty: The Accidental Life of the World's First Supermodel, New York, 2003, p. 216.

298 "spent the entire shoot" and following: Ibid., pp. 218–19.

299 "Look, that bitch" and following: Robert Younger, AI, 10/15/08.

8. ONE FROM THE HART

page

304 Epigraph: AI, 9/8/93.

304 *"You want to"*: Confidential source.

305 *"I'm the biggest narcissist" and following*: Craig McKay, AI, 10/12/05.

305 *"The tenor of that"*: AI, 5/4/05.

305 *"Jack was so good"*: Confidential source.

305 *"You know Jack"*: AI, 5/4/05.

306 *"Warren was a little"*: AI, 10/13/08.

306 *"Jerry came in"*: Confidential source.

306 *"I was shocked" and following*: Confidential source.

306 *"Beatty couldn't handle it"*: Confidential source.

306 *"The big fight"*: AI, 3/4/05.

306 *"a bullet is worth"*: Trevor Griffiths, AI, 10/11/05.

307 *"For me, you will never"*: AI, 1/14/06.

307 *"While we were mixing" and following*: AI, 10/3/05.

308 *"I hated that" and following*: Confidential source.

308 *"Poor Maurice had done"*: AI, 10/3/05.

308 *"It was extraordinarily discouraging"*: AI, 12/4/05.

309 *"they made the film"*: AI, 1/22/08.

309 *"It was frustrating"*: AI, 1/16/08.

309 *"I never liked"*: AI, 6/28/94.

309 *"One of the things"*: AI, 8/8/05.

309 *"Hey, Dil," and following*: Scharf, AI, 12/4/05.

310 *"John Reed definitely left" and following*: AI, 10/11/05.

310 *"Warren made some" and following*: AI, 5/3/05.

311 *"The last night"*: AI, 10/3/05.

311 *"Films are never finished"*: Quoted by Beatty, AI, n.d.

311 *"We were going crazy"*: AI, 10/12/05.

311 *"Oh my God, Communism"*: unsourced.

312 *"Everyone was telling him" and following*: AI, 12/24/05.

313 *"for having financed"*: Carr, "Dick Tracy Speaks."

313 *"I was talking to Walt"*: Avnet, AFI seminar.

313 *"I met Ronnie"*: AI, 12/29/99.

313 *"We used to laugh"*: AI, n.d.

313 *"Ronnie was not"*: AI, 11/29/99.

313 *"We shot in studios"*: AI, 6/7/94.

314 *"no one would ever say"*: AI, 12/24/05.

314 *"I don't know how much"*: AI, 6/11/94.

314 *"lunacy"*: Daily News, 8/19/81, p. 49.

314 *"spanked"*: Village Voice, n.d.

314 *"quaint"*: AI, n.d.

314 *"He had his own"*: AI, 12/24/05.

314 *"His whole approach"*: AI, 5/3/05.

315 *"Warren grilled me"*: AI, 1/16/08.

315 *"That was just a piece"*: AI, 12/29/05.

315 *"an extraordinary film"*: Vincent Canby, *New York Times*, 12/4/81.

315 *"Reds is a big"*: Richard Corliss, *Time,* 12/7/81.

315 *"It isn't really"*: Kael, "Reds," *The New Yorker,* 12/21/81.

316 *"I was the reason"*: AI, 7/27/05.

316 *"Warren betrayed Pauline"*: AI, 3/22/06.

316 *"I haven't spoken"*: AI, n.d.

318 *"Dede was in shock" and following*: AI, 10/12/05.

318 *"It's going to be you"*: Andrew Yule, *Fast Fade: David Puttnam, Columbia Pictures, and the Battle for Hollywood,* New York, 1989, p. 103.

318 *"The character who had"*: AI, 3/16/95.

318 *"I went out of my way"*: Yule, *Fast Fade,* p. 207.

318 *"hated each other"*: AI, 5/26/93.

319 *"A lot of people"*: Confidential source.

319 *"You know, Warren"*: Quoted by Dick Sylbert, AI, 4/9/93.

319 *"Warren doesn't have"*: Confidential source.

319 *"I sent him some sketches"*: AI, 3/20/06.

319 *"Film schools gave us guys"*: AI, 5/26/93.

320 *"Get rid of all that"*: Confidential source.

321 *"In the subject matter" and following*: AI, 1/7/98.

321 *"I think there was"*: AI, 10/2/91.

322 *"It was said"*: AI, 1/12/06.

323 *"was excited by being" and following*: Ronald Brownstein, *The Power and the Glitter: The Hollywood-Washington Connection,* New York, 1990, p. 317.

323 *"Maybe if* Reds *"*: AI, 9/9/04.

323 *"He was disruptive" and following*: Brownstein, *The Power and the Glitter,* p. 321.

324 *"Warren has that manner" and following*: AI, 9/9/04.

325 *"message doctor"*: Peter Goldman, "A Voice for the Yuppie Generation," *Newsweek,* 11/84.

325 *"He owed her"*: AI, 4/14/06.

325 *"I wanted the director"*: AI, 11/29/99.

325 *"Orson couldn't get"*: Jaglom, AI, 3/3/05.

326 *"Elaine wasn't interested"*: AI, 11/29/99.

327 *"In Warren Beatty"*: Brian D. Johnson, *Brave Films, Wild Nights: 25 Years of Festival Fever,* Toronto, 2000, p. 118.

327 *"There was a feeling"*: Ibid., p. 121.

327 *"We got high together"*: Ibid., p. 119.

327 *"They wanted to control"*: Ibid., p. 120.

327 *"We'll take you" and following*: Ibid., p. 121.

328 *"I didn't know"*: AI, 5/5/08.

329 *"Bert, anything she wants"*: Feibleman, AI, 4/14/06.

329 *"nightmare was having" and following*: Confidential source.

329 *"You have to be"*: Blum, "The Road to Ishtar," *New York,* 3/16/87.

330 *"I spent a lot of"*: Pat H. Broeske, "Melting Cost of Ishtar," *L.A. Times,* 5/24/87.

330 *"What happens sometimes" and following*: AI, 10/2/91.

330 *"I originally went" and following*: AI, 1/31/08.

331 *"made Warren tremble" and following*: Paul Mazursky, *Show Me the Magic: My Adventures in Life and Hollywood,* New York, 1999, p. 179.

331 *"Just think of a dirty" and following*: AI, 1/31/08.

332 *"a series" and following:* AI, 1990.

332 *"I'm tired of Hollywood" and following:* G. Mac Brown, AI, 8/7/08.

333 *"acne so bad":* Brad Darrach, "On the Road to Ishtar," *People,* 5/25/87.

333 *"I was sort of self-conscious" and following:* AI, 6/12/05.

336 *"could perhaps be made":* David T. Friendly, "First Look at the Studio," *Los Angeles Times,* 9/4/86.

336 *"I was always aware":* Broeske, "Check the Pulse of Two Movies," *LA Times,* 5/29/87.

337 *"Warren knew" and following:* AI, 3/4/05.

337 *"provocative encounter":* People, 5/18/87.

338 *"An airport-limousine driver":* Tom Mathews, "Election '88. Part 2: The Democrats' Quest, Fatal Attraction," *Newsweek,* 11/21/88.

338 *"We were still":* AI, 9/9/04.

338 *"He [was] always":* Howard Fineman, "Gary Hart: A Candidate in Search of Himself," *Newsweek,* 4/13/87.

338 *"[I had] my problems":* AI, 3/4/05.

338 *"You're in charge" and following:* Bradley, AI, 9/9/04.

338 *"radiant divorcee" and following:* Gail Sheehy, "The Hidden Hart," *Vanity Fair,* 7/84.

339 *"It was bullshit":* AI, 3/4/05.

339 *"You know, people":* Bradley, AI, 9/9/04.

339 *"I didn't want":* AI, 3/4/05.

339 *"Even Warren couldn't":* AI, 9/9/04.

340 *"It's your campaign":* Brownstein, *The Power and the Glitter,* p. 326.

340 *"Warren, to his discredit":* AI, 9/9/04.

340 *"Gary was a lot better" and following:* AI, 3/4/05.

341 *"dark and depressive":* Holly Millea, "Enduring Isabelle," *Premiere,* 4/96.

341 *"I began meeting":* Suzanne Finstad, *Warren Beatty: A Private Man,* New York, 2005, p. 456.

341 *"I think you're" and following:* Fran Drescher, *Enter Whining,* New York, 1996, pp. 70–78.

342 *"She was the hatcheck girl":* AI, 11/8/07.

342 *"Is your name DeLauné?" and following:* DeLauné Michel, AI, 7/25/09.

343 *"This was right before" and following:* AI, 6/4/07.

9. FATAL ATTRACTION

page

346 Epigraph: AI, 6/12/05.

346 *"We had been out looking":* David Blum, "The Road to 'Ishtar,'" *New York,* 3/16/87.

347 *"We heard there were":* AI, n.d.

347 *"Dustin was very nervous":* AI, 8/8/05.

347 *"I was standing" and following:* AI, 12/4/05.

347 *"The Moroccans were":* Peter Biskind, "Inside 'Ishtar,'" *American Film,* 5/87.

348 *"The humps would be":* David Blum, "'The Road to Ishtar,'" *New York,* 3/16/87.

348 *"In New York, before" and following:* AI, 3/20/06.

349 *"None of that happened":* AI, 2/15/08.

349 *"Elaine was nobody's fool"*: Scharf email, 6/16/09.

349 *"She would change"*: AI, 8/8/05.

350 *"Directors control in different"*: Confidential source.

350 *"One problem"*: Wooll, AI, 8/8/05.

350 *"Elaine, I love her" and following*: Dustin Hoffman, AI, 6/12/05.

351 *"We all figured"*: Paul Sylbert, AI, 3/20/06.

351 *"The notion of her eccentricity"*: AI, 2/15/08.

351 *"Warren never pushed"*: Nicola Pecorini, AI, 4/3/09.

351 *"one of the great" and following*: AI, 6/12/05.

352 *"Isabelle's greatest attribute"*: Confidential source.

352 *"You know why"*: AI, 3/20/06.

352 *"There wasn't a lot"*: AI, 6/12/05.

352 *"He was very cold" and following*: Pecorini, AI, 4/4/09.

353 *"Why is this chair"*: Scharf, AI, 12/11/05.

353 *"Then we said" and following*: Pecorini, AI, 4/4/09.

354 *"Warren would never learn"*: AI, 6/12/05.

354 *"she leaned against me" and following*: AI, 3/20/06.

356 *"In any other circumstances"*: Pecorini, AI, 4/4/09.

356 *"Warren did not have"*: AI, 4/14/06.

356 *"Great composers are"*: AI, 3/22/06.

357 *"Warren was going off" and following*: AI, 6/12/05.

358 *"Halfway through the movie"*: Scott Eyman, "The Commish Steps Up to the Plate," *Palm Beach Post*, 4/9/06.

359 *"acting, I had to be" and following*: G. Mac Brown, AI, 8/7/08.

359 *"Do what you do" and following*: Biskind, "Inside 'Ishtar," 5/87.

360 *"So what are"*: G. Mac Brown, AI, 8/7/08.

360 *"She picked up one"*: AI, 3/25/06.

360 *"oozed integrity"*: Margot Dougherty, reported by Richard Natale, "He Rode into Hollywood on a Chariot of Fire, but David Puttnam's Job at Columbia Went Up in Smoke," *Los Angeles Times*, 11/16/87.

360 *"After he went"*: AI, 6/12/05.

361 *"Puttnam was on"*: AI, 6/4/07.

361 *"I don't want"*: Andrew Yule, *Fast Fade: David Puttnam, Columbia Pictures, and the Battle for Hollywood*, New York, 1989, p. 204.

361 *"If your director's not there" and following*: Confidential source.

361 *"Towards the end"*: Schopper, AI, 2/15/08.

361 *"How does this guy" and following*: Julia Phillips, *You'll Never Eat Lunch in This Town Again*, New York, 1992, pp. 526, 528.

362 *"You gotta do me"*: Paul Sylbert, AI, 3/20/06.

362 *"You think he wasn't" and following*: Brown, 8/7/08.

362 *"In terms of preparing" and following*: AI, 7/8/08.

363 *"was like a brother" and following*: Geoff Pevere, *Toronto Star*, quoted by Brian D. Johnson, *Brave Films, Wild Nights: 25 Years of Festival Fever*, Toronto, 2000, excerpted in *Maclean's*, 8/28/2000.

363 *"You're gonna get called"*: Brown, AI, 8/7/08.

363 *"We all got called" and following*: AI, 3/20/06.

363 *"We were in constant contact" and following*: AI, 7/8/08.

364 *"I spent two years"*: AI, 9/8/93.

364 *"Warren really loved"*: AI, 9/8/08.

364 *"he distanced himself"*: AI, 8/7/08.

364 *"Warren was basically in effect"*: AI, 7/27/05.

365 *"I had hoped to work"*: AI, 8/7/08.

365 *"I was staggered"*: Yule, *Fast Fade,* p. 244.

365 *"Who gives a shit"*: Ibid.

365 *"a stern man"*: Shirley MacLaine, *Don't Fall Off the Mountain,* New York, 1971, pp. 2–3.

365 *"My dad internalized"*: Shirley MacLaine, *My Lucky Stars: A Hollywood Memoir,* New York, 1996, p. 7.

365 *"Shaving gel works"*: Michel, AI, 6/4/07.

366 *"I remember my father"*: Douglas Thompson, "Warren Beatty Has It All," *Mail on Sunday,* 7/15/90.

366 *"Before my father died"*: Michael Shelden, "I was always an oddball," *Daily Telegraph,* 2/18/00; Finstad, *Warren Beatty,* p. 459.

366 *"I had zero interest" and following:* AI, 10/13/08.

367 *"It wasn't entirely comforting"*: MacLaine, *My Lucky Stars,* p. 19.

367 *"It was hard for him" and following:* AI, 10/13/08.

369 *"If you don't get"*: Confidential source.

369 *"Elaine's so smart" and following:* Confidential source.

370 *"The idea was"*: Tom Fleischman, AI, 12/3/05.

370 *"Warren and Elaine had"*: AI, 10/13/08.

370 *"Bert Fields had" and following:* Confidential source.

370 *"bullshit"*: AI, 2/26/09.

371 *"It says, 'Use'" and following:* Confidential source.

371 *"Warren kept trying"*: AI, 2/15/08.

371 *"We're doing great"*: Confidential source.

371 *"Elaine finally said"*: AI, 2/15/08.

371 *"We have a movie!" and following:* Confidential source.

372 *"there was a widespread"*: AI, 9/9/04.

373 *"laughed and laughed"*: Jennifer Lee, *Tarnished Angel,* New York, 1991, p. 55.

373 *"A lot of the time" and following:* AI, 9/9/04.

373 *"If anybody wants"*: E. J. Dionne, "The Elusive Front-Runner Gary Hart," *New York Times Magazine,* 5/3/87.

374 *"What do people your age" and following:* Bradley, AI, 9/9/04.

374 *"We knew there was"*: Tom Morganthau et al., "The Sudden Fall of Gary Hart," *Newsweek,* 5/18/87.

375 *"For Gary Hart, the end" and following:* Walter Shapiro, "Fall from Grace," *Time,* 5/18/87.

375 *"angry at everything" and following:* Ronald Brownstein, *The Power and the Glitter: The Hollywood-Washington Connection,* New York, 1990, p. 335.

375 *"It amazed me" and following:* AI, 3/4/05.

375 *"Everyone is telling him" and following:* Brownstein, *The Power and the Glitter,* p. 336.

376 *"You're crazy"*: Tom Mathews, "Election '88. Part 2: The Democrats' Quest, Fatal Attraction," *Newsweek,* 11/21/88.

376 *"Warren, it's raining concrete"*: Brownstein, *The Power and the Glitter,* p. 337.

376 *"Warren told me"*: Hart, AI, 1999.

376 *"The candidate had"*: Caddell, AI, 3/4/05.

376 *"Under the present circumstances"*: Morganthau et al., "The Sudden Fall of Gary Hart."

376 *"I don't think"*: Finstad, *Warren Beatty,* p. 459.

376 *"Warren was right there" and following:* AI, 10/13/08.

377 *"He had poked" and following:* AI, 9/9/04.

377 *"I've assumed since 1961"*: Beatty, AI, n.d.

377 *"Not the Donna Rice part"*: AI, n.d.

377 *"By the time"*: AI, 11/27/99.

378 *"If Gary was going"*: AI, 9/9/04.

378 *"It was a catastrophe" and following:* Nicholson, AI, 1990.

378 *"I didn't even know"*: AI, 6/12/05.

378 *"turn movie production"*: Richard Schickel, "They Got What They Wanted; *Ishtar* Directed and Written by Elaine May," *Time,* 5/18/87.

378 *"the most expensive comedy" and following:* Pat Broeske, "The High Cost of 'Ishtar,'" *Los Angeles Times,* 5/24/87.

378 *"The word went out"*: Ibid.

379 *"Warren started to"*: AI, 10/13/08.

379 *"I can't use you" and following:* Yule, *Fast Fade,* p. 244.

379 *"Warren's friend"*: AI, 6/12/05.

379 *"five-part 'GMA'"*: Tom Shales, "Beatty, on His Terms," *Washington Post,* 5/21/87.

379 *"Mr. Beatty edited"*: Aljean Harmetz, "Figuring Out the Fates of 'Cop' and 'Ishtar,'" *New York Times,* 6/4/87.

379 *"I'd rather ride down"*: D. Dedubovay, "A Couple of Flirts," *Queensland Courier-Mail,* 7/4/87.

380 *"I have never had"*: AI, n.d.

380 *"The movie's not important" and following:* Quoted by MaryLouise Oates, AI, 8/15/07.

380 *"It's a likable"*: Janet Maslin, *New York Times,* 2/15/87.

380 *"vanity production"*: David Denby, *New York,* 5/25/87.

381 *"When you make"*: AI, 3/22/06.

381 *"Elaine was blaming him"*: AI, 10/13/08.

381 *"Who can control Elaine?"*: Confidential source.

381 *"Whenever I see"*: AI, 8/8/06.

381 *"The great producer"*: AI, 3/20/06.

382 *"We probably shouldn't have gone"*: AI, 3/7/09.

382 *"Ishtar was a B minus"*: AI, 6/12/05.

382 *"We were wildly high"*: AI, 8/7/08.

382 *"The man didn't see"*: AI, 1990.

383 *"In some respects"*: Yule, *Fast Fade,* p. 287.

383 *"Could David have gotten involved"*: Ibid.

383 *"It hurt me"*: Eyman, "The Commish Steps Up to the Plate."

383 *"You must remember"*: Craig Modderno, "'Ishtar': It's Unmusic to the Ear," *Los Angeles Times,* 5/10/87.

383 *"With the negative publicity"*: Ronald Grover, "How *Ishtar* Put Columbia on the Road to Merger," *BusinessWeek,* 11/30/87.

383 *"A big problem"*: Gene Siskel, "'Ishtar' the $40 Million Desert Dance," *Chicago Tribune,* 5/10/87.

384 *"I think I'm becoming"*: Marie Helvin, *The Autobiography,* London, 2007, excerpted in *Daily Mail,* n.d.

384 *"I know because"*: Shirley MacLaine, quoted by Joyce Hyser, AI, 10/13/08.

10. MATERIAL BOY

page

385 Epigraph: Fax, 6/28/06.

386 *"You think you've"* and following: AI, 1990.

386 *Bo Goldman:* AI, 7/1/06.

386 "Dick Tracy *has"* and following: Dick Sylbert, AI, 1989.

387 *"I don't like that"*: Beatty, AI, 6/28/94.

387 *"You ask Warren"*: AI, 6/7/94.

388 *"[Gene] is giving me"* and following: Avnet, AFI seminar.

389 *"jihad of terror"*: Entertainment Weekly, 9/21/07.

390 *"Warren Beatty is up there"* and following: Bo Goldman, AI, 5/6/06.

392 *"I don't want to see"* and following: Goldman, AI, n.d., and fax.

392 *"Thank God you"* and following: Joyce Hyser, AI, 10/13/08.

393 *"Warren is Scottish"* and following: AI, 1989.

394 *"There's nothing more important"*: Hyser, AI, 10/13/08.

395 *"Once, a girl's name"*: AI, 1989.

395 *"What do you do?"*: Confidential source.

395 *"If you think"*: George Hackett et al., "The Hart-Beatty Connection," *Newsweek,* 1/25/88.

396 *"I'm back"*: unsourced.

396 *"self-indulgent folly"*: Walter Shapiro, "The Ghost of Gary Past," *Time,* 12/28/87.

396 *"Warren is the kind"*: AI, 6/19/04.

396 *"winning one"*: George Hackett, "Hart: The Invisible Man," *Newsweek,* 2/22/88.

397 *"I saw the A list"*: David Ansen, "Tracymania," *Newsweek,* 6/25/90.

397 *"Everybody said"*: Madonna, AI, 1990.

397 *"I know you've heard"* and following: J. Randy Taraborrelli, *Madonna: An Intimate Biography,* London, 2001, p. 157.

398 *"Warren was very proud"* and following: AI, 6/24/06.

398 *"Jeffrey loved him"*: AI, 6/14/06.

398 *"Warren is not"*: AI, 6/24/06.

398 *"Katzenberg would call"*: AI, 5/6/06; 7/1/06.

399 *"I wanted to try"* and following: Gene Siskel, "Beatty's Dick Tracy," *Chicago Tribune,* 6/10/90.

399 *"This is not some"*: Siskel, "Beatty's Dick Tracy."

399 *"It's about the"* and following: AI, 1989.

399 *"I gave him"* and following: AI, 6/24/06.

399 *"The movie, for me"*: Avnet, AFI Seminar.

400 *"At first he'd say"* and following: AI, 5/6/06.

402 *"Where's my car?" and following:* AI, 10/13/08.

402 *"We made all":* AI, 7/18/06.

402 *"I can't tell you":* AI, 10/13/08.

406 *"I was the world's" and following:* AI, 6/24/06.

406 *"I was under":* AI, 5/5/04.

406 *"Warren Beatty is":* AI, 5/6/06.

406 *"He was terrified":* AI, 10/7/08.

407 *"Hughes would never" and following:* AI, 7/14/06.

407 *"It was a completely":* AI, 6/24/06.

407 *"while Bo wrote up":* AI, 10/7/08.

407 *"Fire him" and following:* Bo Goldman, AI, 7/1/06.

409 *"Madonna and I":* AI, 5/5/08.

409 *"old enough to be":* J. Randy Taraborrelli, "In Bed," London *Daily Mail*, 3/27/99.

409 *"would follow her":* Taraborrelli, *Madonna*, p. 160.

409 *"I'm half a mile":* Taraborrelli, "In Bed."

410 *"You seem to like":* Taraborrelli, *Madonna*, pp. 178–79; Taraborrelli, "In Bed."

410 *"He knows a woman's body":* Taraborrelli, *Madonna*, pp. 179–80.

410 *"a perfectly wonderful size":* Don Shewey, "Madonna: The Saint, the Slut, the Sensation," *The Advocate*, 5/7, 21/91.

410 *"You older guys":* Taraborrelli, *Madonna*, pp. 180–81.

410 *"I sense that":* Christopher Ciccone, *Life with My Sister Madonna*, New York, 2008, p. 170.

411 *"Their relationship was very odd" and following:* AI, 5/5/08.

411 *"I was there":* AI, 11/19/06.

411 *"When we walked":* AI, 7/27/05.

412 *"Don't you think":* Bo Goldman, AI, 6/24/06.

412 *"this guy standing":* AI, 6/12/05.

412 *"Oh, this kid" and following:* Bo Goldman, AI, 7/1/06.

413 *"Warren was a genius":* AI, 8/16/09.

413 *"Warren had to limit":* AI, 1989.

413 *"Warren pisses me off":* AI, 1990.

413 *"is a guy":* AI, 1989.

413 *"I was pissed":* AI, 1990.

414 *"Shit, I turned":* Madonna, on set, 1989.

414 *"War-ren, I'm losing":* Kim Masters, *The Keys to the Kingdom: How Michael Eisner Lost His Grip*, New York, 2000, p. 239.

414 *"I'm here Warren." "I know":* Madonna and Beatty, on set.

414 *"Warren wanted to":* AI, 1990.

414 *"Ya know, you":* Mike Medavoy, AI, 1/25/08.

415 *"Get over here" and following:* Michel, 7/27/09.

415 *"Warren was just" and following:* AI, 6/4/07.

416 *"I don't want":* Michel, AI, 7/27/09.

416 *"Hey, Pussy Man":* Taraborrelli *Madonna*, pp. 183–84.

416 *"I'd never seen Warren":* AI, 4/4/09.

416 *"We would taunt him":* AI, 7/2/09.

417 *"Women with one name" and following:* Mike Nichols, AI, 12/3/99.

417 *"Never, ever fuck":* Glenn Gordon Caron, AI, 5/31/07.

417 *"One morning"*: Ciccone, *Life with My Sister Madonna*, p. 169.

418 *"It was the most peculiar"*: AI, 7/1/06.

419 *"The ax had fallen"*: AI, n.d.

420 *"I beg of you" and following*: Beatty, AI, 10/7/08.

420 *"Well, should we"*: AI, 7/1/06.

420 *"had been"*: AI, 6/24/06.

420 *"Spielberg and Bo"*: AI, 11/8/07.

420 *"Warren was pissed off"*: AI, 6/24/06.

420 *"I want you" and following*: Bo Goldman, AI, 5/6/06.

421 *"The question for me" and following*: AI, 6/14/06.

421 *"He could not"*: AI, 1989.

421 *"I finally realized"*: Ibid.

422 *"There was this"*: Masters, *The Keys to the Kingdom*, p. 240.

422 *"I have a much bigger"*: Ansen, "Tracymania," *Newsweek*, 6/25/90.

422 *"Don't hide back there"*: Christopher Andersen, *Madonna: Unauthorized*, New York, 1991, p. 289.

423 *"And not only" and following*: AI, 5/6/06.

423 *"I just learned"*: Mab Goldman, AI, 7/1/06.

423 *"Somebody of Warren's stature"*: AI, 7/18/06.

424 *"Why did he insist"*: AI, 6/24/06.

424 *"I tried very hard" and following*: AI, 11/8/07.

424 *"He's an amazing person"*: AI, 7/1/06.

11. LETTING GO

page

425 Epigraph: AFI Life Achievement Award, 6/12/08.

425 *"You can't escape" and following*: Jeffrey Katzenberg, AI, 1990.

426 *"The numbers are great"*: Bob Thomas, "Warren Beatty," *The Canadian Press*, 6/22/90.

426 *"has been gloriously reinvented"*: Vincent Canby, *New York Times*, 6/15/90.

426 *"a class act"*: David Ansen, *Newsweek*, 6/25/90.

427 *"The other actors"*: Anthony Lane, "A Blush from Beatty, for the lady is a Vamp," *Independent* (London), 7/8/90.

428 *"somewhat shorter" and following*: Kim Masters, *The Keys to the Kingdom: How Michael Eisner Lost His Grip*, New York, 2000, p. 252.

428 *"You talk to yourself"*: AI, 7/31/09.

429 *"Take his time?"*: AI, 1989.

429 *"Warren hated"*: Confidential source.

429 *"Jeffrey treated me very well"*: AI, 10/1/91.

429 *"I'm told he tried"*: AI, 1989; 10/1/91.

430 *"Go to hell"*: Christopher Andersen, *Madonna: Unauthorized*, New York, 1991, p. 303.

430 *"There's a lot"*: Don Shewey, "Madonna: The Saint, the Slut, the Sensation," *The Advocate*, 5/7, 21/91.

430 *"no scenes"*: AI, 8/10/09.

430 *"He tried to stay" and following*: AI, 4/8/08.

430 *"the sparring chamber" and following:* AI, 11/19/06.

431 *"He's 50 from":* Sally Ogle Davis, "How Many Women Does It Take to Change a Lothario," *Mail on Sunday,* 5/24/92.

431 *"I was in" and following:* AI, 6/27/05.

432 *"That's when I knew" and following:* DeLauné Michel, AI, 6/4/07.

433 *"would hire a hit man":* AI, n.d.

434 *"There's a Didion-Dunne script":* Beatty, AI, n.d.

434 *"master creator" and following:* James Toback, "Divisions and Dislocations: A Journal for 1994," *Projections* 4, p. 75.

434 *"I wouldn't come up with" and following:* AI, 7/27/05.

435 *"There was some caution":* Mike Medavoy, with Josh Young, *You're Only as Good as Your Next One,* New York, 2002, p. 237.

435 *"to lose weight":* Mike Medavoy, AI, 1/25/08.

435 *"He was in love":* AI, 2/20/08.

435 *"I'm in just":* AI, 10/1/91.

435 *"What do you think" and following:* James Toback, AI, 7/27/05.

437 *"came back the next day":* Bugsy, DVD, Making of—Documentary, Road to Damascus.

437 *"It was a mess" and following:* AI, 6/1/07.

437 *"I got this long":* Bugsy, DVD, Making of—Documentary, Road to Damascus.

437 *"When I first met Barry":* AI, 7/27/05.

438 *"Warren is very secretive":* AI, 2/1/08.

438 *"Everything was so secretive":* AI, 2/15/08.

438 *"It got back":* AI, 2/1/08.

438 *"In a way" and following:* AI, 11/29/99.

439 *"By the end" and following:* AI, 11/19/06.

439 *"I didn't have any":* Suzanne Finstad, *Warren Beatty: A Private Man,* New York, p. 478.

439 *"I knew all about":* Garth Pearce, "Mrs. Beatty's Recipe for Success," *London Sunday Times,* 11/14/04.

439 *"I was elated" and following:* AI, 11/29/99.

440 *"He let out":* AI, 7/27/05.

440 *"I had to stop":* "Love Story," *Vanity Fair,* 9/94.

440 *"I didn't fall":* Mal Vincent, "Still Faithful After All Three Years," *Virginian-Pilot,* 10/22/94.

440 *"How did it go?":* Bugsy, DVD, making of—Documentary, Road to Damascus.

440 *"Bugsy, with Warren" and following:* AI, 2/1/08.

441 *"he came up" and following:* AI, 1/30/07.

441 *"Half of him":* AI, 7/27/05.

441 *"There isn't an ounce" and following:* AI, 6/1/07.

442 *"Bugsy was a":* AI, 10/6/91.

442 *"Barry's not a very gregarious":* AI, 1/30/07.

442 *"a shopping list":* AI, 2/1/08.

442 *"The men followed":* AI, 1/30/07.

442 *"It's just more fun":* Beatty, 11/29/99.

443 *"'That's a fucking" and following:* James Toback, AI, 7/27/05.

443 *"Bugsy was a guy":* Bugsy, DVD, Making of—Documentary, Road to Damascus.

443 *"Would you stop":* Toback, AI, 7/27/05.

444 *"So I dropped":* Bugsy, DVD, Making of—Documentary, Road to Damascus.

444 *"I don't have":* AI, 6/1/07.

444 *"Warren loves to mess":* Confidential source.

444 *"We thought":* AI, 6/6/07.

444 *"Warren was insecure":* AI, 1/30/07.

444 *"I'm sure it was":* AI, 2/15/08.

445 *"There's a kind":* Unsourced.

445 *"We have a deal" and following:* James Toback, AI, 7/27/05.

446 *"I don't enjoy":* Avnet, AFI seminar.

447 *"a closet psychopath" and following:* AI, 7/8/08.

447 *"I admit to an":* Shirley MacLaine, *My Lucky Stars: A Hollywood Memoir,* New York, 1996, pp. 81, 110.

447 *"I believe he's":* AI, 7/8/08.

447 *"What other actor" and following:* Bugsy, DVD, Making of—Documentary, Road to Damascus.

448 *"His performance":* Ibid.

448 *"How did you get":* James Toback, AI, 9/28/04.

448 *"Barry gained his trust":* AI, 1/30/07.

448 "Dick Tracy, *with its":* AI, 10/18/91.

448 *"I've worked with" and following:* AI, 2/15/08.

449 *"I hope I get":* Unsourced.

449 *"I don't think Warren":* AI, 2/1/08.

449 *"That was way down":* AI, 11/29/99.

450 *"Barry, Warren, and I":* AI, 7/27/05.

450 *"I used to stay":* AI, 7/27/05.

450 *"They were falling in love":* AI, 2/1/08.

450 *"You ask my dad":* Hilary De Vries, "Regarding Annette," *Los Angeles Times,* 7/7/91.

450 *"My parents are":* AI, 11/29/99.

450 *"It got to be late" and following:* AI, 11/29/99.

451 *"When I met Warren":* Vincent, "Still Faithful."

451 *"I want to have":* Allegra Clegg, AI, 1/30/07.

451 *"very quickly":* AI, 11/29/99.

451 *"It was a wonderful thing":* AI, 11/29/99.

451 *"I think back sometimes":* Michel, AI, 6/4/07.

451 *"The Teamsters told us":* AI, 6/1/07.

451 *"I didn't know":* AI, 2/15/08.

452 *"She was really":* AI, 11/29/99.

452 *"He had no intention":* AI, n.d.

453 *"told stories" and following:* AI, 7/8/08.

453 *"I know Warren felt":* AI, 6/6/07.

454 *"Despite protestations":* AI, 7/27/05.

454 *"That movie was everything":* AI, 6/1/07.

454 *"We were dealing":* Confidential source.

454 *"He called me" and following:* Medavoy with Young, *You're Only as Good as Your Next One,* p. 240.

454 *"He cussed me":* AI, 1/25/08.

455 *"Would he pick up":* AI, 6/6/07.

455 *"Warren obsessed over":* Medavoy with Young, *You're Only as Good as Your Next One,* p. 240.

455 *"The studio spent":* AI, 6/6/07.

455 *"There were lots":* AI, 6/1/07.

455 *"Even if you fell in love":* AI, 6/6/07.

456 *"We had total control":* AI, n.d.

456 *"He can be a bully" and following:* AI, 7/24/09.

456 *"Warren wouldn't talk":* AI, 1/25/08.

456 *"It bothered me" and following:* AI, 6/1/07.

457 *"Warren Beatty . . . has found":* Janet Maslin, *New York Times,* 12/13/91.

457 *"I liked the idea" and following:* AI, 10/1/91.

458 *"Can we do two o'clock":* AI, 6/6/07.

458 *"I know that Warren":* AI, 1/25/08.

458 *"That was one place":* AI, 2/20/08.

458 *"Frankly I'd had enough":* AI, 1/25/08.

458 *"It wasn't that Mike":* AI, 6/6/07.

458 *"What studio head":* AI, 7/27/05.

458 *"I don't know whether":* AI, n.d.

458 *"Warren flipped out":* AI, 1/25/08.

459 *"I don't think he" and following:* AI, 7/27/05.

459 *"Peter got upset":* AI, 1/25/08.

459 *"It isn't as if":* AI, 7/27/05.

459 *"Nobody wanted to be":* Kathy Jones, 6/6/07.

459 *"Too much was made":* AI, 6/1/07.

460 *"Mike's response was":* AI, 7/27/07.

460 *"All you wanted" and following:* AI, 6/6/07.

461 *"Up to then":* AI, 6/1/07.

461 *"I had to go through":* Medavoy with Young, *You're Only as Good as Your Next One,* p. 245.

461 *"You go to dailies":* AI, 6/1/07.

462 *"Is he focused on":* AI, 7/24/09.

462 *"He was as close":* AI, 7/8/08.

462 *"knowledgeable":* Confidential source.

462 *"I'd like to dedicate":* Axl Rose, Paris, 1992 concert, YouTube.

463 *"Warren wanted":* Doug Camilli, "Warren Beatty," *The Gazette* (Montreal), 4/4/07.

463 *"He's very frightened":* unsourced.

463 *"Everything he's done":* Sally Ogle Davis, "How Many Women Does It Take to Change a Lothario?"

463 *"In a weird way":* AI, 6/14/06.

463 *"The only thing":* Sally Ogle Davis, "How Many Women Does It Take to Change a Lothario?"

463 *"Warren has always":* AI, 6/7/94.

463 *"I don't think":* AI, 4/8/08.

12. MR. BEATTY GOES TO WASHINGTON

page

464 Epigraph: Conversation with author, n.d.

464 *"He's never going"*: Sally Ogle Davis, "How Many Women Does It Take to Change a Lothario?," London *Mail on Sunday*, 5/24/98.

465 *"See that guy?"*: A. Scott Berg, *Kate Remembered*, New York, 2003, p. 324.

465 *"This was a"*: AI, 2/95.

465 *"Are you still"*: Corie Brown "No Love Affair," *Premiere*, 2/95.

465 *"I opened it up"*: Michael Sragow, "Return of the Native," *New Times*, 3–9, 9/98.

466 *"Gosh" and following*: Glenn Gordon Caron, AI, 5/31/07.

466 *"Basically, success breeds"*: Curtis Lee Hanson, "Warren Beatty as Producer," in Sandra Wake and Nicola Hayden, eds., *Bonnie and Clyde*, London, 1978, pp. 179, 180.

467 *"Frankly I became"*: Susan King, "Seeking Perfection; Glenn Gordon Caron, Whose *Moonlighting* Turned Heads on TV, Hopes His Current Picture Will Do the Same on the Big Screen," *Los Angeles Times*, 8/7/97.

467 *"Warren really wanted" and following*: AI, 5/31/07.

468 *"But Warren's star" and following*: AI, 5/1/07.

468 *"Warren will make"*: AI, n.d.

468 *"I felt he was" and following*: AI, 5/31/07.

469 *"I'm not sure Connie" and following*: Caron, AI, 5/31/07.

470 *"Oh my God!" and following*: AI, 5/1/07.

471 *"Warren had this"*: AI, 5/31/07.

471 *"nasty word"*: William J. Mann, *Kate: The Woman Who Was Hepburn*, New York, 2006, pp. 520–21.

471 *"Warren was fascinated" and following*: AI, 5/31/07.

472 *"Every day, it was"*: AI, 1/30/08.

472 *"He called her"*: AI, 5/1/07.

472 *"I've always been in love"*: Berg, *Kate Remembered*, p. 321.

473 *"The first day" and following*: AI, 5/31/07.

473 *"I wouldn't be stupid"*: AI, 11/8/07.

473 *"I never saw Warren"*: AI, 5/1/07.

473 *"Glenn did speak" and following*: AI, 1/30/08.

474 *"It's got to"*: AI, 10/13/08.

474 *"Warren seemed to like" and following*: AI, 5/31/07.

475 *"About a week" and following*: Beatty, AI, 11/8/07.

475 *"Very early on" and following*: AI, 5/31/07.

475 *"Connie didn't want"*: AI, 11/9/07.

475 *"Connie didn't respect him"*: AI, 1/30/08.

475 *"Warren is very"*: AI, 5/1/07.

475 *"It was very dark"*: AI, 1/30/08.

475 *"From the moment" and following*: AI, 5/31/07.

476 *"There's the scene"*: AI, 5/1/07.

476 *"A hundred forty takes" and following*: AI, 1/30/08.

477 *"I have a friend"*: AI, 8/8/06.

477 *"I was sitting"*: AI, 1/31/08.

477 *"Most directors come into"*: AI, 5/31/07.

478   *"Narcissism!":* AI, 5/1/07.

478   *"yell at Glenn":* AI, 5/1/07.

478   *"This was the first film":* AI, 5/31/07.

478   *"It sometimes seemed":* Norman Mailer, "The Warren Report," *Vanity Fair,* 11/91.

478   *"Whenever there was":* AI, 5/31/07.

478   *"He was flirting":* AI, 1/30/08.

478   *"two people totally":* AI, 5/1/07.

479   *"My God, Jimmy" and following:* Glenn Gordon Caron, AI, 5/31/07.

479   *"Why would you" and following:* AI, 5/1/07.

479   *"My God, her face":* Berg, *Kate Remembered,* p. 336.

479   *"Is this okay?" and following:* Clegg, AI, 1/30/08.

480   *"opportunity" and following:* Berg, *Kate Remembered,* pp. 342–43.

480   *"Fuck a duck" and following:* Ibid., pp. 341–42.

480   *"I told Warren" and following:* Mann, *Kate,* pp. 520–21.

481   *"Warren was too respectful":* AI, 5/1/07.

481   *"She definitely got cranky":* AI, 1/30/08.

481   *"not allowed on":* Berg, *Kate Remembered,* p. 345.

481   *"We certainly weren't" and following:* AI, 5/31/07.

481   *"If I had only":* Berg, *Kate Remembered,* p. 345.

481   *"What you must":* Ibid., p. 346.

481   *"All the glass":* Davis, AI, 5/1/07.

481   *"I just kept looking":* AI, 5/31/07.

482   *"We were four days" and following:* AI, 5/1/07.

482   *"I shot Love Affair" and following:* AI, 5/31/07.

482   *"How's his skin look?" and following:* AI, 11/9/07.

483   *"It was admittedly":* AI, 5/31/07.

483   *"We can save":* AI, 5/31/07.

483   *"He had his time":* AI, 11/9/07.

483   *"Glenn just abdicated":* AI, 5/1/07.

483   *"I certainly didn't":* AI, 5/31/07.

484   *"The editing on that film":* AI, 11/9/07.

484   *"I know Warren":* AI, 5/31/07.

484   *"the progenitor" and following:* James Toback, *Projections* 4, p. 80.

485   *"I saw this":* AI, 1/15/08.

485   *"Children-izing replaced":* Phillips, AI, 3/4/08.

485   *"He won't let":* AI, 9/8/93.

485   *"I only call him":* Michael Childers, AI, 3/1/05.

485   *"In the Sixties":* Tim Adams, "The Divine Miss Julie," *The Observer* (London), 4/1/07.

485   *"Love Affair fell off":* unsourced.

485   *"This is one":* Roger Ebert, "Love and Warren," *Chicago Sun-Times,* 10/21/94.

485   *"tongue-tied":* Janet Maslin, *New York Times,* 10/21/94.

486   *"will refuse to acknowledge":* Toback, "Divisions and Dislocations," *Projectionist* 4, p. 94.

486   *"The campaign was not" and following:* AI, 5/1/07.

486   *"The Crying Game":* AI, 4/1/93.

486   *"I ran into Connie Hall":* Confidential source.

487 *"I was in movie jail" and following:* AI, 5/31/07.

487 *"Warren and I" and following:* AI, 5/1/07.

488 *"He just can't":* Confidential source.

488 *"a comedy about":* AI, 10/23/06.

488 *"This sounds like":* Jeremy Pikser, AI, 6/27/05.

488 *"What attracted him":* AI, 1/31/08.

489 *"I know what":* Alter, "Beatty Goes Bonkers," *Newsweek,* 5/18/98.

489 *"Where's the party":* Gary Younge, "Rebel with a Cause," ZA@PLAY, 6/10/99.

489 *"doing what's politically expedient":* AI, 11/28/99.

489 *"I have witnessed":* Barry Koltnow, "Bitter Laughter," *Orange County Register,* 5/12/98.

489 *"The underbelly" and following:* Beatty, interview, *The Nation,* n.d.

489 *"He gets off on" and following:* AI, 4/8/08.

490 *"Warren was in":* AI, 11/19/06.

490 *"We're having":* Pikser, AI, 4/8/08.

491 *"was trying to":* AI, 7/8/09.

492 *"Depression is the":* AI, 7/8/08.

492 *"I do remember" and following:* Younge, "Rebel with a Cause."

493 *"ashen and crying":* Shirley MacLaine, *My Lucky Stars: A Hollywood Memoir,* New York, 1996, p. 196.

493 *"curse at the communists":* Ibid., p. 7.

493 *"Warren is from":* Confidential source.

493 *"I don't think" and following:* AI, 5/3/05.

493 *"Jimmy took the":* AI, 5/3/05.

494 *"Warren takes":* AI, 6/27/05.

494 *"My ability to get":* AI, 4/8/08.

494 *"He doesn't whine" and following:* AI, 6/27/05.

495 *"He was always coming in," and following:* AI, 6/27/05.

495 *"The film's hero":* Philip French, "Return to senator: A Jaded Democrat finds himself. Again. And So Does Warren Beatty," *The Observer* (London), 1/24/99.

496 *"Pussy, pussy, pussy":* Pikser, AI, 6/27/05.

496 *"In America that's":* Younge, "Rebel with a Cause."

496 *"I was amazed" and following:* AI, 4/8/08.

497 *"I don't want to do that" and following:* Pikser, AI, 4/8/08.

498 *"Warren Beatty is":* Lynn Hirschberg, "Film Star, Womanizer, Charmer, Man of the People, Warren Beatty for President," *The Observer* Review Page, 5/17/98.

499 *"We need to rewrite" and following:* AI, 4/8/08.

500 *"I'm not an actor":* Michael Lerner, conversation with the author.

500 *"You're one of":* Confidential source.

500 *"God, can you imagine?" and following:* Pikser, AI, 4/8/08.

501 *"Rumor had it":* AI, 5/5/08.

501 *"I could tell that" and following:* Jeremy Pikser, AI, 7/27/05.

502 *"Warren always likes":* AI, 7/27/05.

502 *"Annette once said":* AI, 5/3/05.

13. IN HIS OWN WAY

page

503 Epigraph: AI, 6/24/06.

503 "Reds *was doing*" *and following:* AI, 5/3/05.

504 "*Don thought that*": Pecorini, AI, 4/3/09.

504 "*He knows how*": Pecorini, AI, 4/3/09

504 "*I think he feels*" *and following:* AI, 11/9/07.

505 "*For the two years*" *and following:* AI, n.d.

506 "*If you ask*": Gary Younge, "Rebel with a Cause," ZA@PLAY, 6/10/99.

506 "*I think that*": Beatty interview, *The Nation,* n.d.

507 "*the kind of*": Janet Maslin, *New York Times,* 5/15/98.

507 "*For Warren Beatty*": Joel Siegel, *Good Morning America,* 5/21/98.

507 "*What should we say*": Jeremy Pikser, AI, 6/27/05.

507 "*Spike Lee could make*": *Today,* 5/13/98.

508 "*This makes*": Wills, "Slumming," *New York Review of Books,* 7/16/98.

508 "*We were aware*": AI, 6/27/05.

510 "*Don't do as I did*": AI, n.d.

510 "*Was there something*": AI, n.d.

511 "*It had to do*": AI, 10/23/06.

511 "*When Warren told me*": AI, 7/19/06.

512 "*I felt that*": AI, 11/15/06.

512 "*After* Bulworth": AI, 11/13/06.

513 "*It was clear*": AI, 7/19/06.

513 "*It's a tough thing*": AI, 11/29/99.

513 "*One of his stipulations*" *and following:* AI, 7/19/06.

513 "*approval over*": AI, 11/13/06.

513 "*I feel kind of responsible*" *and following:* AI, 10/23/06.

513 "*We'd all seen*": AI, 7/19/06.

513 "*Leslie spoke highly*": AI, 10/23/06.

513 "*I don't think*": Paul Mazursky, AI, n.d.

514 "*Why doesn't Warren*": Michael Laughlin, AI, 10/23/06.

514 "*Their relationship was*": AI, 12/7/94.

514 "*Not that there*": AI, 7/19/06.

514 "*It's a chancy*": AI, 11/29/99.

514 "*The reason we*": AI, 11/15/06.

515 "*We felt*": AI, 11/13/06.

515 "*I was talking*": AI, 7/19/06.

515 "*Peter would read it*" *and following:* AI, 10/23/06.

515 "*We had stop dates*": AI, 7/19/06.

515 "*Had the original*": AI, 11/13/06.

515 "*It wasn't that*": AI, 7/19/06.

516 "*It seemed as though*": Confidential source.

516 "*I didn't want*" *and following:* AI, 10/23/06.

516 "*I don't think*": AI, 8/8/06.

516 "*corny and objectionable*" *and following:* AI, 11/15/06.

516 "*Warren didn't want*": AI, 7/19/06.

516 "*I don't think that*": Confidential source.

517 *"One of the biggest changes"*: AI, 11/15/06.
517 *"I was in a meeting"*: AI, 10/23/06.
517 *"I'm only trying"*: Confidential source.
517 *"Warren never brought up"*: AI, 11/15/06.
517 *"I was ready to go" and following*: AI, n.d.
518 *"This was not"*: AI, 11/13/06.
518 *"I was going through"*: AI, 7/19/06.
518 *"The keynote of"*: AI, 8/8/06.
518 *"Warren thought it"*: AI, 10/23/06.
518 *"Warren said it was"*: AI, 7/19/06.
519 *"raped"*: Benjamin Svetkey, "X Marks The Spot," *Entertainment Weekly*, 10/23/98.
519 *"New Line was reluctant"*: AI, 7/19/06.
519 *"I was aware"*: AI, 11/15/06.
519 *"You don't know" and following*: Lynn Harris, AI, 11/13/06.
520 *"I worked and worked"*: AI, 7/19/06.
520 *"I've always hated"*: AI, 8/8/06.
520 *" 'Buck, I promise' "*: Andy Karsch, AI, 7/19/06.
520 *"Okay, I'll come out" and following*: Buck Henry, AI, 8/8/06.
521 *"As the budget"*: AI, 7/19/06.
521 *"I had no power"*: AI, 11/13/06.
521 *"Do you know"*: Kim Masters, "New Line Says *Town & Country* Is Just Fine, and Don't Blame Beatty for the Awful Mess," Inside.com, 10/25/00.
521 *"Make no mistake" and following*: Lynn Harris, AI, 11/13/06.
523 *"Garry and Warren were" and following*: AI, 8/8/06.
523 *"The movie should"*: AI, 10/23/06.
523 *"His role was tiny"*: Confidential source.
523 *"When you're an actor"*: AI, 11/13/06.
524 *"Diane said to me"*: AI, 8/8/06.
524 *"I don't know why" and following*: AI, 11/13/06.
524 *"It was Chelsom's" and following*: AI, 8/8/06.
525 *"You cunt"*: Harris, AI, 11/13/06.
525 *"I knew every time" and following*: AI, 8/8/06.
525 *"Warren's guys" and following*: AI, 7/19/06.
526 *"Peter didn't say"*: AI, 11/13/06.
526 *"I don't think"*: Confidential source.
526 *"If you knew MacLeod"*: AI, 7/8/08.
526 *"The struggle over" and following*: AI, 8/8/06.
527 *"That was the day"*: AI, 11/15/06.
528 *"Warren would have liked"*: AI, 10/13/08.
528 *"Easter eggs"*: Bill Bradley, AI, 5/5/04.
528 *"There was definitely"*: AI, 5/23/05.
528 *"Going into 2000"*: AI, 4/22/04.
529 *"Warren knew I"*: AI, 5/23/05.
529 *"The question was"*: AI, 5/5/04.
529 *"It's hard to imagine"*: AI, 12/3/99.
529 *"for about forty-five minutes" and following*: Bradley, AI, 9/9/04.
530 *"We're living in"*: The Nation, n.d.

530 *"That group of four" and following:* AI, 4/22/04.

531 *"Warren would talk" and following:* AI, 5/5/04.

531 *"So I wrote":* AI, 4/22/04.

531 *"We could never":* AI, 5/5/04.

531 *"In the mini-world" and following:* AI, 4/22/04.

532 *"drum majorette" and following:* text of speech, 9/29/99.

532 *"Oh my God!":* Cooper, AI, 4/22/04.

533 *"It was covered" and following:* AI, 5/23/05.

533 *"McCain hates George Bush":* Confidential source.

533 *"I think he was":* AI, 5/23/05.

533 *"The Teamsters are" and following:* AI, 4/22/04.

534 *" 'Well, I just' ":* Bradley, AI, 6/19/04.

534 *"In the end":* Cooper, AI, 4/22/04.

534 *"purgatory":* Confidential source.

534 *"For me, when he" and following:* AI, 4/22/04.

534 *"Warren is an actor":* AI, 5/5/05.

535 *"You can't really":* AI, 11/29/99.

535 *"This [campaign] was" and following:* AI, 4/22/04.

537 *"Hello, John?":* Paul Mazursky, AI, 1/31/08.

537 *"We were into" and following:* AI, 4/22/04.

537 *"I was at one":* AI, 11/15/06.

538 *"to tell me":* Lynn Harris, AI, 11/13/06.

538 *"He was quite loaded":* AI, 8/8/06.

538 *"Postproduction was endless":* AI, 11/13/06.

538 *"It reminds me":* Rick Lyman, "Stumbling Toward a Theater Near You," *New York Times,* 4/15/01.

538 *"It was just us":* AI, 11/15/06.

539 *"Warren was really bitter" and following:* AI, 8/8/06.

539 *"He will live":* AI, 7/19/06.

540 *"All these movies":* Michael Laughlin, AI, 10/23/06.

540 *"Part of it was":* AI, 11/15/06.

540 *"When you move":* Confidential source.

540 *"After* Town & Country*":* Confidential source.

541 *"Now, almost three years later":* Lyman, "Stumbling Toward a Theater Near You."

541 *"The hermetically wealthy":* Lisa Schwarzbaum, *Entertainment Weekly,* 4/26/01.

541 *"patched-together":* Stephen Holden, *New York Times,* 4/27/01.

541 *"In this commencement season":* Dade Hayes, "Inside Move: Really Down 'Town'/ New Line Pic Makes Dubious Grade, *Variety,* 6/5/01.

542 *"It was fun":* Beatty, AI, n.d.

542 *"New Line Says":* Kim Masters, "New Line Says *Town & Country* Is Just Fine, and Don't Blame Beatty for the Awful Mess," Inside.com, 10/25/00.

542 *"As things started" and following:* AI, 11/15/06.

542 *delivered a rant and following:* Patrick Goldstern, "Pater Familias," *Los Angeles Times,* 11/7/99.

542 *"Categorically untrue":* AI, 7/19/06.

542 *"cease and desist":* Goldstein, "Beatty's Troops," *Los Angeles Times,* 1/30/00.

542 *"Bob felt crazy":* AI, 11/15/06.

543 *"They would swear"*: Confidential source.

543 *"I found him" and following*: AI, 7/19/06.

543 *"It is a mess"*: Masters, "New Line Says *Town & Country* Is Just Fine."

543 *"I'm sure Peter"*: AI, 8/8/06.

543 *"It's an incredibly" and following*: AI, 11/13/06.

14. HE'S BEEN UP SO LONG IT LOOKS LIKE DOWN TO ME
page

545 Epigraph: AI, 10/18/91.

545 *"Warren is in trouble"*: AI, 3/15/95.

546 *"[My bosses] wouldn't"*: AI, 4/27/07.

546 *"Warren at the point"*: AI, 7/31/09.

547 *"When you take"*: AI, 4/20/96.

547 *"Warren used to say"*: AI, 9/28/04.

547 *"Stella Adler said"*: Beatty, AI, 10/1/91.

548 *"crackpot"*: Carla Maranucci, "Actor-activist Warren Beatty digs his rhetorical talons into Arnold Schwarzenegger," *San Francisco Chronicle*, 10/9/05.

549 *"Warren is an underachiever"*: AI, 6/24/06.

549 *"that life is short"*: Beatty, AI, 12/11/00.

549 *"stand naked"*: AI, 7/1/06.

550 *"Warren just act" and following*: AI, 4/8/08.

551 *"Why don't you do"*: Andy Karsch, 7/19/06.

551 *"He may still"*: AI, 3/15/95.

552 *"He's preparing"*: John Hiscock, "The Real Housewife Superstar," *The Telegraph*, (London), 9/11/04.

INDEX